Options,
Futures, and
Other Derivative
Securities

SECOND EDITION

Options, Futures, and Other Derivative Securities

JOHN HULL

University of Toronto

PRENTICE HALL

ENGLEWOOD CLIFFS, NEW JERSEY 07632

Library of Congress Cataloging-in-Publication Data

HULL, J. C. (JOHN C.)
   Options, futures, and other derivative securities / John C. Hull.
— 2nd ed.
     p. cm.
   Includes bibliographical references and index.
   ISBN 0-13-639014-5
   1. Futures. 2. Stock options. I. Title.
HG6024.A3H85   1993
332.63′2—dc20   92-25111

Acquisitions editor: *Leah Jewell*
Editorial/production supervision: *Edie Riker*
Cover design: *Anne Ricigliano*
Cover illustration is a sketch of the future and options trading floor
Prepress buyer: *Patrice Fraccio*
Manufacturing buyer: *Trudi Pisciotti*
Editorial assistant: *Eileen DeGuzman*

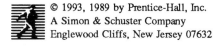

© 1993, 1989 by Prentice-Hall, Inc.
A Simon & Schuster Company
Englewood Cliffs, New Jersey 07632

Printed in the United States of America

10 9 8

ISBN   0-13-639014-5

Prentice-Hall International (UK) Limited, *London*
Prentice-Hall of Australia Pty. Limited, *Sydney*
Prentice-Hall Canada Inc., *Toronto*
Prentice-Hall Hispanoamericana, S.A., *Mexico*
Prentice-Hall of India Private Limited, *New Delhi*
Prentice-Hall of Japan, Inc., *Tokyo*
Simon & Schuster Asia Pte. Ltd., *Singapore*
Editora Prentice-Hall do Brasil, Ltda., *Rio de Janeiro*

To Kathy,
Colin, and Michael

Contents

4   INTEREST RATE FUTURES   80

5   SWAPS   111

6   OPTIONS MARKETS   136

15   INTEREST RATE DERIVATIVE SECURITIES   370

16   EXOTIC OPTIONS   414

Preface

This book is appropriate for graduate and advanced undergraduate elective courses in business and economics. It is also suitable for practitioners who want to acquire a working knowledge of how derivative securities can be analyzed.

One of the key decisions that must be made by an author who is writing in the area of derivative securities concerns the use of mathematics. If the level of mathematical sophistication is too high, the material is likely to be inaccessible to many students and practitioners. If it is too low, some important issues will inevitably be treated in a rather superficial way. In this book, great care has been taken in the use of mathematics. Nonessential mathematical material has been either eliminated or included in end-of-chapter appendices. Concepts that are likely to be new to many readers have been explained carefully and many numerical examples have been included.

The feature of this book that distinguishes it from others in the same area is that it provides a unifying approach to the valuation of all derivative securities—not just futures and options. This book assumes that the reader has taken an introductory course in finance and an introductory course in probability and statistics. No prior knowledge of options, futures contracts, swaps, and so on, is assumed. It is not therefore necessary for students to take an elective course in investments prior to taking a course based on this book.

CHANGES IN THIS EDITION

This edition contains much more material than the previous edition. Also, the material in the previous edition has been updated and the organization of the material has been improved in a number of places. The main changes are:

1. There is more material on futures markets and the way they are used for hedging (chapters 2, 3, and 4). A discussion of duration and duration-based hedging strategies has been included.
2. There is more material on the details of how markets work and the trading strategies that can be used (chapters 2, 4, 6 and 8).
3. The material on interest rate derivatives (Chapter 15) has been completely rewritten to reflect recent developments in this area. It now includes a fuller discussion of no-arbitrage models that provide an exact fit to the current term structure.
4. A new chapter on exotic options (Chapter 16) has been added.
5. A whole chapter has been devoted to the increasingly important area of credit risk (Chapter 18).
6. The chapter concerned with the Cox, Ingersoll, and Ross general approach to pricing derivative securities has been restructured (Chapter 12). Also, a discussion of guaranteed exchange rate foreign index options is now included.
7. New questions and problems have been added at the ends of the chapters. As in the previous edition, those which are more difficult than average have been asterisked.

ACKNOWLEDGMENTS

Many people have played a part in the production of this book. Colleagues who have made excellent and useful suggestions are: George Athanassakos, Giovanni Barone-Adesi, George Blazenko, Laurence Booth, Phelim Boyle, Peter Carayannopoulos, Peter Carr, Dieter Dorp, Jerome Duncan, Steinar Ekern, David Fowler, Mark Garman, Kevin Hebner, Elizabeth Maynes, Paul Potvin, Gordon Roberts, Chris Robinson, John Rumsey, Klaus Schurger, Piet Sercu, Stuart Turnbull, Yisong Tian, P. V. Viswanath, Bob Whaley, and Alan White. I am particularly grateful to Eduardo Schwartz, who read the original manuscript for the first edition and made many comments which have led to significant improvements.

The students in my elective courses on derivative securities at York University and the University of Toronto have made many useful suggestions on how the book can be improved. I would particularly like to thank Scott Drabin, Cheryl Rosen, and Jason Wei. These three students read my original manuscript very carefully and had a number of good ideas as to how (from a student's perspective) it could be improved.

The first edition of my book was very popular with practitioners. Many have provided me with ideas and suggestions for improvements. I would particularly like to thank Kannan Ayyar (Renaissance Software), Alex Bergier (Goldman Sachs), Emanuel Derman (Goldman Sachs), Don Goldman (Bankers Trust), Ian Hawkins (Deutschebank), Nico Meier (Citibank), Isaac Muskat (Royal Bank), Bruce Rogers (Bank of Nova Scotia), Ayesha Shah (Nomura International), Armand Tatevossian (Fuji Capital Markets), Edward Thorp (Edward O. Thorp and Associates), and Cathy Willis (Renaissance Software)

Alan White, a colleague at the University of Toronto (formerly a colleague at York University), deserves a special acknowledgment. Alan and I have been carrying out joint research in the area of derivative securities for many years. During that time we have spent countless hours discussing different issues concerning derivative securities. Many of the new ideas in this book, and many of the new ways used to explain old ideas, are as much Alan's as mine. Alan read the original version of this book very carefully and made many excellent suggestions for improvement.

The staff at Prentice Hall have been a continual source of encouragement to me as this project has progressed. I would particularly like to thank Scott Barr (my original editor), Leah Jewell (my current editor), and Edie Riker (the production editor for this edition).

Last but not least I would like to thank my wife, Kathy. She has been unfailingly supportive and very understanding of the inevitable disruptions to family life caused by a project such as this.

John Hull

Introduction

A *derivative security* is a security whose value depends on the values of other more basic underlying variables. In recent years, derivative securities have become increasingly important in the field of finance. Futures and options are now actively traded on many different exchanges. Forward contracts, swaps, and many different types of options are regularly traded outside of exchanges by financial institutions and their corporate clients in what are termed the *over-the-counter* markets. Other more specialized derivative securities often form part of a bond or stock issue.

Derivative securities are also known as *contingent claims*, and these two terms will be used interchangeably throughout this book. Very often the variables underlying derivative securities are the prices of traded securities. A stock option, for example, is a derivative security whose value is contingent on the price of a stock. However, as we shall see, derivative securities can be contingent on almost any variable, from the price of hogs to the amount of snow falling at a certain ski resort.

This book has two objectives. The first is to explore the properties of those derivative securities that are commonly encountered in practice; the second is to provide a theoretical framework within which all derivative securities can be valued and hedged. In this opening chapter, we take a first look at forward contracts, futures contracts, and options. In later chapters, these securities and the way they are traded will be discussed in more detail.

1.1 FORWARD CONTRACTS

A *forward contract* is a particularly simple derivative security. It is an agreement to buy or sell an asset at a certain future time for a certain price. The contract is usually between two financial institutions or between a financial institution and one of its corporate clients. It is not normally traded on an exchange.

One of the parties to a forward contract assumes a *long position* and agrees to buy the underlying asset on a certain specified future date for a certain specified price. The other party assumes a *short position* and agrees to sell the asset on the same date for the same price. The specified price in a forward contract will be referred to as the *delivery price*. At the time the contract is entered into, the delivery price is chosen so that the value of the forward contract to both parties is zero.[1] This means that it costs nothing to take either a long or a short position.

A forward contract is settled at maturity. The holder of the short position delivers the asset to the holder of the long position in return for a cash amount equal to the delivery price. A key variable determining the value of a forward contract is the market price of the asset. As already mentioned, a forward contract is worth zero when it is first entered into. Later it can have a positive or a negative value depending on movements in the price of the asset. For example, if the price of the asset rises sharply soon after the initiation of the contract, the value of a long position in the forward contract becomes positive and the value of a short position in the forward contract becomes negative.

THE FORWARD PRICE

The *forward price* for a certain contract is defined as the delivery price which would make that contract have zero value. The forward price and the delivery price are therefore equal at the time the contract is entered into. As time passes, the forward price is liable to change while the delivery price, of course, remains the same. The two are not therefore equal, except by chance, at any time after the start of the contract. Generally, the forward price at any given time varies with the maturity of the contract being considered. For example, the forward price for a contract to buy or sell in 3 months is typically different from that for a contract to buy or sell in 6 months.

---

[1]In Chapter 3 we explain the way in which this delivery price can be calculated.

TABLE 1.1 Spot and
Forward Foreign Exchange
Quotes, September 11, 1991

Spot	1.7280
30-day forward	1.7208
90-day forward	1.7090
180-day forward	1.6929

Corporations frequently enter into forward contracts on foreign exchange. Consider the quotes shown in Table 1.1 for the pound sterling–U.S. dollar exchange rate on September 11, 1991. The first quote indicates that, ignoring commissions and other transactions costs, sterling can be bought or sold in the spot market (that is, for virtually immediate delivery) at the rate of $1.7280 per pound; the second quote indicates that the forward price (or forward exchange rate) for a contract to buy or sell sterling in 30 days is $1.7208 per pound; the third quote indicates that the forward price for a contract to buy or sell sterling in 90 days is $1.7090 per pound; and so on.

PAYOFFS FROM FORWARD CONTRACTS

The payoff from a long position in a forward contract on one unit of an asset is

$$S_T - K$$

where K is the delivery price and S_T is the spot price of the asset at maturity of the contract. This is because the holder of the contract is obligated to buy an asset worth S_T for K. Similarly, the payoff from a short position in a forward contract on one unit of an asset is

$$K - S_T$$

These payoffs can be positive or negative. They are illustrated in Figure 1.1. Since it costs nothing to enter into a forward contract, the payoff from the contract is also the investor's total gain or loss from the contract.

1.2 FUTURES CONTRACTS

A *futures contract*, like a forward contract, is an agreement between two parties to buy or sell an asset at a certain time in the future for a certain price. Unlike forward contracts, futures contracts are normally traded on an exchange. To make trading possible, the exchange specifies certain standardized features of the contract. As

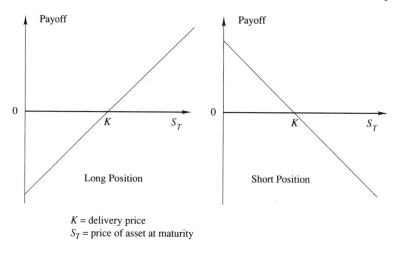

K = delivery price
S_T = price of asset at maturity

Figure 1.1 Payoffs from Forward Contracts.

the two parties to the contract do not necessarily know each other, the exchange also provides a mechanism which gives the two parties a guarantee that the contract will be honored.

The largest exchanges on which futures contracts are traded are the Chicago Board of Trade (CBOT) and the Chicago Mercantile Exchange (CME). On these and other exchanges, a very wide range of commodities and financial assets form the underlying assets in the various contracts. The commodities include pork bellies, live cattle, sugar, wool, lumber, copper, aluminum, gold, and tin. The financial assets include stock indices, currencies, Treasury bills, and bonds.

One way in which a futures contract is different from a forward contract is that an exact delivery date is not usually specified. The contract is referred to by its delivery month, and the exchange specifies the period during the month when delivery must be made. For commodities, the delivery period is often the whole month. The holder of the short position has the right to choose the time during the delivery period when he or she will make delivery. Usually, contracts with several different delivery months are traded at any one time. The exchange specifies the amount of the asset to be delivered for one contract; how the futures price is to be quoted; and, possibly, limits on the amount by which the futures price can move in any one day. In the case of a commodity, the exchange also specifies the product quality and the delivery location. Consider, for example, the wheat futures contract currently traded on the Chicago Board of Trade. The size of the contract is 5,000 bushels. Contracts for five delivery months (March, May, July, September, and December) are available for up to one year into the future. The exchange specifies the grades of wheat that can be delivered and the places where delivery can be made.

Futures prices are regularly reported in the financial press. Suppose that, on September 1, the December futures price of gold is quoted at $500. This is the price, exclusive of commissions, at which investors can agree to buy or sell gold for December delivery. It is determined on the floor of the exchange in the same way as other prices (that is, by the laws of supply and demand). If more investors want to go long than to go short, the price goes up; if the reverse is true, the price goes down.[2]

Further details on issues such as margin requirements, daily settlement procedures, delivery procedures, bid-ask spreads, and the role of the exchange clearinghouse will be given in the next chapter.

1.3 OPTIONS

Options on stocks were first traded on an organized exchange in 1973. Since then, there has been a dramatic growth in options markets. Options are now traded on many different exchanges throughout the world. Huge volumes of options are also traded over the counter by banks and other financial institutions. The underlying assets include stocks, stock indices, foreign currencies, debt instruments, commodities, and futures contracts.

There are two basic types of options. A *call option* gives the holder the right to buy the underlying asset by a certain date for a certain price. A *put option* gives the holder the right to sell the underlying asset by a certain date for a certain price. The price in the contract is known as the *exercise price* or *strike price*; the date in the contract is known as the *expiration date, exercise date,* or *maturity. American options* can be exercised at any time up to the expiration date. *European options* can only be exercised on the expiration date itself.[3] Most of the options that are traded on exchanges are American. However, European options are generally easier to analyze than American options, and some of the properties of an American option are frequently deduced from those of its European counterpart.

It should be emphasized that an option gives the holder the right to do something. The holder does not have to exercise this right. This fact distinguishes options from forwards and futures where the holder is obligated to buy or sell the underlying asset. Note that, whereas it costs nothing to enter into a forward or futures contract, an investor must pay to purchase an option contract.

---

[2]As we will see in Chapter 3, a futures price can sometimes be related to the price of the underlying asset (gold, in this case).

[3]Note that the terms *American* and *European* do not refer to the location of the option or the exchange. Some options trading on North American exchanges are European.

EXAMPLES

Consider the situation of an investor who buys 100 European call options on IBM stock with a strike price of $140. Suppose that the current stock price is $138, the expiration date of the option is in 2 months, and the option price is $5. Since the options are European, the investor can exercise only on the expiration date. If the stock price on this date is less than $140, he or she will clearly choose not to exercise. (There is no point in buying for $140 a stock that has a market value of less than $140.) In these circumstances the investor loses the whole of the initial investment of $500. If the stock price is above $140 on the expiration date, the options will be exercised. Suppose, for example, that the stock price is $155. By exercising the options, the investor is able to buy 100 shares for $140 per share. If the shares are sold immediately, the investor makes a gain of $15 per share or $1,500, ignoring transactions costs. When the initial cost of the options is taken into account, the net profit to the investor is $10 per option, or $1,000. (This calculation ignores the time value of money.) Figure 1.2 shows the way in which the investor's net profit or loss per option varies with the terminal stock price. Note that in some cases the investor exercises the options but takes a loss overall. Consider the situation when the stock price is $142 on the expiration date. The investor exercises the options but takes a loss of $300 overall. This is better than the loss of $500 that would be incurred if the options were not exercised.

Whereas the purchaser of a call option is hoping that the stock price will increase, the purchaser of a put option is hoping that it will decrease. Consider an investor who buys 100 European put options on Exxon with a strike price of $90. Suppose that the current stock price is $86, the expiration date of the option is in

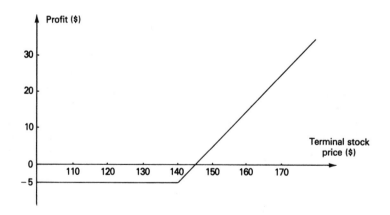

Figure 1.2 Profit from Buying an IBM European Call Option. Option Price = $5; Strike Price = $140.

3 months, and the option price is $7. Since the options are European, they will be exercised only if the stock price is below $90 at the expiration date. Suppose that the stock price is $65 on this date. The investor can buy 100 shares for $65 per share and, under the terms of the put option, sell the same stock for $90 to realize a gain of $25 per share, or $2,500. (Again, transactions costs are ignored.) When the initial cost of the option is taken into account, the investor's net profit is $18 per option, or $1,800. Of course, if the final stock price is above $90, the put option expires worthless and the investor loses $7 per option, or $700. Figure 1.3 shows the way in which the investor's profit or loss per option varies with the terminal stock price.

As already mentioned, stock options are generally American rather than European. This means that the investors in the examples just given do not have to wait until the expiration date before exercising the options. We will see later that there are some circumstances under which it is optimal to exercise American options prior to maturity.

OPTION POSITIONS

There are two sides to every option contract. On one side is the investor who has taken the long position (i.e., has bought the option). On the other side is the investor who has taken a short position (i.e., has sold or *written* the option). The writer of an option receives cash up front but has potential liabilities later. His or her profit or loss is the reverse of that for the purchaser of the option. Figures 1.4 and 1.5 show the variation of the profit and loss with the final stock price for writers of the options considered in figures 1.2 and 1.3.

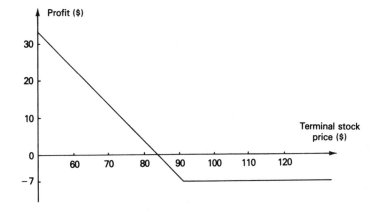

Figure 1.3   Profit from Buying an Exxon European Put Option. Option Price = $7; Strike Price = $90.

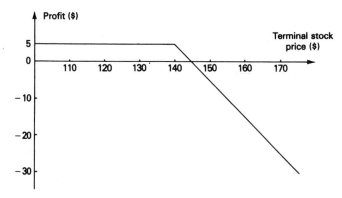

Figure 1.4 Profit from Writing an IBM European Call Option. Option Price = $5; Strike Price = $140.

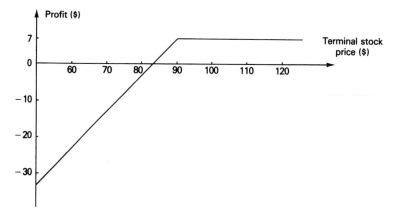

Figure 1.5 Profit from Writing an Exxon European Put Option. Option Price = $7; Strike Price = $90.

Four basic option positions are possible:

1. A long position in a call option
2. A long position in a put option
3. A short position in a call option
4. A short position in a put option

PAYOFFS

It is often useful to characterize European option positions in terms of the payoff to the investor at maturity. The initial cost of the option is then not included in the calculation. If X is the strike price and S_T is the final price of the underlying asset, the payoff from a long position in a European call option is

$$\max (S_T - X, 0)$$

This reflects the fact that the option will be exercised if $S_T > X$ and will not be exercised if $S_T \leq X$. The payoff to the holder of a short position in the European call option is

$$- \max (S_T - X, 0)$$

or

$$\min (X - S_T, 0)$$

The payoff to the holder of a long position in a European put option is

$$\max (X - S_T, 0)$$

and the payoff from a short position in a European put option is

$$- \max (X - S_T, 0)$$

or

$$\min (S_T - X, 0)$$

Figure 1.6 illustrates these payoffs graphically.

1.4 OTHER DERIVATIVE SECURITIES

In recent years, banks and other financial institutions have been very imaginative in designing nonstandard derivative securities to meet the needs of clients. Sometimes these are sold by financial institutions directly to their corporate clients. On other occasions, they are added to bond or stock issues to make these issues more attractive to investors. Some of the securities are simply combinations of simpler contracts, such as forwards and options. Others are far more complex. The possibilities for designing new interesting derivative securities seems to be virtually limitless. In this section, we give a few examples.

INTEREST RATE CAPS

An interest rate cap is designed to provide corporate borrowers with protection against the rate of interest on a floating-rate loan going above some level. This level is known as the *cap rate*. If the rate of interest on the loan does go above the cap rate, the seller of the cap provides the difference between the interest on the loan and the interest that would be required if the cap rate applied. Suppose

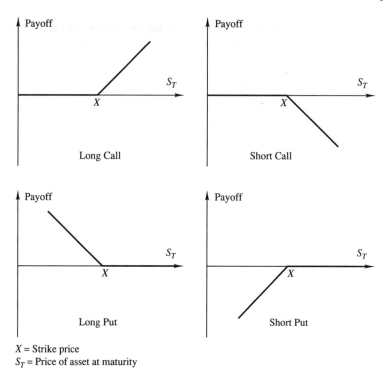

X = Strike price
S_T = Price of asset at maturity

Figure 1.6   Payoffs from Positions in European Options

the loan is for $10 million, the cap rate is 12 percent per annum, and that for a particular 3-month period during the life of the cap, the floating rate applicable to the loan turns out to be 14 percent per annum. The purchaser of the cap would receive $50,000 (= 1/4 of 2% of $10 million) from the seller of the cap at the end of the 3-month period. Occasionally caps are structured to guarantee that the average rate paid during the life of the loan (rather than the rate at any particular time) will not go above a certain level. Caps will be discussed further in Chapter 15.

Standard Oil's Bond Issue

An example of a derivative security added to a bond issue is provided by Standard Oil's issue of zero-coupon bonds in 1986. In addition to the bond's $1,000 maturity value, the company promised to pay an amount based on the price of oil at maturity of the bond. This additional amount was equal to the product of 170 and the excess (if any) of the price of a barrel of oil at maturity over $25. However, the maximum additional amount paid was restricted to $2,550 (which corresponds to a price of \$40 per barrel). The bonds provided holders with a stake in a commodity that was critically important to the fortunes of the company. If the price of the commodity went up, the company was in a good position to provide the bondholder with the additional payment.

ICONs

In 1985, Bankers Trust developed *index currency option notes* or ICONs. These are bonds in which the amount received by the holder at maturity varies with a foreign exchange rate. Two exchange rates, X_1 and, X_2, are specified with $X_1 > X_2$. If the exchange rate at the bond's maturity is above X_1, the bondholder receives the full face value. If it is less than X_2, the bondholder receives nothing. Between X_2 and X_1, a portion of the full face value is received. Bankers Trust's first issue of an ICON was for the Long Term Credit Bank of Japan. The ICON specified that if the yen–U.S. dollar exchange rate, S, is greater than 169 yen per dollar at maturity (in 1995), the holder of the bond receives \$1,000. If it is less than 169 yen per dollar, the amount received by holder of the bond is reduced by

$$\max \left[0, \ 1000 \left(\frac{169}{S} - 1 \right) \right]$$

When the exchange rate is below 84.5, nothing is received by the holder at maturity.

RANGE FORWARD CONTRACTS

A *range forward contract* (or flexible forward contract) is another interesting example of a derivative security. Suppose that on September 11, 1991, a U.S. company finds that it will require sterling in 90 days' time and faces the exchange rates shown in Table 1.1. It could enter into a 90-day forward contract to buy at \$1.7090 per pound. Alternatively, a range forward exchange band could be set from, say, \$1.6700 per pound to \$1.7500 per pound. At maturity, if the spot rate is less than \$1.6700 per pound, the company pays \$1.6700 per pound; if it is between \$1.6700 and \$1.7500, the company pays the spot rate; if it is greater than \$1.7500, the company pays \$1.7500. Like a regular forward contract, a range forward contract is normally structured so that it is initially worth zero to both parties.

OTHER EXAMPLES

As mentioned earlier, there is virtually no limit to the innovations that are possible in the derivative securities area. Some of the options traded over the counter have payoffs dependent on maximum value attained by a variable during a period of time; some have exercise prices which are functions of time; some have features where exercising one option automatically gives the holder another option; and so on. Up to now, the variables underlying options and other derivative securities have usually been stock prices, stock indices, interest rates, exchange rates, and commodity prices. However, other variables can be, and on occasion have been, used. For example, ski slope operators have been known to issue bonds where the payoff depends on the total snow falling at a certain resort, and banks have been known to create deposit instruments where the interest paid depends on the performance of the local football team.

1.5 TYPES OF TRADERS

Traders of derivative securities can be categorized as hedgers, speculators, or arbitrageurs. We now take a first look at each each of these.

HEDGERS

Hedgers are interested in reducing a risk that they already face. Suppose that a U.S. company knows that it is due to pay £1,000,000 to one of its British suppliers in 90 days. It is faced with a significant foreign exchange risk. The cost, in U.S. dollars, of making the payment depends on the sterling exchange rate in 90 days. Using the rates quoted in Table 1.1, the company can choose to hedge by entering into a long forward contract to buy £1,000,000 in 90 days for $1,709,000. The effect is to lock in the exchange rate that will apply to the sterling it requires.

This hedge using forward exchange rates requires no initial payment. In some circumstances it saves the company a significant amount of money. For example, if the exchange rate rises to 1.8000, the company ends up $91,000 better off if it hedges. In other circumstances, the company may wish it had not hedged. For example, if the exchange rate falls to 1.6000, hedging leads to an outcome that is $109,000 worse than no hedging. This emphasizes that the purpose of hedging is to make the outcome more certain. It does not necessarily improve the outcome.

As an alternative to a forward contract, the company could buy a call option to acquire £1,000,000 at a certain exchange rate, say 1.7000, in 90 days. If the actual exchange rate in 90 days proves to be above 1.7000, the company exercises the option and buys the sterling it requires for $1,700,000. If the actual exchange rate proves to be below 1.7000, the company buys the sterling in the market in the usual way. This option strategy enables the company to insure itself against adverse exchange rate movements while still benefitting from favorable movements. Of course this insurance is achieved at a cost. Whereas forward contracts require no initial payment, option contracts can be quite expensive.

SPECULATORS

Whereas hedgers want to eliminate an exposure to movements in the price of an asset, speculators wish to take a position in the market. Either they are betting that a price will go up or they are betting that it will go down.

Forward contracts can be used for speculation. An investor who thinks that sterling will increase in value relative to the U.S. dollar can speculate by taking a long position in a forward contract on sterling. Suppose that in the situation depicted in Table 1.1, the actual spot sterling exchange rate in 90 days proves to be 1.7600. An investor who enters into a long position in a 90-day forward contract will be able to purchase pounds for $1.7090 when they are worth $1.7600. He or she will realize a gain of $0.0510 per pound.

There is an important difference between speculating using forward markets and speculating by buying the underlying asset (in this case, a currency) in the spot market. Buying a certain amount of the underlying asset in the spot market requires an initial cash payment equal to the total value of what is bought. Entering into a forward contract on the same amount of the asset requires no initial cash payment.[4] Speculating using forward markets therefore provides an investor with a much higher level of leverage than speculating using spot markets.

Options when used for speculation also give extra leverage. To illustrate this point, suppose that a stock price is $32 and an investor who feels that it will rise buys call options with a strike price of $35 for $0.50 per option. If the price does not go above $35 during the life of the option, the investor will lose $0.50 per option (or 100 percent of the investment). However, if the price rises to $40, the investor will realize a profit of $4.50 per option (or 900 percent of the original investment).

ARBITRAGEURS

Arbitrageurs are a third important group of participants in derivative securities markets. Arbitrage involves locking in a riskless profit by simultaneously entering into transactions in two or more markets. In later chapters, we will show how arbitrage is sometimes possible when the futures price of an asset gets out of line with its cash price. We will also discuss how arbitrage arguments can be used in option pricing. In this section, we illustrate the concept of arbitrage with a very simple example.

---

[4]In practice, a financial institution when entering into a forward contract with a speculator may require the speculator to deposit some funds up front. These funds, which usually earn interest, are generally a relatively small proportion of the value of the assets underlying the contract. They serve as a guarantee that the contract will be honored by the speculator.

Consider a stock that is traded in both New York and London. Suppose that the stock price is \$172 in New York and £100 in London at a time when the exchange rate is \$1.7500 per pound. An arbitrageur could simultaneously buy 100 shares of the stock in New York and sell them in London to obtain risk-free profit of

$$100 \times (\$1.75 \times 100 - \$172)$$

or \$300 in the absence of transactions costs. Transactions costs would probably eliminate the profit for a small investor. However, large investment houses face very low transactions costs in both the stock market and the foreign exchange market. They would find the arbitrage opportunity very attractive and would try to take as much advantage of it as possible.

Arbitrage opportunities such as the one that has just been described cannot last for long. As arbitrageurs buy the stock in New York, the forces of supply and demand will cause the dollar price to rise. Similarly, as they sell the stock in London, the sterling price will be driven down. Very quickly, the two prices will become equivalent at the current exchange rate. Indeed, the existence of profit-hungry arbitrageurs makes it unlikely that a major disparity between the sterling price and the dollar price could ever exist in the first place.

Generalizing from this example, we can say that the very existence of arbitrageurs means that, in practice, only very small arbitrage opportunities are observed in the prices that are quoted in most financial markets. In this book, most of our arguments concerning futures prices and the values of option contracts will be based on the assumption that there are no arbitrage opportunities.

1.6 SUMMARY

One of the interesting developments in financial markets over the last 15 to 20 years has been the growing popularity of derivative securities or contingent claims. In many situations, both hedgers and speculators find it more attractive to trade a derivative security on an asset than to trade the asset itself. Some derivative securities are traded on exchanges. Others are made available to corporate clients by financial institutions or added to new issues of securities by underwriters. There seems to be no shortage of new ideas in this area. Much of this book is concerned with the valuation of derivative securities. The aim is to present a unifying framework within which all derivative securities—not just options or futures—can be valued.

In this chapter, we have taken a first look at forward, futures, and options contracts. A forward or futures contract involves an obligation to buy or sell an asset at a certain time in the future for a certain price. There are two types of options: calls and puts. A call option gives the holder the right to buy an asset by a certain date for a certain price. A put option gives the holder the right to sell an asset by a certain date for a certain price. Forwards, futures, and options are now traded on a wide range of different assets.

Derivative securities have been very successful innovations in capital markets. Three main types of traders can be identified: hedgers, speculators, and arbitrageurs. Hedgers are in the position where they face risk associated with the price of an asset. They use derivative securities to reduce or eliminate this risk. Speculators wish to bet on future movements in the price of an asset. They use derivative securities to get extra leverage. Arbitrageurs are in business to take advantage of a discrepancy between prices in two different markets. If, for example, they see the futures price of an asset getting out of line with the cash price, they will take offsetting positions in the two markets to lock in a profit.

QUESTIONS AND PROBLEMS

1.1. What is the difference between a long forward position and a short forward position?

1.2. Explain carefully the difference between (a) hedging; (b) speculation; and (c) arbitrage.

1.3. What is the difference between
  (a) entering into a long forward contract when the forward price is $50 and
  (b) taking a long position in a call option with a strike price of $50?

1.4. An investor enters into a short cotton futures contract when the futures price is 50 cents per pound. The contract is for the delivery of 50,000 pounds. How much does the investor gain or lose if the cotton price at the end of the contract is (a) 48.20 cents per pound; and (b) 51.30 cents per pound?

1.5. Suppose that you write a put option contract on 100 IBM shares with a strike price of $120 and an expiration date in 3 months. The current price of IBM stock is $121. What have you committed yourself to? How much could you gain or lose?

1.6. You would like to speculate on a rise in the price of a certain stock. The current stock price is $29 and a 3-month call with a strike of $30 costs $2.90. You have $5,800 to invest. Identify two alternative strategies, one involving an investment in the stock and the other involving investment in the option. What are the potential gains and losses from each?

1.7. Suppose you own 5,000 shares worth $25 each. How can put options be used to provide you with insurance against a decline in the value of your holding over the next 4 months?

1.8. A stock, when it is first issued, provides funds for a company. Is the same true of a stock option? Discuss.

1.9. Explain why a forward contract can be used for either speculation or hedging.

1.10. Suppose that a European call option to buy a share for $50 costs $2.50 and is held until maturity. Under what circumstances will the holder of the option make a profit?

Under what circumstances will the option be exercised? Draw a diagram illustrating how the profit from a long position in the option depends on the stock price at maturity of the option.

1.11. Suppose that a European put option to sell a share for $60 costs $4.00 and is held until maturity. Under what circumstances will the seller of the option (i.e., the party with the short position) make a profit? Under what circumstances will the option be exercised? Draw a diagram illustrating how the profit from a short position in the option depends on the stock price at maturity of the option.

1.12. An investor writes a September call option with a strike price of $20. It is now May, the stock price is $18, and the option price is $2. Describe the investor's cash flows if the option is held until September and the stock price is $25 at this time.

1.13. An investor writes a December European put option with a strike price of $30. The price of the option is $4. Under what circumstances does the investor make a gain?

1.14. Interest rate caps are described in Section 1.4. Which of the following is more valuable,
   (a) a cap which guarantees that the rate of interest paid on a floating-rate loan never goes above 10% or
   (b) a cap which guarantees that the average rate of interest paid on a floating-rate loan during its life is below 10%?
   Explain your answer.

1.15. Show that the Standard Oil bond described in the Section 1.4 is a combination of a regular bond, a long position in call options on oil with a strike price of $25, and a short position in call options on oil with a strike price of $40.

1.16. A company knows it is due to receive a certain amount of a foreign currency in 4 months. What type of option contract is appropriate for hedging?

1.17. The price of gold is currently $500 per ounce. The futures price for delivery in one year is $700. An arbitrageur can borrow money at 10% per annum. What should the arbitrageur do? Assume that the cost of storing gold is zero.

1.18. The Chicago Board of Trade offers a futures contract on long-term Treasury bonds. Characterize the investors likely to use this contract.

1.19. The current price of a stock is $94 and 3-month call options with a strike price of $95 currently sell for $4.70. An investor who feels that the price of the stock will increase is trying to decide between buying 100 shares and buying 2,000 call options (= 20 contracts). Both strategies involve an investment of $9,400. What advice would you give? How high does the stock price have to rise for the option strategy to be more profitable?

1.20. "Options and futures are zero-sum games." What do you think is meant by this statement?

1.21. Describe the payoff from the following portfolio: a long forward contract on an asset and a long European put option on the asset with the same maturity as the forward contract and a strike price that is equal to the forward price of the asset at the time the portfolio is set up.

1.22. Show that a range forward contract, such as the one described in Section 1.4, is a combination of two options. How can a range forward contract be constructed so that it has zero value?

1.23. Show that an ICON, such as the one described in Section 1.4, is a combination of a regular bond and two options.

1.24. On July 1, 1992, a company enters into a forward contract to buy 10 million Japanese yen on January 1, 1993. On September 1, 1992, it enters into a forward contract to sell 10 million Japanese yen on January 1, 1993. Describe the payoff from this strategy.

1.25. Suppose that sterling–U.S. dollar spot and forward exchange rates are as given in Table 1.1. What opportunities are open to an investor in the following situations?
(a) A 180-day European call option to buy £1 for $1.6700 costs 2 cents.
(b) A 90-day European put option to sell £1 for $1.73 costs 2 cents.

1.26. "A long forward contract is equivalent to a long position in a European call option and a short position in a European put option." Explain this statement.

2 Futures Markets and the Use of Futures for Hedging

Futures contracts were introduced in Chapter 1. They are agreements to buy or sell an asset in the future for a certain price. Unlike forward contracts they are usually traded on an exchange. In this chapter, we explain the way in which exchanges organize the trading of futures contracts. We discuss issues such as the specification of contracts, the operation of margin accounts, and the way in which quotes are made. We also discuss how futures contracts are used for hedging purposes.

2.1 TRADING FUTURES CONTRACTS

Suppose it is March and you call your broker with instructions to buy, at the market price, one July corn futures contract (5,000 bushels) on the Chicago Board of Trade (CBOT) at the current market price. What happens? As a first step in the process, the broker passes your instructions on to a representative at the CBOT. From there, the instructions are sent by messenger to a trader on the floor of the exchange. This trader assesses the best price currently available and uses hand signals to indicate to other traders that he or she is willing to buy one contract at that price. If another trader indicates a willingness to take the other side of the position (i.e., short one July contract), the deal will be done. If not, the trader representing you will have to signal a willingness to trade at a higher price. Eventually someone will be found to take the other side of the transaction. Confirmation that your instructions have been carried out and a notification of the price obtained are sent back to you through your broker.

There are two types of traders in the trading pits on the floor of an exchange. These are *commission brokers*, who execute trades for other people and earn commissions; and *locals*, who trade for their own account. There are many different types of orders that can be passed on to a commission broker. In the example just given, the instructions were to take a long position in one July corn contract at the current market price. This is a *market order*. Another popular type of order is a *limit order*. This specifies a certain price and requests that the transaction be executed only if that price or a better one is obtained.

CLOSING OUT POSITIONS

Closing out a position involves entering into an opposite trade to the original one. For example, if an investor goes long one July corn futures contract on March 6, he or she can close out the position on April 20 by shorting one July corn futures contract. If an investor shorts one July contract on March 6, he or she can close out the position on April 20 by going long one July contract. In each case, the investor's total gain or loss reflects the change in the futures price between March 6 and April 20.

The vast majority of the futures contracts that are initiated are closed out in this way. The delivery of the underlying asset is relatively rare. In spite of this, it is important to understand the delivery arrangements. This is because it is the possibility of final delivery that ties the futures price to the cash price.

2.2 THE SPECIFICATION OF THE FUTURES CONTRACT

When developing a new contract, an exchange must specify in some detail the exact nature of the agreement between the two parties. In particular, it must specify the asset, the contract size (i.e., exactly how much of the asset will be delivered under one contract), how prices will be quoted, where delivery will be made, when delivery will be made, and how the price paid will be determined. Sometimes alternatives are specified for the asset that will be delivered and for the delivery arrangements. It is the party with the short position (the party that has agreed to sell) that chooses between these alternatives.

The Asset

When the asset is a commodity there may be quite a variation in the quality of what is available in the marketplace. When specifying the asset, it is therefore important that the exchange stipulate the grade or grades of the commodity that are acceptable. The New York Cotton Exchange has specified the asset in its orange juice futures contract as

> US Grade A, with Brix value of not less than 57 degrees, having a Brix value to acid ratio of not less than 13 to 1 nor more than 19 to 1, with factors of color and flavor each scoring 37 points or higher and 19 for defects, with a minimum score 94.

The Chicago Mercantile Exchange in its random-length lumber futures contract has specified that

> Each delivery unit shall consist of nominal 2×4s of random lengths from 8 feet to 20 feet, grade-stamped Construction and Standard, Standard and better, or #1 and #2; however, in no case may the quantity of Standard grade or #2 exceed 50 percent. Each delivery unit shall be manufactured in California, Idaho, Montana, Nevada, Oregon, Washington, Wyoming, or Alberta or British Columbia, Canada, and contain lumber produced from and grade-stamped Alpine fir, Englemann spruce, hem-fir, lodgepole pine and/or spruce pine fir.

In the case of some commodities, a range of grades can be delivered but the price received is adjusted depending on the grade chosen. For example, in the Chicago Board of Trade corn futures contract, the standard grade is "No. 2 Yellow," but substitutions are allowed at differentials established by the exchange.

The financial assets in futures contracts are generally well defined and unambiguous. For example, there is no need to specify the grade of a Japanese yen. However, there are some interesting features of the Treasury bond and Treasury note futures contracts traded on the Chicago Board of Trade. The underlying asset in the Treasury bond contract is any long-term U.S. Treasury bond which has a maturity of greater than 15 years and is not callable within 15 years. In the Treasury note futures contract, the underlying asset is any long-term Treasury note with a maturity no less than 6.5 years and not greater than 10 years. In both of these cases, the exchange has a formula for adjusting the price received according to the coupon and maturity date of the bond delivered. This will be discussed in Chapter 4.

The Contract Size

The contract size specifies the amount of the asset that has to be delivered under one contract. This is an important decision for the exchange. If the contract size is too large, many investors who wish to hedge relatively small exposures or who wish to take relatively small speculative positions will be unable to use the exchange. On the other hand, if the contract size is too small, trading may be expensive since there is a cost associated with each contract traded.

The correct size for a contract clearly depends on the likely user. Whereas the value of what is delivered under a futures contract on an agricultural product might be $10,000 to $20,000, it is much higher for some financial futures. For example, under the Treasury bond futures contract traded on the Chicago Board of Trade, instruments with face value of $100,000 are delivered.

DELIVERY ARRANGEMENTS

The place where delivery will be made must be specified by the exchange. This is particularly important for commodities where there may be significant transportation costs. In the case of the Chicago Mercantile Exchange random-length lumber contract, the delivery location is specified as

> On track and shall either be unitized in double-door boxcars or, at no additional cost to the buyer, each unit shall be individually paper-wrapped and loaded on flatcars. Par delivery of hem-fir in California, Idaho, Montana, Nevada, Oregon, and Washington, and in the province of British Columbia.

When alternative delivery locations are specified, the price received by the party with the short position is sometimes adjusted according to the location chosen by that party. For example, in the case of the corn futures contract traded by the Chicago Board of Trade, delivery can be made at Chicago, Burns Habor, Toledo, or St. Louis. Deliveries at Toledo and St. Louis are made at a discount of 4 cents per bushel from the Chicago contract price.

A futures contract is referred to by its delivery month. The exchange must specify the precise period during the month when delivery can be made. For many futures contracts, the delivery period is the whole month.

The delivery months vary from contract to contract and are chosen by the exchange to meet the needs of market participants. For example, currency futures on the International Monetary Exchange (IMM) have delivery months of March, June, September, and December; corn futures traded on the Chicago Board of Trade have delivery months of March, May, July, September, and December. At any given time, contracts trade for the closest delivery month and a number of subsequent delivery months. The exchange specifies when trading in a particular month's contract will begin. The exchange also specifies the last day on which trading can take place for a given contract. This is generally a few days before the last day on which delivery can be made.

PRICE QUOTES

The futures price is quoted in a way that is convenient and easy to understand. For example, crude oil futures prices on the New York Mercantile Exchange

(NYMEX) are quoted in dollars per barrel to two decimal places (i.e., to the nearest cent). Treasury bond and Treasury note futures prices on the Chicago Board of Trade are quoted in dollars and 32nds of a dollar. The minimum price movement that can occur in trading is consistent with the way in which the price is quoted. Thus, it is $0.01 (or 1 cent per barrel) for the oil futures and one-32nd of a dollar for the Treasury bond and Treasury note futures.

DAILY PRICE MOVEMENT LIMITS

For most contracts, daily price movement limits are specified by the exchange. For example, at the time of writing, the daily price movement limit for oil futures is $1. If the price moves down by an amount equal to the daily price limit, the contract is said to be *limit down*. If it moves up by the limit, it is said to be *limit up*. A *limit move* is a move in either direction equal to the daily price limit. Normally, trading on a contract ceases for the day once the contract is limit up or limit down, but in some instances, the exchange has the authority to step in and change the limits.

The purpose of daily price limits is to prevent large price movements occurring because of speculative excesses. However, these limits can become an artificial barrier to trading when the price of the underlying commodity is advancing or declining rapidly. Whether price limits are, on balance, good for futures markets is controversial.

POSITION LIMITS

Position limits are the maximum number of contracts that a speculator may hold. In the Chicago Mercantile Exchange random-length lumber contract, for example, the position limit (at the time of writing) is 1,000 contracts with no more than 300 in any one delivery month. Bona fide hedgers are not affected by position limits. The purpose of the limits is to prevent speculators from exercising undue influence on the market.

2.3 THE OPERATION OF MARGINS

If two investors get in touch with each other directly and agree to trade an asset in the future for a certain price, there are obvious risks. One of the investors may regret the deal and try to back out. Alternatively, the investor simply may not have the financial resources to honor the agreement. One of the key roles of the exchange is to organize trading so that contract defaults are minimized. This is where margins come in.

MARKING TO MARKET

To illustrate how margins work consider an investor who contacts his or her broker on Monday, June 1, 1992, to buy two December 1992 gold futures contracts on the New York Commodity Exchange (COMEX). We suppose that the current futures price is $400 per ounce. Since the contract size is 100 ounces, the investor has contracted to buy a total of 200 ounces at this price. The broker will require the investor to deposit funds in what is termed a *margin account*. The amount that must be deposited at the time the contract is first entered into is known as the *initial margin*. This is determined by the broker. We will suppose this is $2,000 per contract, or $4,000 in total. At the end of each trading day, the margin account is adjusted to reflect the investor's gain or loss. This is known as *marking to market* the account.

Suppose, for example, that by the end of the June 1, the futures price has dropped from $400 to $397. The investor has a loss of 200 × $3 or $600. This is because the 200 ounces of December gold, which he or she contracted to buy at $400, can now be sold for only $397. The balance in the margin account would therefore be reduced by $600 to $3,400. Similarly, if the price of December gold rose to $403 by the end of the first day, the balance in the margin account would be increased by $600 to $4,600. A trade is first marked to market at the close of the day on which it takes place. It is then marked to market at the close of trading on each subsequent day. It the delivery period is reached and delivery is made by the party with the short position, the price received is generally the futures price at the time the contract was last marked to market.

Note that marking to market is not merely an arrangement between broker and client. When there is a $600 decrease in the futures price so that the margin account of an investor with a long position is reduced by $600, the investor's broker has to pay the exchange $600 and the exchange passes the money on to the broker of an investor with a short position. Similarly, when there is an increase in the futures price, brokers for parties with short positions pay money to the exchange, and brokers for parties with long positions receive money from the exchange. We will give more details of the mechanism by which this happens later in this section.

MAINTENANCE MARGIN

The investor is entitled to withdraw any balance in the margin account in excess of the initial margin. To ensure that the balance in the margin account never becomes negative, a *maintenance margin*, which is somewhat lower than the initial margin, is set. If the balance in the margin account falls below the maintenance margin, the investor receives a *margin call* and is requested to top up the margin account to the initial margin level within a very short period of time. The extra funds deposited are known as a *variation margin*. If the investor does not provide the variation margin, the broker closes out the position by selling the contract. In the case of the investor in the previous example, closing out the position would involve neutralizing the existing contract by selling 200 ounces of gold for delivery in December.

Table 2.1 illustrates the operation of the margin account for one possible sequence of futures prices in the case of the investor considered here. The maintenance margin is assumed for the purpose of the illustration to be $1,500 per contract or $3,000 in total. On June 9, the balance in the margin account falls $340 below the maintenance margin level. This triggers a margin call from the broker for additional margin of $1,340. The table assumes that the investor does in

TABLE 2.1   Operation of Margins for a Long
Position in Two Gold Futures Contracts

The initial margin is $2,000 per contract or $4,000 in total; the
maintenance margin is $1,500 per contract or $3,000 in total.
The contract is entered into on June 1 at $400 and closed out on
June 22 at $392.30. The numbers in the second column, except
for the first and last numbers, are the futures price at the close
of trading.

Day	Futures Price (dollars)	Daily Gain (Loss) (dollars)	Cumulative Gain (Loss) (dollars)	Margin Account Balance (dollars)	Margin Call (dollars)
	400.00			4,000	
June 1	397.00	(600)	(600)	3,400	
June 2	396.10	(180)	(780)	3,220	
June 3	398.20	420	(360)	3,640	
June 4	397.10	(220)	(580)	3,420	
June 5	396.70	(80)	(660)	3,340	
June 8	395.40	(260)	(920)	3,080	
June 9	393.30	(420)	(1,340)	2,660	1,340
June 10	393.60	60	(1,280)	4,060	
June 11	391.80	(360)	(1,640)	3,700	
June 12	392.70	180	(1,460)	3,880	
June 15	387.00	(1,140)	(2,600)	2,740	1,260
June 16	387.00	0	(2,600)	4,000	
June 17	388.10	220	(2,380)	4,220	
June 18	388.70	120	(2,260)	4,340	
June 19	391.00	460	(1,800)	4,800	
June 22	392.30	260	(1,540)	5,060	

fact provide this margin by close of trading on June 10. On June 15, the balance in the margin account again falls below the maintenance margin level and a margin call for $1,260 is sent out. The investor provides this margin by close of trading on June 16. On the June 22, the investor decides to close out the position by shorting the two contracts. The futures price on that day is 392.30 and the investor has made a cumulative loss of $1,540. Note that the investor has excess margin on June 10, 17, 18, and 19. The table assumes that this is not withdrawn.

FURTHER DETAILS

Some brokers allow an investor to earn interest on the balance in his or her margin account. The balance in the account does not therefore represent a true cost, providing the interest rate is competitive with that which could be earned elsewhere. To satisfy the initial margin requirements (but not subsequent margin calls), an investor can sometimes deposit securities with the broker. Treasury bills are usually accepted in lieu of cash, at about 90 percent of their face value. Shares are also sometimes accepted in lieu of cash—but at about 50 percent of their face value.

The effect of the marking to market is that a futures contract is settled daily rather than all at the end of its life. At the end of each day, the investor's gain (loss) is added to (subtracted from) the margin account. This brings the value of the contract back to zero. A futures contract is, in effect, closed out and rewritten at a new price each day.

Minimum levels for initial and maintenance margins are set by the exchange. Individual brokers may require greater margins from their clients than those specified by the exchange. However, brokers cannot require lower margins than those specified by the exchange. Margin levels are determined by the variability of the price of the underlying asset. The higher this variability, the higher the margin levels. A maintenance margin is usually about 75 percent of the initial margin.

Margin requirements may depend on the objectives of the trader. A bona fide hedger, such as a company that produces the commodity on which the futures contract is written, is often subject to lower margin requirements than a speculator. This is because there is deemed to be less risk of default. What are known as day trades and spread transactions often give rise to lower margin requirements than hedge transactions. A *day trade* is a trade where the trader announces to the broker that he or she plans to close out the position in the same day. Thus, if the trader has taken a long position, the plan is to take an offsetting short position later in the day; if the trader has taken a short position, the plan is to take an offsetting long position later in the day. A *spread transaction* is one where the trader simultaneously takes a long position in the contract with one delivery month and a short position in a contract with another delivery month.

Note that margin requirements are the same on short futures positions as they are on long futures positions. It is just as easy to take a short futures position as it is to take a long futures position. The cash market does not have this symmetry. Taking a long position in the cash market involves buying the asset and presents no problems. Taking a short position involves selling an asset that you do not own. This is a more complex transaction that may or may not be possible in a particular market. It will be discussed further in the next chapter.

THE CLEARINGHOUSE AND CLEARING MARGINS

The *exchange clearinghouse* is an adjunct of the exchange and acts as an intermediary or middleman in futures transactions. It guarantees the performance of the parties to each transaction. The clearinghouse has a number of members all of which have offices close to the clearinghouse. Brokers who are not clearinghouse members themselves must channel their business through a member. The main task of the clearinghouse is to keep track of all the transactions that take place during a day so that it can calculate the net position of each of its members.

Just as an investor is required to maintain a margin account with his or her broker, a clearinghouse member is required to maintain a margin account with the clearinghouse. This is known as a *clearing margin*. The margin accounts for clearinghouse members are adjusted for gains and losses at the end of each trading day in the same way as the margin accounts of investors. However, in the case of the clearinghouse member, there is an original margin but no maintenance margin. Every day, the account balance for each contract must be maintained at an amount equal to the original margin times the number of contracts outstanding. Thus, depending on transactions during the day and price movements, the clearinghouse member may have to add funds to its margin account at the end of the day. Alternatively, it may find it can remove funds from the account at this time. Brokers who are not clearinghouse members must maintain a margin account with a clearinghouse member.

In the calculation of clearing margins, the exchange clearinghouse calculates the number of contracts outstanding on either a gross or a net basis. The *gross basis* adds the total of all long positions entered into by clients to the total of all the short positions entered into by clients. The *net basis* allows these to be offset against each other. Suppose a clearinghouse member has two clients, one with a long position in 20 contracts, the other with a short position in 15 contracts. Gross margining would calculate the clearing margin on the basis of 35 contracts; net margining would calculate the clearing margin on the basis of 5 contracts. Most exchanges currently use net margining.

It should be stressed that the whole purpose of the margining system is to reduce the possibility of market participants sustaining losses because of defaults. Overall, the system has been very successful. Losses arising from defaults have been almost nonexistent.

2.4 NEWSPAPER QUOTES

Many newspapers carry futures quotations. In *The Wall Street Journal*, futures quotations can currently be found under the headings "Commodities," "Interest Rate Instruments," "Index Trading," and "Foreign Exchange" in the Money and Investing section. Table 2.2 shows the quotations for commodities as they appeared in *The Wall Street Journal* on Friday, October 18, 1991. These refer to the trading that took place on the previous day (Thursday, October 17, 1991). The quotations for index futures and currency futures are given in Chapter 3. The quotations for interest rate futures are given in Chapter 4.

The asset underlying the futures contract, the exchange it is traded on, the contract size, and how the price is quoted are all shown at the top of each section. The first asset in Table 2.2 is corn, traded on the Chicago Board of Trade. The contract size is 5,000 bushels and the price is quoted in cents per bushel. The months in which particular contracts are traded are shown in the first column. Corn contracts with maturities in December 1991, March 1992, May 1992, July 1992, September 1992, and December 1992 were traded on October 17, 1991.

PRICES

The first three numbers in each row show the opening price, the highest price achieved in trading during the day, and the lowest price achieved in trading during the day. The opening price is representative of the prices at which contracts were trading immediately after the opening bell. For December corn on October 17, 1991, the opening price was $247\frac{1}{4}$ cents per bushel; during the day, the price traded between $246\frac{3}{4}$ cents and $249\frac{1}{4}$ cents.

SETTLEMENT PRICE

The fourth number in the row is the *settlement price*. This is the average of the prices at which the contract traded immediately before the bell signaling the end of trading for the day. The fifth number is the change in the settlement price from the previous day. In the case of the December 1991 corn futures contract, the settlement price was 248 cents on October 17, 1991, up 2 cents from October 16, 1991.

The settlement price is important because it is used for calculating daily gains and losses and margin requirements. In the case of the December 1991 corn futures contract, an investor with a long position in one contract would find that his or her margin account balance increased by $100 (= 5,000 × 2 cents) between October 16 and October 17, 1991. Similarly, an investor with a short position in one contract would find that the margin balance decreased by $100 between October 16, 1991 and October 17, 1991.

TABLE 2.2 Commodity Futures Quotes from *The Wall Street Journal*, October 18, 1991

COMMODITIES FUTURES PRICES

Thursday, October 17, 1991.

Open Interest Reflects Previous Trading Day.

	Open	High	Low	Settle	Change	Lifetime High	Lifetime Low	Open Interest
–GRAINS AND OILSEEDS–								
CORN (CBT) 5,000 bu.; cents per bu.								
Dec	247¼	249¼	246¾	248	+ 2	275	220	121,226
Mr92	256½	258¼	256	257¼	+ 1¾	277¼	228½	66,974
May	263	264¾	262¼	263½	+ 1¾	279½	234¾	24,144
July	267¼	269½	266¾	268	+ 1¾	282	239½	15,280
Sept	259½	260¾	259½	260	+ 1	265	236½	2,529
Dec	257¼	257½	256	256¾	+ ⅛	262½	236½	6,905
Est vol 33,000; vol Wed 34,250; open int 237,082, +1,880.								
OATS (CBT) 5,000 bu.; cents per bu.								
Dec	134¾	135	133	133¼	– ¾	151½	118½	9,237
Mr92	143½	144	141¾	142¼	– ½	157	126½	1,968
May	149	149	148½	147	– 1	159½	132	216
July	152	152½	151¼	150	– 1	161½	139¾	185
Est vol 1,250; vol Wed 1,549; open int 11,649, +113.								
SOYBEANS (CBT) 5,000 bu.; cents per bu.								
Nov	554½	556½	546½	547¼	– 4¾	675	517	46,939
Ja92	566	568	558	558½	– 4¾	659	527½	26,160
Mar	576½	579	569	569¾	– 4½	666	538	20,226
May	586½	589	578	578¼	– 6¼	668	547	8,245
July	593½	596½	586½	586¾	– 5½	668	554	8,703
Aug	597	597½	589	589	– 4¾	660	565	739
Sept	589	589	585	582	– 3	628	557	651
Nov	589½	591½	582¼	582½	– 6½	620¾	552	4,806
Est vol 37,000; vol Wed 26,970; open int 116,471, –340.								
SOYBEAN MEAL (CBT) 100 tons; $ per ton.								
Oct	183.50	184.00	181.40	181.40	– .80	201.00	159.90	2,041
Dec	180.70	181.20	178.70	178.70	– 1.30	198.50	160.00	32,996
Ja92	180.30	180.30	178.00	178.10	– 1.20	197.00	161.30	10,054
Mar	179.00	179.00	176.70	176.70	– 1.10	197.00	163.50	11,445
May	176.50	177.00	175.20	175.20	– 1.10	194.00	164.50	5,992
July	176.20	177.00	175.10	175.20	– .90	196.00	166.00	2,918
Aug	176.50	176.70	175.00	175.00	– 1.00	188.50	172.00	1,015
Sept	176.00	176.50	176.00	175.50	– .50	186.00	172.00	860
Oct	189.00	189.00	187.50	187.50	– .50	194.00	186.00	324
Dec	189.00	189.00	188.00	188.00	-1.20	199.00	187.00	435
Est vol 18,000; vol Wed 18,081; open int 68,080, +1,833.								
May	44.90	45.00	43.15	43.50	– 1.62	59.00	43.15	1,003
July	45.10	45.10	43.55	43.90	– 1.42	59.00	43.55	228
Est vol 4,936; vol Wed 2,668; open int 10,872, +271.								
–FOOD & FIBER–								
COCOA (CSCE)–10 metric tons; $ per ton.								
Dec	1,211	1,227	1,211	1,219	+ 8	1,535	953	18,040
Mr92	1,277	1,285	1,274	1,277	+ 7	1,538	997	15,380
May	1,312	1,315	1,308	1,311	+ 8	1,385	1,036	6,236
July	1,338	1,342	1,338	1,341	+ 11	1,410	1,056	4,213
Sept	1,366	1,370	1,365	1,365	+ 7	1,420	1,080	3,337
Dec	1,403	1,403	1,396	1,402	+ 10	1,460	1,119	2,495
Mr93	1,437	1,437	1,430	1,434	+ 9	1,490	1,272	2,585
May	....	....	....	1,459	+ 9	1,450	1,210	1,117
July	....	....	....	1,484	+ 9	1,447	1,320	842
Est vol 3,723; vol Wed 6,166; open int 54,245, –365.								
COFFEE (CSCE)–37,500 lbs.; cents per lb.								
Dec	82.00	83.75	82.00	82.80	+ .30	116.00	78.90	27,347
Mr92	86.15	87.60	86.15	86.65	+ .20	107.50	80.10	12,571
May	88.65	90.10	88.65	89.15	+ .35	106.00	85.40	2,856
July	91.50	91.90	91.50	91.65	+ 1.15	108.00	87.85	907
Sept	93.70	94.70	93.70	94.15	+ 1.15	108.00	90.50	719
Dec	97.00	97.00	96.95	96.95	– 2.05	107.25	93.90	109
Est vol 10,008; vol Wed 7,739; open int 44,509, –187.								
SUGAR–WORLD (CSCE)–112,000 lbs.; cents per lb.								
Mar	8.79	8.89	8.79	8.80	– .02	10.14	7.56	53,748
May	8.69	8.78	8.69	8.70	– .01	9.77	7.67	18,993
July	8.68	8.72	8.67	8.68	– .02	9.16	7.85	9,353
Oct	8.67	8.68	8.64	8.64	– .04	9.06	8.05	6,877
Mar	....	....	....	8.62	+ .04	8.45	8.37	215
Est vol 6,985; vol Wed 14,128; open int 89,186, –1,047.								
SUGAR–DOMESTIC (CSCE)–112,000 lbs.; cents per lb.								
Jan	21.75	21.75	21.70	21.71	+ .01	23.01	21.68	3,260
Mar	21.80	21.82	21.80	21.80	....	22.80	21.74	3,219
July	....	....	....	456.9	+ 1.1	470.5	439.0	1,383
Est vol 8,000; vol Wed 10,704; open int 92,152, +1,676.								
SILVER (CBT)–1,000 troy oz.; cents per troy oz.								
Oct	407.0	410.0	405.0	410.0	....	537.0	380.0	2
Dec	414.0	415.0	408.0	412.0	– 1.0	575.0	374.0	4,277
Fb92	419.0	419.0	415.0	416.5	– 0.5	476.0	384.0	123
Apr	424.0	424.0	419.0	421.0	....	485.0	385.0	123
June	429.0	429.0	424.0	425.0	– 1.0	494.0	400.0	839
Est vol 50; vol Wed 82; open int 5,389, –7.								
CRUDE OIL, Light Sweet (NYM) 1,000 bbls.; $ per bbl.								
Nov	23.78	23.96	23.72	23.93	+ .26	28.10	17.20	40,068
Dec	23.53	23.68	23.48	23.66	+ .23	27.70	17.10	82,651
Ja92	23.25	23.38	23.22	23.36	+ .21	27.60	17.25	44,203
Feb	22.96	23.05	22.91	23.06	+ .18	27.00	17.50	23,465
Mar	22.68	22.70	22.62	22.74	+ .14	26.75	17.25	15,170
Apr	22.38	22.38	22.31	22.42	+ .10	26.50	17.50	24,906
May	22.14	22.14	22.03	22.17	+ .08	24.60	17.30	9,133
June	21.93	21.93	21.82	21.97	+ .06	24.50	17.70	9,997
July	21.79	21.79	21.70	21.80	+ .04	23.59	17.90	7,897
Aug	21.67	21.67	21.54	21.66	+ .03	21.48	17.75	5,727
Sept	21.42	21.42	21.42	21.54	+ .02	24.00	17.78	2,448
Oct	....	....	....	21.43	....	22.00	18.85	2,586
Nov	21.25	21.25	21.25	21.36	– .01	21.45	19.70	2,235
Dec	21.25	21.25	21.25	21.31	– .02	24.00	18.25	8,459
Ja93	21.25	21.25	21.25	21.24	– .02	21.25	20.10	2,559
Feb	....	....	....	21.19	– .02	20.91	20.50	1,103
Mar	....	....	....	21.16	– .02	21.25	18.64	3,002
June	....	....	....	21.14	– .02	23.00	18.60	9,199
Sept	....	....	....	21.15	– .02	21.05	20.85	620
Dec	....	....	....	21.16	– .02	23.00	18.70	6,844
Ju94	....	....	....	21.26	– .02	21.35	20.60	6,969
Est vol 88,860; vol Wed 133,188; open int 309,246, +3,722.								
HEATING OIL NO. 2 (NYM) 42,000 gal.; $ per gal.								
Nov	.6880	.6955	.6870	.6940	+.0096	.7800	.5230	24,422
Dec	.6995	.7060	.6980	.7044	+.0082	.8262	.5330	47,506
Ja92	.7010	.7065	.7000	.7052	+.0069	.8200	.5340	28,438
Feb	.6835	.6870	.6820	.6862	+.0064	.6870	.5225	17,725
Mar	.6500	.6525	.6490	.6520	+.0057	.6525	.5415	6,590
Apr	.6175	.6220	.6175	.6225	+.0057	.6220	.5000	7,805

TABLE 2.2 Commodity Futures Quotes from *The Wall Street Journal*, October 18, 1991 (*continued*)

SOYBEAN OIL (CBT) 60,000 lbs.; cents per lb.								
Oct	19.44	19.54	19.33	19.34	+ .04	24.90	18.50	1,216
Dec	19.70	19.79	19.55	19.55	....	24.75	18.81	27,637
Ja92	19.84	19.95	19.73	19.74	....	24.15	19.00	13,140
Mar	20.16	20.28	20.03	20.05	– .02	24.10	19.31	11,499
May	20.52	20.60	20.32	20.33	– .04	24.00	19.60	4,158
July	20.83	20.85	20.58	20.59	– .09	24.30	19.88	1,790
Aug	20.70	20.70	20.70	20.70	– .11	22.20	20.70	557
Sept	20.85	20.85	20.75	20.75	– .20	22.30	20.90	419
Oct	20.70	20.75	20.70	20.72	– .23	22.30	20.65	426
Dec	21.07	21.07	21.07	21.05	– .20	22.60	21.00	144
Est vol 17,000; vol Wed 12,019; open int 60,986, +521.								
WHEAT (CBT) 5,000 bu.; cents per bu.								
Dec	349½	353	349	352¾	+ 3¼	353	272½	32,039
Mr92	351½	355	351½	354½	+ 2¾	355	279	17,002
May	344	346½	344	345¼	+ 1½	346½	280½	4,372
July	331	332½	330	330	+ ¾	332½	279	6,545
Sept	335½	337¼	335½	335½	+ 1	337¼	292	350
Dec	346	346½	345	345	+ ½	346½	338	180
Est vol 10,000; vol Wed 11,215; open int 60,488, +540.								
WHEAT (KC) 5,000 bu.; cents per bu.								
Dec	355	357	354	356	+ 2¾	357	272¼	19,002
Mr92	354½	357	354	356¼	+ 2½	357	275½	14,193
May	344½	348	344½	347½	+ 3¾	348	273	3,868
July	337	340	336½	339¼	+ 3¾	340	272	3,639
Est vol 5,255; vol Wed 8,593; open int 40,708, –47.								
WHEAT (MPLS) 5,000 bu.; cents per bu.								
Dec	335	338¼	335	337¾	+ 3	338¼	269½	10,104
Mr92	343	345¾	343	344½	+ 2½	345¾	279½	3,963
May	346	347	346	346½	+ 2½	347	284	697
Est vol 2,595; vol Wed 3,653; open int 14,897, –59.								
BARLEY (WPG) 20 metric tons; Can. $ per ton								
Oct	83.80	83.80	83.50	83.80	+ .50	94.50	74.70	502
Dec	85.80	85.80	85.60	85.60	....	95.80	77.20	2,407
Mr92	90.50	90.60	90.00	90.00	– .10	97.50	81.00	2,178
May	92.50	92.70	92.40	92.40	....	96.00	85.70	486
Est vol 420; vol Wed 359; open int 5,593, +127.								
FLAXSEED (WPG) 20 metric tons; Can. $ per ton								
Oct	....	....	....	194.00	– 1.10	292.00	183.00	10
Dec	199.90	200.10	197.00	197.20	– 2.70	272.50	187.10	3,688
Mr92	207.50	207.50	205.00	205.20	– 1.90	234.50	193.20	1,928
May	....	....	....	210.00	– 2.10	232.00	200.70	594
Est vol 1,725; vol Wed 385; open int 6,299, +170.								
May	21.95	21.95	21.95	21.95	– .04	22.30	21.81	1,121
July	....	....	....	22.04	– .04	22.39	21.93	1,699
Sept	....	....	....	22.05	– .03	22.39	21.95	294
Est vol 118; vol Wed 189; open int 9,588, +129.								
COTTON (CTN)–50,000 lbs.; cents per lb.								
Dec	64.00	64.05	63.28	63.29	– .66	76.35	63.28	19,798
Mr92	65.90	66.00	65.43	65.44	– .41	77.15	64.70	10,234
May	66.60	66.60	66.25	66.30	– .20	77.30	65.10	4,252
July	67.25	67.25	67.00	67.12	– .13	77.70	65.50	3,767
Oct	65.90	66.10	65.90	66.00	+ .05	70.60	65.60	461
Dec	65.85	66.05	65.81	65.85	– .12	69.00	65.30	1,636
Est vol 3,950; vol Wed 3,246; open int 40,208, –26.								
ORANGE JUICE (CTN)–15,000 lbs.; cents per lb.								
Nov	161.50	165.25	161.25	163.60	+ 2.80	166.20	111.00	3,493
Ja92	157.60	157.60	156.70	156.70	+ 8.00	157.60	113.40	5,606
Mar	158.70	158.70	158.00	158.70	+ 8.00	158.70	113.60	2,600
May	158.95	158.95	158.00	158.95	+ 8.00	158.95	115.00	634
July	158.95	158.95	158.95	158.95	+ 8.00	158.95	115.25	120
Est vol 1,800; vol Wed 1,788; open int 12,499, –252.								
–METALS & PETROLEUM–								
COPPER-HIGH (CMX)–25,000 lbs.; cents per lb.								
Oct	106.70	107.20	106.20	107.00	+ .90	109.50	95.30	1,505
Nov	106.00	106.70	105.60	106.75	+ 1.30	107.80	95.10	1,493
Dec	105.10	106.10	104.70	105.95	+ 1.30	108.50	94.50	24,915
Ja92	....	....	....	104.80	+ 1.25	105.50	95.00	938
Feb	....	....	....	104.05	+ 1.15	105.10	95.00	290
Mar	102.70	103.40	102.40	103.35	+ 1.10	106.80	93.90	4,684
Apr	....	....	....	102.80	+ 1.00	103.00	93.50	235
May	101.40	101.70	101.40	102.20	+ .95	106.20	93.30	1,915
June	....	....	....	101.85	+ .95	102.00	94.80	130
July	....	....	....	101.30	+ .85	103.80	92.80	1,591
Sept	....	....	....	100.65	+ .80	103.45	92.80	1,284
Dec	....	....	....	99.65	+ .80	100.50	91.60	1,708
Mr93	98.50	98.60	98.50	98.70	+ .75	99.50	92.80	389
Est vol 6,000; vol Wed 4,879; open int 41,291, –359.								
GOLD (CMX)–100 troy oz.; $ per troy oz.								
Oct	358.50	359.10	358.50	360.00	+ 1.80	476.00	343.00	327
Dec	360.80	362.60	360.00	362.30	+ 1.80	483.00	346.00	50,054
Fb92	363.60	365.30	363.00	365.20	+ 1.90	456.50	349.80	11,252
Apr	366.50	368.30	366.10	367.90	+ 2.00	446.00	354.00	11,252
June	368.60	369.00	368.50	370.60	+ 2.10	467.00	355.00	8,356
Aug	....	....	....	373.50	+ 2.20	426.50	359.60	4,446
Oct	....	....	....	376.20	+ 2.20	410.80	364.20	1,384
May	.6010	.6025	.6000	.6035	+ .0057	.6025	.4875	4,884
June	.5865	.5900	.5865	.5905	+ .0057	.5900	.4800	1,365
July	.5820	.5840	.5820	.5860	+ .0057	.5840	.5160	5,805
Aug	.5860	.5860	.5860	.5915	+ .0062	.5870	.5070	2,098
Sept	....	....	....	.6015	+ .0062	.5980	.5375	100
Oct	....	....	....	.6100	+ .0062	.6065	.5450	126
Dec	....	....	....	.6270	+ .0067	....	....	230
Est vol 33,364; vol Wed 40,477; open int 147,104, +1,303.								
GASOLINE, Unleaded (NYM) 42,000 gal.; $ per gal.								
Nov	.6380	.6480	.6380	.6450	+ .0124	.8675	.4860	13,942
Dec	.6355	.6400	.6345	.6390	+ .0104	.7525	.4775	19,960
Ja92	.6270	.6330	.6270	.6320	+ .0097	.6415	.4700	14,474
Feb	.6280	.6320	.6280	.6330	+ .0087	.6320	.5070	15,313
Mar	.6380	.6405	.6380	.6420	+ .0075	.6405	.5050	7,077
Apr	.6775	.6790	.6775	.6800	+ .0070	.6790	.5500	8,042
May	.6730	.6735	.6715	.6730	+ .0065	.6735	.5525	5,422
June	....	....	....	.6610	+ .0060	.6580	.5500	3,984
July	....	....	....	.6480	+ .0060	.6500	.5270	3,226
Aug	.6325	.6325	.6325	.6350	+ .0060	.6335	.5070	4,272
Est vol 21,097; vol Wed 18,810; open int 95,712, –376.								
NATURAL GAS, (NYM) 10,000 MMBtu.; $ per MMBtu's								
Nov	2.010	2.020	2.010	2.014	+ .013	2.040	1.430	2,426
Dec	2.185	2.190	2.175	2.186	+ .006	2.360	1.665	5,124
Ja92	2.315	2.315	2.305	2.314	+ .004	2.360	1.790	5,933
Feb	1.930	1.930	1.925	1.927	....	2.040	1.535	4,664
Mar	1.625	1.625	1.620	1.620	+ .004	1.675	1.350	2,120
Apr	1.460	1.461	1.460	1.461	+ .011	1.500	1.250	1,084
May	1.465	1.465	1.465	1.465	+ .005	1.495	1.250	994
June	1.475	1.475	1.473	1.475	+ .010	1.510	1.250	1,089
July	1.480	1.480	1.480	1.480	+ .005	1.510	1.270	724
Aug	1.485	1.485	1.485	1.485	....	1.520	1.420	735
Sept	....	....	....	1.510	....	1.550	1.440	589
Est vol 2,109; vol Wed 3,774; open int 25,568, +500.								
BRENT CRUDE (IPE) 1,000 net bbls.; $ per bbl.								
Dec	22.15	22.45	22.15	22.42	+ .25	22.55	18.45	29,884
Ja92	22.05	22.10	21.96	21.88	+ .79	22.17	19.40	44,775
Feb	21.72	21.75	21.62	21.72	+ .22	21.87	19.33	10,664
Mar	21.35	21.40	21.31	21.35	+ .02	21.50	19.10	2,608
Apr	21.08	21.10	21.08	20.98	+ .18	21.10	19.20	3,359
May	20.84	20.85	20.70	20.70	+ .40	20.85	19.05	2,404
June	....	....	....	20.60	+ .40	19.76	19.53	1,547
July	....	....	....	20.55	+ .40	20.28	19.45	2,795
Est vol 22,218; vol Wed 43,970; open int 98,936, –1,462.								

TABLE 2.2 Commodity Futures Quotes from *The Wall Street Journal*, October 18, 1991 *(continued)*

CANOLA (WPG) 20 metric tons; Can. $ per ton
Nov	274.10	275.50	274.40	+ .30	326.50	247.10	10,620
Ja92	280.40	281.70	280.60	+ .20	317.50	253.40	11,153
Mar	286.40	287.50	286.40	....	321.50	261.60	1,006
June	295.80	296.60	295.50	+ .90	326.40	267.00	3,258

Est vol 2,050; vol Wed 3,257; open int 1,029.

WHEAT (WPG) 20 metric tons; Can. $ per ton
Oct	99.00	99.00	98.00	-1.00	111.60	84.10	570
Dec	96.00	96.30	94.80	-1.00	104.50	86.00	4,868
Mr92	98.50	98.90	97.80	-.10	106.60	89.00	4,316
May	100.70	101.00	100.00	-.20	104.00	92.00	1,081
July	102.60	102.90	102.50	+.50	102.90	100.30	143

Est vol 1,460; vol Wed 1,260; open int 10,978, +393.

—LIVESTOCK & MEAT—

CATTLE-FEEDER (CME) 44,000 lbs.; cents per lb.
Oct	85.85	85.85	85.45	85.67	-.17	88.10	80.20	2,484
Nov	86.35	86.35	85.65	85.82	-.45	88.00	80.90	3,846
Ja92	85.37	85.37	84.90	85.07	-.25	87.80	80.80	2,171
Mar	83.52	83.65	83.25	83.60	-.20	87.00	79.90	952
Apr	83.20	83.20	83.00	83.17	-.22	87.00	79.90	461
May	82.05	82.25	82.02	82.10	-.02	86.50	78.95	390
Aug	81.85	81.95	81.70	81.70	+.10	83.00	80.50	85

Est vol 1,548; vol Wed 1,741; open int 10,410, -232.

CATTLE-LIVE (CME) 40,000 lbs.; cents per lb.
Oct	73.90	74.25	73.75	74.20	-.27	74.90	68.62	5,957
Dec	76.95	77.00	76.65	76.95	+.10	77.27	71.15	24,981
Fb92	75.75	75.95	75.67	75.67	+.07	76.70	71.10	14,263
Apr	75.75	75.75	75.45	75.45	-.05	77.00	72.10	9,705
June	72.55	72.55	72.30	72.47	-.07	75.95	70.25	3,915
Aug	70.75	70.75	70.30	70.30	-.20	72.60	69.25	958
Oct	71.10	71.10	71.00	71.00	-.02	72.10	69.80	135

Est vol 10,962; vol Wed 16,125; open int 69,914, -606.

HOGS (CME) 40,000 lbs.; cents per lb.
Oct	44.60	44.60	44.00	44.00	-.60	49.55	42.05	1,751
Dec	44.10	44.10	43.52	43.57	-.57	48.92	42.00	8,519
Fb92	43.32	43.32	42.80	42.90	-.45	48.35	41.60	3,779
Apr	41.80	41.87	41.35	41.37	-.40	46.62	40.70	2,650
June	46.30	46.30	46.10	46.10	-.17	50.60	45.55	416
July	46.20	46.45	46.15	46.20	-.17	48.20	45.55	267
Aug				44.87	-.10	46.85	44.10	185

Est vol 4,112; vol Wed 3,780; open int 17,618, -141.

PORK BELLIES (CME) 40,000 lbs.; cents per lb.
Feb	44.45	44.60	42.57	42.57	-2.00	63.15	42.42	8,017
Mar	44.15	44.22	42.50	42.42	-1.70	63.05	42.42	1,528

Dec	376.70	376.70	376.70	379.20	+2.20	431.00	366.00	2,495
Fb93				382.30	+2.30	404.20	378.00	957
Apr				385.40	+2.40	410.00	375.00	1,006
June				388.70	+2.50	418.50	376.40	2,519
Aug				392.10	+2.60			600
Oct				398.90	+2.60			100

Est vol 40,000; vol Wed 23,221; open int 94,760, +2,608.

PLATINUM (NYM)—50 troy oz.; $ per troy oz.
Oct	371.50	371.50	370.50	370.70	-1.90	513.00	330.00	516
Ja92	371.50	373.50	370.60	372.70	-1.40	451.50	334.50	13,253
Apr	374.00	376.00	374.00	376.20	-1.40	438.50	339.50	1,533
July	380.00	380.00	378.50	379.80	-1.40	427.50	342.00	771
Oct				386.80	-1.40	404.00	356.50	460

Est vol 1,568; vol Wed 1,810; open int 16,533, +40.

PALLADIUM (NYM) 100 troy oz.; $ per troy oz.
Dec	85.25	86.50	85.25	86.30	-.90	114.50	78.00	2,840
Mr92	86.50	86.50	86.50	87.20	-.90	103.50	80.30	1,139

Est vol 165; vol Wed 309; open int 4,016, +154.

SILVER (CMX)—5,000 troy oz.; cents per troy oz.
Oct	410.0	410.0	410.0	409.7	-.1	421.0	398.0	557
Dec	414.0	416.0	408.5	412.5	-.2	623.5	374.0	56,962
Mr92	421.0	422.5	415.0	419.0	-.1	613.0	382.0	11,502
May	422.0	422.0	421.0	423.4	-.1	589.0	385.0	6,001
July	430.0	430.0	426.0	427.7	-.5	557.0	395.0	4,794
Sept	429.5	429.5	429.5	432.2	-.5	483.0	408.0	1,393
Dec	436.0	436.0	436.0	438.8	+.7	507.0	408.0	6,283
Mr93				446.0	+.8	513.0	429.0	1,698
May				451.6	+1.0	473.0	438.0	1,554

EXCHANGE ABBREVIATIONS
(for commodity futures and futures options)

CBT-Chicago Board of Trade; CME-Chicago Mercantile Exchange; CMX-Commodity Exchange, New York; CRCE-Chicago Rice & Cotton Exchange; CTN-New York Cotton Exchange; CSCE-Coffee, Sugar & Cocoa Exchange, New York; FOX-London Futures and Options Exchange; IPE-International Petroleum Exchange; KC-Kansas City Board of Trade; MCE-MidAmerica Commodity Exchange; MPLS-Minneapolis Grain Exchange; NYM-New York Mercantile Exchange; PBOT-Philadelphia Board of Trade; WPG-Winnipeg Commodity Exchange.

GAS OIL (IPE) 100 metric tons; $ per ton
Nov	220.75	223.00	218.75	222.75	+2.75	235.00	169.00	28,408
Dec	210.00	223.00	219.00	223.00	+2.50	232.00	172.00	27,797
Ja92	216.00	219.75	216.00	219.50	+2.25	231.00	174.50	13,778
Feb	210.00	211.50	209.50	211.00	+2.00	220.00	175.75	5,849
Mar	200.00	202.50	200.00	202.00	+2.00	204.00	174.25	3,914
Apr	191.00	195.00	194.25	194.75	+1.50	195.00	171.00	2,728
May	188.00	188.00	188.00	188.00	+1.00	195.00	172.00	830
June				185.00	+3.00	184.00	173.00	478

Est Vol 16,030; vol Wed 21,536; open int 83,832, +1,759.

OTHER COMMODITY FUTURES

Settlement prices of selected contracts. Volume and open interest of all contract months.

	Vol.	High	Low	Close	Net Change	Lifetime High	Low	Open Interest
BROILERS (CME) 40,000 lb.; ¢ per lb.								
Dec	0		49.75	52.05			46.50	357
CATTLE-LIVE (MCE) 20,000 lb.; ¢ per lb.								
Dec	90	77.00	76.65	76.95	+ .10	77.27	71.15	296
CORN (MCE) 1,000 bu.; cents per bu.								
Dec	1,400	249¼	245¾	248	+ 2	275	220	12,258
GOLD-KILO (CBT) 32.15 troy oz.; $ per troy oz.								
Dec	50	362.5	360.5	362.3	+1.80	424.0	346.0	414
HOGS (MCE) 20,000 lb.; ¢ per lb.								
Dec	70	44.10	43.52	43.57	-.57	48.92	42.00	229
LUMBER (CME) 160,000 bd. ft.; $ per 1,000 bd.ft.								
Nov	461	194.7	189.8	190.9	+ .40	233.4	165.0	2,474
PROPANE (NYM) 42,000 gal.; ¢ per gal.								
Nov	284	42.75	41.50	42.50	+ .80	45.00	25.25	2,945
RICE-ROUGH (CRCE) 2000 cwt.; $ per cwt								
Nov	325	8.850	8.590	8.710	+.110	8.940	7.500	2,211
SILVER (MCE) 1,000 troy oz.; cents per troy oz.								
Dec	25			410.7	- 0.1	408.6	384.5	605
SORGHUM (KC) 5,000 bu.; cents per bu.								
Dec	0		235½	1		252½	206	100
SOYBEANS (MCE) 1,000 bu.; cents per bu.								
Nov	5,400	556½	545½	547¼	- 4¾	674	517	17,941
SOYBEAN MEAL (MCE) 20 tons; $ per ton								
Dec	20	181.2	178.7	178.7	- 1.30	198.5	160.0	307
WHEAT (MCE) 1,000 bu.; cents per bu.								
Dec	300	353	349	352¾	+ 3¼	353	272½	3,075

Lifetime Highs and Lows

The sixth and seventh numbers show the highest futures price and the lowest futures price achieved in the trading of the particular contract. The highest and lowest prices for the December 1991 corn futures contract were 275 cents and 220 cents. (The contract had traded for over a year on October 17, 1991.)

Open Interest and Volume of Trading

The final column in Table 2.2 shows the *open interest* for each contract. This is the total number of the contracts outstanding. It is the sum of all the long positions or, equivalently, it is the sum of all the short positions. Because of the problems in compiling the data, the open interest information is one trading day older than the price information. Thus, in *The Wall Street Journal* of October 18, 1991, the open interest is for the close of trading on October 16, 1991. In the case of the December 1991 corn futures contract, the open interest was 121,226 contracts.

At the end of each commodity's section, Table 2.2 shows the estimated volume of trading in contracts of all maturities on October 17, 1991 and the actual volume of trading in these contracts on October 16, 1991. It also shows the total open interest for all contracts on October 16, 1991 and the change in this open interest from October 15, 1991. For all corn futures contracts, the estimated trading volume was 33,000 contracts on October 17, 1991 and the actual trading volume was 34,250 contracts on October 16, 1991. The open interest for all contracts was 237,082 on October 16, 1991—up 1,880 from the previous day.

It sometimes happens that the volume of trading in a day is greater than the open interest at the end of the day. This is indicative of a large number of day trades.

Patterns of Futures Prices

A number of different patterns of futures prices can be picked out from Table 2.2. The futures price of platinum on the New York Mercantile Exchange increases as the time to maturity increases. This is known as a *normal market*. By contrast, the futures price of copper on the New York Commodity Exchange is a decreasing function of the time to maturity. This is known as an *inverted market*. For cotton, the pattern is mixed. The futures price first increases and then decreases as the time to maturity increases. The factors determining the pattern observed for a commodity will be discussed in Chapter 3.

2.5 CONVERGENCE OF FUTURES PRICE TO SPOT PRICE

As the delivery month of a futures contract is approached, the futures price converges to the spot price of the underlying asset. When the delivery period is reached, the futures price equals—or is very close to—the spot price.

To show why this is so, suppose first that the futures price is above the spot price during the delivery period. This gives rise to a clear arbitrage opportunity for traders:

1. Short a futures contract.
2. Buy the asset.
3. Make delivery.

This is certain to lead to a profit equal to the amount by which the futures price exceeds the spot price. As traders exploit this arbitrage opportunity, the futures price will fall. Suppose next that the futures price is below the spot price during the delivery period. Companies interested in acquiring the asset will find it attractive to enter into a long futures contract and then wait for delivery to be made. As they do this, the futures price will tend to rise.

Figure 2.1 illustrates the convergence of the futures price to the spot price. In Figure 2.1(a) the futures price is above the spot price prior to the delivery month.

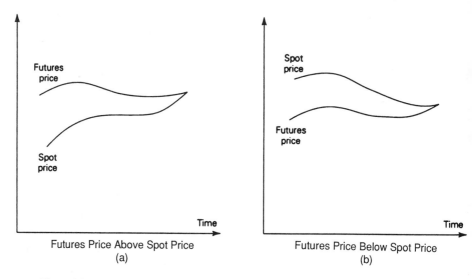

Futures Price Above Spot Price
(a)

Futures Price Below Spot Price
(b)

Figure 2.1   Relationship Between Futures Price and Spot Price as the Delivery Month is Approached

(This corresponds to platinum in Table 2.2.) In Figure 2.1(b) the futures price is below the spot price prior to the delivery month. (This corresponds to copper in Table 2.2.)

2.6 CASH SETTLEMENT

Some financial futures, such as those on stock indices, are settled in cash. This is because it is inconvenient or impossible to deliver the underlying asset. In the case of the futures contract on the S&P 500, for example, delivering the underlying asset would involve delivering a portfolio of 500 stocks. When a contract is settled in cash, it is marked to market at the end of the last trading day and all positions are declared closed. The settlement price on the last trading day is the closing spot price of the underlying asset. This ensures that the futures price converges to the spot price.

One exception to the rule that the settlement price on the last trading day equals the closing spot price is the S&P 500 futures contract. This bases the final settlement price on the opening price of the index the morning after the last trading day. This procedure is designed to avoid some of the problems connected with the fact that stock index futures, stock index options, and options on stock index futures all expire on the same day. Arbitrageurs often take large offsetting positions in these three contracts and there may be chaotic trading and significant price movements toward the end of an expiration day as they attempt to close out their positions. The media has coined the term *triple witching hour* to describe trading during the last hour of an expiration day.

2.7 HEDGING USING FUTURES

A company that knows it is due to sell an asset at a particular time in the future can hedge by taking a short futures position. This is known as a *short hedge*. If the price of the asset goes down, the company does not fare well on the sale of the asset, but makes a gain on the short futures position. If the price of the asset goes up, the company gains from the sale of the asset, but makes a loss on the futures position. Similarly, a company that knows it is due to buy an asset in the future can hedge by taking a long futures position. This is known as a *long hedge*. It is important to recognize that futures hedging does not necessarily improve the overall financial outcome. In fact, we can expect a futures hedge to make the outcome worse roughly 50 percent of the time. What the futures hedge does do is reduce risk by making the outcome more certain.

There are a number of reasons why hedging using futures contracts works less than perfectly in practice.

1. The asset whose price is to be hedged may not be exactly the same as the asset underlying the futures contract.
2. The hedger may be uncertain as to the exact date when the asset will be bought or sold.
3. The hedge may require the futures contract to be closed out well before its expiration date.

These problems give rise to what is termed *basis risk*.

BASIS RISK

The *basis* in a hedging situation is defined as follows:[1]

Basis = Spot price of asset to be hedged − Futures price of contract used

If the asset to be hedged and the asset underlying the futures contract are the same, the basis should be zero at the expiration of the futures contract. Prior to expiration, as shown in Table 2.2 and illustrated in Figure 2.1, the basis may be positive or negative.

When the spot price increases by more than the futures price, the basis increases. This is referred to as a *strengthening of the basis*. When the futures price increases by more than the spot price, the basis declines. This is referred to as a *weakening of the basis*.

To examine the nature of basis risk we will use the following notation:

S_1: Spot price at time t_1
S_2: Spot price at time t_2
F_1: Futures price at time t_1
F_2: Futures price at time t_2
b_1: Basis at time t_1
b_2: Basis at time t_2

We will assume that a hedge is put in place at time t_1 and closed out at time t_2. As an example we will consider the case where the spot and futures price at the time the hedge is initiated are \$2.50 and \$2.20, respectively, and that at the time the hedge is closed out they are \$2.00 and \$1.90, respectively. This means that $S_1=2.50$, $F_1=2.20$, $S_2=2.00$, and $F_2=1.90$.

---

[1]This is the usual definition. However the alternative definition

$$\text{Basis} = \text{Futures price} - \text{Spot price}$$

is sometimes used, particularly when the futures contract is on a financial asset.

From the definition of the basis:

$$b_1 = S_1 - F_1$$

$$b_2 = S_2 - F_2$$

In our example, b_1=0.30 and b_2=0.10.

Consider first the situation of a hedger who knows that the asset will be sold at time t_2 and takes a short futures position at time t_1. The price realized for the asset is S_2 and the profit on the futures position is $F_1 - F_2$. The effective price that is obtained for the asset with hedging is therefore

$$S_2 + F_1 - F_2 = F_1 + b_2$$

In our example, this is $2.30. The value of F_1 is known at time t_1. If b_2 were also known at this time, a perfect hedge (that is, a hedge eliminating all uncertainty about the price obtained) would result. The hedging risk is the uncertainty associated with b_2. This is known as *basis risk*. Consider next a situation where a company knows it will buy the asset at time t_2 and initiates a long hedge at time t_1. The price paid for the asset is S_2 and the loss on the hedge is $F_1 - F_2$. The effective price that is paid with hedging is therefore

$$S_2 + F_1 - F_2 = F_1 + b_2$$

This is the same expression as before; it is $2.30 in the example. The value of F_1 is known at time t_1 and the term b_2 represents basis risk.

For investment assets such as currencies, stock indices, gold, and silver, the basis risk tends to be fairly small . This is because, as we will see in Chapter 3, arbitrage arguments lead to a well-defined relationship between the futures price and the spot price of an investment asset. The basis risk for an investment asset arises mainly from uncertainty as to the level of the risk-free interest rate in the future. In the case of a commodity such as oil, corn, or copper, imbalances between supply and demand and the difficulties sometimes associated with storing the commodity can lead to large variations in the basis and therefore a much higher basis risk.

The asset that gives rise to the hedger's exposure is sometimes different from the asset underlying the hedge.[2] The basis risk is then usually greater. Define S_2^* as the price of the asset underlying the futures contract at time t_2. As before, S_2 is the price of the asset being hedged at time t_2. By hedging, a company ensures that the price that will be paid (or received) for the asset is

$$S_2 + F_1 - F_2$$

This can be written

---

[2]For example, airlines sometimes use the NYMEX heating oil futures contract to hedge their exposure to the price of jet fuel. See the article by Nikkhah referenced at the end of this chapter for a description of this.

$$F_1 + (S_2^* - F_2) + (S_2 - S_2^*)$$

The terms $S_2^* - F_2$ and $S_2 - S_2^*$ represent the two components of the basis. The $S_2^* - F_2$ term is the basis that would exist if the asset being hedged were the same as the asset underlying the futures contract. The $S_2 - S_2^*$ term is the basis arising from the difference between the two assets.

Note that basis risk can lead to an improvement or a worsening of a hedger's position. Consider a short hedge. If the basis strengthens unexpectedly, the hedger's position improves, whereas if the basis weakens unexpectedly, the hedger's position worsens. For a long hedge, the reverse holds. If the basis strengthens unexpectedly, the hedger's position worsens whereas if the basis weakens unexpectedly, the hedger's position improves.

CHOICE OF CONTRACT

One key factor affecting basis risk is the choice of the futures contract to be used for hedging. This choice has two components:

1. The choice of the asset underlying the futures contract.
2. The choice of the delivery month.

If the asset being hedged exactly matches an asset underlying a futures contract, the first choice is generally fairly easy. In other circumstances, it is necessary to carry out a careful analysis to determine which of the available futures contracts has futures prices that are most closely correlated with the price of the asset being hedged.

The choice of the delivery month is likely to be influenced by several factors. It might be assumed that, when the expiration of the hedge corresponds to a delivery month, the contract with that delivery month is chosen. In fact, a contract with a later delivery month is usually chosen in these circumstances. This is because futures prices are in some instances quite erratic during the delivery month. Also, a long hedger runs the risk of having to take delivery of the physical asset if he or she holds the contract during the delivery month. This can be expensive and inconvenient.

In general, basis risk increases as the time difference between the hedge expiration and the delivery month increases. A good rule of thumb is therefore to choose a delivery month that is as close as possible to, but later than, the expiration of the hedge. Suppose delivery months are March, June, September, and December for a particular contract. For hedge expirations in December, January, and February, the March contract will be chosen; for hedge expirations in March, April, and May, the June contract will be chosen; and so on. This rule of thumb assumes that there is sufficient liquidity in all contracts to meet the hedger's requirements. In

practice, liquidity tends to be greatest in short maturity futures contracts. Therefore, in some situations the hedger may be inclined to use short maturity contracts
and roll them forward. This strategy is explained at the end of this chapter.

Example 2.1

It is March 1. A U.S. company expects to receive 50 million Japanese yen at the end
of July. Yen futures contracts on the International Monetary Exchange (IMM) have delivery
months of March, June, September, and December. One contract is for the delivery of
12.5 million yen. The company therefore shorts four September yen futures contracts on
March 1. When the yen are received at the end of July, the company closes out its position.
We suppose that the futures price on March 1 in cents per yen is 0.7800 and that the spot
and futures prices when the contract is closed out are 0.7200 and 0.7250, respectively. This
means that the basis is –0.0050 when the contract is closed out. The effective price obtained
in cents per yen is the final spot price plus the gain on the futures:

$$0.7200 + 0.0550 = 0.7750$$

This can also be written as the initial futures price plus the final basis:

$$0.7800 - 0.0050 = 0.7750$$

The company receives a total of 50×0.00775 million dollars or $387,500.

Example 2.2

It is June 8 and a company knows that it will need to purchase 20,000 barrels crude
oil at some time in October or November. Oil futures contracts are currently traded for
delivery every month on NYMEX and the contract size is 1,000 barrels. The company
therefore decides to use the December contract for hedging and takes a long position in
20 December contracts. The futures price on June 8 is $18.00 per barrel. The company
finds that it is ready to purchase the crude oil on November 10. It therefore closes out its
futures contract on that date. The spot price and futures price on November 10 are $20.00
per barrel and $19.10 per barrel, respectively, so that the basis is $0.90. The effective price
paid is $18.90 per barrel or $378,000 in total. This can be calculated as the final spot price
of $20.00 less the gain on the futures of $1.10; or as the initial futures price, $18.00, plus
the final basis, $0.90.

2.8 OPTIMAL HEDGE RATIO

The hedge ratio is the ratio of the size of the position taken in futures contracts
to the size of the exposure. Up to now we have always assumed a hedge ratio of
1.0. We now show that, if the objective of the hedger is to minimize risk, a hedge
ratio of 1.0 is not necessarily optimal.

Define:

ΔS: Change in spot price, S, during a period of time equal to the life of the hedge

ΔF: Change in futures price, F, during a period of time equal to the life of the hedge

σ_S: Standard deviation of ΔS

σ_F: Standard deviation of ΔF

ρ: Coefficient of correlation between ΔS and ΔF

h: Hedge ratio

When the hedger is long the asset and short futures, the change in the value of the hedger's position during the life of the hedge is

$$\Delta S - h \Delta F$$

For a long hedge it is

$$h \Delta F - \Delta S$$

In either case the variance, v, of the change in value of the hedged position is given by

$$v = \sigma_S^2 + h^2 \sigma_F^2 - 2h\rho\sigma_S\sigma_F$$

so that

$$\frac{\partial v}{\partial h} = 2h\sigma_F^2 - 2\rho\sigma_S\sigma_F$$

Setting this equal to zero, and noting that $\partial^2 v/\partial h^2$ is positive, we see that the value of h that minimizes the variance is

$$h = \rho \frac{\sigma_S}{\sigma_F} \tag{2.1}$$

The optimal hedge ratio is therefore the product of the coefficient of correlation between ΔS and ΔF and the ratio of the standard deviation of ΔS to the standard deviation of ΔF. Figure 2.2 shows how the variance of the value of the hedger's position depends on the hedge ratio chosen.

If $\rho = 1$ and $\sigma_F = \sigma_S$, the optimal hedge ratio, h, is 1.0. This is to be expected since in this case the futures price mirrors the spot price perfectly. If $\rho = 1$ and $\sigma_F = 2\sigma_S$, the optimal hedge ratio h is 0.5. This result is also as expected since in this case the futures price always changes by twice as much as the spot price.

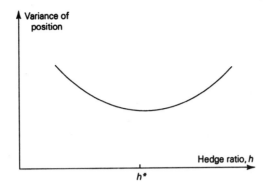

Figure 2.2   Dependence of Variance of Hedger's Position on Hedge Ratio

Example 2.3

A company knows that it will buy 1 million gallons of jet fuel in 3 months. The standard deviation of the change in the price per gallon of jet fuel over a 3-month period is calculated as 0.032. The company chooses to hedge by buying futures contracts on heating oil. The standard deviation of the change in the futures price over a 3-month period is 0.040 and the coefficient of correlation between the 3-month change in the price of jet fuel and the 3-month change in the futures price is 0.8. The optimal hedge ratio is therefore

$$0.8 \times \frac{0.032}{0.040} = 0.64$$

One heating oil futures contract is on 42,000 gallons. The company should therefore buy

$$0.64 \times \frac{1,000,000}{42,000} = 15.2$$

contracts. Rounding to the nearest whole number 15 contracts are required.

2.9 ROLLING THE HEDGE FORWARD

Sometimes, the expiration date of the hedge is later than the delivery dates of all the futures contracts that can be used. The hedger must then roll the hedge forward. This involves closing out one futures contract and taking the same position in a futures contract with a later delivery date. Hedges can be rolled forward many times. Consider a company that wishes to use a short hedge to reduce the risk associated with the price to be received for an asset at time T. If there are futures contracts 1, 2, 3, $\ldots$, n (not all necessarily in existence at the present time) with progressively later delivery dates, the company can use the following strategy:

Time t_1: Short futures contract 1

Time t_2: Close out futures contract 1
       Short futures contract 2
Time t_3: Close out futures contract 2
       Short futures contract 3
       ⋮   ⋮
Time t_n: Close out futures contract $n - 1$
       Short futures contract n
Time T: Close out futures contract n

In this strategy there are n basis risks or sources of uncertainty. At time T, there is uncertainty about the difference between the futures price for contract n and the spot price of the asset being hedged. In addition, on each of the $n - 1$ occasions when the hedge is rolled forward, there is uncertainty about the difference between the futures price for the contract being closed out and the futures price for the new contract being entered into.

Example 2.4

In April 1992, a company realizes that it will have 100,000 barrels of oil to sell in June 1993 and decides to hedge its risk with a hedge ratio of 1.0. The current spot price is $19. Although futures contracts are traded for every month of the year up to 1 year in the future, we suppose that only the first 6 delivery months have sufficient liquidity to meet the company's needs. The company therefore shorts 100 October 1992 contracts. In September 1992, it rolls the hedge forward into the March 1993 contract. In February 1993, it rolls the hedge forward again into the July 1993 contract.

One possible outcome, is that the price of oil drops from $19 to $16 per barrel between April 1992 and June 1993. Suppose that the October 1992 futures contract is shorted at $18.20 per barrel and closed out at $17.40 per barrel for a profit of $0.80 per barrel; the March 1993 contract is shorted at $17.00 per barrel and closed out at $16.50 per barrel for a profit of $0.50 per barrel; the July 1993 contract is shorted at $16.30 per barrel and closed out at $15.90 per barrel for a profit of $0.40 per barrel. In this case, the futures contracts provide a total of $1.70 per barrel compensation for the $3 per barrel oil price decline.

2.10 SUMMARY

In this chapter, we have looked at how futures markets operate. In futures markets, contracts are traded on an exchange, and it is necessary for the exchange to define carefully the precise nature of what it is that is traded, the procedures that will be followed, and the regulations that will govern the market. By contrast, forward contracts are negotiated directly over the telephone by two relatively sophisticated individuals. As a result, there is no need to standardize the product, and an extensive set of rules and procedures is not required.

A very high proportion of futures contracts that are initiated do not lead to the delivery of the underlying asset. They are closed out prior to the delivery period being reached. But it is the possibility of final delivery that drives the determination of the futures price. For each futures contract, there is a range of days during which delivery can be made and a well-defined delivery procedure. Some contracts, such as those on stock indices, are settled in cash rather than by delivery of the underlying asset.

The specification of contracts is an important activity for a futures exchange. The two sides to any contract must know what can be delivered, where delivery can take place, and when delivery can take place. They also need to know such details as the trading hours, how prices will be quoted, maximum price movements, and so on.

Margins are an important aspect of futures markets. An investor keeps a margin account with his or her broker. This is adjusted daily to reflect gains or losses, and the broker may require the account to be topped up from time to time if adverse price movements have taken place. The broker must either be a clearinghouse member or must maintain a margin account with a clearinghouse member. Each clearinghouse member maintains a margin account with the exchange clearinghouse. The balance in the account is adjusted daily to reflect gains and losses on the business for which the clearinghouse member is responsible.

The exchange ensures that information on prices is collected in a systematic way and relayed within a matter of seconds to investors throughout the world. Many newspapers, such as *The Wall Street Journal*, carry each day a summary of the previous day's trading.

Futures contracts can be used to hedge a company's exposure to a price of a commodity. A position in futures markets is taken to offset the effect of the price of the commodity on the rest of the company's business. An important concept in futures hedging is basis. This is the difference between the spot price of an asset and its futures price. The risk in a hedge is the uncertainty about the value of the basis at the maturity of the hedge. This is known as basis risk.

The hedge ratio is the ratio of the size of the position taken in futures contracts to the size of the exposure. It is not always optimal to use a hedge ratio of 1.0. If the hedger wishes to minimize the variance of his or her total position, a hedge ratio different from 1.0 may be appropriate. When there is no liquid futures contract that matures later than the expiration of the hedge, a strategy known as rolling the hedge forward is sometimes used. This involves entering into a sequence of futures contracts. When the first futures contract is near expiration, it is closed out and the hedger enters into a second contract with a later delivery month. When the second contract is close to expiration, it is closed out and the hedger enters into a third contract with a later delivery month; and so on. Rolling the hedge works well if there is a close correlation between changes in the futures prices and changes in the spot prices.

SUGGESTIONS FOR FURTHER READING

On Futures Markets

Chance, D., *An Introduction to Options and Futures*. Orlando, Fla.: Dryden Press, 1989.

Chicago Board of Trade, *Commodity Trading Manual*. Chicago: 1989.

Duffie, D., *Futures Markets*. Englewood Cliffs, NJ.: Prentice Hall, 1989.

Horn, F. F., *Trading in Commodity Futures*. New York: New York Institute of Finance, 1984.

Kolb, R., *Understanding Futures Markets*. Glenview, Ill.: Scott, Foresman, 1985.

Schwarz, E. W., J. M. Hill, and T. Schneeweis, *Financial Futures*. Homewood, Ill.: Richard D. Irwin, 1986.

Teweles, R. J., and F. J. Jones, *The Futures Game*. New York: McGraw-Hill, 1987.

On Hedging

Chicago Board of Trade, *Introduction to Hedging*. Chicago: 1984.

Ederington, L. H., "The Hedging Performance of the New Futures Market," *Journal of Finance*, 34 (March 1979), 157–70.

Frankcle, C. T., "The Hedging Performance of the New Futures Market: Comment," *Journal of Finance*, 35 (December 1980), 1273–79.

Johnson, L. L., "The Theory of Hedging and Speculation in Commodity Futures Markets." *Review of Economics Studies*, 27 (October 1960), 139–51.

Nikkhah, S., "How End Users Can Hedge Fuel Costs in Energy Markets," *Futures* (October 1987), 66–67.

Stulz, R. M., "Optimal Hedging Policies," *Journal of Financial and Quantitative Analysis*, 19 (June 1984), 127–40.

QUESTIONS AND PROBLEMS

2.1. Distinguish between the terms "open interest" and "trading volume."

2.2. What is the difference between a "local" and a "commission broker"?

2.3. What is the difference between the operation of the margin accounts administered by the clearinghouse and those administered by a broker?

2.4. What are the most important aspects of the design of a new futures contract?

2.5. Explain how margins protect investors against the possibility of default.

2.6. Under what circumstances are (a) a short hedge and (b) a long hedge appropriate?

2.7. Explain what is meant by basis risk when futures contracts are used for hedging.

2.8. Does a perfect hedge always lead to a better outcome than an imperfect hedge? Explain your answer.

2.9. Under what circumstances does a minimum variance hedge portfolio lead to no hedging at all?

2.10. Suppose that you enter into a short futures contract to sell July silver for $5.20 per ounce on the New York Commodity Exchange. The size of the contract is 5,000 ounces. The initial margin is $4,000 and the maintenance margin is $3,000. What change in the futures price will lead to a margin call? What happens if you do not meet the margin call?

2.11. The party with a short position in a futures contract sometimes has options as to the precise asset that will be delivered, where delivery will take place, when delivery will take place, and so on. Do these options increase or decrease the futures price? Explain your reasoning.

2.12. A company enters into a short futures contract to sell 5,000 bushels of wheat for 250 cents per bushel. The initial margin is $3,000 and the maintenance margin is $2,000. What price change would lead to a margin call? Under what circumstances could $1,500 be withdrawn from the margin account?

2.13. An investor enters into two long futures contracts on frozen orange juice. Each contract is for the delivery of 15,000 pounds. The current futures price is 160 cents per pound; the initial margin is $6,000 per contract; and the maintenance margin is $4,500 per contract. What price change would lead to a margin call? Under what circumstances could $2,000 be withdrawn from the margin account?

2.14. At the end of one day, a clearinghouse member is long 100 contracts and the settlement price is $50,000 per contract. The original margin is $2,000 per contract. On the following day, the member becomes responsible for clearing an additional 20 long contracts. These were entered into at a price of $51,000 per contract. The settlement price at the end of this day is $50,200. How much does the member have to add to its margin account with the exchange clearinghouse?

2.15. Suppose that the standard deviation of quarterly changes in the prices of a commodity is $0.65; the standard deviation of quarterly changes in a futures price on the commodity is $0.81; and the coefficient of correlation between the two changes is 0.8. What is the optimal hedge ratio for a 3-month contract? What does it mean?

2.16. "Speculation in futures markets is pure gambling. It is not in the public interest to allow speculators to buy seats on a futures exchange." Discuss this viewpoint.

2.17. Identify the most actively traded contracts in Table 2.2. Consider each of the following sections separately: grains and oilseeds, livestock and meat, food & fiber, and metals and petroleum.

2.18. What do you think would happen if an exchange started trading a contract where the quality of the underlying asset was incompletely specified?

2.19. "When a futures contract is traded on the floor of the exchange, it may be the case that the open interest increases by one, stays the same, or decreases by one." Explain this statement.

2.20. In the Chicago Board of Trade's corn futures contract, the following delivery months are available: March, May, July, September, and December. Which contract should be used for hedging when the expiration of the hedge is in
(a) June?
(b) July?

(c) January?

2.21. Does a perfect hedge always succeed in locking in the current spot price of an asset for a future transaction? Explain your answer.

2.22. Explain why a short hedger's position improves when the basis strengthens unexpectedly and worsens when the basis weakens unexpectedly.

2.23. Imagine you are the treasurer of a Japanese company exporting electronic equipment to the United States. Discuss how you would design a foreign exchange hedging strategy and the arguments you would use to sell the strategy to your fellow executives.

2.24. "If the minimum variance hedge ratio is calculated as 1.0, the hedge must be perfect." Is this statement true? Explain your answer.

2.25. "If there is no basis risk, the minimum variance hedge ratio is always 1.0." Is this statement true? Explain your answer.

2.26. The standard deviation of monthly changes in the spot price of live cattle is (in cents per pound) 1.2. The standard deviation of monthly changes in the futures price of live cattle for the closest contract is 1.4. The correlation between the futures price changes and the spot price changes is 0.7. It is now October 15. A beef producer is committed to purchasing 200,000 pounds of live cattle on November 15. The producer wants to use the December live cattle futures contracts to hedge its risk. Each contract is for the delivery of 40,000 pounds of cattle. What strategy should the beef producer follow?

2.27. A pig farmer expects to have 90,000 pounds of live hogs to sell in 3 months. The live hogs futures contract on the Chicago Mercantile Exchange is for the delivery of 30,000 pounds of hogs. How can the farmer use this for hedging? From the farmer's viewpoint, what are the pros and cons of hedging?

2.28. It is now July 1992. A mining company has just discovered a small deposit of gold. It will take 6 months to construct the mine. The gold will then be extracted on a more or less continuous basis for one year. Futures contracts on gold are available on the New York Commodity Exchange. The delivery months range from August 1992 to April 1994 and are at 2-month intervals. Each contract is for the delivery of 100 ounces. Discuss how the mining company might use futures markets for hedging.

2.29. An airline executive has argued: "There is no point in our using oil futures. There is just as much chance that the price of oil in the future will be less than the futures price as there is that it will be greater than this price." Discuss this viewpoint.

2.30. What is the effect of using a hedge ratio of 1.5 instead of 1.0 in Example 2.4 of Section 2.9?

2.31. "Shareholders can hedge the risks faced by a company. There is no need for the company itself to hedge." Discuss this viewpoint.

2.32. "A company that uses a certain commodity in its manufacturing operations should pass price changes on to its customers. Hedging is then unnecessary." Discuss this viewpoint.

2.33. "Company treasurers should not hedge. They will be blamed when a loss is experienced on the position taken in the hedging instrument." Discuss this viewpoint.

3

Forward and Futures Prices

In this chapter, we discuss how forward prices and futures prices are related to the price of the underlying asset. Forward contracts are generally easier to analyze than futures contracts because there is no daily settlement. Consequently, most of the analysis in the first part of the chapter is directed toward determining forward prices rather than futures prices. Luckily, it can be shown that the forward price and futures price of an asset are generally very close to each other when the maturities of the two contracts are the same. This means that results obtained for forward prices can be assumed to be true for futures prices as well.

In the first part of the chapter, key results are provided for forward contracts on

1. Securities providing no income
2. Securities providing a known cash income
3. Securities providing a known dividend yield

The second part of the chapter uses these results to calculate futures prices for contracts on stock indices, foreign exchange, gold, and silver.

This chapter draws an important distinction between assets that are held solely for investment by a significant number of investors and those which are held almost exclusively for consumption. Futures and forward prices on the former can be determined in a relatively straightforward way, whereas those on the latter cannot. Later in this book we will find it necessary to make the same distinction when valuing options and other more complicated derivative securities.

3.1 SOME PRELIMINARIES

Before we get into the calculation of forward prices, it is useful to present some preliminary material.

CONTINUOUS COMPOUNDING

In this book, the interest rates used will be continuously compounded except where otherwise stated. Readers used to working with interest rates that are compounded annually, semiannually, or in some other way may find this frustrating. However, continuously compounded interest rates are used to such a great extent when options and other complex derivative securities are being priced that it makes sense to get used to working with them now.

Consider an amount A invested for n years at an interest rate of R per annum. If the rate is compounded once per annum, the terminal value of the investment is

$$A(1 + R)^n$$

If it is compounded m times per annum, the terminal value of the investment is

$$A \left(1 + \frac{R}{m} \right)^{mn} \tag{3.1}$$

Suppose $A = \$100$, $R = 10\%$ per annum, and $n = 1$ so that we are considering 1 year. When we compound once per annum ($m = 1$), this formula shows that the $100 grows to

$$\$100 \times 1.1 = \$110$$

When we compound twice a year ($m = 2$), the formula shows that the $100 grows to

$$\$100 \times 1.05 \times 1.05 = \$110.25$$

When we compound four times a year ($m = 4$), the formula shows that the $100 grows to

$$\$100 \times 1.025^4 = \$110.38$$

Table 3.1 shows the effect of increasing the compounding frequency further (i.e., of increasing m). The limit as m tends to infinity is known as *continuous compounding*. With continuous compounding, it can be shown that an amount A invested for n years at rate R grows to

$$Ae^{Rn} \tag{3.2}$$

where e is the mathematical constant, 2.71828. In the example in Table 3.1, $A = 100$, $n = 1$, and $R = 0.1$ so that the value to which A grows with continuous compounding is

$$100\,e^{0.1} = 110.52$$

This is (to two decimal places) the same as the value using daily compounding. For most practical purposes, continuous compounding can be thought of as being equivalent to daily compounding. Compounding a sum of money at a continuously compounded rate R for n years involves multiplying it by e^{Rn}. Discounting it at a continuously compounded rate R for n years involves multiplying by e^{-Rn}.

Suppose that R_1 is a rate of interest with continuous compounding and R_2 is the equivalent rate with compounding m times per annum. From the results in (3.1) and (3.2), we must have

$$Ae^{R_1 n} = A\left(1 + \frac{R_2}{m}\right)^{mn}$$

or

$$e^{R_1} = \left(1 + \frac{R_2}{m}\right)^{m}$$

TABLE 3.1   Compounding Frequency

The effect of increasing the compounding frequency on the value of $100 at the end of 1 year when the interest rate is 10% per annum

Compounding Frequency	Value of $100 at End of 1 Year (dollars)
Annually ($m = 1$)	110.00
Semiannually ($m = 2$)	110.25
Quarterly ($m = 4$)	110.38
Monthly ($m = 12$)	110.47
Weekly ($m = 52$)	110.51
Daily ($m = 365$)	110.52

This means that

$$R_1 = m \ln \left(1 + \frac{R_2}{m} \right) \qquad (3.3)$$

and

$$R_2 = m(e^{R_1/m} - 1) \qquad (3.4)$$

These equations can be used to convert a rate where the compounding frequency is m times per annum to a continuously compounded rate and vice versa. The function ln is the natural logarithm function. It is defined so that if $y = \ln x$, then $x = e^y$

Example 3.1

Consider an interest rate that is quoted as 10% per annum with semiannual compounding. From using Equation (3.3) with $m = 2$ and $R_2 = 0.1$, the equivalent rate with continuous compounding is

$$2 \ln (1 + 0.05) = 0.09758$$

or 9.758% per annum.

Example 3.2

Suppose that a lender quotes the interest rate on loans as 8% per annum with continuous compounding and that interest is actually paid quarterly. From using Equation (3.4) with $m = 4$ and $R_1 = 0.08$, the equivalent rate with quarterly compounding is

$$4(e^{0.02} - 1) = 0.0808$$

or 8.08% per annum This means that on a $1,000 loan, interest payments of $20.20 would be required each quarter.

SHORT SELLING

Some of the arbitrage strategies presented in this chapter involve short selling. This is a trading strategy that yields a profit when the price of a security goes down and a loss when it goes up. It involves selling securities that are not owned and buying them back later.

To explain the mechanics of short selling, we suppose that an investor contacts a broker to short 500 IBM shares. The broker immediately borrows 500 IBM shares from another client and sells them in the open market in the usual way, depositing the sale proceeds to the investor's account. Providing there are shares that can be borrowed, the investor can continue to maintain the short position for as long as desired. At some stage, however, the investor will choose to instruct the broker to close out the position. The broker then uses funds in the investor's account to purchase 500 IBM shares and replaces them in the account of the client from which the shares were borrowed. The investor makes a profit if the stock price has declined and a loss if it has risen. If, at any time while the contract is open, the broker runs out of shares to borrow, the investor is what is known as *short-squeezed* and must close out the position immediately even though he or she may not be ready to do so.

Regulators currently only allow shares to be sold short on an *uptick*, that is, when the most recent movement in the price of the security was an increase. A broker requires significant initial margins from clients with short positions, and, as with futures contracts, if there are adverse movements (i.e., increases) in the price of the security, additional margin may be required. The proceeds of the initial sales of the security normally form part of the initial margin requirement. Some brokers pay interest on margin accounts and marketable securities such as Treasury bills can be deposited with a broker to meet initial margin requirements. As in the case of futures contracts, the margin does not therefore represent a real cost.

An investor with a short position must pay to his or her broker any income, such as dividends or interest, that would normally be received on the securities that have been shorted. The broker will transfer this to the account of the client from whom the securities have been borrowed. Consider the position of an investor who shorts 500 IBM shares in April when the price per share is $120 and closes out his or her position by buying them back in July when the price per share is $100. Suppose that a dividend of $4 per share is paid in May. The investor receives $500 \times \$120 = \$60,000$ in April when the short position is initiated. The dividend leads to a payment of $500 \times \$4 = \$2,000$ in May. The investor also pays $500 \times \$100 = \$50,000$ when the position is closed out in July. The net gain is, therefore,

$$\$60,000 - \$2,000 - \$50,000 = \$8,000$$

ASSUMPTIONS

In this chapter, we will assume that the following are all true for some market participants:

1. There are no transactions costs.
2. All trading profits (net of trading losses) are subject to the same tax rate.
3. The market participants can borrow money at the same risk-free rate of interest as they can lend money.
4. The market participants take advantage of arbitrage opportunities as they occur.

Note that we do not require these assumptions to be true for all market participants. All that we require is that they be true for a subset of all market participants, for example, large investment houses. This is not unreasonable. As discussed in Chapter 1, the fact that these market participants are prepared to take advantage of arbitrage opportunities as they occur means that in practice arbitrage opportunities disappear almost as soon as they arise. It is reasonable therefore to assume for the purposes of our analyses that there are no arbitrage opportunities.

THE REPO RATE

The relevant risk-free rate of interest for many arbitrageurs operating in the futures market is what is known as the *repo rate*. A *repo* or *repurchase agreement* is an agreement where the owner of securities agrees to sell them to a counterparty and buy them back at a slightly higher price later. The counterparty is providing a loan. The difference between the price at which the securities are sold and the price at which they are repurchased is the interest earned by the counterparty. The loan has virtually no risk since, if the borrowing company does not keep to its side of the agreement, the lender simply keeps the securities.

The repo rate is only slightly higher than the Treasury bill rate. The most common type of repo is an *overnight repo* where the agreement is renegotiated each day. However, longer-term arrangements, known as *term repos*, of up to two weeks are sometimes used.

NOTATION

Some of the notation that will be used in this chapter is as follows:

T: Time when forward contract matures (years)

t: Current time (years)

S: Price of asset underlying forward contract at time t

S_T: Price of asset underlying forward contract at time T (unknown at the current time, t)

K: Delivery price in forward contract

f: Value of a long forward contract at time t

F: Forward price at time t

r: Risk-free rate of interest per annum at time t, with continuous compounding, for an investment maturing at time T

The variables T and t are measured in years from some date (it does not matter when) prior to the start of the contract. The variable of interest for the purposes of our current analysis is of course $T - t$, which is the time remaining, measured in years, in the forward contract. There is a reason for defining two separate variables, t and T. This will become apparent in later chapters when we consider the effect on the price of a derivative security of time passing. At this stage, the reader can conveniently think in terms of $T - t$ as a single variable.

It is important to realize that the forward price, F, is quite different from the value of the forward contract, f. As explained in Chapter 1, the forward price at any given time is the delivery price that would make the contract have a zero value. When a contract is initiated, the delivery price is normally set equal to the forward price so that $F = K$ and $f = 0$. As time passes, both f and F change. The analysis and the examples in the next few sections should make clear the distinction between the two variables.

3.2 FORWARD CONTRACTS ON A SECURITY THAT PROVIDES NO INCOME

The easiest forward contract to value is one written on a security that provides the holder with no income. Non-dividend-paying stocks and discount bonds are examples of such securities.[1]

For there to be no arbitrage opportunities, the relationship between the forward price, F, and the spot price, S, for a no-income security must be

$$F = Se^{r(T-t)} \qquad (3.5)$$

To show this, suppose first that $F > Se^{r(T-t)}$. An investor can borrow S dollars for a period of time $T - t$ at the risk-free interest rate, buy the asset, and take a short position in the forward contract. At time T, the asset is sold under the terms of the forward contract for F, and $Se^{r(T-t)}$ is used to repay the loan. A profit of $F - Se^{r(T-t)}$ is therefore realized at time T.

Suppose next that $F < Se^{r(T-t)}$. An investor can short the asset, invest the proceeds for a period of time $T - t$ at rate r, and take a long position in the forward contract. At time T, the asset is purchased under the terms of the forward contract for F, the short position is closed out, and a profit of $Se^{r(T-t)} - F$ is realized.

Example 3.3

Consider a forward contract on a non-dividend-paying stock that matures in 3 months. Suppose that the stock price is $40, and the 3-month risk-free rate of interest is 5% per annum. In this case $T - t = 0.25$, $r = 0.05$, and $S = 40$ so that

$$F = 40e^{0.05 \times 0.25} = 40.50$$

This would be the delivery price in a contract negotiated today. If the actual forward price is greater than $40.50, an arbitrageur can borrow money, buy the stock, and short the forward

---

[1] Some of the contracts that are used as examples in the first half of this chapter (e.g., forward contracts on non-dividend-paying stocks) do not normally arise in practice. However, they form useful examples for developing our ideas.

contract for a net profit. If the forward price is less than \$40.50, an arbitrageur can short the stock, invest the proceeds, and take a long forward position. Again a net profit is realized.

To express our arguments more formally, consider the following two portfolios:

> ***Portfolio A***: one long forward contract on the security plus an amount of cash equal to $Ke^{-r(T-t)}$
>
> ***Portfolio B***: one unit of the security

In portfolio A, the cash, assuming that it is invested at the risk-free rate, will grow to an amount K at time T. It can then be used to pay for the security at the maturity of the forward contract. Both portfolios will therefore consist of one unit of the security at time T. It follows that they must be equally valuable at the earlier time, t. If this were not true, an investor could make a riskless profit by buying the less expensive portfolio and shorting the more expensive one.

It follows that

$$f + Ke^{-r(T-t)} = S$$

or

$$f = S - Ke^{-r(T-t)} \tag{3.6}$$

When a forward contract is initiated, the forward price equals the delivery price specified in the contract and is chosen so that the value of the contract is zero. The forward price, F, is therefore that value of K which makes $f = 0$ in Equation (3.6), that is,

$$F = Se^{r(T-t)}$$

This is in agreement with Equation (3.5)

Example 3.4

Consider a long 6-month forward contract on a 1-year discount bond when the delivery price is \$950. We assume that the 6-month risk-free rate of interest (continuously compounded) is 6% per annum and that the current bond price is \$930. In this case $T - t = 0.50$, $r = 0.06$, $K = 950$, $S = 930$, and Equation (3.6) shows that the value, f, of the long forward contract is given by

$$f = 930 - 950\,e^{-0.5 \times 0.06} = 8.08$$

Similarly, the value of a short forward is -8.08.

3.3 FORWARD CONTRACTS ON A SECURITY THAT PROVIDES A KNOWN CASH INCOME

In this section we consider a forward contract on a security that will provide a perfectly predictable cash income to the holder. Examples are stocks paying known dividends and coupon-bearing bonds. Define I as the present value, using the risk-free discount rate, of income to be received during the life of the forward contract.

For there to be no arbitrage, the relationship between F and S must be

$$F = (S - I)e^{r(T-t)} \tag{3.7}$$

To show this, suppose first that $F > (S - I)e^{r(T-t)}$. An arbitrageur can borrow money, buy the asset, and short a forward contract. The asset is sold for F at time T under the terms of the forward contract. Assuming that the income received is used to pay off part of the loan, an amount $(S - I)e^{r(T-t)}$ of the loan remains to be repaid at time T. A profit of $F - (S - I)e^{r(T-t)}$ is therefore realized at time T.

Suppose next that $F < (S - I)e^{r(T-t)}$. An arbitrageur can short the asset, invest the proceeds, and take a long position in the forward contract. In this case, a profit of $(S - I)e^{r(T-t)} - F$ is realized at time T.

Example 3.5

Consider a 10-month forward contract on a stock with a price of $50. We assume that the risk-free rate of interest (continuously compounded) for all maturities is 8% per annum and the term structure is flat. We also assume that dividends of $0.75 per share are expected after 3 months, 6 months, and 9 months. The present value of the dividends, I, is given by

$$I = 0.75e^{-0.02} + 0.75e^{-0.04} + 0.75e^{-0.06} = 2.162$$

The variable $T - t$ is 0.8333 year so that the forward price, F, is given by

$$F = (50 - 2.162)e^{0.08 \times 0.8333} = 51.14$$

If the forward price were less than this, an arbitrageur would short the stock and buy forward contracts. If the forward price were greater than this, an arbitrageur would short forward contracts and buy the stock.

To express our arguments more formally, we change portfolio B in the preceding section to:

Portfolio B: one unit of the security plus borrowings of amount I at the risk-free rate

The income from the security can be used to repay the borrowings so that this portfolio has the same value as one unit of the security at time T. Portfolio A also has this value at time T. The two portfolios must therefore have the same value at time t, that is,

$$f + Ke^{-r(T-t)} = S - I$$

or

$$f = S - I - Ke^{-r(T-t)} \qquad (3.8)$$

The forward price, F, is, as before, the value of K that makes f zero. Using Equation (3.8) we obtain

$$F = (S - I)e^{r(T-t)}$$

which is in agreement with Equation (3.7).

Example 3.6

Consider a 5-year bond with a price of \$900. Suppose that a forward contract on the bond with a delivery price of \$910 has a maturity of 1 year. Coupon payments of \$60 are expected after 6 months and after 12 months. The second coupon payment is immediately prior to the delivery date in the forward contract. The continuously compounded risk-free rates of interest for 6 months and 1 year are 9% per annum and 10% per annum. In this case $S = 900$, $K = 910$, $r = 0.10$, $T - t = 1$, and

$$I = 60e^{-0.09 \times 0.5} + 60e^{-0.10} = 111.65$$

and the value, f, of a long position in the forward contract, using Equation (3.8), is given by

$$f = 900 - 111.65 - 910\,e^{-0.1} = -35.05$$

The value of a short position is $+35.05$. Note that there is no accrued interest at the beginning and end of the contract in this example. Complications arising from accrued interest are discussed in Chapter 4.

3.4 FORWARD CONTRACTS ON A SECURITY THAT PROVIDES A KNOWN DIVIDEND YIELD

As will be explained in later sections, both currencies and stock indices can be regarded as securities that provide known dividend yields. In this section, we provide a general analysis of forward contracts on such securities.

A known dividend yield means that the income when expressed as a percentage of the security price is known. We will assume that the dividend yield is paid continuously at an annual rate q. To illustrate what this means, suppose that $q = 0.05$ so that the dividend yield is 5 percent per annum. When the security price is \$10, dividends in the next small interval of time are paid at the rate of 50 cents per annum; when the security price is \$100, dividends in the next small interval of time are paid at the rate of \$5 per annum; and so on.

To value the forward contract, portfolio B in Section 3.2 can be replaced by:

Portfolio B: $e^{-q(T-t)}$ of the security with all income being reinvested in the security

The security holding in portfolio B grows as a result of the dividends which are paid, so that at time T exactly one unit of the security is held. Portfolios A and B are therefore worth the same at time T. From equating their values at time, t, we obtain

$$f + Ke^{-r(T-t)} = Se^{-q(T-t)}$$

or

$$f = Se^{-q(T-t)} - Ke^{-r(T-t)} \tag{3.9}$$

and the forward price, F, is given by the value of K that makes f zero:

$$F = Se^{(r-q)(T-t)} \tag{3.10}$$

Note that if the dividend yield rate varies during the life of the forward contract, Equation (3.10) is still correct with q equal to the average dividend yield rate.

Example 3.7

Consider a 6-month forward contract on a security that is expected to provide a continuous dividend yield of 4% per annum. The risk-free rate of interest (with continuous compounding) is 10% per annum. The stock price is \$25 and the delivery price is \$27. In this case $S = 25$, $K = 27$, $r = 0.10$, $q = 0.04$, and $T - t = 0.5$. From Equation (3.9) the value of a long position, f, is given by

$$f = 25e^{-0.04 \times 0.5} - 27e^{-0.1 \times 0.5} = -1.18$$

From Equation (3.10) the forward price, F, is given by

$$F = 25e^{0.06 \times 0.5} = 25.76$$

3.5 A GENERAL RESULT

A result that is true for all assets (both those held for investment purposes and those held for consumption purposes) is

$$f = (F - K)e^{-r(T-t)} \tag{3.11}$$

This is because, if $f > (F-K)e^{-r(T-t)}$ or $f < (F-K)e^{-r(T-t)}$, there are arbitrage opportunities.

Consider first the $f > (F - K)e^{-r(T-t)}$ situation. We take a long position in a forward contract with delivery price F maturing at time T and a short position in a forward contract with delivery price K maturing at time T. Since the first contract has a value of zero, this strategy generates an initial cash flow equal to f. The final cash flow is

$$(S_T - F) + (K - S_T) = -(F - K)$$

The investment therefore locks in cash flows with a positive present value of

$$f - (F - K)e^{-r(T-t)}$$

Similarly, if $f < (F - K)e^{-r(T-t)}$, we take a short position in a forward contract with delivery price F maturing at time T and a long position in a forward contract with delivery price K maturing at time T. This locks in cash flows with a positive present value of

$$(F - K)e^{-r(T-t)} - f$$

It is easy to verify that the relationship in Equation (3.11) is consistent with the formulas derived for F and f in each of Section 3.2, Section 3.3, and Section 3.4.

3.6 FORWARD PRICES VERSUS FUTURES PRICES

Appendix 3A provides an arbitrage argument to show that, when the risk-free interest rate is constant and the same for all maturities, the forward price for a contract with a certain delivery date is the same as the futures price for a contract with the same delivery date. The argument in Appendix 3A can be extended to cover situations where the interest rate is a known function of time.

When interest rates vary unpredictably (as they do in the real world), forward and futures prices are in theory no longer the same. The proof of the relationship between the two is beyond the scope of this book. However, we can get a sense of the nature of the relationship by considering the situation where the price of the underlying asset, S, is strongly positively correlated with interest rates. When S increases, an investor who holds a long futures position makes an immediate gain because of the daily settlement procedure. Since increases in S tend to occur at the same time as increases in interest rates, this gain will tend to be invested at a higher-than-average rate of interest. Similarly, when S decreases, the investor will make an immediate loss. This loss will tend to be financed at a lower-than-average rate of interest. An investor holding a forward contract rather than a futures contract is not affected in this way by interest rate movements. It follows that, *ceteris paribus*, a long futures contract will be more attractive than a long forward contract. Hence, when S is strongly positively correlated with interest rates, futures prices will tend to be higher than forward prices. When S is strongly negatively correlated with interest rates, a similar argument shows that forward prices will tend to be higher than futures prices.

The theoretical differences between forward and futures prices for contracts which last only a few months are in most circumstances sufficiently small to be ignored. As the life of the contracts increase these differences become greater. In practice, there are a number of factors, not reflected in theoretical models, that may cause forward and futures prices to be different. These factors include taxes, transaction costs, and the treatment of margins. Also, in some instances, futures contracts are more liquid and easier to trade than are forward contracts. Despite all these points, in most circumstances it is reasonable to assume that forward and futures prices are the same. This is the assumption that will be made throughout this book. The symbol F will be used to represent both the futures price and the forward price of an asset.

EMPIRICAL RESEARCH

Some empirical research that has been carried out comparing forward and futures contracts is listed at the end of this chapter. Cornell and Reinganum studied forward and futures prices on the British pound, Canadian dollar, German mark, Japanese yen, and Swiss franc between 1974 and 1979. They found very few statistically significant differences between the two prices. Their results were confirmed by Park and Chen who as part of their study looked at the British pound, German mark, Japanese yen, and Swiss franc between 1977 and 1981.

French studied copper and silver during the period 1968 to 1980. The results for silver show that the futures price and the forward price are significantly different (at the 5% confidence level) with the futures price generally above the forward price. The results for copper are less clear cut. Park and Chen looked at gold, silver, silver coin, platinum, copper, and plywood between 1977 and 1981. Their results are similar to those of French for silver. The forward and futures prices are significantly different with the futures price above the forward price. Rendleman and Carabini studied the Treasury bill market between 1976 and 1978. They also found statistically significant differences between futures and forward prices.

3.7 STOCK INDEX FUTURES

A *stock index* tracks the changes in the value of a hypothetical portfolio of stocks. The weight of a stock in the portfolio equals the proportion of the portfolio invested in the stock. The stocks in the portfolio can have equal weights or weights that change in some way over time. The percentage increase in the value of a stock index over a small interval of time is usually defined so that it is equal to the percentage increase in the total value of the stocks comprising the portfolio at that time. A stock index is not usually adjusted for cash dividends. In other words, any cash dividends received on the portfolio are ignored when percentage changes in most indices are being calculated.

It is worth noting that if the hypothetical portfolio of stocks remains fixed, the weights assigned to individual stocks in the portfolio do not remain fixed. If the price of one particular stock in the portfolio rises more sharply than others, more weight is automatically given to that stock. A corollary to this is that, if the weights of the stocks in the portfolio are specified as constant over time, the hypothetical portfolio will change each day. If the price of one particular stock in the portfolio rises more sharply than others, the holding of the stock must be reduced to maintain the weightings.

STOCK INDICES

Table 3.2 shows futures prices for contracts on four different stock indices as they were reported in *The Wall Street Journal* of October 18, 1991. The prices refer to the close of trading on October 17, 1991. The stock indices are as follows:

1. *The Standard & Poor's 500 (S&P 500) Index.* This trades on the Chicago Mercantile Exchange (CME) and is based on a portfolio of 500 different stocks: 400 industrials, 40 utilities, 20 transportation companies, and 40 financial institutions. The weights of the stocks in the portfolio at any given time reflect the stock's total market capitalization (= stock price × number of shares outstanding). The index accounts for 80 percent of the market capitalization of all the stocks listed on the New York Stock Exchange. One futures contract, traded on the Chicago Mercantile Exchange, is on 500 times the index.

2. *The Nikkei 225 Stock Average.* This is based on a portfolio of 225 of the largest stocks trading on the Tokyo Stock Exchange. Stocks are weighted according to their prices. One futures contract, traded on the Chicago Mercantile Exchange, is on 5 times the index.

3. *The New York Stock Exchange (NYSE) Composite Index.* This is based on a portfolio of all the stocks listed on the New York Stock Exchange. As with the S&P 500, weights reflect market capitalizations. One futures contract, traded on the New York Futures Exchange, is on 500 times the index.

4. *The Major Market Index (MMI).* This is based on a portfolio of 20 blue-chip stocks listed on the New York Stock Exchange. The stocks are weighted according to their prices with adjustments being made to reflect the effects of stock splits and stock dividends. The MMI is very closely correlated to

the widely quoted Dow Jones Industrial Average, which is also based on relatively few stocks. One futures contract, traded on the Chicago Board of Trade, is on 500 times the index.

As mentioned in Chapter 2, futures contracts on stock indices are settled in cash, not by delivery of the underlying asset. All contracts are marked to market on the last trading day and the positions are deemed to be closed. For most contracts, the settlement price on the last trading day is set at the closing value of the index on that day. But, as discussed in Chapter 2, for the S&P 500 it is set as the value of the index based on opening prices the next day. For the futures on the NYSE composite and MMI, the last trading day is the third Friday of the delivery month. For the S&P 500, it is the Thursday before the third Friday of the delivery month.

FUTURES PRICES OF STOCK INDICES

Most indices can be thought of as securities that pay dividends. The security is the portfolio of stocks underlying the index and the dividends paid by the security are the dividends that would be received by the holder of this portfolio. To a

TABLE 3.2   Stock Index Futures
Quotes from *The Wall Street
Journal*, October 18, 1991

FUTURES

S&P 500 INDEX (CME) 500 times index

	Open	High	Low	Settle	Chg	Open High	Low	Open Interest
Dec	393.50	395.85	391.75	393.75	− .85	401.50	316.50	139,641
Mr92	395.70	398.50	394.10	396.15	− .75	404.00	374.70	3,170
June	....	....	....	398.40	− .70	407.00	379.00	781

Est vol 48,495; vol Wed 45,886; open int 143,623, +662.
Indx prelim High 393.81; Low 390.32; Close 391.92 −.88

NIKKEI 225 Stock Average (CME)−$5 times NSA

	Open	High	Low	Settle	Chg	High	Low	Open Interest
Dec	24900.	24950.	24870.	24930.	+160.0	28900.	22380.	11,272
Mr92	....	....	....	25440.	+170.0	26725.	23000.	292

Est vol 380; vol Wed 362; open int 11,564, +64.
The index: High 24643.11; Low 24344.68; Close 24439.85 +105.18

NYSE COMPOSITE INDEX (NYFE) 500 times index

	Open	High	Low	Settle	Chg	High	Low	Open Interest
Dec	216.45	217.70	215.60	216.75	− .35	219.70	175.50	4,762
Mr92	218.40	217.95	217.40	217.85	− .35	220.35	207.60	685

Est vol 4,764; vol Wed 5,686; open int 5,488, −150.
The index: High 216.54; Low 215.07; Close 215.81 −.24

MAJOR MKT INDEX (CBT) $500 times index

	Open	High	Low	Settle	Chg	High	Low	Open Interest
Oct	323.70	325.70	322.20	324.05	− .90	325.70	314.90	4,010
Nov	323.75	325.70	322.40	324.10	− .95	325.70	315.20	1,888
Dec	324.80	326.20	323.00	324.75	− .95	326.20	315.75	195

Est vol 3,500; vol Wed 2,018; open int 6,104, +167.
The index: High 325.88; Low 322.55; Close 323.79 −1.09

reasonable approximation, the dividends can be assumed to be paid continuously. If q is the dividend yield rate, Equation (3.10) gives the futures price, F, as

$$F = Se^{(r-q)(T-t)} \qquad (3.12)$$

Example 3.8

Consider a 3-month futures contract on the S&P 500. Suppose that the stocks underlying the index provide a dividend yield of 3% per annum, that the current value of the index is 400, and that the continuously compounded risk-free interest rate is 8% per annum. In this case, $r = 0.08$, $S = 400$, $T - t = 0.25$, and $q = 0.03$ and the futures price, F, is given by

$$F = 400e^{0.05 \times 0.25} = 405.03$$

In practice, the dividend yield on the portfolio underlying an index varies week by week throughout the year. For example, a large proportion of the dividends on NYSE stocks are paid in the first week of February, May, August, and November of each year. The value of q that is used should represent the average annualized dividend yield during the life of the contract. The dividends used for estimating q should be those for which the ex-dividend date is during the life of the futures contract. Looking at Table 3.2, we see that the futures prices for the S&P 500 appear to be increasing with maturity at about 2.4 percent per annum. This corresponds to the situation where the risk-free interest rate exceeds the dividend yield by about 2.4 percent per annum.

If an analyst is unhappy working in terms of dividend yields, he or she can estimate the dollar amount of dividends that will be paid by the portfolio underlying the index and the timing of those dividends. The index can then be considered to be a security providing known income, and the result in Equation (3.7) can be used to calculate the futures price. This approach is useful for indices in countries such as Japan, France, and Germany where all stocks tend to pay dividends on the same dates.

INDEX ARBITRAGE

If $F > Se^{(r-q)(T-t)}$, profits can be made by buying the stocks underlying the index and shorting futures contracts. If $F < Se^{(r-q)(T-t)}$, profits can be made by doing the reverse, that is, shorting or selling the stocks underlying the index and taking a long position in futures contracts. These strategies are known as *index arbitrage*. When $F < Se^{(r-q)(T-t)}$, index arbitrage is often done by a pension fund that owns an indexed portfolio of stocks. When $F > Se^{(r-q)(T-t)}$, it is often done by a corporation holding short-term money market investments. For indices involving many stocks, index arbitrage is sometimes accomplished by trading a relatively small representative sample of stocks whose movements closely mirror those of the index. Often index arbitrage is implemented using *program trading*. This means that a computer system is used to generate the trades.

In normal market conditions, F is very close to $Se^{(r-q)(T-t)}$. However, it is interesting to note what happened on October 19, 1987, when the market fell by over 20 percent and the volume of shares traded on the New York Stock Exchange (604 million) easily exceeded all previous records. For most of the day, futures prices were at a significant discount to the underlying index. For example, at the close of trading, the S&P 500 index was at 225.06 (down 57.88 on the day) while the futures price for December delivery on the S&P 500 was 201.50 (down 80.75 on the day). This was largely because the delays in processing orders to sell equity made index arbitrage too risky. On the next day, October 20, 1987, the New York Stock Exchange placed temporary restrictions on the way in which program trading could be done. The result was that the breakdown of the traditional linkage between stock indices and stock index futures continued. At one point, the futures price for the December contract was 18 percent less than the S&P 500 index!

THE NIKKEI INDEX

Equation (3.12) does not apply to the futures contract on the Nikkei 225. The reason for this is quite subtle. Define S_F as the value of the Nikkei 225 index. This is the value of a portfolio measured in yen. The variable underlying the CME futures contract on the Nikkei 225 is a variable with a *dollar value* of $5S_F$. In other words, the futures contract takes a variable which is measured in yen and treats it as though it were dollars. We cannot invest in a portfolio whose value will always be $5S_F$ dollars. The best we can do is to invest in one that is always worth $5S_F$ yen or in one that is always worth $5QS_F$ dollars where Q is the dollar value of 1 yen. The variable underlying the Nikkei 225 is therefore a dollar amount that does not equal the price of a traded security. Consequently, we cannot derive a theoretical futures price using arbitrage arguments. In Chapter 12 we will show how other arguments can be used to produce a formula for the CME Nikkei 225 futures price.

HEDGING USING INDEX FUTURES

Stock index futures can be used to hedge the risk in a well-diversified portfolio of stocks. Readers familiar with the capital asset pricing model will know that the relationship between the return on a portfolio of stocks and the return on the market is described by a parameter β (= beta). This is the slope of the best fit line obtained when the excess return on the portfolio over the risk-free rate is regressed against the excess return on the market over the risk-free rate. When $\beta = 1.0$, the return on the portfolio tends to mirror the return on the market; when

$\beta = 2.0$, the excess return on the portfolio tends to be twice as great as the excess return on the market; when $\beta = 0.5$, it tends to be half as great; and so on.

Suppose we wish to hedge against changes in the value of a portfolio during a period of time, $T - t$. Define

Δ_1: Change in the value of $1 during time $T - t$ if it is invested in the portfolio

Δ_2: Change in the value of $1 during time $T - t$ if it is invested in the market index

S: Current value of the portfolio

F: Current value of one futures contract

N: Optimal number of contracts to short when hedging the portfolio

The value of one futures contract, F, is the futures price multiplied by the contract size. In the case of the S&P 500, one contract is on 500 times the index. If the futures price of the S&P 500 is 400, the value of one contract is therefore $400 \times 500 = \$200,000$.

From the definition of β, it is approximately true that

$$\Delta_1 = \alpha + \beta \Delta_2$$

where α is a constant. The change in the value of the portfolio between times t and T is $S\Delta_1$ or

$$\alpha S + \beta S \Delta_2$$

The change in the value of one futures contract price during this time is approximately $F\Delta_2$. The uncertain component of the change in the value of the portfolio is therefore approximately

$$\beta \frac{S}{F}$$

times the change in the value of one futures contract. It follows that

$$N = \beta \frac{S}{F}$$

Example 3.9

A company wishes to hedge a portfolio worth $2,100,000 using an S&P 500 index futures contract with 4 months to maturity. The current futures price is 300 and the β of the portfolio is 1.5. The value of one futures contract is $300 \times 500 = \$150,000$. The correct number of futures contracts to short, therefore, is

$$1.5 \times \frac{2,100,000}{150,000} = 21$$

A stock index hedge, if effective, should result in the hedger's position growing at approximately the risk-free interest rate. It is natural to ask why the hedger should go to the trouble of using futures contracts. If the hedger's objective is to earn the risk-free interest rate, he or she can simply sell the portfolio and invest the proceeds in Treasury bills.

One possibility is that the hedger feels that the stocks in the portfolio have been chosen well. He or she might be very uncertain about the performance of the market as a whole but confident that the stocks in the portfolio will outperform the market (after appropriate adjustments have been made for the β of the portfolio). A hedge using index futures removes the risk arising from market moves and leaves the hedger exposed only to the performance of the portfolio relative to the market. Another possibility is that the hedger is planning to hold a portfolio for a long period of time and requires short-term protection in an uncertain market situation. The alternative strategy of selling the portfolio and buying it back later might involve unacceptably high transaction costs.

CHANGING BETA

Stock index futures can be used to change the beta of a portfolio. Consider the situation in Example 3.9. To reduce the beta of the portfolio from 1.5 to 0, 21 contracts are required. To reduce the beta to 1.0, it is necessary to short only one-third of 21 or 7 contracts; to increase the beta from 1.5 to 3.0 a long position in 21 contracts is required; and so on. In general, to change the beta of the portfolio from β to β^* where $\beta > \beta^*$, a short position in

$$(\beta - \beta^*)\frac{S}{F}$$

contracts is required. When $\beta < \beta^*$, a long position in

$$(\beta^* - \beta)\frac{S}{F}$$

is required.

3.8 FORWARD AND FUTURES CONTRACTS ON CURRENCIES

We now move on to consider forward and futures contracts on foreign currencies. The variable, S, is the current price in dollars of one unit of the foreign currency; K is the delivery price agreed to in the forward contract. A foreign currency has the property that the holder of the currency can earn interest at the risk-free interest rate prevailing in the foreign country. (For example, the holder can invest the currency in a foreign denominated bond.) We define r_f as the value of this foreign risk-free interest rate with continuous compounding.

The two portfolios that enable us to price a forward contract on a foreign currency are

Portfolio A: One long forward contract plus an amount of cash equal to $Ke^{-r(T-t)}$

Portfolio B: An amount $e^{-r_f(T-t)}$ of the foreign currency

Both portfolios will become worth the same as one unit of the foreign currency at time T. They must therefore be equally valuable at time t. Hence,

$$f + Ke^{-r(T-t)} = Se^{-r_f(T-t)}$$

or

$$f = Se^{-r_f(T-t)} - Ke^{-r(T-t)} \tag{3.13}$$

The forward price (or forward exchange rate), F, is the value of K that makes $f = 0$ in Equation (3.13). Hence,

$$F = Se^{(r-r_f)(T-t)} \tag{3.14}$$

This is the well-known interest rate parity relationship from the field of international finance. From the discussion earlier in this chapter, F is, to a reasonable approximation, also the futures price.

Note that equations (3.13) and (3.14) are identical to equations (3.9) and (3.10), respectively, with q replaced by r_f. This is because a foreign currency is analogous to a security paying a known dividend yield. The "dividend yield" is the risk-free rate of interest in the foreign currency. To see why this is so, note that interest earned on a foreign currency holding is denominated in the foreign currency. Its value when measured in the domestic currency is therefore proportional to the value of the foreign currency.

Table 3.3 shows futures prices on October 17, 1991 for contracts trading on the Japanese yen, Deutschemark, Canadian dollar, British pound, Swiss franc, and Australian dollar in the International Monetary Market of the Chicago Mercantile Exchange. The futures exchange rate is quoted as the value of the foreign currency in U.S. dollars (or, in the case of the yen, the value of the foreign currency in U.S. cents). This can be confusing because spot and forward rates on most currencies are quoted the other way around, that is, as the number of units of the foreign currency per U.S. dollar. A forward quote on the Canadian dollar of 1.2000 would become a futures quote of 0.8333.

When the foreign interest rate is greater than the domestic interest rate ($r_f > r$), Equation (3.14) shows that F is always less than S and that F decreases as the maturity of the contract, T, increases. Similarly, when the domestic interest rate is greater than the foreign interest rate ($r > r_f$), Equation (3.14) shows that F is always greater than S and that F increases as T increases. On October 17, 1991, interest rates in Japan, Germany, Canada, Britain, Switzerland, and Australia were

TABLE 3.3 Foreign Exchange
Futures Quotes from *The Wall
Street Journal*, October 18, 1991

FUTURES

	Open	High	Low	Settle	Change	Lifetime High	Low	Open Interest
JAPAN YEN (IMM)—12.5 million yen; $ per yen (.00)								
Dec	.7700	.7720	.7675	.7707	+ .0041	.7770	.6997	75,304
Mr92	.7693	.7700	.7670	.7698	+ .0043	.7718	.7000	1,446
June	....	....		.7699	+ .0046	.7705	.7015	378
Sept	....	....		.7707	+ .0050	.7710	.7265	658
Dec	....	....		.7718	+ .0056	.7700	.7512	1,147
Est vol 20,149; vol Wed 17,021; open Int 78,933, −2,332.								
DEUTSCHEMARK (IMM)—125,000 marks; $ per mark								
Dec	.5838	.5850	.5818	.5840	+ .0021	.6770	.5365	57,712
Mr92	.5785	.5800	.5763	.5785	+ .0021	.5923	.5353	2,819
June	....	....		.5733	+ .0021	.5868	.5322	234
Est vol 40,793; vol Wed 33,283; open Int 60,767, +518.								
CANADIAN DOLLAR (IMM)—100,000 dlrs.; $ per Can $								
Dec	.8797	.8818	.8791	.8817	+ .0022	.8818	.8175	25,502
Mr92	.8739	.8768	.8739	.8766	+ .0022	.8768	.8253	2,649
June	.8720	.8725	.8718	.8720	+ .0022	.8725	.8330	463
Est vol 5,140; vol Wed 3,371; open Int 28,736, +282.								
BRITISH POUND (IMM)—62,500 pds.; $ per pound								
Dec	1.6970	1.6990	1.6900	1.6986	+.0068	1.7900	1.5670	20,112
Mr92	1.6770	1.6810	1.6730	1.6804	+.0072	1.7200	1.5560	1,377
Est vol 12,808; vol Wed 10,072; open Int 21,498, −123.								
SWISS FRANC (IMM)—125,000 francs; $ per franc								
Dec	.6692	.6700	.6655	.6696	+ .0027	.8090	.6235	24,063
Mr92	.6647	.6649	.6620	.6650	+ .0029	.6995	.6225	570
Est vol 17,700; vol Wed 14,402; open Int 24,681, −22.								
AUSTRALIAN DOLLAR (IMM)—100,000 dlrs.; $ per A.$								

all higher than in the United States. This corresponds to the $r_f > r$ situation and explains why futures prices for these currencies decline with maturity.

Example 3.10

The futures price of the Canadian dollar in Table 3.3 appears to be decreasing at a rate of about 2.2% per annum with the maturity. For example, the June 1992 settlement price is about 1.1% lower than the December 1991 settlement price. This suggests that the short-term risk-free interest rate was about 2.2% per annum lower in the United States than in Canada.

3.9 FUTURES ON COMMODITIES

We now move on to consider commodity futures contracts. Here it will prove to be important to distinguish between commodities that are held solely for investment by a significant number of investors (e.g., gold and silver) and those that are held primarily for consumption. Arbitrage arguments can be used to obtain exact futures prices in the case of investment commodities. However, it turns out that they can only be used to give an upper bound to the futures price in the case of consumption commodities.

GOLD AND SILVER

Gold and silver are held by a significant number of investors solely for investment. If storage costs are zero, they can be considered as being analogous to securities paying no income. Using the notation introduced earlier, S is the current spot price of gold. As shown by Equation (3.5), the futures price, F, should be given by

$$F = Se^{r(T-t)} \tag{3.15}$$

Storage costs can be regarded as negative income. If U is the present value of all the storage costs that will be incurred during the life of a futures contract, it follows from Equation (3.7) that

$$F = (S + U)e^{r(T-t)} \tag{3.16}$$

If the storage costs incurred at any time are proportional to the price of the commodity, they can be regarded as providing a negative dividend yield. In this case, from Equation (3.10),

$$F = Se^{(r+u)(T-t)} \tag{3.17}$$

where u is the storage costs per annum as a proportion of the spot price.

If we return to Table 2.2, we see that the futures price of gold increases at about 4.5 percent per annum with the maturity of the contract. This is close to the risk-free interest rate on October 17, 1991 and is consistent with the formulas just given.

Example 3.11

Consider a 1-year futures contract on gold. Suppose that it costs $2 per ounce per year to store gold, with the payment being made at the end of the year. Assume that the spot price is $450 and the risk-free rate is 7% per annum for all maturities. This corresponds to $r = 0.07$, $S = 450$, $T - t = 1$, and

$$U = 2e^{-0.07} = 1.865$$

The futures price, F, is given by

$$F = (450 + 1.865)e^{0.07} = 484.6$$

Other Commodities

For commodities that are not held primarily for investment purposes, the arbitrage arguments leading to equations (3.15), (3.16), and (3.17) need to be reviewed carefully.

Suppose that instead of Equation (3.16), we have

$$F > (S + U)e^{r(T-t)} \qquad\qquad (3.18)$$

To take advantage of this, an arbitrageur should implement the following strategy:

1. Borrow an amount $S + U$ at the risk-free rate and use it to purchase one unit of the commodity and to pay storage costs.
2. Short a futures contract on one unit of the commodity.

If we regard the futures contract as a forward contract, this is certain to lead to a profit of $F - (S + U)e^{r(T-t)}$ at time T. There is no problem with implementing the strategy for any commodity. However, as arbitrageurs do so, there will be a tendency for S to increase and F to decrease until Equation (3.18) is no longer true. We conclude that Equation (3.18) cannot hold for any significant length of time.

Suppose next that

$$F < (S + U)e^{r(T-t)} \qquad\qquad (3.19)$$

We might try to take advantage of this using a strategy analogous to that for a forward contract on a non-dividend-paying stock when the forward price is too low. However, this would involve shorting the commodity in such a way that the storage costs are paid to the person with the short position. This is not usually possible.

For gold and silver, we can argue that there are many investors who hold the commodity solely for investment. When they observe the inequality in Equation (3.19), they will find it profitable to

1. Sell the commodity, save the storage costs, and invest the proceeds at the risk-free interest rate.
2. Buy the futures contract.

The result is a riskless profit at maturity of $(S + U)e^{r(T-t)} - F$ relative to the position the investors would have been in if they had held the gold or silver. It follows that Equation (3.19) cannot hold for long. Since neither Equation (3.18) nor Equation (3.19) can hold for long, we must have $F = (S + U)e^{r(T-t)}$.

For commodities that are not, to any significant extent, held for investment, this argument cannot be used. Individuals and companies who keep the commodity in inventory do so because of its consumption value—not because of its value as an investment. They are reluctant to sell the commodity and buy futures contracts since futures contracts cannot be consumed. There is therefore nothing to stop Equation (3.19) from holding. Since Equation (3.18) cannot hold, all we can assert for a consumption commodity is

$$F \leq (S + U)e^{r(T-t)} \tag{3.20}$$

If storage costs are expressed as a proportion, u, of the spot price, the equivalent result is

$$F \leq Se^{(r+u)(T-t)} \tag{3.21}$$

CONVENIENCE YIELDS

When $F < Se^{(r+u)(T-t)}$, users of the commodity must feel that there are benefits from ownership of the physical commodity that are not obtained by the holder of a futures contract. These benefits may include the ability to profit from temporary local shortages or the ability to keep a production process running. The benefits are sometimes referred to as the *convenience yield* provided by the product. If the dollar amount of storage costs is known and has a present value, U, the convenience yield, y, is defined so that

$$Fe^{y(T-t)} = (S + U)e^{r(T-t)}$$

If the storage costs per unit are a constant proportion, u, of the spot price, y is defined so that

$$Fe^{y(T-t)} = Se^{(r+u)(T-t)}$$

or

$$F = Se^{(r+u-y)(T-t)} \tag{3.22}$$

The convenience yield simply measures the extent to which the left-hand side is less than the right-hand side in Equation (3.20) or in Equation (3.21). For investment assets, the convenience yield must be zero; otherwise, there are arbitrage opportunities. Table 2.2 of Chapter 2 shows that the futures prices of copper and crude oil decrease as the maturity of the contract increases. This indicates that the convenience yield, y, is greater than $r + u$.

The convenience yield reflects the market's expectations concerning the future availability of the commodity. The greater the possibility that shortages will occur during the life of the futures contract, the higher the convenience yield. If users of the commodity have high inventories, there is very little chance of shortages in the near future and the convenience yield tends to be low. On the other hand, low inventories tend to lead to high convenience yields.

3.10 THE COST OF CARRY

The relationship between futures prices and spot prices can be summarized in terms of what is known as the *cost of carry*. This measures the storage cost plus the interest that is paid to finance the asset less the income earned on the asset. For a non-dividend-paying stock, the cost of carry is r since there are no storage costs and no income is earned; for a stock index, it is $r - q$ since income is earned at rate q on the asset; for a currency, it is $r - r_f$; for a commodity with storage costs that are a proportion u of the price, it is $r + u$; and so on.

Define the cost of carry as c. For an investment asset, the futures price is

$$F = Se^{c(T-t)} \tag{3.23}$$

For a consumption asset, it is

$$F = Se^{(c-y)(T-t)} \tag{3.24}$$

where y is the convenience yield.

3.11 DELIVERY OPTIONS

Whereas a forward contract normally specifies that delivery is to take place on a particular day, a futures contract often allows the party with the short position to choose to deliver at any time during a certain period. (Typically, the party has to give a few days notice of its intention to deliver.) This introduces a complication into the determination of futures prices. Should the maturity of the futures contract be assumed to be the beginning, middle, or end of the delivery period? Even though most futures contracts are closed out prior to maturity, it is important to know when delivery would have taken place, in order to calculate the theoretical futures price.

If the futures price is an increasing function of the time to maturity, it can be seen from Equation (3.24) that the benefits from holding the asset (including convenience yield and net of storage costs) are less than the risk-free rate. It is then usually optimal for the party with the short position to deliver as early as possible. This is because the interest earned on the cash received outweighs the benefits of holding the asset. As a general rule, futures prices in these circumstances should therefore be calculated on the basis that delivery will take place at the beginning of the delivery period. If futures prices are decreasing as maturity increases, the reverse is true: it is usually optimal for the party with the short position to deliver as late as possible and futures prices should, as a general rule, be calculated on the assumption that this will happen.

3.12 FUTURES PRICES AND THE EXPECTED FUTURE SPOT PRICE

One question that is often raised is whether the futures price of an asset is equal to its expected future spot price. If you had to guess what the price of an asset will be in 3 months, is the futures price an unbiased estimate? John Maynard Keynes and John Hicks in the 1930s argued that, if hedgers tend to hold short positions and speculators tend to hold long positions, the futures price will be below the expected future spot price. This is because speculators require compensation for the risks they are bearing. They will trade only if there is an expectation that the futures price will rise over time. (Hedgers, on the other hand, because they are reducing their risks, are prepared to enter into contracts where the expected payoff is slightly negative.) If hedgers tend to hold long positions while speculators hold short positions, Keynes and Hicks argue that the futures price must be above the expected future spot price. The reason is similar. To compensate speculators for the risks they are bearing, there must be an expectation that the futures prices will decline over time.

The situation where the futures price is below the expected future spot price is known as *normal backwardation*; the situation where the futures price is above the expected future spot price is known as *contango*. We now consider the factors determining normal backwardation and contango from the point of view of the trade-offs that have to be made between risk and return in capital markets.

RISK AND RETURN

In general, the higher the risk of an investment, the higher the expected return demanded by an investor. Readers familiar with the capital asset pricing model will know that there are two types of risk in the economy: systematic and nonsystematic. Nonsystematic risk should not be important to an investor. This is because it can be almost completely eliminated by holding a well-diversified portfolio. An investor should not therefore require a higher expected return for bearing nonsystematic risk. Systematic risk, by contrast, cannot be diversified away. It arises from a correlation between returns from the investment and returns from the stock market as a whole. An investor in general requires a higher expected return than the risk-free interest rate for bearing positive amounts of systematic risk. Also, an investor is prepared to accept a lower expected return than the risk-free interest rate when the systematic risk in an investment is negative.

THE RISK IN A FUTURES POSITION

Consider a speculator who takes a long futures position in the hope that the price of the asset will be above the futures price at maturity. We suppose that the speculator puts the present value of the futures price into a risk-free investment while simultaneously taking a long futures position. We assume that the futures contract can be treated as a forward contract. The proceeds of the risk-free investment are used to buy the asset on the delivery date. The asset is then immediately sold for its market price. This means that the cash flows to the speculator are

Time t : $-Fe^{-r(T-t)}$

Time T : $+S_T$

where S_T is the price of the asset at time T.

The present value of this investment is

$$-Fe^{-r(T-t)} + E(S_T)e^{-k(T-t)}$$

where k is the discount rate appropriate for the investment (that is, it is the expected return required by investors on the investment) and E denotes expected value. Assuming that all investment opportunities in securities markets have zero net present value,

$$-Fe^{-r(T-t)} + E(S_T)e^{-k(T-t)} = 0$$

or

$$F = E(S_T)e^{(r-k)(T-t)} \qquad (3.25)$$

The value of k depends on the systematic risk of the investment. If S_T is uncorrelated with the level of the stock market, the investment has zero systematic risk. In this case, $k = r$ and Equation (3.25) shows that $F = E(S_T)$. If S_T is positively correlated with the stock market as a whole, the investment has positive systematic risk. In this case, $k > r$ and Equation (3.25) shows that $F < E(S_T)$. Finally, if S_T is negatively correlated with the stock market, the investment has negative systematic risk. This means that $k < r$ and Equation (3.25) shows that $F > E(S_T)$.

EMPIRICAL EVIDENCE

If $F = E(S_T)$, the futures price will drift up or down only if the market changes its views about the expected future spot price. Over a long period of time, we can reasonably assume that the market revises its expectations about future spot prices upward as often as it does so downward. It follows that, when $F = E(S_T)$, the average profit from holding futures contracts over a long period of time should be zero. The $F < E(S_T)$ situation corresponds to the positive systematic risk situation. Since the futures price and the spot price must be equal at maturity of the futures contract, it implies that a futures price should, on average, drift up and a trader should over a long period of time make positive profits from consistently holding long futures positions. Similarly, the $F > E(S_T)$ situation implies that a trader should over a long period of time make positive profits from consistently holding short futures positions.

How do futures prices behave in practice? Some of the empirical work that has been carried out is listed at the end of this chapter. The results are mixed. Houthakker's study looked at futures prices for wheat, cotton, and corn during the period 1937 to 1957. It showed that it was possible to earn significant profits from taking long futures positions. This suggests that an investment in corn has positive systematic risk and $F < E(S_T)$. Telser's study contradicted the findings of Houthakker. His data covered the period 1926 to 1950 for cotton and 1927 to 1954 for wheat and gave rise to no significant profits for traders taking either long or short positions. To quote from Telser, "The futures data offer no evidence to contradict the simple ... hypothesis that the futures price is an unbiased estimate of the expected future spot price." Gray's study looked at corn futures prices during the 1921 to 1959 period and resulted in similar findings to those of Telser. Dusak's study used data on corn, wheat, and soybeans during 1952 to 1967 and took a different approach. It attempted to estimate the systematic risk of an investment in these commodities by calculating the correlation of movements in the commodity prices with movements in the S&P 500. The results suggest that there is no systematic risk and lend support to the $F = E(S_T)$ hypothesis. However, more recent work by Chang using the same commodities and more advanced statistical techniques supports the $F < E(S_T)$ hypothesis.

3.13 SUMMARY

For most purposes, the futures price of a contract with a certain delivery date can be considered to be the same as the forward price for a contract with the same delivery date. It can be shown that, in theory, the two should be exactly the same when interest rates are perfectly predictable, and should be close to each other when interest rates vary unpredictably.

For the purposes of understanding futures (or forward) prices, it is convenient to divide futures contracts into two categories: those where the underlying asset is held for investment by a significant number of investors and those where the underlying investment is held primarily for consumption purposes.

In the case of investment assets, we have considered three different situations:

1. The asset provides no income.
2. The asset provides a known dollar income.
3. The asset provides a known dividend yield.

TABLE 3.4 Forward/Futures Price on Investment Assets

Summary of results for a contract with maturity T on an asset with price S when the risk-free interest rate for a T-year period is r:

Asset	Value of Long Forward Contract with Delivery Price K	Forward/Futures Price
Provides no income	$S - Ke^{-r(T-t)}$	$Se^{r(T-t)}$
Provides known income with present value, I	$S - I - Ke^{-r(T-t)}$	$(S - I)e^{r(T-t)}$
Provides known dividend yield, q	$Se^{-q(T-t)} - Ke^{-r(T-t)}$	$Se^{(r-q)(T-t)}$

The results are summarized in Table 3.4. They enable futures prices to be obtained for contracts on stock indices, currencies, gold, and silver.

In the case of consumption assets, it is not possible to obtain the futures price as a function of the spot price and other observable variables. A parameter known as the asset's convenience yield becomes important. This measures the extent to which users of the commodity feel that there are benefits from ownership of the physical asset that are not obtained by the holders of the futures contract. These benefits may include the ability to profit from temporary local shortages or the ability to keep a production process running. It is possible to obtain only an upper bound for the futures price of consumption assets using arbitrage arguments.

The concept of a cost of carry is sometimes useful. The cost of carry is the storage cost of the underlying asset plus the cost of financing it minus the income received from it. In the case of investment assets, the futures price is greater than the spot price by an amount reflecting the cost of carry. In the case of consumption assets, the futures price is greater than the spot price by an amount reflecting the cost of carry net of the convenience yield.

If we assume the capital asset pricing model is true, the relationship between the futures price and the expected future spot price depends on whether the spot price is positively or negatively correlated with the level of the stock market. Positive correlation will tend to lead to a futures price lower than the expected future spot price. Negative correlation will tend to lead to a futures price higher than the expected future spot price. Only when the correlation is zero will the theoretical futures price be equal to the expected future spot price.

SUGGESTIONS FOR FURTHER READING

On Empirical Research Concerning Forward and Futures Prices

CORNELL, B., and M. REINGANUM, "Forward and Futures Prices: Evidence from Foreign Exchange Markets," *Journal of Finance*, 36 (December 1981), 1035–45.

FRENCH, K., "A Comparison of Futures and Forward Prices," *Journal of Financial Economics*, 12 (November 1983), 311–42.

PARK, H. Y., and A. H. CHEN, "Differences between Futures and Forward Prices: A Further Investigation of Marking to Market Effects," *Journal of Futures Markets*, 5 (February 1985), 77–88.

RENDLEMAN, R., and C. CARABINI, "The Efficiency of the Treasury Bill Futures Markets," *Journal of Finance*, 34 (September 1979), 895–914.

VISWANATH, P. V., "Taxes and the Futures-Forward Price Difference in the 91-day T-Bill Market," *Journal of Money Credit and Banking*, 21, 2 (May 1989), 190–205.

On Empirical Research Concerning the Relationship Between Futures Prices and Expected Future Spot Prices

CHANG, E. C., "Returns to Speculators and the Theory of Normal Backwardation," *Journal of Finance*, 40 (March 1985), 193–208.

DUSAK, K., "Futures Trading and Investor Returns: An Investigation of Commodity Risk Premiums," *Journal of Political Economy*, 81 (December 1973), 1387–1406.

GRAY, R. W., "The Search for a Risk Premium," *Journal of Political Economy*, 69 (June 1961), 250–60.

HOUTHAKKER, H. S., "Can Speculators Forecast Prices?" *Review of Economics and Statistics*, 39 (1957), 143–51.

TELSER, L. G., "Futures Trading and the Storage of Cotton and Wheat," *Journal of Political Economy*, 66 (June 1958), 233–55.

On the Theoretical Relationship Between Forward and Futures Prices

COX, J. C., J. E. INGERSOLL, and S. A. ROSS, "The Relation between Forward Prices and Futures Prices," *Journal of Financial Economics*, 9 (December 1981), 321–46.

JARROW, R. A., and G. S. OLDFIELD, "Forward Contracts and Futures Contracts," *Journal of Financial Economics*, 9 (December 1981), 373–82.

KANE, E. J., "Market Incompleteness and Divergences between Forward and Futures Interest Rates," *Journal of Finance*, 35 (May 1980), 221–34.

MARGRABE, W., "A Theory of Forward and Futures Prices," working paper, The Wharton School, University of Pennsylvania, 1976.

RICHARD, S., and M. SUNDARESAN, "A Continuous Time Model of Forward and Futures Prices in a Multigood Economy," *Journal of Financial Economics*, 9 (December 1981), 347–72.

Other

HICKS, J. R., *Value and Capital.* Oxford, England: Clarendon Press, 1939.

KEYNES, J. M., *A Treatise on Money.* London: Macmillan, 1930.

QUESTIONS AND PROBLEMS

3.1. A bank quotes you a rate of interest of 14% per annum with quarterly compounding. What is the equivalent rate with (a) continuous compounding and (b) annual compounding?

3.2. Explain what happens when an investor shorts a certain share.

3.3. Suppose that you enter into a 6-month forward contract on a non-dividend-paying stock when the stock price is $30 and the risk-free interest rate (with continuous compounding) is 12% per annum. What is the forward price?

3.4. A stock index currently stands at 350. The risk-free interest rate is 8% per annum (with continuous compounding) and the dividend yield on the index is 4% per annum. What should the futures price for a 4-month contract be?

3.5. Explain carefully why the futures price of gold can be calculated from its spot price and other observable variables, while the futures price of copper cannot.

3.6. Explain carefully the meaning of the terms "convenience yield" and "cost of carry". What is the relationship between the futures price, the spot price, the convenience yield, and the cost of carry?

3.7. Is the futures price of a stock index greater than or less than the expected future value of the index? Explain your answer.

3.8. An individual receives $1,100 in 1 year in return for an investment of $1,000 now. What is the percentage return per annum with
  (a) annual compounding?
  (b) semiannual compounding?
  (c) monthly compounding?
  (d) continuous compounding?

3.9. What rate of interest with continuous compounding is equivalent to 15% per annum with monthly compounding?

3.10. A deposit account pays 12% per annum with continuous compounding, but interest is actually paid quarterly. How much interest will be paid each quarter on a $10,000 deposit?

3.11. A 1-year-long forward contract on a non-dividend-paying stock is entered into when the stock price is $40 and the risk-free rate of interest is 10% per annum with continuous compounding.
  (a) What are the forward price and the initial value of the forward contract?
  (b) Six months later, the price of the stock is $45 and the risk-free interest rate is still 10%. What are the forward price and the value of the forward contract?

3.12. A stock is expected to pay a dividend of $1 per share in 2 months and again in 5 months. The stock price is $50 and the risk-free rate of interest is 8% per annum with continuous compounding for all maturities. An investor has just taken a short position in a 6-month forward contract on the stock.

    (a) What are the forward price and the initial value of the forward contract?

    (b) Three months later, the price of the stock is $48 and the risk-free rate of interest is still 8% per annum. What are the forward price and the value of the short position in the forward contract?

3.13. The risk-free rate of interest is 7% per annum with continuous compounding and the dividend yield on a stock index is 3.2% per annum. The current value of an index is 150. What is the 6-month futures price?

3.14. Assume that the risk-free interest rate is 9% per annum with continuous compounding and that the dividend yield on a stock index varies throughout the year. In February, May, August, and November, the dividend yield is 5% per annum. In other months, it is 2% per annum. Suppose that the value of the index on July 31, 1992 is 300. What is the futures price for a contract deliverable on December 31, 1992?

3.15. Suppose that the risk-free interest rate is 10% per annum with continuous compounding and the dividend yield on a stock index is 4% per annum. The index is standing at 400 and the futures price for a contract deliverable in 4 months is 405. What arbitrage opportunities does this create?

3.16. Estimate the difference between risk-free rates of interest in Germany and the United States from the information in Table 3.3.

3.17. The 2-month interest rates in Switzerland and the United States with continuous compounding are 3% and 8% per annum, respectively. The spot price of the Swiss franc is $0.6500. The futures price for a contract deliverable in 2 months is $0.6600. What arbitrage opportunities does this create?

3.18. The current price of silver is $9 per ounce. The storage costs are $0.24 per ounce per year payable quarterly in advance. Assuming a flat term structure with a continuously compounded interest rate of 10%, calculate the futures price of silver for delivery in 9 months.

3.19. A bank offers a corporate client a choice between borrowing cash at 11% per annum and borrowing gold at 2% per annum. (If gold is borrowed, interest and principal must be repaid in gold. Thus 100 ounces borrowed today would require 102 ounces to be repaid in 1 year.) The risk-free interest rate is 9.25% per annum and storage costs are 0.5% per annum. Discuss whether the rate of interest on the gold loan is too high or too low in relation to the rate of interest on the cash loan. The interest rates on the two loans are expressed with annual compounding. The risk-free interest rate and storage cost are expressed with continuous compounding.

3.20. Suppose that F_1 and F_2 are two futures contracts on the same commodity with maturity dates of t_1 and t_2 and $t_2 > t_1$. Prove that

$$F_2 \leq (F_1 + U)e^{r(t_2 - t_1)}$$

where r is the risk-free interest rate (assumed to be constant) between t_1 and t_2 and U is the cost of storing the commodity between times t_1 and t_2 discounted to time t_1

at the risk-free rate. For the purposes of this problem, assume that a futures contract is the same as a forward contract.

3.21. When a known cash outflow in a foreign currency is hedged by a company using a forward contract, there is no foreign exchange risk. When it is hedged using futures contracts, the marking to market process does leave the company exposed to some risk. Explain the nature of this risk. In particular, consider whether the company is better off using a futures contract or a forward contract when
   (a) the value of the foreign currency falls rapidly during the life of the contract
   (b) the value of the foreign currency rises rapidly during the life of the contract
   (c) the value of the foreign currency first rises and then falls back to its initial level
   (d) the value of the foreign currency first falls and then rises back to its initial level
   Assume that the forward price equals the futures price.

3.22. It is sometimes argued that a forward exchange rate is an unbiased predictor of future exchange rates. Under what circumstances is this so?

3.23. A company that is uncertain about the exact date when it will pay a foreign currency sometimes wishes to negotiate with its bank a forward contract where there is a period during which delivery can be made. The company wants to reserve the right to choose the exact delivery date to fit in with its own cash flows. Put yourself in the position of the bank. How would you price the product that the client wants?

3.24. What is the difference between the way in which prices are quoted in the foreign exchange futures market, the foreign exchange spot market, and the foreign exchange forward market?

3.25. The forward price on the German mark for delivery in 45 days is quoted as 1.8204. The futures price for a contract that will be delivered in 45 days is 0.5479. Explain these two quotes. Which is more favorable for an investor wanting to sell marks?

3.26. The Value Line Index is designed to reflect changes in the value of a portfolio of over 1,600 equally weighted stocks. Prior to March 9, 1988, the change in the index from one day to the next was calculated as the *geometric* average of the changes in the prices of the stocks underlying the index. In these circumstances, does Equation (3.12) correctly relate the futures price of the index to its cash price? If not, does the equation overstate or understate the futures price?

3.27. A company has a $10 million portfolio with a beta of 1.2. How can it use futures contracts on the Major Market Index to hedge its risk? The index is currently standing at 270.

3.28. "When the convenience yield is high, long hedges are likely to be particularly attractive to a company that knows it will require a certain quantity of a commodity on a certain future date." Discuss.

3.29. A U.S. company is interested in using the futures contracts traded on the IMM to hedge its German mark exposure. Define r as the interest rate (all maturities) on the U.S. dollar and r_f as the interest rate (all maturities) on the mark. Assume that r and r_f are constant and suppose that the company uses a contract expiring at time T to hedge an exposure at time t ($T > t$). Show that the optimal hedge ratio is

$$e^{(r_f - r)(T - t)}$$

APPENDIX 3A: A PROOF THAT FORWARD AND FUTURES PRICES ARE EQUAL WHEN INTEREST RATES ARE CONSTANT

In this appendix, we show that forward and futures prices are equal when interest rates are constant. Suppose that a futures contract lasts for n days and that F_i is the futures price at the end of day i $(0 < i < n)$. Define δ as the risk-free rate per day (assumed constant). Consider the following strategy.[2]

1. Take a long futures position of e^{δ} at the end of day 0 (i.e., at the beginning of the contract).

2. Increase long position to $e^{2\delta}$ at the end of day 1.

3. Increase long position to $e^{3\delta}$ at the end of day 2.

And so on.

This strategy is summarized in Table 3.5. By the beginning of day i, the investor has a long position of $e^{\delta i}$. The profit (possibly negative) from the position on day i is

$$(F_i - F_{i-1})e^{\delta i}$$

Assume that this is compounded at the risk-free rate until the end of day n. Its value at the end of day n is

$$(F_i - F_{i-1})e^{\delta i}e^{(n-i)\delta} = (F_i - F_{i-1})e^{n\delta}$$

The value at the end of day n of the entire investment strategy is therefore

$$\sum_{i=1}^{n}(F_i - F_{i-1})e^{n\delta}$$

This is

$$[(F_n - F_{n-1}) + (F_{n-1} - F_{n-2}) + \cdots + (F_1 - F_0)]e^{n\delta}$$

$$= (F_n - F_0)e^{n\delta}$$

Since F_n is the same as the terminal asset price, S_T, the terminal value of the investment strategy can be written

$$(S_T - F_0)e^{n\delta}$$

---

[2] This strategy was proposed by J. C. Cox, J. E. Ingersoll, and S. A. Ross, "The Relationship between Forward Prices and Futures Prices," *Journal of Financial Economics*, 9 (December 1981), 321–46.

TABLE 3.5 The Investment Strategy to Show
that Futures and Forward Prices Are Equal

Day	0	1	2	... $n-1$	n
Futures price	F_0	F_1	F_2	... F_{n-1}	F_n
Futures position	e^δ	$e^{2\delta}$	$e^{3\delta}$	... $e^{n\delta}$	0
Gain/loss	0	$(F_1 - F_0)e^\delta$	$(F_2 - F_1)e^{2\delta}$	... ...	$(F_n - F_{n-1})e^{n\delta}$
Gain/loss compounded to day n	0	$(F_1 - F_0)e^{n\delta}$	$(F_2 - F_1)e^{n\delta}$	... ...	$(F_n - F_{n-1})e^{n\delta}$

An investment of F_0 in a risk-free bond combined with the strategy just given yields

$$F_0 e^{n\delta} + (S_T - F_0)e^{n\delta} = S_T e^{n\delta}$$

at time T. No investment is required for all the long futures positions described. It follows that an amount F_0 can be invested to give an amount $S_T e^{n\delta}$ at time T.

Suppose next that the forward price at the end of day 0 is G_0. By investing G_0 in a riskless bond and taking a long forward position of $e^{n\delta}$ forward contracts, an amount $S_T e^{n\delta}$ is also guaranteed at time T. Thus, there are two investment strategies, one requiring an initial outlay of F_0, the other requiring an initial outlay of G_0, both of which yield $S_T e^{n\delta}$ at time T. It follows that in the absence of arbitrage opportunities

$$F_0 = G_0$$

In other words, the futures price and the forward price are identical. Note that in this proof there is nothing special about the time period of one day. The futures price based on a contract with weekly settlements is also the same as the forward price when corresponding assumptions are made.

4 Interest Rate Futures

An interest rate futures contract is a futures contract on an asset whose price is dependent solely on the level of interest rates. In this chapter, we describe the mechanics of how interest rate futures contracts work and how prices are quoted. We also explain the way in which futures prices can be related to spot prices, discuss the concept of duration, and consider hedging strategies involving interest rate futures.

Hedging a company's exposure to interest rates is more complicated than hedging its exposure to, say, the price of copper. This is because a whole term structure is necessary to provide a full description of the level of interest rates, whereas the price of copper can be described by a single number. A company, when wishing to hedge its interest rate exposure, must decide not only the maturity of the hedge it requires but also the maturity of the interest rate to which it is exposed. It must then find a way of using available interest rate futures contracts so that an appropriate hedge is obtained.

4.1 SOME PRELIMINARIES

Before we describe the nature of interest rate futures contracts, it is appropriate to review a few topics concerned with the term structure of interest rates.

SPOT AND FORWARD INTEREST RATES

The n-year spot interest rate is the interest rate on an investment that is made for a period of time starting today and lasting for n years. Thus, the 3-year spot rate is the rate of interest on an investment lasting 3 years, the 5-year spot rate is the rate of interest on an investment lasting 5 years, and so on. The investment considered should be a "pure" n-year investment with no intermediate payments. This means that all the interest and the principal is repaid to the investor at the end of year n. The n-year spot rate is also referred to as the *n-year zero-coupon yield*. This is because it is, by definition, the yield on a bond that pays no coupons.

Forward interest rates are the rates of interest implied by current spot rates for periods of time in the future. To illustrate how they are calculated, we suppose that the spot rates are as shown in the second column of Table 4.1. The rates are assumed to be continuously compounded. Thus, the 10 percent per annum rate for 1 year means that, in return for an investment of $100 today, the investor receives $100e^{0.1} = \$110.52$ in one year; the 10.5 percent per annum rate for 2 years means that, in return for an investment of $100 today, the investor receives $100e^{0.105 \times 2} = \$123.37$ in two years; and so on.

The forward interest rate in Table 4.1 for year 2 is 11 percent per annum. This is the rate of interest that is implied by the spot rates for the period of time between the end of the first year and the end of the second year. It can be calculated from the 1-year spot interest rate of 10 percent per annum and the 2-year spot interest rate of 10.5 percent per annum. It is the rate of interest for year 2 that, when combined with 10 percent per annum for year 1, gives 10.5 percent per annum overall for the 2 years. To show that the correct answer is 11 percent per annum,

TABLE 4.1   Calculation of Forward Rates

Year (n)	Spot rate for an n-year investment (% per annum)	Forward rate for nth year (% per annum)
1	10.0	
2	10.5	11.0
3	10.8	11.4
4	11.0	11.6
5	11.1	11.5

suppose that $100 is invested. A rate of 10 percent for the first year and 11 percent for the second year yields

$$100e^{0.1}e^{0.11} = \$123.37$$

at the end of the second year. A rate of 10.5 percent per annum for 2 years yields

$$100e^{0.105 \times 2}$$

which is also $123.37. This example illustrates the general result that when interest rates are continuously compounded and rates in successive time periods are combined, the overall equivalent rate is simply the arithmetic average of the rates (10.5 percent is the average of 10 percent and 11 percent). The result is only approximately true when the rates are not continuously compounded.

The forward rate for the third year is the rate of interest that is implied by a 10.5 percent per annum 2-year spot rate and a 10.8 percent per annum 3-year spot rate. It is 11.4 percent per annum. This is because an investment for 2 years at 10.5 percent per annum averaged with an investment for 1 year at 11.4 percent per annum gives an overall return for the 3 years of 10.8 percent per annum. The other forward rates can be calculated similarly and are shown in the third column of the table. In general, if r is the spot rate of interest applying for T years and r^* is the spot rate of interest applying to T^* years where $T^* > T$, the forward interest rate for the period of time between T and T^*, $\hat{r}$, is given by

$$\hat{r} = \frac{r^*T^* - rT}{T^* - T} \tag{4.1}$$

To illustrate the use of this formula consider the calculation of the year 4 forward rate from the data in Table 4.1: $T = 3$, $T^* = 4$, $r = 0.108$, and $r^* = 0.11$, and the formula gives $\hat{r} = 0.116$.

THE ZERO-COUPON YIELD CURVE

The *zero-coupon yield curve* is a curve showing the relationship between spot rates (i.e., zero-coupon yields) and maturity. Figure 4.1 shows the zero-coupon yield curve for the data in Table 4.1. It is important to distinguish between the zero-coupon yield curve and a yield curve for coupon-bearing bonds. In a situation such as that shown in Figure 4.1 where the yield curve is upward sloping, the zero-coupon yield curve will always be above the yield curve for coupon-bearing bonds. This is because the yield on a coupon-bearing bond is affected by the fact that the investor gets some payments before the maturity of the bond and the discount rates corresponding to these payment dates are lower than the discount rate corresponding to the final payment date.

Analysts sometimes also look at the curve relating forward rates to the maturity of the forward contract. The forward rates can be defined so that they corre-

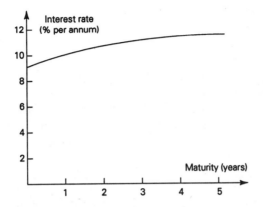

Figure 4.1   Zero-coupon Yield Curve for the Data in Table 4.1

spond to 3 months or 6 months or any other convenient time period. Equation (4.1) can be rewritten

$$\hat{r} = r^* + (r^* - r)\frac{T}{T^* - T}$$

This shows that if the yield curve is upward sloping with $r^* > r$, then $\hat{r} > r^* > r$ so that forward rates are higher than zero-coupon yields. Taking limits as T^* approaches T (so that r^* approaches r) we see that the forward rate for a very short period of time beginning at time T is

$$r + T\frac{\partial r}{\partial T}$$

This is known as the *instantaneous forward rate* for a maturity T.

Figure 4.2 shows the zero-coupon yield curve, coupon-bearing-bond yield curve, and forward rate curve when the yield curve is upward sloping. For the

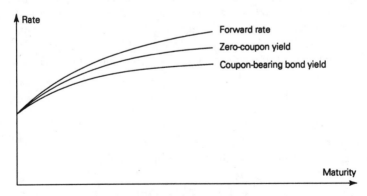

Figure 4.2   Situation When Yield Curve Is Upward Sloping

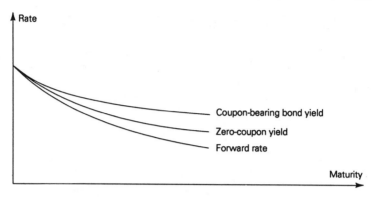

Figure 4.3   Situation When Yield Curve Is Downward Sloping

reasons just given, the forward rate curve is above the zero-coupon yield curve, which is in turn above the coupon-bearing bond yield curve. Figure 4.3 shows the situation when the yield curve is downward sloping. Arguments similar to those for the upward-sloping yield curve show that in this situation the coupon-bearing bond yield curve is above the zero-coupon yield curve which is in turn above the forward rate curve.

DETERMINATION OF ZERO-COUPON YIELD CURVE

In practice, spot rates (or zero-coupon yields) cannot always be observed directly. What can be observed are the prices of coupon-bearing bonds. An important issue, therefore, is how the zero-coupon yield curve can be extracted from the prices of coupon-bearing bonds.

One commonly used approach is known as the *bootstrap method*. To illustrate it, consider the data in Table 4.2 on the prices of 6 bonds. Since the first 3 bonds pay no coupons, the continuously compounded spot rates corresponding to the maturities of these bonds can easily be calculated. The first bond provides a return of 2.5 on an investment of 97.5 over 3 months. The 3-month rate with continuous compounding is

$$4\ln\left(1 + \frac{2.5}{97.5}\right) = 0.1012$$

or 10.12 percent per annum. Similarly, the 6-month rate is

$$2\ln\left(1 + \frac{5.1}{94.9}\right) = 0.1047$$

or 10.47 percent per annum. The 1-year rate is

$$\ln\left(1 + \frac{10}{90.0}\right) = 0.1054$$

or 10.54 percent per annum.

The fourth bond lasts 1.5 years. The payments are as follows:

6 months: $4
1 year: $4
1.5 years: $104

From our earlier calculations, we know that the discount rate for the payment at the end of 6 months is 10.47 percent and the discount rate for the payment at the end of 1 year is 10.54 percent. We also know that the bond's price, $96, must equal the present value of all the payments received by the bondholder. Suppose the 1.5-year spot rate is denoted by R. It follows that

$$4e^{-0.1047 \times 0.5} + 4e^{-0.1054} + 104e^{-1.5R} = 96$$

This reduces to

$$e^{-1.5R} = 0.85196$$

or

$$R = -\frac{\ln(0.85196)}{1.5} = 0.1068$$

The 1.5-year spot rate is therefore 10.68 percent. This is the only spot rate that is consistent with the 6-month and 1-year spot rate and consistent with the data in Table 4.2.

TABLE 4.2 Data for Bootstrap Method

Bond Principal ($)	Time to Maturity (yrs.)	Annual Coupon ($)*	Bond Price ($)
100	0.25	0	97.5
100	0.50	0	94.9
100	1.00	0	90.0
100	1.50	8	96.0
100	2.00	12	101.6
100	2.75	10	99.8

*Half of the stated coupon is assumed to be paid every 6 months.

The 2-year spot rate can be calculated similarly from the 6-month, 1-year, and 1.5-year spot rates and the information on the fifth bond in Table 4.2. If R is the 2-year spot rate

$$6e^{-0.1047 \times 0.5} + 6e^{-0.1054 \times 1.0} + 6e^{-0.1068 \times 1.5} + 106e^{-2R} = 101.6$$

This gives $R = 0.1081$ or 10.81 percent.

So far we have points on the zero-coupon curve corresponding to 5 different maturities. Points corresponding to other intermediate maturities are obtained by linear interpolation. The sixth bond provides cash flows as follows:

3 months:	$5
9 months:	$5
1.25 years:	$5
1.75 years:	$5
2.25 years:	$5
2.75 years:	$105

The discount rate corresponding to the first cash flow has already been determined as 10.12 percent. Using linear interpolation, the discount rates for the next three cash flows are 10.505 percent, 10.61 percent, and 10.745 percent. The present value of the first four cash flows is therefore:

$$5e^{-0.1012 \times 0.25} + 5e^{-0.10505 \times 0.75} + 5e^{-0.1061 \times 1.25} + 5e^{-0.10745 \times 1.75} = 18.018$$

The present value of the last two cash flows is therefore

$$99.8 - 18.018 = 81.782$$

Suppose that the 2.75-year spot rate is R. Using linear interpolation, the 2.25-year spot rate is

$$0.1081 \times \frac{2}{3} + \frac{R}{3}$$

or $0.0721 + R/3$. An equation for R is, therefore,

$$5e^{-2.25 \times (0.0721 + R/3)} + 105e^{-2.75 \times R} = 81.782$$

This can be solved by trial and error or by using a numerical procedure such as Newton–Raphson to give $R = 0.1087$.[1] The 2.75-year interest rate is 10.87 percent.

Figure 4.4 plots the zero-coupon yield curve that is constructed from the prices of the six bonds in Table 4.2. If other longer maturity bonds were available, a complete term structure could be obtained.

---

[1] The Newton–Raphson procedure is designed to solve an equation of the form $f(x) = 0$. It starts with a guess of the solution: $x = x_0$. It then produces successively better estimates of the solution: $x = x_1$, $x = x_2$, $x = x_3$, ... using the formula $x_{i+1} = x_i - f(x_i)/f'(x_i)$. Usually x_2 is extremely close to the true solution.

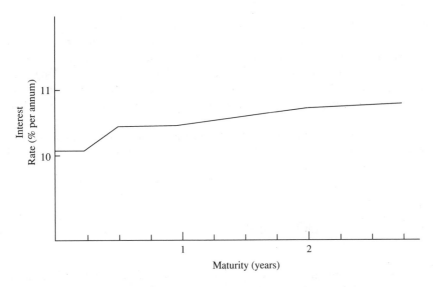

Figure 4.4   Zero-coupon Yield Curve for Data in Table 4.2

THEORIES OF THE TERM STRUCTURE

A number of different theories of the term structure have been proposed. The simplest is the *expectations theory*. This conjectures that long-term interest rates should reflect expected future short-term interest rates. More precisely, it argues that a forward interest rate corresponding to a certain period is equal to the expected future spot interest rate for that period. Another theory is known as the *market segmentation theory*. This conjectures that there need be no relationship between short-, medium-, and long-term interest rates. Under the theory, different institutions invest in bonds of different maturity and do not switch maturities. The short-term interest rate is determined by supply and demand in the short-term bond market, the medium-term interest rate is determined by supply and demand in the medium-term bond market, and so on.

The theory that is in some ways most appealing is known as *liquidity prefer-ence theory*. This argues that forward rates should always be higher than expected future spot interest rates. The basic assumption underlying the theory is that investors prefer to preserve their liquidity and invest funds for short periods of time. Borrowers, on the other hand, usually prefer to borrow at fixed rates for long periods of time. If the interest rates offered by banks and other financial intermediaries were such that the forward rate equaled the expected future spot rate, long-term interest rates would equal the average of expected future short-term interest rates. In the absence of any incentive to do otherwise, investors would tend to deposit their funds for short time periods and borrowers would tend to choose to borrow for long time periods. Financial intermediaries would then find themselves financing substantial amounts of long-term fixed rate loans with short-term deposits. This would involve excessive interest rate risk. In practice, in order to match depositors with borrowers and avoid interest rate risk, financial intermediaries raise long-term interest rates relative to expected future short-term interest rates. This reduces the demand for long-term fixed rate borrowing and encourages investors to deposit their funds for long terms.

Liquidity preference theory leads to a situation in which long rates are greater than the average of expected future short rates. It is also consistent with the empirical result that yield curves tend to be upward sloping more often than they are downward sloping.

4.2 TREASURY BOND AND TREASURY NOTE FUTURES

Table 4.3 shows interest rate futures quotes as they appeared in *The Wall Street Journal* on October 18, 1991. The most popular long-term interest rate futures contracts is the Treasury bond futures contract traded on the Chicago Board of Trade (CBOT). In this contract, any government bond with more than 15 years to maturity on the first day of the delivery month and not callable within 15 years from that day can be delivered. As will be explained later, the exchange has developed a procedure for adjusting the price received by the party with the short position according to the particular bond delivered.

The Treasury note and 5-year Treasury note futures contract are also actively traded. In the Treasury note futures contract, any government bond (or note) with a maturity between $6\frac{1}{2}$ and 10 years can be delivered. As in the case of the Treasury bond futures contract, there is a way of adjusting the price received by the party with the short position according to the particular note delivered. In the 5-year Treasury note futures contract, any of the four most recently auctioned Treasury notes can be delivered.

The rest of our discussion will focus on Treasury bond futures. However, many of the points made are applicable to other contracts.

QUOTES

Treasury bond prices are quoted in dollars and 32nds of a dollar. The quoted price is for a bond with a face value of $100. Thus, a quote of 90-05 means that the indicated price for a bond with a face value of $100,000 is $90,156.25.

The quoted price is not the same as the cash price that is paid by the purchaser. The relationship between the cash price and the quoted price is

Cash price = Quoted price + Accrued interest since last coupon date

TABLE 4.3 Interest Rate Futures Quotes from
The Wall Street Journal, October 18, 1991

FUTURES

	Open	High	Low	Settle	Yield Chg	Open Settle Chg	Open Interest
TREASURY BONDS (CBT)–$100,000; pts. 32nds of 100%
Dec	99-27	100-03	98-19	98-20 −	41	8.140 + .131	276,491
Mr92	99-00	99-08	97-26	97-26 −	41	8.225 + .133	17,282
June	97-16	97-16	96-31	96-31 −	41	8.313 + .134	9,433
Sept	96-15	96-17	96-06	96-06 −	41	8.397 + .136	2,439
Dec	95-24	95-24	95-15	95-15 −	41	8.474 + .137	2,981
Mr93	....	....	....	94-26 −	41	8.546 + .139	232
Est vol 400,000; vol Wed 190,068; op int 308,889, −3,712.
TREASURY BONDS (MCE)–$50,000; pts. 32nds of 100%
Dec	100-01	100-03	98-18	98-21 −	38	8.137 + .121	16,628
Est vol 7,500; vol Wed 4,513; open int 16,673, −106.
T–BONDS (LIFFE) U.S. $100,000; pts of 100%
Dec	100-00	100-02	98-25	98-30 −	1-03	100-20 96-24	4,401
Est vol 1,246; vol Wed 999; open int 4,401, +305.
GERMAN GOV'T. BOND (LIFFE)
250,000 marks; $ per mark (.01)
Dec	86.24	86.35	86.21	86.32 +	.07	86.38 83.73	83,113
Mr92	86.55	86.59	86.50	86.57 +	.06	86.63 85.39	1,530
Est vol 37,158; vol 33,460; open int 84,643, +1,539.
TREASURY NOTES (CBT)–$100,000; pts. 32nds of 100%
Dec	102-27	102-31	102-04	102-04 −	23	7.692 + .103	91,105
Mr92	102-07	102-07	101-13	101-14 −	23	7.790 + .103	3,616
Est vol 30,000; vol Wed 13,950; open int 94,721, +536.
5 YR TREAS NOTES (CBT)–$100,000; pts. 32nds of 100%
Dec	04-065	04-075	03-225	103-25 −	12.5	7.089 + .092	91,659
Mr92	03-035	103-04	03-025	103-03 −	12.5	7.251 + .092	434
Est vol 14,124; vol Wed 11,249; open int 92,093, −1,972.
2 YR TREAS NOTES (CBT)–$200,000; pts. 32nds of 100%
Dec	103-11	103-11	103-05	103-062 −	4¼	6.275 + .070	14,760
Est vol 800; vol Wed 582; open int 14,764, −121.
30–DAY INTEREST RATE (CBT)–$5 million; pts. of 100%
Oct	94.82	94.82	94.77	94.78 −	.03	5.22 + .03	1,250
Nov	94.90	94.90	94.82	94.83 −	.06	5.17 + .06	1,245
Dec	94.75	94.76	94.75	94.75 −	.05	5.25 + .05	1,103
Ja92	94.78	94.78	94.78	94.78 −	.05	5.22 + .05	693
Feb	94.85	94.86	94.85	94.85 −	.06	5.15 + .06	757
Mar	94.82	94.82	94.81	94.81 −	.06	5.19 + .06	304
June	....	....	....	94.61 −	.05	5.39 + .05	113
Est vol 281; vol Wed 408; open int 5,557, +105.
TREASURY BILLS (IMM)–$1 mil.; pts. of 100%
					Discount		Open
	Open	High	Low	Settle	Chg	Settle Chg	Interest
Dec	95.08	95.08	94.98	95.02 −	.05	4.98 + .05	27,859
Mr92	95.17	95.17	95.06	95.08 −	.08	4.92 + .08	20,046
June	94.98	94.98	94.88	94.89 −	.10	5.11 + .10	2,107
Sept	94.60	94.62	94.60	94.63 −	.12	5.37 + .12	251
Est vol 7,844; vol Wed 3,781; open int 50,359, −461.
LIBOR–1 MO. (IMM)–$3,000,000; points of 100%
Nov	94.78	94.78	94.69	94.69 −	.09	5.31 + .09	9,535
Dec	94.22	94.22	94.16	94.16 −	.06	5.84 + .06	5,614
Ja92	94.74	94.74	94.66	94.68 −	.06	5.32 + .06	6,062
Feb	94.65	94.65	94.64	94.65 −	.06	5.35 + .06	1,069
Mar	94.61	94.69	94.59	94.61 −	.07	5.39 + .07	674
Est vol 2,347; vol Wed 1,922; open int 22,955, +124.

	Open	High	Low	Settle	Chg	High	Low	Open Interest
MUNI BOND INDEX (CBT)–$1,000; times Bond Buyer MBI
Dec	94-30	94-30	94-05	94-10 −	18	95-09	88-16	10,469
Mr92	93-26	93-26	93-16	93-20 −	19	94-18	88-00	123
Est vol 2,500; vol Wed 1,313; open int 10,592, +175.
The Index: Close 95-01; Yield 6.87.
EURODOLLAR (IMM)–$1 million; pts of 100%
	Open	High	Low	Settle	Chg	Yield Settle Chg	Open Interest
Dec	94.56	94.56	94.46	94.47 −	.07	5.53 + .07	264,211
Mr92	94.64	94.65	94.52	94.55 −	.08	5.45 + .08	216,583
June	94.44	94.46	94.31	94.32 −	.11	5.68 + .11	124,299
Sept	94.15	94.17	94.00	94.01 −	.13	5.99 + .13	79,395
Dec	93.60	93.61	93.45	93.45 −	.14	6.55 + .14	59,271
Mr93	93.44	93.44	93.30	93.30 −	.12	6.70 + .12	51,833
June	93.12	93.12	93.00	93.00 −	.10	7.00 + .10	36,057
Sept	92.83	92.83	92.72	92.73 −	.08	7.27 + .08	23,889
Dec	92.47	92.47	92.36	92.38 −	.06	7.62 + .06	20,078
Mr94	92.44	92.46	92.36	92.37 −	.06	7.63 + .06	16,782
June	92.28	92.28	92.18	92.19 −	.06	7.81 + .06	14,520
Sept	92.10	92.10	92.00	92.01 −	.06	7.99 + .06	10,224
Dec	91.79	91.79	91.71	91.73 −	.06	8.27 + .06	9,544
Mr95	91.78	91.78	91.69	91.72 −	.06	8.28 + .06	6,308
June	91.70	91.70	91.60	91.63 −	.06	8.37 + .06	5,679
Sept	91.61	91.62	91.52	91.55 −	.06	8.45 + .06	5,230
Est vol 206,438; vol Wed 63,709; open int 942,822, −1,721.
EURODOLLAR (LIFFE)–$1 million; pts of 100%
	Open	High	Low	Settle	Change	Lifetime High Low	Open Interest
Dec	94.55	94.56	94.47	94.48 −	.07	94.56 90.58	18,088
Mr92	94.65	94.65	94.54	94.56 −	.08	94.65 90.60	7,734
June	94.45	94.45	94.33	94.35 −	.09	94.45 90.97	3,723
Sept	94.15	94.17	94.04	94.06 −	.11	94.17 90.97	1,423
Dec	93.60	93.60	93.60	93.50 −	.11	93.60 91.54	467
Mr93	....	....	....	93.33 −	.11	93.35 91.55	405
June	....	....	....	93.03 −	.08	92.80 92.60	330
Est vol 2,973; vol Wed 1,510; open int 32,242, +314.
STERLING (LIFFE)–£500,000; pts of 100%
Dec	89.95	89.97	89.92	89.96 +	.02	90.35 86.52	53,360
Mr92	90.34	90.37	90.32	90.35 +	.02	90.49 86.68	35,435
June	90.38	90.40	90.36	90.39 +	.02	90.46 87.45	29,134
Sept	90.34	90.37	90.34	90.36 +	.02	90.40 87.46	10,238
Dec	90.26	90.27	90.24	90.27 +	.02	90.32 87.55	6,654
Mr93	90.11	90.12	90.10	90.12 +	.02	90.16 87.50	3,819
June	89.98	90.00	89.98	89.99 +	.01	90.09 87.58	1,822
Sept	89.93	89.97	89.93	89.96	....	90.08 88.20	1,595
Dec	....	....	....	89.86	....	90.02 88.95	1,708
Est vol 33,465; vol Wed 30,309; open int 143,765, −594.
LONG GILT (LIFFE)–£50,000; 32nds of 100%
Dec	94-25	94-25	94-10	94-17 −	0-06	97-17 89-10	52,997
Mr92	94-22	94-22	94-22	94-20 −	0-06	96-06 96-00	228
Est vol 35,445; vol Wed 26,424; open int 53,225, +29.

To illustrate this formula, suppose that it is March 5, 1990 and the bond under consideration is an 11 percent coupon bond maturing on July 10, 2010 with a quoted price of 95-16 (or $95.50). Since coupons are paid semiannually on government bonds, the most recent coupon date is January 10, 1990 and the next coupon date is July 10, 1990. The number of days between January 10, 1990 and March 5, 1990 is 54 while the number of days between January 10, 1990 and July 10, 1990 is 181. On $100 face value of bonds, the coupon payment is $5.50 on January 10 and July 10. The accrued interest on March 5, 1990 is the share of the July 10 coupon accruing to the bondholder and is calculated as

$$\frac{54}{181} \times \$5.5 = \$1.64$$

The cash price per $100 face value for the July 10, 2010 bond is therefore

$$\$95.5 + \$1.64 = \$97.14$$

The cash price of a $100,000 bond is $97,140.

Treasury bond futures prices are quoted in the same way as the Treasury bond prices themselves. Table 4.3 shows that the settlement price for the December contract on October 17, 1991 was 98-20 or $98\frac{20}{32}$. One contract involves the delivery of $100,000 of face value of bond. Thus a $1 change in the quoted futures price would lead to a $1,000 change in the value of the futures contract. Delivery can take place at any time during the delivery month.

CONVERSION FACTORS

As mentioned, there is a provision in the Treasury bond futures contract for the party with the short position to choose to deliver any bond with a maturity over 15 years and not callable within 15 years. When a particular bond is delivered, a parameter known as its *conversion factor* defines the price received by the party with the short position. The quoted price applicable to the delivery is the product of the conversion factor and the quoted futures price. Taking accrued interest into account, we have the following relationship for each $100 face value of the bond delivered:

$$
\begin{array}{ccc}
\text{Cash received by party} \\
\text{with short position}
\end{array}
=
\begin{array}{c}
\text{Quoted futures} \\
\text{price}
\end{array}
\times
\begin{array}{c}
\text{Conversion factor} \\
\text{for bond delivered}
\end{array}
$$

$$
+
\begin{array}{c}
\text{Accrued interest} \\
\text{on bond delivered}
\end{array}
$$

Each contract is for the delivery of $100,000 face value of bonds. Suppose the quoted futures price is 90-00, the conversion factor for the bond delivered is 1.3800, and the accrued interest on this bond at the time of delivery is $3.00 per $100 face value. The cash received by the party with the short position when it delivers the bond (and is paid by the party with the long position when it takes delivery) is

$$(1.38 \times 90.00) + 3.00 = \$127.20$$

per $100 face value. A party with the short position in one contract would therefore deliver bonds with face value of $100,000 and receive $127,200.

The conversion factor for a bond is equal to the value of the bond on the first day of the delivery month on the assumption that the interest rate for all maturities equals 8 percent per annum (with semiannual compounding). The bond maturity and the times to the coupon payment dates are rounded down to the nearest 3 months for the purposes of the calculation. This enables the CBOT to produce comprehensive tables. If, after the rounding, the bond lasts for an exact number of half years, the first coupon is assumed to be paid in 6 months. If after rounding the bond does not last for an exact number of 6 months (i.e., there is an extra 3 months), the first coupon is assumed to be paid after 3 months and accrued interest is subtracted.

Example 4.1

Consider a 14% coupon bond with 20 years and 2 months to maturity. For the purposes of calculating the conversion factor, the bond is assumed to have exactly 20 years to maturity. The first coupon payment is assumed to be made after 6 months. Coupon payments are then assumed to be made at 6-month intervals until the end of the 20 years when the principal payment is made. We will work in terms of a $100 face value bond. On the assumption that the discount rate is 8% per annum with semiannual compounding (or 4% per 6 months), the value of the bond is

$$\sum_{i=1}^{40} \frac{7}{1.04^i} + \frac{100}{1.04^{40}} = 159.38$$

Dividing by the face value, the credit conversion factor is 1.5938.

Example 4.2

Consider a 14% coupon bond with 18 years and 4 months to maturity. For the purposes of calculating the conversion factor, the bond is assumed to have exactly 18 years and 3 months to maturity. Discounting all the payments back to a point in time 3 months from today gives a value of

$$\sum_{i=0}^{36} \frac{7}{1.04^i} + \frac{100}{1.04^{36}} = 163.73$$

The interest rate for a 3-month period is $\sqrt{1.04} - 1$ or 1.9804%. Hence discounting back to the present gives the bond's value as $163.73/1.019804 = 160.55$. Subtracting the accrued interest of 3.5, this becomes 157.05. The conversion factor is therefore 1.5705.

CHEAPEST-TO-DELIVER BOND

At any given time, there are about 30 bonds that can be delivered in the CBOT Treasury bond futures contract. These vary widely as far as coupon and maturity is concerned. The party with the short position can choose which of the available bonds is "cheapest" to deliver. Since the party with the short position receives

(Quoted futures price × Conversion factor) + Accrued interest and the cost of purchasing a bond is

$$\text{Quoted price} + \text{Accrued interest}$$

the cheapest-to-deliver bond is the one for which

$$\genfrac{}{}{0pt}{}{\text{Quoted}}{\text{price}} - \left(\genfrac{}{}{0pt}{}{\text{Quoted futures}}{\text{price}} \times \genfrac{}{}{0pt}{}{\text{Conversion}}{\text{factor}} \right)$$

is least. This can be found by examining each of the bonds in turn.

Example 4.3

The party with the short position has decided to deliver and is trying to choose between the three bonds in Table 4.4. Assume the current quoted futures price is 93-08 or 93.25. The cost of delivering each of the bonds is as follows:

> **Bond 1:** $99.50 - (93.25 \times 1.0382) = 2.69$
> **Bond 2:** $143.50 - (93.25 \times 1.5188) = 1.87$
> **Bond 3:** $119.75 - (93.25 \times 1.2615) = 2.12$

The cheapest-to-deliver bond is bond 2.

A number of factors determine the cheapest-to-deliver bond. When yields are in excess of 8 percent, there is a tendency for the conversion factor system to favor the delivery of low-coupon long-maturity bonds. When yields are less than 8 percent, there is a tendency for it to favor the delivery of high-coupon, short-maturity bonds. Also, when the yield curve is upward sloping, there is a tendency for bonds with a long time to maturity to be favored; whereas when it is downward sloping, there is a tendency for bonds with a short time to maturity to be delivered. Finally, some bonds tend to sell for more than their theoretical value. Examples are low-coupon bonds and bonds where the coupons can be stripped from the interest. These bonds are unlikely to prove to be cheapest to deliver in any circumstances.

TABLE 4.4 Deliverable
Bonds in Example 4.3

Bond	Quoted Price	Conversion Factor
1	99.50	1.0382
2	143.50	1.5188
3	119.75	1.2615

THE WILD CARD PLAY

Trading in the CBOT Treasury bond futures contracts ceases at 2 p.m. (Chicago time). However, Treasury bonds themselves continue trading until 4 p.m. Furthermore, the party with the short position has until 8 p.m. to issue to the clearinghouse a notice of intention to deliver. If the notice is issued, the invoice price is calculated on the basis of the settlement price that day. This is the price at which trading was being done just before the bell at 2 p.m.

This gives the party with the short position an option known as the *wild card play*. If bond prices decline after 2 p.m., he or she can issue a notice of intention to deliver and proceed to buy cheapest-to-deliver bonds in preparation for delivery. If the bond price does not decline, the party with the short position keeps the position open and waits until the next day when the same strategy can be used.

Like the other options open to the party with the short position, the wild card option is not free. Its value is reflected in the futures price, which is lower than it would be without the option.

DETERMINING THE FUTURES PRICE

An exact theoretical futures price for the Treasury bond contract is difficult to determine because the short party's options concerned with the timing of delivery and choice of the bond that is delivered cannot easily be valued. However, if we assume that both the cheapest-to-deliver bond and the delivery date are known, the Treasury bond futures contract is a futures contract on a security providing the holder with known income. Equation (3.7) from Chapter 3 then shows that futures price, F, is related to the spot price, S, by

$$F = (S - I)e^{r(T-t)} \qquad (4.2)$$

where I is the present value of the coupons during the life of the futures contract, T is the time when the futures contract matures, t is the current time, and r is the risk-free interest rate applicable to the period between times t and T.

In Equation (4.2), F is the cash futures price and S is the cash bond price. The correct procedure is therefore as follows:

1. Calculate cash price of the cheapest-to-deliver bond from quoted price.
2. Calculate cash futures price from cash bond price using Equation (4.2).
3. Calculate the quoted futures price from the cash futures price.
4. Divide the quoted futures price by the conversion factor to allow for difference between the cheapest-to-deliver bond and the standard 15-year 8% bond.

The procedure is best illustrated with an example.

Figure 4.5   Time Chart for Example 4.4

Example 4.4

Suppose that in a T-bond futures contract, it is known that the cheapest-to-deliver bond will be a 12% coupon bond with a conversion factor of 1.4000. Suppose also that it is known that delivery will take place in 270 days' time. Coupons are payable semiannually on the bond. As illustrated in Figure 4.5, the last coupon date was 60 days ago, the next coupon date is in 122 days' time, and the next-but-one coupon date is in 305 days' time. The term structure is flat and the rate of interest (with continuous compounding) is 10% per annum. We assume that the current quoted bond price is $120. The cash price of the bond is obtained by adding to this quoted price the proportion of the next coupon payment that accrues to the holder. The cash price is therefore

$$120 + \frac{60}{182} \times 6 = 121.978$$

A coupon payment of $6 will be received after 122 days (= 0.3342 year). The present value of this is

$$6e^{-0.3342 \times 0.1} = 5.803$$

The futures contract lasts for 270 days (= 0.7397 year). The cash futures price if the contract were written on the 12% bond would therefore be

$$(121.978 - 5.803)e^{0.7397 \times 0.1} = 125.094$$

At delivery, there are 148 days of accrued interest. The quoted futures price if the contract were written on the 12% bond would therefore be

$$125.094 - 6 \times \frac{148}{183} = 120.242$$

The contract is in fact written on a standard 8% bond, and 1.4000 standard bonds are considered equivalent to each 12% bond. The quoted futures price should therefore be

$$\frac{120.242}{1.4000} = 85.887$$

4.3 TREASURY BILL FUTURES

We now move on to consider futures contracts dependent on the short rate. In the Treasury bill futures contract, the underlying asset is a 90-day Treasury bill. Under the terms of the contract, the party with the short position must deliver $1 million of Treasury bills on one of 3 successive business days. The first delivery day is the first day of the delivery month on which a 13-week Treasury bill is issued and a 1-year Treasury bill has 13 weeks remaining to maturity. In practice this means that the Treasury bill may have 89 or 90 or 91 days to expiration when it is delivered.

A Treasury bill is what is known as a *discount instrument*. It pays no coupons, and the investor receives the face value at maturity. Prior to maturity of the futures contract, the underlying asset is a Treasury bill with a maturity longer than 90 days. For example, if the futures contract matures in 160 days, the underlying asset is a 250-day Treasury bill.

To present a general analysis, we suppose that we are at time 0, the futures contract matures in T years and the Treasury bill underlying the futures contract matures in T^* years. (The difference between T^* and T is 90 days.) We suppose further that r and r^* are the continuously compounded interest rates for risk-free investments maturing at times T and T^*, respectively. Assuming the Treasury bill underlying the futures contract has a face value of $100, its current value, V^* is given by

$$V^* = 100e^{-r^*T^*}$$

Since no income is paid on the instrument, we know from Equation (3.5) that the futures price, F, is e^{rT} times this; that is,

$$F = 100e^{-r^*T^*}e^{rT} = 100e^{rT-r^*T^*} \tag{4.3}$$

From Equation (4.1), this reduces to

$$F = 100e^{-\hat{r}(T^*-T)}$$

where $\hat{r}$ is the forward rate for the time period between T and T^*. This expression shows that the futures price of a Treasury bill is the price it will have if the 90-day interest rate on the delivery date proves to be equal to the current forward rate.

ARBITRAGE OPPORTUNITIES

If the forward interest rate implied by the Treasury bill futures price is different from that implied by the rates on Treasury bills themselves, there is a potential arbitrage opportunity. Suppose that the 45-day Treasury bill rate is 10 percent, the 135-day Treasury bill rate is 10.5 percent, and the rate corresponding to the Treasury bill futures prices for a contract maturing in 45 days is 10.6 percent with all rates being continuously compounded. The forward rate for the period between 45 days and 135 days implied by the Treasury bill rates is from Equation (4.1)

$$\frac{135 \times 10.5 - 45 \times 10}{90} = 10.75\%$$

This is greater than the 10.6 percent forward rate implied by the futures price. An arbitrageur should attempt to borrow for the period of time between 45 days and 135 days at 10.6 percent and invest at 10.75 percent. This is achieved by the following strategy

1. Short the futures contract.
2. Borrow 45-day money at 10 percent per annum.
3. Invest the borrowed money for 135 days at 10.5 percent per annum.

We will refer to this as a *Type 1 arbitrage*. The first trade ensures that a Treasury bill yielding 10.6 percent can be sold after 45 days have elapsed. It in effect locks in a rate of interest of 10.6 percent on borrowed funds for this time period. The second and third trades ensure that a rate of interest of 10.75 percent is earned during the time period.

If instead, the rate of interest corresponding to the Treasury bill futures were greater than 10.75 percent, the opposite strategy would be appropriate:

1. Take a long position in the futures contract.
2. Borrow 135-day money at 10.5 percent per annum.
3. Invest the borrowed money for 45 days at 10.5 percent per annum.

We will refer to this as a *Type 2 arbitrage*.

Both of these arbitrage possibilities involve borrowing at, or close to, the Treasury bill rate. As discussed in Chapter 3, repos provide a way in which companies that own portfolios of marketable securities can do this for short periods of time. In testing for arbitrage opportunities in the Treasury bill market, traders frequently calculate what is known as the *implied repo rate*. This is the rate of interest on a short-term Treasury bill implied by the futures price for a contract maturing at the same time as the short-term Treasury bill and the price of a Treasury bill maturing 90 days later than the short-term Treasury bill. If the implied repo rate is greater than the actual short-term Treasury bill rate, a Type 1 arbitrage is in principle possible. If the implied repo rate is less than the short-term Treasury bill rate, a Type 2 arbitrage is in principle possible.

Example 4.5

The cash price (per $100 face value) of a Treasury bill maturing in 146 days is $95.21 and the cash futures price for a 90-day Treasury bill futures contract maturing in 56 days is $96.95. Since 90 days is 0.2466 year and 146 days is 0.4000 year, the continuously compounded 146-day rate, r^*, is

$$-\frac{1}{0.4000} \ln 0.9521 = 0.1227$$

or 12.27% and the continuously compounded forward rate, $\hat{r}$, implied by the futures price, is

$$-\frac{1}{0.2466} \ln 0.9695 = 0.1256$$

or 12.56%. Rearranging Equation (4.1), we see that the continuously compounded 56-day rate, r, implied by r^* and $\hat{r}$ is

$$r = \frac{r^* T^* - \hat{r}(T^* - T)}{T}$$

This is the implied repo rate. In this case it is

$$\frac{12.27 \times 146 - 12.56 \times 90}{56} = 11.80\%$$

If the 56-day rate is less than 11.80% per annum, a Type 1 arbitrage is indicated. If it is greater than 11.80%, a Type 2 arbitrage is indicated.

QUOTES

Treasury bill price quotes are for a Treasury bill with a face value of \$100. Suppose that Y is the cash price of a Treasury bill that has a face value of \$100 and n days to maturity. The price is quoted as

$$\frac{360}{n}(100 - Y)$$

This is referred to as the *discount rate*. It is the annualized dollar return provided by the Treasury bill expressed as a percentage of the face value. If, for a 90-day Treasury bill, the cash price, Y, were 98, the quoted price would be 8.00.

The discount rate is not the same as the rate of return earned on the Treasury bill. The latter is calculated as the dollar return divided by the cost. In the previous example, where the quoted price is 8.00, the rate of return would be 2/98 or 2.04 percent per 90 days. This amounts to

$$\frac{2}{98} \times \frac{365}{90} = 0.0828$$

or 8.28 percent per annum with compounding every 90 days.[2] This rate of return is sometimes referred to as the *bond equivalent yield*.

A 90-day Treasury bill futures contract is for delivery of \$1 million of Treasury bills. Treasury bill futures prices are not quoted in the same way as the prices

---

[2]It is interesting to note that the compounding frequency used when a yield on a money market instrument such as a Treasury bill is quoted is generally equal to the life of the instrument. This means that the yields on money market instruments of different maturities are not directly comparable.

of Treasury bills themselves. The following relationship is used:[3]

$$\text{Treasury bill futures price quote} = 100 - \text{Corresponding Treasury bill price quote}$$

If Z is the quoted futures price and Y is the cash futures price, this means that

$$Z = 100 - 4(100 - Y)$$

or, equivalently,

$$Y = 100 - 0.25(100 - Z)$$

Thus the closing quote of 95.02 for December 1991 Treasury bills in Table 4.3 corresponds to a price of $100 - 0.25(100 - 95.02) = \$98.755$ per $100 of 90-day Treasury bills or a contract price of $987,550.

If the Treasury bills that are delivered have 89 days to maturity, the price received is calculated by replacing the 0.25 in the preceding formula by 89/360 or 0.2472. If they have 91 days to maturity, the 0.25 in the formula becomes 91/360 or 0.2528.

Example 4.6

Suppose that the 140-day interest rate is 8% per annum and the 230-day rate is 8.25% per annum with continuous compounding being used for both rates. The forward rate for the time period between day 140 and day 230 is

$$\frac{0.0825 \times 230 - 0.08 \times 140}{90} = 0.0864$$

or 8.64%. Since 90 days = 0.2466 year, the futures price for $100 of 90-day Treasury bills deliverable in 140 days is

$$100e^{-0.0864 \times 0.2466} = 97.89$$

This would be quoted as $100 - 4(100 - 97.89) = 91.56$

4.4 EURODOLLAR FUTURES

The Eurodollar futures contract is a very popular contract. It is traded on the International Monetary Market (IMM) and the London International Financial Futures Exchange (LIFFE). A Eurodollar is a dollar deposited in a U.S. or foreign bank outside the United States. The Eurodollar interest rate is the rate of interest earned on Eurodollars deposited by one bank with another bank and is also known as the 3-month London Interbank Offer Rate (LIBOR). Eurodollar interest rates are generally higher than the corresponding Treasury bill interest rates. This is because

---

[3] The reason for quoting Treasury bill futures prices in this way is to ensure that the bid quote is below the ask quote.

the Eurodollar interest rate is a commercial lending rate whereas the Treasury bill rate is the rate at which governments borrow.

On the surface, a Eurodollar futures contract appears to be structurally the same as the Treasury bill futures contract. The formula for calculating the value of one contract from the quoted futures price is the same as the formula used for Treasury bill futures. The quote of 94.47 for the December contract in Table 4.3 corresponds to a Eurodollar interest rate quote of 5.53 and a contract price of

$$10,000[100 - 0.25(100 - 94.47)] = \$986,175$$

However, there are some important differences between the Treasury bill and Eurodollar futures contracts. For a Treasury bill, the contract price converges at maturity to the price of a 90-day $1 million face value Treasury bill and, if a contract is held until maturity, this is the instrument delivered. A Eurodollar futures contract is settled in cash on the second London business day before the third Wednesday of the month. The final marking to market sets the contract price equal to

$$10,000(100 - 0.25R)$$

where R is the quoted Eurodollar rate at that time. This quoted Eurodollar rate is the actual 90-day rate on Eurodollar deposits with quarterly compounding. It is not a discount rate. The Eurodollar futures contract is therefore a futures contract on an interest rate, whereas the Treasury bill futures contract is a futures contract on the price of a Treasury bill.

4.5 DURATION

Duration is an important concept in the use of interest rate futures for hedging. The duration of a bond is a measure of how long, on average, the holder of the bond has to wait before receiving cash payments. A zero-coupon bond that matures in n years has a duration of n years. However, a coupon-bearing bond maturing in n years has a duration of less than n years. This is because some of the cash payments are received by the holder prior to year n.

Suppose that the current time is 0 and a bond provides the holder with payments c_i at time t_i $(1 \le i \le n)$. The price, B, and yield, y, (continuously compounded) are related by

$$B = \sum_{i=1}^{n} c_i e^{-yt_i} \qquad (4.4)$$

The duration, D, of the bond is defined as

$$D = \frac{\sum_{i=1}^{n} t_i c_i e^{-yt_i}}{B} \qquad (4.5)$$

This can be written

$$D = \sum_{i=1}^{n} t_i \left[\frac{c_i e^{-yt_i}}{B} \right]$$

The term in square brackets is the ratio of the present value of the payment at time t_i to the bond price. The bond price is the present value of all payments. The duration is therefore a weighted average of the times when payments are made with the weight applied to time t_i being equal to the proportion of the bond's total present value provided by the payment at time t_i. The sum of the weights is 1.0. We now show why duration is an important concept in hedging.

From Equation (4.4)

$$\frac{\partial B}{\partial y} = -\sum_{i=1}^{n} c_i t_i e^{-yt_i} \tag{4.6}$$

and from Equation (4.5) this can be written

$$\frac{\partial B}{\partial y} = -BD \tag{4.7}$$

If we make a small parallel shift to the yield curve increasing all interest rates by a small amount Δy, the yields on all bonds also increase by Δy. Equation (4.7) shows that the bond's price increases by ΔB where

$$\frac{\Delta B}{\Delta y} = -BD \tag{4.8}$$

or

$$\frac{\Delta B}{B} = -D\Delta y$$

This shows that the percentage change in a bond price is equal to its duration multiplied by the size of the parallel shift in the yield curve.

Example 4.7

Consider a 3-year 10% coupon bond with a face value of $100. Suppose that the yield on the bond is 12% per annum with continuous compounding. This means that $y = 0.12$. Coupon payments of $5 are made every 6 months. Table 4.5 shows the calculations necessary to determine the bond's duration. The present values of the payments using the yield as the discount rate are shown in column 3. (For example, the present value of the first payment is $5e^{-0.12 \times 0.5} = 4.709$.) The sum of the numbers in column 3 give the bond's price as $94.213. The weights are calculated by dividing the numbers in column 3 by 94.213. The sum of the numbers in column 5 gives the duration as 2.654 years. From Equation (4.8)

$$\Delta B = -94.213 \times 2.654\Delta y$$

that is

$$\Delta B = -250.04\Delta y$$

TABLE 4.5 Calculation of Duration

Time	Payment	Present Value	Weight	Time × Weight
0.5	5	4.709	0.050	0.025
1.0	5	4.435	0.047	0.047
1.5	5	4.176	0.044	0.066
2.0	5	3.933	0.042	0.084
2.5	5	3.704	0.039	0.098
3.0	105	73.256	0.778	2.334
Total	130	94.213	1.000	2.654

If $\Delta y = +0.001$ so that y increases to 0.121, this formula indicates that we expect ΔB to be -0.25. In other words, we expect the bond price to go down to $94.213 - 0.250 = 93.963$. By recomputing the bond price for a yield of 12.1%, the reader can verify that this is indeed what happens.

The duration of a bond portfolio can be defined as a weighted average of the durations of the individual bonds in the portfolio with the weights being proportional to the bond prices. Equation (4.8) then shows that the proportional effect of a parallel shift of Δy in the yield curve is the duration of the portfolio multiplied by the Δy.

This analysis is based on the assumption that y is expressed with continuous compounding. If y is expressed with annual compounding, it can be shown that Equation (4.8) becomes

$$\Delta B = -\frac{BD\Delta y}{1 + y}$$

4.6 DURATION-BASED HEDGING STRATEGIES

Consider the situation where a position in an interest rate dependent asset such as a bond portfolio or a money market security is being hedged using an interest rate futures contract. Define

F: Contract price for the interest rate futures contract

D_F: Duration of asset underlying futures contract

S: Value of asset being hedged

D_S: Duration of asset being hedged

We assume that the change in the yield, Δy, is the same for all maturities—which means that only parallel shifts in the yield curve can occur. From Equation (4.8) it is approximately true that

$$\Delta S = -SD_S \Delta y \tag{4.9}$$

To a reasonable approximation, it is also true that

$$\Delta F = -FD_F \Delta y \tag{4.10}$$

The number of contracts required to hedge against an uncertain Δy is therefore

$$N^* = \frac{SD_S}{FD_F} \tag{4.11}$$

This is the *duration-based hedge ratio*.[4] It is sometimes also called the *price sensitivity hedge ratio*. Using it has the effect of making the duration of the whole position zero.

Example 4.8

On May 20, a corporate treasurer learns that $3.3 million will be received on August 5. The funds will be needed for a major capital investment the following February. The treasurer therefore plans to invest the funds in 6-month Treasury bills as soon as they are received. The current yield on 6-month Treasury bills, expressed with semiannual compounding, is 11.20%. The treasurer is concerned that this may decline between May 20 and August 5 and decides to hedge using Treasury bill futures. The quoted price for the September T-bill futures contract is 89.44. In this case, the company will lose money if interest rates go down. The hedge must therefore provide a positive profit when rates go down or, equivalently, when Treasury bill prices go up. This means that a long hedge is required.

To calculate the number T-bill futures contracts that should be purchased, we note that the asset underlying the futures contract lasts for 3 months. Since it is a discount instrument, its duration is also 3 months or 0.25 years. Similarly, the 6-month Treasury bill investment planned by the treasurer has a duration of 6 months or 0.50 years. Each T-bill futures contract is for the delivery of $1 million of T-bills. The contract price is

$$10,000[100 - 0.25(100 - 89.44)] = \$973,600$$

---

[4]If y is defined with annual compounding, Equation (4.11) becomes

$$N^* = [SD_S(1 + y_F)]/[FD_F(1 + y_S)]$$

where y_S and y_F are the yields on S and F. This is not the same as Equation (4.11) except when $y_S = y_F$. The reason for the difference is that the assumption that $\Delta y_S = \Delta y_F$ when yields are continuously compounded is not quite the same assumption as $\Delta y_S = \Delta y_F$ when yields are compounded once a year.

The number of contracts that should be purchased is, using Equation (4.11),

$$\frac{3,300,000}{973,600} \times \frac{0.5}{0.25} = 6.78$$

Rounding to the nearest whole number, the treasurer should purchase 7 contracts.

Example 4.9

It is August 2 and a fund manager with $10 million invested in government bonds is concerned that interest rates are expected to be highly volatile over the next 3 months. The fund manager decides to use the December T-bond futures contract to hedge the value of the portfolio. The current futures price is 93-02 or 93.0625. Since each contract is for the delivery of $100,000 face value of bonds, the futures contract price is $93,062.50.

The average duration of the bond portfolio over the next 3 months will be 6.80 years. The cheapest-to-deliver bond in the T-bond contract is expected to be a 20-year 12% per annum coupon bond. The yield on this bond is currently 8.80% per annum, and the duration will be 9.20 years at maturity of the futures contract.

The fund manager requires a short position in T-bond futures to hedge the bond portfolio. If interest rates go up, a gain will be made on the short futures position and a loss will be made on the bond portfolio. If interest rates decrease, a loss will be made on the short position, but there will be a gain on the bond portfolio. The number of bond futures contracts that should be shorted can be calculated from Equation (4.11) as

$$\frac{10,000,000}{93,062.50} \times \frac{6.80}{9.20} = 79.42$$

Rounding to the nearest whole number, the portfolio manager should short 79 contracts.

4.7 LIMITATIONS OF DURATION

The duration concept provides a simple approach to interest rate risk management. However, the hedge to which it gives rise is far from perfect. There are two main reasons for this. The first concerns a concept known as *convexity*. The second concerns the underlying assumption of parallel shifts in the yield curve.

CONVEXITY

For very small parallel shifts in the yield curve, the change in value of a portfolio depends solely on its duration. When moderate or large changes in interest rates are considered, a factor known as convexity is sometimes important. Figure 4.6 shows the relationship between the percentage change in value and change in yield for two portfolios having the same duration. The gradients of the two curves are the same for the current yield. This means that both portfolios change in value by the same percentage for small yield changes and is consistent with Equation (4.8). For large interest rate changes, the portfolios behave differently.

Portfolio A has more convexity or curvature than portfolio B. Its value increases by a greater percentage amount than that of portfolio B when yields decline, and its value decreases by less than that of portfolio B when yields increase.

The convexity of a bond portfolio tends to be greatest when the portfolio provides payments evenly over a long period of time. It is least when the payments are concentrated around one particular point in time. For long positions in bond portfolios, it is clear from Figure 4.6 that a high-convexity portfolio with a certain duration is always more attractive than a low-convexity bond portfolio with the same duration. Not surprisingly, it is generally also more expensive.

A measure of convexity is

$$\frac{\partial^2 B}{\partial y^2} = \sum_{i=1}^{n} c_i t_i^2 e^{-y t_i}$$

This is a measure of the curvature of the relationship between ΔB and Δy in Figure 4.6. Some financial institutions when managing portfolios of assets and liabilities try to match both duration and this convexity measure.

NONPARALLEL SHIFTS

One serious problem with the duration concept is that it assumes all interest rate change by the same amount. In practice, short-term rates are usually more

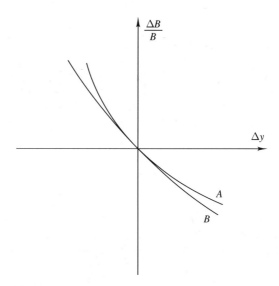

Figure 4.6   Bond Portfolios with Different Convexities

volatile than, and are not closely correlated with, long-term rates. Sometimes it even happens that short- and long-term rates move in opposite directions to each other. For this reason, financial institutions often hedge their interest rate exposure by dividing the zero-coupon yield curve up into segments and ensuring that they are hedged against a movement in each segment. Suppose that the ith segment is the part of the zero-coupon yield curve between time t_i and t_{i+1}. A financial institution would examine the effect of a small increase Δy in all the zero-coupon yields for maturities between t_i and t_{i+1} while keeping the rest of the zero-coupon yield curve unchanged. If the exposure were unacceptable, further trades would be undertaken in carefully selected instruments to reduce it. In the context of a bank managing a portfolio of assets and liabilities, this approach is sometimes referred to as *GAP management*.

4.8 SUMMARY

In this chapter, we have discussed three of the most popular interest rate futures contracts: the Treasury bond, Treasury bill, and Eurodollar contracts. We have also considered different ways in which these contracts can be used for hedging. Since bond prices are inversely related to interest rates, a short hedge provides protection against a increase in interest rates; a long hedge provides protection against an decrease in interest rates.

In the Treasury bond futures contract, the party with the short position has a number of interesting delivery options:

1. Delivery can be made on any day during the delivery month.
2. There are a number of alternative bonds that can be delivered.
3. On any day during the delivery month, the notice of intention to deliver at the 2 p.m. settlement price can be made any time up to 8 p.m.

These options all tend to reduce the futures price.

The concept of duration is important in hedging interest rate risk. Duration measures how long, on average, an investor has to wait before receiving payments. It is a weighted average of the times until payments are received, with the weight for a particular payment time being proportional to the present value of the payment.

A key result underlying the duration-based hedging scheme described in this chapter is

$$\Delta B = -BD\Delta y$$

where B is a bond price, D is its duration, Δy is a small change in its yield (continuously compounded), and ΔB is the resultant small change in B. The equation enables a hedger to assess the sensitivity of a bond to small changes in its yield. It also enables the hedger to assess the sensitivity of an interest rate futures price to small changes in the yield of the underlying bond. If the hedger is prepared to assume that Δy is the same for all bonds, the result enables the hedger to calculate the number of futures contracts necessary to protect a bond or bond portfolio against small changes in interest rates.

The key assumption underlying the duration-based hedging scheme is that all interest rates change by the same amount. This means that only parallel shifts in the term structure are allowed for. In practice, short-term interest rates are generally more volatile than long-term interest rates, and hedge performance is liable to be poor if the duration of the bond underlying the futures contract and the duration of the asset being hedged are markedly different.

SUGGESTIONS FOR FURTHER READING

CHICAGO BOARD OF TRADE, *Interest Rate Futures for Institutional Investors*. Chicago: 1987.

FIGLEWSKI, S., *Hedging with Financial Futures for Institutional Investors*. Cambridge, Mass.: Ballinger, 1986.

GAY, G. D., R. W. KOLB, and R. CHIANG, "Interest Rate Hedging: An Empirical Test of Alternative Strategies," *Journal of Financial Research*, 6 (Fall 1983), 187–97.

KLEMKOSKY, R. C., and D. J. LASSER, "An Efficiency Analysis of the T-Bond Futures Market," *Journal of Futures Markets*, 5 (1985), 607–20.

KOLB, R. W., *Interest Rate Futures: A Comprehensive Introduction*. Richmond, Va.: R. F. Dame, 1982.

KOLB, R. W., and R. CHIANG, "Improving Hedging Performance Using Interest Rate Futures," *Financial Management*, 10 (Autumn 1981), 72–79.

RESNICK, B. G., "The Relationship between Futures Prices for U.S. Treasury Bonds," *Review of Research in Futures Markets*, 3 (1984), 88–104.

RESNICK, B. G., and E. HENNIGAR, "The Relationship between Futures and Cash Prices for U.S. Treasury Bonds," *Review of Research in Futures Markets*, 2 (1983), 282–99.

SENCHAK, A. J., and J. C. EASTERWOOD, "Cross Hedging CDs with Treasury Bill Futures," *Journal of Futures Markets*, 3 (1983), 429–38.

VEIT, W. T., and W. W. REIFF, "Commercial Banks and Interest Rate Futures: A Hedging Survey," *Journal of Futures Markets*, 3 (1983), 283–93.

QUESTIONS AND PROBLEMS

4.1. Suppose that spot interest rates with continuous compounding are as follows:

Maturity (years)	Rate (% per annum)
1	8.0
2	7.5
3	7.2
4	7.0
5	6.9

Calculate forward interest rates for the second, third, fourth, and fifth years.

4.2. The term structure is upward sloping. Put the following in order of magnitude:
(a) The 5-year spot rate
(b) The yield on a 5-year coupon-bearing bond
(c) The forward rate corresponding to the period between 5 and $5\frac{1}{4}$ years in the future
What is the answer to this question when the term structure is downward sloping?

4.3. The 6-month and the 1-year spot rates are both 10% per annum. For a bond that lasts 18 months and pays a coupon of 8% per annum (with a coupon payment having just been made), the yield is 10.4% per annum. What is the bond's price? What is the 18-month spot rate? All rates are quoted with semiannual compounding.

4.4. It is January 9, 1990. The price of a Treasury bond with a 12% coupon that matures on October 12, 1999 is quoted as 102-07. What is the cash price?

4.5. The price of a 90-day Treasury bill is quoted as 10.00. What continuously compounded return does an investor earn on the Treasury bill for the 90-day period?

4.6. What assumptions does a duration-based hedging scheme make about the way in which the term structure moves?

4.7. It is January 30. You are managing a bond portfolio worth $6 million. The average duration of the portfolio is 8.2 years. The September Treasury bond futures price is currently 108-15 and the cheapest-to-deliver bond has a duration of 7.6 years. How should you hedge against changes in interest rates over the next 7 months?

4.8. Suppose that spot interest rates with continuous compounding are as follows:

Maturity (years)	Rate (% per annum)
1	12.0
2	13.0
3	13.7
4	14.2
5	14.5

Calculate forward interest rates for the second, third, fourth, and fifth years.

4.9. Suppose that spot interest rates with continuous compounding are as follows:

Maturity (months)	Rate (% per annum)
3	8.0
6	8.2
9	8.4
12	8.5
15	8.6
18	8.7

Calculate forward interest rates for the second, third, fourth, fifth, and sixth quarters.

4.10. The cash prices of 6-month and 1-year Treasury bills are 94.0 and 89.0. A $1\frac{1}{2}$-year, bond that will pay coupons of $4 every 6 months currently sells for $94.84. A 2-year bond that will pay coupons of $5 every 6 months currently sells for $97.12. Calculate the 6-month, 1-year, $1\frac{1}{2}$-year, and 2-year spot rates.

4.11. A 10-year 8% coupon bond currently sells for $90. A 10-year 4% coupon bond currently sells for $80. What is the 10-year spot rate? (Hint: Consider taking a long position in two of the 4% coupon bonds and a short position in one of the 8% coupon bonds.)

4.12. Explain carefully why liquidity preference theory is consistent with the observation that the term structure tends to be upward sloping more often than it is downward sloping.

4.13. It is May 5, 1990. The quoted price of a government bond with a 12% coupon that matures on July 27, 2001 is 110-17. What is the cash price?

4.14. Suppose that the T-bond futures price is 101-12. Which of the following four bonds is cheapest to deliver?

Bond	Price	Conversion Factor
1	125-05	1.2131
2	142-15	1.3792
3	115-31	1.1149
4	144-02	1.4026

4.15. It is July 30, 1992. The cheapest-to-deliver bond in a September 1992 Treasury bond futures contract is a 13 percent coupon bond, and delivery is expected to be made on September 30, 1992. Coupon payments on the bond are made on February 4 and August 4 each year. The term structure is flat and the rate of interest with semiannual compounding is 12% per annum The conversion factor for the bond is 1.5. The current quoted bond price is $110. Calculate the quoted futures price for the contract.

4.16. An investor is looking for arbitrage opportunities in the Treasury bond futures market. What complications are created by the fact that the party with a short position can choose to deliver any bond with a maturity of over 15 years?

4.17. Suppose that the Treasury bill futures price for a contract maturing in 33 days is quoted as 90.04 and the discount rate for a 123-day Treasury bill is 10.03. What is the implied repo rate? How can it be used?

4.18. Suppose that the 9-month interest rate is 8% per annum and the 6-month interest rate is 7.5% per annum (both with continuous compounding). Estimate the futures price of 90-day Treasury bills with a face value of $1 million for delivery in 6 months. How would the price be quoted?

4.19. Assume that a bank can borrow or lend money at the same interest rate in Euromarkets. The 90-day rate is 10% per annum and the 180-day rate is 10.2% per annum both expressed with continuous compounding. The Eurodollar futures price for a contract maturing in 90 days is quoted as 89.5. What arbitrage opportunities are open to the bank?

4.20. A Canadian company wishes to create a Canadian T-bill futures contract from a U.S. Treasury bill futures contract and forward contracts on foreign exchange. Using an example, explain how this can be done. For the purposes of this problem, assume that a futures contract is the same as a forward contract.

4.21. A 5-year bond with a yield of 11% (continuously compounded) pays an 8% coupon at the end of each year.
   (a) What is the bond's price?
   (b) What is the bond's duration?
   (c) Use the duration to calculate the effect on the bond's price of a 0.2% decrease in its yield.
   (d) Recalculate the bond's price on the basis of a 10.8% per annum yield and verify that the result is in agreement with your answer to (c).

4.22. Portfolio A consists of a 1-year discount bond with a face value of $2,000 and a 10-year discount bond with a face value of $6,000. Portfolio B consists of a 5.95 year discount bond with a face value of $5,000. The current yield on all bonds is 10% per annum
   (a) Show that both portfolios have the same duration.
   (b) Show that the percentage changes in the values of the two portfolios for a 10-basis-point increase in yields is the same.
   (c) What are the percentage changes in the values of the two portfolios for a 5% per annum increase in yields?
   (d) Which portfolio has the higher convexity?

4.23. Suppose that a bond portfolio with a duration of 12 years is hedged using a futures contract where the underlying asset has a duration of 4 years. What is likely to be the impact on the hedge of the fact that the 12-year rate is less volatile than the 4-year rate?

4.24. Suppose that it is February 20 and a treasurer realizes that on July 17, the company will have to issue $5 million of commercial paper with a maturity of 180 days. If the paper were issued today, it would realize $4,520,000. (In other words, the company would receive $4,520,000 for its paper and have to redeem it at $5,000,000 in 180 days time.) The September Eurodollar futures price is quoted as 92.00. How should the treasurer hedge the company's exposure?

4.25. On August 1, a portfolio manager has a bond portfolio worth $10 million. The duration of the portfolio is 7.1 years. The December Treasury bond futures price is currently 91-12 and the cheapest-to-deliver bond has a duration of 8.8 years. How should the portfolio manager immunize the portfolio against changes in interest rates over the next 2 months?

4.26. How can the portfolio manager change the duration of the portfolio to 3.0 years in Problem 4.25?

5

Swaps

Swaps are private agreements between two companies to exchange cash flows in the future according to a prearranged formula. They can be regarded as portfolios of forward contracts. The study of swaps is therefore a natural extension of the study of forward and futures contracts.

The first swap contracts were negotiated in 1981. Since then, the market has grown very rapidly. Hundreds of billions of dollars of contracts are currently negotiated each year. In this chapter, we discuss how swaps are designed, how they are used, and how they can be valued. We also briefly consider the nature of the credit risk facing financial institutions when they trade swaps and other similar financial contracts.

5.1 MECHANICS OF INTEREST RATE SWAPS

The most common type of swap is a "plain vanilla" interest rate swap. In this, one party, B, agrees to pay to the other party, A, cash flows equal to interest at a predetermined fixed rate on a notional principal for a number of years. At the same time, party A agrees to pay party B cash flows equal to interest at a floating rate on the same notional principal for the same period of time. The currencies of the two sets of interest cash flows are the same. The life of the swap can range from 2 years to over 15 years.

Why should A and B enter into such an agreement? The reason most commonly put forward concerns comparative advantages. Some companies appear to have a comparative advantage in fixed rate markets, while other companies have a comparative advantage in floating rate markets. When obtaining a new loan, it makes sense for a company to go to the market where it has a comparative advantage. However, this may lead to a company borrowing fixed when it wants floating, or borrowing floating when it wants fixed. This is where a swap comes in. A swap has the effect of transforming a fixed rate loan into a floating rate loan or vice versa.

LONDON INTERBANK OFFER RATE

The floating rate in many interest rate swap agreements is the London Interbank Offer Rate (LIBOR). We have already mentioned this in Chapter 4. LIBOR is the rate of interest offered by banks on deposits from other banks in eurocurrency markets. One-month LIBOR is the rate offered on 1-month deposits, 3-month LIBOR is the rate offered on 3-month deposits, and so on. LIBOR rates are determined by trading between banks and change continuously as economic conditions change. Just as prime is often the reference rate of interest for floating rate loans in the domestic financial market, LIBOR is frequently a reference rate of interest for loans in international financial markets. To understand how it is used, consider a loan where the rate of interest is specified as 6-month LIBOR plus 0.5 percent per annum. The life of the loan is divided into 6-month time periods. For each period, the rate of interest is set 0.5 percent per annum above the 6-month LIBOR rate at the beginning of the period. Interest is paid at the end of the period.

AN EXAMPLE OF AN INTEREST RATE SWAP

We now give an example of how comparative advantages can lead to an interest rate swap.[1] We suppose that two companies, A and B, both wish to borrow $10 million for 5 years and have been offered the rates shown in Table 5.1. We assume that company B wants to borrow at a fixed rate of interest, while company A wants to borrow floating funds at a rate linked to 6-month LIBOR. Company B clearly has a lower credit rating than company A since it pays a higher rate of interest than company A in both fixed and floating markets.

---

[1] The comparative advantage argument is a useful way of introducing swaps but, as we will discuss later in this chapter, perceived comparative advantages may be largely illusory.

TABLE 5.1 Borrowing Rates
Motivating Interest Rate Swap

	Fixed	Floating
Company A	10.00%	6-month LIBOR + 0.30%
Company B	11.20%	6-month LIBOR + 1.00%

A key feature of the rates offered to companies A and B is that the difference between the two fixed rates is greater than the difference between the two floating rates. Company B pays 1.20 percent more than company A in fixed rate markets, and only 0.70 percent more than company A in floating rate markets.

Company B appears to have a comparative advantage in floating rate markets, while company A appears to have a comparative advantage in fixed rate markets.[2] It is this apparent anomaly that allows a profitable swap to be negotiated. Company A borrows fixed rate funds at 10 percent per annum. Company B borrows floating rate funds at LIBOR plus 1.00 percent per annum. They then enter into a swap agreement to ensure that A ends up with floating rate funds and B ends up with fixed rate funds.

As a first step in understanding how the swap might work, we assume that A and B get in touch with each other directly. The sort of swap they might negotiate is shown in Figure 5.1. Company A agrees to pay company B interest at 6-month LIBOR on $10 million. In return, company B agrees to pay company A interest at a fixed rate of 9.95 percent per annum on $10 million.

When the external borrowings of A and B are taken into account, we obtain Figure 5.2. Company A has three sets of interest rate cash flows:

1. It pays 10.00% per annum to outside lenders.
2. It receives 9.95% per annum from B.
3. It pays LIBOR to B.

The first two cash flows taken together cost A 0.05 percent per annum. It follows that the net effect of the three cash flows is that A pays LIBOR plus 0.05 percent

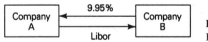

Figure 5.1 A Direct Swap Agreement Between A and B

---

[2]Note that B's comparative advantage in floating rate markets does not imply that B pays less than A in this market. It means that the extra amount that B pays over the amount paid by A is less in this market. One of my students summarized the situation as follows: "A pays more less in fixed rate markets; B pays less more in floating rate markets."

Figure 5.2   Direct Swap Agreement with Outside Borrowing

per annum. This is 0.25 percent per annum less than it would pay if it went directly to floating rate markets. Company B also has three sets of interest rate cash flows:

1. It pays LIBOR + 1.00% per annum to outside lenders.
2. It receives LIBOR from A.
3. It pays 9.95% per annum to A.

The first two cash flows taken together cost B 1.00 percent per annum. It follows that the net effect of the three cash flows is that B pays 10.95 percent per annum. This is 0.25 percent per annum less than it would pay if it went directly to fixed rate markets.

The swap arrangement improves the position of both A and B by 0.25 percent per annum. The total gain is therefore 0.50 percent per annum. This could have been calculated in advance. The total potential gain from an interest rate swap agreement is always $a - b$ where a is the difference between the interest rates facing the two companies in fixed rate markets, and b is the difference between the interest rates facing the two companies in floating rate markets. In this case, $a = 1.20\%$ and $b = 0.70\%$.

ROLE OF FINANCIAL INTERMEDIARY

Usually, two companies do not get in touch with each other directly to arrange a swap. They each deal with a financial intermediary such as a bank. This means that the total potential gain (0.5 percent per annum in our example) has to be split three ways between A, B, and the financial intermediary. One possible arrangement is shown in Figure 5.3.

When the external borrowings of A and B are taken into account, we obtain Figure 5.4. Company A has three sets of interest rate cash flows

1. It pays 10.00% per annum to outside lenders.

Figure 5.3   Interest Rate Swap Using Financial Intermediary

2. It receives 9.9% per annum from the financial institution.

3. It pays LIBOR to the financial institution.

The net effect of these three cash flows is that company A pays LIBOR plus 0.10 percent, which is a 0.20 percent per annum improvement over the rate it could get by going directly to floating rate markets. Company B also has three sets of interest rate cash flows:

1. It pays LIBOR + 1.00% per annum to outside lenders.

2. It receives LIBOR from the financial institution.

3. It pays 10.0% per annum to the financial institution.

The net effect of these three cash flows is that company B pays 11.0 percent per annum, which is a 0.20 percent per annum improvement over the rate it could get by going directly to fixed rate markets. The financial institution's net gain is 0.10 percent per annum. (The floating rate it receives is the same as the floating rate it pays, but the fixed rate it receives is 0.10 percent higher than the fixed rate it pays.) The total gain to all parties is as before 0.50 percent per annum.

Note that the financial institution has two separate contracts, one with company A and the other with company B. If one of the companies defaults, the financial institution still has to honor its agreement with the other company. In most instances, company A will not even know that the financial institution has entered into an offsetting swap with company B and vice versa.

THE EXCHANGE OF PAYMENTS

In the swap that has been described, interest payment dates would occur every 6 months, and all interest rates would be quoted with semiannual compounding. (This is because the swap is based on 6-month LIBOR.) The terms of the swap agreement would specify that one party should send a check for the difference between the fixed and floating interest payments to the other party every 6 months. Suppose that in Figure 5.3, the 6-month LIBOR rate applicable to a particular payment date is 12.0 percent. Company A pays the financial institution

$$0.5 \times (12.0 - 9.9)\% \text{ of } \$10 \text{ million}$$

Figure 5.4   Interest Rate Swap Using Financial Intermediary and Including Outside Borrowings

or \$105,000. The financial institution pays company B

$$0.5 \times (12.0 - 10.0)\% \text{ of } \$10 \text{ million}$$

or \$100,000.

Principal payments are not exchanged in an interest rate swap. This is because the dollar value of the principal remains the same throughout the contract for both the floating rate loan and the fixed rate loan. The 6-month LIBOR rate applicable to a payment date is the rate prevailing 6 months earlier. This reflects the way in which interest is paid on LIBOR-based loans. The first payment date is 6 months after the start of the swap contract. The exchange of cash flows that will take place on that date is based on the 6-month LIBOR rate at the start of the swap. The second payment date is 12 months after the start of the swap. The exchange of payments that will take place on that date is based on the 6-month LIBOR rate prevailing six months after the swap begins.

VALIDITY OF THE COMPARATIVE ADVANTAGE ARGUMENT

The comparative advantage argument, although a good way of introducing swaps, is open to question. Why in Table 5.1 should the spreads between the rates offered to A and B be different in fixed and floating markets? Now that the swap market has been in existence for some time we might reasonably expect these types of differences to have been arbitraged away.

The reason why spread differentials appear to continue to exist may in part be due to the nature of the contracts available to companies in fixed and floating markets. The 10.0 percent and 11.2 percent rates available to A and B in fixed rate markets are likely to be the rates at which the companies can issue 5-year fixed-rate bonds. The LIBOR + 0.3 percent and LIBOR + 1.0 percent rates available to A and B in floating rate markets are 6-month rates. The lender usually has the opportunity to review the rates every six months. If the creditworthiness of A or B has declined, the lender has the option of increasing the spread over LIBOR that is charged. In extreme circumstances the lender can refuse to roll over the loan at all. The providers of fixed rate finance do not have the option to change the terms on the loan in this way.

The spreads between the rates offered to A and B are a reflection of the extent to which B is more likely to default than A. During the next 6 months there is very little chance that either A or B will default. As we look further ahead the probability of a default by B increases faster than the probability of a default by A. This is why the spread between the 5-year rates is greater than the spread between the 6-month rates.

After negotiating a floating rate loan at LIBOR + 1.0 percent and entering into the swap shown in Figure 5.3 we argued that B obtained a fixed rate loan at 11.0 percent. The arguments we are now presenting show that this is not really the case. In practice, the rate paid is 11.0 percent only if B can continue to borrow floating rate funds at a spread of 1.0 percent over LIBOR. For example, if the credit rating of B declines so that the floating rate loan is rolled over at LIBOR + 2.0 percent, the rate paid by B increases to 12.0 percent. The relatively high 5-year borrowing rate offered to B in Table 5.1 suggests that the market considers that B's spread over 6-month LIBOR for borrowed funds is expected to rise. Assuming this is so, B's expected total borrowing rate if it enters into the swap is greater than 11.0 percent and possibly greater than the 11.2 percent B could get by going to fixed rate markets directly.

Assuming that there is no chance of default by the financial institution, the swap in Figure 5.1 locks in LIBOR + 0.1 percent for company A for the whole of the next 5 years, not just for the next 6 months. Unless there is a strong reason for supposing that A's credit rating will improve, this must be a good deal for A. Later in this chapter and in chapter 18 we will look at the swap from the point of view of the financial institution.

PRICING SCHEDULES

The most common interest rate swap is similar to the one described above in that it involves an exchange of 6-month LIBOR for a fixed rate of interest. The fixed rate of interest is usually expressed as a certain number of basis points above the Treasury note yield. (A basis point is 0.01 percent.) Table 5.2 shows what is termed an *indication pricing schedule*. This would be used for reference purposes by a swap trader working for a bank. For example, it indicates that when the bank is negotiating a 5-year swap where it will pay fixed and receive 6-month LIBOR, the fixed rate should be set 44 basis points above the current 5-year Treasury note rate of 7.90 percent. In other words, the bank should set the fixed rate at 8.34 percent. When the bank is negotiating a 5-year swap where it will receive fixed

TABLE 5.2   Indication Pricing for Interest Rate Swaps

Maturity	Bank Pays Fixed Rate	Bank Receives Fixed Rate	Current TN Rate (%)
2 years	2-yr. TN + 30 bps	2-yr. TN + 38 bps	7.52
3 years	3-yr. TN + 35 bps	3-yr. TN + 44 bps	7.71
4 years	4-yr. TN + 38 bps	4-yr. TN + 48 bps	7.83
5 years	5-yr. TN + 44 bps	5-yr. TN + 54 bps	7.90
6 years	6-yr. TN + 48 bps	6-yr. TN + 60 bps	7.94
7 years	7-yr. TN + 50 bps	7-yr. TN + 63 bps	7.97
10 years	10-yr. TN + 60 bps	10-yr. TN + 75 bps	7.99

and pay 6-month LIBOR for 5 years, the schedule indicates that it should set the fixed rate at 54 basis points above the current 5-year Treasury note rate, or at 8.44 percent. The bank's profit or its bid-asked spread from negotiating two offsetting 5-year swaps would be 10 basis points (= 0.1%) per annum.[3]

Table 5.2 would be updated regularly as market conditions changed. One point to note is that 6-month LIBOR is quoted with semiannual compounding on the basis of a 360-day year, whereas the Treasury note rate is quoted with semiannual compounding on the basis of a 365-day year. This can be confusing. To make a 6-month LIBOR rate comparable with a Treasury note rate, either the 6-month LIBOR rate must be multiplied by 365/360 or the Treasury note rate must be multiplied by 360/365.[4]

The CBOT trades futures contracts on the 3- and 5-year swap rates. The contracts are cash settled to a swap rate which is the median of the average of the bid and offer quotes of seven dealers randomly selected from an approved list. The CBOT also trades options on swap futures.

WAREHOUSING

In practice, it is unlikely that two companies will contact a financial institution at exactly the same time and want to take opposite positions in exactly the same swap. For this reason, most large financial institutions are prepared to warehouse interest rate swaps. This involves entering into a swap with one counterparty and then hedging the interest rate risk until a counterparty wanting to take an opposite position is found. The interest rate futures contracts discussed in Chapter 4 are one way of carrying out the hedging.

5.2 VALUATION OF INTEREST RATE SWAPS

If we assume no possibility of default, an interest rate swap can be valued either as a long position in one bond combined with a short position in another bond, or as a portfolio of forward contracts.

---

[3]In the early days of swaps, bid-asked spreads as high as 100 basis points were common. By the late 1980s, bid-asked spreads on interest rate swaps had narrowed to less than 10 basis points.

[4]Some of the numbers calculated earlier in this chapter are not perfectly accurate because they do not take into account these differences between the ways of quoting fixed and floating rates. For example, in the swap in Figure 5.4, we stated that company A ends up borrowing at LIBOR + 0.1% per annum. The 0.1% spread over LIBOR is the difference between two fixed interest rates and is likely to be expressed on the basis of a 365-day year with semiannual compounding. To be compatible with LIBOR we should convert it to a 360-day year. The rate paid by company A then becomes

$$\text{LIBOR} + 0.1 \times \frac{360}{365} = \text{LIBOR} + 0.0986\% \text{ per annum}$$

Consider the swap between company B and the financial institution in Figure 5.3. Although the principal is not exchanged, we can assume without changing the value of the swap that, at the end of its life, A pays B the notional principal of $10 million and B pays A the same notional principal. The swap is then the same as an arrangement in which

1. Company B has lent the financial institution $10 million at the 6-month LIBOR rate.
2. The financial institution has lent company B $10 million at a fixed rate of 10% per annum.

To put this another way, the financial institution has sold a $10 million floating rate (LIBOR) bond to company B and has purchased a $10 million fixed rate (10% per annum) bond from company B. The value of the swap is therefore the difference between the values of two bonds.

In general, suppose that it is now time zero and that under the terms of a swap, a financial institution receives fixed payments of k dollars at times t_i $(1 \leq i \leq n)$ and makes floating payments at the same times. Define

V: Value of swap
B_1: Value of fixed rate bond underlying the swap
B_2: Value of floating rate bond underlying the swap
Q: Notional principal in swap agreement

It follows that

$$V = B_1 - B_2 \qquad\qquad (5.1)$$

The discount rates used in valuing the bonds should reflect the riskiness of the cash flows. We suppose that it is appropriate to use a discount rate with a risk level corresponding to the floating rate underlying the swap. In our example, the floating rate underlying the swap is LIBOR, and so our assumption means that the appropriate risk level is the risk associated with loans in the interbank market. The assumption that the floating basis rate underlying the swap is the appropriate rate to use for discounting is a very common one and considerably simplifies the valuation procedure. In some cases, however, it is clearly inappropriate. For example, the cash flows in a LIBOR-based swap with the Federal government have no risk; the cash flows in a T-bill based swap with a BBB-rated counterparty are subject to some risk.

It is reasonable to assume that a swap, if entered into at the average of the bid and offer quotes in Table 5.2, has a value of zero. Given our assumption about discount rates, $B_2 = Q$. It follows from Equation (5.1) that $B_1 = Q$. An indication pricing schedule such as the one in Table 5.2, therefore, defines a number of bonds that are worth their par value. (These are known as par yield bonds.) The bootstrap procedure described in Section 4.1 can be used to determine a zero-coupon yield curve from these par yield bonds. This zero-coupon yield curve defines the appropriate discount rates for swap cash flows and can be used in conjunction with Equation (5.1) to determine the values of swaps that were negotiated some time ago.

Define r_i as the discount rate corresponding to a maturity t_i. Since B_1 is the present value of the fixed rate bond's future cash flows,

$$B_1 = \sum_{i=1}^{n} ke^{-r_i t_i} + Qe^{-r_n t_n}$$

Consider next the floating rate bond, B_2. Immediately after a payment date, B_2 is always equal to notional principal, Q. Between payment dates, we can use the fact that B_2 will equal Q immediately after the next payment date. In our notation, the time until the next payment date is t_1 so that

$$B_2 = Qe^{-r_1 t_1} + k^* e^{-r_1 t_1}$$

where k^* is the floating rate payment (already known) that will be made at time t_1.

In the situation where the financial institution is paying fixed and receiving floating, B_1 and B_2 are calculated in the same way and

$$V = B_2 - B_1$$

It is interesting to note that the value of the swap is zero when it is first negotiated and zero at the end of its life. During its life it may have a positive or negative value.

Example 5.1

Suppose that under the terms of a swap, a financial institution has agreed to pay 6-month LIBOR and receive 8% per annum (with semiannual compounding) on a notional principal of $100 million. The swap has a remaining life of 1.25 years. The relevant discount rates with continuous compounding for 3-month, 9-month, and 15-month maturities are 10.0%, 10.5%, and 11.0%, respectively. The 6-month LIBOR rate at the last payment date was 10.2% (with semiannual compounding). In this case, $k = \$4$ million and $k^* = \$5.1$ million so that

$$B_1 = 4e^{-0.25 \times 0.1} + 4e^{-0.75 \times 0.105} + 104e^{-1.25 \times 0.11}$$

$$= \$98.24 \text{ million}$$

$$B_2 = 5.1e^{-.25 \times 0.1} + 100e^{-0.25 \times 0.1}$$

$$= \$102.51 \text{ million}$$

Hence, the value of the swap is

$$98.24 - 102.51 = -\$4.27 \text{ million}$$

If the bank has been in the opposite position of paying fixed and receiving floating the value of the swap would be +$4.27 million.

RELATIONSHIP TO FORWARD CONTRACTS

In the absence of default risk, an interest rate swap can be decomposed into a series of forward contracts. This is best illustrated by returning to the example in Figure 5.3. Consider the swap agreement between the financial institution and company A. Since the principal amount is $10 million and payments are exchanged every 6 months, the cash flow to the financial institution on a payment date is (in millions of dollars)

$$10 \times (0.5 \times \text{LIBOR} - 0.5 \times 0.099)$$

or

$$5 \times (\text{LIBOR} - 0.099)$$

This is the payoff from a forward contract on LIBOR with a "delivery price" of 9.9 percent and a principal of $5 million. The only difference between this and a regular forward contract is that it is the value of LIBOR 6 months prior to the maturity date that determines the payoff.

Suppose that $\hat{R}_i$ is the forward interest rate (expressed with semiannual compounding) for the 6-month period prior to a payment date i ($i \geq 2$). Section 3.5 in Chapter 3 shows that the value of a long forward contract is the present value of the amount by which the current forward price exceeds the delivery price. Using the notation introduced earlier, the value of the forward contract corresponding the payment number i ($i \geq 2$) for the party receiving fixed and paying floating is therefore

$$(k - 0.5\hat{R}_i Q)e^{-r_i t_i}$$

The exchange that will take place on the first payment date (at time t_1) involves a payment k^* and receipt k. The value of this is

$$(k - k^*)e^{-r_1 t_1}$$

The total value of the swap is therefore

$$(k - k^*)e^{-r_1 t_1} + \sum_{i=2}^{n}(k - 0.5\hat{R}_i Q)e^{-r_i t_i}$$

For the party receiving floating and paying fixed the value is

$$(k^* - k)e^{-r_1t_1} + \sum_{i=2}^{n}(0.5\hat{R}_i Q - k)e^{-r_it_i}$$

Example 5.2

Consider again the situation in the previous example. In millions of dollars, $k = 4.0, k^* = 5.1$ and $Q = 100$. Also, $r_1 = 0.10$, $r_2 = 0.105$, $r_3 = 0.11$, $t_1 = 0.25$, $t_2 = 0.75$, and $t_3 = 1.25$. Equation (4.1) gives the values of $\hat{R}_2$ and $\hat{R}_3$ with continuous compounding as

$$\hat{R}_2 = \frac{r_2t_2 - r_1t_1}{t_2 - t_1} = \frac{0.75 \times 0.105 - 0.25 \times 0.10}{0.5} = 0.1075$$

$$\hat{R}_3 = \frac{r_3t_3 - r_2t_2}{t_3 - t_2} = \frac{1.25 \times 0.11 - 0.75 \times 0.105}{0.5} = 0.1175$$

These can be converted to semiannual compounding using Equation (3.4): $\hat{R}_2 = 0.1104$, $\hat{R}_3 = 0.1210$. The value of the swap is therefore

$$(4.0 - 5.1)e^{-0.1 \times 0.25} + (4.0 - 0.5 \times 0.1104 \times 100)e^{-0.105 \times 0.75}$$

$$+ \ (4.0 - 0.5 \times 0.1210 \times 100)e^{-0.11 \times 1.25} = -4.27$$

or –\$4.27 million. This is in agreement with the calculation based on bond prices in the previous example.

At the time the swap is entered into, it is worth zero. This means that the sum of the value of the forward contracts underlying the swap is zero at this time. However, it does not mean that the value of each individual forward contract is zero. In general, some will have positive values while others have negative values.

For the forward contracts underlying the swap between the financial institution and company A in Figure 5.3

Value of forward contract > 0 when forward interest rate $> 9.9\%$

Value of forward contract $= 0$ when forward interest rate $= 9.9\%$

Value of forward contract < 0 when forward interest rate $< 9.9\%$

Suppose the term structure is upward sloping at the time the swap is negotiated. This means that the forward interest rates increase as the maturity of the forward contract increases. Since the sum of the values of the forward contracts is zero, this must mean that the forward interest rate is less than 9.9 percent for the early payment dates and greater than 9.9 percent for the later payment dates. The value to the financial institution of the forward contracts corresponding to early payment dates are therefore negative, while those corresponding to later payment dates are positive. If the term structure is downward sloping at the time the swap is negotiated, the reverse is true. This argument is illustrated in Figure 5.5.

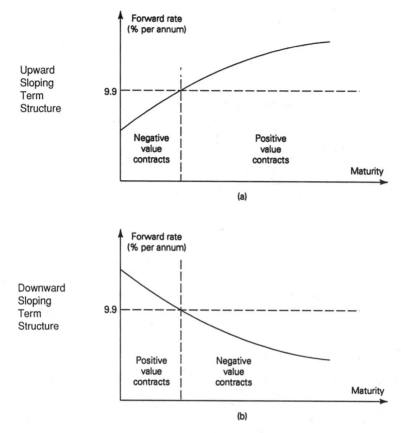

Figure 5.5   Value of Forward Contracts Underlying Financial Institution's Swap with Company A in Figure 5.3 When Term Structure Is Upward Sloping and Downward Sloping

5.3 CURRENCY SWAPS

Another popular type of swap is known as a *currency swap*. In its simplest form, this involves exchanging principal and fixed rate interest payments on a loan in one currency for principal and fixed rate interest payments on an approximately equivalent loan in another currency.

AN EXAMPLE

Like interest rate swaps, currency swaps can be motivated by comparative advantage. Suppose that company A and company B are offered the fixed rates of interest in U.S. dollars and sterling, shown in Table 5.3. This table shows that

TABLE 5.3 Borrowing Rates
Motivating Currency Swap

	Dollars	Sterling
Company A	8.0%	11.6%
Company B	10.0%	12.0%

sterling interest rates are generally higher than U.S. interest rates. Company A is clearly more creditworthy than company B since it is offered a more favorable rate of interest in both currencies. However, the differences between the rates offered to A and B in the two markets are not the same. Company B pays 2.0 percent more than company A in the U.S. dollar market and only 0.4 percent more than company A in the sterling markets.

Company A has a comparative advantage in the U.S. dollar market while company B has a comparative advantage in the sterling market. This might be because A is an American company that is better known to U.S. investors, while B is a U.K. company that is better known to British investors. Tax considerations may also play an important role in determining the rates. We suppose that A wants to borrow sterling while B wants to borrow dollars. This creates a perfect situation for a currency swap. Company A and company B each borrow in the market where they have a comparative advantage; that is, company A borrows dollars while company B borrows sterling. They then use a currency swap to transform A's loan into a sterling loan and B's loan into a dollar loan.

As already mentioned, the difference between the dollar interest rates is 2.0 percent while the difference between the sterling interest rates is 0.4 percent. By analogy with the interest rate swap case, we expect the total gain to all parties to be 2.0% − 0.4% = 1.6% per annum.

There are many ways in which the swap can be organized. Figure 5.6 shows one possible arrangement. Company A borrows dollars while company B borrows sterling. The effect of the swap is to transform the U.S. dollar interest rate of 8.0 percent per annum to a sterling interest rate of 11.0 percent per annum for company A. This makes company A 0.6 percent per annum better off than it would be if it went directly to dollar markets. The financial intermediary gains 1.4 percent per annum on its dollar cash flows and loses 1.0 percent per annum on its sterling cash

Figure 5.6   A Currency Swap

flows. Ignoring the difference between the two currencies, it makes a net gain of 0.4 percent per annum. As predicted, the total gain to all parties is 1.6 percent per annum.

A currency swap agreement requires the principal to be specified in each of the two currencies. The principal amounts are exchanged at the beginning and at the end of the life of the swap. They are chosen so that they are approximately equal at the exchange rate at the beginning of the swap's life. In the example in Figure 5.6, the principal amounts might be $15 million and £10 million. Initially, the principal amounts flow in the opposite direction to the arrows in Figure 5.6. The interest payments during the life of the swap and the final principal payment flow in the same direction as the arrows. Thus, at the outset of the swap, company A pays $15 million and receives £10 million. Each year during the life of the swap contract, company A receives $1.20 million (= 8% of $15 million) and pays £1.10 million (= 11% of £10 million). At the end of the life of the swap, it pays a principal of £10 million and receives a principal of $15 million.

The reader may feel that the swap in Figure 5.6 is unsatisfactory because the financial institution is exposed to foreign exchange risk. Each year, it makes a gain of $210,000 (= 1.4% of $15 million) and a loss of £100,000 (= 1% of £10 million). However, the financial institution can avoid this risk by buying £100,000 per annum in the forward market for each year of the life of the swap. This will lock in a net gain in U.S. dollars. If we tried to redesign the swap so that the financial institution makes 0.4 percent spread in dollars and zero spread in sterling, we might come up with the arrangement in Figure 5.7 or Figure 5.8. In Figure 5.7, company B bears some foreign exchange risk because it pays 1.0 percent per annum in sterling and 8.4 percent in dollars. In Figure 5.8, company A bears some foreign exchange risk because it receives 1.0 percent per annum in dollars and pays 12.0 percent in sterling. In general, it makes sense for the financial institution to bear the foreign exchange risk because it is in the best position to hedge it.

Figure 5.7   Alternative Arrangement for Currency Swap; Company B Bears Some Foreign Exchange Risk

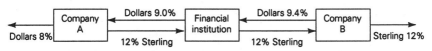

Figure 5.8   Alternative Arrangement for Currency Swap; Company A Bears Some Foreign Exchange Risk

Like interest rate swaps, currency swaps are frequently warehoused by financial institutions. The financial institution then carefully monitors its exposures to different currencies so that it can hedge its risk.

5.4 VALUATION OF CURRENCY SWAPS

In the absence of default risk, a currency swap can be decomposed into a position in two bonds in a similar way to an interest rate swap. Consider the position of company B in Figure 5.6. It is long a sterling bond that pays interest at 12.0 percent per annum and short a dollar bond that pays interest at 9.4 percent per annum. In general, if V is the value of a swap such as the one in Figure 5.6 to the party paying U.S. dollar interest rates,

$$V = SB_F - B_D$$

where B_F is the value, measured in the foreign currency, of the foreign denominated bond underlying the swap, B_D is the value of the U.S. dollar bond underlying the swap, and S is the spot exchange rate (expressed as number of units of domestic currency per unit of foreign currency). The value of a swap can therefore be determined from the term structure of interest rates in the domestic currency, the term structure of interest rates in the foreign currency, and the spot exchange rate.

Example 5.3

Suppose that the term structure of interest rates is flat in both Japan and the United States. The Japanese rate is 4% per annum and the U.S. rate is 9% per annum (both with continuous compounding). A financial institution has entered into a currency swap where it receives 5% per annum in yen and pays 8% per annum in dollars once a year. The principals in the two currencies are $10 million and 1,200 million yen. The swap will last for another 3 years and the current exchange rate is 110 yen = $1. In this case

$$B_D = 0.8e^{-0.09} + 0.8e^{-0.09 \times 2} + 10.8e^{-0.09 \times 3}$$

$$= \$9.64 \text{ million}$$

$$B_F = 60e^{-0.04} + 60e^{-0.04 \times 2} + 1260e^{-0.04 \times 3}$$

$$= 1,230.55 \text{ million yen}$$

The value of the swap is

$$\frac{1230.55}{110} - 9.64 = \$1.55 \text{ million}$$

If the financial institution had been paying yen and receiving dollars, the value of the swap would have been –$1.55 million.

DECOMPOSITION INTO FORWARD CONTRACTS

An alternative decomposition of the currency swap is into a series of forward contracts. Suppose that in Figure 5.6 there is one payment date per year. On each payment date company B has agreed to exchange an inflow of £1.2 million (= 12% of £10 million) for an outflow of $1.41 million (= 9.4% of $15 million). In addition, at the final payment date, it has agreed to exchange a £10 million inflow for a $15 million outflow. Each of these exchanges represents a forward contract. Suppose t_i ($1 \leq i \leq n$) is the time of the ith settlement date, r_i ($1 \leq i \leq n$) is the continuously compounded U.S. dollar interest rate applicable to a time period of length t_i, and F_i ($1 \leq i \leq n$) is the forward exchange rate applicable to time t_i. In Chapter 3, we showed that the value of a long forward contract is in all circumstances the present value of the amount by which the forward price exceeds the delivery price. The value to company B of the forward contract corresponding to the exchange of interest payments at time t_i is, therefore,

$$(1.2F_i - 1.41)e^{-r_i t_i}$$

for $1 \leq i \leq n$. The value to company B of the forward contract corresponding to the exchange of principal payments at time t_n is

$$(10F_n - 15)e^{-r_n t_n}$$

This shows that the value of a currency swap can always be calculated from the term structure of forward rates and the term structure of domestic interest rates.

Example 5.4

Consider again the situation in the previous example. The current spot rate is 110 yen per dollar or 0.009091 dollar per yen. Since the difference between the dollar and yen interest rates is 5% per annum, Equation (3.14) can be used to give the 1-year, 2-year, and 3-year forward exchange rates as

$$0.009091e^{0.05 \times 1} = 0.0096$$

$$0.009091e^{0.05 \times 2} = 0.0100$$

$$0.009091e^{0.05 \times 3} = 0.0106$$

respectively. The exchange of interest involves receiving 60 million yen and paying $0.8 million. The risk-free interest rate in dollars is 9% per annum The value of the forward contracts corresponding to the exchange of interest are therefore (in millions of dollars)

$$(60 \times 0.0096 - 0.8)e^{-0.09 \times 1} = -0.21$$

$$(60 \times 0.0101 - 0.8)e^{-0.09 \times 2} = -0.16$$

$$(60 \times 0.0106 - 0.8)e^{-0.09 \times 3} = -0.13$$

The final exchange of principal involves receiving 1,200 million yen and paying $10 million. The value of the forward contract corresponding to this is (in millions of dollars)

$$(1,200 \times 0.0106 - 10)e^{-0.09 \times 3} = 2.04$$

The total value of the swap is $2.04 - 0.13 - 0.16 - 0.21 = \$1.54$ million which (allowing for rounding errors) is in agreement with the result of the calculations in the previous example.

Assume that the principal amounts in the two currencies are exactly equivalent at the start of a currency swap. At this time, the total value of the swap is zero. However, as in the case of interest rate swaps, this does not mean that each of the individual forward contracts underlying the swap has zero value. It can be shown that, when interest rates in two currencies are significantly different, the payer of the low-interest-rate currency is in the position where the forward contracts corresponding to the early exchanges of cash flows have positive values and the forward contract corresponding to final exchange of principals has a negative expected value. The payer of the high-interest-rate currency is likely to be in the opposite position; that is, the early exchanges of cash flows have negative values and the final exchange has a positive expected value.

For the payer of the low-interest-rate currency, there will be a tendency for the swap to have a negative value during most of its life. This is because the forward contracts corresponding to the early exchanges of payments have positive values, and, once these exchanges have taken place, there is a tendency for the remaining forward contracts to have, in total, a negative value. For the payer of the high-interest-rate currency, the reverse is true. There is a tendency for the value of the swap to be positive during most of its life. These results are important when the credit risk in the swap is being evaluated.

5.5 OTHER SWAPS

A swap in its most general form is a security that involves the exchange of cash flows according to a formula that depends on the value of one or more underlying variables. There is therefore no limit to the number of different types of swaps that can be invented. In this section, we discuss a few of the variants on the plain vanilla interest rate swap and currency swap that have been described so far.

In an interest rate swap, a number of different floating reference rates can be used. Six-month LIBOR is the most common. Among the others used are: the 3-month LIBOR, the 1-month commercial paper rate, the T-bill rate, and the tax-exempt rate. The particular reference rate chosen by a company will depend on the nature of its exposure. Swaps can be constructed to swap one floating rate (say, LIBOR) for another floating rate (say, prime). This allows a financial institution to hedge an exposure arising from assets and liabilities that are subject to different floating rates.

The principal in a swap agreement can be varied throughout the term of the swap to meet the needs of a counterparty. In an *amortizing swap*, the principal reduces in a way that corresponds to the amortization schedule on a loan. In a *step-up swap*, the principal increases in a way that corresponds to the drawdowns on a loan agreement. *Deferred swaps* or *forward swaps* in which parties do not begin to exchange interest payments until some future date can also be arranged.

One popular swap is an agreement to exchange a fixed interest rate in one currency for a floating interest rate in another currency. As such, it is a combination of a plain vanilla interest rate swap and a plain deal currency swap.

Swaps can be extendable or puttable. In an *extendable swap*, one party has the option to extend the life of the swap beyond the specified period. In a *puttable swap*, one party has the option to terminate the swap early. Options on swaps or *swaptions* are also available. An option on an interest rate swap is, in essence, an option to exchange a fixed rate bond for a floating rate bond. Since the floating rate bond is worth close to its face value, swaptions can be considered as options on the value of the fixed rate bond. Swaptions will be discussed further in Chapter 15.

Swaps are now becoming increasingly available on commodities. A company that consumes 100,000 barrels of oil per year could agree to pay $2 million each year for the next 10 years and to receive in return $100,000S$, where S is the current market price of oil per barrel. This would in effect lock in its oil cost at $20 per barrel. Similarly, an oil producer might agree to the opposite exchange. This would have the effect of locking in the price it realized for its oil at $20 per barrel.

5.6 CREDIT RISK

Contracts such as swaps that are private arrangements between two companies entail credit risks. Consider a financial institution that has entered into offsetting contracts with two companies, A and B. (See Figure 5.3 or Figure 5.6.) If neither party defaults, the financial institution remains fully hedged. A decline in the value of one contract will always be offset by an increase in the value of the other contract. However, there is a chance that one party will get into financial difficulties and default. The financial institution would then still have to honor the contract it has with the other party.

Suppose that some time after the initiation of the contracts in Figure 5.3, the contract with company B has a positive value to the financial institution while the contract with company A has a negative value. If company B defaults, the financial institution would lose the positive value it has in this contract. To maintain a hedged position, it would have to find a third party willing to take company B's position. To induce the third party to take the position, it would have to pay the third party an amount roughly equal to the value of the financial institution's contract with B prior to the default.

A financial institution only has credit risk exposure from a swap when the value of the swap to the financial institution is positive. What happens when this value is negative and the counterparty gets into financial difficulties? In theory, the financial institution could realize a windfall gain since a default would lead to it getting rid of a liability. In practice, it is likely that the counterparty would choose to sell the contract to a third party or rearrange its affairs in some way so that its positive value in the contract is not lost. The most realistic assumption for the financial institution is therefore as follows. If the counterparty goes bankrupt, there will be a loss if the value of the swap to the financial institution is positive and there will be no effect on the financial institution's position if the value of the swap to the financial institution is negative. This situation is summarized in Figure 5.9.

Sometimes a financial institution can predict in advance which of two off-setting contracts is likely to have a positive value. Consider the currency swap in Figure 5.6. Sterling interest rates are higher than U.S. interest rates. As mentioned earlier, this means that as time passes the financial institution is likely to find that its swap with A has a negative value while its swap with B has a positive value. The creditworthiness of B is therefore far more important than the creditworthiness of A. In general, the expected loss from a default on a currency swap is greater than the expected loss from a default on an interest rate swap. This is because, in the case of a currency swap, principal amounts in different currencies are exchanged. In the case of both types of swaps, the expected loss from a default is much less

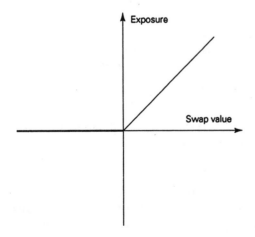

Figure 5.9 The Credit Exposure in a Swap

than the expected loss from a default on a regular loan with approximately the same principal as the swap.

It is important to distinguish between the credit risk and market risk to a financial institution in any contract. As discussed earlier, the credit risk arises from the possibility of a default by the counterparty when the value of the contract to the financial institution is positive. The market risk arises from the possibility that market variables such as interest rates and exchange rates will move in such a way that the value of a contract to the financial institution becomes negative. Market risks can be hedged by entering into offsetting contracts; credit risks cannot be hedged. Credit risk issues will be discussed further in Chapter 18.

5.7 SUMMARY

The two most common types of swaps are interest rate swaps and currency swaps. In an interest rate swap, one party agrees to pay the other party interest at a fixed rate on a notional principal for a number of years. In return, it receives interest at a floating rate on the same notional principal for the same period of time. In a currency swap, one party agrees to pay interest on a principal amount in one currency. In return, it receives interest on a principal amount in another currency.

Principal amounts are not exchanged in an interest rate swap. In a currency swap, principal amounts are exchanged at both the beginning and the end of the life of the swap. For a party paying interest in the foreign currency, the foreign principal is received and the domestic principal is paid at the beginning of the life of the swap. At the end of the life of the swap, the foreign principal is paid and the domestic principal is received.

An interest rate swap can be used to transform a floating rate loan into a fixed rate loan or vice versa. A currency swap can be used to transform a loan in one currency into a loan in another currency. In essence, a swap is a long position in one bond combined with a short position in another bond. Alternatively, it can be considered as a portfolio of forward contracts.

Swaps are usually arranged by financial institutions. Ideally, in order to eliminate interest rate or exchange rate risk, a financial institution would like to enter into offsetting swap agreements with two parties at the same time. In practice, financial institutions frequently warehouse swaps. This means that they enter into a swap agreement with one party and then hedge their risk on a day-to-day basis while they attempt to find a party wanting to take the opposite position.

When a financial institution enters into a pair of offsetting swaps with different counterparties, it is exposed to credit risk. If one of the counterparties defaults when the financial institution has positive value in its swap with that counterparty, the financial institution loses money since it still has to honor its swap agreement with the other counterparty.

SUGGESTIONS FOR FURTHER READING

BICKSLER, J., and A. H. CHEN, "An Economic Analysis of Interest Rate Swaps," *The Journal of Finance*, 41, 3 (1986), 645–55.

HULL, J., "Assessing Credit Risk in a Financial Institutions Off-balance Sheet Commitments," *Journal of Financial and Quantitative Analysis*, 24 (December 1989), 489–502.

INTERNATIONAL SWAP DEALER'S ASSOCIATION, "Code of Standard Working, Assumptions and Provisions for Swaps." New York: 1986.

LAYARD-LIESCHING, R., "Swap Fever," *Euromoney*, Supplement (January 1986), 108–13.

MARSHALL, J. F., and K. R. KAPNER, *Understanding Swap Finance*. Cincinnati, Ohio: South-Western, 1990.

SMITH, C. W., C. W. SMITHSON, and L. M. WAKEMAN, "The Evolving Market for Swaps," *Midland Corporate Finance Journal*, 3 (Winter 1986), 20–32.

TURNBULL, S. M., "Swaps: A Zero Sum Game," *Financial Management*, 16 (Spring 1987), 15–21.

WALL, L. D., and J. J. PRINGLE, "Alternative Explanations of Interest Rate Swaps: A Theoretical and Empirical Analysis," *Financial Management*, 18, 2 (Summer 1989), 59–73.

QUESTIONS AND PROBLEMS

5.1. Companies A and B have been offered the following rates per annum on a $20 million 5-year loan:

	Fixed Rate	Floating Rate
Company A	12.0%	LIBOR + 0.1%
Company B	13.4%	LIBOR + 0.6%

Company A requires a floating rate loan; company B requires a fixed rate loan. Design a swap that will net a bank, acting as intermediary, 0.1% per annum and appear equally attractive to both companies.

5.2. Company X wishes to borrow U.S. dollars at a fixed rate of interest. Company Y wishes to borrow Japanese yen at a fixed rate of interest. The amounts required by the two companies are roughly the same at the current exchange rate. The companies have been quoted the following interest rates:

	Yen	Dollars
Company X	5.0%	9.6%
Company Y	6.5%	10.0%

Design a swap that will net a bank, acting as intermediary, 50 basis points per annum. Make the swap appear equally attractive to the two companies and ensure that all foreign exchange risk is assumed by the bank.

5.3. A $100 million interest rate swap has a remaining life of 10 months. Under the terms of the swap, 6-month LIBOR is exchanged for 12% per annum (compounded semi-annually). The average of the bid and ask rate being exchanged for 6-month LIBOR in swaps of all maturities is currently 10% per annum with continuous compounding. The 6-month LIBOR rate was 9.6% per annum 2 months ago. What is the current value of the swap to the party paying floating? What is its value to the party paying fixed?

5.4. What is meant by warehousing swaps?

5.5. A currency swap has a remaining life of 15 months. It involves exchanging interest at 14% on £20 million for interest at 10% on $30 million once a year. The term structure of interest rates in both the United Kingdom and the United States is currently flat and if the swap were negotiated today, the interest rates exchanged would be 8% in dollars and 11% in sterling. All interest rates are quoted with annual compounding. The current exchange rate is 1.6500. What is the value of the swap to the party paying sterling? What is the value of the swap to the party paying dollars?

5.6. Explain the difference between the credit risk and the market risk in a financial contract. Which of the risks can be hedged?

5.7. Explain why a bank is subject to credit risk when it enters into two offsetting swap contracts.

5.8. Companies X and Y have been offered the following rates per annum on a $5 million 10-year loan:

	Fixed Rate	Floating Rate
Company X	7.0%	LIBOR + 0.5%
Company Y	8.8%	LIBOR + 1.5%

Company X requires a floating rate loan; company Y requires a fixed rate loan. Design a swap that will net a bank, acting as intermediary, 0.2% per annum and which will appear equally attractive to X and Y.

5.9. Company A, a British manufacturer, wishes to borrow U.S. dollars at a fixed rate of interest. Company B, a U.S. multinational, wishes to borrow sterling at a fixed rate of interest. They have been quoted the following rates per annum:

	Sterling	U.S. Dollars
Company A	11.0%	7.0%
Company B	10.6%	6.2%

Design a swap that will net a bank, acting as intermediary, 10 basis points per annum and which will produce an apparent gain of 15 basis points per annum for each of the two companies.

5.10. Under the terms of an interest rate swap, a financial institution has agreed to pay 10% per annum and to receive 3-month LIBOR in return on a notional principal of $100 million with payments being exchanged every 3 months. The swap has a remaining life of 14 months. The average of the bid and ask fixed rate currently being swapped for 3-month LIBOR is 12% per annum for all maturities. The 3-month LIBOR rate one month ago was 11.8% per annum. All rates are compounded quarterly. What is the value of the swap?

5.11. Suppose that the term structure of interest rates is flat in the United States and Germany. The dollar interest rate is 11% per annum while the mark interest rate is 8% per annum The current exchange rate is 2.1 marks = $1. Under the terms of a swap agreement, a financial institution pays 5% per annum in marks and receives 10% per annum in dollars. The principals in the two currencies are $10 million and 20 million marks. Payments are exchanged every year with one exchange having just taken place. The swap will last 2 more years. What is the value of the swap to the financial institution? Assume all interest rates are continuously compounded.

5.12. A financial institution has entered into an interest rate swap with company X. Under the terms of the swap, it receives 10% per annum and pays 6-month LIBOR on a principal of $10 million for 5 years. Payments are made every 6 months. Suppose that company X defaults on the sixth payment date (end of year 3) when the interest rate (with semiannual compounding) is 8% per annum for all maturities. What is the loss to the financial institution? Assume that 6-month LIBOR was 9% per annum half way through year 3.

5.13. A financial institution has entered into a 10-year currency swap with company Y. Under the terms of the swap, it receives interest at 3% per annum in Swiss francs and pays interest at 8% per annum in U.S. dollars. Interest payments are exchanged once a year. The principal amounts are $7 million and 10 million francs. Suppose that company Y defaults at the end of year 6 when the exchange rate is $0.80 per franc. What is the cost to the financial institution? Assume that at the end of year 6, the interest rate is 3% per annum in Swiss francs and 8% per annum in U.S. dollars for all maturities. All interest rates are quoted with annual compounding.

5.14. Companies A and B face the following interest rates:

	A	B
U.S. dollars (floating rate)	LIBOR + 0.5%	LIBOR + 1.0%
German marks (fixed rate)	5.0%	6.5%

Assume that A wants to borrow dollars at a floating rate of interest and B wants to borrow marks at a fixed rate of interest. A financial institution is planning to arrange · a swap and requires a 50 basis point spread. If the swap is to appear equally attractive to A and B, what rates of interest will A and B end up paying?

5.15. Company X is based in the United Kingdom and would like to borrow U.S. $50 million at a fixed rate of interest for 5 years in U.S. funds. As the company is not well known in the United States, this has proved to be impossible. However, the company has been quoted 12% per annum on fixed rate 5-year sterling funds. Company Y is based in the United States and would like to borrow the equivalent of $U.S. 50 million in sterling funds for 5 years at a fixed rate of interest. It has been unable to get a quote, but has been offered U.S.$ funds at 10.5% per annum. Five-year government bonds currently yield 9.5% per annum in the United States and 10.5% in the United Kingdom. Suggest an appropriate currency swap which will net the financial intermediary 0.5% per annum.

5.16. After it hedges its foreign exchange risk using forward contracts, is the financial institution's average spread in Figure 5.6 likely to be greater than or less than 40 basis points. Explain your answer.

5.17. How can a deferred swap be created from two other swaps?

5.18. "Companies with high credit risks are the ones that cannot access fixed rate markets directly. They are the companies that are most likely to be paying fixed and receiving floating in an interest rate swap." Assume that this is true. Do you think it increases or decreases the risk of a financial institution's swap portfolio? Assume that companies are most likely to default when interest rates are high.

5.19. How can a financial institution that warehouses interest rate swaps monitor its exposure to interest rate changes?

5.20. Why is the expected loss from a default on a swap less than the expected loss from the default on a loan with the same principal?

5.21. A bank finds that its assets are not matched with its liabilities. It is taking floating rate deposits and making fixed rate loans. How can swaps be used to offset the risk?

Options Markets

Options were introduced in Chapter 1. It will be recalled that a call option is the right to buy an asset for a certain price; a put option is the right to sell an asset for a certain price. A European option can be exercised only at the end of its life; an American option can be exercised at any time during its life. In this chapter, we explain the way in which options markets are organized, the terminology used, how the contracts are traded, how margin requirements are set, and so on. Options are fundamentally different from the forward, futures, and swap contracts discussed in the last few chapters. An option gives the holder of the option the right to do something. The holder does not have to exercise this right. By contrast, in a forward, futures, or swap contract, the two parties have entered into a binding commitment.

6.1 EXCHANGE-TRADED OPTIONS

Options trade on many different exchanges throughout the world. The underlying assets include stocks, foreign currencies, stock indices, and many different futures contracts.

STOCK OPTIONS

The exchanges trading stock options in the United States are the Chicago Board Options Exchange (CBOE), the Philadelphia Exchange (PHLX), the American Stock Exchange (AMEX), the Pacific Stock Exchange (PSE), and the New York Stock Exchange (NYSE). Options trade on over 500 different stocks. Among the most actively traded options contracts are those on IBM, Kodak, and General Motors. One contract gives the holder the right to buy or sell 100 shares at the specified strike price. This is convenient since the shares themselves are normally traded in lots of 100.

FOREIGN CURRENCY OPTIONS

The major exchange for trading foreign currency options is the Philadelphia Exchange. It offers both European and American contracts on the Australian dollar, British pound, Canadian dollar, German mark, French franc, Japanese yen, and Swiss franc. The size of one contract depends on the currency. For example, in the case of the British pound, one contract gives the holder the right to buy or sell £31,250; in the case of the Japanese yen, one contract gives the holder the right to buy or sell 6.25 million yen.

INDEX OPTIONS

Many different index options trade in the United States. The two most popular are those on the S&P 100 and S&P 500 traded on the CBOE. The S&P 500 option is European whereas the S&P 100 option is American. One contract is to buy or sell 100 times the index at the specified strike price. Settlement is in cash rather than by delivering the portfolio underlying the index. Consider, for example, one call contract on the S&P 100 with a strike price of 280. If it is exercised when the value of the index is 292, the writer of the contract pays the holder $(292 - 280) \times 100 = \$1,200$. This cash payment is based on the index value at the end of the day on which exercise instructions are issued. Not surprisingly, investors usually wait until the end of a day before issuing these instructions.

FUTURES OPTIONS

In a futures option (or options on futures), the underlying asset is a futures contract. The futures contract normally matures shortly after the expiration of the option. Futures options are now available for most of the assets on which futures contracts are traded. When the holder of a call option exercises, he or she acquires from the writer a long position in the underlying futures contract plus a cash amount equal to the excess of the futures price over the strike price. When the holder of a put option exercises, he or she acquires a short position in the underlying futures contract plus a cash amount equal to the excess of the strike price over the futures price. In both cases, the futures contracts have zero value and can be closed out immediately. The payoff from a futures option is therefore the same as the payoff from a stock option with the stock price replaced by the futures price. The most actively traded futures option is the Treasury bond futures option traded on the Chicago Board of Trade. The contracts on corn, soybeans, crude oil, live cattle, gold, Eurodollars, and some currencies are also popular.

6.2 OVER-THE-COUNTER OPTIONS

Not all options are traded on exchanges. Over-the-counter options markets, where financial institutions and corporations trade directly with each other, are becoming increasingly popular. Trading is particularly active in over-the-counter options on foreign exchange and interest rates.

The main advantage of an over-the-counter option is that it can be tailored by a financial institution to meet the needs of a corporate client. The strike price and maturity do not have to correspond to those of exchange-traded options. Also, nonstandard features can be incorporated into the design of the option. Two examples of options involving nonstandard features are Bermudan and Asian options. A *Bermudan option* is exercisable on certain specified days of its life. In an *Asian* option, the payoff is defined in terms of the average value of the underlying asset during a certain time period rather than in terms of its final value. Both types of options are sometimes traded over the counter.

6.3 SPECIFICATION OF STOCK OPTIONS

In the rest of this chapter, we will focus on exchange-traded stock options. The contract specifications and trading of index options, currency options, and futures options are discussed further in Chapter 11.

As already mentioned, a stock option contract is an American-style option contract to buy or sell 100 shares of the stock. Details of the contract, such as the expiration date, the strike price, what happens when dividends are declared, how large a position investors can hold, and so on, are specified by the exchange.

EXPIRATION DATES

One of the items used to describe a stock option is the month in which the expiration date occurs. Thus, a January call on IBM is a call option on IBM with an expiration date in January. The precise expiration date is 10:59 p.m. Central Time on the Saturday immediately following the third Friday of the expiration month. The last day on which options trade is the third Friday of the expiration month. An investor with a long position in an option normally has until 4:30 p.m. Central Time on that Friday to instruct his or her broker to exercise the option. The broker then has until 10:59 p.m. the next day to complete the paperwork notifying the exchange that exercise is to take place.

Stock options are on a January, February, or March cycle. The January cycle consists of the months of January, April, July, and October. The February cycle consists of the months of February, May, August, and November. The March cycle consists of the months of March, June, September, and December. If the expiration date for the current month has not yet been reached, options trade with expiration dates in the current month, the following month, and the next two months in its cycle. If the expiration date of the current month has passed, options trade with expiration dates in the next month, the next-but-one month, and the next two months of the expiration cycle. For example, IBM is on a January cycle. At the beginning of January, options are traded with expiration dates in January, February, April, and July; at the end of January, they are traded with expiration dates in February, March, April, and July; at the beginning of May, they are traded with expiration dates in May, June, July, and October; and so on. When one option reaches expiration, trading in another is started. Longer dated stock options known as LEAPS also trade on exchanges. They will be discussed in more detail in Chapter 11.

STRIKE PRICES

The exchange chooses the strike prices at which options can be written. For stock options, strike prices are normally spaced $2\frac{1}{2}$, $5, or $10 apart. (An exception occurs when there has been a stock split or a stock dividend, as will be described shortly.) The usual rule followed by exchanges is to use a $2\frac{1}{2}$ spacing for strike prices when the stock price is less than $25, a $5 spacing when it is between $25 and $200, and a $10 spacing when it is greater than $200. For example, at the time of writing, Citicorp has a stock price of 12 and the options traded have strike prices of 10, $12\frac{1}{2}$, 15, $17\frac{1}{2}$, and 20. IBM has a stock price of $99\frac{7}{8}$ and the options traded have strike prices of 90, 95, 100, 105, 110, and 115.

When a new expiration date is introduced, the two strike prices closest to the current stock price are usually selected by the exchange. If one of these is very close to the existing stock price, the third strike price closest to the current stock price may also be selected. If the stock price moves outside the range defined by the highest and lowest strike price, trading is usually introduced in an option with a new strike price. To illustrate these rules, suppose that the stock price is $53 when

trading in the October options start. Call and put options would first be offered
with strike prices of 50 and 55. If the stock price rose above $55, a strike price
of 60 would be offered; if it fell below $50, a strike price of 45 would be offered;
and so on.

TERMINOLOGY

For any given asset at any given time, there may be many different option
contracts trading. Consider a stock where there are four expiration dates and five
strike prices. If call and put options trade with every expiration date and every
strike price, there are a total of 40 different contracts. All options of the same type
(calls or puts) are referred to as an *option class*. For example, IBM calls are one
class while IBM puts are another class. An *option series* consists of all the options
of a given class with the same expiration date and strike price. In other words, an
option series refers to a particular contract that is traded. The IBM 110 January
calls are an option series.

Options are referred to as *in the money*, *at the money*, or *out of the money*.
An in-the-money option is one that would lead to a positive cash flow to the holder
if it were exercised immediately. Similarly, an at-the-money option would lead to
zero cash flow if it were exercised immediately, and an out-of-the-money option
would lead to a negative cash flow if it were exercised immediately. If S is the
stock price and X is the strike price, a call option is in the money when $S > X$,
at the money when $S = X$, and out of the money when $S < X$. A put option is in
the money when $S < X$, at the money when $S = X$, and out of the money when
$S > X$. Clearly, an option will only be exercised if it is in the money. In the
absence of transaction costs, an in-the-money option will always be exercised on
the expiration date if it has not been exercised previously.

The *intrinsic value* of an option is defined as the maximum of zero and the
value it would have if it were exercised immediately. For a call option, the intrinsic
value is therefore $\max(S - X, 0)$. For a put option, it is $\max(X - S, 0)$. An in-
the-money American option must be worth at least as much as its intrinsic value
since the holder can realize the intrinsic value by exercising immediately. Often
it is optimal for the holder of an in-the-money American option to wait rather
than exercise immediately. The option is then said to have *time value*. The total
value of an option can be thought of as the sum of its intrinsic value and its time
value.

DIVIDENDS AND STOCK SPLITS

The early over-the-counter options were dividend protected. If a company
declared a cash dividend, the strike price for options on the company's stock was
reduced on the ex-dividend day by the amount of the dividend. Exchange-traded

options are not generally adjusted for cash dividends. As we will see in Chapter 10, this has significant implications for the way in which options are valued.

Exchange-traded options are adjusted for stock splits. A stock split occurs when the existing shares are "split" into more shares. For example, in a 3-for-1 stock split, 3 new shares are issued to replace each existing share. Since a stock split does not change the assets or the earning ability of a company, we should not expect it to have any effect on the wealth of the company's shareholders. All else being equal, the 3-for-1 stock split just referred to should cause the stock price to go down to one-third of its previous value. In general, an n-for-m stock split should cause the stock price to go down to m/n of its previous value. The terms of option contracts are adjusted to reflect expected changes in a stock price arising from a stock split. After an n-for-m stock split, the exercise price is reduced to m/n of its previous value and the number of shares covered by one contract is increased to n/m of its previous value. If the stock price reduces in the way expected, the positions of both the writer and the purchaser of a contract remain unchanged.

Example 6.1

Consider a call option to buy 100 shares of a company for $30 per share. Suppose that the company makes a 2-for-1 stock split. The terms of the option contract are then changed so that it gives the holder the right to purchase 200 shares for $15 per share.

Stock options are adjusted for stock dividends. A stock dividend involves a company issuing more shares to its existing shareholders. For example, a 20 percent stock dividend means that investors receive 1 new share for each 5 already owned. A stock dividend, like a stock split, has no effect on either the assets or the earning power of a company. The stock price can be expected to go down as a result of a stock dividend. The 20 percent stock dividend referred to is essentially the same as a 6-for-5 stock split. All else being equal, it should cause the stock price to decline to 5/6 of its previous value. The terms of an option are adjusted to reflect the expected price decline arising from a stock dividend in the same way as they are for that arising from a stock split.

Example 6.2

Consider a put option to sell 100 shares of a company for $15 per share. Suppose that the company declares a 25% stock dividend. This is equivalent to a 5-for-4 stock split. The terms of the option contract are changed so that it gives the holder the right to sell 125 shares for $12.

Position Limits and Exercise Limits

The exchange specifies a *position limit* for each stock upon which options are traded. This defines the maximum number of option contracts that an investor can hold on one side of the market. For this purpose, long calls and short puts are considered to be on the same side of the market. Also, short calls and long puts are considered to be on the same side of the market. The *exercise limit* equals the position limit. It defines the maximum number of contracts that can be exercised by any individual (or group of individuals acting together) in any period of 5 consecutive business days. For Digital Equipment, the position limit/exercise limit is at the time of writing 8,000 contracts.

Position limits and exercise limits are designed to prevent the market from being unduly influenced by the activities of an individual investor or group of investors. However, whether they are really necessary is a controversial issue.

6.4 NEWSPAPER QUOTES

Many newspapers carry option quotations. In *The Wall Street Journal*, stock option quotations can currently be found under the heading "Listed Options" in the Money and Investing section. Table 6.1 shows the quotations as they appeared in *The Wall Street Journal* of Friday October 18, 1991. These refer to trading that took place on the previous day (i.e., Thursday, October 17, 1991).

The company on whose stock the option is written together with the closing stock price is listed in the first column. The strike price appears in the second column. The next three columns show the prices of the call options with the closest three expiration months. The last three columns show the prices of the put options with the closest three expiration months. Since at least four expiration months are active at any given time, *The Wall Street Journal* does not provide quotes on all available options at any given strike price. The letter *r* indicates that the option was not traded on October 17, 1991. The letter *s* indicates that the option is not offered by the exchange.

The quoted price is the price of an option to buy or sell 1 share. As mentioned earlier, one contract is for the purchase or sale of 100 shares. A contract therefore costs 100 times the price shown. Since most options are priced at less than $10 and some are priced at less than $1, individuals do not have to be extremely wealthy to trade options.

From Table 6.1, it appears that there were arbitrage opportunities on October 17, 1991. For example, an October call on Dow Chemical with a strike price of 50 could be bought for 2. Since the stock price is $52\frac{1}{8}$, it appears that this call could be purchased and then exercised immediately for a profit of $\frac{1}{8}$. In fact, these arbitrage opportunities almost certainly did not exist. For both options and stocks, Table 6.1 gives the prices at which the last trade took place on October 17, 1991. The last trade for the October Dow Chemical call with a strike price of 50 almost certainly occurred much earlier in the day than the last trade on the stock. If an option trade had been attempted at the time of the last trade on the stock, the call price would have been higher than $2\frac{1}{8}$.

TABLE 6.1 Stock Option Quotations from *The Wall Street Journal*, October 18, 1991

Thursday, October 17, 1991

Options closing prices. Sales unit usually is 100 shares.
Stock close is New York or American exchange final price.

CHICAGO BOARD

Option & NY Close	Strike Price	Calls-Last Oct	Calls-Last Nov	Calls-Last Dec	Puts-Last Oct	Puts-Last Nov	Puts-Last Dec
APwrCv	30	6	5 1/2	6 3/8	r	r	r
35 1/2	35	5/8	3	3 1/2	r	1 3/4	r
BergBr	25	r	r	3/16	r	r	r
Blkbst	10	2 5/8	2 13/16	2 7/8	1/16	1/16	r
12 3/4	12 1/2	1/4	7/8	1 1/8	1/16	9/16	13/16
12 3/4	15	1/16	1/4	1/2	r	r	r
BrMSq	75	r	r	8	r	r	1/2
82 1/8	80	1 5/8	3 1/2	4 3/8	1/16	1	1 7/8
82 1/8	85	1/16	15/16	2	3 1/8	3 3/4	3 7/8
82 1/8	90	r	r	3/4	r	r	r
Bruns	15	r	r	1/4	r	r	r
Chamln	25	1 1/8	r	r	r	7/16	r
26 3/8	30	r	r	1/4	r	r	r
CompSc	55	r	r	13 1/4	r	r	r
67 5/8	60	r	8	r	r	r	r
67 5/8	65	2 1/2	r	r	r	1 1/8	r
67 5/8	70	r	1 1/2	2 1/2	r	3 7/8	r
67 5/8	75	s	s	1 1/8	s	s	r
ContBk	10	1	r	1 1/2	r	5/16	r
10 7/8	12 1/2	r	r	1/2	1 11/16	1 7/8	r
CypSem	17 1/2	3	r	r	r	r	r
20 3/8	20	1/2	1 1/2	2 1/8	r	r	1 5/8
20 3/8	22 1/2	r	r	1	r	r	r
Dow Ch	45	r	r	r	r	r	3/8
52 1/8	50	2	2 1/2	3 5/8	1/16	7/8	1 1/4
52 1/8	55	1/16	1/2	1 1/16	r	3 3/8	r
52 1/8	60	r	s	3/8	r	s	r
Duracl	30	r	r	r	r	15/16	1 5/16
30 5/8	35	r	3/16	r	r	r	r
FHP s	15	r	3/8	1/2	3 1/4	r	r
12 3/4	17 1/2	r	r	3/16	r	r	r
12 3/4	22 1/2	r	r	1/4	r	r	r
12 3/4	30	r	r	1/8	r	r	r
FtBkSy	20	2	r	r	r	r	r
22	22 1/2	r	1/2	1 1/16	r	r	r
FFB	35	r	r	11/16	r	r	r
Ford	25	4 1/4	r	r	r	r	1/4
29 1/4	30	1/16	11/16	1 1/8	7/8	1 5/8	2
29 1/4	35	r	r	3/16	r	r	r
29 1/4	40	s	s	1/16	s	s	r
Fuqua	12 1/2	r	r	1/2	r	r	r
11 5/8	15	r	s	3/16	r	s	r
Gap	27 1/2	s	s	20 1/4	s	s	r
46 1/8	30	s	s	17 1/2	s	s	r
46 1/8	35	r	s	r	r	s	3/8
46 1/8	40	6 3/4	7 1/4	8	r	5/16	1
46 1/8	45	1 1/4	3	3 3/4	1/16	1 1/4	2 1/4
46 1/8	50	r	1	1 13/16	r	4 1/2	5
Gen El	65	6 5/8	7 1/4	7 3/8	r	1/4	7/8
71 1/2	70	1 5/8	2 7/8	3 5/8	1/16	1 1/16	2
71 1/2	75	1/16	9/16	1 1/4	3 1/2	3 3/4	4 1/2
71 1/2	80	r	s	5/16	r	s	8 1/2
G M	35	2 1/2	r	3 1/8	r	3/8	r
37 1/2	40	r	5/16	11/16	2 1/2	3 1/8	3 1/8
37 1/2	45	r	s	3/16	r	s	r
GtLCh	90	6	7	r	r	1	r
96 1/8	95	s	r	r	s	2 1/8	r
96 1/8	100	s	1 1/2	r	s	r	r
Hanson	20	r	1/4	1/2	r	1	r
Heinz	35	3	3 5/8	4	r	r	1/2
38 1/8	40	1/16	5/8	1 1/8	2	2 1/4	2 5/8
38 1/8	45	r	r	7/16	6 3/4	r	r
38 1/8	50	r	s	1/8	r	s	r
I T T	55	r	2 3/4	3 1/4	r	r	1 1/4
57 1/8	60	r	7/16	7/8	r	r	r
IntelE	22 1/2	2 7/16	r	r	r	r	r

Option & NY Close	Strike Price	Calls-Last Oct	Calls-Last Nov	Calls-Last Jan	Puts-Last Oct	Puts-Last Nov	Puts-Last Jan
12	12 1/2	1/16	7/16	13/16	1/2	15/16	1 1/16
12	15	r	1/16	1/4	2 7/8	3	3 1/4
12	17 1/2	r	r	1/8	5 5/8	r	5 1/2
12	20	r	s	1/16	r	s	r
CmprsL	15	r	r	10 1/2	r	r	1/4
24 7/8	20	5	4 7/8	r	r	3/8	1
24 7/8	22 1/2	2 1/8	3 5/8	4 5/8	r	r	r
24 7/8	25	r	2	3 1/4	r	r	r
24 7/8	30	s	7/16	s	s	r	s
CmpAsc	7 1/2	3/8	1	r	r	r	1/2
8 1/8	10	1/16	3/16	3/8	2 1/8	2	r
8 1/8	12 1/2	r	s	r	4 5/8	s	4 5/8
CyprMn	17 1/2	r	r	5	r	r	r
22	20	1 3/4	r	2 3/4	r	r	r
22	22 1/2	1/8	11/16	1 1/4	15/16	r	r
22	25	r	s	11/16	r	s	r
Delta	60	r	9 1/2	r	1/16	r	3/4
68 1/2	65	3 5/8	5 3/4	6 1/8	r	7/8	1 15/16
68 1/2	70	1/16	1 5/8	3 1/2	1 11/16	2 1/2	4 3/8
68 1/2	75	r	r	1 3/4	5 3/8	r	8
68 1/2	80	r	s	3/4	r	s	r
DlaSrk	20	r	11/16	r	r	r	1 3/8
Dryfus	35	r	r	1 7/8	r	1 1/4	r
34 3/4	40	r	r	r	5 3/4	r	r
EKodak	35	r	s	r	r	s	1/8
45 3/8	40	5 3/8	5 1/8	5 3/8	r	3/16	7/16
45 3/8	45	7/16	1 1/2	2 1/8	1/8	1 1/8	2 1/4
45 3/8	50	r	1/4	1/2	r	r	r
Eaton	60	1 1/4	r	r	r	r	r
61 1/4	65	r	r	1 1/4	r	r	6 1/4
Elan	40	7 1/2	6 7/8	8 3/4	r	r	15/16
47 5/8	45	2 5/8	r	4 3/4	r	1 5/16	2 1/4
47 5/8	50	s	1 1/4	2 3/4	s	4 1/4	r
Engelh	30	2 5/16	r	r	r	r	13/16
Enron	60	r	r	11 1/2	r	r	r
71 1/2	65	6 3/8	r	r	r	r	r
71 1/2	75	s	r	1 3/4	s	r	r
Exxon	50	r	s	r	1/16	s	r
61	55	6	6 1/8	6	r	r	r
61	60	7/8	1 3/16	2 1/2	1/16	13/16	r
61	65	r	1/8	1/2	4 1/2	r	4 5/8
FedExp	35	r	r	6 1/8	r	1/4	3/4
40 1/2	40	3/8	1 7/8	2 1/2	3/16	1 1/4	2 1/4
40 1/2	45	r	3/16	1	4 3/4	r	r
FstChl	22 1/2	3 3/4	r	r	r	r	r
26 1/2	25	1 5/16	r	r	r	1/2	1 3/16
26 1/2	30	r	r	1/2	r	r	r
Flntste	25	r	r	5	1/16	r	r
28 7/8	30	1/16	1	2	1 1/4	1 3/4	3
28 7/8	35	r	r	7/8	6 1/2	r	r
28 7/8	40	r	s	1/2	10 3/4	s	r
Fluor	35	9 1/4	s	r	r	s	r
45 1/4	40	5 1/4	4 3/4	6 1/4	1/8	r	3/4
45 1/4	45	1/4	1 1/2	2 5/8	1/2	1 3/4	2 1/4
45 1/4	50	1/16	s	1	r	s	6
GrtWF	15	1 1/8	r	1 3/4	r	r	r
16 1/4	17 1/2	r	3/8	11/16	1 3/8	r	r
16 1/4	20	r	r	r	4	r	r
Grumm	15	5	s	r	r	s	r
20 1/8	17 1/2	2 5/8	r	r	r	r	r
20 1/8	20	1/4	13/16	1 1/16	r	r	r
Halbtn	30	5 1/8	r	r	r	r	11/16
35 1/4	35	3/8	1 1/8	2	1/4	r	2 1/4
35 1/4	40	r	1/4	r	5	r	5 3/8
35 1/4	45	1/16	r	r	r	r	r
Hitachi	80	r	r	r	2 11/16	r	4 7/8
77 1/2	85	r	r	1 13/16	r	r	r
Homfed	5	1/16	s	s	r	s	s

Option & NY Close	Strike Price	Calls-Last Oct	Calls-Last Nov	Calls-Last Feb	Puts-Last Oct	Puts-Last Nov	Puts-Last Feb
152	175	r	r	r	r	21 3/4	r
Cadenc	15	r	5 7/8	r	r	r	r
20 3/4	17 1/2	r	3 3/8	r	r	1/4	r
20 3/4	20	1 1/16	1 3/4	r	1/4	r	r
20 3/4	22 1/2	1/8	3/4	1 3/4	1 7/8	r	r
CapClt	110	10 1/8	15 1/4	r	1 1/16	r	r
414 1/2	400	r	r	r	r	4	r
414 1/2	420	3/4	8 1/4	r	r	13 1/8	r
414 1/2	430	r	4 3/4	r	r	r	r
414 1/2	440	r	2 3/8	r	r	r	34 3/8
414 1/2	470	r	r	r	r	54 1/4	r
Coke	50	s	r	13 7/8	s	r	3/16
62 7/8	60	3 1/8	3 3/4	5 1/2	r	1/2	1 7/8
62 7/8	65	1/16	15/16	2 5/8	2 3/8	3	4 1/8
62 7/8	70	r	r	7/8	r	r	r
CocaCE	15	r	r	3/8	r	r	r
ColgPl	35	r	8 3/8	r	r	r	r
42 5/8	40	3	2 7/8	3 3/4	r	1/2	1
42 5/8	42 1/2	s	1 1/4	s	s	r	s
42 5/8	45	r	1/4	1	2 7/16	2 3/4	r
Cmw Ed	35	r	r	r	r	r	3/8
39 7/8	40	r	r	r	r	3/4	1 7/8
Corng	60	15 1/8	r	15 1/2	r	r	r
74 3/4	70	4 3/4	5 1/4	7 3/8	r	r	2 3/16
74 3/4	75	r	2	4 1/2	r	r	r
CrCare	45	15/16	r	r	9/16	r	r
Diebld	50	1 5/8	2 1/4	r	r	r	r
52	55	r	3/4	r	r	r	r
Edwrd o	25	r	9 1/2	s	r	1/16	s
34 1/2	30	4 3/8	4 5/8	s	r	r	s
34 1/2	35	r	1	s	r	r	s
Exabyt	20	5 1/8	r	r	r	r	r
25 5/8	25	r	1 7/8	r	r	1 3/16	r
ForstL	25	8 1/4	r	r	r	r	r
33 3/8	30	r	4 1/8	r	r	r	r
33 3/8	35	r	1 1/16	2 7/8	7/8	2 1/8	r
33 3/8	40	r	1/4	1 3/8	r	r	r
33 3/8	45	r	1/8	r	r	r	r
FptMc	35	5 3/4	5 1/2	5 3/4	r	r	r
40 7/8	40	3/4	1 5/8	2 5/8	r	r	r
40 7/8	45	r	1/4	7/8	r	r	r
GnCine	20	r	r	1 1/2	1/8	r	r
Gn Dyn	45	3 3/4	4 7/8	r	r	1/2	r
49 3/4	50	7/16	2	4	3/4	2 1/2	r
Gdrich	40	r	3 1/8	r	r	11/16	r
42 1/8	45	r	3/8	1 11/16	2 7/8	3	r
42 1/8	50	r	1/8	r	r	r	r
Harris	22 1/2	r	1 1/8	r	r	r	r
23 1/8	25	r	r	r	r	2 1/4	r
Hewlet	45	4 5/8	5 1/4	r	r	1/2	1 11/16
49 5/8	50	3/8	1 13/16	3 7/8	1/2	2	3 3/4
49 5/8	55	1/16	1/2	2	5 1/8	5 7/8	6 7/8
49 5/8	60	r	r	1 1/8	r	r	r
Honwll	50	5 1/4	5 3/4	r	r	r	r
55 3/8	55	3/8	r	r	1/8	1 5/8	r
55 3/8	60	r	3/8	r	r	5	r
Humana	25	2 3/4	r	r	r	7/16	3/4
28	30	r	r	r	2	r	r
In Flv	80	r	11 3/8	r	r	r	11/16
91 5/8	85	r	7 1/2	r	r	3/8	r
91 5/8	90	r	4 1/4	5 5/8	r	1 3/4	r
Limitd	20	s	r	r	s	3/16	r
24 1/8	22 1/2	1 1/2	1 7/8	2 7/8	r	1/2	1 3/8
24 1/8	25	1/16	5/8	2	1 1/8	1 1/2	2 3/4
24 1/8	30	r	1/16	5/8	6 1/4	r	r
Medtrn	65	r	r	14	r	3/8	r
76 1/4	67 1/2	r	r	r	r	r	2
76 1/4	70	6	7	10	r	5/8	r

6.5 TRADING

Options trading is in many respects similar to futures trading (see Chapter 2). An exchange has a number of members (individuals and firms) who are referred to as having seats on the exchange. Membership of an exchange entitles one to go on the floor of the exchange and trade with other members.

MARKET MAKERS

Most options exchanges (including the CBOE) use a market maker system to facilitate trading. A *market maker* for a certain option is an individual who will quote both a bid and an ask price on the option whenever he or she is asked to do so. The bid is the price at which the market maker is prepared to buy and the ask is the price at which the market maker is prepared to sell. At the time the bid and the ask are quoted, the market maker does not know whether the trader who asked for the quotes wants to buy or sell the option. The ask is of course higher than the bid and the amount by which the ask exceeds the bid is referred to as the *bid-ask spread*. The exchange sets upper limits for the bid-ask spread. It must be no more than $0.25 for options priced at less than $0.50; $0.50 for options priced between $0.50 and $10, $0.75 for options priced between $10 and $20, and $1 for options priced over $20.

The existence of the market maker ensures that buy and sell orders can always be executed at some price without any delays. Market makers therefore add liquidity to the market. The market makers themselves make their profits from the bid-ask spread. They use some of the schemes that will be discussed later in this book to hedge their risks.

THE FLOOR BROKER

Floor brokers execute trades for the general public. When an investor contacts his or her broker to buy or sell an option, the broker relays the order to the firm's floor broker in the exchange on which the option trades. If the brokerage house does not have its own floor broker, it generally has an arrangement whereby it uses either an independent floor broker or the floor broker of another firm.

The floor broker trades either with another floor broker or with the market maker. A floor broker may be on commission or may be paid a salary by the brokerage house for which he or she executes trades.

THE ORDER BOOK OFFICIAL

Many orders that are relayed to floor brokers are limit orders. This means that they can only be executed at the specified price or a more favorable price. Often when a limit order reaches a floor broker, it cannot be executed immediately. (For example, a limit order to buy a call at $5 cannot be executed immediately when the market maker is quoting a bid of $$4\frac{3}{4}$$ and an ask of $$5\frac{1}{4}$$.) In most exchanges, the floor broker will then pass the order to an individual known as the *order book official* (or board broker). This person enters the order into a computer along with other public limit orders. This ensures that as soon as the limit price is reached, the order is executed. The information on all outstanding limit orders is available to all traders.

The market marker/order book official system can be contrasted with the specialist system which is used in a few options exchanges (e.g., AMEX and PHLX) and is the most common system for trading stocks. Under the specialist system, an individual known as the specialist is responsible for being a market maker and keeping a record of limit orders. Unlike the order book official, the specialist does not make information on limit orders available to other traders.

OFFSETTING ORDERS

An investor who has purchased an option can close out his or her position by issuing an offsetting order to sell the same option. Similarly, an investor who has written an option can close out his or her position by issuing an offsetting order to buy the same option.

If, when an options contract is traded, neither investor is offsetting an existing position, the open interest increases by one contract. If one investor is offsetting an existing position and the other is not, the open interest stays the same. If both investors are offsetting existing positions, the open interest goes down by one contract.

6.6 MARGINS

When shares are purchased, an investor can either pay cash or use a margin account. The initial margin is usually 50 percent of the value of the shares and the maintenance margin is usually 25 percent of the value of the shares. The margin account operates in the same way as it does for an investor entering into a futures contract (see Chapter 2). When call and put options are purchased, the option price must be paid in full. Investors are not allowed to buy options on margin. This is because options already contain substantial leverage. Buying on margin would raise this leverage to an unacceptable level.

When an investor writes options, he or she is required to maintain funds in a margin account. This is because the investor's broker and the exchange want to be satisfied that the investor will not default if the option is exercised. The size of the margin required depends on the circumstances.

WRITING NAKED OPTIONS

Consider first the situation where the option is naked. This means that the option position is not combined with an offsetting position in the underlying stock. If the option is in the money, the initial margin is 30 percent of the value of the stocks underlying the option plus the amount by which the option is in the money. If the option is out of the money, the initial margin is 30 percent of the value of the stocks underlying the option minus the amount by which the option is out of the money. The option price received by the writer can be used to partially fulfil this margin requirement.

Example 6.3

An investor writes four naked call option contracts. The option price is $5, the strike price is $40, and the stock price is $42. The first part of the margin requirement is 30% of $42 × 400 or $5,040. The option is $2 in the money. The second part of the margin requirement is therefore $2 × 400 or $800. The price received for the option contracts is $5 × 400 or $2,000. The additional margin required is therefore

$$\$5,040 + \$800 - \$2,000 = \$3,840$$

Note that if the option had been a put, it would be $2 out of the money and the additional margin requirement would be

$$\$5,040 - \$800 - \$2,000 = \$2,240$$

A calculation similar to the initial margin calculation is repeated every day. Funds can be withdrawn from the margin account when the calculation indicates that the margin required is less than the current balance in the margin account. When the calculation indicates that a significantly greater margin is required, a margin call will be made.

WRITING COVERED CALLS

Writing covered calls involves writing call options when the shares that might have to be delivered are already owned. Covered calls are far less risky than naked calls since the worst that can happen is that the investor is required to sell shares already owned at below their market value. If covered call options are out of the money, no margin is required. The shares owned can be purchased using a margin account as just described, and the price received for the option can be used to partially fulfil this margin requirement. If the options are in the money, no margin is required for the options. However, the extent to which the shares can be margined is reduced by the extent to which the option is in the money.

Example 6.4

An investor decides to buy 200 shares of a certain stock on margin and to write 2 call option contracts on the stock. The stock price is $63, the strike price is $60 and the price of the option is $7. The margin account allows the investor to borrow 50% of the price of the stock less the amount by which the option is in the money. In this case, the option is $3 in the money so that the investor is able to borrow

$$0.5 \times \$63 \times 200 - \$3 \times 200 = \$5,700$$

The investor is also able to use the price received for the option, $7 × 200 or $1,400, to finance the purchase of the shares. The shares cost $63 × 200 = $12,600. The minimum cash initially required from the investor for his or her trades is therefore

$$\$12,600 - \$5,700 - \$1,400 = \$5,500$$

In Chapter 8 we will discuss more complicated option trading strategies such as spreads, combinations, straddles, strangles, and so on. There are special rules for determining the margin requirements when these trading strategies are used.

6.7 THE OPTIONS CLEARING CORPORATION

The Options Clearing Corporation (OCC) performs much the same sort of function for options markets as the clearinghouse does for futures markets (see Chapter 2). It guarantees that the option writer will fulfil his or her obligations under the terms of the option contract and keeps a record of all long and short positions. The OCC has a number of members, and all option trades must be cleared through a member. If a brokerage house is not itself a member of an exchange's OCC, it must arrange to clear its trades with a member. Members are required to have a certain minimum amount of capital and to contribute to a special fund that can be used if any member defaults on an option obligation.

When purchasing an option, the buyer must pay for it in full by the morning of the next business day. These funds are deposited with the OCC. The writer of the option maintains a margin account with his or her broker, as described earlier. The broker maintains a margin account with the OCC member that clears its trades. The OCC member, in turn, maintains a margin account with the OCC. The margin requirements described in the previous section are the margin requirements imposed by the OCC on its members. A brokerage house may require higher margins from its clients. However, it cannot require lower margins.

EXERCISING AN OPTION

When an investor wishes to exercise an option, the investor notifies his or her broker. The broker in turn notifies the OCC member that clears its trades. This member then places an exercise order with the OCC. The OCC randomly selects a member with an outstanding short position in the same option. The member, using a procedure established in advance, selects a particular investor who has written the option. If the option is a call, this investor is required to sell stock at the strike price. If it is a put, the investor is required to buy stock at the strike price. The investor is said to be *assigned*. When an option is exercised, the open interest goes down by one.

At the expiration of the option, all in-the-money options should be exercised unless the transactions costs are so high as to wipe out the payoff from the option. Some brokerage firms will automatically exercise options for their clients at expiration when it is in their clients' interest to do so. The OCC automatically exercises stock options owned by individuals that are in the money by more than $0.75 and stock options owned by institutions that are in the money by more than $0.25.

6.8 WARRANTS AND CONVERTIBLES

For the exchange-traded options that have been described so far, the writers and purchasers meet on the floor of the exchange and, as trading takes place, the number of contracts outstanding fluctuates. A warrant is an option that arises in a quite different way. *Warrants* are issued (i.e., written) by a company or a financial institution. In some cases they are subsequently traded on an exchange. The number of contracts outstanding is determined by the size of the original issue and changes only when options are exercised or expire. Warrants are bought and sold in much the same way as stocks and there is no need for an Options Clearing Corporation to become involved. When a warrant is exercised, the original issuer settles up with the current holder of the warrant.

Call warrants are frequently issued by companies on their own stock. For example, in a debt issue a company might offer investors a package consisting of bonds plus call warrants on its stock. If the warrants are exercised, the company issues new treasury stock to the warrant holders in return for the strike price specified in the contract. The strike price and exercise date of the warrants do not have to correspond to those of the regular exchange-traded call options. Typically, warrants have longer maturities than regular exchange-traded call options.

Put and call warrants are also sometimes issued by financial institutions to satisfy a demand in the market. The underlying asset is typically an index, a currency, or a commodity. For example, at the end of the 1980s there was a great deal of interest in put warrants on the Japanese Nikkei 225 index. Once a warrant like this has been issued, it is often traded on an exchange. The financial institution typically settles in cash when the warrant is exercised. The financial institution is paid for the warrant up front, but must hedge its risk. The techniques for doing this will be described in Chapter 13.

Convertible bonds are debt instruments with embedded options issued by corporations. The holder has the right to exchange a convertible bond for equity in the issuing company at certain times in the future according to a certain exchange ratio. Very often, the convertible is *callable*. This means that it can be repurchased by the issuer at a certain price at certain times in the future. Once the bonds have been called, the holder can always choose to convert prior to repurchase. Thus the effect of a call provision is often to give the issuer the right to force conversion of the bonds into equity at an earlier time than the holders would otherwise choose. The company provides the holder with new treasury stock in exchange for the bonds when the convertible is converted. If, as a rough approximation, interest rates are assumed constant and call provisions are ignored, a convertible can be regarded as a regular debt instrument plus call warrants.

6.9 SUMMARY

Options trade on a wide range of different assets on exchanges and in the over-the-counter market. An exchange must specify the terms of the option contracts it trades. In particular, it must specify the size of the contract, the precise expiration time, and the strike price. Over-the-counter options can be tailored to the particular needs of corporations and do not have to correspond to those traded on exchanges.

The terms of a stock option are not adjusted for cash dividends. However, they are adjusted for stock dividends and stock splits. The aim of the adjustment is to keep the positions of both the writer and the buyer of a contract unchanged.

Most options exchanges use a market maker system. A market maker is an individual who is prepared to quote both a bid (price at which he or she is prepared to buy) and an ask (price at which he or she is prepared to sell). Market makers improve the liquidity of the market and ensure that there is never any delay in executing market orders. They themselves make a profit from the difference between their bid and ask prices (known as their bid-ask spread). The exchange has rules specifying upper limits for the bid-ask spread.

Writers of options have potential liabilities and are required to maintain margins with their brokers. The broker, if not a member of the Options Clearing Corporation, will maintain a margin account with a firm that is a member. This firm will in turn maintain a margin account with the Options Clearing Corporation. The Options Clearing Corporation is responsible for keeping a record of all outstanding contracts, handling exercise orders, and so on.

SUGGESTIONS FOR FURTHER READING

CHANCE, D. M., *An Introduction to Options and Futures Markets*. Orlando, Fla.: Dryden Press, 1989.

CHICAGO BOARD OPTIONS EXCHANGE, *Reference Manual*. Chicago: 1982.

CHICAGO BOARD OPTIONS EXCHANGE, *Understanding Options*. Chicago: 1985.

CLASING, H. K., *The Dow Jones–Irwin Guide to Put and Call Trading*. Homewood, Ill.: Dow Jones–Irwin, 1978.

COX, J. C., and M. RUBINSTEIN, *Options Markets*. Englewood Cliffs, N.J.: Prentice Hall, 1985.

GASTINEAU, G., *The Stock Options Manual*. New York: McGraw-Hill, 1979.

MCMILLAN, L. G., *Options as a Strategic Investment*. New York: New York Institute of Finance, 1986.

QUESTIONS AND PROBLEMS

6.1. Explain why brokers require margins from clients when they write options, but not when they buy options.

6.2. A stock option is on a February, May, August, November cycle. What options trade on (a) April 1 and (b) May 30?

6.3. A company declares a 3-for-1 stock split. Explain how the terms of a call option with a strike price of $60 change.

6.4. Explain the difference between the specialist system and the market maker/order book official system for the organization of trading at an exchange.

6.5. Explain carefully the difference between writing a call option and buying a put option.

6.6. The treasurer of a corporation is trying to choose between the use of options and forward contracts to hedge the corporation's foreign exchange risk. Discuss the advantages and disadvantages of each.

6.7. Consider an exchange-traded call option contract to buy 500 shares with exercise price $40 and maturity in 4 months. Explain how the terms of the option contract change when there is
   (a) A 10% stock dividend.
   (b) A 10% cash dividend.
   (c) A 4-for-1 stock split.

6.8. "If most of the call options on a stock are in the money, it is likely that the stock price has risen rapidly in the last few months." Discuss this statement.

6.9. What is the effect of an unexpected cash dividend on (a) a call option price and (b) a put option price?

6.10. Options on General Motors' stock are on a March, June, September, and December cycle. What options trade on (a) March 1; (b) June 30; and (c) August 5?

6.11. Explain why the market maker's bid-ask spread represents a real cost to options' investors.

6.12. An investor writes 5 naked call option contracts. The option price is $3.50, the strike price is $60.00, and the stock price is $57.00. What is the initial margin requirement?

6.13. An investor buys 500 shares of a stock and sells 5 call option contracts on the stock. The strike price is $30. The price of the option is $3. What is the investor's minimum cash investment (a) if the stock price is $28 and (b) if the stock price is $32?

7

Properties of Stock Option Prices

In this chapter, we discuss the factors affecting stock option prices. We use a number of different arbitrage arguments to explore the relationships between European option prices, American option prices, and the underlying asset price. We show that it is never optimal to exercise an American call option on a non-dividend-paying stock prior to expiration, but that there are some circumstances under which the early exercise of an American put option on such a stock is optimal.

7.1 FACTORS AFFECTING OPTION PRICES

There are six factors affecting the price of a stock option:

1. The current stock price
2. The strike price
3. The time to expiration
4. The volatility of the stock price
5. The risk-free interest rate
6. The dividends expected during the life of the option

In this section, we consider what happens to option prices when one of these factors changes with all the others remaining fixed. The results are summarized in Table 7.1.

STOCK PRICE AND STRIKE PRICE

If it is exercised at some time in the future, the payoff from a call option will be the amount by which the stock price exceeds the strike price. Call options therefore become more valuable as the stock price increases and less valuable as the strike price increases. For a put option, the payoff on exercise is the amount by which the strike price exceeds the stock price. Put options therefore behave in the opposite way to call options. They become less valuable as the stock price increases and more valuable as the strike price increases.

TIME TO EXPIRATION

Consider next the effect of the expiration date. Both put and call American options become more valuable as the time to expiration increases. To see this, consider two options that differ only as far as the expiration date is concerned. The owner of the long-life option has all the exercise opportunities open to the owner of the short-life option—and more. The long-life option must therefore always be worth at least as much as the short-life option.

European put and call options do not necessarily become more valuable as the time to expiration increases. This is because it is not true that the owner of a long-life European option has all the exercise opportunities open to the owner of a short-life European option. The owner of the long-life European option can only exercise at the maturity of that option. Consider two European call options on a stock, one with an expiration date in 1 month, the other with an expiration date in 2 months. Suppose that a very large dividend is expected in 6 weeks. The

TABLE 7.1   Summary of the Effect on the Price of a Stock Option of Increasing One Variable While Keeping All Others Fixed

Variable	European Call	European Put	American Call	American Put
Stock Price	+	−	+	−
Strike Price	−	+	−	+
Time to Expiration	?	?	+	+
Volatility	+	+	+	+
Risk-free Rate	+	−	+	−
Dividends	−	+	−	+

dividend will cause the stock price to decline. It is possible that this will lead to the short-life option being worth more than the long-life option.

VOLATILITY

The precise way in which the volatility is defined will be discussed in Chapter 10. Roughly speaking, the volatility of a stock price is a measure of how uncertain we are about future stock price movements. As volatility increases, the chance that the stock will do very well or very poorly increases. For the owner of a stock, these two outcomes tend to offset each other. However, this is not so for the owner of a call or put. The owner of a call benefits from price increases but has limited downside risk in the event of price decreases since the most that he or she can lose is the price of the option. Similarly, the owner of a put benefits from price decreases but has limited downside risk in the event of price increases. The values of both calls and puts therefore increase as volatility increases.

RISK-FREE INTEREST RATE

The risk-free interest rate affects the price of an option in a less clear-cut way. As interest rates in the economy increase, the expected growth rate of the stock price tends to increase. However, the present value of any future cash flows received by the holder of the option decreases. These two effects both tend to decrease the value of a put option. Hence, put option prices decline as the risk-free interest rate increases. In the case of calls, the first effect tends to increase the price while the second effect tends to decrease it. It can be shown that the first effect always dominates the second effect; that is, the prices of calls always increase as the risk-free interest rate increases.

It should be emphasized that these results assume all other variables remain fixed. In practice when interest rates rise (fall), stock prices tend to fall (rise). The net effect of an interest rate change and the accompanying stock price change may therefore be the opposite of that just given.

DIVIDENDS

Dividends have the effect of reducing the stock price on the ex-dividend date. This is bad news for the value of call options and good news for the value of put options. The values of call options are therefore negatively related to the sizes of any anticipated dividends and the values of put options are positively related to the sizes of any anticipated dividends.

7.2 ASSUMPTIONS AND NOTATION

We now move on to derive some relationships between option prices that do not require any assumptions about volatility and the probabilistic behavior of stock prices. The assumptions we do make are similar to those we made when deriving forward and futures prices in Chapter 3. We assume that there are some market participants, such as large investment banks, for which

1. There are no transaction costs.
2. All trading profits (net of trading losses) are subject to the same tax rate.
3. Borrowing and lending at the risk-free interest rate is possible.

We assume that these market participants are prepared to take advantage of arbitrage opportunities as they arise. As discussed in chapters 1 and 3, this means that any available arbitrage opportunities disappear very quickly. For the purposes of our analyses, it is therefore reasonable to assume that there are no arbitrage opportunities.

We will use the following notation:

S: Current stock price

X: Strike price of option

T: Time of expiration of option

t: Current time

S_T: Stock price at time T

r: Risk-free rate of interest for an investment maturing at time T

C: Value of American call option to buy one share

P: Value of American put option to sell one share

c: Value of European call option to buy one share

p: Value of European put option to sell one share

σ: Volatility of stock price

It should be noted that r is the nominal rate of interest, not the real rate of interest. We can assume that $r > 0$. Otherwise, a risk-free investment would provide no advantages over cash. (Indeed, if $r < 0$, cash would be preferable to a risk-free investment.)

7.3 UPPER AND LOWER BOUNDS FOR OPTION PRICES

In this section, we derive upper and lower bounds for option prices. These do not depend on any particular assumptions about the factors mentioned in the previous section (except $r > 0$). If the option price is above the upper bound or below the lower bound, there are profitable opportunities for arbitrageurs.

UPPER BOUNDS

An American or European call option gives the holder the right to buy one share of a stock for a certain price. No matter what happens, the option can never be worth more than the stock. Hence, the stock price is an upper bound to the option price:

$$c \leq S \text{ and } C \leq S$$

If these relationships are not true, an arbitrageur can easily make a riskless profit by buying the stock and selling the call option.

An American or European put option gives the holder the right to sell one share of a stock for X. No matter how low the stock price becomes, the option can never be worth more than X. Hence,

$$p \leq X \text{ and } P \leq X$$

For European options, we know that at time T, the option will not be worth more than X. It follows that it must now not be worth more than the present value of X:

$$p \leq Xe^{-r(T-t)} \quad PV \ NOTATION$$

If this were not true, an arbitrageur could make a riskless profit by writing the option and investing the proceeds of the sale at the risk-free interest rate.

LOWER BOUND FOR CALLS ON NON-DIVIDEND-PAYING STOCKS

A lower bound for the price of a European call option on a non-dividend-paying stock is

$$S - Xe^{-r(T-t)}$$

We first illustrate this with a numerical example and then present a more formal argument.

Suppose that $S = \$20$, $X = \$18$, $r = 10\%$ per annum, and $T - t = 1$ year. In this case,

$$S - Xe^{-r(T-t)} = 20 - 18e^{-0.1} = 3.71$$

or $3.71. Consider the situation where the European call price is $3.00, which is less than the theoretical minimum of $3.71. An arbitrageur can buy the call and short the stock. This provides a cash inflow of $20.00 - \$3.00 = \$17.00$. If invested for 1 year at 10 percent per annum, the $17.00 grows to $17e^{0.1} = \$18.79$. At the end of the year, the option expires. If the stock price is greater than $18, the arbitrageur exercises the option for $18, closes out the short position and makes a profit of

$$\$18.79 - \$18.00 = \$0.79$$

If the stock price is less than \$18, the stock is bought in the market and the short position is closed out. The arbitrageur then makes an even greater profit. For example, if the stock price is \$17, the arbitrageur's profit is

$$\$18.79 - \$17.00 = \$1.79$$

For a more formal argument, we consider the following two portfolios:

Portfolio A: One European call option plus an amount of cash equal to $Xe^{-r(T-t)}$

Portfolio B: One share

In portfolio A, the cash, if it is invested at the risk-free interest rate, will grow to X at time T. If $S_T > X$, the call option is exercised at time T and portfolio A is worth S_T. If $S_T < X$, the call option expires worthless and the portfolio is worth X. Hence, at time T, portfolio A is worth

$$\max(S_T, X)$$

Portfolio B is worth S_T at time T. Hence, portfolio A is always worth as much as, and is sometimes worth more than, portfolio B at time T. It follows that, in the absence of arbitrage opportunities this must also be true today. Hence,

$$c + Xe^{-r(T-t)} > S$$

or

$$c > S - Xe^{-r(T-t)}$$

Since the worst than can happen to a call option is that it expires worthless, its value must be positive. This means that $c > 0$ and therefore

$$c > \max(S - Xe^{-r(T-t)}, 0) \tag{7.1}$$

Example 7.1

Consider an American call option on a non-dividend-paying stock when the stock price is \$51, the exercise price is \$50, the time to maturity is 6 months, and the risk-free rate of interest is 12% per annum. In this case, $S = 51$, $X = 50$, $T - t = 0.5$, and $r = 0.12$. From Equation (7.1), a lower bound for the option price is $S - Xe^{-r(T-t)}$ or

$$51 - 50e^{-0.12 \times 0.5} = \$3.91$$

Lᴏᴡᴇʀ Bᴏᴜɴᴅ ғᴏʀ Eᴜʀᴏᴘᴇᴀɴ Pᴜᴛs ᴏɴ Nᴏɴ-Dɪᴠɪᴅᴇɴᴅ-Pᴀʏɪɴɢ Sᴛᴏᴄᴋs

For a European put option on a non-dividend paying stock, a lower bound for the price is

$$Xe^{-r(T-t)} - S$$

Again, we first illustrate this with a numerical example and then present a more formal argument.

Suppose that $S = \$37$, $X = \$40$, $r = 5\%$ per annum, and $T - t = 0.5$ years. In this case,

$$Xe^{-r(T-t)} - S = 40e^{-0.05 \times 0.5} - 37 = 2.01$$

or $2.01. Consider the situation where the European put price is $1.00, which is less than the theoretical minimum of $2.01. An arbitrageur can borrow $38.00 for 6 months to buy both the put and the stock. At the end of the 6 months, the arbitrageur will be required to repay $38e^{0.05 \times 0.5} = \$38.96$. If the stock price is below $40.00, the arbitrageur exercises the option to sell the stock for $40.00, repays the loan, and makes a profit of

$$\$40.00 - \$38.96 = \$1.04$$

If the stock price is greater than $40.00, the arbitrageur discards the option, sells the stock, and repays the loan for an even greater profit. For example, if the stock price is $42.00, the arbitrageur's profit is

$$\$42.00 - \$38.96 = \$3.04$$

For a more formal argument, we consider the following two portfolios:

Portfolio C: One European put option plus one share
Portfolio D: An amount of cash equal to $Xe^{-r(T-t)}$

If $S_T < X$, the option in portfolio C is exercised at time T and the portfolio becomes worth X. If $S_T > X$, the put option expires worthless and the portfolio is worth S_T at time T. Hence, portfolio C is worth

$$\max(S_T, X)$$

at time T. Assuming the cash is invested at the risk-free interest rate, portfolio D is worth X at time T. Hence, portfolio C is always worth as much as, and is sometimes worth more than, portfolio D at time T. It follows that, in the absence of arbitrage opportunities, portfolio C must be worth more than portfolio D today. Hence,

$$p + S > Xe^{-r(T-t)}$$

or

$$p > Xe^{-r(T-t)} - S$$

Since the worst that can happen to a put option is that it expires worthless, its value must be positive. This means that

$$p > \max(Xe^{-r(T-t)} - S, 0) \qquad (7.2)$$

Example 7.2

Consider a European put option on a non-dividend-paying stock when the stock price is $38, the exercise price is $40, the time to maturity is 3 months, and the risk-free rate of interest is 10% per annum. In this case, $S = 38$, $X = 40$, $T - t = 0.25$, and $r = 0.10$. From Equation (7.2), a lower bound for the option price is $Xe^{-r(T-t)} - S$ or

$$40e^{-0.1 \times 0.25} - 38 = \$1.01$$

7.4 EARLY EXERCISE: CALLS ON A NON-DIVIDEND-PAYING STOCK

In this section, we show that it is never optimal to exercise an American call option on a non-dividend-paying stock early.

To illustrate the general nature of the argument, consider an American call option on a non-dividend-paying stock with one month to expiration when the stock price is $50 and the strike price is $40. The option is deep in the money and the investor who owns the option might well be tempted to exercise it immediately. However, if the investor plans to hold the stock for more than one month, this is not the best strategy. A better course of action is to keep the option and exercise it at the end of the month. The $40 strike price is then paid out one month later than it would be if the option were exercised immediately. This means that interest is earned on the $40 for one month. Since the stock pays no dividend, no income from the stock is sacrificed. A further advantage of waiting rather than exercising immediately is that there is some chance (however remote) that the stock price will be below $40 in one month. In this case, the investor will not exercise and will be glad that the decision to exercise early was not taken!

This argument shows that there are no advantages to exercising early if the investor plans to keep the stock for the rest of the life of the option (one month, in this case). What if the investor thinks the stock is currently overpriced and is wondering whether to exercise the option and sell the stock? In this case, the investor is better off selling the option than exercising it.[1] The option will be bought by another investor who does want to hold the stock. Such investors must exist. Otherwise the current stock price would not be $50. The price obtained for the option will be greater than its intrinsic value of $10 for the reasons just mentioned. In fact, Equation (7.1) shows that the market price of the option must always be greater than

$$50 - 40e^{-0.1 \times 0.08333} = \$10.33$$

Otherwise there are arbitrage opportunities.

---

[1] As an alternative strategy, the investor can keep the option and short the stock. This locks in a better profit than $10.

To present a more formal argument, consider again the following two portfolios:

Portfolio E: One American call option plus an amount of cash equal to $Xe^{-r(T-t)}$

Portfolio F: One share

The value of the cash in portfolio E at expiration of the option is X. At some earlier time τ, it is $Xe^{-r(T-\tau)}$. If the call option is exercised at time τ, the value of portfolio E is

$$S - X + Xe^{-r(T-\tau)}$$

This is always less than S when $\tau < T$ since $r > 0$. Portfolio E is therefore always worth less than portfolio F if the call option is exercised prior to maturity. If the call option is held to expiration, the value of portfolio E at time T is

$$\max(S_T, X)$$

The value of portfolio F is S_T. There is always some chance that $S_T < X$. This means that portfolio E is always worth as much as, and is sometimes worth more than, portfolio F.

We have shown that portfolio E is worth less than portfolio F if the option is exercised immediately, but is worth at least as much as portfolio F if the holder of the option delays exercise until the expiration date. It follows that a call option on a non-dividend-paying stock should never be exercised prior to the expiration date. An American call option on a non-dividend-paying stock is therefore worth the same as the corresponding European option on the same stock:

$$C = c$$

For a quicker proof, we can use Equation (7.1):

$$c > S - Xe^{-r(T-t)}$$

Since the owner of an American call has all the exercise opportunities open to the owner of the corresponding European call, we must have

$$C \geq c$$

Hence,

$$C > S - Xe^{-r(T-t)}$$

Since $r > 0$, it follows from this that $C > S - X$. If it were optimal to exercise early, C would equal $S - X$. We deduce that it can never be optimal to exercise early.

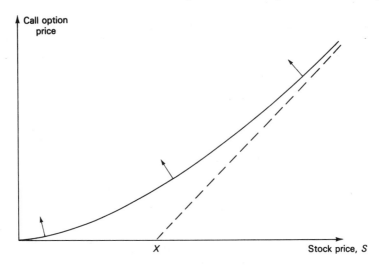

Figure 7.1 Variation of Price of an American or European Call Option on a Non-Dividend-Paying Stock with the Price, S

Figure 7.1 shows the general way in which the call price varies with S and X. It indicates that the call price is always above its intrinsic value of max $(S - X, 0)$. As r, σ, or $T - t$ increase, the call price moves in the direction indicated by the arrows (i.e., farther away from the intrinsic value).

To summarize, one reason why a call option should not be exercised early can be considered as being due to the insurance that it provides. A call option, when held instead of the stock itself, in effect insures the holder against the stock price falling below the exercise price. Once the option has been exercised and the exercise price has been exchanged for the stock price, this insurance vanishes. Another reason is concerned with the time value of money. The later the strike price is paid out the better.

7.5 EARLY EXERCISE: PUTS ON A NON-DIVIDEND-PAYING STOCK

It can be optimal to exercise an American put option on a non-dividend-paying stock early. Indeed, at any given time during its life, a put option should always be exercised early if it is sufficiently deeply in the money.

To illustrate this, consider an extreme situation. Suppose that the strike price is $10 and the stock price is virtually zero. By exercising immediately, an investor makes an immediate gain of $10. If the investor waits, the gain from exercise might be less than $10 but it cannot be more than $10 since negative stock prices are impossible. Furthermore, receiving $10 now is preferable to receiving $10 in the future. It follows that the option should be exercised immediately.

It is instructive to consider the following two portfolios:

Portfolio G: One American put option plus one share
Portfolio H: An amount of cash equal to $Xe^{-r(T-t)}$

If the option is exercised at time $\tau < T$, portfolio G becomes worth X while portfolio H is worth $Xe^{-r(T-\tau)}$. Portfolio G is therefore worth more than portfolio H. If the option is held to expiration, portfolio G becomes worth

$$\max(X, S_T)$$

while portfolio H is worth X. Portfolio G is therefore worth at least as much as, and possibly more than, portfolio H. Note the difference between this situation and the one in the previous section. Here, we cannot argue that early exercise is undesirable since portfolio G looks more attractive than portfolio H regardless of the decision on early exercise.

Like a call option, a put option can be viewed as providing insurance. A put option, when held in conjunction with the stock, insures the holder against the stock price falling below a certain level. However, a put option is different from a call option in that it may be optimal for an investor to forgo this insurance and exercise early in order to realize the strike price immediately. In general, the early exercise of a put option becomes more attractive as S decreases, as r increases, and as σ decreases.

It will be recalled from Equation (7.2) that

$$p > Xe^{-r(T-t)} - S$$

For an American put with price P, the stronger condition

$$P \geq X - S$$

must always hold since immediate exercise is always possible.

Figure 7.2 shows the general way in which the price of an American put varies with S. Provided that $r > 0$, it is always optimal to exercise an American put immediately when the stock price is sufficiently low. When early exercise is optimal, the value of the option is $X - S$. The curve representing the value of the put therefore merges into the put's intrinsic value, $X - S$, for a sufficiently small value of S. In Figure 7.2, this value of S is shown as point A. The value of the put moves in the direction indicated by the arrows when r decreases, when σ increases, and when T increases.

Since there are some circumstances when it is desirable to exercise an American put option early, it follows that an American put option is always worth more than the corresponding European put option. Since an American put is sometimes

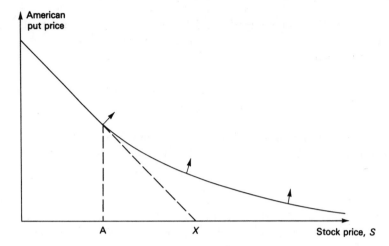

Figure 7.2 Variation of Price of an American Put Option with the Stock Price, S

worth its intrinsic value (see Figure 7.2), it follows that a European put option must sometimes be worth less than its intrinsic value. Figure 7.3 shows the variation of the European put price with the stock price. Note that point B in Figure 7.3, at which the price of the option is equal to its intrinsic value, must represent a higher value of the stock price than point A in Figure 7.2. Point E in Figure 7.3 is where $S = 0$ and the European put price is $Xe^{-r(T-t)}$.

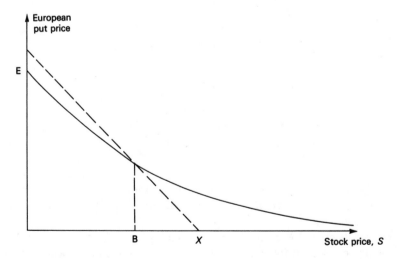

Figure 7.3 Variation of Price of a European Put Option with the Stock Price, S

7.6 PUT-CALL PARITY

It will be recalled that P and C are the prices of American put and call options, while p and c are the prices of European put and call options. The variables, P, p, C, and c are all functions of S, X, r, $T - t$, and σ. We have shown that for a non-dividend-paying stock,

$$C = c$$

$$P > p \text{ when } r > 0$$

We now derive an important relationship between p and c. Consider the following two portfolios:

> ***Portfolio A:*** One European call option plus an amount of cash equal to $Xe^{-r(T-t)}$
>
> ***Portfolio C:*** One European put option plus one share

Both are worth

$$\max(S_T, X)$$

at expiration of the options. Since the options are European, they cannot be exercised prior to the expiration date. The portfolios must therefore have identical values today. This means that

$$c + Xe^{-r(T-t)} = p + S \tag{7.3}$$

This relationship is known as *put-call parity*. It shows that the value of a European call with a certain exercise price and exercise date can be deduced from the value of a European put with the same exercise price and date, and vice versa.

If Equation (7.3) does not hold, there are arbitrage opportunities. Suppose that the stock price is \$31, the exercise price is \$30, the risk-free interest rate is 10 percent per annum, the price of a 3-month European call option is \$3, and the price of a 3-month European put option is \$2.25. In this case,

$$c + Xe^{-r(T-t)} = 3 + 30e^{-0.1 \times 0.25} = 32.26$$

$$p + S = 2.25 + 31 = 33.25$$

Portfolio C is overpriced relative to portfolio A. The correct arbitrage strategy is to buy the securities in portfolio A and short the securities in portfolio C. This involves buying the call and shorting both the put and the stock. The strategy generates a positive cash flow of

$$-3 + 2.25 + 31 = \$30.25$$

upfront. When invested at the risk-free interest rate, this grows to $30.25e^{0.1\times0.25} =$ 31.02 in 3 months. If the stock price at expiration of the option is greater than $30, the call will be exercised. If it is less than $30, the put will be exercised. In either case the investor ends up buying one share for $30. This share can be used to close out the short position. The net profit is therefore

$$\$31.02 - \$30.00 = \$1.02$$

For an alternative situation, suppose that the call price is $3 and the put price is $1. In this case

$$c + Xe^{-r(T-t)} = 3 + 30e^{-0.1\times0.25} = 32.25$$

$$p + S = 1 + 31 = 32.00.$$

Portfolio A is overpriced relative to portfolio C. An arbitrageur can short the securities in portfolio A and buy the securities in portfolio C to lock in a profit. This involves shorting the call and buying both the put and the stock. The strategy involves an initial investment of

$$\$31 + \$1 - \$3 = \$29$$

at time zero. When financed at the risk-free interest rate, a repayment of $29e^{0.1\times0.25} = \$29.73$ is required at the end of the 3 months. As in the previous case, either the call or the put will be exercised. The short call and long put option position therefore leads to the stock being sold for $30.00. The net profit is therefore

$$\$30.00 - \$29.73 = \$0.27.$$

Relationship Between American Call and Put Prices

Put-call parity holds only for European options. However, it is possible to derive some relationships between American option prices for a non-dividend-paying stock.

Since $P > p$, it follows from Equation (7.3) that

$$P > c + Xe^{-r(T-t)} - S$$

and since $c = C$,

$$P > C + Xe^{-r(T-t)} - S$$

or

$$C - P < S - Xe^{-r(T-t)} \tag{7.4}$$

For a further relationship between C and P consider

Portfolio I: European call option plus an amount of cash equal to X
Portfolio J: American put option plus one share

Both options have the same exercise price and expiration date. Assume that the cash in portfolio I is invested at the risk-free interest rate. If the put option is not exercised early portfolio J is worth

$$\max(S_T, X)$$

at time T. Portfolio I is worth

$$\max(S_T, X) + Xe^{r(T-t)} - X$$

at this time. Portfolio I is therefore worth more than portfolio J. Suppose next that the put option in portfolio J is exercised early, say, at time τ. This means that portfolio J is worth X at time τ. However, even if the call option were worthless, portfolio I would be worth $Xe^{r(\tau-t)}$ at time τ. It follows that portfolio I is worth more than portfolio J in all circumstances. Hence,

$$c + X > P + S$$

Since $c = C$,

$$C + X > P + S$$

or

$$C - P > S - X$$

Combining this with Equation (7.4), we obtain

$$S - X < C - P < S - Xe^{-r(T-t)} \tag{7.5}$$

Example 7.3

Consider the situation where an American call option on a non-dividend-paying stock with exercise price \$20.00 and maturity in 5 months is worth \$1.50. This must also be the value of a European call option on the same stock with the same exercise price and maturity. Suppose that the current stock price is \$19.00 and the risk-free interest rate is 10% per annum. From a rearrangement of Equation (7.3), the price of a European put with exercise price \$20 and maturity in 5 months is

$$1.50 + 20e^{-0.1\times0.4167} - 19 = \$1.68$$

From Equation (7.5)

$$19 - 20 < C - P < 19 - 20e^{-0.1\times0.4167}$$

or

$$1 > P - C > 0.18$$

showing that $P - C$ lies between $1.00 and $0.18. Since C is $1.50, P must lie between $1.68 and $2.50. In other words, upper and lower bounds for the price of an American put with the same strike price and expiration date as the American call are $2.50 and $1.68.

7.7 EFFECT OF DIVIDENDS

The results produced in sections 7.3 to 7.6 have assumed that we are dealing with options on a non-dividend-paying stock. In this section, we discuss the impact of dividends. In the United States, exchange-traded stock options generally have less than 8 months to maturity. The dividends payable during the life of the option can usually be predicted with reasonable accuracy. We will use D to denote the present value of the dividends during the life of the option. For this purpose a dividend is assumed to occur at the time of its ex-dividend date.

<small>LOWER BOUND FOR CALLS AND PUTS</small>

We can redefine portfolios A and B as follows:

Portfolio A: One European call option plus an amount of cash equal to $D + Xe^{-r(T-t)}$

Portfolio B: One share

A similar argument to the one used to derive Equation (7.1) shows that

$$c > S - D - Xe^{-r(T-t)} \tag{7.6}$$

We can also redefine portfolios C and D as follows:

Portfolio C: One European put option plus one share
Portfolio D: An amount of cash equal to $D + Xe^{-r(T-t)}$

A similar argument to the one used to derive Equation (7.2) shows that

$$p > D + Xe^{-r(T-t)} - S \tag{7.7}$$

<small>EARLY EXERCISE</small>

When dividends are expected, we can no longer assert that an American call option will not be exercised early. Sometimes it is optimal to exercise an American call immediately prior to an ex-dividend date. This is because the dividend will cause the stock price to jump down, making the option less attractive. It is never optimal to exercise a call at other times. This point will be discussed further in Chapter 10.

PUT-CALL PARITY

Comparing the value at time T of the redefined portfolios A and C shows that when there are dividends, put-call parity becomes

$$c + D + Xe^{-r(T-t)} = p + S \qquad (7.8)$$

Dividends cause Equation (7.5) to be modified to

$$S - D - X < C - P < S - Xe^{-r(T-t)} \qquad (7.9)$$

To prove this inequality, consider

Portfolio I: European call option plus an amount of cash equal to $D + X$

Portfolio J: American put option plus a share

Regardless of what happens, it can be shown that portfolio I is worth more than portfolio J. Hence,

$$P + S < c + D + X$$

Since a European call is never worth more than its American counterpart, or $c < C$, it follows that

$$P + S < C + D + X$$

or

$$S - D - X < C - P$$

This proves the first half of the inequality in Equation (7.9). For a non-dividend-paying stock, we showed in Equation (7.5) that

$$C - P < S - Xe^{-r(T-t)}$$

Since dividends decrease the value of a call and increase the value of a put, this inequality must also be true for options on a dividend-paying stock. This proves the second half of the inequality in Equation (7.9).

7.8 EMPIRICAL RESEARCH

Empirical research to test the results in this chapter might seem to be relatively simple to carry out once the appropriate data has been assembled. In fact, there are a number of complications:

1. It is important to be sure that option prices and stock prices are being observed at exactly the same time. For example, testing for arbitrage opportunities by looking at the price at which the last trade is done each day is inappropriate. This point has already been made in connection with the numbers in Table 6.1.

2. It is important to consider carefully whether a trader could have taken advantage of any observed arbitrage opportunity. If the opportunity exists only momentarily, there might, in practice, be no way of exploiting it.

3. Transactions costs must be taken into account when determining whether arbitrage opportunities were possible.

4. Put-call parity only holds for European options. Exchange-traded stock options are American.

5. Dividends to be paid during the life of the option must be estimated.

Some of the empirical research that has been carried out is described in the papers by Bhattacharya, Galai, Gould and Galai, Klemkosky and Resnick, and Stoll that are referenced at the end of this chapter. Galai and Bhattacharya test whether option prices are ever less than their lower bounds; Stoll, Gould and Galai, and the two papers by Klemkosky and Resnick test whether put-call parity holds. We will consider the results of Bhattacharya and of Klemkosky and Resnick.

Bhattacharya's study examined whether the theoretical lower bounds for call options applied in practice. He used data consisting of the transaction prices for options on 58 stocks over a 196-day period between August 1976 and June 1977. The first test examined whether the options satisfied the condition that price be greater than intrinsic value, that is, whether $C > \max(S - X, 0)$. Over 86,000 option prices were examined and about 1.3 percent were found to violate this condition. In 29 percent of the cases, the violation disappeared by the next trade, indicating that in practice traders would not have been able to take advantage of it. When transaction costs were taken into account, the profitable opportunities created by the violation disappeared. Bhattacharya's second test examined whether options sold for less than the lower bound $S - D - Xe^{-r(T-t)}$. [See Equation (7.6).] He found that 7.6 percent of his observations did in fact sell for less than this lower bound. However, when transaction costs were taken into account, these did not give rise to profitable opportunities.

Klemkosky and Resnick's tests of put-call parity used data on option prices taken from trades between July 1977 and June 1978. They subjected their data to several tests to determine the likelihood of options being exercised early and discarded data where early exercise was considered probable. By doing this they felt they were justified in treating Amerian options as European. They identified 540 situations where the call price was too low relative to the put and 540 situations where the call price was too high relative to the put. After allowing for transaction costs, 38 of the first set of situations gave rise to profitable arbitrage opportunities and 147 of the second set of situations did so. The opportunities persisted when either a 5- or a 15-minute delay between the opportunity being noted and trades being executed was assumed. Klemkosky and Resnick's conclusion is that arbitrage opportunities were available to some traders, particularly market makers, during the period they studied.

7.9 SUMMARY

There are six factors affecting the value of a stock option: the current stock price, the strike price, the expiration date, the stock price volatility, the risk-free interest rate, and the dividends expected during the life of the option. The value of a call generally increases as the current stock price, the time to expiration, the volatility, and the risk-free interest rate increase. The value of a call decreases as the strike price and expected dividends increase. The value of a put generally increases as the strike price, the time to expiration, the volatility and the expected dividends increase. The value of a put decreases as the current stock price and the risk-free interest rate increase.

It is possible to reach some conclusions about the values of stock options without making any assumptions about the probabilistic behavior of stock prices. For example, the price of a call option on a stock must always be worth less than the price of the stock itself. Similarly, the price of a put option on a stock must always be worth less than the option's strike price.

A call option on a non-dividend-paying stock must be worth more than

$$\max\left(S - Xe^{-r(T-t)},\, 0\right)$$

where S is the stock price, X is the exercise price, r is the risk-free interest rate, and T is the time to expiration. A put option on a non-dividend-paying stock must be worth more than

$$\max\left(Xe^{-r(T-t)} - S,\, 0\right)$$

When dividends with present value D will be paid, the lower bound for a call option becomes

$$\max\left(S - D - Xe^{-r(T-t)},\, 0\right)$$

and the lower bound for a put option becomes

$$\max\left(Xe^{-r(T-t)} + D - S,\, 0\right)$$

Put-call parity is a relationship between the price, c, of a European call option on a stock and the price, p, of a European put option on a stock. For a non-dividend-paying stock, it is

$$c + Xe^{-r(T-t)} = p + S$$

For a dividend-paying stock, the put-call parity relationship is

$$c + D + Xe^{-r(T-t)} = p + S$$

Put-call parity does not hold for American options. However, it is possible to use arbitrage arguments to obtain upper and lower bounds for the difference between the price of an American call and the price of an American put.

In future chapters, we will carry the analyses in this chapter further by making some specific assumptions about the probabilistic behavior of stock prices. This will enable us to derive exact pricing formulas for European stock options. It will also enable us to derive numerical procedures for pricing American options.

SUGGESTIONS FOR FURTHER READING

BHATTACHARYA, M., "Transaction Data Tests of Efficiency of the Chicago Board Options Exchange," *Journal of Financial Economics*, 12 (1983), 161–85.

GALAI, D., "Empirical Tests of Boundary Conditions for CBOE Options," *Journal of Financial Economics*, 6 (1978), 187–211.

GOULD, J. P., and D. GALAI, "Transactions Costs and the Relationship Between Put and Call Prices," *Journal of Financial Economics*, 1 (1974), 105–29.

KLEMKOSKY, R. C., and B. G. RESNICK, "An Ex-ante Analysis of Put-Call Parity," *Journal of Financial Economics*, 8 (1980), 363–78.

KLEMKOSKY, R. C., and B. G. RESNICK, "Put-Call Parity and Market Efficiency," *Journal of Finance*, 34 (December 1979), 1141–55.

MERTON, R. C., "The Relationship Between Put and Call Prices: Comment," *Journal of Finance*, 28 (March 1973), 183–84.

MERTON, R. C., "Theory of Rational Option Pricing," *Bell Journal of Economics and Management Science*, 4 (Spring 1973), 141–83.

STOLL, H. R., "The Relationship Between Put and Call Option Prices," *Journal of Finance*, 31 (May 1969), 319–32.

QUESTIONS AND PROBLEMS

7.1. An investor buys a call with strike price X and writes a put with the same strike price. Describe the investor's position.

7.2. Explain why an American option is always worth at least as much as a European option on the same asset with the same strike price and exercise date.

7.3. Explain why an American option is always worth at least as much as its intrinsic value.

7.4. List the six factors affecting stock option prices.

7.5. What is a lower bound for the price of a 4-month call option on a non-dividend-paying stock when the stock price is $28, the strike price is $25, and the risk-free interest rate is 8% per annum?

7.6. What is a lower bound for the price of a 1-month European put option on a non-dividend-paying stock when the stock price is $12, the strike price is $15, and the risk-free interest rate is 6% per annum?

7.7. Give two reasons why the early exercise of an American call option on a non-dividend-paying stock is not optimal. The first reason should involve the time value of money. The second reason should apply even if interest rates are zero.

7.8. "The early exercise of an American put is a trade-off between the time value of money and the insurance value of a put." Explain this statement.

7.9. A European call and put option on a stock both have a strike price of $20 and an expiration date in 3 months. Both sell for $3. The risk-free interest rate is 10% per annum, the current stock price is $19, and a $1 dividend is expected in 1 month. Identify the arbitrage opportunity open to a trader.

7.10. Explain why the arguments leading to put-call parity for European options cannot be used to give a similar result for American options.

7.11. What is a lower bound for the price of a 6-month call option on a non-dividend-paying stock when the stock price is $80, the strike price is $75, and the risk-free interest rate is 10% per annum?

7.12. What is a lower bound for the price of a 2-month European put option on a non-dividend-paying stock when the stock price is $58, the strike price is $65, and the risk-free interest rate is 5% per annum?

7.13. A 4-month European call option on a dividend-paying stock is currently selling for $5. The stock price is $64, the strike price is $60, and a dividend of $0.80 is expected in 1 month. The risk-free interest rate is 12% per annum for all maturities. What opportunities are there for an arbitrageur?

7.14. A 1-month European put option on a non-dividend-paying stock is currently selling for 2\frac{1}{2}$. The stock price is $47, the strike price is $50, and the risk-free interest rate is 6% per annum. What opportunities are there for an arbitrageur?

7.15. Give an intuitive explanation of why the early exercise of an American put becomes more attractive as the risk-free rate increases and volatility decreases.

7.16. The price of a European call which expires in 6 months and has a strike price of $30 is $2. The underlying stock price is $29, and a dividend of $0.50 is expected in 2 months and in 5 months. The term structure is flat with all risk-free interest rates being 10%. What is the price of a European put option that expires in 6 months and has a strike price of $30.

7.17. Explain carefully the arbitrage opportunities in Problem 7.16 if the European put price is $3.

7.18. The price of an American call on a non-dividend-paying stock is $4. The stock price is $31, the strike price is $30, and the expiration date is in 3 months. The risk-free interest rate is 8%. Derive upper and lower bounds for the price of an American put on the same stock with the same strike price and expiration date.

7.19. Explain carefully the arbitrage opportunities in Problem 7.18 if the American put price is greater than the calculated upper bound.

7.20. Suppose that c_1, c_2, and c_3 are the prices of European call options with strike prices X_1, X_2, and X_3, respectively, where $X_3 > X_2 > X_1$ and $X_3 - X_2 = X_2 - X_1$. All options have the same maturity. Show that

$$c_2 \leq 0.5(c_1 + c_3)$$

(Hint: Consider a portfolio that is long one option with strike price X_1, long one option with strike price X_3, and short two options with strike price X_2.)

7.21. What is the result corresponding to that in Problem 7.20 for American put options?

7.22. Suppose that you are the manager and sole owner of a highly leveraged company. All the debt will mature in one year. If at that time the value of the company is greater than the face value of the debt, you will pay off the debt. If the value of the company is less than the face value of the debt, you will declare bankruptcy and the debtholders will own the company.

(a) Express your position as an option on the value of the company.

(b) Express the position of the debtholders in terms of options on the value of the company.

(c) What can you do to increase the value of your position?

8

Trading Strategies Involving Options

The profit pattern from an investment in a single stock option was discussed in Chapter 1. In this chapter we cover more fully the range of profit patterns obtainable using options. In the first section we consider what happens when a position in a stock option is combined with a position in the stock itself. We then move on to discuss the profit patterns obtained when an investment is made in two or more different options on the same stock. One of the attractions of options is that they can be used to create a wide range of different payoff functions. Unless otherwise stated the options we consider are all European. Toward the end of this chapter, we will argue that if European options were available with every single possible strike price, any payoff function could in theory be created.

8.1 STRATEGIES INVOLVING A SINGLE OPTION AND A STOCK

There are a number of different trading strategies involving a single option on a stock and the stock itself. The profits from these are illustrated in Figure 8.1. In this figure, and in other figures throughout this chapter, the dashed line shows the

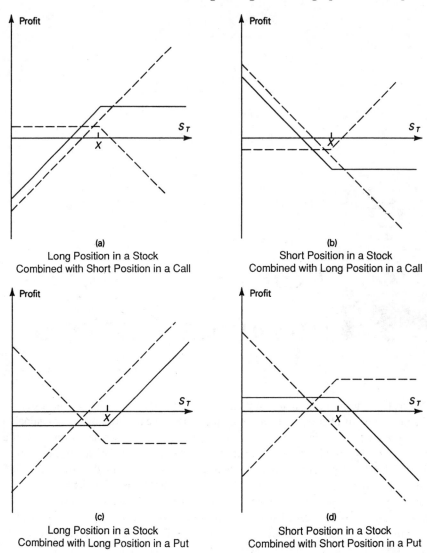

Figure 8.1   Profit from Various Trading Strategies Involving a Single Option and a Stock

relationship between profit and stock price for the individual securities constituting the portfolio, while the solid line shows the relationship between profit and stock price for the whole portfolio.

In Figure 8.1(a), the portfolio consists of a long position in a stock plus a short position in a call option. The investment strategy represented by this portfolio is known as *writing a covered call*. This is because the long stock position "covers" or protects the investor from the possibility of a sharp rise in the stock price. In Figure 8.1(b), a short position in a stock is combined with a long position in a call option. This is the reverse of writing a covered call. In Figure 8.1(c), the investment strategy involves buying a put option on a stock and the stock itself. This is sometimes referred to as a *protective put* strategy. In Figure 8.1(d), a short position in a put option is combined with a short position in the stock. This is the reverse of a protective put.

The profit patterns in Figure 8.1(a), (b), (c), and (d) have the same general shape as the profit patterns discussed in Chapter 1 for short put, long put, long call, and short call, respectively. Put-call parity provides a way of understanding why this is so. It will be recalled from Chapter 7 that the put-call parity relationship is

$$p + S = c + Xe^{-r(T-t)} + D \qquad (8.1)$$

where p is the price of a European put, S is the stock price, c is the price of a European call, X is the strike price of both call and put, r is the risk-free interest rate, T is the maturity date of both call and put, and D is the present value of the dividends anticipated during the life of the option.

Equation 8.1 shows that a long position in a put combined with a long position in the stock is equivalent to a long call position plus an amount $Xe^{-r(T-t)} + D$ of cash. This explains why the profit pattern in Figure 8.1(c) is similar to the profit pattern from a long call position. The position in Figure 8.1(d) is the reverse of that in Figure 8.1(c) and therefore leads to a profit pattern similar to that from a short call position.

Equation 8.1 can be rearranged to become

$$S - c = Xe^{-r(T-t)} + D - p$$

This shows that a long position in a stock combined with a short position in a call is equivalent to a short put position plus an amount $= Xe^{-r(T-t)} + D$ of cash. This explains why the profit pattern in Figure 8.1(a) is similar to the profit pattern from a short put position. The position in Figure 8.1(b) is the reverse of that in Figure 8.1(a) and therefore leads to a profit pattern similar to that from a long put position.

8.2 SPREADS

A spread trading strategy involves taking a position in two or more options of the same type (that is, two or more calls or two or more puts).

BULL SPREADS

One of the most popular types of spreads is a *bull spread*. This can be created by buying a call option on a stock with a certain strike price and selling

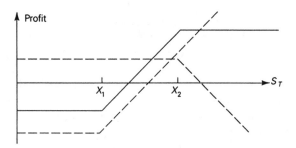

Figure 8.2   Bull Spread Created Using Call Options

a call option on the same stock with a higher strike price. Both options have the same expiration date. The strategy is illustrated in Figure 8.2. The profits from the two option positions taken separately are shown by the dashed lines. The profit from the whole strategy is the sum of the profits given by the dashed lines and is indicated by the solid line. Since a call price always decreases as the strike price increases, the value of the option sold is always less than the value of the option bought. A bull spread, when created from calls, therefore requires an initial investment.

Suppose that X_1 is the strike price of the call option bought, X_2 is the strike price of the call option sold, and S_T is the stock price on the expiration date of the options. Table 8.1 shows the total payoff that will be realized from a bull spread in different circumstances. If the stock price does well and is greater than the higher strike price, the payoff is the difference between the two strike prices, $X_2 - X_1$. If the stock price on the expiration date lies between the two strike prices, the payoff is $S_T - X_1$. If the stock price on the expiration date is below the lower strike price, the payoff is zero. The profit in Figure 8.2 is calculated by subtracting the initial investment from the payoff.

A bull spread strategy limits both the investor's upside potential and his or her downside risk. We can describe the strategy by saying that the investor has a call option with a strike price equal to X_1 and has chosen to give up some upside potential by selling a call option with strike price X_2 ($X_2 > X_1$). In return for giving up the upside potential the investor gets the price of the option with strike

TABLE 8.1   Payoff from a Bull Spread

Stock Price Range	Payoff from Long Call Option	Payoff from Short Call Option	Total Payoff
$S_T \geq X_2$	$S_T - X_1$	$X_2 - S_T$	$X_2 - X_1$
$X_1 < S_T < X_2$	$S_T - X_1$	0	$S_T - X_1$
$S_T \leq X_1$	0	0	0

price X_2. Three types of bull spreads can be distinguished:

1. Both calls initially out of the money
2. One call initially in the money, the other call initially out of the money
3. Both calls initially in the money

The most aggressive bull spreads are those of type 1. They cost very little to set up and have a small probability of giving a relatively high payoff ($= X_2 - X_1$). As we move from type 1 to type 2 and from type 2 to type 3, the spreads become more conservative.

Example 8.1

An investor buys for $3 a call with a strike price of $30 and sells for $1 a call with a strike price of $35. The payoff from this bull spread strategy is $5 if the stock price is above $35 and zero when it is below $30. If the stock price is between $30 and $35 the payoff is the amount by which the stock price exceeds $30. The cost of the strategy is $3 - $1 = $2. The profit is therefore as follows:

Stock Price Range	Profit
$S_T \leq 30$	-2
$30 < S_T < 35$	$S_T - 32$
$S_T \geq 35$	3

Bull spreads can also be created by buying a put with a low strike price and selling a put with a high strike price. This is illustrated in Figure 8.3. Unlike the bull spread created using calls, bull spreads created from puts involve a positive

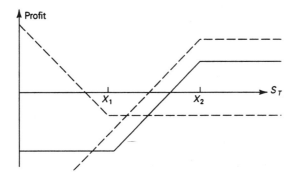

Figure 8.3 Bull Spread Created Using Put Options

cash flow to the investor up front. (This ignores margin requirements.) Needless to say, the final payoffs from bull spreads created using puts are lower than from those created using calls.

BEAR SPREADS

An investor entering into a bull spread is hoping that the stock price will increase. By contrast an investor who enters into a *bear spread* is hoping that the stock price will decline. Like a bull spread, a bear spread can be created by buying a call with one strike price and selling a call with another strike price. However, in the case of a bear spread, the strike price of the option purchased is greater than the strike price of the option sold. This is illustrated in Figure 8.4 where the profit from the spread is shown by the solid line. A bear spread created from calls involves an initial cash inflow (when margin requirements are ignored) since the price of the call sold is greater than the price of the call purchased.

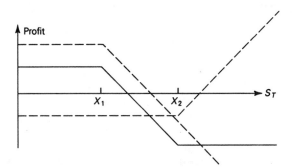

Figure 8.4   Bear Spread Created Using Call Options

Assuming that the strike prices are X_1 and X_2 with $X_1 < X_2$, Table 8.2 shows the payoff that will be realized from a bear spread in different circumstances. If the stock price is greater than X_2, the payoff is negative at $-(X_2 - X_1)$. If the

TABLE 8.2   Payoff from a Bear Spread

Stock Price Range	Payoff from Long Call Option	Payoff from Short Call Option	Total Payoff
$S_T \geq X_2$	$S_T - X_2$	$X_1 - S_T$	$-(X_2 - X_1)$
$X_1 < S_T < X_2$	0	$X_1 - S_T$	$-(S_T - X_1)$
$S_T \leq X_1$	0	0	0

stock price is less than X_1, the payoff is zero. If the stock price is between X_1 and X_2, the payoff is $-(S_T - X_1)$. The profit is calculated by adding the initial cash inflow to the payoff.

Example 8.2

An investor buys for \$1 a call with a strike price of \$35 and sells for \$3 a call with a strike price of \$30. The payoff from this bear spread strategy is –\$5 if the stock price is above \$35 and zero if it is below \$30. If the stock price is between \$30 and \$35 the payoff is $-(S_T - 30)$. The investment generates $\$3 - \$1 = \$2$ up front. The profit is therefore as follows:

Stock Price Range	Profit
$S_T \leq 30$	$+2$
$30 < S_T < 35$	$32 - S_T$
$S_T \geq 35$	-3

Like bull spreads, bear spreads limit both the upside profit potential and the downside risk. Bear spreads can be created using puts instead of calls. The investor buys a put with a high strike price and sells a put with a low strike price. This is illustrated in Figure 8.5. Bear spreads created with puts require an initial investment. In essence, the investor has bought a put with a certain strike price and chosen to give up some of the profit potential by selling a put with a lower strike price. In return for the profit given up, the investor gets the price of the option sold.

BUTTERFLY SPREADS

A butterfly spread involves positions in options with three different strike prices. It can be created by buying a call option with a relatively low strike price,

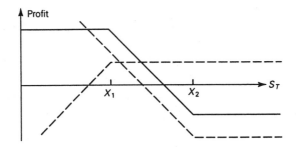

Figure 8.5   Bear Spread Created Using Put Options

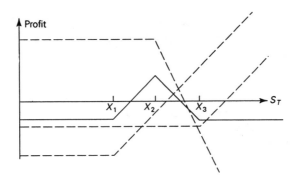

Figure 8.6   Butterfly Spread Using Call Options

X_1; buying a call option with a relatively high strike price, X_3; and selling two call options with a strike price, X_2, halfway between X_1 and X_3. Generally, X_2 is close to the current stock price. The pattern of profits from the strategy is shown in Figure 8.6. A butterfly spread leads to a profit if the stock price stays close to X_2 but gives rise to a small loss if there is a significant stock price move in either direction. It is therefore an appropriate strategy for an investor who feels that large stock price moves are unlikely. The strategy requires a small investment initially. The payoff from a butterfly spread is shown in Table 8.3.

TABLE 8.3   Payoff from a Butterfly Spread

Stock Price Range	Payoff from First Long Call	Payoff from Second Long Call	Payoff from Short Calls	Total Payoff*
$S_T < X_1$	0	0	0	0
$X_1 < S_T < X_2$	$S_T - X_1$	0	0	$S_T - X_1$
$X_2 < S_T < X_3$	$S_T - X_1$	0	$-2(S_T - X_2)$	$X_3 - S_T$
$S_T > X_3$	$S_T - X_1$	$S_T - X_3$	$-2(S_T - X_2)$	0

*These payoffs are calculated using the relationship $X_2 = 0.5(X_1 + X_3)$.

Suppose that a certain stock is currently worth \$61. Consider an investor who feels that it is unlikely that there will be a significant price move in the next 6 months. Suppose that the market prices of 6-month calls are as follows:

Strike Price (\$)	Call Price (\$)
55	10
60	7
65	5

The investor could create a butterfly spread by buying one call with a $55 strike price, buying one call with a $65 strike price, and selling two calls with a $60 strike price. It costs $10 + $5 − (2 × $7) = $1 to create the spread. If the stock price in 6 months is greater than $65 or less than $55, there is no payoff and the investor makes a net loss of $1. If the stock price is between $56 and $64, a profit is made. The maximum profit, $5, occurs when the stock price in 6 months is $60. Butterfly spreads can be created using put options. The investor buys a put with a low strike price, buys a put with a high strike price and sells two puts with an intermediate strike price. This is illustrated in Figure 8.7. The butterfly spread in the example just considered would be created by buying a put with a strike price of $55, buying a put with a strike price of $65, and selling two puts with a strike price of $60. If all options are European, the use of put options results in exactly the same spread as the use of call options. Put-call parity can be used to show that the initial investment is the same in both cases.

A butterfly spread can be sold or shorted by following the reverse strategy to that described earlier. Options are sold with strike prices of X_1 and X_3, and two options with the middle strike price X_2 are purchased. This strategy produces a modest profit if there is a significant movement in the stock price.

CALENDAR SPREADS

Up to now we have assumed that the options used to create a spread all expire at the same time. We now move on to discuss calendar spreads where the options used have the same strike price and different expiration dates.

A calendar spread can be created by selling a call option with a certain strike price and buying a longer-maturity call option with the same strike price. The longer the maturity of an option, the more expensive it is. A calendar spread therefore requires an initial investment. Assuming that the long-maturity option is sold when the short-maturity option expires, the profit pattern given by a calendar

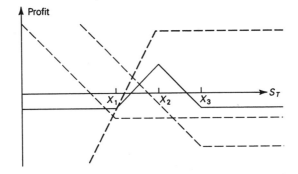

Figure 8.7   Butterfly Spread Using Put Options

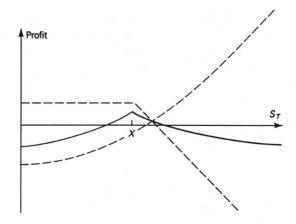

Figure 8.8   Calendar Spread Created Using Two Calls

spread is as shown in Figure 8.8. This is similar to the profit pattern from the butterfly spread in Figure 8.6. The investor makes a profit if the stock price at the expiration of the short-maturity option is close to the strike price of the short-maturity option. However, a loss is incurred when the stock price is significantly above or significantly below this strike price.

To understand the profit pattern from a calendar spread, first consider what happens if the stock price is very low when the short-maturity options expires. The short-maturity option is worthless and the value of the long-maturity option is close to zero. The investor therefore incurs a loss that is only a little less than the cost of setting up the spread initially. Consider next what happens if the stock price, S_T, is very high when the short-maturity option expires. The short-maturity option costs the investor $S_T - X$ and the long-maturity option (assuming early exercise is not optimal) is worth a little more than $S_T - X$, where X is the strike price of the options. Again the investor makes a net loss that is a little less than the cost of setting up the spread initially. If S_T is close to X, the short-maturity option costs the investor either a small amount or nothing at all. However, the long-maturity option is still quite valuable. In this case, a significant net profit is made.

In a *neutral calendar spread*, a strike price close to the current stock price is chosen. A *bullish calendar spread* would involve a higher strike price while a *bearish calendar spread* would involve a lower strike price.

Calendar spreads can be created with put options as well as call options. The investor buys a long-maturity put option and sells a short-maturity put option. As shown in Figure 8.9, the profit pattern is similar to that obtained from using calls.

A *reverse calendar spread* is the opposite to that in Figure 8.8 or Figure 8.9. The investor buys a short-maturity option and sells a long-maturity option. This creates a small profit if the stock price at the expiration of the short-maturity option

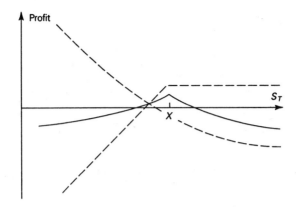

Figure 8.9   Calendar Spread Created Using Two Puts

is well above or well below the strike price of the short-maturity option. However, it leads to a significant loss if it is close to the strike price.

DIAGONAL SPREADS

Bull, bear, and calendar spreads can all be created from a long position in one call and a short position in another call. In the case of bull and bear spreads, the calls have different strike prices and the same expiration date. In the case of calendar spreads, the calls have the same strike price and different expiration dates. A *diagonal spread* is a spread which is such that both the expiration date and the strike price of the calls are different. There are several different types of diagonal spreads. Their profit patterns are generally variations on the profit patterns from the corresponding bull or bear spreads.

8.3 COMBINATIONS

A combination is an option trading strategy that involves taking a position in both calls and puts on the same stock. We will consider what are known as *straddles*, *strips*, *straps*, and *strangles*.

STRADDLE

One popular combination is a *straddle*. This involves buying a call and put with the same strike price and expiration date. The profit pattern is shown in Figure 8.10. The strike price is denoted by X. If the stock price is close to this strike price at expiration of the options, the straddle leads to a loss. However, if

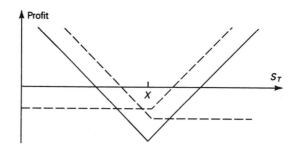

Figure 8.10 A Straddle

there is a sufficiently large move in either direction, a significant profit will result. The payoff from a straddle is calculated in Table 8.4.

A straddle is appropriate when an investor is expecting a large move in a stock price but does not know in which direction the move will be. Consider an investor who feels that the price of a certain stock, currently valued at $69 by the market, will move significantly in the next 3 months. The investor could create a straddle by buying both a put and a call with a strike price of $70 and an expiration date in 3 months. Suppose that the call costs $4 and the put costs $3. If the stock price stays at $69 it is easy to see that the strategy costs the investor $6. (An up-front investment of $7 is required, the call expires worthless, and the put expires worth $1.) If the stock price moves to $70, a loss of $7 is experienced. (This is the worst that can happen.) However, if the stock price jumps up to $90, a profit of $13 is made; if the stock moves down to $55, a profit of $8 is made; and so on.

A straddle would seem to be a natural strategy for the stock of a company that is subject to a takeover bid. If the bid is successful, the stock price can be expected to move up sharply. If it is unsuccessful, the stock price can be expected to move down sharply. In practice it is not quite that easy to make money! Option prices for a stock whose price is expected to exhibit a large jump tend to be significantly higher than for a similar stock where no jump is expected.

The straddle in Figure 8.10 is sometimes referred to as a *bottom straddle* or *straddle purchase*. A *top straddle* or *straddle write* is the reverse position. It is

TABLE 8.4　Payoff from a Straddle

Range of Stock Price	Payoff from Call	Payoff from Put	Total Payoff
$S_T \leq X$	0	$X - S_T$	$X - S_T$
$S_T > X$	$S_T - X$	0	$S_T - X$

created by selling a call and a put with the same exercise price and expiration date. It is a highly risky strategy. If the stock price on the expiration date is close to the strike price, it leads to a significant profit. However, the loss arising from a large move in either direction is unlimited.

STRIPS AND STRAPS

A *strip* consists of a long position in one call and two puts with the same strike price and expiration date. A *strap* consists of a long position in two calls and one put with the same strike price and expiration date. The profit patterns from strips and straps are shown in Figure 8.11. In a strip, the investor is betting that there will be a big stock price move and considers a decrease in the stock price to be more likely than an increase. In a strap, the investor is also betting that there will be a big stock price move. However, in this case, an increase in the stock price is considered to be more likely than a decrease.

STRANGLES

In a *strangle*, sometimes called a *bottom vertical combination*, an investor buys a put and a call with the same expiration date and different strike prices. The profit pattern that is obtained is shown in Figure 8.12. The call strike price, X_2, is higher than the put strike price, X_1. The payoff function for a strangle is calculated in Table 8.5.

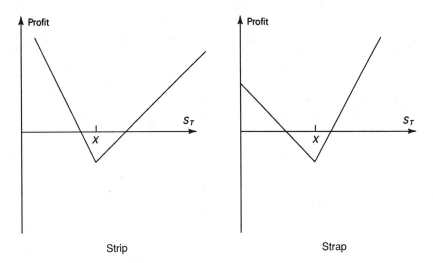

Figure 8.11 Profit Patterns from Strips and Straps

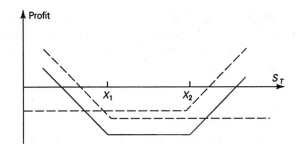

Figure 8.12   A Strangle

TABLE 8.5   Payoff from a Strangle

Range of Stock Price	Payoff from Call	Payoff from Put	Total Payoff
$S_T \leq X$	0	$X_1 - S_T$	$X_1 - S_T$
$X_1 < S_T < X_2$	0	0	0
$S_T \geq X_2$	$S_T - X_2$	0	$S_T - X_2$

A strangle is a similar strategy to a straddle. The investor is betting that there will be a large price move but is uncertain whether it will be an increase or a decrease. Comparing figures 8.12 and 8.10 we see that the stock price has to move farther in a strangle than in a straddle for the investor to make a profit. However, the downside risk if the stock price ends up at a central value is less with a strangle.

The profit pattern obtained with a strangle depends on how close the strike prices are together. The farther they are apart, the less the downside risk and the farther the stock price has to move for a profit to be realized.

The sale of a strangle is sometimes referred to as a *top vertical combination*. It can be appropriate for an investor who feels that large stock price moves are unlikely. However, like the sale of a straddle, it is a risky strategy since the investor's potential loss is unlimited.

8.4 OTHER PAYOFFS

This chapter has demonstrated just a few of the ways in which options can be used to produce an interesting relationship between profit and stock price. If European options expiring at time T were available with every single possible strike price, any payoff function at time T could in theory be obtained. The easiest way to see this is in terms of butterfly spreads. It will be recalled that a butterfly spread is created by buying options with strike prices X_1 and X_3 and selling two options with strike price X_2 where $X_1 < X_2 < X_3$ and $X_3 - X_2 = X_2 - X_1$. Figure 8.13 shows the payoff from a butterfly spread. This could be described as a "spike." As X_1 and X_3 become closer together, the spike becomes smaller. By judiciously combining together a large number of very small spikes, any payoff function can be approximated.

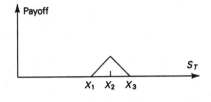

Figure 8.13   Payoff from a Butterfly Spread

8.5 SUMMARY

A number of common trading strategies involve a single option and the underlying stock. For example, writing a covered call involves buying the stock and selling a call option on the stock; a protective put involves buying a put option and buying the stock. The former is similar to selling a put option; the latter is similar to buying a call option.

Spreads involve either taking a position in two or more calls or taking a position in two or more puts. A bull spread can be created by buying a call (put) with a low strike price and selling a call (put) with a high strike price. A bear spread can be created by buying a call (put) with a high strike price and selling a call (put) with a low strike price. A butterfly spread involves buying calls (puts) with a low and high strike price and selling two calls (puts) with some intermediate strike price. A calendar spread involves selling a call (put) with a short time to expiration and buying a call (put) with a longer time to expiration. A diagonal spread involves a long position in one option and a short position in another option where both the strike price and expiration date are different.

Combinations involve taking a position in both calls and puts on the same stock. A straddle combination involves taking a long position in a call and a long position in a put with the same strike price and expiration date. A strip consists of a long position in one call and two puts with the same strike price and expiration date. A strap consists of a long position in two calls and one put with the same strike price and expiration date. A strangle consists of a long position in a call and a put with different strike prices and the same expiration date. There are many other ways in which options can be used to produce interesting payoffs. It is not surprising that option trading has steadily increased in popularity and continues to fascinate investors.

SUGGESTIONS FOR FURTHER READING

BOOKSTABER, R. M., *Option Pricing and Strategies in Investing*. Reading, Mass.: Addison-Wesley, 1981.

CHANCE, D. M., *An Introduction to Options and Futures*. Orlando, Fla.: Dryden Press, 1989.

DEGLER, W. H., and H. P. BECKER, "19 Option Strategies and When to Use Them," *Futures*, June 1984.

GASTINEAU, G., *The Stock Options Manual* (2nd ed.). New York: McGraw-Hill, 1979.

McMILLAN, L. G., *Options as a Strategic Investment* (2nd ed.). New York: New York Institute of Finance, 1986.

SLIVKA, R., "Call option spreading," *Journal of Portfolio Management*, 7 (Spring 1981), 71–76.

WELCH, W. W., *Strategies for Put and Call Option Trading*. Cambridge, Mass.: Winthrop, 1982.

YATES, J. W., and R. W. KOPPRASCH, "Writing Covered Call Options: Profits and Risks," *Journal of Portfolio Management*, 6 (Fall 1980), 74–80.

QUESTIONS AND PROBLEMS

8.1. What is meant by a protective put? What position in call options is equivalent to a protective put?

8.2. Explain two ways in which a bear spread can be created.

8.3. When is it appropriate for an investor to purchase a butterfly spread?

8.4. Call options on a stock are available with strike prices of $15, 17\frac{1}{2}$, and $20 and expiration dates in 3 months. Their prices are $4, $2, and $$\frac{1}{2}$, respectively. Explain how the options can be used to create a butterfly spread. Construct a table showing how profit varies with stock price for the butterfly spread.

8.5. What trading strategy creates a reverse calendar spread?

8.6. What is the difference between a strangle and a straddle?

8.7. A call option with a strike price of $50 costs $2. A put option with a strike price of $45 costs $3. Explain how a strangle can be created from these two options. What is the pattern of profits from the strangle?

8.8. Analyze carefully the difference between a bull spread created from puts and a bull spread created from calls.

8.9. Explain how an aggressive bear spread can be created using put options.

8.10. Suppose that put options on a stock with strike price $30 and $35 cost $4 and $7, respectively. How can the options be used to create (a) a bull spread and (b) a bear spread? Construct a table that shows the profit and payoff for both spreads.

8.11. Three put options on a stock have the same expiration date, and strike prices of $55, $60, and $65. The market prices are $3, $5, and $8, respectively. Explain how a butterfly spread can be created. Construct a table showing the profit from the strategy. For what range of stock prices would the butterfly spread lead to a loss?

8.12. Use put-call parity to show that the cost of a butterfly spread created from European puts is identical to the cost of a butterfly spread created from European calls.

8.13. A diagonal spread is created by buying a call with strike price X_2 and exercise date T_2, and selling a call with strike price X_1 and exercise date T_1 ($T_2 > T_1$). Draw a diagram showing the profit when (a) $X_2 > X_1$ and (b) $X_2 < X_1$.

8.14. A call with a strike price of $50 costs $6. A put with the same strike price and expiration date costs $4. Construct a table that shows the profits from a straddle. For what range of stock prices would the straddle lead to a loss?

8.15. Construct a table showing the payoff from a bull spread when puts with strike prices X_1 and X_2 are used ($X_2 > X_1$).

8.16. An investor believes that there will be a big jump in a stock price but is uncertain as to the direction. Identify six different strategies the investor can follow and explain the differences between them.

8.17. How can a forward contract on a stock with a certain delivery price and delivery date be created from options?

8.18. A box spread is a combination of a bull call spread with strike prices X_1 and X_2 and a bear put spread with the same strike prices. The expiration dates of all options are the same. What are the characteristics of a box spread?

8.19. What is the result if the strike price of the put is higher than the strike price of the call in a strangle?

8.20. Draw a diagram showing the variation of an investor's profit and loss with the terminal stock price for a portfolio consisting of
(a) One share and a short position in one call option
(b) Two shares and a short position in one call option
(c) One share and a short position in two call options
(d) One share and a short position in four call options
In each case, assume that the call option has an exercise price equal to the current stock price.

9

A Model of the Behavior of Stock Prices

Any variable whose value changes over time in an uncertain way is said to follow a *stochastic process*. Stochastic processes can be classified as "discrete time" or "continuous time." A discrete-time stochastic process is one where the value of the variable can only change at certain fixed points in time, whereas a continuous-time stochastic process is one where changes can take place at any time. Stochastic processes can also be classified as "continuous variable" or "discrete variable." In a continuous-variable process, the underlying variable can take any value within a certain range, whereas in a discrete-variable process, only certain discrete values are possible.

In this chapter we derive a continuous-variable, continuous-time stochastic process for stock prices. An understanding of this process is the first step to understanding the pricing of options and other more complicated derivative securities. It should be pointed out that in practice we do not observe stock prices following continuous-variable, continuous-time processes. Stock prices are restricted to discrete values (usually multiples of $\$\frac{1}{8}$) and changes can be observed only when the exchange is open. Nevertheless, the continuous-variable, continuous-time process proves to be a useful model for most purposes.

In this chapter and the next we introduce the reader to what is known as *stochastic calculus*. This is an extension of regular calculus that deals with continuous-time stochastic processes. Many people feel that continuous-time stochastic processes are so complicated that they must be left entirely to "rocket scientists." This is not so. The biggest hurdle to understanding these processes is the notation. In this chapter we present a step-by-step approach aimed at getting the reader over this hurdle.

9.1 THE MARKOV PROPERTY

A *Markov process* is a particular type of stochastic process where only the present value of a variable is relevant for predicting the future. The past history of the variable and the way in which the present has emerged from the past are irrelevant.

Stock prices are usually assumed to follow a Markov process. Suppose that the price of IBM stock is $100 now. If the stock price follows a Markov process, our predictions for the future should be unaffected by the price 1 week ago, 1 month ago, or 1 year ago. The only relevant piece of information is the fact that the price is now $100.[1] Predictions for the future are uncertain and must be expressed in terms of probability distributions. The Markov property implies that the probability distribution of the price at any particular future time depends only on the current stock price of $100.

The Markov property of stock prices is consistent with the weak form of market efficiency. This states that the present price of a stock impounds all the information contained in a record of past prices. If the weak form of market efficiency were not true, technical analysts could make above-average returns by interpreting charts of the past history of stock prices. There is very little evidence that they are in fact able to do this.

It is competition in the marketplace which tends to ensure that weak-form market efficiency holds. The very fact that there are many, many investors watching the stock market closely and trying to make a profit from it leads to a situation where a stock price at any given time impounds the information in past prices. Suppose that it is discovered that a particular pattern in past stock prices always gives a 65 percent chance of price rises in the near future. Investors would attempt to buy a stock as soon as the pattern was observed, and demand for the stock would immediately rise. This would lead to an immediate rise in its price and the observed effect would be eliminated—as would any profitable trading opportunities.

---

[1] Statistical properties of the stock price history of IBM may be useful in determining the characteristics of the stochastic process followed by the stock price (e.g., its volatility). The point which is being made here is that the particular path followed by the stock in the past is irrelevant.

9.2 WIENER PROCESSES

Models of stock price behavior are usually expressed in terms of what are known as *Wiener processes*. A Wiener process is a particular type of Markov stochastic process. It has been used in physics to describe the motion of a particle that is subject to a large number of small molecular shocks and is sometimes referred to as Brownian motion.

The behavior of a variable, z, which follows a Wiener process, can be understood by considering the changes in its value in small intervals of time. Consider a small interval of time of length Δt and define Δz as the change in z during Δt. There are two basic properties Δz must have for z to be following a Wiener process:

PROPERTY 1

Δz is related to Δt by the equation

$$\Delta z = \epsilon \sqrt{\Delta t} \tag{9.1}$$

where ϵ is a random drawing from a standardized normal distribution (i.e., a normal distribution with a mean of zero and a standard deviation of 1.0).

PROPERTY 2

The values of Δz for any two different short intervals of time Δt are independent.

It follows from the property 1 that Δz itself has a normal distribution with

$$\text{mean of } \Delta z = 0$$

$$\text{standard deviation of } \Delta z = \sqrt{\Delta t}$$

$$\text{variance of } \Delta z = \Delta t$$

Property 2 implies that z follows a Markov process.

Consider next the increase in the value of z during a relatively long period of time, T. We will denote this by $z(T) - z(0)$. It can be regarded as the sum of the increases in z in N small time intervals of length Δt, where

$$N = \frac{T}{\Delta t}$$

Thus

$$z(T) - z(0) = \sum_{i=1}^{N} \epsilon_i \sqrt{\Delta t} \tag{9.2}$$

where the ϵ_i ($i = 1, 2, \ldots, N$) are random drawings from a standardized normal distribution. From property 2 the ϵ_i's are independent of each other. It follows from Equation (9.2) that $z(T) - z(0)$ is normally distributed with[2]

$$\text{mean of } [z(T) - z(0)] = 0$$

$$\text{variance of } [z(T) - z(0)] = N \Delta t = T$$

$$\text{standard deviation of } [z(T) - z(0)] = \sqrt{T}$$

Thus in any time interval of length T, the increase in the value of a variable that follows a Wiener process is normally distributed with a mean of zero and a standard deviation of $\sqrt{T}$. It should now be clear why Δz is defined as the product of ϵ and $\sqrt{\Delta t}$ rather than as the product of ϵ and Δt. Variances are additive for independent normal distributions; standard deviations are not. It makes sense to define the stochastic process so that the variance rather than the standard deviation of changes is proportional to the length of the time interval considered.

Example 9.1

Suppose that the value, z, of a variable which follows a Wiener process is initially 25 and that time is measured in years. At the end of 1 year the value of the variable is normally distributed with a mean of 25 and a standard deviation of 1.0. At the end of 2 years it is normally distributed with a mean of 25 and a standard deviation of $\sqrt{2}$, or 1.414. Note that our uncertainty about the value of the variable at a certain time in the future, as measured by its standard deviation, increases as the square root of how far we are looking ahead.

In ordinary calculus, it is usual to proceed from small changes to the limit as the small changes become closer to zero. Thus $\Delta y / \Delta x$ becomes dy/dx in the limit, and so on. We can proceed similarly when dealing with continuous-time stochastic processes. A Wiener process is the limit as $\Delta t \longrightarrow 0$ of the process described above for z. Figure 9.1 illustrates what happens to the path followed by z as the limit $\Delta t \longrightarrow 0$ is taken. Analogously to ordinary calculus, we write the limiting case of Equation (9.1) as

$$dz = \epsilon \sqrt{dt}$$

GENERALIZED WIENER PROCESS

The basic Wiener process that has been developed so far has a drift rate of zero and a variance rate of 1.0. The drift rate of zero means that the expected

---

[2]This result is based on the following well-known property of normal distributions. If a variable Y is equal to the sum of N independent normally distributed variables X_i ($1 \leq i \leq N$), Y is itself normally distributed. The mean of Y is equal to the sum of the means of the X_i's. The variance of Y is equal to the sum of the variances of the X_i's.

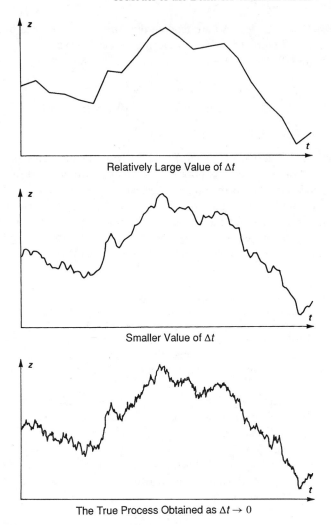

Relatively Large Value of Δ*t*

Smaller Value of Δ*t*

The True Process Obtained as Δ*t* → 0

Figure 9.1   Illustration of How a Wiener Process is Obtained when Δ*t* ⟶ 0 in Equation (9.1)

value of z at any future time is equal to its current value. The variance rate of 1.0 means that the variance of the change in z in a time interval of length T is $1.0 \times T$. A *generalized Wiener process* for a variable x can be defined in terms of dz as follows:

$$dx = a\,dt + b\,dz \qquad (9.3)$$

where a and b are constants.

To understand Equation (9.3) it is useful to consider the two components on the right-hand side separately. The $a\,dt$ term implies that x has an expected drift rate of a per unit time. Without the $b\,dz$ term, the equation is

$$dx = a\,dt$$

which implies that

$$\frac{dx}{dt} = a$$

or

$$x = x_0 + at$$

where x_0 is the value of x at time zero. In a time interval of length T, x increases by an amount aT. The $b\,dz$ term on the right-hand side of Equation (9.3) can be regarded as adding noise or variability to the path followed by x. The amount of this noise or variability is b times a Wiener process. In a small time interval Δt, the change in the value of x, Δx, is from equations (9.1) and (9.3) given by:

$$\Delta x = a\,\Delta t + b\epsilon\,\sqrt{\Delta t}$$

where, as before, ϵ is a random drawing from a standardized normal distribution. Thus Δx has a normal distribution with

$$\text{mean of } \Delta x = a\,\Delta t$$

$$\text{standard deviation of } \Delta x = b\,\sqrt{\Delta t}$$

$$\text{variance of } \Delta x = b^2\,\Delta t$$

Similar arguments to those just given show that the change in the value of x in any time interval T is normally distributed with

$$\text{mean of change in } x = aT$$

$$\text{standard deviation of change in } x = b\,\sqrt{T}$$

$$\text{variance of change in } x = b^2 T$$

Thus the generalized Wiener process given in Equation (9.3) has an expected drift rate (i.e., average drift per unit time) of a and a variance rate (i.e., variance per unit of time) of b^2. It is illustrated in Figure 9.2.

Example 9.2

Consider the situation where the cash position of a company, measured in thousands of dollars, follows a generalized Wiener process with a drift of 20 per year and a variance rate of 900 per year. Initially, the cash position is 50. At the end of 1 year the cash position will have a normal distribution with a mean of 70 and a standard deviation of $\sqrt{900}$ or 30. At the end of 6 months it will have a normal distribution with a mean of 60 and a standard

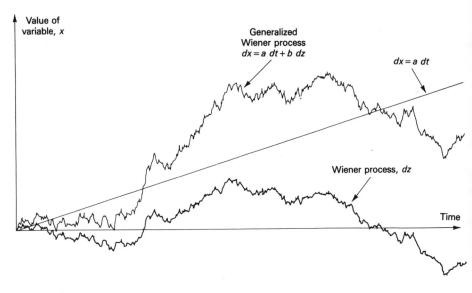

Figure 9.2   Generalized Wiener Process; $a=0.3$, $b=1.5$

deviation of $30\sqrt{0.5} = 21.21$. Note that our uncertainty about the cash position at some time in the future, as measured by its standard deviation, increases as the square root of how far ahead we are looking. Also, note that the cash position can become negative (which we can interpret as a situation where the company is borrowing funds).

ITO PROCESS

A further type of stochastic process can be defined. This is known as an *Ito process*. It is a generalized Wiener process where the parameters a and b are functions of the value of the underlying variable, x, and time, t. Algebraically, an Ito process can be written

$$dx = a(x, t)dt + b(x, t)dz \qquad (9.4)$$

Both the expected drift rate and variance rate of an Ito process are liable to change over time.

9.3 THE PROCESS FOR STOCK PRICES

In this section we discuss the stochastic process followed by the price of a non-dividend-paying stock. The effects of dividends on the process will be discussed in Chapter 10.

It is tempting to suggest that a stock price follows a generalized Wiener process; that is, that it has a constant expected drift rate and a constant variance rate. However, this model fails to capture a key aspect of stock prices. This is that the expected percentage return required by investors from a stock is independent of the stock's price. If investors require a 14 percent per annum expected return when the stock price is $10, then, *ceteris paribus*, they will also require a 14 percent per annum expected return when it is $50.

Clearly, the constant expected drift-rate assumption is inappropriate and needs to be replaced by the assumption that the expected drift, expressed as a proportion of the stock price, is constant. The latter implies that if S is the stock price, the expected drift rate in S is μS for some constant parameter, μ. Thus, in a short interval of time, Δt, the expected increase in S is $\mu S \, \Delta t$. The parameter, μ, is the expected rate of return on the stock, expressed in decimal form.

If the variance rate of the stock price is always zero, this model implies that

$$dS = \mu S \, dt$$

or

$$\frac{dS}{S} = \mu \, dt$$

so that

$$S = S_0 e^{\mu t} \tag{9.5}$$

where S_0 is the stock price at time zero. Equation (9.5) shows that, when the variance rate is zero, the stock price grows at a continuously compounded rate of μ per unit time.

In practice, of course, a stock price does exhibit volatility. A reasonable assumption is that the variance of the percentage return in a short period of time, Δt, is the same regardless of the stock price. In other words, an investor is just as uncertain as to his or her percentage return when the stock price is $50 as when it is $10. Define σ^2 as the variance rate of the proportional change in the stock price. This means that $\sigma^2 \, \Delta t$ is the variance of the proportional change in the stock price in time Δt and that $\sigma^2 S^2 \, \Delta t$ is the variance of the actual change in the stock price, S, during Δt. The instantaneous variance rate of S is therefore $\sigma^2 S^2$.

These arguments suggest that S can be represented by an Ito process which has instantaneous expected drift rate μS and instantaneous variance rate $\sigma^2 S^2$. This can be written as

$$dS = \mu S \, dt + \sigma S \, dz$$

or:

$$\frac{dS}{S} = \mu \, dt + \sigma \, dz \tag{9.6}$$

Equation (9.6) is the most widely used model of stock price behavior. The variable σ is usually referred to as the *stock price volatility*. The variable μ is its expected rate of return.

Example 9.3

Consider a stock that pays no dividends, has a volatility of 30% per annum, and provides an expected return of 15% per annum with continuous compounding. In this case $\mu = 0.15$ and $\sigma = 0.30$. The process for the stock price is

$$\frac{dS}{S} = 0.15\,dt + 0.30\,dz$$

If S is the stock price at a particular time and ΔS is the increase in the stock price in the next small interval of time,

$$\frac{\Delta S}{S} = 0.15\,\Delta t + 0.30\epsilon\,\sqrt{\Delta t}$$

where ϵ is a random drawing from a standardized normal distribution. Consider a time interval of 1 week or 0.0192 year and suppose that the initial stock price is $100. Then $\Delta t = 0.0192$, $S = 100$, and

$$\Delta S = 100(0.00288 + 0.0416\epsilon)$$

showing that the price increase is a random drawing from a normal distribution with mean $0.288 and standard deviation $4.16.

9.4 A REVIEW OF THE MODEL

The model of stock price behavior that has been developed in this chapter [see Equation (9.6)] is sometimes known as *geometric Brownian motion*. The discrete-time version of the model is

$$\frac{\Delta S}{S} = \mu\,\Delta t + \sigma\epsilon\,\sqrt{\Delta t} \tag{9.7}$$

The variable ΔS is the change in the stock price, S, in a small interval of time, Δt; and ϵ is a random drawing from a standardized normal distribution (i.e., a normal distribution with a mean of zero and standard deviation of 1.0). The parameter μ is the expected rate of return per unit time from the stock and the parameter σ is the volatility of the stock price. Both of these parameters are assumed constant.

The left-hand side of Equation (9.7) is the proportional return provided by the stock in a short period of time Δt. The term $\mu\,\Delta t$ is the expected value of this return, while the term $\sigma\epsilon\,\sqrt{\Delta t}$ is the stochastic component of the return. The variance of the stochastic component (and therefore of the whole return) is $\sigma^2\,\Delta t$.

Equation (9.7) shows that $\Delta S/S$ is normally distributed with mean $\mu \, \Delta t$ and standard deviation $\sigma \sqrt{\Delta t}$. In other words,

$$\frac{\Delta S}{S} \sim \phi(\mu \, \Delta t, \, \sigma \sqrt{\Delta t}) \tag{9.8}$$

where $\phi(m, s)$ denotes a normal distribution with mean m and standard deviation s.

MONTE CARLO SIMULATION

Suppose that the expected return from the stock is 14 percent per annum and that the standard deviation of the return (i.e., the volatility) is 20 percent per annum. If time is measured in years, it follows that

$$\mu = 0.14$$

$$\sigma = 0.20$$

Suppose that $\Delta t = 0.01$ so that we are considering changes in the stock price in time intervals of length 0.01 year (or 3.65 days). It follows that $\Delta S/S$ is normal with mean 0.0014 (= 0.14×0.01) and standard deviation 0.02 (= $0.2 \times \sqrt{0.01}$), that is,

$$\frac{\Delta S}{S} \sim \phi(0.0014, \, 0.02) \tag{9.9}$$

A path for the stock price can be simulated by sampling repeatedly from $\phi(0.0014, 0.02)$. One procedure for doing this is to sample values, v_1, from a standardized normal distribution [i.e., $\phi(0, 1)$] and then convert these to samples, v_2, from $\phi(0.0014, 0.02)$ using

$$v_2 = 0.0014 + 0.02v_1 \tag{9.10}$$

Table 9.1 shows one particular simulation of stock price movements. The initial stock price is assumed to be \$20. For the first period the random number, v_1, sampled from $\phi(0, 1)$ is 0.52. Using Equation (9.10) this gives a random sample of 0.0118 from $\phi(0.0014, 0.02)$. Using Equation (9.9), $\Delta S = 20 \times 0.0118$, or 0.236. At the beginning of the next period the stock price is therefore \$20.236, and so on. Note that the samples, v_2, must be independent of each other. Otherwise, the Markov property, discussed in Section 9.1, does not hold.

Table 9.1 assumes that stock prices are measured to the nearest 0.001, which of course is not the case. To get the stock price that would be quoted, the figures in the first column of the table should be rounded to the nearest \$$\frac{1}{8}$. It is important to realize that the table shows only one possible pattern of stock price movements. Different random samples would lead to different price movements. Any small time interval Δt can be used in the simulation. However, only in the limit as $\Delta t \longrightarrow 0$ is a true description of geometric Brownian motion obtained. The final stock price

TABLE 9.1 Simulation of Stock Price when $\mu = 0.14$
and $\sigma = 0.20$ During Periods of Length 0.01 Year

Stock Price at Start of Period	Random Sample, v_1, from $\phi(0, 1)$	Corresponding Random Sample, v_2, from $\phi(0.0014, 0.02)$	Change in Stock Price During Period
20.000	0.52	0.0118	0.236
20.236	1.44	0.0302	0.611
20.847	−0.86	−0.0158	−0.329
20.518	1.46	0.0306	0.628
21.146	−0.69	−0.0124	−0.262
20.883	−0.74	−0.0134	−0.280
20.603	0.21	0.0056	0.115
20.719	−1.10	−0.0206	−0.427
20.292	0.73	0.0160	0.325
20.617	1.16	0.0246	0.507
21.124	2.56	0.0526	1.111

of 21.124 in Table 9.1 can be regarded as a random sample from the distribution of stock prices at the end of 10 time intervals or one-tenth of a year. By repeatedly simulating movements in the stock price, as in Table 9.1, a complete probability distribution of the stock price at the end of one-tenth of a year is obtained.

9.5 THE PARAMETERS

The process for stock prices that has been developed in this chapter involves two parameters, μ and σ. The values of those parameters depend on the units in which time is measured. Here and elsewhere in this book, we assume that time is measured in years.

The parameter μ is the expected proportional return earned by an investor in a short period of time. It is annualized and expressed as a proportion. Most investors require higher expected returns to induce them to take higher risks. It follows that the value of μ should depend on the risk of the return from the stock.[3] It should also depend on the level of interest rates in the economy. The higher the level of interest rates, the higher the expected return required on any given stock. On average, μ is about 8 percent greater than the return on a risk-free investment such as a Treasury bill.[4] Thus when the return on Treasury bills is 8 percent per

---

[3]More precisely, μ depends on that part of the risk which cannot be diversified away by the investor.

[4]See R. G. Ibbotson and R. A. Sinquefield, *Stocks, Bonds, Bills and Inflation: The Past and the Future* (Charlotteville, Va.: Financial Analyst Research Foundation, 1982), Exhibit 29, p. 71.

annum, or 0.08, a typical value of μ is 0.16; that is, a typical expected return on a stock is 16 percent per annum.

Fortunately, we do not have to concern ourselves with the determinants of μ in any detail because the value of a derivative security dependent on a stock is in general independent of μ. The parameter σ, the stock price volatility, is, by contrast, critically important to the determination of the value of most contingent claims. Procedures for estimating σ empirically are discussed in Chapter 10. Typical values of σ for a stock are in the range 0.20 to 0.40 (i.e., 20 percent to 40 percent).

The standard deviation of the proportional change in the stock price in a small interval of time Δt is $\sigma \sqrt{\Delta t}$. As a rough approximation, the standard deviation of the proportional change in the stock price in a relatively long period of time, T, is $\sigma \sqrt{T}$. This means that, as an approximation, volatility can be interpreted as the standard deviation of the change in the stock price in one year.

Note that the standard deviation of the proportional change in the stock price in a relatively long time interval, T, is not exactly $\sigma \sqrt{T}$. This is because proportional changes are not additive. (For example, a 10 percent increase in a stock price followed by a 20 percent increase leads to a total increase of 32 percent, not 30 percent.) In Chapter 10, the probability distribution of the change in the stock price in a relatively long time period T will be shown to be lognormal. Also, the volatility of a stock price will be shown to be exactly equal to the standard deviation of the continuously compounded return provided by the stock in one year.

9.6 A BINOMIAL MODEL

At various points in this book we will use a binomial model as a discrete-time representation of the continuous-time model for stock prices which has been described in this chapter. Suppose that the stock price starts at S. Under the binomial model, the stock price follows the process illustrated in Figure 9.3 in the next small time interval of length Δt. It moves up to Su with probability p and down to Sd with probability $1 - p$. Figure 9.4 illustrates how the binomial model leads to

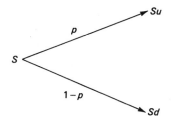

Figure 9.3   Binomial Model

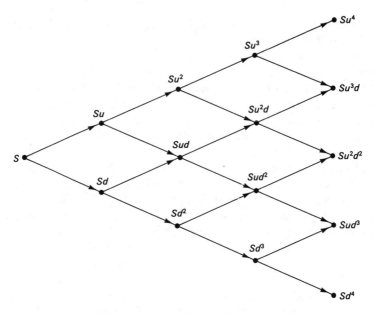

Figure 9.4   Stock Price Movements over Four Time Periods Using Binomial Model

three alternative stock prices at the end of two time intervals, four alternative stock prices at the end of three time intervals, and so on.

The variables u, d, and p must be chosen so that, for a small Δt, the expected return from the stock price in time Δt is $\mu \, \Delta t$ and the variance of the return in time Δt is $\sigma^2 \, \Delta t$. One way of doing this is by setting[5]

$$u = e^{\sigma \sqrt{\Delta t}}, \qquad d = \frac{1}{u}, \qquad p = \frac{e^{\mu \Delta t} - d}{u - d}$$

[5]To demonstrate that these values of u, d, and p have the right properties, note that the expected stock price at time Δt is

$$p Su + (1 - p)Sd = Se^{\mu \Delta t}$$

The variance of the stock price at time Δt is

$$p S^2 u^2 + (1 - p)S^2 d^2 - (Se^{\mu \Delta t})^2$$

This equals

$$S^2 \left[e^{\mu \Delta t} (e^{\sigma \sqrt{\Delta t}} + e^{-\sigma \sqrt{\Delta t}}) - 1 - e^{2\mu \Delta t} \right]$$

Expanding e^x in series form $e^x = 1 + x + x^2/2 + x^3/6 + \ldots$, the variance of the stock price is $S^2 \sigma^2 \, \Delta t$ when terms of order Δt^2 and higher are ignored.

It can be shown that in the limit as $\Delta t \longrightarrow 0$, this binomial model of stock price movements becomes the geometric Brownian motion model which has been developed in this chapter.

Example 9.4

Consider a stock price that provides an expected return of 12% per annum and has a volatility of 30% per annum. Suppose that the binomial model is used to represent movements in time periods of 0.04 year (approximately 2 weeks). In this case $\mu = 0.12$, $\sigma = 0.30$, and $\Delta t = 0.04$ and, from the previous equations:

$$u = e^{0.30 \times \sqrt{0.04}} = 1.0618$$

$$d = \frac{1}{u} = 0.9418$$

$$p = \frac{e^{0.12 \times 0.04} - 0.9418}{1.0618 - 0.9418} = 0.525$$

If the stock price starts at \$100, possible movements over four time intervals of length Δt are as illustrated in Figure 9.5. The probability of an up movement is always 0.525 and the probability of a down movement is always 0.475. For the stock price of \$112.7 to occur at the end of the four time intervals there must be three up movements and one down movement. There are four ways that this can happen. These are $DUUU, UDUU, UUDU,$ and $UUUD$, where U denotes an up movement and D denotes a down movement. Hence

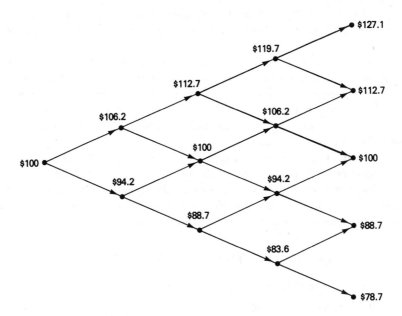

Figure 9.5   Stock Price Movements in Example 9.4

the probability of the stock price being \$112.7 at the end of four time intervals is

$$4 \times 0.525^3 \times 0.475 = 0.275$$

The probabilities of stock prices of \$127.1, \$100.0, \$88.7, and \$78.7 can similarly be shown to be 0.076, 0.373, 0.225, and 0.051, respectively.

9.7 SUMMARY

Stochastic processes describe the probabilistic evolution of the value of a variable through time. A Markov process is one where only the present value of the variable is relevant for predicting the future. The past history of the variable and the way in which the present has emerged from the past is irrelevant.

A Wiener process, dz, is a process describing the evolution of a normally distributed variable. The drift of the process is zero and the variance rate is 1 per unit time. This means that, if the value of the variable is x at time zero, at time T it is normally distributed with mean x and standard deviation $\sqrt{T}$.

A generalized Wiener process describes the evolution of a normally distributed variable with a drift of a per unit time and a variance rate of b^2 per unit time where a and b are constants. This means that if the value of the variable is x at time zero, at time T it is normally distributed with a mean of $x + aT$ and a standard deviation of $b\sqrt{T}$.

An Ito process is a process where the drift and variance rate of x can be a function of both x itself and time. The change in x in a very short period of time is normally distributed but its change over longer periods of time is liable to be non-normal.

In this chapter we have developed a plausible Markov stochastic process for the behavior of a stock price over time. The process is widely used in the valuation of derivative securities. It is known as geometric Brownian motion. Under this process, the proportional rate of return to the holder of the stock in any small interval of time is normally distributed and the returns in any two different small intervals of time are independent.

One way of gaining an intuitive understanding of a stochastic process for a variable is to simulate the behavior of the variable. This involves dividing a time interval into many small time steps and randomly sampling possible paths for the variable. The future probability distribution for the variable can then be calculated. Monte Carlo simulation will be discussed further in Chapter 14.

SUGGESTIONS FOR FURTHER READING

On the Markov Property of Stock Prices

BREALEY, R. A., *An Introduction to Risk and Return from Common Stock* (2nd ed.). Cambridge, Mass.: MIT Press, 1983.

COOTNER, P. H., ed., *The Random Character of Stock Market Prices*. Cambridge, Mass.: MIT Press, 1964.

On Stochastic Processes

COX, D. R., and H. D. MILLER, *The Theory of Stochastic Processes*. London: Chapman & Hall, 1965.

FELLER, W., *Probability Theory and its Applications*, vols. 1 and 2. New York: John Wiley, 1950.

QUESTIONS AND PROBLEMS

9.1. What would it mean to assert that the temperature at a certain place follows a Markov process? Do you think that temperatures do, in fact, follow a Markov process?

9.2. Can a trading rule based on the past history of a stock's price ever produce returns which are consistently above average? Discuss.

*9.3. A company's cash position, measured in millions of dollars, follows a generalized Wiener process with a drift rate of 0.1 per month and a variance rate of 0.16 per month. The initial cash position is 2.0.

(a) What are the probability distributions of the cash position after 1 month, 6 months, and 1 year?

(b) What are the probabilities of a negative cash position at the end of 6 months and 1 year?

(c) At what time in the future is the probability of a negative cash position greatest?

*9.4. A company's cash position, measured in millions of dollars, follows a generalized Wiener process with a drift rate of 1.5 per quarter and a variance rate of 4.0 per quarter. How high does the company's initial cash position have to be for the company to have a less than 5% chance of a negative cash position by the end of 1 year?

*9.5. Variables X_1 and X_2 follow generalized Wiener processes with drift rates μ_1 and μ_2 and variances σ_1^2 and σ_2^2. What process does $X_1 + X_2$ follow if:

(a) The changes in X_1 and X_2 in any short interval of time are uncorrelated?

(b) There is a correlation ρ between the changes in X_1 and X_2 in any short interval of time?

9.6. Consider a variable, S, which follows the process

$$dS = \mu \, dt + \sigma \, dz$$

For the first 3 years, $\mu = 2$ and $\sigma = 3$; for the next 3 years, $\mu = 3$ and $\sigma = 4$. If the initial value of the variable is 5, what is the probability distribution of the value of the variable at the end of year 6?

9.7. Suppose that a stock price has an expected return of 16% per annum and a volatility of 30% per annum. When the stock price at the end of a certain day is $50, calculate the following:

(a) The expected stock price at the end of the next day.

(b) The standard deviation of the stock price at the end of the next day.

(c) The 95% confidence limits for the stock price at the end of the next day.

9.8. Stock A and stock B both follow geometric Brownian motion. Changes in any short interval of time are uncorrelated with each other. Does the value of a portfolio consisting of one of stock A and one of stock B follow geometric Brownian motion? Explain your answer.

9.9. Equation (9.7) can be written as

$$\Delta S = \mu S \, \Delta t + \sigma S \epsilon \sqrt{\Delta t}$$

where μ and σ are constant. Explain carefully the difference between this model and each of the following:

$$\Delta S = \mu \, \Delta t + \sigma \epsilon \sqrt{\Delta t}$$

$$\Delta S = \mu S \, \Delta t + \sigma \epsilon \sqrt{\Delta t}$$

$$\Delta S = \mu \, \Delta t + \sigma S \epsilon \sqrt{\Delta t}$$

Why is the model in Equation (9.7) a more appropriate model of stock price behavior than any of these three alternatives?

9.10. It has been suggested that the short-term interest rate, r, follows the stochastic process:

$$dr = (a - r)b \, dt + rc \, dz$$

where a, b, and c are positive constants and dz is a Wiener process. Describe the nature of this process.

9.11. Consider a stock price that provides an expected return of 15% per annum and has a volatility of 40% per annum. Suppose that a time interval of 0.01 year is used for the binomial model. Calculate u, d, and p. Show that they give correct values for the expected return and variance of the return during the time interval. Suppose that the stock price starts at $50. What are the possible stock prices at the end of 0.03 year? What is the probability of each one occurring?

10

The Black–Scholes Analysis

In the early 1970s, Black and Scholes made a major breakthrough by deriving a differential equation that must be satisfied by the price of any derivative security dependent on a non-dividend-paying stock.[1] They used the equation to obtain values for European call and put options on the stock. In this chapter we explain the Black–Scholes analysis. We also discuss the properties of the stochastic process for stock prices developed in Chapter 9 and explain a powerful tool known as risk-neutral valuation.

Before we start, it is appropriate to mention one point concerning the notation that will be used. When valuing forward contracts in Chapter 3, no assumptions were made about interest rates and the variable, r, was used to denote the risk-free rate of interest for an investment maturing at time T. In this chapter and the next few chapters, we continue to denote the risk-free interest rate by r. However, except where otherwise stated, we assume that interest rates are constant and the same for all maturities. In Chapter 17 we will discuss how this constant interest rate assumption can be relaxed.

---

[1] See F. Black and M. Scholes, "The Pricing of Options and Corporate Liabilities," *Journal of Political Economy*, 81 (May–June 1973), 637–54.

10.1 ITO'S LEMMA

The price of a stock option is a function of the underlying stock's price and time. More generally, we can say that the price of any derivative security is a function of the stochastic variables underlying the derivative security and time. A serious student of derivative securities must therefore acquire some understanding of the behavior of functions of stochastic variables. An important result in this area was discovered by a mathematician, Ito, in 1951.[2] It is known as *Ito's lemma*.

Suppose that the value of a variable x follows an Ito process:

$$dx = a(x, t)\, dt + b(x, t)\, dz \tag{10.1}$$

where dz is a Wiener process and a and b are functions of x and t. The variable x has a drift rate of a and a variance rate of b^2. Ito's lemma shows that a function, G, of x and t follows the process

$$dG = \left(\frac{\partial G}{\partial x} a + \frac{\partial G}{\partial t} + \frac{1}{2} \frac{\partial^2 G}{\partial x^2} b^2 \right) dt + \frac{\partial G}{\partial x} b\, dz \tag{10.2}$$

where the dz is the same Wiener process as in Equation (10.1). Thus G also follows an Ito process. It has a drift rate of

$$\frac{\partial G}{\partial x} a + \frac{\partial G}{\partial t} + \frac{1}{2} \frac{\partial^2 G}{\partial x^2} b^2$$

and a variance rate of

$$\left(\frac{\partial G}{\partial x} \right)^2 b^2$$

A completely rigorous proof of Ito's lemma is beyond the scope of this book. In Appendix 10A we show that the lemma can be viewed as an extension of well-known results in differential calculus.

In Chapter 9 we argued that

$$dS = \mu S\, dt + \sigma S\, dz \tag{10.3}$$

with μ and σ constant is a reasonable model of stock price movements. From Ito's lemma, it follows that the process followed by a function, G, of S and t is

$$dG = \left(\frac{\partial G}{\partial S} \mu S + \frac{\partial G}{\partial t} + \frac{1}{2} \frac{\partial^2 G}{\partial S^2} \sigma^2 S^2 \right) dt + \frac{\partial G}{\partial S} \sigma S\, dz \tag{10.4}$$

Note that both S and G are affected by the same underlying source of uncertainty, dz. This proves to be very important in the derivation of the Black–Scholes results.

---

[2] See K. Ito, "On Stochastic Differential Equations," *Memoirs, American Mathematical Society*, no. 4 (1951), 1–51.

APPLICATION TO FORWARD CONTRACTS

To illustrate Ito's lemma consider a forward contract on a non-dividend-paying stock. Assume that the risk-free rate of interest is constant and equal to r for all maturities. Define F as the forward price. From Equation (3.5):

$$F = Se^{r(T-t)}$$

so that

$$\frac{\partial F}{\partial S} = e^{r(T-t)}, \qquad \frac{\partial^2 F}{\partial S^2} = 0, \qquad \frac{\partial F}{\partial t} = -rSe^{r(T-t)}$$

Assume that S follows geometric Brownian motion with expected return μ and volatility σ. [This is the process in Equation (10.3).] The process for F is, from Equation (10.4), given by

$$dF = \left[e^{r(T-t)}\mu S - rSe^{r(T-t)} \right] dt + e^{r(T-t)}\sigma S\, dz$$

Substituting $F = Se^{r(T-t)}$, this becomes

$$dF = (\mu - r)F\, dt + \sigma F\, dz \qquad (10.5)$$

Like S, F follows geometric Brownian motion. It has an expected growth rate of $\mu - r$ rather than μ.

APPLICATION TO THE LOGARITHM OF THE STOCK PRICE

We now use Ito's lemma to derive the process followed by $\ln S$. Define:

$$G = \ln S$$

Since

$$\frac{\partial G}{\partial S} = \frac{1}{S}, \qquad \frac{\partial^2 G}{\partial S^2} = -\frac{1}{S^2}, \qquad \frac{\partial G}{\partial t} = 0$$

it follows from Equation (10.4) that the process followed by G is

$$dG = \left(\mu - \frac{\sigma^2}{2} \right) dt + \sigma\, dz$$

Since μ and σ are constant, this equation indicates that G follows a generalized Wiener process. It has constant drift rate $\mu - \sigma^2/2$ and constant variance rate σ^2. From the results in Chapter 9, this means that the change in G between the current time, t, and some future time, T, is normally distributed with mean

$$\left(\mu - \frac{\sigma^2}{2} \right)(T - t)$$

and variance

$$\sigma^2(T - t)$$

The value of G at time t is $\ln S$. Its value at time T is $\ln S_T$, where S_T is the stock price at time T. Its change during the time interval $T - t$ is therefore

$$\ln S_T - \ln S$$

Hence

$$\ln S_T - \ln S \sim \phi\left[(\mu - \frac{\sigma^2}{2})(T - t), \sigma\sqrt{T - t}\right]$$

10.2 THE LOGNORMAL PROPERTY OF STOCK PRICES

A variable has a lognormal distribution if the natural logarithm of the variable is normally distributed. It has just been shown that the model of stock price behavior developed in Chapter 9 implies that

$$\ln S_T - \ln S \sim \phi[(\mu - \frac{\sigma^2}{2})(T - t), \sigma\sqrt{T - t}] \tag{10.6}$$

where S_T is the stock price at a future time T; S is the stock price at the current time, t; and $\phi(m, s)$ denotes a normal distribution with mean m and standard deviation s. From the properties of the normal distribution, it follows from Equation (10.6) that

$$\ln S_T \sim \phi[\ln S + (\mu - \frac{\sigma^2}{2})(T - t), \sigma\sqrt{T - t}] \tag{10.7}$$

This shows that S_T has a lognormal distribution. The standard deviation of $\ln S_T$ is proportional to $\sqrt{T - t}$. This means that our uncertainty about the logarithm of the stock price, as measured by its standard deviation, is proportional to the square root of how far ahead we are looking.

Example 10.1

Consider a stock with an initial price of $40, an expected return of 16% per annum, and a volatility of 20% per annum. From Equation (10.7), the probability distribution of the stock price, S_T, in 6 months' time is given by

$$\ln S_T \sim \phi[\ln 40 + (0.16 - \frac{0.04}{2})0.5, 0.2\sqrt{0.5}]$$

$$\ln S_T \sim \phi(3.759, 0.141)$$

There is a 95% probability that a normally distributed variable has a value within two standard deviations of its mean. Hence, with 95% confidence,

$$3.477 < \ln S_T < 4.041$$

This can be written

$$e^{3.477} < S_T < e^{4.041}$$

or

$$32.36 < S_T < 56.88$$

Thus there is a 95% probability that the stock price in 6 months will lie between 32.36 and 56.88.

A variable that has a lognormal distribution can take any value between zero and infinity. Figure 10.1 illustrates the shape of a lognormal distribution. Unlike the normal distribution, it is skewed so that the mean, median, and mode are all different. From Equation (10.7) and the properties of the lognormal distribution, it can be shown that the expected value of S_T, $E(S_T)$, is given by[3]

$$E(S_T) = Se^{\mu(T-t)} \tag{10.8}$$

This fits in with the definition of μ as the expected rate of return. The variance of S_T, $\text{var}(S_T)$, can be shown to be given by

$$\text{var}(S_T) = S^2 e^{2\mu(T-t)} \left(e^{\sigma^2(T-t)} - 1 \right) \tag{10.9}$$

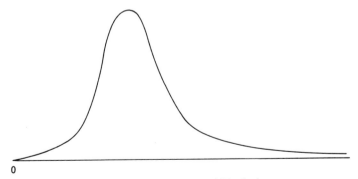

0

Figure 10.1   The Lognormal Distribution

[3]For a discussion of the properties of the lognormal distribution, see J. Aitchison and J. A. C. Brown, *The Lognormal Distribution* (Cambridge: Cambridge University Press, 1966).

Example 10.2

Consider a stock where the current price is $20, the expected return is 20% per annum, and the volatility is 40% per annum. The expected stock price in 1 year, $E(S_T)$, and the variance of the stock price in 1 year, var (S_T), are given by

$$E(S_T) = 20e^{0.2} = 24.43$$

$$\text{var}(S_T) = 400e^{0.4}(e^{0.16} - 1) = 103.54$$

The standard deviation of the stock price in 1 year is $\sqrt{103.54}$ or 10.18.

10.3 THE DISTRIBUTION OF THE RATE OF RETURN

The lognormal property of stock prices can be used to provide information on the probability distribution of the continuously compounded rate of return earned on a stock between times t and T. Define the annualized continuously compounded rate of return between t and T as η.[4] It follows that

$$S_T = Se^{\eta(T-t)}$$

and

$$\eta = \frac{1}{T - t} \ln \frac{S_T}{S} \qquad (10.10)$$

Since

$$\ln S_T - \ln S = \ln \frac{S_T}{S}$$

Equation (10.6) implies that

$$\ln \frac{S_T}{S} \sim \phi \left[(\mu - \frac{\sigma^2}{2})(T - t), \, \sigma\sqrt{T - t} \right] \qquad (10.11)$$

From the properties of normal distributions, it follows from Equation (10.10) that

$$\eta \sim \phi \left(\mu - \frac{\sigma^2}{2}, \, \frac{\sigma}{\sqrt{T - t}} \right) \qquad (10.12)$$

---

[4]It is important to distinguish between the continuously compounded rate of return, η, and the annualized return with no compounding (see Section 3.1). The latter is

$$\frac{1}{T - t} \left(\frac{S_T - S}{S} \right)$$

and is always greater than η.

Thus the continuously compounded rate of return is normally distributed with mean $\mu - \sigma^2/2$ and standard deviation $\sigma/\sqrt{T - t}$.

Example 10.3

Consider a stock with an expected return of 17% per annum and a volatility of 20% per annum. The probability distribution for the actual rate of return (continuously compounded) realized over 3 years is normal with mean

$$0.17 - \frac{0.04}{2} = 0.15$$

or 15% per annum and standard deviation

$$\frac{0.2}{\sqrt{3}} = 0.115$$

or 11.5% per annum. Since there is a 95% chance that a normally distributed variable will lie within two standard deviations of its mean, we can be 95% confident that the actual return realized over 3 years will be between −8% and +38% per annum.

WHAT IS THE EXPECTED RATE OF RETURN?

The result in Equation (10.12) shows that the expected continuously compounded rate of return in time $T - t$ is $\mu - \sigma^2/2$. This may seem strange since in Chapter 3, μ was defined as the expected value of the rate of return in any short interval. How can this be different from the expected value of the continuously compounded rate of return in a longer time interval? To understand the difference between the two, we consider a numerical example. Suppose that the following is a sequence of returns per annum on a stock, measured using annual compounding:

$$15\%, \quad 20\%, \quad 30\%, \quad -20\%, \quad 25\%$$

The arithmetic mean of the returns is calculated by taking the sum of the returns and dividing by 5. It is 14 percent. However, an investor would actually earn less than 14 percent per annum if he or she left money invested in the stock for 5 years. The dollar value of $100 at the end of the 5 years would be

$$100 \times 1.15 \times 1.20 \times 1.30 \times 0.80 \times 1.25 = 179.40$$

By contrast a 14 percent return with annual compounding would give

$$100 \times 1.14^5 = 192.54$$

This example illustrates the general result that the mean of the returns earned in different years is not necessarily the same as the mean return per annum over several years with annual compounding. It can be shown that unless the returns happen to be the same in each year, the former is always greater than the latter.[5] The actual average return earned by the investor, with annual compounding, is

$$(1.7940)^{1/5} - 1 = 0.124$$

or 12.4 percent per annum.

There is, of course, nothing magical about the time period of 1 year in this example. Suppose that the time period over which returns are measured is made progressively shorter and the number of observations is increased. We can calculate the following two estimates:

1. The expected rate of return in a very short period of time. (This is obtained by calculating the arithmetic average of the returns realized in many very short periods of time.)
2. The expected continuously compounded rate of return over a longer period of time (This is obtained by calculating the return with continuous compounding realized over the whole period covered by the data.)

Analogously to the example just given, we would expect estimate 1 to be greater than estimate 2. Our earlier results show that this is in fact the case. The expected rate of return in an infinitesimally short period of time is μ. The expected continuously compounded rate of return is $\mu - \sigma^2/2$.

These arguments show that the term "expected return" is ambiguous. It can refer to either μ or to $\mu - \sigma^2/2$. Unless otherwise stated, we will use it to refer to μ throughout this book.

10.4 ESTIMATING VOLATILITY FROM HISTORICAL DATA

To estimate the volatility of a stock price empirically, the stock price is usually observed at fixed intervals of time (e.g., every day, every week, or every month).
Define:

$n+1$: Number of observations

S_i: Stock price at end of ith interval ($i = 0, 1, \ldots, n$)

τ: Length of time interval in years

---

[5]Some readers may recognize this as equivalent to the statement that the arithmetic mean of a set of numbers is always greater than the geometric mean if the numbers are not all equal to each other.

and let

$$u_i = \ln\left(\frac{S_i}{S_{i-1}}\right)$$

for $i = 1, 2, \ldots n$.

Since $S_i = S_{i-1}e^{u_i}$, u_i is the continuously compounded return (not annualized) in the ith interval. The usual estimate, s, of the standard deviation of the u_i's is given by

$$s = \sqrt{\frac{1}{n-1} \sum_{i=1}^{n} (u_i - \bar{u})^2}$$

or

$$s = \sqrt{\frac{1}{n-1} \sum_{i=1}^{n} u_i^2 - \frac{1}{n(n-1)} \left(\sum_{i=1}^{n} u_i\right)^2}$$

where $\bar{u}$ is the mean of the u_i's.

From Equation (10.11), the standard deviation of the u_i's is $\sigma\sqrt{\tau}$. The variable, s, is therefore an estimate of $\sigma\sqrt{\tau}$. It follows that σ itself can be estimated as s^*, where

$$s^* = \frac{s}{\sqrt{\tau}}$$

The standard error of this estimate can be shown to be approximately $s^*/\sqrt{2n}$.

Choosing an appropriate value for n is not easy. *Ceteris paribus*, more data generally lead to more accuracy. However, σ does change over time and data that are too old may not be relevant for predicting the future. A compromise which seems to work reasonably well is to use closing prices from daily data over the most recent 90 to 180 days. There is an important issue concerned with whether time should be measured in calendar days or trading days when volatility parameters are being estimated and used. Later in this chapter we will show that the empirical research carried out to date indicates that trading days should be used. In other words, days when the exchange is closed should be ignored for the purposes of the volatility calculation.

Example 10.4

Table 10.1 shows a possible sequence of stock prices over a 20-day period. Since

$$\sum u_i = 0.09531 \quad \text{and} \quad \sum u_i^2 = 0.00333$$

an estimate of the standard deviation of the daily return is

$$\sqrt{\frac{0.00333}{19} - \frac{0.09531^2}{380}} = 0.0123$$

TABLE 10.1 Computation of Volatility

Day	Closing Stock Price (dollars)	Price Relative, S_i/S_{i-1}	Daily Return, $u_i = \ln(S_i/S_{i-1})$
0	20		
1	$20\frac{1}{8}$	1.00625	0.00623
2	$19\frac{7}{8}$	0.98758	−0.01250
3	20	1.00629	0.00627
4	$20\frac{1}{2}$	1.02500	0.02469
5	$20\frac{1}{4}$	0.98781	−0.01227
6	$20\frac{7}{8}$	1.03086	0.03040
7	$20\frac{7}{8}$	1.00000	0.00000
8	$20\frac{7}{8}$	1.00000	0.00000
9	$20\frac{3}{4}$	0.99401	−0.00601
10	$20\frac{3}{4}$	1.00000	0.00000
11	21	1.01205	0.01198
12	$21\frac{1}{8}$	1.00595	0.00593
13	$20\frac{7}{8}$	0.98817	−0.01190
14	$20\frac{7}{8}$	1.00000	0.00000
15	$21\frac{1}{4}$	1.01796	0.01780
16	$21\frac{3}{8}$	1.00588	0.00587
17	$21\frac{3}{8}$	1.00000	0.00000
18	$21\frac{1}{4}$	0.99415	−0.00587
19	$21\frac{3}{4}$	1.02353	0.02326
20	22	1.01149	0.01143

Assuming that time is measured in trading days, and that there are 250 trading days per year, $\tau = 1/250$ and the data give an estimate for the volatility per annum of $0.0123\sqrt{250} = 0.194$. The estimated volatility is 19.4% per annum. The standard error of this estimate is

$$\frac{0.194}{\sqrt{2 \times 20}} = 0.031$$

or 3.1 percent per annum.

This analysis assumes that the stock pays no dividends, but it can be adapted to accommodate dividend-paying stocks. The return, u_i, during a time interval that includes an ex-dividend day is given by

$$u_i = \ln \frac{S_i + D}{S_{i-1}}$$

where D is the amount of the dividend. The return in other time intervals is still

$$u_i = \ln \frac{S_i}{S_{i-1}}$$

However, as tax factors play a part in determining returns around an ex-dividend date, it is probably best to discard altogether data for intervals that include an ex-dividend date.

10.5 OPTION VALUATION USING A SIMPLE BINOMIAL MODEL

In this section we provide an example showing how a European call option can be valued in a particularly simple situation. The example gives some insights into the arguments underlying the Black–Scholes differential equation.

Suppose that a stock price is currently $20 and that it is known that at the end of one month the price will be either $22 or $18. Consider a European call option to buy the stock for $21 in 1 month. If the stock price turns out to be $22, the value of the option is $1; if the stock price turns out to be $18, the value of the option is zero. This situation is illustrated in Figure 10.2.

Consider a portfolio consisting of a long position in α shares of the stock and a short position in one call option. The value of this portfolio is $22\alpha - 1$ if the stock price moves up and 18α if it moves down. When α is chosen equal to 0.25, these two values are the same:

$$18\alpha = 22\alpha - 1 = 4.5$$

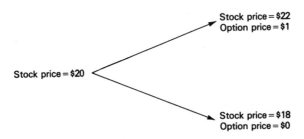

Figure 10.2   Stock Price Movements

For this value of α the portfolio is therefore riskless. Regardless of what happens it is worth \$4.5 in 1 month. The current value of the portfolio when $\alpha = 0.25$ is

$$20 \times 0.25 - f = 5 - f$$

where f is the current value of the call option. Riskless portfolios must, in the absence of arbitrage opportunities, earn the risk-free rate of interest. Suppose that risk-free rate is 1 percent per month (with monthly compounding). It follows that

$$1.01(5 - f) = 4.5$$

or

$$f = 5 - \frac{4.5}{1.01} = 0.5445$$

that is, the current value of the option is \$0.5445.

The reader may be surprised that the probabilities of the stock moving up to \$22 and down to \$18 were not used in arriving at this answer. This point will be returned to in Section 10.8.

10.6 CONCEPTS UNDERLYING THE BLACK–SCHOLES DIFFERENTIAL EQUATION

The Black–Scholes differential equation is an equation that must be satisfied by the price, f, of any derivative security dependent on a non-dividend-paying stock. The equation is derived in the next section. Here we consider the nature of the arguments used.

In essence, the argument is very similar to the argument used to value the option in the simple situation in the previous section. A riskless portfolio consisting of a position in the derivative security and a position in the stock is set up, and the return on the portfolio is then set equal to the risk-free rate of interest. In the Black–Scholes analysis, the portfolio that is set up remains riskless for only a very short period of time. Nevertheless, it can be argued that the return during this short period of time must be the risk-free rate of interest if arbitrage opportunities are to be avoided.

The reason why a riskless portfolio can be set up is because the stock price and the derivative security price are both affected by a single underlying source of uncertainty. This means that in any short period of time, the two are perfectly correlated. When an appropriate portfolio of the stock and the derivative security is set up, the gain (loss) from the stock position always offsets the loss (gain) from the derivative security position so that the overall value of the portfolio at the end of the short period of time is known with certainty.

The assumptions we will use to derive the Black–Scholes differential equation are as follows:

1. The stock price follows the process developed in Chapter 9 with μ and σ constant.
2. The short selling of securities with full use of proceeds is permitted.
3. There are no transactions costs or taxes. All securities are perfectly divisible.
4. There are no dividends during the life of the derivative security.
5. There are no riskless arbitrage opportunities.
6. Security trading is continuous.
7. The risk-free rate of interest, r, is constant and the same for all maturities.

As will be discussed in Chapter 17, some of these assumptions can be relaxed. For example, μ, r, and σ can be known functions of t.

10.7 DERIVATION OF THE BLACK–SCHOLES DIFFERENTIAL EQUATION

We now derive the Black–Scholes differential equation. We assume that the stock price S follows the process discussed in Chapter 9:

$$dS = \mu S\, dt + \sigma S\, dz \tag{10.13}$$

Suppose that f is the price of a derivative security contingent on S. The variable f must be some function of S and t. Hence from Equation (10.4),

$$df = \left(\frac{\partial f}{\partial S} \mu S + \frac{\partial f}{\partial t} + \frac{1}{2} \frac{\partial^2 f}{\partial S^2} \sigma^2 S^2 \right) dt + \frac{\partial f}{\partial S} \sigma S\, dz \tag{10.14}$$

The discrete versions of equations (10.13) and (10.14) are

$$\Delta S = \mu S\, \Delta t + \sigma S\, \Delta z \tag{10.15}$$

and

$$\Delta f = \left(\frac{\partial f}{\partial S} \mu S + \frac{\partial f}{\partial t} + \frac{1}{2} \frac{\partial^2 f}{\partial S^2} \sigma^2 S^2 \right) \Delta t + \frac{\partial f}{\partial S} \sigma S\, \Delta z \tag{10.16}$$

where ΔS and Δf are the changes in f and S in a small time interval Δt. It will be recalled from the discussion of Ito's lemma in Section 10.1 that the Wiener processes underlying f and S are the same. In other words, the Δz $(= \epsilon \sqrt{\Delta t})$ in equations (10.15) and (10.16) are the same. It follows that by choosing a portfolio of the stock and the derivative security, the Wiener process can be eliminated.

The appropriate portfolio is

$$-1: \qquad \text{derivative security}$$

$$+\frac{\partial f}{\partial S}: \qquad \text{shares}$$

The holder of this portfolio is short one derivative security and long an amount $\partial f/\partial S$ of shares. Define Π as the value of the portfolio. By definition

$$\Pi = -f + \frac{\partial f}{\partial S} S \tag{10.17}$$

The change $\Delta\Pi$ in the value of the portfolio in time Δt is given by

$$\Delta\Pi = -\Delta f + \frac{\partial f}{\partial S} \Delta S \tag{10.18}$$

Substituting equations (10.15) and (10.16) into Equation (10.18) yields

$$\Delta\Pi = \left(-\frac{\partial f}{\partial t} - \frac{1}{2}\frac{\partial^2 f}{\partial S^2}\sigma^2 S^2 \right) \Delta t \tag{10.19}$$

Since this equation does not involve Δz, the portfolio Π must be riskless during time Δt. The assumptions listed in the preceding section imply that the portfolio must instantaneously earn the same rate of return as other short-term risk-free securities. If it earned more than this return, arbitrageurs could make a riskless profit by shorting the risk-free securities and using the proceeds to buy the portfolio; if it earned less, they could make a riskless profit by shorting the portfolio and buying risk-free securities. It follows that

$$\Delta\Pi = r\Pi\,\Delta t$$

where r is the risk-free interest rate. Substituting from equations (10.17) and (10.19) this becomes

$$\left(\frac{\partial f}{\partial t} + \frac{1}{2}\frac{\partial^2 f}{\partial S^2}\sigma^2 S^2 \right) \Delta t = r\left(f - \frac{\partial f}{\partial S} S \right) \Delta t$$

so that

$$\frac{\partial f}{\partial t} + rS\frac{\partial f}{\partial S} + \frac{1}{2}\sigma^2 S^2\frac{\partial^2 f}{\partial S^2} = rf \tag{10.20}$$

Equation (10.20) is the Black–Scholes differential equation. It has many solutions, corresponding to all the different derivative securities that can be defined with S as the underlying variable. The particular derivative security that is obtained when the equation is solved depends on the *boundary conditions* that are used. These specify the values of the derivative security at the boundaries of possible values of S and t. In the case of a European call option, the key boundary condition is

$$f = \max(S - X, 0) \qquad \text{when } t = T$$

In the case of a European put option, it is

$$f = \max(X - S, 0) \qquad \text{when } t = T$$

One point that should be emphasized about the portfolio Π in the derivation of Equation (10.20) is that it is not permanently riskless. It is riskless only for an infinitesimally short period of time. As S and t change, $\partial f/\partial S$ also changes. To keep the portfolio riskless, it is therefore necessary to change continuously the relative proportions of the derivative security and the stock in the portfolio.

Example 10.5

A forward contract on a non-dividend-paying stock is a derivative security dependent on the stock. As such, it should satisfy Equation (10.20). From Equation (3.6), the value of the forward contract, f, is given by

$$f = S - Ke^{-r(T-t)}$$

where K is the delivery price. This means that

$$\frac{\partial f}{\partial t} = -rKe^{-r(T-t)}, \qquad \frac{\partial f}{\partial S} = 1, \qquad \frac{\partial^2 f}{\partial S^2} = 0$$

When these are substituted into the left-hand side of Equation (10.20), we obtain

$$-rKe^{-r(T-t)} + rS$$

This equals rf, showing that Equation (10.20) is indeed satisfied.

10.8 RISK–NEUTRAL VALUATION

Risk-neutral valuation is without doubt the single most important tool for the analysis of derivative securities. It arises from one key property of the Black–Scholes differential equation (10.20). This property is that the equation does not involve any variables that are affected by the risk preferences of investors. The variables that do appear in the equation are the current stock price, time, stock price volatility, and the risk-free rate of interest. All are independent of risk preferences.

The Black–Scholes differential equation would not be independent of risk preferences if it involved the expected return on the stock, μ. This is because the value of μ does depend on risk preferences. The higher the level of risk aversion by investors, the higher μ will be for any given stock. It is fortunate that μ happens to drop out in the derivation of the equation.

The fact that the Black–Scholes differential equation is independent of risk preferences enables an ingenious argument to be used. If risk preferences do not enter into the equation, they cannot affect its solution. Any set of risk preferences can therefore be used when evaluating f. In particular, the very simple assumption that all investors are risk neutral can be made.

In a world where investors are risk neutral, the expected return on all securities is the risk-free rate of interest, r. This is because risk-neutral investors do not require a premium to induce them to take risks. It is also true that the present value of any cash flow in a risk-neutral world can be obtained by discounting its expected value at the risk-free rate. The assumption that the world is risk neutral does therefore considerably simplify the analysis of derivative securities. Consider a derivative security such as a European option that pays off some function of the stock price at time T. First, the expected value of the derivative security at time T is calculated on the assumption that the expected return from the stock is r rather than μ. This expected value is then discounted to the present time using a discount rate of r.

It is important to realize that the risk-neutrality assumption is merely an artificial device for obtaining solutions to the Black–Scholes differential equation. The solutions that are obtained are valid in all worlds—not just those where investors are risk neutral. When we move from a risk-neutral world to a risk-averse world, two things happen. The expected growth rate in the stock price changes and the discount rate that must be used for any payoffs from the derivative security changes. It happens that these two effects always offset each other exactly.

THE BINOMIAL MODEL REVISITED

In this section we return to the example considered in Section 10.5. It will be recalled that this concerns a stock price which is currently $20 and which will either move up to $22 or down to $18 at the end of 1 month. The derivative security in the example is a call option with an exercise price of $21.

It is instructive that the probabilities of the stock price moving up to $22 and down to $18 were never used in deriving the option price of $0.5445 in Section 10.5. This can be interpreted as meaning that the option price is independent of the expected return on the stock. It is consistent with the observation, made in the Section 10.9, that the Black–Scholes differential equation is independent of the expected return on the stock.

We now show that the call option price can be derived using risk-neutral valuation. In a risk-neutral world, the expected return on the stock must be the risk-free rate of interest of 1 percent per month. The probability, p, of an upward movement must therefore satisfy

$$22p + 18(1 - p) = 20 \times 1.01$$

that is, p must be 0.55. The expected value of the call option in 1 month using this value of p is

$$0.55 \times 1 + 0.45 \times 0 = \$0.55$$

This is the expected terminal value of the call option in a risk-neutral world. The present value of this expected value when discounted at the risk-free rate of interest is

$$\frac{0.55}{1.01} = 0.5445$$

or \$0.5445. This is the same as the value obtained in Section 10.5. Thus riskless arbitrage arguments and risk-neutral valuation give the same answer. It can be shown that this is always the case for a binomial model. As discussed in Section 9.6, geometric Brownian motion can be regarded as a limiting case of the binomial model. Showing that risk-neutral valuation always holds for the binomial model is therefore one way of showing that it holds when stock prices follow geometric Brownian motion.

APPLICATION TO FORWARD CONTRACTS ON A STOCK

Forward contracts on a non-dividend-paying stock have already been valued in Section 3.2. They will be valued again in this section to provide a simple illustration of risk-neutral valuation. We make the assumption that interest rates are constant and equal to r. This is somewhat more restrictive than the assumption in Section 3.2. Consider a long forward contract that matures at time T with delivery price, K. As described in Chapter 1, the value of the contract at maturity is

$$S_T - K$$

where S_T is the stock price at time T. From the risk-neutral valuation argument, the value of the forward contract at time t ($< T$) is its expected value at time T in a risk-neutral world, discounted to time t at the risk-free rate of interest. Denoting the value of the forward contract at time t by f, this means that

$$f = e^{-r(T-t)} \hat{E}(S_T - K) \tag{10.21}$$

where $\hat{E}$ denotes expected value in a risk-neutral world. Since K is a constant, Equation (10.21) becomes

$$f = e^{-r(T-t)} \hat{E}(S_T) - K e^{-r(T-t)} \tag{10.22}$$

The growth rate of the stock price, μ, becomes r in a risk-neutral world. Hence from Equation (10.8),

$$\hat{E}(S_T) = S e^{r(T-t)} \tag{10.23}$$

Substituting Equation (10.23) into Equation (10.22) gives

$$f = S - K e^{-r(T-t)} \tag{10.24}$$

This is in agreement with Equation (3.6). Example 10.5 shows that this expression for f satisfies the Black–Scholes differential equation.

10.9 THE BLACK–SCHOLES PRICING FORMULAS

In their pathbreaking paper, Black and Scholes succeeded in solving their differential equation to obtain exact formulas for the prices of European call and put options. These formulas are presented in equations (10.27) and (10.28). In this section we indicate how a similar analysis to that just used for forward contracts can be used to derive the formulas.

The expected value of a European call option at maturity in a risk-neutral world is

$$\hat{E}[\max(S_T - X, 0)]$$

where as before $\hat{E}$ denotes expected value in a risk-neutral world. From the risk-neutral valuation argument the European call option price, c, is the value of this discounted at the risk-free rate of interest, that is,

$$c = e^{-r(T-t)}\hat{E}[\max(S_T - X, 0)] \tag{10.25}$$

In a risk-neutral world, $\ln S_T$ has the probability distribution in Equation (10.7) with μ replaced by r; that is,

$$\ln S_T \sim \phi[\ln S + (r - \frac{\sigma^2}{2})(T - t), \sigma\sqrt{T - t}] \tag{10.26}$$

Evaluating the right-hand side of Equation (10.25) is an application of integral calculus.[6] The result is

$$c = SN(d_1) - Xe^{-r(T-t)}N(d_2) \tag{10.27}$$

where

$$d_1 = \frac{\ln(S/X) + (r + \sigma^2/2)(T - t)}{\sigma\sqrt{T - t}}$$

$$d_2 = \frac{\ln(S/X) + (r - \sigma^2/2)(T - t)}{\sigma\sqrt{T - t}} = d_1 - \sigma\sqrt{T - t}$$

and $N(x)$ is the cumulative probability distribution function for a standardized normal variable (i.e., it is the probability that such a variable will be less than x).

---

[6]If g is the probability density function of S_T in a risk-neutral world given by (10.26), Equation (10.25) becomes

$$c = e^{-r(T-t)}\int_X^\infty (S_T - X)g(S_T)\,dS_T$$

Substituting $S_T = e^w$ converts this to an integral involving the normal rather than the lognormal distribution. The rest is tedious algebra!

Since $c = C$, Equation (10.27) also gives the value of an American call option on a non-dividend-paying stock. The value of a European put can be calculated in a similar way to a European call. Alternatively, put-call parity (see Chapter 7) can be used. The result is

$$p = Xe^{-r(T-t)}N(-d_2) - SN(-d_1) \qquad (10.28)$$

Unfortunately, no exact analytic formula for the value of an American put option on a non-dividend-paying stock has been produced. Numerical procedures and analytic approximations for calculating American put values are discussed in Chapter 14.

Note that to derive equations (10.27) and (10.28), it has been assumed that r is constant. In practice when the equations are used, r is set equal to the risk-free rate of interest on an investment lasting for $T - t$, the life of the option.

PROPERTIES OF THE BLACK–SCHOLES FORMULAS

We now show that the Black–Scholes formulas have the right general properties by considering what happens when some of the parameters take extreme values.

When the stock price, S, becomes very large, a call option is almost certain to be exercised. It then becomes very similar to a forward contract with delivery price X. From Equation (3.6) we therefore expect the call price to be

$$S - Xe^{-rT}$$

This is in fact the call price given by Equation (10.27) since, when S becomes very large, both d_1 and d_2 become very large and $N(d_1)$ and $N(d_2)$ are both close to 1.0.

When the stock price becomes very large, the price of a European put option, p, approaches zero. This is consistent with Equation (10.28) since $N(-d_1)$ and $N(-d_2)$ are both close to zero.

Consider next what happens when the volatility σ approaches zero. Since the stock is virtually riskless, its price will grow at rate r to Se^{rT} at time T and the payoff from a call option is

$$\max(Se^{rT} - X, 0)$$

Discounting at rate r, the value of the call today is

$$e^{-rT} \max(Se^{rT} - X, 0)$$

$$= \max(S - Xe^{-rT}, 0)$$

To show that this is consistent with Equation (10.27), consider first the case where $S > Xe^{-rT}$. This implies $\ln(S/X) + rT > 0$. As σ tends to zero, d_1 and d_2 tend to $+\infty$ so that $N(d_1)$ and $N(d_2)$ tend to 1.0 and Equation (10.27) becomes

$$c = S - Xe^{-rT}$$

When $S < Xe^{-rT}$, it follows that $\ln(S/X) - rT < 0$. As σ tends to zero, d_1 and d_2 tend to $-\infty$ so that $N(d_1)$ and $N(d_2)$ tend to zero and Equation (10.27) gives a call price of zero. The call price is therefore always max $(S - Xe^{-rT}, 0)$ as σ tends to zero. Similarly, it can be shown that the put price is always max $(Xe^{-rT} - S, 0)$ as σ tends to zero.

10.10 THE CUMULATIVE NORMAL DISTRIBUTION FUNCTION

The only problem in applying equations (10.27) and (10.28) is in calculating the cumulative normal distribution function, N. Tables for $N(x)$ are provided at the end of this book. The function can also be evaluated directly using numerical procedures. Alternatively, a polynomial approximation can be used.[7] One such approximation that can easily be obtained using a hand calculator is

$$N(x) = \begin{cases} 1 - N'(x)(a_1 k + a_2 k^2 + a_3 k^3) & \text{when } x \geq 0 \\ 1 - N(-x) & \text{when } x < 0 \end{cases}$$

where

$$k = \frac{1}{1 + \gamma x}$$

$$\gamma = 0.33267$$

$$a_1 = 0.4361836$$

$$a_2 = -0.1201676$$

$$a_3 = 0.9372980$$

and

$$N'(x) = \frac{1}{\sqrt{2\pi}} e^{-x^2/2}$$

This provides values for $N(x)$ that are usually accurate to four decimal places and are always accurate to 0.0002. For six decimal place accuracy the following can be used

$$N(x) = \begin{cases} 1 - N'(x)(a_1 k + a_2 k^2 + a_3 k^3 + a_4 k^4 + a_5 k^5) & \text{when } x \geq 0 \\ 1 - N(-x) & \text{when } x < 0 \end{cases}$$

[7]See M. Abramowitz and I. Stegun, *Handbook of Mathematical Functions* (New York: Dover Publications, 1972.)

where

$$k = \frac{1}{1 + \gamma x}$$

$$\gamma = 0.2316419$$

$$a_1 = 0.319381530$$

$$a_2 = -0.356563782$$

$$a_3 = 1.781477937$$

$$a_4 = -1.821255978$$

$$a_5 = 1.330274429$$

and $N'(x)$ is defined as above.

Example 10.6

Consider the situation where the stock price 6 months from the expiration of an option is $42, the exercise price of the option is $40, the risk-free interest rate is 10% per annum, and the volatility is 20% per annum. This means that $S = 42$, $X = 40$, $r = 0.1$, $\sigma = 0.2$, $T - t = 0.5$,

$$d_1 = \frac{\ln 1.05 + 0.12 \times 0.5}{0.2 \sqrt{0.5}} = 0.7693$$

$$d_2 = \frac{\ln 1.05 + 0.08 \times 0.5}{0.2 \sqrt{0.5}} = 0.6278$$

and

$$Xe^{-r(T-t)} = 40e^{-0.05} = 38.049$$

Hence if the option is a European call, its value, c, is given by

$$c = 42N(0.7693) - 38.049N(0.6278)$$

If the option is a European put, its value, p, is given by

$$p = 38.049N(-0.6278) - 42N(-0.7693)$$

Using one of the polynomial approximations,

$$N(0.7693) = 0.7791, \qquad N(-0.7693) = 0.2209$$

$$N(0.6278) = 0.7349, \qquad N(-0.6278) = 0.2651$$

so that

$$c = 4.76, \qquad p = 0.81$$

The stock price has to rise by \$2.76 for the purchaser of the call to break even. Similarly, the stock price has to fall by \$2.81 for the purchaser of the put to break even.

10.11 WARRANTS ISSUED BY A COMPANY ON ITS OWN STOCK

The Black–Scholes formula, with some adjustments for the impact of dilution, can be used to value European warrants issued by a company on its own stock.[8] Consider a company with N outstanding shares and M outstanding European warrants. Suppose that each warrant entitles the holder to purchase γ shares from the company at time T at a price of X per share.

If V_T is the value of the company's equity at time T and the warrant holders exercise, the company receives a cash inflow from the payment of the exercise price of $M\gamma X$ and the value of the company's equity increases to $V_T + M\gamma X$. This value is distributed among $N + M\gamma$ shares so that the share price immediately after exercise becomes

$$\frac{V_T + M\gamma X}{N + M\gamma}$$

The payoff to the warrant holder is therefore

$$\gamma \left[\frac{V_T + M\gamma X}{N + M\gamma} - X \right]$$

or

$$\frac{N\gamma}{N + M\gamma} \left[\frac{V_T}{N} - X \right]$$

The warrants should be exercised only if this payoff is positive. The payoff to the warrant holder is therefore

$$\frac{N\gamma}{N + M\gamma} \max \left[\frac{V_T}{N} - X, 0 \right]$$

This shows that the value of the warrant is the value of

$$\frac{N\gamma}{N + M\gamma}$$

regular call options on V/N where V is the value of the company's equity.

---

[8] See F. Black and M. Scholes, "The Pricing of Options and Corporate Liabilities," *Journal of Political Economy*, 81 (May–June 1973), 637–59; D. Galai and M. Schneller, "Pricing Warrants and the Value of the Firm," *Journal of Finance*, 33 (1978), 1339–42; B. Lauterbach and P. Schultz, "Pricing Warrants: An Empirical Study of the Black–Scholes Model and its Alternatives," *Journal of Finance*, 45 (1990), 1181–1209.

The value of V is given by

$$V = NS + MW$$

where S is the stock price and W is the warrant price so that

$$\frac{V}{N} = S + \frac{M}{N}W$$

The Black–Scholes formula in Equation (10.27) therefore gives the warrant price W if

1. The stock price S is replaced by $S + (M/N)W$
2. The volatility σ is the volatility of the equity of the company (i.e., it is the volatility of the value of the stocks plus warrants, not just the stocks).
3. The formula is multiplied by $(N\gamma)/(N + M\gamma)$.

When these adjustments are made we end up with a formula for W in terms of W. This can be solved numerically.

10.12 IMPLIED VOLATILITIES

The one parameter in the Black–Scholes pricing formulas that cannot be observed directly is the volatility of the stock price. In Section 10.4 we discussed how this can be estimated from a history of the stock price. At this stage it is appropriate to mention an alternative approach that uses what is termed an *implied volatility*. This is the volatility implied by an option price observed in the market.

To illustrate the basic idea, suppose that the value of a call on a non-dividend-paying stock is 1.875 when $S = 21$, $X = 20$, $r = 0.1$, and $T - t = 0.25$. The implied volatility is the value of σ, which when substituted into Equation (10.27) gives $c = 1.875$. Unfortunately, it is not possible to invert Equation (10.27) so that σ is expressed as a function of S, X, r, $T - t$, and c. However, an iterative search procedure can be used to find the implied σ. We could start by trying $\sigma = 0.20$. This gives a value of c equal to 1.76, which is too low. Since c is an increasing function of σ, a higher value of σ is required. We could next try a value of 0.30 for σ. This gives a value of c equal to 2.10, which is too high and means that σ must lie between 0.20 and 0.30. Next, a value of 0.25 can be tried for σ. This also proves to be too high, showing that σ lies between 0.20 and 0.25. Proceeding in this way the range for σ can be halved at each iteration and the correct value of σ can be calculated to any required accuracy.[9] In this example, the implied volatility is 0.235 or 23.5 percent per annum.

---

[9]This method is presented for illustration. Other more powerful methods, such as the Newton–Raphson method, are often used in practice. (See footnote 1 in Chapter 4 for further information on the Newton–Raphson method.)

Implied volatilities can be used to monitor the market's opinion about the volatility of a particular stock. This does change over time. They can also be used to estimate the price of one option from the price of another option. Very often, several implied volatilities are obtained simultaneously from different options on the same stock and a composite implied volatility for the stock is then calculated by taking a suitable weighted average of the individual implied volatilities. The amount of weight given to each implied volatility in this calculation should reflect the sensitivity of the option price to the volatility. To illustrate this point, suppose that two implied volatility estimates are available. The first is 21 percent per annum and is based on an at-the-money option; the second is 26 percent per annum and is based on a deep-out-of-the-money option with the same maturity. The price of the at-the-money option is far more sensitive to volatility than the price of the deep-out-of-the-money option. It is therefore providing more information about the "true" implied volatility. We might therefore choose a weight of 0.9 for the at-the-money implied volatility and a weight of 0.1 for the deep-out-of-the-money option. The weighted-average implied volatility would then be

$$0.9 \times 0.21 + 0.1 \times 0.26 = 0.215$$

or 21.5 percent per annum. Different weighting schemes are discussed by Latane and Rendleman, by Chiras and Manaster, and by Whaley.[10] Beckers, after examining various weighting schemes, concluded that best results are obtained by using only the option whose price is most sensitive to σ.[11] Thus the Beckers approach would estimate 21 percent for the volatility in the example just mentioned.

10.13 THE CAUSES OF VOLATILITY

Proponents of the efficient markets hypothesis have traditionally claimed that the volatility of a stock price is caused solely by the random arrival of new information about the future returns from the stock. Others have claimed that volatility is caused largely by trading. An interesting question, therefore, is whether volatility is the same when the exchange is open as when it is closed.

---

[10] See H. Latane and R. J. Rendleman, "Standard Deviation of Stock Price Ratios Implied by Option Premia," *Journal of Finance*, 31 (May 1976), 369–82; D. P. Chiras and S. Manaster, "The Information Content of Option Prices and a Test of Market Efficiency," *Journal of Financial Economics*, 6 (1978), 213–34; R. E. Whaley, "Valuation of American Call Options on Dividend-Paying Stocks: Empirical Tests," *Journal of Financial Economics*, 10 (March 1982), 29–58.

[11] See S. Beckers, "Standard Deviations in Option Prices as Predictors of Future Stock Price Variability," *Journal of Banking and Finance*, 5 (September 1981), 363–82. The sensitivity of an option with respect to σ is measured by the partial derivative of its price with respect to σ. See Chapter 13 for how this can be calculated.

Fama and K. French have tested this question empirically.[12] They collected data on the stock price at the close of each trading day over a long period of time, and then calculated:

1. The variance of stock price returns between the close of trading on one day and the close of trading on the next trading day when there are no intervening nontrading days
2. The variance of the stock price returns between the close of trading on Fridays and the close of trading on Mondays

If trading and nontrading days are equivalent, the variance in situation 2 should be three times as great as the variance in situation 1. Fama found that it was only 22 percent higher. French's results were similar. He found that is was 19 percent higher.

These results suggest that volatility is far larger when the exchange is open than when it is closed. Proponents of the traditional view that volatility is caused only by new information might be tempted to argue that most new information on stocks arrives during trading hours.[13] However, studies of futures prices on agricultural commodities, which depend largely on the weather, have shown that they exhibit much the same behavior as stock prices; that is, they are much more volatile during trading hours. Presumably, news about the weather is equally likely to arise on any day. The only reasonable conclusion seems to be that volatility is to some extent caused by trading itself.[14]

What are the implications of all of this for the measurement of volatility and the Black–Scholes model? If daily data are used to measure volatility, the results suggest that days when the exchange is closed can be ignored. The volatility per annum is calculated from the volatility per trading day using the formula

$$\text{volatility per annum} = \frac{\text{volatility per}}{\text{trading day}} \times \sqrt{\frac{\text{number of trading}}{\text{days per annum}}}$$

This is the approach that was used in Section 10.4.

---

[12] See E. E. Fama, "The Behavior of Stock Market Prices," *Journal of Business*, 38 (January 1965), 34–105; K. R. French, "Stock Returns and the Weekend Effect,"*Journal of Financial Economics*, 8 (March 1980), 55–69.

[13] In fact, this is questionable. Often important announcements (e.g., those concerned with sales and earnings) are made when exchanges are closed.

[14] For a discussion of this, see K. French and R. Roll, "Stock Return Variances: The Arrival of Information and the Reaction of Traders," *Journal of Financial Economics*, 17 (September 1986), 5–26. We will consider one way in which trading can generate volatility when we discuss portfolio insurance schemes in Chapter 13.

Although volatility appears to be a phenomenon that is related largely to trading days, interest is paid by the calendar day. This has led D. French[15] to suggest that, when options are being valued, two time measures should be calculated:

$$\tau_1 : \frac{\text{trading days until maturity}}{\text{trading days per year}}$$

$$\tau_2 : \frac{\text{calendar days until maturity}}{\text{calendar days per year}}$$

and that the Black–Scholes formulas should be adjusted to

$$c = SN(d_1) - Xe^{-r\tau_2}N(d_2)$$

and

$$p = Xe^{-r\tau_2}N(-d_2) - SN(-d_1)$$

where

$$d_1 = \frac{\ln(S/X) + r\tau_2 + (\sigma^2/2)\tau_1}{\sigma\sqrt{\tau_1}}$$

$$d_2 = \frac{\ln(S/X) + r\tau_2 - (\sigma^2/2)\tau_1}{\sigma\sqrt{\tau_1}} = d_1 - \sigma\sqrt{\tau_1}$$

In practice, this adjustment makes little difference except for very short life options.

10.14 DIVIDENDS

Up to now we have assumed that the stock upon which the option is written pays no dividends. In practice, this is not usually true. In this section we assume that the dividends that will be paid during the life of an option can be predicted with certainty. As traded options typically last for less than 9 months, this is not an unreasonable assumption.

A dividend-paying stock can reasonably be expected to follow the stochastic process developed in Chapter 9 except when the stock goes ex-dividend. At this point the stock's price goes down by an amount reflecting the dividend paid per share. For tax reasons, the stock price may go down by somewhat less than the cash amount of the dividend. To take account of this, the word "dividend" in this section should be interpreted as the reduction in the stock price on the ex-dividend date caused by the dividend. Thus, if a dividend of $1 per share is anticipated

---

[15] See D. W. French, "The Weekend Effect on the Distribution of Stock Prices: Implications for Option Pricing,"*Journal of Financial Economics*, 13 (September 1984), 547–59.

and the share price normally goes down by 80 percent of the dividend on the ex-dividend date, the dividend should be assumed to be $0.80 for the purposes of the analysis.

EUROPEAN OPTIONS

European options can be analyzed by assuming that the stock price is the sum of two components: a riskless component that will be used to pay the known dividends during the life of the option and a risky component. The riskless component at any given time is the present value of all the dividends during the life of the option discounted from the ex-dividend dates to the present at the risk-free rate. The dividends will cause the riskless component to disappear by the time the option matures. The Black–Scholes formula is therefore correct if S is put equal to the risky component of the stock price and σ is the volatility of the process followed by the risky component.[16] Operationally, this means that the Black–Scholes formula can be used provided that the stock price is reduced by the present value of all the dividends during the life of the option, the discounting being done from the ex-dividend dates at the risk-free rate. A dividend is included in calculations only if its ex-dividend date occurs during the life of the option.

Example 10.7

Consider a European call option on a stock when there are ex-dividend dates in 2 months and 5 months. The dividend on each ex-dividend date is expected to be $0.50. The current share price is $40, the exercise price is $40, the stock price volatility is 30% per annum, the risk-free rate of interest is 9% per annum, and the time to maturity is 6 months. The present value of the dividends is

$$0.5e^{-0.1667\times0.09} + 0.5e^{-0.4167\times0.09} = 0.9741$$

The option price can therefore be calculated from the Black–Scholes formula with $S = 39.0259$, $X = 40$, $r = 0.09$, $\sigma = 0.3$, and $T - t = 0.5$.

$$d_1 = \frac{\ln 0.9756 + 0.135 \times 0.5}{0.3\sqrt{0.5}} = 0.2017$$

$$d_2 = \frac{\ln 0.9756 + 0.045 \times 0.5}{0.3\sqrt{0.5}} = -0.0104$$

Using the polynomial approximation in Section 10.10 gives us

$$N(d_1) = 0.5800, \qquad N(d_2) = 0.4959$$

---

[16]In theory this is not quite the same as the volatility of the stochastic process followed by the whole stock price. The volatility of the risky component is approximately equal to the volatility of the whole stock price multiplied by $S/(S - V)$, where V is the present value of the dividends. In practice, the two are often assumed to be the same.

and from Equation (10.27), the call price is

$$39.0259 \times 0.5800 - 40e^{-0.09 \times 0.5} \times 0.4959 = 3.67$$

or $3.67.

AMERICAN OPTIONS

Consider next American call options. Earlier in this chapter we presented an argument to show that these should never be exercised early in the absence of dividends. An extension to the argument shows that when there are dividends, it can only be optimal to exercise at a time immediately before the stock goes ex-dividend. We assume that n ex-dividend dates are anticipated and that t_1, t_2, ..., t_n are moments in time immediately prior to the stock going ex-dividend with $t_1 < t_2 < t_3 < \ldots < t_n$. The dividends at these times will be denoted by D_1, D_2, ..., D_n, respectively.

We start by considering the possibility of early exercise just prior to the final ex-dividend date (i.e., at time t_n). If the option is exercised at time t_n, the investor receives

$$S(t_n) - X$$

If the option is not exercised, the stock price drops to $S(t_n) - D_n$. As shown by Equation (7.6), the value of the option is then greater than

$$S(t_n) - D_n - Xe^{-r(T-t_n)}$$

It follows that if

$$S(t_n) - D_n - Xe^{-r(T-t_n)} \geq S(t_n) - X$$

that is,

$$D_n \leq X(1 - e^{-r(T-t_n)}) \tag{10.29}$$

it cannot be optimal to exercise at time t_n. On the other hand, if

$$D_n > X(1 - e^{-r(T-t_n)}) \tag{10.30}$$

it can be shown that it is always optimal to exercise at time t_n for a sufficiently high value of $S(t_n)$. The inequality in (10.30) will tend to be satisfied when the final ex-dividend date is fairly close to the maturity of the option (i.e., $T - t_n$ is small) and the dividend is large.

Consider next, time t_{n-1}, the penultimate ex-dividend date. If the option is exercised at time t_{n-1}, the investor receives

$$S(t_{n-1}) - X$$

If the option is not exercised at time t_{n-1}, the stock price drops to $S(t_{n-1}) - D_{n-1}$ and the earliest subsequent time at which exercise could take place is t_n. Hence from Equation (7.6) a lower bound to the option price if it is not exercised at time t_{n-1} is

$$S(t_{n-1}) - D_{n-1} - Xe^{-r(t_n - t_{n-1})}$$

It follows that if

$$S(t_{n-1}) - D_{n-1} - Xe^{-r(t_n - t_{n-1})} \geq S(t_{n-1}) - X$$

or

$$D_{n-1} \leq X(1 - e^{-r(t_n - t_{n-1})})$$

it is not optimal to exercise at time t_{n-1}. Similarly, for any $i < n$, if

$$D_i \leq X(1 - e^{-r(t_{i+1} - t_i)}) \tag{10.31}$$

it is not optimal to exercise at time t_i.

The inequality in (10.31) is approximately equivalent to

$$D_i \leq Xr(t_{i+1} - t_i)$$

Assuming that X is fairly close to the current stock price, the dividend yield on the stock would have to be either close to or above the risk-free rate of interest for this inequality not to be satisfied. This is not usually the case.

We can conclude from this analysis that, in most circumstances, the only time that needs to be considered for the early exercise of an American call is the final ex-dividend date, t_n. Furthermore, if inequality (10.31) holds for $i = 1, 2, \ldots, n-1$ and inequality (10.29) holds, we can be certain that early exercise is never optimal.

BLACK'S APPROXIMATION

Black suggests an approximate procedure for taking account of early exercise.[17] This involves calculating, as described earlier in this section, the prices of European options that mature at times T and t_n, and then setting the American price equal to the greater of the two. This approximation seems to work well in most cases. A more exact procedure suggested by Roll, Geske, and Whaley is given in Appendix 10B.[18]

---

[17] See F. Black, "Fact and Fantasy in the Use of Options," *Financial Analysts Journal*, 31 (July–August 1975), 36–41, 61–72.

[18] See R. Roll, "An Analytic Formula for Unprotected American Call Options on Stocks with Known Dividends," *Journal of Financial Economics*, 5 (1977), 251–58; R. Geske, "A Note on an Analytic Valuation Formula for Unprotected American Call Options on Stocks with Known Dividends," *Journal of Financial Economics*, 7 (1979), 375–80; R. Whaley, "On the Valuation of American Call Options on Stocks with Known Dividends," *Journal of Financial Economics*, 9 (June 1981), 207–11; R. Geske, "Comments on Whaley's Note," *Journal of Financial Economics*, 9 (June 1981), 213–15.

Example 10.8

Consider the situation in Example 10.7, but suppose that the option is American rather than European. In this case $D_1 = D_2 = 0.5$, $S = 40$, $X = 40$, $r = 0.09$, t_1 occurs after 2 months and t_2 occurs after 5 months.

$$X(1 - e^{-r(t_2 - t_1)}) = 40(1 - e^{-0.09 \times 0.25}) = 0.89$$

Since this is greater than 0.5, it follows [see inequality (10.31)] that the option should never be exercised on the first ex-dividend date.

$$X(1 - e^{-r(T - t_2)}) = 40(1 - e^{-0.09 \times 0.0833}) = 0.30$$

Since this is less than 0.5, it follows [see inequality (10.29)] that when it is sufficiently deeply in-the-money, the option should be exercised on its second ex-dividend date.

We now use Black's approximation to value the option. The present value of the first dividend is

$$0.5e^{-0.1667 \times 0.09} = 0.4926$$

so that the value of the option on the assumption that it expires just before the final ex-dividend date can be calculated using the Black–Scholes formula with $S = 39.5074$, $X = 40$, $r = 0.09$, $\sigma = 0.30$, and $T - t = 0.4167$. It is \$3.52. Black's approximation involves taking the greater of this and the value of the option when it can only be exercised at the end of 6 months. From Example 10.7 we know that the latter is \$3.67. Black's approximation therefore gives the value of the American call as \$3.67.

Whaley[19] has tested empirically three models for the pricing of American calls on dividend-paying stocks: (1) the formula in Appendix 10B; (2) Black's model; and (3) the European option pricing model described at the beginning of this section. He used 15,582 Chicago Board options. The models produced pricing errors with means of 1.08 percent, 1.48 percent, and 2.15 percent, respectively. The typical bid-ask spread on a call option is greater than 2.15 percent of the price. On average, therefore, all three models work well and within the tolerance imposed on the options market by trading imperfections.

Up to now, our discussion has centered around American call options. The results for American put options are less clear cut. Dividends make it less likely that an American put option will be exercised early. It can be shown that it is never worth exercising an American put for a period immediately prior to an ex-dividend date.[20] Indeed, if

$$D_i \geq X(1 - e^{-r(t_{i+1} - t_i)})$$

---

[19]See R. E. Whaley, "Valuation of American Call Options on Dividend Paying Stocks: Empirical Tests," *Journal of Financial Economics*, 10 (March 1982), 29–58.

[20]See H. E. Johnson, "Three Topics in Option Pricing," Ph.D. thesis, University of California, Los Angeles, 1981, p. 42.

for all $i < n$ and

$$D_n \geq X(1 - e^{-r(T - t_n)})$$

an argument analogous to that just given shows that the put option should never be exercised early. In other cases, numerical procedures must be used to value a put.

10.15 SUMMARY

In this chapter we started by examining the properties of the process for stock prices introduced in Chapter 9. The process implies that the price of a stock at some future time, given its price today, is lognormal. It also implies that the continuously compounded return from the stock in a period of time is normally distributed. Our uncertainty about future stock prices increases as we look further ahead. The standard deviation of the logarithm of the stock price is proportional to the square root of how far ahead we are looking.

To estimate the volatility, σ, of a stock price empirically, the stock price is observed at fixed intervals of time (for example, every day, every week, or every month). For each time period, the natural logarithm of the ratio of the stock price at the end of the time period to the stock price at the beginning of the time period is calculated. The volatility is estimated as the standard deviation of these numbers divided by the square root of the length of the time period in years. Usually, days when the exchanges are closed are ignored in measuring time for the purposes of volatility calculations.

The differential equation for the price of any derivative security dependent on a stock can be obtained by setting up a position in the option and the stock that is riskless. Since the derivative security and the option price both depend on the same underlying source of uncertainty this can always be done. The position that is set up remains riskless for only a very short period of time. However, the return on a riskless position must always be the risk-free interest rate if there are to be no arbitrage opportunities.

The expected return on the stock does not enter into the Black–Scholes differential equation. This leads to a useful result known as risk-neutral valuation. This result states that, when valuing a derivative security dependent on a stock price, we can assume that the world is risk neutral. This means that we can assume that the expected return from the stock is the risk-free interest rate and then discount expected payoffs at the risk-free interest rate. The Black–Scholes equations for European call and put options can be derived by either solving their differential equation or by using risk-neutral valuation.

An implied volatility is the volatility which, when used in conjunction with the Black–Scholes option pricing formula, gives the market price of the option.

Traders monitor implied volatilities and sometimes use the implied volatility from one stock option price to calculate the price of another option on the same stock. Empirical results show that the volatility of a stock is much higher when the exchange is open than when it is closed. This suggests that to some extent trading itself causes stock price volatility.

The Black–Scholes results can easily be extended to cover European call and put options on dividend-paying stocks. The procedure is to use the Black–Scholes formula with the stock price reduced by the present value of the dividends anticipated during the life of the option, and the volatility equal to the volatility of the stock price net of the present value of these dividends.

In theory, American call options are liable to be exercised early immediately before any ex-dividend date. In practice, only the final ex-dividend date usually needs to be considered. Fischer Black has suggested an approximation. This involves setting the American call option price equal to the greater of two European call option prices. The first European call option expires at the same time as the American call option; the second expires immediately prior to the final ex-dividend date. A more exact approach involving bivariate normal distributions is explained in Appendix 10B.

SUGGESTIONS FOR FURTHER READING

On the Distribution of Stock Price Changes

BLATTBERG, R., and N. GONEDES, "A Comparison of the Stable and Student Distributions as Statistical Models for Stock Prices," *Journal of Business*, 47 (April 1974), 244–80.

FAMA, E. F., "The Behavior of Stock Prices," *Journal of Business*, 38 (January 1965), 34–105.

KON, S. J., "Models of Stock Returns—A Comparison," *Journal of Finance*, 39 (March 1984), 147–65.

On the Black-Scholes Differential Equation

BLACK, F., and M. SCHOLES, "The Pricing of Options and Corporate Liabilities," *Journal of Political Economy*, 81 (May–June 1973), 637–59.

MERTON, R. C., "Theory of Rational Option Pricing," *Bell Journal of Economics and Management Science*, 4 (Spring 1973), 141–83.

On Risk-neutral Valuation

COX, J. C., and S. A. ROSS, "The Valuation of Options for Alternative Stochastic Processes," *Journal of Financial Economics*, 3 (1976), 145–66.

SMITH, C. W., "Option Pricing: A Review," *Journal of Financial Economics*, 3 (1976), 3–54.

On the Black–Scholes Formula and its Extensions

BLACK, F., "Fact and Fantasy in the Use of Options and Corporate Liabilities," *Financial Analysts Journal*, 31 (July–August 1975), 36–41, 61–72.

BLACK, F., and M. SCHOLES, "The Pricing of Options and Corporate Liabilities," *Journal of Political Economy*, 81 (May–June 1973), 637–59.

MERTON, R. C., "Theory of Rational Option Pricing," *Bell Journal of Economics and Management Science*, 4 (Spring 1973), 141–83.

SMITH, C. W., "Option Pricing: A Review," *Journal of Financial Economics*, 3 (March 1976), 3–51.

On Analytic Solutions to the Pricing of American Calls

GESKE, R., "Comments on Whaley's Note," *Journal of Financial Economics*, 9 (June 1981), 213–15.

GESKE, R., "A Note on an Analytic Valuation Formula for Unprotected American Call Options on Stocks with Known Dividends," *Journal of Financial Economics*, 7 (1979), 375–80.

ROLL, R., "An Analytical Formula for Unprotected American Call Options on Stocks with Known Dividends," *Journal of Financial Economics*, 5 (1977), 251–58.

WHALEY, R., "On the Valuation of American Call Options on Stocks with Known Dividends," *Journal of Financial Economics*, 9 (June 1981), 207–11.

QUESTIONS AND PROBLEMS

10.1. What does the Black–Scholes stock option pricing model assume about the probability distribution of the stock price in 1 year?

10.2. The volatility of a stock price is 30% per annum. What is the standard deviation of the proportional price change in one trading day?

10.3. A stock price is currently $40. It is known that at the end of 1 month it will be either $42 or $38. The risk-free rate of interest is 8% per annum. What is the value of a European call option with a strike price of $39?

10.4. Explain what is meant by risk-neutral valuation.

10.5. Calculate the price of a 3-month European put option on a non-dividend-paying stock with a strike price of $50 when the current stock price is $50, the risk-free interest rate is 10% per annum, and the volatility is 30% per annum.

10.6. What difference does it make to your calculations in the previous question if a dividend of $1.50 is expected in 2 months?

10.7. What is meant by implied volatility? How can it be calculated?

10.8. A stock price is currently $50. Assume that the expected return from the stock is 18% and its volatility is 30%. What is the probability distribution for the stock price in 2 years? Calculate the mean and standard deviation of the distribution. Determine 95% confidence intervals.

10.9. A stock price is currently $40. Assume that the expected return from the stock is 15% and that its volatility is 25%. What is the probability distribution for the rate of return (with continuous compounding) earned over a 2-year period?

10.10. A stock price follows geometric Brownian motion with an expected return of 16% and a volatility of 35%. The current price is $38.
    (a) What is the probability that a European call option on the stock with an exercise price of $40 and a maturity date in 6 months will be exercised?
    (b) What is the probability that a European put option on the stock with the same exercise price and maturity will be exercised?

*10.11. Suppose that x is the yield to maturity with continuous compounding on a discount bond that pays off $1 at time T. Assume that x follows the process:

$$dx = a(x_0 - x)\,dt + sx\,dz$$

where a, x_0, and s are positive constants and dz is a Wiener process. What is the process followed by the bond price?

*10.12. Suppose that x is the yield on a perpetual government bond which pays interest at the rate of $1 per annum. Assume that x is expressed with continuous compounding, that interest is paid continuously on the bond, and that x follows the process

$$dx = a(x_0 - x)\,dt + sx\,dz$$

where a, x_0, and s are positive constants and dz is a Wiener process. What is the process followed by the bond price? What is the expected instantaneous return (including interest and capital gains) to the holder of the bond?

10.13. Prove that with the notation in the chapter, a 95% confidence interval for S_T is between

$$Se^{(\mu - \sigma^2/2)(T-t) - 2\sigma\sqrt{T-t}} \quad \text{and} \quad Se^{(\mu - \sigma^2/2)(T-t) + 2\sigma\sqrt{T-t}}$$

10.14. A portfolio manager announces that the average of the returns realized in each year of the last 10 years is 20% per annum. In what respect is this statement misleading?

10.15. Suppose that observations on a stock price (in dollars) at the end of each of 15 consecutive weeks are as follows: $30\frac{1}{4}$, 32, $31\frac{1}{8}$, $30\frac{1}{8}$, $30\frac{1}{4}$, $30\frac{3}{8}$, $30\frac{5}{8}$, 33, $32\frac{7}{8}$, 33, $33\frac{1}{2}$, $33\frac{1}{2}$, $33\frac{3}{4}$, $33\frac{1}{2}$, $33\frac{1}{4}$. Estimate the stock price volatility. What is the standard error of your estimate?

10.16. A stock price is currently $50. It is known that at the end of 6 months it will be either $60 or $42. The risk-free rate of interest with continuous compounding is 12% per annum. Calculate the value of a 6-month European call option on the stock with exercise price $48.

10.17. A stock price is currently $40. It is known that at the end of 3 months it will be either $45 or $35. The risk-free rate of interest with quarterly compounding is 8% per annum. Calculate the value of a 3-month European put option on the stock with an exercise price of $40. Show that this value is consistent with risk-neutral valuation.

*10.18. Assume that a non-dividend-paying stock has an expected return of μ and a volatility of σ. An innovative financial institution has just announced that it will trade a security which pays off a dollar amount equal to $\ln S_T$ at time T where S_T denotes the value of the stock price at time T.
    (a) Use risk-neutral valuation to calculate the price of the security at time t in terms of the stock price, S, at time t.
    (b) Confirm that your price satisfies the differential equation (10.20).

*10.19. If the security in Problem 10.18 is a success, the financial institution plans to offer another security which pays off a dollar amount equal to S_T^2 at time T.
    (a) Use risk-neutral valuation to calculate the price of the security at time t in terms of the stock price, S, at time t. (*Hint:* The expected value of S_T^2 can be calculated from the mean and variance of S_T given in Section 10.2.)
    (b) Confirm that your price satisfies the differential equation (10.20).

10.20. Suppose that S and f are the current values of a stock price and a derivative security dependent on the stock price. Assume that in the next small interval of time, Δt, the stock price will either move up to Su or down to Sd. If the stock price moves up to Su, the value of the derivative security will be f_u. If it moves down to Sd, its value will be f_d. The risk-free rate of interest with continuous compounding is r.
    (a) Using an argument similar to that in Section 10.5, show that

$$f = e^{-r\Delta t}\left[\frac{(f_u - f_d)e^{r\Delta t} + f_d u - f_u d}{u - d}\right]$$

    (b) Show that in a risk-neutral world the probability of an upward stock price movement is

$$\frac{e^{r\Delta t} - d}{u - d}$$

    (c) Derive the result in part (a) using risk-neutral valuation.

10.21. What is the price of a European call option on a non-dividend-paying stock when the stock price is \$52, the strike price is \$50, the risk-free interest rate is 12% per annum, the volatility is 30% per annum, and the time to maturity is 3 months?

10.22. What is the price of a European put option on a non-dividend-paying stock when the stock price is \$69, the strike price is \$70, the risk-free interest rate is 5% per annum, the volatility is 35% per annum, and the time to maturity is 6 months?

10.23. Consider an option on a non-dividend-paying stock when the stock price is \$30, the exercise price is \$29, the risk-free interest rate is 5%, the volatility is 25% per annum, and the time to maturity is 4 months.
    (a) What is the price of the option if it is a European call?
    (b) What is the price of the option if it is an American call?
    (c) What is the price of the option if it is a European put?
    (d) Verify that put-call parity holds.

10.24. Assume that the stock in Problem 10.23 is due to go ex-dividend in $1\frac{1}{2}$ months. The expected dividend is 50 cents.
   (a) What is the price of the option if it is a European call?
   (b) What is the price of the option if it is a European put?
   (c) If the option is an American call, are there any circumstances under which it will be exercised early?

10.25. A call option on a non-dividend-paying stock has a market price of $2\frac{1}{2}$. The stock price is \$15, the exercise price is \$13, the time to maturity is 3 months, and the risk-free interest rate is 5% per annum. What is the implied volatility?

*10.26. With the notation used in this chapter
   (a) What is $N'(x)$?
   (b) Show that $SN'(d_1) = Xe^{-r(T-t)}N'(d_2)$.
   (c) Calculate $\partial d_1/\partial S$ and $\partial d_2/\partial S$.
   (d) Show that

$$\frac{\partial c}{\partial t} = -rXe^{-r(T-t)}N(d_2) - SN'(d_1)\frac{\sigma}{2\sqrt{T-t}}$$

   where c is the price of a call option on a non-dividend-paying stock.
   (e) Show that $\partial c/\partial S = N(d_1)$.
   (f) Show that the Black–Scholes formula for the price of a call option on a non-dividend-paying stock does satisfy the Black–Scholes differential equation.

*10.27. Show that the Black–Scholes formula for the price of a call option gives a price which tends to $\max[S-X, 0]$ as $t \longrightarrow T$.

10.28. Consider an American call option when the stock price is \$18, the exercise price is \$20, the time to maturity is 6 months, the volatility is 30% per annum, and the risk-free interest rate is 10% per annum. Two equal dividends are expected during the life of the option with ex-dividend dates at the end of 2 months and 5 months. How high can the dividends be without the American option being worth more than the corresponding European option?

10.29. Suppose that in Problem 10.28 each dividend is 40 cents per share. Use Black's approximation to value the option.

10.30. Explain carefully why Black's approach to evaluating an American call option on a dividend-paying stock may give an approximate answer even when only one dividend is anticipated. Does the answer given by Black's approach understate or overstate the true option value? Explain your answer.

10.31. Consider an American call option on a stock. The stock price is \$70, the time to maturity is 8 months, the risk-free rate of interest is 10% per annum, the exercise price is \$65, and the volatility is 32%. Dividends of \$1 are expected after 3 months and 6 months. Show that it can never be optimal to exercise the option on either of the two dividend dates. Calculate the price of the option.

10.32. Show that the probability that a European call option will be exercised in a risk-neutral world is, with the notation introduced in this chapter, $N(d_2)$. Derive an expression for the value of a derivative security which pays off \$100 if the price of a stock at time T is greater than X.

APPENDIX 10A: DERIVATION OF ITO'S LEMMA

In this appendix we show how Ito's lemma can be regarded as a natural extension of other, simpler results. Consider a continuous and differentiable function G of a variable x. If Δx is a small change in x and ΔG is the resulting small change in G, it is well known that

$$\Delta G \approx \frac{dG}{dx} \Delta x \qquad (10A.1)$$

In other words, ΔG is approximately equal to the rate of change of G with respect to x multiplied by Δx. The error involves terms of order Δx^2. If more precision is required, a Taylor series expansion of ΔG can be used:

$$\Delta G = \frac{dG}{dx} \Delta x + \frac{1}{2} \frac{d^2 G}{dx^2} \Delta x^2 + \frac{1}{6} \frac{d^3 G}{dx^3} \Delta x^3 + \ldots$$

For a continuous and differentiable function G of two variables, x and y, the result analogous to Equation (10A.1) is

$$\Delta G \approx \frac{\partial G}{\partial x} \Delta x + \frac{\partial G}{\partial y} \Delta y \qquad (10A.2)$$

and the Taylor series expansion of ΔG is

$$\Delta G = \frac{\partial G}{\partial x} \Delta x + \frac{\partial G}{\partial y} \Delta y + \frac{1}{2} \frac{\partial^2 G}{\partial x^2} \Delta x^2 + \frac{\partial^2 G}{\partial x \, dy} \Delta x \, \Delta y + \frac{1}{2} \frac{\partial^2 G}{\partial y^2} \Delta y^2 + \ldots \quad (10A.3)$$

In the limit as Δx and Δy tend to zero, Equation 10A.3 gives

$$dG = \frac{\partial G}{\partial x} dx + \frac{\partial G}{\partial y} dy \qquad (10A.4)$$

A derivative security is a function of a variable that follows a stochastic process. We now extend Equation (10A.4) to cover such functions. Suppose that a variable x follows the general Ito process in Equation (9.4)

$$dx = a(x, t) \, dt + b(x, t) \, dz \qquad (10A.5)$$

and that G is some function of x and of time, t. By analogy with Equation (10A.3), we can write

$$\Delta G = \frac{\partial G}{\partial x} \Delta x + \frac{\partial G}{\partial t} \Delta t + \frac{1}{2} \frac{\partial^2 G}{\partial x^2} \Delta x^2 + \frac{\partial^2 G}{\partial x \, \partial t} \Delta x \, \Delta t + \frac{1}{2} \frac{\partial^2 G}{\partial t^2} \Delta t^2 + \ldots \quad (10A.6)$$

Using the notation in Chapter 9, Equation (10A.5) can be discretized to

$$\Delta x = a(x, t) \, \Delta t + b(x, t) \epsilon \sqrt{\Delta t}$$

or if arguments are dropped

$$\Delta x = a\, \Delta t + b\epsilon\, \sqrt{\Delta t} \tag{10A.7}$$

This equation reveals an important difference between the situation in Equation (10A.6) and the situation in Equation (10A.3). When limiting arguments were used to move from Equation (10A.3) to Equation (10A.4), terms in Δx^2 were ignored because they were second-order terms. From Equation (10A.7),

$$\Delta x^2 = b^2\epsilon^2\, \Delta t + \text{ terms of higher order in } \Delta t \tag{10A.8}$$

which shows that the term involving Δx^2 in Equation (10A.6) has a component that is of order Δt and cannot be ignored.

The variance of a standardized normal distribution is 1.0. This means that

$$E(\epsilon^2) - [E(\epsilon)]^2 = 1$$

where E denotes expected value. Since $E(\epsilon) = 0$, it follows that $E(\epsilon^2) = 1$. The expected value of $\epsilon^2\, \Delta t$ is therefore Δt. It can be shown that the variance of $\epsilon^2\, \Delta t$ is of order Δt^2 and that, as a result of this, $\epsilon^2\, \Delta t$ becomes nonstochastic and equal to its expected value of Δt as Δt tends to zero. It follows that the first term on the right-hand side of Equation (10A.8) becomes nonstochastic and equal to $b^2\, dt$ as Δt tends to zero. Taking limits as Δx and Δt tend to zero in Equation (10A.6) and using this last result, we therefore obtain

$$dG = \frac{\partial G}{\partial x}dx + \frac{\partial G}{\partial t}dt + \frac{1}{2}\frac{\partial^2 G}{\partial x^2}b^2\, dt \tag{10A.9}$$

This is Ito's lemma. Substituting for dx from Equation (10A.5), Equation (10A.9) becomes

$$dG = \left(\frac{\partial G}{\partial x}a + \frac{\partial G}{\partial t} + \frac{1}{2}\frac{\partial^2 G}{\partial x^2}b^2\right)dt + \frac{\partial G}{\partial x}b\, dz$$

APPENDIX 10B: AN EXACT PROCEDURE FOR CALCULATING THE VALUES OF AMERICAN CALLS ON DIVIDEND-PAYING STOCKS

The Roll, Geske, and Whaley formula for the value of an American call option on a stock paying a single dividend D_1 at time t_1 is

$$C = (S - D_1 e^{-r\tau_1})N(b_1) + (S - D_1 e^{-r\tau_1})M\left(a_1, -b_1; -\sqrt{\frac{\tau_1}{\tau}}\right)$$

$$- Xe^{-r\tau}M\left(a_2, -b_2; -\sqrt{\frac{\tau_1}{\tau}}\right) - (X - D_1)e^{-r\tau_1}N(b_2) \tag{10B.1}$$

where

$$a_1 = \frac{\ln[(S - D_1 e^{-r\tau_1})/X] + (r + \sigma^2/2)\tau}{\sigma\sqrt{\tau}}$$

$$a_2 = a_1 - \sigma\sqrt{\tau}$$

$$b_1 = \frac{\ln[(S - D_1 e^{-r\tau_1})/\overline{S}] + (r + \sigma^2/2)\tau_1}{\sigma\sqrt{\tau_1}}$$

$$b_2 = b_1 - \sigma\sqrt{\tau_1}$$

$$\tau_1 = t_1 - t$$

$$\tau = T - t$$

The function, $M(a, b; \rho)$, is the cumulative probability in a standardized bivariate normal distribution that the first variable is less than a and the second variable is less than b, when the coefficient of correlation between the variables is ρ. The variable $\overline{S}$ is the solution to

$$c(\overline{S}, t_1) = \overline{S} + D_1 - X$$

where $c(\overline{S}, t_1)$ denotes the Black–Scholes option price given by Equation (10.27) when $S = \overline{S}$ and $t = t_1$. When early exercise is never optimal, $\overline{S} = \infty$. In this case $b_1 = b_2 = -\infty$ and Equation (10B.1) reduces to the Black–Scholes equation with S replaced by $S - D_1 e^{-r\tau_1}$. In other situations $\overline{S} < \infty$ and the option should be exercised at time t_1 when $S(t_1) > \overline{S} + D_1$.

When several dividends are anticipated, early exercise is normally only ever optimal on the final ex-dividend date (see Section 10.14). It follows that the Roll, Geske, and Whaley formula can be used with S reduced by the present value of all dividends except the final one. The variable, D_1, should be set equal to the final dividend and t_1 should be set equal to the final ex-dividend date.

Drezner provides a fairly easy way to program a computer to calculate $M(a, b; \rho)$ to four-decimal-place accuracy.[21] If $a \leq 0$, $b \leq 0$, and $\rho \leq 0$,

$$M(a, b; \rho) = \frac{\sqrt{1 - \rho^2}}{\pi} \sum_{i,j=1}^{4} A_i A_j f(B_i, B_j)$$

where

$$f(x, y) = \exp[a'(2x - a') + b'(2y - b') + 2\rho(x - a')(y - b')]$$

$$a' = \frac{a}{\sqrt{2(1 - \rho^2)}}, \qquad b' = \frac{b}{\sqrt{2(1 - \rho^2)}}$$

[21]Z. Drezner, "Computation of the Bivariate Normal Integral," *Mathematics of Computation*, 32 (January 1978), 277–79. Note that the presentation here corrects a typo in Drezner's paper.

$A_1 = 0.3253030,$ $A_2 = 0.4211071,$ $A_3 = 0.1334425,$ $A_4 = 0.006374323$

$B_1 = 0.1337764,$ $B_2 = 0.6243247,$ $B_3 = 1.3425378,$ $B_4 = 2.2626645$

In other circumstances where the product of a, b, and ρ is negative or zero, one of the following identities can be used:

$$M(a, b; \rho) = N(a) - M(a, -b; -\rho)$$

$$M(a, b; \rho) = N(b) - M(-a, b; -\rho)$$

$$M(a, b; \rho) = N(a) + N(b) - 1 + M(-a, -b; \rho)$$

In circumstances where the product of a, b, and ρ is positive, the identity

$$M(a, b; \rho) = M(a, 0; \rho_1) + M(b, 0; \rho_2) - \delta$$

can be used in conjunction with the previous results, where

$$\rho_1 = \frac{(\rho a - b)\, \text{sgn}\,(a)}{\sqrt{a^2 - 2\rho ab + b^2}}, \qquad \rho_2 = \frac{(\rho b - a)\, \text{sgn}\,(b)}{\sqrt{a^2 - 2\rho ab + b^2}}$$

$$\delta = \frac{1 - \text{sgn}\,(a)\, \text{sgn}\,(b)}{4}, \qquad \text{sgn}\,(x) = \begin{cases} +1 & \text{when } x \geq 0 \\ -1 & \text{when } x < 0 \end{cases}$$

11 Options on Stock Indices, Currencies, and Futures Contracts

In this chapter we tackle the problem of valuing options on stock indices, currencies, and futures contracts. As a first step, the analysis in Chapter 10 is extended to cover European options on a stock paying a continuous dividend yield. It is then argued that stock indices, currencies, and many futures prices are analogous to stocks paying continuous dividend yields. The basic results for options on a stock paying a continuous dividend yield can therefore be extended to value options on these other assets.

11.1 OPTIONS ON STOCKS PAYING KNOWN DIVIDEND YIELDS

Consider a stock that pays a continuous dividend yield at a constant annualized rate of q. To understand how an option on the stock is valued, we compare the stock to a similar stock that pays no dividends. As explained in Section 10.14, the payment of a dividend causes a stock price to drop by an amount equal to the dividend. It follows that the payment of a continuous dividend yield at rate q causes the growth rate in the stock price to be less than it would otherwise be by an amount q. If, with a continuous dividend yield of q, the stock price grows from S at time t to S_T at time T, it follows that with no dividends it would grow from S at time t to $S_T e^{q(T-t)}$ at time T. Alternatively it would grow from $Se^{-q(T-t)}$ at time t to S_T at time T.

From this we can argue that a European option on a stock with price S paying a continuous dividend yield of q has the same value as the corresponding European option on a stock with price $Se^{-q(T-t)}$ that pays no dividend. This is because the terminal value of the stock price is the same in both cases. To value a European option on a stock paying a known dividend yield, we can therefore reduce the current stock price from S to $Se^{-q(T-t)}$ and use the Black–Scholes formulas. Replacing S by $Se^{-q(T-t)}$ in equations (10.27) and (10.28) we obtain

$$c = Se^{-q(T-t)} N(d_1) - Xe^{-r(T-t)} N(d_2) \qquad (11.1)$$

$$p = Xe^{-r(T-t)} N(-d_2) - Se^{-q(T-t)} N(-d_1) \qquad (11.2)$$

Since

$$\ln\left(\frac{Se^{-q(T-t)}}{X}\right) = \ln\frac{S}{X} - q(T-t)$$

d_1 and d_2 are given by

$$d_1 = \frac{\ln(S/X) + (r - q + \sigma^2/2)(T-t)}{\sigma\sqrt{T-t}}$$

and

$$d_2 = \frac{\ln(S/X) + (r - q - \sigma^2/2)(T-t)}{\sigma\sqrt{T-t}} = d_1 - \sigma\sqrt{(T-t)}$$

These results were first derived by Merton.[1] As discussed in Section 10.14, the word "dividend" should, for the purposes of option valuation, be defined as the reduction in the stock price on the ex-dividend date arising from the dividend. If the dividend yield rate is not constant during the life of the option, equations (11.1) and (11.2) are still true, with q equal to the average annualized dividend yield during the life of the option.

Appendix 11A derives, in a similar way in Section 10.7, the differential equation that must be satisfied by any derivative security whose price, f, depends on a stock paying a continuous dividend yield. Like the basic differential equation, it does not involve any variable affected by risk preferences. The risk-neutral valuation procedure, described in Section 10.8, can therefore be used. In a risk-neutral world, the total return from the stock must be r. The dividends provide a return of q. The expected proportional growth rate in the stock price must therefore be $r - q$. To value a derivative security dependent on a stock paying a continuous

---

[1] See R. Merton, "Theory of Rational Option Pricing," *Bell Journal of Economics and Management Science*, 4 (Spring 1973), 141–83.

dividend we therefore set the expected growth rate of the stock equal to $r - q$ and discount the expected payoff at rate r. This approach can be used to derive equations (11.1) and (11.2).

11.2 OPTIONS ON STOCK INDICES

Several exchanges trade options on stock indices. Some of the indices used track the movement of the U.S. stock market as a whole. Some are based on the performance of a particular sector (e.g., mining, computer technology, and utilities). Some are designed to track the performance of a foreign stock market.

Table 11.1 shows the closing prices of options on February 3, 1992, as they appeared in *The Wall Street Journal* the following day. The S&P 500, NYSE Composite, and Major Market Index were discussed in Section 3.7. The S&P 100 is similar to the S&P 500 but based on only 100 stocks: 92 industrials, 1 utility, 2 transportation companies, and 5 financial institutions.

The acronym LEAPS in Table 11.1 stands for Long-term Equity AnticiPation Securities and was originated by the CBOE. LEAPS are long-term exchange-traded options. They last up to 3 years. Table 11.1 shows quotes for LEAPS on the S&P 500, the S&P 100, and the Major Market Index. The index is divided by 10 for the purposes of quoting the strike price and the option price. One contract is an option on 100 times one-tenth of the index (or 10 times the index). LEAPS on indices have expiration dates in December. LEAPS on the S&P 100 and Major Market Index are American while those on the S&P 500 are European. The CBOE and several other exchanges also trade LEAPS on many individual stocks. These have expirations in January.

Another innovation of the CBOE is CAPS. These trade on the S&P 100 and S&P 500. These are options where the payout is capped so that it cannot exceed $30. The options are European except for the following: a call cap is automatically exercised on a day when the index closes more than $30 above the strike price; a put cap is automatically exercised on a day when the index closes more than $30 below the cap level.

The indices underlying other options in Table 11.1 are as follows:

Institutional Index: 75 stocks most widely held by institutions, weighted by market value

Japan Index: 210 stocks traded on the Tokyo Stock Exchange, weighted by price

Gold/Silver Index: 7 mining stocks, weighted by market value

Value Line Index: Approximately 1,700 U.S. stocks, equally weighted

Utilities Index: 20 electric utility stocks, weighted by market value

Financial News Composite Index: 30 blue-chip stocks, weighted by price

TABLE 11.1 Closing Prices of Stock Index Options, February 3, 1992

INDEX TRADING

Monday, February 3, 1992

OPTIONS CHICAGO BOARD

S&P 100 INDEX-$100 times index

Strike Price	Calls—Last Feb	Calls—Last Mar	Calls—Last Apr	Puts—Last Feb	Puts—Last Mar	Puts—Last Apr
330	....	....	....	3/16	¾	....
335	....	46⅝	....	3/16	⅞	....
340	....	....	....	5/16	1⅛	2 1/16
345	....	....	....	7/16	1½	2⅝
350	32	32⅜	....	½	2	3⅛
355	26⅞	....	....	¾	2½	....
360	21¼	24	....	1	3⅛	5
365	17	18¾	21½	1½	3⅞	5⅝
370	13	15¼	17¾	2¼	5¼	7⅛
375	9⅜	12	....	3⅜	6⅝	8¾
380	5⅞	9½	11¾	5⅛	8½	10⅝
385	3½	6¾	8½	7¾	11	13¼
390	1⅞	4⅝	6½	11¼	14	16⅝
395	⅞	3	4⅝	15¼	17¾	18½
400	⅜	1⅞	3⅜	20⅛	20⅞	22½
405	⅜	1 1/16	....	25⅛	....	....
410	⅛	⅝	1¼	30½	30¾	....

Total call volume 64,120 Total call open int. 337,404
Total put volume 75,560 Total put open int. 444,854
The index: High 381.95; Low 379.08; Close 381.71, +1.70

S&P 500 INDEX-$100 times index

Strike Price	Calls—Last Feb	Calls—Last Mar	Calls—Last Apr	Puts—Last Feb	Puts—Last Mar	Puts—Last Apr
310	97½	....	....	....	....	....
325	....	....	84⅛	....	¼	....
350	....	....	....	....	⅝	....
360	....	....	....	....	⅞	....
365	....	....	....	....	1 5/16	....
370	....	....	....	7/16	....	....
375	....	....	....	....	2⅛	....
380	....	....	....	....	2½	....
385	....	....	....	⅞	3⅛	....
390	....	22¼	....	1½	3⅞	....
395	....	18¼	....	2⅛	4⅞	....
400	11¼	14⅜	....	3¼	6¼	8⅛
405	8⅛	....	....	4⅝	7⅞	9¾
410	5	8¾	....	6⅝	10⅜	12½
415	3¼	6⅜	9	9½	12	14½
420	1⅝	4⅛	....	14	15½	17½
425	⅞	3⅛	....	17⅛	18⅝	....
430	⅜	2	....	22⅞	23	23½
435	¼	1 3/16	....	26	26½	....
440	1/16	¾	....	31½	....	31¼
450	....	....	....	....	....	40¼
460	....	1/16	....	....	51¾	....

Total call volume 3,368 Total call open int. 352,711
Total put volume 14,070 Total put open int. 477,482
The index: High 409.95; Low 407.45; Close 409.53, +0.74

LEAPS-S&P 100 INDEX

Strike Price	Calls—Last Dec 92	Calls—Last Dec 93	Puts—Last Dec 92	Puts—Last Dec 93
30	....	....	....	1 1/16
32½	....	....	¾	1 9/16
35	4½	....	1 5/16	....
37½	2¾	....	2⅛	3⅛
40	1 9/16	....	3⅛	....

Total call volume 40 Total call open int. 31,454
Total put volume 188 Total put open int. 121,169
The index: High 38.20; Low 37.91; Close 38.19, +0.17

Strike Price	Calls—Last Dec 92	Calls—Last Dec 93	Calls—Last Dec 94	Puts—Last Dec 92	Puts—Last Dec 93	Puts—Last Dec 94
35	....	....	....	2 1/16	2⅝	2⅞
37½	....	....	....	....	....	3¾

Total call volume 0 Total call open int. 78,037
Total put volume 2,202 Total put open int. 157,907
The index: High 34.82; Low 34.56; Close 34.72, +0.06

INSTITUTIONAL INDEX

Strike Price	Calls—Last Feb	Calls—Last Mar	Calls—Last Apr	Puts—Last Feb	Puts—Last Mar	Puts—Last Apr
330	....	....	....	....	3/16	....
350	....	....	....	....	7/16	....
375	....	....	....	¼	....	....
380	....	....	....	....	1¼	....
385	....	....	....	9/16	....	....
395	....	....	....	¾	....	....
400	....	....	....	1	....	....
405	....	....	....	....	4	....
410	....	....	....	2	4⅞	....
415	....	....	....	3⅛	6⅜	....
420	8⅛	12⅛	....	4⅛	8⅛	....
425	6	....	12⅞	6	....	12
430	3¾	....	10⅛	8⅞	11¾	14⅝
435	2⅛	....	....	....	16	....
440	1	3⅜	....	....	....	....
445	½	2 5/16	....	....	....	....
450	¼	1⅜	....	....	....	....
455	⅛	15/16	....	29⅞	30	....
490	....	1/16	⅛	....	....	....

Total call volume 1,887 Total call open int. 63,959
Total put volume 4,759 Total put open int. 76,402
The index: High 426.39; Low 423.48; Close 425.69, +0.86

JAPAN INDEX

Strike Price	Calls—Last Feb	Calls—Last Mar	Calls—Last Apr	Puts—Last Feb	Puts—Last Mar	Puts—Last Apr
190	....	....	....	¼	1⅝	....
200	....	....	....	⅞	2¾	....
205	....	....	....	1 7/16	3⅝	....
210	....	....	....	2⅜	5⅛	6⅝
215	....	....	....	3¾	6⅝	....
220	6½	10	....	5⅝	....	9⅞
225	4¼	7⅞	....	8	10¾	....
230	2½	5⅝	7¾	11¼	....	....
245	....	1⅝	2¾	....	....	....
250	3/16	....	1⅞	....	....	....

Total call volume 264 Total call open int. 11,205
Total put volume 563 Total put open int. 20,934
The index: Close 222.42, +1.19

PHILADELPHIA

GOLD/SILVER INDEX

Strike Price	Calls—Last Feb	Calls—Last Mar	Calls—Last Apr	Puts—Last Feb	Puts—Last Mar	Puts—Last Apr
75	....	....	....	....	1⅛	....
80	5¼	....	....	1 7/16	2⅛	....
85	2 5/16	3⅝	....	....	....	....
90	¾	1 15/16	2½	....	....	....

Total call volume 127 Total call open int. 1,298
Total put volume 25 Total put open int. 905
The index: High 84.24; Low 82.62; Close 83.72, +0.19

VALUE LINE INDEX OPTIONS

Strike Price	Calls—Last Feb	Calls—Last Mar	Calls—Last Apr	Puts—Last Feb	Puts—Last Mar	Puts—Last Apr
325	27	29	....	....	....	....
335	....	....	....	1 5/16	....	....
345	9¾	....	....	....	....	....
355	3⅜	6½	....	6⅛	....	....
360	1⅝	4	6⅛	10	....	13

TABLE 11.1 (*cont.*) Closing Prices of Stock Index Options, February 3, 1992

LEAPS-S&P 500 INDEX

Strike Price	Calls—Last Dec 92	Calls—Last Dec 93	Puts—Last Dec 92	Puts—Last Dec 93
30	....	12	....	....
40	....	....	....	3

Total call volume 1 Total call open int. 30,740
Total put volume 10 Total put open int. 94,919
The index: High 41.00; Low 40.75; Close 40.95, +0.07

CAPS-S&P 100 INDEX

Strike Price	Calls—Last Feb 92	Calls—Last Apr 92	Puts—Last Feb 92	Puts—Last Apr 92
360	....	....	1	4½
380	....	10⅛	5¼	....
400	....	3⅛	....	....

Total call volume 55 Total call open int. 956
Total put volume 682 Total put open int. 5,629
The index: High 381.95; Low 379.08; Close 381.91, +1.70

AMERICAN

MAJOR MARKET INDEX

Strike Price	Calls—Last Feb	Calls—Last Mar	Calls—Last Apr	Puts—Last Feb	Puts—Last Mar	Puts—Last Apr
310	....	....	....	....	1 3/16	....
320	....	....	....	9/16	....	....
325	....	24⅛	....	11/16	2¼	....
330	17⅜	....	....	1	3¼	....
335	13⅜	....	....	1⅝	4⅛	....

Total call volume 2,517 Total call open int. 32,478
Total put volume 2,918 Total put open int. 45,459
The index: High 348.16; Low 345.56; Close 347.22, +0.63

LEAPS-MAJOR MARKET INDEX

Strike Price	Calls—Last Dec 92	Calls—Last Dec 93	Calls—Last Dec 94	Puts—Last Dec 92	Puts—Last Dec 93	Puts—Last Dec 94
27½	....	....	....	5/16	....	....
32½	....	....	....	1 1/16	1⅞	....

Total call volume 79 Total call open int. 10,514
Total put volume 29 Total put open int. 5,647
The index: High 352.43; Low 351.14; Close 352.43, +1.02

UTILITIES INDEX

Strike Price	Calls—Last Feb	Calls—Last Mar	Calls—Last Apr	Puts—Last Feb	Puts—Last Mar	Puts—Last Apr
255	1⅜	2⅝	....	....	6½	....
260	....	....	....	9⅛	....	....
265	¼	....	1 3/16	....	....	....

Total call volume 305 Total call open int. 1,704
Total put volume 30 Total put open int. 8,297
The index: High 253.69; Low 251.80; Close 252.28, −1.48

PACIFIC

FINANCIAL NEWS COMPOSITE INDEX

Strike Price	Calls—Last Feb	Calls—Last Mar	Calls—Last Apr	Puts—Last Feb	Puts—Last Mar	Puts—Last Apr
260	....	....	....	½	....	....
265	....	....	....	⅝	....	....
270	....	....	....	1 1/16	....	....
280	4	....	....	3½	6⅛	....
285	2 3/16	....	....	6⅜	....	....
290	¾	....	....	10	....	....
295	....	....	....	14½	....	....

Total call volume 99 Total call open int. 2,071
Total put volume 145 Total put open int. 1,415
The index: High 281.56; Low 279.42; Close 281.16, +1.40

NEW YORK

NYSE INDEX OPTIONS

Total call volume 20 Total call open int. 854
Total put volume 126 Total put open int. 1,783
The index: High 226.79; Low 225.59; Close 226.61, +0.41

The options on the Institutional Index, the Japan Index, and the Financial News Composite Index are European. The rest are American.

Index options are settled in cash rather than by delivering the securities underlying the index. This means that upon exercise of the option, the holder of a call option receives $S - X$ in cash and the writer of the option pays this amount in cash, where S is the value of the index and X is the strike price. Similarly, the holder of a put option receives $X - S$ in cash and the writer of the option pays this amount in cash. Each contract is for \$100 times the value of the index. Thus, from Table 11.1, one April call option contract on the S&P 100 with strike price 370 cost \$1,775 on Februry 3, 1992. The value of the index was 381.71, so that the option was in the money. If the option contract was exercised on February 3, the holder would receive $(381.71 - 370) \times 100 = \$1{,}171$ in cash.

The precise maturity date of stock index options is generally calculated in the same way as for stock options; that is, it is the Saturday following the third Friday in the expiration month.

Portfolio Insurance

Index options can be used by portfolio managers to limit their downside risk. Suppose that the value of an index is S. Consider a manager in charge of a well-diversified portfolio which has a β of 1.0 so that its value mirrors the value of the index. (See Section 3.7 for a discussion of β.) If for each $100S$ dollars in the portfolio, the manager buys one put option contract with exercise price X, the value of the portfolio is protected against the possibility of the index falling below X. For instance, suppose that the manager's portfolio is worth $500,000 and the value of the index is 250. The portfolio is worth 2,000 times the index. The manager can obtain insurance against the value of the portfolio dropping below $480,000 in the next 3 months by buying 20 put option contracts with a strike price of 240. To illustrate how this would work, consider the situation where the index drops to 225 in 3 months. The portfolio will be worth about $450,000. However, the payoff from the options will be $20 \times (\$240 - \$225) \times 100 = \$30,000$, bringing the total value of the portfolio up to the insured value of $480,000.

WHEN THE PORTFOLIO'S BETA IS NOT 1.0

Consider next a portfolio that has a β of 2.0 and is not therefore expected to mirror the index. Suppose that it currently has a value of $1 million. Suppose also that the current risk-free interest rate is 12 percent per annum, the dividend yield on both the portfolio and the index is expected to be 4 percent per annum, and the current value of the index is 250.

Table 11.2 shows the expected relationship between the level of the index and the value of the portfolio in 3 months. To illustrate the sequence of calculations necessary to derive the table, consider what happens when the value of the index in 3 months proves to be 260:

Value of index in 3 months	260
Return from change in index	10/250 or 4% per 3 months
Dividends from index	$0.25 \times 4 = 1\%$ per 3 months
Total return from index	$4 + 1 = 5\%$ per 3 months
Risk-free interest rate	$0.25 \times 12 = 3\%$ per 3 months
Excess return from index over risk-free interest rate	$5 - 3 = 2\%$ per 3 months
Excess return from portfolio over risk-free interest rate	$2 \times 2 = 4\%$ per 3 months
Return from portfolio	$3 + 4 = 7\%$ per 3 months
Dividends from portfolio	$0.25 \times 4 = 1\%$ per 3 months
Increase in value of portfolio	$7 - 1 = 6\%$ per 3 months
Value of portfolio	$1 \times 1.06 = \$1.06$ million

If S is the value of the index, β put contracts should be purchased for each $100S$ dollars in the portfolio. The strike price should be the value the index is expected to have when the value of the portfolio reaches the insured value. Suppose

TABLE 11.2 Relation
between Value of Index and
Value of Portfolio for a
Situation where $\beta = 2$

Value of Index in 3 Months	Value of Portfolio in 3 Months ($ millions)
270	1.14
260	1.06
250	0.98
240	0.90
230	0.82

that the insured value is $0.90 million in our example. Table 11.2 shows that the appropriate strike price for the put options purchased is 240. In this case $100S = \$25,000$ and the value of the portfolio is $1 million. Since $1,000,000/25,000 = 40$ and $\beta = 2$, the correct strategy is to buy 80 put contracts with a strike price of 240.

To illustrate that this gives the required result, consider what happens if the value of the index falls to 230. As shown in Table 11.2, the value of the portfolio is $0.82 million. The put options pay off $(240 - 230) \times 80 \times 100 = \$80,000$ and this is exactly what is necessary to move the total value of the portfolio manager's position up from $0.82 million to the required level of $0.90 million.

VALUATION

When options on stock indices are valued, it is usual to assume that the stock index follows geometric Brownian motion.[2] This means that equations (11.1) and (11.2) can be used to value European call and put option on an index with S equal to the value of the index, σ equal to the volatility of the index, and q equal to the dividend yield on the index.

Equations (11.1) and (11.2) were presented on the assumption that dividends are paid continuously and that the rate at which they are paid is constant. In fact, both of these assumptions can be relaxed. All that is required is that we be able to estimate the dividend yield in advance. The variable q should be set equal to the average annualized dividend yield during the life of the option. For the purposes

---

[2]This presents a theoretical problem since it is inconsistent to assume that both stock prices and a weighted average of stock prices follow geometric Brownian motion. For practical purposes, however, this inconsistency is not really important. Neither individual stocks nor stock indices follow geometric Brownian motion exactly, but for both it is a convenient approximation.

of calculating this average dividend yield, a dividend is considered as occurring during the life of the option if the ex-dividend date is during its life.

In the United States, there is a tendency for dividends to be paid during the first week of February, May, August, and November. At any given time the correct value of q is therefore likely to depend on the life of the option. This is even more true for some foreign indices. For example, in Japan all companies tend to have the same ex-dividend days.

Example 11.1

Consider a European call option on the S&P 500 which is 2 months from maturity. The current value of the index is 310, the exercise price is 300, the risk-free interest rate is 8% per annum, and the volatility of the index is 20% per annum. Dividend yields of 0.2% and 0.3% are expected in the first month and the second month, respectively. In this case, $S = 310$, $X = 300$, $r = 0.08$, $\sigma = 0.2$, and $T - t = 0.1667$. The average dividend yield is 0.5% per 2 months or 3% per annum. Hence $q = 0.03$ and Equation (11.1) gives

$$d_1 = \frac{\ln 1.03333 + 0.07 \times 0.1667}{0.2\sqrt{0.1667}} = 0.5444$$

$$d_2 = \frac{\ln 1.03333 + 0.03 \times 0.1667}{0.2\sqrt{0.1667}} = 0.4628$$

$$N(d_1) = 0.7069, \qquad N(d_2) = 0.6782$$

so that the call price, c, is given by

$$c = 310 \times 0.7069e^{-0.03 \times 0.1667} - 300 \times 0.6782e^{-0.08 \times 0.1667} = 17.28$$

One contract would cost $1,728.

As an alternative to estimating future dividend yields, we can attempt to predict the absolute amounts of the dividend that will be paid. The basic Black–Scholes formula can be used with the initial stock price being reduced by the present value of the dividends. This is the approach recommended in Section 10.14 for a stock paying known dividends. It is difficult to implement for a broadly based stock index since it requires a prediction of the dividends expected on every stock underlying the index.

In some circumstances it is optimal to exercise American put options on an index prior to the exercise date. To a lesser extent this is also true of American call options on an index. American stock index option prices are therefore always worth slightly more than the corresponding European stock index option prices. Numerical procedures and analytic approximations for valuing American index options are discussed in Chapter 14.

11.3 CURRENCY OPTIONS

The Philadelphia Exchange commenced trading in currency options in 1982. Since then the size of the market has grown very rapidly. By 1992 the currencies traded included the Australian dollar, British pound, Canadian dollar, German mark, Japanese yen, French franc, Swiss franc, and European currency unit. For most of these currencies, the Philadelphia Exchange trades both European and American options. It also trades an option German mark–Japanese yen exchange rate.

A significant amount of trading in foreign currency options is also done outside the organized exchanges. Many banks and other financial institutions are prepared to sell or buy foreign currency options that have exercise prices and exercise dates tailored to meet the needs of their corporate clients. For a corporate client wishing to hedge a foreign exchange exposure, foreign currency options are an interesting alternative to forward contracts. A company due to receive sterling at a known time in the future can hedge its risk by buying put options on sterling which mature at that time. This guarantees that the value of the sterling will not be less than the exercise price, while allowing the company to benefit from any favorable exchange-rate movements. Similarly, a company due to pay sterling at a known time in the future can hedge by buying calls on sterling which mature at that time. This guarantees that the cost of the sterling will not be greater than a certain amount while allowing the company to benefit from favorable exchange-rate movements. Whereas a forward contract locks in the exchange rate for a future transaction, an option provides a type of insurance. Of course, insurance is not free. It costs nothing to enter into a forward transaction, while options require a premium to be paid up front.

QUOTES

Table 11.3 shows the closing prices of some of the currency options traded on the Philadelphia Exchange on February 3, 1992. Options are traded with maturity dates in March, June, September, and December for up to 9 months into the future. They are also traded with maturity dates in each of the next 2 months. The precise expiration date is the Saturday preceding the third Wednesday of the month. Table 11.3 shows only the three contracts with the shortest time to maturity.

The sizes of contracts are indicated at the beginning of each section in Table 11.3. The option prices are for the purchase or sale of one unit of a foreign currency with U.S. dollars. For the Japanese yen, the prices are in hundredths of a cent. For the other currencies they are in cents. Thus one call option contract on the British pound with exercise price 185 cents and exercise month March would give the holder the right to purchase £31,250 for U.S. $57,812.50. The indicated price of the contract is 31,250 × 0.0103 or $321.875. The spot exchange rate on sterling is shown as 178.73 cents per pound.

TABLE 11.3 Currency Option
Prices on the Philadelphia
Exchange, February 3, 1992

Option & Underlying	Strike Price	Calls—Last			Puts—Last		
		Feb	Mar	Jun	Feb	Mar	Jun
50,000 Australian Dollars-European Style.							
ADollr.....	76	r	0.42	r	r	r	r
50,000 Australian Dollars-cents per unit.							
ADollr.....	74	1.21	r	r	0.15	r	r
75.18	75	0.50	0.86	r	0.47	0.83	r
31,250 British Pounds-cents per unit.							
BPound ..	170	r	r	r	0.12	0.67	r
178.73 ..	172½	r	r	r	r	1.20	r
178.73 ..	175	r	r	r	0.55	2.00	r
178.73 ..	177½	r	3.88	r	1.08	r	r
178.73 ..	180	1.30	r	r	2.72	4.00	r
178.73 ..	182½	0.81	r	r	r	r	r
178.73 ..	185	0.28	1.03	r	r	8.10	r
178.73 ..	187½	r	r	r	8.85	r	r
178.73 ..	190	0.06	r	r	r	r	r
50,000 Canadian Dollars-European Style.							
CDollar....	83½	r	r	r	r	r	0.80
50,000 Canadian Dollars-cents per unit.							
CDollr.....	83½	r	r	r	r	r	0.80
85.16	84½	r	r	r	0.15	0.43	r
85.16	85½	r	0.43	r	r	r	r
62,500 European Currency Units-cents per unit.							
ECU......	126	r	r	r	r	r	4.95
1,000,000 GermanMark-JapaneseYen cross.							
GMk-JYn .	78	0.79	r	r	0.58	1.02	r
62,500 German Marks-European Style.							
DMark	58	4.18	4.01	r	r	r	r
62.08	60	r	r	r	r	0.50	r
62,500 German Marks-cents per unit.							
DMark	57	r	r	r	r	r	0.55
62.08	58	r	r	r	r	r	0.73
62.08	59	r	r	r	0.04	r	1.09
62.08	60	2.45	r	r	0.10	0.47	1.40
62.08	60½	r	r	s	0.15	0.55	s
62.08	61	1.40	r	r	0.26	0.80	r
62.08	61½	r	1.60	s	0.46	1.02	s
62.08	62	0.88	1.14	r	0.55	1.29	2.49
62.08	62½	0.53	0.90	s	0.72	r	s
62.08	63	0.46	r	1.36	1.27	r	r
62.08	63½	0.30	r	s	r	r	s
62.08	64	0.21	0.50	0.98	r	r	s
62.08	64½	0.15	0.32	s	r	r	s
62.08	66	r	r	0.55	r	r	s
6,250,000 Japanese Yen-100ths of a cent per unit.							
JYen......	76	r	r	r	r	0.15	r
79.59	78	1.70	r	r	0.13	r	r
79.59	78½	r	r	s	0.29	r	r
79.59	79	r	1.00	r	r	0.97	r
79.59	79½	r	r	s	0.59	r	s
79.59	80	0.40	r	r	r	r	r
79.59	81½	0.04	r	s	r	r	s
79.59	82	0.07	r	r	r	r	r
79.59	83	0.03	r	r	r	r	s
62,500 Swiss Francs-cents per unit.							
SFranc....	68	r	r	r	0.18	r	r
69.82	69	r	r	r	0.41	r	r
69.82	70	r	1.16	r	r	r	r
69.82	70½	0.63	r	s	r	r	s
69.82	72	r	0.48	r	r	r	r
69.82	73	r	r	0.99	r	r	r
Total Call Vol	11,884			Call Open Int	353,827		
Total Put Vol	10,112			Put Open Int	441,509		

Reprinted by permission of *The Wall Street Journal*, February 4, 1992. Copyright ©1992, Dow Jones & Company, Inc. All rights reserved worldwide.

VALUATION

To value currency options, we define S as the spot exchange rate, that is, the value of 1 unit of the foreign currency in U.S. dollars. We assume that exchange rates follow the same type of stochastic process as a stock: geometric Brownian motion. We define σ as the volatility of the exchange rate and r_f as the risk-free rate of interest in the foreign country.

As noted in Section 3.8, a foreign currency is analogous to a stock paying a known dividend yield. The owner of foreign currency receives a "dividend yield" equal to the risk-free interest rate, r_f, in the foreign currency. Since we are assuming the same stochastic process for stocks and foreign currencies, the formulas derived in Section 11.1 are correct with q replaced by r_f. The European call price, c, and put price, p, are therefore given by

$$c = Se^{-r_f(T-t)}N(d_1) - Xe^{-r(T-t)}N(d_2) \tag{11.3}$$

$$p = Xe^{-r(T-t)}N(-d_2) - Se^{-r_f(T-t)}N(-d_1) \tag{11.4}$$

where

$$d_1 = \frac{\ln(S/X) + (r - r_f + \sigma^2/2)(T - t)}{\sigma\sqrt{T - t}}$$

and

$$d_2 = \frac{\ln(S/X) + (r - r_f - \sigma^2/2)(T - t)}{\sigma\sqrt{T - t}} = d_1 - \sigma\sqrt{T - t}$$

Both the domestic interest rate, r, and the foreign interest rate, r_f, are assumed to be constant and the same for all maturities. Put and call options on a currency are symmetrical in that a put option to sell X_A units of currency A for X_B units of currency B is the same as a call option to buy X_B units of currency B for X_A units of currency A.

From Equation (3.14) the forward rate, F, for a maturity T is given by

$$F = Se^{(r-r_f)(T-t)}$$

This enables equations (11.3) and (11.4) to be simplified to

$$c = e^{-r(T-t)}[FN(d_1) - XN(d_2)] \tag{11.5}$$

$$p = e^{-r(T-t)}[XN(-d_2) - FN(-d_1)] \tag{11.6}$$

where

$$d_1 = \frac{\ln(F/X) + (\sigma^2/2)(T - t)}{\sigma \sqrt{T - t}}$$

$$d_2 = \frac{\ln(F/X) - (\sigma^2/2)(T - t)}{\sigma \sqrt{T - t}} = d_1 - \sigma \sqrt{T - t}$$

Note that the maturities of the forward contract and the option must be the same for equations (11.5) and (11.6) to apply.

Example 11.2

Consider a 4-month European call option on the British pound. Suppose that the current exchange rate is 1.6000, the exercise price is 1.6000, the risk-free interest rate in the United States is 8% per annum, the risk-free interest rate in Britain is 11% per annum, and the option price is 4.3 cents. In this case $S = 1.6$, $X = 1.6$, $r = 0.08$, $r_f = 0.11$, $T - t = 0.3333$, and $c = 0.043$. The implied volatility can be calculated by trial and error. A volatility of 20% gives an option price of 0.0639; a volatility of 10% gives an option price of 0.0285; and so on. The implied volatility is 14.1%.

In some circumstances, it is optimal to exercise American currency options prior to maturity. Thus American currency options are worth more than their European counterparts. In general, call options on high-interest currencies and put options on low-interest currencies are the most likely to be exercised prior to maturity. This is because a high-interest currency is expected to depreciate relative to the U.S. dollar and a low-interest currency is expected to appreciate relative to the U.S. dollar. Unfortunately, analytic formulas do not exist for the evaluation of American currency options. Numerical procedures and analytic approximations are discussed in Chapter 14.

11.4 FUTURES OPTIONS

Options on futures contracts or futures options are now traded on many different exchanges. They require the delivery of an underlying futures contract when exercised. If a call futures option is exercised, the holder acquires a long position in the underlying futures contract plus a cash amount equal to the current futures price minus the exercise price. If a put futures option is exercised, the holder acquires a short position in the underlying futures contract plus a cash amount equal to the exercise price minus the current futures price.

Example 11.3

Consider an investor who has a September futures call option on 25,000 pounds of copper with an exercise price of 70 cents per pound. Suppose that the current futures price of copper for delivery in September is 80 cents. If the option is exercised, the investor receives $2,500

(= 25,000 × 10 cents) plus a long position in a futures contract to buy 25,000 pounds of copper in September. If desired, the position in the futures contract can be immediately closed out at no cost. This would leave the investor with the $2,500 cash payoff.

Example 11.4

Consider an investor who has a December futures put option on 5,000 bushels of corn with an exercise price of 200 cents per bushel. Suppose that the current futures price of corn for delivery in December is 180 cents. If the option is exercised, the investor receives $1,000 (= 5,000 × 20 cents) plus a short position in a futures contract to sell 5,000 bushels of corn in December. If desired, the position in the futures contract can be closed out immediately at no cost. This would leave the investor with the $1,000 cash payoff.

Futures options are written on both financial futures and commodity futures. Table 11.4 shows the closing prices of a variety of futures options on February 3, 1992. The month shown is the expiration month of the underlying futures contract. The maturity date of the options contract is generally on, or a few days before, the earliest delivery date of the underlying futures contract. For example, the NYSE index futures option and the S&P index futures options both expire on the same day as the underlying futures contract; the IMM currency futures options expire 2 business days prior to the expiration of the futures contract; the CBT T-bond futures option expires on the first Friday preceding by at least 5 business days the end of the month just prior to the futures contract expiration month.

It can be seen from Table 11.4 that the most popular futures options contracts are the T-bond futures option traded on CBOT and the Eurodollar futures options contract traded on the IMM. The open interest on calls and puts totaled over 700,000 contracts. Other futures contracts with open interest greater than 100,000 contracts are on corn (CBOT), sugar (CSCE), crude oil (NYM), gold (CMX), Japanese yen (IMM), Deutschemark (IMM), and Eurodollar (IMM). Futures options are more attractive to investors than options on the underlying asset when it is cheaper or more convenient to deliver futures contracts on the asset rather than the asset itself. In the case of T-bonds, for example, trading options on futures contracts rather than options on the asset ensures that a highly liquid asset will be delivered and that problems associated with accrued interest and the determination of the cheapest-to-deliver bond are avoided. Another advantage is that price information about bond futures is much more readily available than price information about bonds themselves, since the latter can be obtained only by canvassing bond dealers.

BLACK'S MODEL

The analysis in Chapter 3 shows that the futures price, F, of an asset can be related to its spot price by an expression of the form

$$F = Se^{\alpha(T-t)} \tag{11.7}$$

TABLE 11.4 Closing Prices of Futures Options, February 3, 1992

FUTURES OPTIONS PRICES

Monday, February 3, 1992.

AGRICULTURAL

CORN (CBT)
5,000 bu.; cents per bu.

Strike Price	Calls–Settle Mar	May	Jly	Puts–Settle Mar	May	Jly
250	17¾	25	31	⅜	1¼	3½
260	8¾	16½	24½	1¼	3¼	6½
270	2⅞	10½	19½	5¼	7	10¾
280	⅝	6½	15	13	13	16
290	⅛	4	11	22¼	20	22
300	c6	2	8½	62¼	....	29

Est. vol. 12,000;
Fri vol. 6,061 calls; 2,329 puts
Op. int. Fri 91,349 calls; 54,433 puts

SOYBEANS (CBT)
5,000 bu.; cents per bu.

Strike Price	Calls–Settle Mar	May	Jly	Puts–Settle Mar	May	Jly
525	52½	58¾	68¼	¼	1½	4¼
550	28	38	48¾	1⅛	5¼	9½
575	10	22	34	7¾	13½	18
600	2¼	12¼	23	24	29½	32
625	½	7	17	48	48¼	50
650	¼	3¾	12½	72½	....	....

Est. vol. 5,800;
Fri vol. 3,528 calls; 965 puts
Op. int. Fri 56,846 calls; 26,266 puts

SOYBEAN MEAL (CBT)
100 tons; $ per ton

Strike Price	Calls–Settle Mar	May	Jly	Puts–Settle Mar	May	Jly
165	12.20	13.75	16.35	.15	.85	1.65
170	7.50	9.75	12.80	.40	1.65	3.00
175	3.75	6.60	9.95	1.50	3.35	5.00
180	1.60	4.50	7.70	4.25	6.15	7.65
185	.60	2.90	5.95	8.30	9.60	10.75
190	.25	2.00	4.65	13.00	13.55	....

Est. vol. 250;
Fri vol. 66 calls; 92 puts
Op. int. Fri 6,208 calls; 5,659 puts

SOYBEAN OIL (CBT)
60,000 lbs.; cents per lb.

Strike Price	Calls–Settle Mar	May	Jly	Puts–Settle Mar	May	Jly
1800	....	....	....	.030	.150	.270
1850	....	....	....	.100	.250	....
1900	.450	.980	....	.220	.420	.600
1950	.200	.650	....	....	....	....
2000	.100	.600	.950	.870	1.000	1.130
2050	.070	.370	....	....	....	....

Est. vol. 200;
Fri vol. 109 calls; 2 puts
Op. int. Fri 5,502 calls; 2,751 puts

WHEAT (CBT)
5,000 bu.; cents per bu.

Strike Price	Calls–Settle Mar	May	Jly	Puts–Settle Mar	May	Jly
430	20⅞	19	14	3⅛	19	47
440	13½	15¼	11¼	5¾	24¾	....
450	8¼	12¼	....	10¼	32	....
460	5⅜	9¾	8	....	....	....
470	2¾	....	....	....	....	....
480	1	....	4⅞	....	....	....

Est. vol. 7,500;
Fri vol. 3,441 calls; 2,168 puts
Op. int. Fri 50,367 calls; 42,429 puts

Strike Price	Calls–Settle Mar	Apr	May	Puts–Settle Mar	Apr	May
76	3.00	2.22	1.77	0.70	1.85	2.40
78	1.75	1.10	1.10	1.45	2.72	3.72
80	0.75	0.50	0.45	2.45	4.12	5.07
82	0.25	0.20	0.20	3.95	5.82	6.82
84	0.07	0.10	0.10	5.77	6.77	8.67

Est. vol. 231;
Fri vol. 277 calls; 263 puts
Op. int. Fri 3,302 calls; 6,485 puts

CATTLE-LIVE (CME)
40,000 lbs.; cents per lb.

Strike Price	Calls–Settle Feb	Apr	Jun	Puts–Settle Feb	Apr	Jun
72	4.85	5.45	2.20	0.00	0.40	2.07
74	2.92	3.80	1.17	0.07	0.72	3.00
76	1.12	2.25	0.62	0.27	1.20	....
78	0.12	1.17	0.25	1.27	2.10	....
80	0.00	0.42	0.10	3.15	....	....
82	....	0.15	....	....	....	....

Est. vol. 1,931;
Fri vol. 2,513 calls; 4,053 puts
Op. int. Fri 26,414 calls; 36,345 puts

HOGS–LIVE (CME)
40,000 lbs.; cents per lb.

Strike Price	Calls–Settle Feb	Apr	Jun	Puts–Settle Feb	Apr	Jun
38	3.15	2.55	....	0.05	0.40	0.15
40	1.22	1.25	4.45	0.10	1.25	0.30
42	0.15	0.45	2.90	1.02	2.25	0.70
44	0.00	0.12	1.65	2.87	3.90	1.45
46	0.00	0.02	0.85	4.87	5.80	2.65
48	0.00	0.02	0.32	....	....	....

Est. vol. 202;
Fri vol. 201 calls; 81 puts
Op. int. Fri 7,039 calls; 3,249 puts

METALS

COPPER (CMX)
25,000 lbs.; cents per lb.

Strike Price	Calls–Settle Mar	May	Jly	Puts–Settle Mar	May	Jly
94	3.75	4.65	5.35	0.15	1.25	1.90
96	2.05	3.40	4.20	0.45	1.90	2.65
98	0.90	2.25	3.15	1.30	2.75	3.70
100	0.35	1.65	2.25	2.75	4.15	4.75
102	0.10	1.10	1.70	4.50	5.50	6.20
104	0.05	0.70	1.30	6.35	7.20	7.75

Est. vol. 450;
Fri vol. 414 calls; 284 puts
Op. int. Fri 8,825 calls; 8,256 puts

GOLD (CMX)
100 troy ounces; $ per troy ounce

Strike Price	Calls–Settle Mar	Apr	Jun	Puts–Settle Mar	Apr	Jun
340	18.50	19.30	22.70	0.20	1.00	2.40
350	9.20	10.80	15.00	0.80	2.50	4.50
360	2.60	4.80	8.90	4.20	6.40	8.30
370	0.50	2.10	5.10	12.00	13.50	14.40
380	0.20	1.10	3.00	21.70	22.60	22.20
390	0.10	0.60	2.00	31.60	31.80	30.90

Est. vol. 5,800;
Fri vol. 9,153 calls; 1,140 puts
Op. int. Fri 81,423 calls; 20,271 puts

Strike Price	Calls–Settle Feb	Mar	Apr	Puts–Settle Feb	Mar	Apr
6300	0.16	0.68	0.74	1.14	1.65	....
6350	0.09	0.52	0.61	1.57	1.99	....

Est. vol. 14,442;
Fri vol. 11,513 calls; 6,613 puts
Op. int. Fri 117,660 calls; 110,267 puts

CANADIAN DOLLAR (IMM)
100,000 Can.$, cents per Can.$

Strike Price	Calls–Settle Feb	Mar	Apr	Puts–Settle Feb	Mar	Apr
8400	....	1.14	....	0.03	0.27	0.64
8450	0.48	0.80	....	0.12	0.44	0.87
8500	0.18	0.54	....	0.32	0.67	1.17
8550	0.04	0.33	....	0.68	0.96	1.50
8600	0.01	0.19	0.20	1.13	1.31	1.88
8650	.0000	0.10	0.13	1.63	1.71	2.29

Est. vol. 1,489;
Fri vol. 938 calls; 194 puts
Op. int. Fri 11,841 calls; 14,630 puts

BRITISH POUND (IMM)
62,500 pounds; cents per pound

Strike Price	Calls–Settle Feb	Mar	Apr	Puts–Settle Feb	Mar	Apr
1725	5.76	6.62	....	0.10	0.98	2.54
1750	3.46	4.82	4.08	0.30	1.68	3.62
1775	1.62	3.34	2.94	0.94	2.66	....
1800	0.58	2.18	2.08	2.40	4.00	....
1825	0.16	1.36	1.42	4.48	5.66	....
1850	0.04	0.80	0.94	6.86	7.60	....

Est. vol. 1,605;
Fri vol. 915 calls; 1,551 puts
Op. int. Fri 15,380 calls; 14,534 puts

SWISS FRANC (IMM)
125,000 francs; cents per franc

Strike Price	Calls–Settle Feb	Mar	Apr	Puts–Settle Feb	Mar	Apr
6850	1.37	1.92	....	0.14	0.69	1.26
6900	0.99	1.60	1.66	0.26	0.88	1.49
6950	0.65	1.33	1.42	0.42	1.09	....
7000	0.40	1.08	1.21	0.67	1.35	2.03
7050	0.23	0.87	1.02	1.00	1.63	....
7100	0.13	0.70	....	1.40	1.95	....

Est. vol. 2,270;
Fri vol. 1,416 calls; 1,390 puts
Op. int. Fri 20,564 calls; 20,354 puts

U.S. DOLLAR INDEX (FINEX)
500 times index

Strike Price	Calls–Settle Feb	Mar	Apr	Puts–Settle Feb	Mar	Apr
86	1.95	2.45	....	0.06	0.57	0.58
87	1.13	1.80	....	0.22	0.91	....
88	0.51	1.26	2.40	0.60	1.36	....
89	0.19	0.84	....	1.23	1.93	....
90	0.07	0.54	....	2.14	2.62	....
91	0.02	0.33	....	....	3.40	....

Est. vol. 1,950;
Fri vol. 879 calls; 1,452 puts
Op. int. Fri 25,195 calls; 22,605 puts

INTEREST RATE

T-BONDS (CBT)
$100,000; points and 64ths of 100%

Strike Price	Calls–Settle Mar	Jun	Sep	Puts–Settle Mar	Jun	Sep
96	4-35	4-10	4-06	0-03	0-52	1-51
98	2-45	2-53	2-63	0-13	1-31	2-42

TABLE 11.4 (cont.)   Closing Prices of Futures Options, February 3, 1992

WHEAT (KC)
5,000 bu.; cents per bu.

Strike	Calls—Settle			Puts—Settle		
Price	Mar	May	Jly	Mar	May	Jly
430	19	16¼	14	3	....	....
440	12	....	10½	5½	....	....
450	7	....	....	....	....	....
460	....	8¼	....	....	....	....
470	....	....	....	....	....	....
480	....	....	....:	....	....	....

Est. vol. 631;
Fri vol. 97 calls; 78 puts
Op. Int. Fri 3,380 calls; 4,301 puts

COTTON (CTN)
50,000 lbs.; cents per lb.

Strike	Calls—Settle			Puts—Settle		
Price	Mar	May	Jly	Mar	May	Jly
51	....	....	....	.10	.89	....
52	....	....	....	.20	1.00	....
53	.72	....	....	.49	1.20	....
54	.81	....	....	1.08	1.60	2.00
55	.11	2.10	....	1.88	2.00	2.40
56	.05	1.65	3.25	2.82	2.55	2.85

Est. vol. 1,400;
Fri vol. 1,196 calls; 567 puts
Op. Int. Fri 35,190 calls; 15,428 puts

ORANGE JUICE (CTN)
15,000 lbs.; cents per lb.

Strike	Calls—Settle			Puts—Settle		
Price	Mar	May	Jly	Mar	May	Jly
135	8.55	....	....	.15	3.60	6.70
140	4.20	8.50	....	.80	5.00	8.50
145	1.55	5.75	....	2.65	7.40	12.00
150	.50	4.00	....	6.75	10.90	13.85
155	.35	2.60	4.75	11.50	13.65	18.95
160	.25	2.05	3.65	16.50	18.00	20.05

Est. vol. 105;
Fri vol. 49 calls; 155 puts
Op. Int. Fri 3,840 calls; 4,329 puts

COFFEE (CSCE)
37,500 lbs.; cents per lb.

Strike	Calls—Settle			Puts—Settle		
Price	Mar	May	Jly	Mar	May	Jly
65.00	5.56	8.85	11.80	0.06	0.35	0.70
67.50	3.00	6.60	....	0.13	0.60	....
70.00	1.15	4.75	7.40	0.65	1.25	1.30
72.50	0.33	3.20	....	2.33	2.20	....
75.00	0.13	2.08	4.20	4.63	3.58	3.10
77.50	0.09	1.35	....	7.09	5.35	....

Est. vol. 3,927;
Fri vol. 1,355 calls; 1,378 puts
Op. Int. Fri 27,830 calls; 14,419 puts

SUGAR—WORLD (CSCE)
112,000 lbs.; cents per lb.

Strike	Calls—Settle			Puts—Settle		
Price	Mar	Apr	May	Mar	Apr	May
7.00	1.01	1.16	1.19	0.04	0.13	0.16
7.50	0.58	0.81	0.82	0.11	0.28	0.29
8.00	0.25	0.42	0.53	0.26	0.39	0.49
8.50	0.09	0.23	0.33	0.57	0.68	0.78
9.00	0.03	0.12	0.20	1.03	1.09	1.18
9.50	0.01	0.07	0.14	1.51	1.54	1.61

Est. vol. 6,570;
Fri vol. 3,693 calls; 5,047 puts
Op. Int. Fri 80,288 calls; 46,137 puts

SILVER (CMX)
5,000 troy ounces; cts per troy ounce

Strike	Calls—Settle			Puts—Settle		
Price	Mar	Apr	May	Mar	Apr	May
375	42.2	46.0	49.0	0.2	1.3	3.0
400	18.5	25.1	28.0	1.5	5.2	8.0
425	4.5	11.5	15.0	12.5	16.4	20.0
450	1.3	5.5	8.8	34.3	35.5	38.7
475	0.3	2.8	5.3	58.3	57.5	60.5
500	0.2	1.7	3.8	83.0	81.0	83.5

Est. vol. 2,300;
Fri vol. 2,027 calls; 1,236 puts
Op. Int. Fri 66,540 calls; 19,675 puts

OTHER OPTIONS

Final or settlement prices of selected contracts. Volume and open interest are totals in all contract months.

AUSTRALIAN DOLLAR (IMM)
$100,000; $ per $

Strike	Calls—Settle			Puts—Settle		
Price	Feb	Mar	Apr	Feb	Mar	Apr
7500	0.28	0.72	....	0.48	0.92	....

Est. vol. 10; Fri 0 calls, 0 puts
Op. Int. Fri 1,326 calls, 1,486 puts

LUMBER (CME)
160,000 bd .ft., $ per 1,000 bd.ft.

Strike	Calls—Settle			Puts—Settle		
Price	Mar	May	Jly	Mar	May	Jly
245	....	....	....	....	....	....

Est. vol. 64; Fri 2 calls, 74 puts
Op. Int. Fri 83 calls, 451 puts

MAJOR MKT INDEX (CBT)
$500 times premium

Strike	Calls—Settle			Puts—Settle		
Price	Feb	Mar	Apr	Feb	Mar	Apr
345	6.10	....	....	4.50	....	....

Est. vol. 25; Fri 6 calls, 1 puts
Op. Int. Fri 24 calls, 45 puts

MORTGAGE-BACKED (CBT) Cpn 8.0
$100,000; pts. and 64ths of 100%

Strike	Calls—Settle			Puts—Settle		
Price	Feb	Mar	Apr	Feb	Mar	Apr
99	0-36	0-44	....	0-22	....	....

Est. vol. 0; Fri 10 calls, 0 puts
Op. Int. Fri 45 calls, 35 puts

NYSE COMPOSITE INDEX (NYFE)
$500 times premium

Strike	Calls—Settle			Puts—Settle		
Price	Feb	Mar	Apr	Feb	Mar	Apr
226	3.35	5.15	6.60	3.00	4.95	6.05

Est. vol. 46; Fri 45 calls, 4 puts
Op. Int. Fri 795 calls, 711 puts

NIKKEI 225 STOCK AVG. (CME)
$5 times NSA

Strike	Calls—Settle			Puts—Settle		
Price	Feb	Mar	Jun	Feb	Mar	Jun
22000	550	....	....	....	....	800

Est. vol. 8; Fri 44 calls, 10 puts
Op. Int. Fri 204 calls, 290 puts

PLATINUM (NYM)
50 troy oz.; $ per troy oz.

Strike	Calls—Settle			Puts—Settle		
Price	Mar	Apr	May	Mar	Apr	May
360	....	10.00	....	....	13.10	....

Est. vol. 101; Fri 109 calls, 32 puts
Op. Int. Fri n.a. calls, n.a. puts

100	1-15	1-50	2-07	0-47	2-25	3-46
102	0-26	1-04	1-28	1-58	3-43	5-00
104	0-07	0-38	0-62	3-39	5-11	....
106	0-02	0-20	0-42	5-34	6-58	8-08

Est. vol. 90,000;
Fri vol. 50,198 calls; 42,863 puts
Op. Int. Fri 408,241 calls; 305,571 puts

T-NOTES (CBT)
$100,000; points and 64ths of 100%

Strike	Calls—Settle			Puts—Settle		
Price	Mar	Jun	Sep	Mar	Jun	Sep
101	2-21	....	....	0-10	1-09	....
102	1-33	1-43	....	0-20	1-35	....
103	0-54	1-13	....	0-43	2-07	....
104	0-27	0-54	....	1-15	2-44	....
105	0-12	0-37	....	2-00	3-26	....
106	0-05	0-25	....	2-56	4-14	....

Est. vol. 6,500;
Fri vol. 1,532 calls; 6,875 puts
Op. Int. Fri 41,882 calls; 46,379 puts

MUNICIPAL BOND INDEX (CBT)
$100,000; pts. & 64ths of 100%

Strike	Calls—Settle			Puts—Settle		
Price	Mar	Jun	Sep	Mar	Jun	Sep
92	....	....	....	0-14	....	....
93	1-54	1-48	....	0-21	1-01	....
94	1-06	....	....	0-36	1-21	....
95	0-31	0-41	....	0-61	1-54	....
96	0-13	0-24	....	1-41	2-36	....
97	0-07	....	....	2-36	....	....

Est. vol. 500;
Fri vol. 50 calls; 0 puts
Op. Int. Fri 6,961 calls; 6,625 puts

5 YR TREAS NOTES (CBT)
$100,000; points and 64ths of 100%

Strike	Calls—Settle			Puts—Settle		
Price	Mar	Jun	Sep	Mar	Jun	Sep
10350	1-35	....	....	0-05	....	....
10400	1-07	....	....	0-10	1-02	....
10450	0-48	....	....	0-17	....	....
10500	0-29	0-39	....	0-31	1-37	....
10550	0-16	0-28	....	0-49	....	....
10600	0-08	0-21	....	1-09	....	....

Est. vol. 787;
Fri vol. 257 calls; 342 puts
Op. Int. Fri 9,562 calls; 10,714 puts

EURODOLLAR (IMM)
$ million; pts. of 100%

Strike	Calls—Settle			Puts—Settle		
Price	Mar	Jun	Sep	Mar	Jun	Sep
9525	0.58	0.48	0.34	0.02	0.13	0.36
9550	0.34	0.30	0.23	0.03	0.20	0.49
9575	0.14	0.18	0.14	0.08	0.33	0.64
9600	0.05	0.09	0.08	0.24	0.49	0.83
9625	0.01	0.05	0.05	0.45	0.69	....
9650	.0004	0.03	0.03	0.69	....	....

Est. vol. 19,591;
Fri vol. 15,313 calls; 8,703 puts
Op. Int. Fri 370,147 calls; 484,953 puts

LIBOR — 1 Mo. (IMM)
$3 million; pts. of 100%

Strike	Calls—Settle			Puts—Settle		
Price	Feb	Mar	Apr	Feb	Mar	Apr
9525	0.61	0.57	....	.0004	.0004	....
9550	0.36	0.33	0.37	.0004	0.01	0.03
9575	0.13	0.13	0.18	0.02	0.06	0.09
9600	0.01	0.02	0.07	0.15	0.20	0.23
9625	.0004	0.01	0.02	....	0.44	0.42
9650						

Est. vol. 0;
Fri vol. 0 calls; 0 puts
Op. Int. Fri 3,988 calls; 2,400 puts

TABLE 11.4 (cont.) Closing Prices of Futures Options, February 3, 1992

COCOA (CSCE)
10 metric tons; $ per ton

Strike	Calls–Settle			Puts–Settle		
Price	Mar	May	Jly	Mar	May	Jly
1050	95	142	....	2	10	....
1100	47	102	148	4	20	30
1150	13	70	....	20	38	....
1200	4	48	86	61	65	68
1250	2	30	....	109	98	....
1300	1	22	51	158	140	133

Est. vol. 2,260;
Fri vol. 1,407 calls; 260 puts
Op. int. Fri 14,657 calls; 14,670 puts

OIL

CRUDE OIL (NYM)
1,000 bbls.; $ per bbl.

Strike	Calls–Settle			Puts–Settle		
Price	Mar	Apr	May	Mar	Apr	May
17	1.97	....	....	.01	.14	.23
18	1.00	1.46	1.65	.04	.32	.42
19	.21	.80	1.02	.24	.65	.78
20	.04	.37	.55	1.08	1.21	1.30
21	.01	.15	.27	....	1.99	2.03
22	.01	.06	.14	....	2.90	2.88

Est. vol. 20,783;
Fri vol. 7,517 calls; 7,279 puts
Op. int. Fri 122,927 calls; 144,651 puts

HEATING OIL No.2 (NYM)
42,000 gal.; $ per gal.

Strike	Calls–Settle			Puts–Settle		
Price	Mar	Apr	May	Mar	Apr	May
50	.0372	.0384	.0366	.0020	.0077	.0105
52	.0213	.0243	.0243	.0100	.0135	.0180
54	.0093	.0140	.0155	.0060	.0232	.0291
56	.0030	.0075	.0095	.0270	.0366	....
58	.0010	.0035	.0050	.0456	.0525	....
80	.0004	.0020	.0033	.0650	.0709	....

Est. vol. 1,524;
Fri vol. 886 calls; 1,073 puts
Op. int. Fri 22,451 puts

GASOLINE–Unlead (NYM)
42,000 gal.; $ per gal.

Strike	Calls–Settle			Puts–Settle		
Price	Mar	Apr	May	Mar	Apr	May
54	.0394	....	....	.0016	.0030	.0042
56	.0224	.0542	.0631	.0045	.0055	.0075
58	.0110	.0388	.0482	.0131	.0100	.0125
60	.0045	.0259	.0360	.0266	.0170	.0200
62	....	.0165	.0255	.0438	.0276	.0295
64	....	.0100	.0180	.0627	.0410	....

· Est. vol. 3,244;
Fri vol. 2,240 calls; 2,491 puts
Op. int. Fri 25,997 calls; 22,791 puts

LIVESTOCK

CATTLE-FEEDER (CME)
44,000 lbs.; cents per lb.

Strike	Calls–Settle			Puts–Settle		
Price	Mar	Apr	May	Mar	Apr	May
74	4.70	3.47	2.97	0.40	1.10	1.60

PORK BELLIES (CME)
40,000 lbs.; cents per lb.

Strike	Calls–Settle			Puts–Settle		
Price	Mar	May	Jly	Mar	May	Jly
34	1.25	3.32	4.47	1.20	1.90	2.10

Est. vol. 160; Fri 69 calls, 39 puts
Op. int. Fri 5,501 calls, 388 puts

SILVER (CBT)
1,000 troy oz.; cents per troy oz.

Strike	Calls–Settle			Puts–Settle		
Price	Apr	Jun	Aug	Apr	Jun	Aug
425	11.0	21.0	25.0	13.0	....	....

Est. vol. 0; Fri 28 calls, 0 puts
Op. int. Fri 823 calls, 8 puts

SOYBEANS (MCE)
1,000 bu.; cents per bu.

Strike	Calls–Settle			Puts–Settle		
Price	Mar	May	Jly	Mar	May	Jly
575	10	22	34	7¾	13½	18

Est. vol. 110; Fri 79 calls, 8 puts
Op. int. Fri 4,803 calls, 178 puts

WHEAT (MPLS)
5,000 bu.; cents per bu.

Strike	Calls–Settle			Puts–Settle		
Price	Mar	May	Jly	Mar	May	Jly
430	9	....	....	....	....	....

Est. vol. 6; Fri 24 calls, 0 puts
Op. int. Fri 528 calls, 878 puts

WHITE WHEAT (MPLS)
5,000 bu.; cents per bu.

Strike	Calls–Settle			Puts–Settle		
Price	Mar	May	Jly	Mar	May	Jly
480	....	....	....	....	....	....

Est. vol. 5; Fri 7 calls, 0 puts
Op. int. Fri 106 calls, 144 puts

CURRENCY

JAPANESE YEN (IMM)
12,500,000 yen; cents per 100 yen

Strike	Calls–Settle			Puts–Settle		
Price	Feb	Mar	Apr	Feb	Mar	Apr
7800	1.11	1.51	....	0.10	0.51	0.86
7850	0.70	1.20	....	0.19	0.69	1.06
7900	0.39	0.92	1.18	0.38	0.91	1.31
7950	0.21	0.71	0.97	0.70	1.19	1.58
8000	0.11	0.53	0.76	1.10	1.51	1.90
8050	0.06	0.39	0.63	1.55	1.51	2.23

Est. vol. 6,723;
Fri vol. 5,329 calls; 6,852 puts
Op. int. Fri 74,411 calls; 65,603 puts

DEUTSCHEMARK (IMM)
125,000 marks; cents per mark

Strike	Calls–Settle			Puts–Settle		
Price	Feb	Mar	Apr	Feb	Mar	Apr
6100	1.17	1.68	1.52	0.15	0.66	1.31
6150	0.79	1.35	1.28	0.27	0.83	1.56
6200	0.50	1.09	1.07	0.48	1.07	1.84
6250	0.29	0.86	0.89	0.79	1.33	2.16

TREASURY BILLS (IMM)
$1 million; pts. of 100%

Strike	Calls–Settle			Puts–Settle		
Price	Mar	Jun	Sep	Mar	Jun	Sep
9575	0.43	0.39	....	.0004	0.10	....
9600	0.19	0.22	....	0.01	0.19	0.44
9625	0.03	0.13	....	0.10	0.36	0.63
9650	.0004	....	....	....	0.56	....
9675	....	....	....	....	....	....
9700	....	....	....	....	....	....

Est. vol. 30;
Fri vol. 25 calls; 5 puts
Op. int. Fri 2,406 calls; 1,430 puts

EURODOLLAR (LIFFE)
$1 million; pts. of 100%

Strike	Calls–Settle			Puts–Settle		
Price	Mar	Jun	Sep	Mar	Jun	Sep
9525	0.60	0.49	0.36	0.02	0.12	0.36
9550	0.36	0.32	0.24	0.03	0.20	0.49
9575	0.16	0.19	0.14	0.03	0.32	0.64
9600	0.06	0.10	0.08	0.23	0.48	0.83
9625	0.02	0.05	0.04	0.44	0.68	1.04
9650	0.01	0.02	0.02	0.68	0.90	1.47

Est. vol. Mon, 0 calls; 0 puts
Op. int. Fri , 5,180 calls; 5,806 puts

LONG GILT (LIFFE)
£50,000; 64ths of 100%

Strike	Calls–Settle			Puts–Settle		
Price	Mar	Jun	....	Mar	Jun	....
95	2-35	3-30	....	0-03	0-48	....
96	1-41	2-49	....	0-09	1-03	....
97	0-57	2-10	....	0-25	1-28	....
98	0-24	1-41	....	0-56	1-59	....
99	0-09	1-14	....	1-41	2-32	....
100	0-04	0-57	....	2-36	3-11	....

Est. vol. Mon, 2,070 calls; 755 puts
Op. int. Fri, 41,175 calls; 28,077 puts

INDEX

S&P 500 STOCK INDEX (CME)
$500 times premium

Strike	Calls–Settle			Puts–Settle		
Price	Feb	Mar	Jun	Feb	Mar	Jun
400	12.30	15.35	22.60	2.70	5.80	11.75
405	8.70	11.95	19.40	4.10	7.40	13.50
410	5.65	9.00	16.40	6.05	9.40	15.45
415	3.35	6.55	13.70	8.75	11.90	17.70
420	1.80	4.60	11.35	12.20	14.95	20.25
425	0.90	3.05	9.20	16.25	18.35	23.05

Est. vol. 3,777;
Fri vol. 1,888 calls; 3,859 puts
Op. int. Fri 27,912 calls; 62,999 puts

In the case of a financial asset, α is the risk-free rate of interest less the yield on the asset; in the case of commodities, α is the risk-free rate of interest plus the storage costs per dollar per unit time less the convenience yield. It is shown in Appendix 11B that if α is a function of time (but not a function of S or any other stochastic variables) and the volatility of S is constant, the volatility of F is constant and equal to the volatility of S. In these circumstances, Appendix 11B shows that a futures price can be treated in the same way as a security paying a continuous dividend yield at rate r.[3] The European call price, c, and European put price, p, for a futures option are therefore given by equations (11.1) and (11.2) with S replaced by F and $q = r$:

$$c = e^{-r(T-t)}[FN(d_1) - XN(d_2)] \tag{11.8}$$

$$p = e^{-r(T-t)}[XN(-d_2) - FN(-d_1)] \tag{11.9}$$

where

$$d_1 = \frac{\ln(F/X) + (\sigma^2/2)(T-t)}{\sigma\sqrt{T-t}}$$

$$d_2 = \frac{\ln(F/X) - (\sigma^2/2)(T-t)}{\sigma\sqrt{T-t}} = d_1 - \sigma\sqrt{T-t}$$

These results were derived by Black.[4] We have shown that they hold when:

1. The variable, α, in Equation (11.7) is only a function of time.
2. The volatility of the asset underlying the futures contract is constant.

These assumptions are a reasonable approximation for futures contracts on stocks, stock indices, and currencies. They are also reasonable for most commodity futures. However, they are questionable when the asset underlying the futures contract is an interest-rate-dependent security such as a Treasury bond or Treasury bill. Interest-rate derivatives will be discussed in Chapter 15.

Example 11.5

Consider a European put futures option on crude oil. Suppose that the time to maturity is 4 months, the current futures price is $20, the exercise price is $20, the risk-free interest rate is 9% per annum, and the volatility of the futures price is 25% per annum. In this case, $F = 20$, $X = 20$, $r = 0.09$, $T - t = 0.3333$, and $\sigma = 0.25$. Since $\ln(F/X) = 0$,

$$d_1 = \frac{\sigma\sqrt{T-t}}{2} = 0.07216$$

$$d_2 = -\frac{\sigma\sqrt{T-t}}{2} = -0.07216$$

---

[3]In Section 11.1 it was argued that the expected growth rate in the price of a stock, which pays continuous dividends at rate q, is $r - q$ in a risk-neutral world. It follows that the expected growth rate in a futures price in a risk-neutral world should be zero. This is as might be expected. It costs nothing to enter into a futures contract. The expected gain to the holder of a futures contract in a risk-neutral world must therefore be zero.

[4]See F. Black, "The Pricing of Commodity Contracts," *Journal of Financial Economics*, 3 (March 1976), 167–79.

$$N(-d_1) = 0.4712, \qquad N(-d_2) = 0.5288$$

and the put price, p, is given by

$$p = e^{-0.09 \times 0.3333}(20 \times 0.5288 - 20 \times 0.4712) = 1.12$$

or $1.12.

PUT-CALL PARITY

A put-call parity relationship for European futures options can be derived in a similar way as for ordinary options (see Section 7.6). If F_T is the futures price at maturity, a European call plus an amount of cash equal to $Xe^{-r(T-t)}$ has the terminal value

$$\max(F_T - X, 0) + X = \max(F_T, X)$$

An amount of cash equal to $Fe^{-r(T-t)}$ plus a futures contract plus a European put option has terminal value[5]

$$F + (F_T - F) + \max(X - F_T, 0) = \max(F_T, X)$$

Since the two portfolios are equivalent at maturity, it follows that they are worth the same today. The futures contract is worth zero today. Hence

$$c + Xe^{-r(T-t)} = p + Fe^{-r(T-t)} \tag{11.10}$$

Example 11.6

Suppose that the price of a European call option on silver futures for delivery in 6 months is 56 cents per ounce when the exercise price is $8.50. Assume that the silver futures price for delivery in 6 months is currently $8.00 and the risk-free interest rate for an investment which matures in 6 months is 10% per annum. From a rearrangement of equation (11.10), the price of a European put option on silver futures with the same maturity and exercise date as the call option is

$$0.56 + 8.50e^{-0.5 \times 0.1} - 8.00e^{-0.5 \times 0.1} = 1.04$$

EUROPEAN FUTURES OPTIONS VERSUS EUROPEAN SPOT OPTIONS

The futures price of any asset equals its spot price at maturity of the futures contract. It follows that a European futures option is worth the same as the corresponding European option on the underlying asset if the futures contract has the same maturity as the option. This explains why the formulas in equations (11.5)

---

[5]This assumes no difference between forward and futures contracts.

and (11.6) for a European call option on spot foreign exchange in terms of the forward rate are identical to equations (11.8) and (11.9).

AMERICAN FUTURES OPTIONS VERSUS AMERICAN SPOT OPTIONS

Traded futures options are in practice usually American. Assuming that the risk-free rate of interest, r, is positive, there is always some chance that it will be optimal to exercise an American futures option early. American futures options are therefore worth more than their European counterparts. Unfortunately, no analytic formulas are available for valuing American futures options. Numerical procedures and analytic approximations are discussed in Chapter 14.

It is not generally true that an American futures option is worth the same as the corresponding American option on the underlying asset when the futures and options contract have the same maturity. Suppose, for example, that there is a normal market with futures prices consistently higher than spot prices prior to maturity. This is the case with most indices, gold, silver, low-interest currencies, and some commodities. An American call futures option must be worth more than the corresponding American call option on the underlying asset. This is because there are some situations when it will be exercised early, and in these situations, it will provide a greater profit to the holder. Similarly, an American put futures option must be worth less than the corresponding American put option on the underlying asset. If there is an inverted market with futures prices consistently lower than spot prices, as is the case with high-interest currencies and some commodities, the reverse must be true. American call futures options are worth less than the corresponding American call option on the underlying asset, while American put futures options are worth more than the corresponding American put option on the underlying asset.

The differences between American futures options and American asset options that have just been outlined are true when the futures contract expires later than the options contract as well as when the two expire at the same time. In fact, the differences tend to be greater, the later the futures contract expires. They are also true regardless of the assumptions that are made about the processes followed by the spot price and the futures price.

11.5 SUMMARY

The Black–Scholes formula for valuing European options on a non-dividend-paying stock can be extended to cover European options on a stock paying a continuous known dividend yield. In practice stocks do not pay continuous dividend yields. However, a number of other assets upon which options are written can be considered to be analogous to a stock paying a continous dividend yield. In particular,

1. An index is analogous to a stock paying a continuous dividend yield. The dividend yield is the average dividend yield on the stocks comprising the index.

2. A foreign currency is analogous to a stock paying a continuous dividend yield where the dividend yield is the foreign risk-free interest rate.

3. A futures price is analogous to a stock paying a continuous dividend yield where the dividend is equal to the domestic risk-free interest rate.

The extension to Black–Scholes can therefore be used to value European options on indices, foreign currencies, and futures contracts. As we will see in Chapter 14, these analogies are also useful in valuing numerically American options on indices, currencies, and futures contracts.

Index options are settled in cash. Upon exercise of an index call option, the holder receives the amount by which the index exceeds the strike price at close of trading. Similarly, upon exercise of an index put option, the holder receives the amount by which the strike price exceeds the index at close of trading. Index options can be used for portfolio insurance. If the portfolio has a β of 1.0, it is appropriate to buy one put option for each $100S$ dollars in the portfolio where S is the value of the index; otherwise β put options should be purchased for each $100S$ dollars in the portfolio where β is the beta of the portfolio calculated using the capital asset pricing model. The strike price of the put options purchased should reflect the level of insurance required.

Currency options are traded both on organized exchanges and over the counter. They can be used by corporate treasurers to hedge foreign exchange exposure. For example, a U.S. corporate treasurer who knows sterling will be received by his or her company at a certain time in the future can hedge by buying put options that mature at that time. Similarly a U.S. corporate treasurer who knows sterling will be paid at a certain time in the future can hedge by buying call options that mature at that time.

Futures options require the delivery of the underlying futures contract upon exercise. When a call is exercised, the holder acquires a long futures position plus a cash amount equal to the excess of the futures price over the strike price. Similarly when a put is exercised the holder acquires a short position plus a cash amount equal to the excess of the strike price over the futures price. The futures contract that is delivered typically expires slightly later than the option. If we assume that the two expiration dates are the same, a European futures options is worth exactly the same as the corresponding European option on the underlying asset. However, this is not true of American options. If the futures market is normal, an American call futures is worth more than the American call on the underlying asset, while an American put futures is worth less than the American put on the underlying asset. If the futures market is inverted, the reverse is true.

SUGGESTIONS FOR FURTHER READING

General

MERTON, R. C., "Theory of Rational Option Pricing," *Bell Journal of Economics and Management Science*, 4 (Spring 1973), 141–83.

STOLL, H. R., and R. E. WHALEY, "New Option Instruments; Arbitrageable Linkages and Valuation," *Advances in Futures and Options Research,* 1, pt. A (1986), 25–62.

On Options on Stock Indices

CHANCE, D. M., "Empirical Tests of the Pricing of Index Call Options," *Advances in Futures and Options Research*, 1, pt. A (1986), 141–66.

On Options on Currencies

BIGER, N., and J. HULL, "The Valuation of Currency Options," *Financial Management*, 12 (Spring 1983), 24–28.

BODURTHA, J. N., and G. R. COURTADON, "Tests of an American Option Pricing Model on the Foreign Currency Options Market," *Journal of Financial and Quantitative Analysis*, 22 (June 1987), 153–67.

GARMAN, M. B., and S. W. KOHLHAGEN, "Foreign Currency Option Values," *Journal of International Money and Finance*, 2 (December 1983), 231–37.

GRABBE, J. O., "The Pricing of Call and Put Options on Foreign Exchange," *Journal of International Money and Finance*, 2 (December 1983), 239–53.

On Options on Futures

BLACK, F., "The Pricing of Commodity Contracts," *Journal of Financial Economics*, 3 (March 1976), 167–79.

BRENNER, M., G. COURTADON, and M. SUBRAHMANYAM, "Options on the Spot and Options on Futures," *Journal of Finance*, 40 (December 1985), 1303–17.

RAMASWAMY, K., and S. M. SUNDARESAN, "The Valuation of Options on Futures Contracts," *Journal of Finance*, 40 (December 1985), 1319–40.

WOLF, A., "Fundamentals of Commodity Options on Futures," *Journal of Futures Markets*, 2 (1982), 391–408.

QUESTIONS AND PROBLEMS

11.1. A portfolio is currently worth $10 million and has a beta of 1.0. The S&P 100 is currently standing at 250. Explain how a put option on the S&P 100 with a strike of 240 can be used to provide portfolio insurance.

11.2. "Once we know how to value options on a stock paying a continuous dividend yield, we know how to value options on stock indices, currencies, and futures." Explain this statement.

11.3. Explain the difference between a call option on yen and a call option on yen futures.

11.4. Explain how currency options can be used for hedging.

11.5. Calculate the value of a 3-month at-the-money European call option on a stock index when the index is at 250, the risk-free interest rate is 10% per annum, the volatility of the index is 18% per annum, and the dividend yield on the index is 3% per annum.

11.6. Consider an American futures call option where the futures contract and the option contract expire at the same time. Under what circumstances is the futures option worth more than the corresponding American option on the underlying asset?

11.7. Calculate the value of a 5-month European put futures option when the futures price is $19, the strike price is $20, the risk-free interest rate is 12% per annum, and the volatility of the futures price is 20% per annum.

11.8. Suppose that an exchange constructs a stock index which tracks the return, including dividends, on a certain portfolio. Explain how you would value (a) futures contracts; and (b) European options on the index.

11.9. The S&P index currently stands at 348 and has a volatility of 30% per annum. The risk-free rate of interest is 7% per annum and the index provides a dividend yield of 4% per annum. Calculate the value of a 3-month European put with exercise price 350.

11.10. Suppose that the spot price of the Canadian dollar is U.S. $0.75 and that the Canadian dollar–U.S. dollar exchange rate has a volatility of 4% per annum. The risk-free rates of interest in Canada and the United States are 9% and 7% per annum, respectively. Calculate the value of a European call option with exercise price 0.75 and exercise date in 9 months.

11.11. Calculate the implied volatility of soybean futures prices from the following information concerning a European put on soybean futures:

Current futures price	525
Exercise price	525
Risk-free rate	6% per annum
Time to maturity	5 months
Put price	20

11.12. Show that the put-call parity relationship for European index options is

$$c + Xe^{-r(T-t)} = p + Se^{-q(T-t)}$$

where q is the dividend yield on the index, c is the price of a European call option, p is the price of a European put option, and both options have exercise price X and maturity T.

11.13. What is the put-call parity relationship for European currency options?

11.14. Show that if C is the price of an American call with exercise price X and maturity T on a stock paying a dividend yield of q, and P is the price of an American put on the same stock with the same strike price and exercise date:

$$Se^{-q(T-t)} - X < C - P < S - Xe^{-r(T-t)}$$

where S is the stock price, r is the risk-free interest rate, and $r > 0$. (*Hint*: To obtain the first half of the inequality, consider possible values of:

Portfolio A: A European call option plus an amount X invested at the risk-free rate

Portfolio B: An American put option plus $e^{-q(T-t)}$ of stock with dividends being reinvested in the stock

To obtain the second half of the inequality consider possible values of:

Portfolio C: An American call option plus an amount $Xe^{-r(T-t)}$ invested at the risk-free rate

Portfolio D: A European put option plus one stock with dividends being reinvested in the stock)

11.15. Show that if C is the price of an American call option on a futures contract when the exercise price is X and the maturity is T, and P is the price of an American put on the same futures contract with the same exercise price and exercise date,

$$Fe^{-r(T-t)} - X < C - P < F - Xe^{-r(T-t)}$$

where F is the futures price and r is the risk-free rate. Assume that $r > 0$ and that there is no difference between forward and futures contracts. (*Hint*: Use an analogous approach to that indicated for Problem 11.14.)

*11.16. If the price of currency A expressed in terms of the price of currency B follows the process assumed in Section 11.3, what is the process followed by the price of currency B expressed in terms of currency A?

11.17. Would you expect the volatility of a stock index to be greater or less than the volatility of a typical stock? Explain your answer.

11.18. A mutual fund announces that the salaries of its fund managers will depend on the performance of the fund. If the fund loses money, the salaries will be zero. If the fund makes a profit, the salaries will be proportional to the profit. Describe the salary of a fund manager as a derivative security. How is a fund manager motivated to behave with this type of remuneration package?

11.19. Does the cost of portfolio insurance increase or decrease as the beta of the portfolio increases? Explain your answer.

11.20. Suppose that a portfolio is worth $60 million and the S&P 500 is at 300. If the value of the portfolio mirrors the value of the index, what options should be purchased to provide protection against the value of the portfolio falling below $54 million in one year's time?

11.21. Consider again the situation in Problem 11.20. Suppose that the portfolio has a beta of 2.0, that the risk-free interest rate is 5% per annum, and that the dividend yield on both the portfolio and the index is 3% per annum. What options should be purchased to provide protection against the value of the portfolio falling below $54 million?

11.22. Consider
  (a) A call CAP on the S&P 500 (traded on the CBOT) with a strike price of 300; and
  (b) A bull spread created from European calls on the S&P 500 with strike prices of 300 and 330 and the same maturity as the CAP.
  What is the difference between the two? Which is worth more?

*11.23. In Section 11.4 it is noted that a futures price is analogous to a security paying a continuous dividend yield at rate r. By considering a forward contract on the futures price and using results from Chapter 3, show that the forward price equals the futures price when interest rates are constant.

11.24. Can an option on the deutschemark-yen exchange rate be created from two options, one on the dollar-deutschemark exchange rate the other on the dollar-yen exchange rate? Explain your answer.

APPENDIX 11A: DERIVATION OF DIFFERENTIAL EQUATION SATISFIED BY A DERIVATIVE SECURITY DEPENDENT ON A STOCK PAYING A CONTINUOUS DIVIDEND YIELD

Define f as the price of a derivative security dependent on a stock paying a continuous dividend yield at rate q. We suppose that the stock price, S, follows the process

$$dS = \mu S \, dt + \sigma S \, dz$$

where dz is a Wiener process. The variables μ and σ are the the expected proportional growth rate in the stock price and the volatility of the stock price. Since the stock price provides a continuous dividend yield, μ is not equal to the expected return on the stock.

Since f is a function of S and t, it follows from Ito's lemma that

$$df = \left(\frac{\partial f}{\partial S} \mu S + \frac{\partial f}{\partial t} + \frac{1}{2} \frac{\partial^2 f}{\partial S^2} \sigma^2 S^2 \right) dt + \frac{\partial f}{\partial S} \sigma S \, dz$$

Similarly to Section 10.7, we can set up a portfolio consisting of

$$-1: \quad \text{derivative securities}$$

$$+\frac{\partial f}{\partial S}: \quad \text{stock}$$

If Π is the value of the portfolio,

$$\Pi = -f + \frac{\partial f}{\partial S} S \tag{11A.1}$$

and the change, $\Delta \Pi$, in the value of the portfolio in time Δt is as given by Equation (10.19):

$$\Delta \Pi = \left(-\frac{\partial f}{\partial t} - \frac{1}{2}\frac{\partial^2 f}{\partial S^2}\sigma^2 S^2 \right) \Delta t$$

In time Δt the holder of the portfolio earns capital gains equal to $\Delta \Pi$ and dividends equal to

$$qS\frac{\partial f}{\partial S}\Delta t$$

Define ΔW as the change in the wealth of the portfolio holder in time Δt. It follows that

$$\Delta W = \left(-\frac{\partial f}{\partial t} - \frac{1}{2}\frac{\partial^2 f}{\partial S^2}\sigma^2 S^2 + qS\frac{\partial f}{\partial S} \right) \Delta t \tag{11A.2}$$

Since this expression is independent of the Wiener process, the portfolio is instantaneously riskless. Hence

$$\Delta W = r\Pi \Delta t \tag{11A.3}$$

Substituting from Equation (11A.1) and Equation (11A.2) into Equation (11A.3) gives

$$\left(-\frac{\partial f}{\partial t} - \frac{1}{2}\frac{\partial^2 f}{\partial S^2}\sigma^2 S^2 + qS\frac{\partial f}{\partial S} \right) \Delta t = r\left(-f + \frac{\partial f}{\partial S}S \right) \Delta t$$

so that

$$\frac{\partial f}{\partial t} + (r-q)S\frac{\partial f}{\partial S} + \frac{1}{2}\sigma^2 S^2\frac{\partial^2 f}{\partial S^2} = rf \tag{11A.4}$$

This is the differential equation that must be satisfied by f.

APPENDIX 11B: DERIVATION OF DIFFERENTIAL EQUATION SATISFIED BY A DERIVATIVE SECURITY DEPENDENT ON A FUTURES PRICE

Suppose the relationship between the futures price, F, and the spot price, S, is

$$F = Se^{\alpha(T-t)}$$

where α is a function only of time. Suppose further that S follows the process

$$dS = \mu S\,dt + \sigma S\,dz$$

where σ is a constant. It follows from Ito's lemma that the volatility of F is given by σ_F, where

$$\sigma_F F = \sigma S \frac{\partial F}{\partial S} = \sigma S e^{\alpha(T-t)} = \sigma F$$

Hence

$$\sigma_F = \sigma$$

that is, the volatility of F is therefore the same as the volatility of S. This is the first result referred to in Section 11.4.

Suppose that F does in fact follow the process

$$dF = \mu_F F \, dt + \sigma F \, dz \tag{11B.1}$$

where dz is a Wiener process and σ is constant.

Since f is a function of F and t, it follows from Ito's lemma that

$$df = \left(\frac{\partial f}{\partial F} \mu_F F + \frac{\partial f}{\partial t} + \frac{1}{2} \frac{\partial^2 f}{\partial F^2} \sigma^2 F^2 \right) dt + \frac{\partial f}{\partial F} \sigma F \, dz \tag{11B.2}$$

Consider a portfolio consisting of

$$-1: \qquad \text{derivative securities}$$

$$+\frac{\partial f}{\partial F}: \qquad \text{futures contracts}$$

Define Π as the value of the portfolio and let $\Delta \Pi$, Δf, and ΔF be the change in Π, f, and F in time Δt, respectively. Since it costs nothing to enter into a futures contract,

$$\Pi = -f \tag{11B.3}$$

In time Δt, the holder of the portfolio earns capital gains equal to $-\Delta f$ from the derivative security and income of

$$\frac{\partial f}{\partial F} \Delta F$$

from the futures contract. Define ΔW as the total change in wealth of the portfolio holder in time Δt. It follows that

$$\Delta W = \frac{\partial f}{\partial F} \Delta F - \Delta f$$

The discrete versions of equations (11B.1) and (11B.2) are

$$\Delta F = \mu_F F \, \Delta t + \sigma F \, \Delta z$$

and

$$\Delta f = \left(\frac{\partial f}{\partial F} \mu_F F + \frac{\partial f}{\partial t} + \frac{1}{2} \frac{\partial^2 f}{\partial F^2} \sigma^2 F^2 \right) \Delta t + \frac{\partial f}{\partial F} \sigma F \Delta z$$

where $\Delta z = \epsilon \sqrt{\Delta t}$ and ϵ is a random sample from a standardized normal distribution. It follows that

$$\Delta W = \left(-\frac{\partial f}{\partial t} - \frac{1}{2}\frac{\partial^2 f}{\partial F^2}\sigma^2 F^2 \right) \Delta t \tag{11B.4}$$

This is riskless. Hence it must also be true that

$$\Delta W = r\Pi \, \Delta t \tag{11B.5}$$

Substituting for Π from Equation (11B.3), equations (11B.4) and (11B.5) give

$$\left[-\frac{\partial f}{\partial t} - \frac{1}{2}\frac{\partial^2 f}{\partial F^2}\sigma^2 F^2 \right] \Delta t = -rf \, \Delta t$$

Hence

$$\frac{\partial f}{\partial t} + \frac{1}{2}\frac{\partial^2 f}{\partial F^2}\sigma^2 F^2 = rf$$

This has the same form as Equation (11A.4) with q set equal to r. We deduce that a futures price can be treated in the same way as a stock paying a dividend yield at rate r for the purpose of valuing derivative securities.

12 A General Approach to Pricing Derivative Securities

In this chapter we extend the ideas in chapters 10 and 11 to present a general approach to pricing derivative securities. It can be used when there are several underlying variables following continuous-time stochastic processes and does not require these variables to be the prices of traded securities.

The term "traded security" is here used to describe a traded asset that is held solely for investment by a significant number of individuals. Stocks, bonds, gold, and silver are all traded securities. However, interest rates, inflation rates, and most commodities are not. The distinction between underlying variables that are the prices of traded securities and those that are not is an important one in the valuation of derivative securities. We have already seen this in the context of forward and futures contracts in Chapter 3. In general, when an underlying variable is the price of a traded security, the risk-neutral valuation result shows that investor attitudes to risk are irrelevant to the relationship between the price of the derivative security and value of the underlying variable. When the underlying variable is not the price of a traded security, these risk attitudes become important.

12.1 A SINGLE UNDERLYING VARIABLE

In this section we consider the properties of derivative securities dependent on the value of a variable θ that follows a stochastic process

$$\frac{d\theta}{\theta} = m\,dt + s\,dz \qquad (12.1)$$

where dz is a Wiener process. The parameters m and s are the expected growth rate in θ and the volatility of θ, respectively. We assume that they depend only on θ and t. We do not assume that θ is the price of a trade security. It could be something as far removed from financial markets as the temperature in the center of New Orleans.

Suppose that f_1 and f_2 are the prices of two derivative securities dependent only on θ and time. These could be options or other securities that are defined so that they provide a payoff equal to some function of θ at some future time. The processes followed by f_1 and f_2 can be determined from Ito's lemma. We suppose they are

$$\frac{df_1}{f_1} = \mu_1\,dt + \sigma_1\,dz$$

and

$$\frac{df_2}{f_2} = \mu_2\,dt + \sigma_2\,dz$$

where μ_1, μ_2, σ_1, and σ_2 are functions of θ and t, and dz is the same Wiener process as in Equation (12.1). The discrete versions of these processes are

$$\Delta f_1 = \mu_1 f_1\,\Delta t + \sigma_1 f_1\,\Delta z \qquad (12.2)$$

$$\Delta f_2 = \mu_2 f_2\,\Delta t + \sigma_2 f_2\,\Delta z \qquad (12.3)$$

We can eliminate the Δz by forming an instantaneously riskless portfolio consisting of $\sigma_2 f_2$ of the first derivative security and $-\sigma_1 f_1$ of the second derivative security. If Π is the value of the portfolio,

$$\Pi = (\sigma_2 f_2) f_1 - (\sigma_1 f_1) f_2 \qquad (12.4)$$

and

$$\Delta\Pi = \sigma_2 f_2\,\Delta f_1 - \sigma_1 f_1\,\Delta f_2$$

Substituting from equations (12.2) and (12.3), this becomes

$$\Delta\Pi = (\mu_1 \sigma_2 f_1 f_2 - \mu_2 \sigma_1 f_1 f_2)\,\Delta t \qquad (12.5)$$

Since Π is instantaneously riskless, it must earn the risk-free rate. Hence

$$\Delta\Pi = r\Pi\,\Delta t$$

Substituting into this equation from equations (12.4) and (12.5) gives

$$\mu_1 \sigma_2 - \mu_2 \sigma_1 = r\sigma_2 - r\sigma_1$$

or

$$\frac{\mu_1 - r}{\sigma_1} = \frac{\mu_2 - r}{\sigma_2} \tag{12.6}$$

THE MARKET PRICE OF RISK

Define λ as the value of each side in Equation (12.6) so that

$$\frac{\mu_1 - r}{\sigma_1} = \frac{\mu_2 - r}{\sigma_2} = \lambda$$

Dropping subscripts we have shown that if f is the price of a security dependent only on θ and t with

$$df = \mu f dt + \sigma f dz \tag{12.7}$$

then

$$\frac{\mu - r}{\sigma} = \lambda \tag{12.8}$$

The parameter λ is, in general, dependent on both θ and t but it is not dependent on the nature of the derivative security f. It is known as the *market price of risk* of θ.

The variable μ is the expected return from f. Either σ or $-\sigma$ may be the volatility of f. If f is positively related to θ (so that $\partial f / \partial \theta$ is positive), σ is positive and equals the volatility of f. But, if f is negatively related to θ, then σ is negative and the volatility of f equals $-\sigma$.[1]

The market price of risk of θ measures the trade-offs between risk and return that are made for securities dependent on θ. Equation (12.8) can be written

$$\mu - r = \lambda \sigma \tag{12.9}$$

For an intuitive understanding of this equation we note that the variable σ can be loosely interpreted as the quantity of θ-risk present in f. On the right-hand side of the equation we are therefore multiplying the amount of θ-risk by the price of θ-risk. The left-hand side is the expected return in excess of the risk-free interest rate that is required to compensate for this risk. Many readers will notice an analogy between Equation (12.9) and the capital asset pricing model which relates the expected excess return on a stock to its risk.

---

[1]When σ is negative we can change the underlying Wiener process from dz to $dz' = -dz$. The process for f is then

$$df = \mu f dt + (-\sigma) f dz'$$

Example 12.1

Consider a security whose price is positively related to the price of oil, but depends on no other stochastic variables. Suppose it provides an expected return of 12% per annum and has a volatility of 20% per annum. Assume that the risk-free interest rate is 8% per annum. It follows that the market price of risk of oil is

$$\frac{0.12 - 0.08}{0.2} = 0.2$$

Note that oil is not a traded security. Therefore, its market price of risk cannot be calculated from Equation (12.8) by setting μ equal to the expected return from an investment in oil and σ equal to the volatility of oil prices.

THE DIFFERENTIAL EQUATION

Using Ito's lemma, the parameters μ and σ in Equation (12.7) are given by

$$\mu f = \frac{\partial f}{\partial t} + m\theta \frac{\partial f}{\partial \theta} + \frac{1}{2}s^2\theta^2 \frac{\partial^2 f}{\partial \theta^2}$$

and

$$\sigma f = s\theta \frac{\partial f}{\partial \theta}$$

Substituting these into Equation (12.9) we obtain the following differential equation that must be satisfied by f

$$\frac{\partial f}{\partial t} + \theta \frac{\partial f}{\partial \theta}(m - \lambda s) + \frac{1}{2}s^2\theta^2 \frac{\partial^2 f}{\partial \theta^2} = rf \tag{12.10}$$

Equation (12.10) is structurally very similar to the Black–Scholes differential equation (10.20). With S replaced by θ and $q = r - m + \lambda s$ it is the same as the differential equation (11A.4) for valuing a derivative security dependent on an asset providing a known dividend yield, q. This observation leads to a way of extending the risk-neutral valuation result in Section 10.8 so that it applies when the variables underlying a derivative security are not the prices of traded securities.

RISK-NEUTRAL VALUATION

Any solution to Equation (11A.4) for S is a solution to (12.10) for θ and vice versa when the substitution

$$q = r - m + \lambda s$$

is made. We know how to solve (11A.4) using risk-neutral valuation. This involves setting the drift of S equal to $r - q$ and discounting expected payoffs at the risk-free interest rate. It follows that we can solve Equation (12.10) by setting the drift of θ equal to

$$r - (r - m + \lambda s) = m - \lambda s$$

and discounting expected payoffs at the risk-free interest rate.

The approach to valuing a derivative security is therefore to reduce the drift of θ by λs, from m to $m - \lambda s$, and then behave as though the world is risk neutral. Suppose θ is the price of a non-dividend-paying stock. From Equation (12.9),

$$m - r = \lambda s$$

or

$$m - \lambda s = r$$

which shows that changing the expected growth rate of θ to $m - \lambda s$ is the same as setting the return from the security equal to the risk-free rate of interest. This shows that the risk-neutral-valuation result in Chapter 10 is a particular case of the more general result presented here.

Example 12.2

The current price of copper is 80 cents per pound and the risk-free interest rate is 5% per annum. The expected growth rate in the price of copper is 2% per annum and its volatility is 20% per annum. The market price of the risk associated with copper is 0.5. Assume that a contract is traded which allows the holder to receive 1,000 pounds of copper at no cost in 6 months' time. In this case $m = 0.02$, $\lambda = 0.5$, and $s = 0.2$. The expected growth rate of the price of copper in a risk-neutral world is

$$m - \lambda s = 0.02 - 0.5 \times 0.2 = -0.08$$

or -8% per annum. The expected payoff from the contract in a risk-neutral world is therefore

$$800e^{-0.08 \times 0.5} = 768.63$$

Discounting for 6 months at 5% per annum, we estimate the current value of the contract to be 749.65.

12.2 INTEREST RATE RISK

In this section we outline an argument that indicates that the market price of interest rate risk is negative.

The returns on the stocks and bonds in a typical portfolio are negatively related to changes in interest rates. As interest rates decrease, bond and stock prices tend to increase; as interest rates increase, bond and stock prices tend to decrease. Consider adding to the portfolio a security whose price is positively related to one particular interest rate, say, the 1-year interest rate. This security will tend to have the effect of reducing rather than increasing the risk in the portfolio. This is because, as interest rates rise, the fall in the value of the stocks and bonds in the portfolio is offset by an increase in the value of the security; as interest rates fall, the rise in the value of the stocks and bonds in the portfolio is offset by a decrease in the value of the security. This means that the holder of the portfolio will be happy with an expected return from the security which is less than the risk-free interest rate.

Suppose that the interest rate is denoted by θ and follows the process in Equation (12.1), while the security under consideration has a price f and follows the process in Equation (12.7). Since θ and f are positively related, σ is positive. From the argument just given, $\mu < r$. It follows from Equation (12.8) that the market price of risk of the interest rate is negative.

Example 12.3

Consider two securities, both of which are positively dependent on the 90-day interest rate. Suppose that the first one has an expected return of 3% per annum and a volatility of 20% per annum, and the second one has a volatility of 30% per annum. Assume that the instantaneous risk-free rate of interest is 6% per annum. The market price of interest rate risk is, using the return and volatility for the first security,

$$\frac{0.03 - 0.06}{0.2} = -0.15$$

From a rearrangement of Equation (12.9), the expected return from the second security is therefore

$$0.06 - 0.15 \times 0.3 = 0.015$$

or 1.5% per annum.

12.3 SECURITIES DEPENDENT ON SEVERAL STATE VARIABLES

Appendices 12A and 12B extend the results in Section 12.1 to securities whose prices depend on several underlying variables. Appendix 12A provides a version of Ito's lemma that covers functions of several variables. Appendix 12B derives a differential equation that must be satisfied by all derivative securities dependent on a set of state variables that follow Ito processes.

Suppose that n variables, θ_1, θ_2, ..., θ_n, follow stochastic processes of the form

$$\frac{d\theta_i}{\theta_i} = m_i\,dt + s_i\,dz_i \tag{12.11}$$

for $i = 1, 2, \ldots, n$ where the dz_i are Wiener processes. The parameters m_i and s_i are expected growth rates and volatilities and may be functions of the θ_i and time. Appendix 12A shows that the process for the price, f, of a security that is dependent on the θ_i has the form

$$\frac{df}{f} = \mu \, dt + \sum_{i=1}^{n} \sigma_i \, dz_i \tag{12.12}$$

In this equation, μ is the expected return from the security and $\sigma_i \, dz_i$ is the component of the risk of this return attributable to θ_i.

Appendix 12B shows that

$$\mu - r = \sum_{i=1}^{n} \lambda_i \sigma_i \tag{12.13}$$

where λ_i is the market price of risk for θ_i. This equation relates the expected excess return that investors require on the security to the λ_i and σ_i. The term $\lambda_i \sigma_i$ measures the extent to which the return required by investors on a security is affected by the dependence of the security on θ_i. If $\lambda_i \sigma_i = 0$, there is no effect; if $\lambda_i \sigma_i > 0$, investors require a higher return to compensate them for the risk arising from θ_i; if $\lambda_i \sigma_i < 0$, the dependence of the security on θ_i causes investors to require a lower return than would otherwise be the case. The $\lambda_i \sigma_i < 0$ situation occurs when the variable has the effect of reducing rather than increasing the risks in the portfolio of a typical investor.

Example 12.4

A stock price depends on three underlying variables: the price of oil, the price of gold, and the performance of the stock market as a whole. Suppose that the market prices of risk for these variables are 0.2, -0.1, and 0.4, respectively. Suppose also that the σ_i factors in Equation (12.12) corresponding to the three variables have been estimated as 0.05, 0.1, and 0.15, respectively. The excess return on the stock over the risk-free rate is

$$0.2 \times 0.05 - 0.1 \times 0.1 + 0.4 \times 0.15 = 0.06$$

or 6.0% per annum. If variables other than those considered affect f, this result is still true provided that the market price of risk for each of these other variables is zero.

Equation (12.13) is closely related to arbitrage pricing theory, which was developed by Ross in 1976.[2] The continuous-time version of the capital asset pricing model (CAPM) can be regarded as a particular case of the equation. CAPM argues that an investor requires excess returns to compensate for any risk that is correlated to the risk in the return from the stock market as a whole, but requires no excess return for other risks. Risks that are correlated with the return from the stock

[2]See S. A. Ross, "The Arbitrage Theory of Capital Asset Pricing," *Journal of Economic Theory*, 13 (December 1976), 343–62.

market are referred to as systematic; other risks are referred to as nonsystematic. If CAPM is true, λ_i is proportional to the instantaneous correlation between changes in θ_i and the return from the market. When θ_i is instantaneously uncorrelated with the return from the market, λ_i is zero.

RISK–NEUTRAL VALUATION

Our risk-neutral-valuation arguments in Section 12.1 concerning differential equation (12.10) can be extended to cover the more general differential equation (12B.11) in Appendix 12B. A derivative security can always be valued as if the world were risk neutral, provided that the expected growth rate of each underlying variable is assumed to be $m_i - \lambda_i s_i$ rather than m_i. The volatility of the variables and the coefficient of correlation between variables are not changed. This result was first developed by Cox, Ingersoll, and Ross and represents an important extension to the basic risk-neutral valuation argument.[3]

It is worth noting that our extension of the risk-neutral valuation argument is more subtle than it first appears. When θ_i is not a price of a traded security we cannot assert that its expected growth rate in a risk-neutral world would be $m_i - \lambda_i s_i$. We also cannot assert that a derivative security that is dependent on θ_i would have the same value in a risk-neutral world as it has in a risk-averse world. What we can assert is that changing the expected growth rate of θ_i from m_i to $m_i - \lambda_i s_i$ and then behaving as though the world is risk neutral gives the correct values for derivative securities.[4] For convenience, however, we will refer to a world where expected growth rates are changed from m_i to $m_i - \lambda_i s_i$ as a risk-neutral world.

Suppose that a derivative security which is dependent on θ_i $(1 \leq i \leq n)$ provides a payoff at time T. To value the derivative security, it is necessary to set the expected growth rate of each θ_i equal to $m_i - \lambda_i s_i$ while keeping the volatility of each θ_i equal to s_i and the instantaneous correlation between θ_i and θ_k equal to ρ_{ik} for all i and k. The value of the derivative security is then the expected payoff discounted to the present at the risk-free rate of interest. Thus the value f of a security that pays off f_T at time T is given by

$$f = e^{-r(T-t)} \hat{E}(f_T) \tag{12.14}$$

where $\hat{E}$ denotes expected value in a risk-neutral world (i.e., a world where the growth rate in θ_i is $m_i - \lambda_i s_i$).

---

[3] See lemma 4 in J. C. Cox, J. E. Ingersoll, and S. A. Ross, "An Intertemporal General Equilibrium Model of Asset Prices," *Econometrica*, 53 (1985), 363–84.

[4] To illustrate this point, suppose that θ_i is in fact the temperature in the center of New Orleans. The process followed by θ_i clearly does not depend on the risk preferences of human beings!

If r is a stochastic variable, it is treated in the same way as the other θ_i's. The growth rate (or proportional drift rate) in r is, for the purposes of all calculations, reduced by $\lambda_r s_r$, where λ_r is the market price of the risk associated with r and s_r is the volatility of r.[5] To value a derivative security, it is necessary to calculate the expected payoff in a risk-neutral world conditional on the particular path followed by r. This expected payoff is then discounted at the average value of r on the path and the expected value is taken over all possible paths. Thus the value, f, of a derivative security that pays off f_T at time T is given by

$$f = \hat{E}[e^{-\bar{r}(T-t)} f_T] \tag{12.15}$$

where $\bar{r}$ is the average risk-free interest rate between t and T.

Equations (12.14) and (12.15) are true when the payoff, f_T, is some function of the paths followed by the underlying variables as well as when the payoff depends only on the final values of the variables. In the former situation, f is termed a *history-dependent derivative security*. A number of types of history-dependent securities will be discussed in Chapter 16.

Example 12.5

Consider a security that pays off \$100 at time T if the price of stock A is above X_A and the price of stock B is above X_B. We assume that prices of the two stocks are uncorrelated and that no dividends are paid. Using risk-neutral valuation, the value of the security is $100 Q_A Q_B e^{-r(T-t)}$ where Q_A is the probability of stock A's price being above X_A at time T in a risk-neutral world and Q_B is the probability of stock B's price being above X_B at time T in a risk-neutral world. It can be shown that

$$Q_A = N\left[\frac{\ln(S_A/X_A) + (r - \sigma_A^2/2)(T-t)}{\sigma_A \sqrt{T-t}}\right]$$

$$Q_B = N\left[\frac{\ln(S_B/X_B) + (r - \sigma_B^2/2)(T-t)}{\sigma_B \sqrt{T-t}}\right]$$

where S_A and S_B are the current prices of stock A and stock B, and σ_A and σ_B are the volatilities of stock A and stock B.

12.4 DERIVATIVE SECURITIES DEPENDENT ON COMMODITY PRICES

Most commodities are held primarily for consumption and cannot be considered as traded securities. Their market prices of risk are therefore liable to enter into the pricing of derivative securities. Luckily it turns out that we can finesse the

---

[5]As discussed in Section 12.2, λ_r can be expected to be negative, so that the growth rate is higher in a risk-neutral world.

problem of estimating the market price of risk by using futures prices. Consider first the valuation of a European option on a commodity.

Define:

S: Commodity price

F: Futures price for a contract on the commodity that matures at the same time as the option

At the maturity of the option $S = F$. Instead of assuming that the variable underlying the option is the commodity price, we can assume that it is the futures price and use the results in Chapter 11. The same approach can be used when valuing any security dependent on the commodity price that provides a payoff at only one time.

More generally, we can argue that the futures price of a commodity provides information about the process the commodity price would follow in a risk-neutral world. To show this, consider a forward contract with delivery price K. Assuming interest rates are constant, the value of the forward contract, f, is from Equation (12.14) given by

$$f = e^{-r(T-t)} \hat{E}(S_T - K)$$

or

$$f = e^{-r(T-t)} [\hat{E}(S_T) - K]$$

where $\hat{E}$ denotes expected value in a risk-neutral world. The forward or futures price, F, is the value of K that makes f equal to zero in this equation. Hence

$$F = \hat{E}(S_T) \tag{12.16}$$

This shows that the futures price is the expected future spot price in a risk-neutral world at time T. Assume that the expected growth rate of the commodity price is a function only of time, and does not depend on the commodity price itself or any other variables. The expected growth rates of the commodity price at different times in a risk-neutral world can then be estimated from successive futures prices. These expected growth rates together with an estimate of the volatility of the commodity price define the stochastic process followed by the commodity price in a risk-neutral world. In principle, this is all that is necessary to value any derivative security dependent on the commodity price.

Example 12.6

Suppose that the futures prices of live cattle at the end of July 1992 are as follows:

August 1992	62.20
October 1992	60.60
December 1992	62.70

February 1993   63.37
April 1993   64.42
June 1993   64.40

These can be used to estimate the expected growth rate in live cattle prices in a risk-neutral world. For example, the expected growth rate in live cattle prices between October and December 1992 in a risk-neutral world is

$$\ln \frac{62.70}{60.60} = 0.034$$

or 3.4% with continuous compounding. On an annualized basis this is 20.4% per annum.

As a simple illustration of the valuation of a derivative security, consider one that will pay off at the end of July 1993 an amount equal to the average price of live cattle during the preceding year. As an approximation, the average price of live cattle during the previous year in a risk-neutral world is the average of the six futures prices just given (i.e., it is 62.95 cents). Assuming that the risk-free rate of interest is 10% per annum, this means that the value of the derivative security is

$$62.95e^{-0.1} = 56.96 \text{ cents}$$

CONVENIENCE YIELDS

The convenience yield for a commodity was introduced in Chapter 3. It is a measure of the benefits realized from ownership of the physical commodity that are not realized by the holders of a futures contract. If y is the convenience yield and u is the storage cost, the commodity behaves like a traded security that provides a return equal to $y - u$. In a risk-neutral world its growth is therefore

$$r - (y - u) = r - y + u$$

The convenience yield of a commodity can be related to its market price of risk. From the analysis in the first part of this chapter, the expected growth of the commodity price in a risk-neutral world is $m - \lambda s$ where m is its expected growth in the real world, s its volatility, and λ is its market price of risk. It follows that

$$m - \lambda s = r - y + u$$

or

$$y = r + u - m + \lambda s$$

12.5 CROSS-CURRENCY FUTURES AND OPTIONS

An interesting application of the concepts in this chapter is to cross-currency derivative securities. Consider a forward contract maturing at time T on the Nikkei 225 stock average.

Define:

$S(t)$: Nikkei index measured in yen at time t

$Q(t)$: Value of U.S. $1 in yen at time t

   K: Delivery price measured in yen

   q: Dividend yield on the Nikkei index

   r: Domestic (U.S. dollar) risk-free rate

  r_f: Risk-free rate in Japan

   F: Forward price for the contract

If the payoff from the forward contract is

$$S(T) - K \quad \text{yen}$$

the forward price is $S(t)e^{(r_f - q)(T - t)}$ yen, as explained in Section 3.7. This is because $S(t)$ is the yen price of a traded security and, in a risk-neutral world, it grows at an expected rate of $r_f - q$.

A situation which is more difficult to analyze is one where the payoff is defined as

$$S(T) - K \quad \text{dollars}$$

This corresponds to the CME futures contract on the Nikkei Stock Average that was discussed in Section 3.7. It is tempting to argue that the futures price is $S(t)e^{(r - q)(T - t)}$ dollars. This is not correct. The Nikkei index, when regarded as a dollar number, is not the price of a traded security. To make this point clear, suppose the Nikkei index is 23,000; 23,050; and 23,025 on three successive days. We can trade a portfolio which is worth 23,000 yen; 23,050 yen; and 23,025 yen on the three days. But we cannot trade a portfolio which is worth $23,000; $23,050; and $23,025 on the three days.

The problem in valuing a security that pays off $S(T) - K$ dollars is that we do not know the process followed in a risk-neutral world by the variable $S(t)$ dollars. To determine this, we first note that to a Japanese investor the payoff from the security is

$$[S(T) - K]Q(T) \quad \text{yen}$$

The value of the security is

$$e^{-r_f(T - t)}\hat{E}[S(T)Q(T) - KQ(T)] \quad \text{yen}$$

or

$$e^{-r_f(T - t)}\{\hat{E}[S(T)Q(T)] - K\hat{E}[Q(T)]\} \quad \text{yen}$$

The forward price is the value of K that makes this zero. Hence

$$F = \frac{\hat{E}[S(T)Q(T)]}{\hat{E}[Q(T)]} \tag{12.17}$$

We know that, from the point of view of a Japanese investor, $Q(t)$ grows in a risk-neutral world at an expected rate of $r_f - r$ so that

$$\hat{E}[Q(T)] = Q(t)e^{(r_f-r)(T-t)} \tag{12.18}$$

To evaluate $\hat{E}[S(t)Q(t)]$ we note that

$$dS(t) = (r_f - q)S(t)\,dt + \sigma_S S(t)\,dz_S$$

$$dQ(t) = (r_f - r)Q(t)\,dt + \sigma_Q Q(t)\,dz_Q \tag{12.19}$$

where σ_S and σ_Q are the volatilities of S and Q, and dz_S and dz_Q are Wiener processes. From Ito's lemma in Appendix 12A, the process followed by $S(t)Q(t)$ is

$$d[S(t)Q(t)] = [r_f - q + r_f - r + \rho\sigma_S\sigma_Q]S(t)Q(t)dt + S(t)Q(t)[\sigma_S\,dz_S + \sigma_Q\,dz_Q]$$

where ρ is the instantaneous correlation between S and Q. This shows that the variable $S(t)Q(t)$ follows geometric Brownian motion with an expected drift in a risk-neutral world of $2r_f - q - r + \rho\sigma_S\sigma_Q$. Hence

$$\hat{E}[S(T)Q(T)] = S(t)Q(t)e^{(2r_f-q-r+\rho\sigma_S\sigma_Q)(T-t)} \tag{12.20}$$

From equations (12.17), (12.18), and (12.20)[6]

$$F = S(t)e^{(r_f-q+\rho\sigma_S\sigma_Q)(T-t)} \tag{12.21}$$

Using the result in Equation (12.16), the process followed by $S(t)$ dollars in a risk-neutral world has drift $r_f - q + \rho\sigma_S\sigma_Q$. From the point of view of a U.S. investor it behaves like a dollar-denominated stock that pays a continuous dividend yield of q^* where

$$r - q^* = r_f - q + \rho\sigma_S\sigma_Q$$

or

$$q^* = r - r_f + q - \rho\sigma_S\sigma_Q$$

This observation enables us to value other derivative securities dependent on the Nikkei index that pay off in dollars. For example, equations (11.1) and (11.2) show

---

[6]Note that if the exchange rate, $Q(t)$, had been defined as the number of dollars per yen then the sign of ρ would be reversed and Equation (12.21) would be

$$F = S(t)e^{(r_f-q-\rho\sigma_S\sigma_Q)(T-t)}$$

that the prices of a European call paying off $S(T) - X$ dollars at time T is

$$S(t)e^{-q^*(T-t)}N(d_1) - Xe^{-r(T-t)}N(d_2)$$

and the price of a European put paying off $X - S(T)$ dollars at time T is

$$Xe^{-r(T-t)}N(-d_2) - S(t)e^{-q^*(T-t)}N(-d_1)$$

where

$$d_1 = \frac{\ln(S/X) + (r - q^* + \sigma^2/2)(T - t)}{\sigma\sqrt{T-t}}$$

and

$$d_2 = \frac{\ln(S/X) + (r - q^* - \sigma^2/2)(T - t)}{\sigma\sqrt{T-t}} = d_1 - \sigma\sqrt{(T-t)}$$

These options correspond to several foreign index options and warrants that are traded over the counter and on exchanges.

12.6 SUMMARY

In Chapter 3 we showed that there is an important difference between valuing forward or futures contracts on an asset that is held primarily for investment by a significant number of investors, and valuing forward and futures contracts on an asset that is held primarily for consumption. In this chapter we have shown that the same distinction is important for other derivative securities. The value of a derivative security is independent of an underlying variable's growth rate and its market price of risk when the variable is a traded security. However, it is liable to depend on both of these parameters for other variables.

The key result in this chapter is the extension of risk-neutral valuation. We have shown that when valuing derivative securities, we can always behave as though the world is risk neutral providing we also reduce the expected growth rate of each underlying variable by the product of its volatility and its market price of risk. This adjusted growth rate can be loosely referred to as the risk-neutral growth rate.

Luckily, the risk-neutral growth rate can be estimated in many situations without first estimating the actual growth rate and the market price of risk. When a variable is the price of a traded security, its risk-neutral growth rate is the risk-free interest rate less the dividend yield on the security. When a variable is the price of a commodity, estimates of its risk-neutral growth rate can be calculated from futures prices. When a variable is a function of one or more underlying variables that are the prices of traded securities and commodities, Ito's lemma can be used to calculate the risk-neutral growth rate from the risk-neutral growth rates of these underlying variables. We have shown how this last idea can be used to price futures and options contracts on foreign indices.

SUGGESTIONS FOR FURTHER READING

On the General Theory

Cox J. C., J. E. Ingersoll, and S. A. Ross, "An Intertemporal General Equilibrium Model of Asset Prices," *Econometrica*, 53 (1985), 363–84.

Garman, M., "A General Theory of Asset Valuation Under Diffusion State Processes," Working Paper no. 50, University of California, Berkeley, 1976.

Hull, J. C., and A. White, "An Overview of the Pricing of Contingent Claims," *Canadian Journal of Administrative Sciences*, 5 (September 1988), 55–61.

On Complex Derivative Securities

Boyle, P. P., and E. Kirzner, "Pricing Complex Options: Echo Bay Ltd. Gold Purchase Warrants," *Canadian Journal of Administrative Sciences*, 2 (December 1985), 294–306.

Hull, J. C., and A. White, "The Pricing of Options on Assets with Stochastic Volatilities," *Journal of Finance*, 42 (June 1987), 281–300.

Stulz, R. M., "Options on the Minimum or Maximum of Two Risky Assets," *Journal of Financial Economics*, 10 (1982), pp. 161–85.

Wei, J., "Pricing Forward Contracts and Options on Foreign Assets" Working Paper, University of Toronto, 1991.

QUESTIONS AND PROBLEMS

12.1. How is the market price of risk defined for a variable that is not the price of a traded security?

12.2. Suppose that the market price of risk for gold is zero. If the storage costs are 1% per annum and the risk-free rate of interest is 6% per annum, what is the expected growth rate in the price of gold?

12.3. A security's price is positively dependent on two variables: the price of copper and the yen-dollar exchange rate. Suppose that the market price of risk for these variables is 0.5 and 0.1, respectively. If the price of copper were held fixed, the volatility of the security would be 8% per annum; if the yen-dollar exchange rate were held fixed, the volatility of the security would be 12% per annum. The risk-free interest rate is 7% per annum. What is the expected rate of return from the security? If the two variables are uncorrelated with each other, what is the volatility of the security?

12.4. An oil company is set up solely for the purpose of exploring for oil in a certain small area of Texas. Its value depends primarily on two stochastic variables: the price of oil and the quantity of proven oil reserves. Discuss whether the market price of risk for the second of these two variables is likely to be positive, negative, or zero.

*12.5. Deduce the differential equation for a derivative security dependent on the prices of two non-dividend-paying traded securities by forming a riskless portfolio consisting of the derivative security and the two traded securities. Verify that the differential equation is the same as the one given in Equation (12B.11).

12.6. A forward contract provides a payoff of $(S_T - K)$ yen where S_T is the dollar price of gold at time T. Assuming storage costs for gold are zero and defining other variables as necessary, calculate the forward price.

12.7. The convenience yield for soybean oil is 5% per annum, the storage costs are 1% per annum, the risk-free interest rate is 6% per annum, and the expected growth in the price of soybean oil is zero. What is the relationship between the 6-month futures price and the expected price in 6 months?

12.8. The market price of risk for copper is 0.5, the volatility of copper prices is 20% per annum, the spot price is 80 cents per pound, and the 6-month futures price is 75 cents per pound. What is the expected proportional growth rate in copper prices over the next 6 months?

*12.9. Suppose that an interest rate, x, follows the process

$$dx = a(x_0 - x) dt + c \sqrt{x} \, dz$$

where a, x_0, and c are positive constants. Suppose further that the market price of risk for x is λ. How should the drift rate in x be adjusted when the extension of the risk-neutral valuation argument is used to value a derivative security?

12.10. A security pays off $S_1 S_2$ at time T, where S_1 is the level of the S&P 500 index and S_2 is the price of oil. Assume that both S_1 and S_2 follow geometric Brownian motion and are uncorrelated. Defining other variables as necessary, calculate the value of the security at time t.

*12.11. Using risk-neutral valuation arguments, show that an option to exchange one IBM share for two Kodak shares in 6 months has a value that is independent of the level of interest rates.

12.12. Show that a call option on gold should never be exercised early. Should an option which pays of max $(\overline{S} - X, 0)$ ever be exercised early, where $\overline{S}$ is the average of the prices of gold at close of trading on each of the preceding 5 days?

12.13. Consider a commodity with constant volatility, σ. Assuming that the risk-free interest rate is constant, show that in a risk-neutral world:

$$\ln S_T \sim \phi[\ln F - \frac{\sigma^2}{2}(T - t), \sigma\sqrt{T - t}]$$

where S_T is the value of the commodity at time T and F is the futures price for a contract maturing at time T.

*12.14. What is the formula for the price of a European call option on a foreign index when the strike price is in dollars and the index is translated into dollars at a predetermined exchange rate. What difference does it make if the index is translated into dollars at the exchange rate prevailing at the time of exercise?

APPENDIX 12A: A GENERALIZATION OF ITO'S LEMMA

Ito's lemma as presented in Appendix 10A provides the process followed by a function of a single stochastic variable. Here we present a generalized version of Ito's lemma for the process followed by a function of several stochastic variables.

Suppose that a function, f, depends on the n variables $x_1, x_2, \ldots, x_n$ and time, t. Suppose further that x_i follows an Ito process with instantaneous drift a_i and instantaneous variance b_i^2 ($1 \leq i \leq n$), that is,

$$dx_i = a_i \, dt + b_i \, dz_i \qquad (12A.1)$$

where dz_i is a Wiener process ($1 \leq i \leq n$). Each a_i and b_i may be any function of all the x_i's and t. A Taylor series expansion of f gives

$$\Delta f = \sum_i \frac{\partial f}{\partial x_i} \Delta x_i + \frac{\partial f}{\partial t} \Delta t + \frac{1}{2} \sum_i \sum_j \frac{\partial^2 f}{\partial x_i \partial x_j} \Delta x_i \, \Delta x_j + \frac{1}{2} \sum_j \frac{\partial^2 f}{\partial x_i \partial t} \Delta x_i \Delta t + \cdots$$
$$(12A.2)$$

Equation (12A.1) can be discretized as

$$\Delta x_i = a_i \, \Delta t + b_i \epsilon_i \sqrt{\Delta t}$$

where ϵ_i is a random sample from a standardized normal distribution. The correlation, ρ_{ij}, between dz_i and dz_j is defined as the correlation between ϵ_i and ϵ_j. In Appendix 10A, it was argued that

$$\lim_{\Delta t \to 0} \Delta x_i^2 = b_i^2 \, dt$$

Similarly

$$\lim_{\Delta t \to 0} \Delta x_i \, \Delta x_j = b_i b_j \rho_{ij} \, dt$$

As $\Delta t \to 0$, the first three terms in the expansion of Δf in Equation (12A.2) are of order Δt. All other terms are of higher order. Hence

$$df = \sum_i \frac{\partial f}{\partial x_i} dx_i + \frac{\partial f}{\partial t} dt + \frac{1}{2} \sum_i \sum_j \frac{\partial^2 f}{\partial x_i \partial x_j} b_i b_j \rho_{ij} \, dt$$

This is the generalized version of Ito's lemma. Substituting for dx_i from Equation (12A.1) gives

$$df = \left(\sum_i \frac{\partial f}{\partial x_i} a_i + \frac{\partial f}{\partial t} + \frac{1}{2} \sum_i \sum_j \frac{\partial^2 f}{\partial x_i \partial x_j} b_i b_j \rho_{ij} \right) dt + \sum_i \frac{\partial f}{\partial x_i} b_i \, dz_i$$
$$(12A.3)$$

APPENDIX 12B: DERIVATION OF THE GENERAL DIFFERENTIAL EQUATION SATISFIED

Consider a certain derivative security that depends on n state variables and time, t. We make the assumption that there are a total of at least $n + 1$ traded securities (including the one under consideration) whose prices depend on some or all of the n state variables. In practice this is not unduly restrictive. The traded securities may be options with different strike prices and exercise dates, forward contracts, futures contracts, bonds, stocks, and so on. We assume that no dividends or other income is paid by the $n + 1$ traded securities.[7] Other assumptions are similar to those made in Chapter 10:

1. The short selling of securities with full use of proceeds is permitted.
2. There are no transactions costs and taxes.
3. All securities are perfectly divisible.
4. There are no riskless arbitrage opportunities.
5. Security trading is continuous.

The n state variables are assumed to follow continuous-time Ito diffusion processes. We denote the ith state variable by θ_i $(1 \le i \le n)$ and suppose that

$$d\theta_i = m_i \theta_i \, dt + s_i \theta_i \, dz_i. \tag{12B.1}$$

where dz_i is a Wiener process and the parameters, m_i and s_i, are the expected growth rate in θ_i and the volatility of θ_i. The m_i and s_i can be functions of any of the n state variables and time. Other notation used is as follows:

ρ_{ik}: Correlation between dz_i and dz_k $(1 \le i, k \le n)$

f_j: Price of the jth traded security $(1 \le j \le n + 1)$

r: Instantaneous (i.e., very short term) risk-free rate

One of the f_j is the price of the security under consideration. The short-term risk-free rate, r, may be one of the n state variables.

Since the $n + 1$ traded securities are all dependent on the θ_i, it follows from Ito's lemma in Appendix 12A that the f_j follow diffusion processes:

$$df_j = \mu_j f_j \, dt + \sum_i \sigma_{ij} f_j \, dz_i \tag{12B.2}$$

---

[7]This is not restrictive. A non-dividend-paying security can always be obtained from a dividend-paying security by reinvesting the dividends in the security.

where

$$\mu_j f_j = \frac{\partial f_j}{\partial t} + \sum_i \frac{\partial f_j}{\partial \theta_i} m_i \theta_i + \frac{1}{2} \sum_{i,k} \rho_{ik} s_i s_k \theta_i \theta_k \frac{\partial^2 f_j}{\partial \theta_i \, \partial \theta_k} \qquad (12\text{B}.3)$$

$$\sigma_{ij} f_j = \frac{\partial f_j}{\partial \theta_i} s_i \theta_i \qquad (12\text{B}.4)$$

In these equations, μ_j is the instantaneous mean rate of return provided by f_j and σ_{ij} is the component of the instantaneous standard deviation of the rate of return provided by f_j, which may be attributed to the θ_i.

Since there are $n + 1$ traded securities and n Wiener processes in Equation (12B.2), it is possible to form an instantaneously riskless portfolio, Π, using the securities. Define k_j as the amount of the jth security in the portfolio, so that

$$\Pi = \sum_j k_j f_j \qquad (12\text{B}.5)$$

The k_j must be chosen so that the stochastic components of the returns from the securities are eliminated. From Equation (12B.2) this means that

$$\sum_j k_j \sigma_{ij} f_j = 0 \qquad (12\text{B}.6)$$

for $1 \le i \le n$. The return from the portfolio is then given by

$$d\Pi = \sum_j k_j \mu_j f_j \, dt$$

The cost of setting up the portfolio is $\sum_j k_j f_j$. If there are no arbitrage opportunities, the portfolio must earn the risk-free interest rate, so that

$$\sum_j k_j \mu_j f_j = r \sum_j k_j f_j \qquad (12\text{B}.7)$$

or

$$\sum_j k_j f_j (\mu_j - r) = 0 \qquad (12\text{B}.8)$$

Equations (12B.6) and (12B.8) can be regarded as $n + 1$ linear equations in the k_j's. The k_j's are not all zero. From a well-known theorem in linear algebra, the homogeneous equations (12B.6) and (12B.8) can be consistent only if

$$f_j (\mu_j - r) = \sum_i \lambda_i \sigma_{ij} f_j \qquad (12\text{B}.9)$$

or

$$\mu_j - r = \sum_i \lambda_i \sigma_{ij} \qquad (12\text{B}.10)$$

for some λ_i $(1 \leq i \leq n)$, which are dependent only on the state variables and time. This proves the result in Equation (12.13).

Substituting from equations (12B.3) and (12B.4) into Equation (12B.9), we obtain

$$\frac{\partial f_j}{\partial t} + \sum_i \frac{\partial f_j}{\partial \theta_i} m_i \theta_i + \frac{1}{2} \sum_{i,k} \rho_{ik} s_i s_k \theta_i \theta_k \frac{\partial^2 f_j}{\partial \theta_i \, \partial \theta_k} - r f_j = \sum_i \lambda_i \frac{\partial f_j}{\partial \theta_i} s_i \theta_i$$

which reduces to

$$\frac{\partial f_j}{\partial t} + \sum_i \theta_i \frac{\partial f_j}{\partial \theta_i} (m_i - \lambda_i s_i) + \frac{1}{2} \sum_{i,k} \rho_{ik} s_i s_k \theta_i \theta_k \frac{\partial^2 f_j}{\partial \theta_i \, \partial \theta_k} = r f_j$$

Dropping the subscripts to f, we deduce that any security whose price, f, is contingent on the state variables $\theta_i (1 \leq i \leq n)$ and time, t, satisfies the second-order differential equation

$$\frac{\partial f}{\partial t} + \sum_i \theta_i \frac{\partial f}{\partial \theta_i} (m_i - \lambda_i s_i) + \frac{1}{2} \sum_{i,k} \rho_{ik} s_i s_k \theta_i \theta_k \frac{\partial^2 f}{\partial \theta_i \, \partial \theta_k} = r f \qquad (12B.11)$$

The particular derivative security that is obtained is determined by the boundary conditions which are imposed on Equation (12B.11).

13 Hedging Positions in Options and Other Derivative Securities

A financial institution that sells an option or other derivative security over the counter to a client is faced with the problem of hedging its risk. If the option happens be the same as one that is traded on an exchange, the financial institution can neutralize its exposure by buying on the exchange the same option as it has sold. But, when the option has been tailored to the needs of clients and does not correspond to the standardized products traded by exchanges, hedging the exposure is far more difficult. In this chapter we discuss some of the alternative approaches to this problem. The analysis presented is applicable to market makers in options on an exchange as well as to financial institutions.

One reason why an option is difficult to hedge is that the sensitivity of an option's price to the underlying asset's price changes as time passes and as market conditions change. This means that the appropriate position for a hedger to take in the underlying asset also changes. Another reason is that the value of the option is also sensitive to volatility changes. This second dimension of the option's risk cannot be hedged using the underlying asset.

A problem closely related to hedging option positions is that of creating options synthetically. Portfolio managers are sometimes interested in creating a put option on a portfolio synthetically in order to ensure that the value of the portfolio does not fall below a certain level. The last part of this chapter discusses how this can be done—and the reasons why it does not always work well!

13.1 AN EXAMPLE

In this section and the next two sections, we use as an example the position of a financial institution that has sold for $300,000 a European call option on 100,000 shares of a non-dividend-paying stock. We assume that the stock price is $49, the exercise price is $50, the risk-free interest rate is 5 percent per annum, the stock price volatility is 20 percent per annum, the time to maturity is 20 weeks, and the expected return from the stock is 13 percent per annum.[1] With our usual notation this means that

$$S = 49, \qquad X = 50, \qquad r = 0.05,$$

$$\sigma = 0.20, \qquad T - t = 0.3846, \qquad \mu = 0.13$$

Financial institutions do not normally write call options on individual stocks. However, a call option on a stock is a convenient example with which to develop our ideas. The points that will be made apply to other types of options and to other derivative securities.

The Black–Scholes price of the option is about $240,000. The financial institution has therefore sold the option for $60,000 more than its theoretical value and is faced with the problem of hedging its exposure.

13.2 NAKED AND COVERED POSITIONS

One strategy open to the financial institution is to do nothing. This involves what is known as a *naked position*. If the call is exercised, the financial institution will have to buy 100,000 shares at the current market price to cover the call. The cost to the financial institution will then be 100,000 times the amount by which the stock price exceeds the exercise price. For example, if after 20 weeks the stock price is $60, the option costs the financial institution $1,000,000. This is considerably greater than the $300,000 premium received. A naked position works well if the stock price is below $50 at the end of the 20 weeks. The option then costs the financial institution nothing and it makes a profit of $300,000 on the whole deal.

As an alternative to a naked position, the financial institution can adopt a *covered position*. This involves buying 100,000 shares as soon as the option has been sold. If the option is exercised, this strategy works well, but in other

---

[1]It was shown in Chapter 10 that the expected return is irrelevant to the pricing of the option. However, it can have some bearing on the effectiveness of a particular hedging scheme.

circumstances it could prove to be expensive. For example, if the stock price drops to $40, the financial institution loses $900,000 on its stock position. Again, this is considerably greater than the $300,000 charged for the option. Put-call parity shows that the exposure from writing a covered call is the same as the exposure from writing a naked put.

Neither a naked position nor a covered position provides a satisfactory hedge. If the assumptions underlying the Black–Scholes formula hold, the cost to the financial institution should always be $240,000 on average for both approaches.[2] But, on any one occasion the cost is liable to range from zero to over $1,000,000. A perfect hedge would ensure that the cost is always $240,000, that is, that the standard deviation of the cost of writing the option and hedging it is zero.

13.3 A STOP-LOSS STRATEGY

One hedging idea that is sometimes proposed involves what is known as a *stop-loss strategy*.[3] To illustrate the basic idea, consider an institution that has written a European call option with strike price X to buy one unit of a security. The hedging scheme involves buying the security as soon as its price rises above X, and selling as soon as it falls below X. The objective is to hold a naked position whenever the stock price is less than X and a covered position whenever the stock price is greater than X. The scheme is designed to ensure that the institution owns the security at time T if the option closes in the money, and does not own it if the option closes out of the money. It appears to produce payoffs that are the same as the payoffs on the option. In the situation illustrated in Figure 13.1, the stop-loss strategy involves buying the security at time t_1, selling it at time t_2, buying it at time t_3, selling it at time t_4, buying it at time t_5, and delivering it at time T.

As usual, we denote the initial stock price by S. The cost of setting up the hedge initially is S if $S > X$ and zero otherwise. At first blush, the total cost, Q, of writing and hedging the option would appear to be given by

$$Q = \max (S - X, 0) \qquad (13.1)$$

since all purchases and sales subsequent to time zero are made at price X. If this were in fact correct, the hedging scheme would work perfectly in the absence of transactions costs. Furthermore, the cost of hedging the option would always be less than its Black–Scholes price. Thus, one could earn riskless profits by writing options and hedging them.

---

[2]More precisely, the present value of the expected cost is $240,000 for both approaches assuming that appropriate risk-adjusted discount rates are used.

[3]For a fuller analysis of the scheme, see J. Hull and A. White, "Hedging through the Cap: Implications for Market Efficiency, Hedging, and Option Pricing," *International Options Journal*, 4 (1987), 17–22.

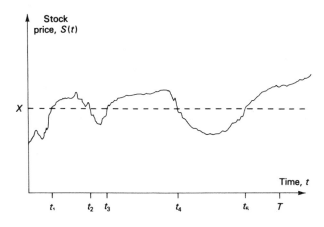

Figure 13.1   A Stop-Loss Strategy

   There are two basic reasons why Equation (13.1) is incorrect. The first is that the cash flows to the hedger occur at different times and must be discounted. The second is that purchases and sales cannot be made at exactly the same price X. This second point is critical. If we assume a risk-neutral world with zero interest rates, we can justify ignoring the time value of money. However, we cannot legitimately assume that both purchases and sales are made at the same price. If markets are efficient, the hedger cannot know whether, when the stock price equals X, it will continue above or below X.

   As a practical matter, purchases will be made at $X + \delta$ and sales will be made at $X - \delta$, for some positive δ. Thus every purchase and subsequent sale includes a cost (apart from transactions costs) of 2δ. A natural response to this on the part of the hedger is to monitor price movements more closely so that δ is reduced. Assuming that stock prices change continuously, δ can be made arbitrarily small by monitoring security prices closely. However, as δ is made smaller, trades tend to occur more frequently. The cost per trade is reduced, but this is offset by the increasing frequency of trading. As $\delta \longrightarrow 0$, the expected number of trades tends to infinity.

   The stop-loss strategy, although superficially attractive, does not work particularly well as a hedging scheme. If the stock price never crosses the line $S(t) = X$, the hedging scheme costs nothing for an out-of-the-money option. But, if the path of the stock price crosses the line $S(t) = X$ many times, the scheme is liable to be quite expensive. Monte Carlo simulation can be used to assess the overall performance of the scheme. Table 13.1 shows the results for the option considered in Section 13.2. It assumes that the stock price is observed at the end of time intervals of length Δt and calculates hedge performance as the ratio of the standard deviation of the cost of hedging the option to the Black–Scholes price of

TABLE 13.1   Performance of Stop-Loss Strategy

Δt (weeks)	5	4	2	1	0.5	0.25
Hedge Performance	1.02	0.93	0.82	0.77	0.76	0.76

the option.[4] Each result is based on 1,000 sample paths for the stock price and has a standard error of about 2 percent. It appears to be impossible to produce a performance measure for the scheme which is below 0.70 regardless of how small Δt is made.

13.4 MORE SOPHISTICATED HEDGING SCHEMES

Most option traders use more sophisticated hedging schemes that those that have been described so far. As a first step, they attempt to make their portfolio immune to small changes in the price of the underlying asset in the next small interval of time. This is known as *delta hedging*. They then look at what are known as *gamma* and *vega*. Gamma is the rate of change of the value of the portfolio with respect to delta; vega is the rate of change of the portfolio with respect to the asset's volatility. By keeping gamma close to zero, a portfolio can be made relatively insensitive to fairly large changes in the price of the asset; by keeping vega close to zero, it can be made insensitive to changes in its volatility. Option traders may also look at *theta* and *rho*. Theta is the rate of change of the option portfolio with the passage of time and rho is its rate of change with respect to the risk-free interest rate.

In the next few sections we will discuss these hedge parameters in more detail.

13.5 DELTA HEDGING

The *delta* of a derivative security, Δ, is defined as the rate of change of its price with respect to the price of the underlying asset.[5] It is the slope of the curve that relates the derivative security price to the underlying asset price.

Consider a call option on a stock. Figure 13.2 shows the relationship between the call price and the underlying stock price. When the stock price corresponds to

---

[4]The precise hedging rule used was as follows. If the stock price moves from below X to above X in a time interval of length Δt, it is bought at the end of the interval. If it moves from above X to below X in the time interval, it is sold at the end of the interval. Otherwise, no action is taken.

[5]More formally, $\Delta = \partial f / \partial S$, where f is the price of the derivative security and S is the price of the underlying asset.

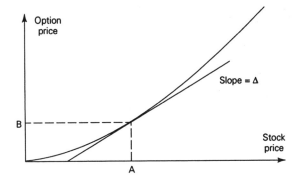

Figure 13.2   Calculation of Delta

point A, the option price corresponds to point B and the Δ of the call is the slope of the line indicated. As an approximation,

$$\Delta = \frac{\Delta c}{\Delta S}$$

where ΔS is a small change in the stock price and Δc is the corresponding change in the call price.

Assume the delta of the call option is 0.6. This means that when the stock price changes by a small amount, the option price changes by about 60 percent of that amount. Suppose that the option price is $10 and the stock price is $100. Imagine an investor who has sold 20 option contracts, that is, options to buy 2,000 shares. The investor's position could be hedged by buying $0.6 \times 2,000 = 1,200$ shares. The gain (loss) on the option position would tend to be offset by the loss (gain) on the stock position. For example, if the stock price goes up by $1 (producing a gain of $1,200 on the shares purchased), the option price will tend to go up by $0.6 \times \$1 = \$0.60$ (producing a loss of $1,200 on the options written); if the stock price goes down by $1 (producing a loss of $1,200 on the shares purchased), the option price will tend to go down by $0.60 (producing a gain of $1,200 on the options written).

In this example, the delta of the investor's option position is $0.6 \times (-2,000) = -1,200$. In other words, the investor loses $1,200\Delta S$ on the options when the stock price increases by ΔS. The delta of the stock is by definition 1.0 and the long position in 1,200 shares has a delta of $+1,200$. The delta of the investor's hedged position is therefore zero. The delta of the asset position offsets the delta of the option position. A position with a delta of zero is referred to as being *delta neutral*.

It is important to realize that the investor's position only remains delta hedged (or delta neutral) for a relatively short period of time. This is because delta changes with both changes in the stock price and the passage of time. In practice when delta hedging is implemented, the hedge has to be adjusted periodically. This is known as *rebalancing*. In our example, at the end of 3 days the stock price might increase to $110. As indicated by Figure 13.2, an increase in the stock price leads to an increase in delta. Suppose that delta rises from 0.60 to 0.65. This would mean that an extra $0.05 \times 2,000 = 100$ shares would have to be purchased to maintain the hedge. Hedging schemes such as this that involve frequent adjustments are known as *dynamic hedging schemes*.

Delta is closely related to the Black–Scholes analysis. Black and Scholes showed that it is possible to set up a riskless portfolio consisting of a position in a derivative security on a stock and a position in the stock. Expressed in terms of Δ, their portfolio was

$$-1 : \quad \text{Derivative security}$$

$$+\Delta : \quad \text{Shares of the stock}$$

Using our new terminology, we can say that Black and Scholes valued options by setting up a delta-neutral position and arguing that the return on the position in a short period of time equals the risk-free interest rate.

DELTA OF FORWARD CONTRACTS

Equation (3.6) shows that when the price of a non-dividend-paying stock changes by ΔS, with all else remaining the same, the value of a forward contract on the stock also changes by ΔS. The delta of a forward contract on one share of a non-dividend-paying stock is therefore 1.0. This means that a short forward contract on one share can be hedged by purchasing one share, while a long forward contract on one share can be hedged by shorting one share. These two hedging schemes are "hedge and forget" schemes in the sense that no changes need to be made to the position in the stock during the life of the contract. As already mentioned, when an option or other more complicated derivative security is being hedged, delta hedging is not a hedge-and-forget scheme. If the hedge is to be effective, the position in the stock must be rebalanced frequently.

DELTAS OF EUROPEAN CALLS AND PUTS

For a European call option on a non-dividend-paying stock, it can be shown that

$$\Delta = N(d_1)$$

where d_1 is defined in Equation 10.27. Using delta hedging for a short position in a European call option therefore involves keeping a long position of $N(d_1)$ shares at any given time. Similarly, using delta hedging for a long position in a European call option involves maintaining a short position of $N(d_1)$ shares at any given time.

For a European put option on a non-dividend-paying stock, delta is given by

$$\Delta = N(d_1) - 1$$

where d_1 is defined as in Equation (10.28). This is negative, which means that a long position in a put option should be hedged with a continuously changing long position in the underlying stock, and a short position in a put option should be hedged with a continuously changing short position in the underlying stock. The variation of the delta of a call option and a put option with the stock price is shown in Figure 13.3. Figure 13.4 shows the variation in delta with time to maturity for an at-the-money, in-the-money, and out-of-the-money option.

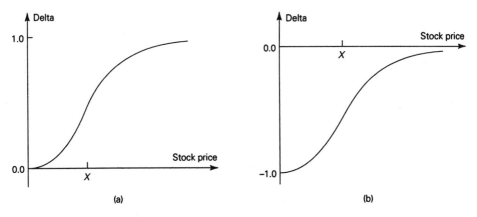

Figure 13.3 Variation of Delta with the Stock Price for (a) a Call Option and (b) a Put Option on a Non-Dividend-Paying Stock

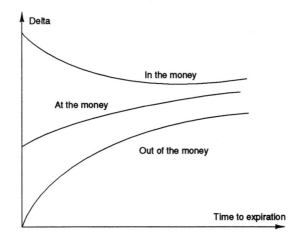

Figure 13.4 Variation of Delta with the Time to Maturity for a Call Option

Tables 13.2 and 13.3 provide two simulations of the operation of delta hedging for the example in Section 13.2. The hedge is assumed to be adjusted or rebalanced weekly. In Table 13.2, delta is initially calculated as 0.522. This means that as soon as the option is written, $2,557,800 must be borrowed to buy 52,200

TABLE 13.2   Simulation of Delta Hedging; Option Closes in the Money; Cost of Hedging = $263,400

Week	Stock Price	Delta	Shares Purchased	Cost of Shares Purchased (thousands of dollars)	Cumulative Cost (incl. interest in thousands of dollars)	Interest Cost (thousands of dollars)
0	49	0.522	52,200	2,557.8	2,557.8	2.5
1	$48\frac{1}{8}$	0.458	(6,400)	(308.0)	2,252.3	2.2
2	$47\frac{3}{8}$	0.400	(5,800)	(274.8)	1,979.7	1.9
3	$50\frac{1}{4}$	0.596	19,600	984.9	2,966.5	2.9
4	$51\frac{3}{4}$	0.693	9,700	502.0	3,471.3	3.3
5	$53\frac{1}{8}$	0.774	8,100	430.3	3,904.9	3.8
6	53	0.771	(300)	(15.9)	3,892.8	3.7
7	$51\frac{7}{8}$	0.706	(6,500)	(337.2)	3,559.3	3.4
8	$51\frac{3}{8}$	0.674	(3,200)	(164.4)	3,398.4	3.3
9	53	0.787	11,300	598.9	4,000.5	3.8
10	$49\frac{7}{8}$	0.550	(23,700)	(1,182.0)	2,822.3	2.7
11	$48\frac{1}{2}$	0.413	(13,700)	(664.4)	2,160.6	2.1
12	$49\frac{7}{8}$	0.542	12,900	643.4	2,806.1	2.7
13	$50\frac{3}{8}$	0.591	4,900	246.8	3,055.6	2.9
14	$52\frac{1}{8}$	0.768	17,700	922.6	3,981.2	3.8
15	$51\frac{7}{8}$	0.759	(900)	(46.7)	3,938.3	3.8
16	$52\frac{7}{8}$	0.865	10,600	560.5	4,502.6	4.3
17	$54\frac{7}{8}$	0.978	11,300	620.1	5,127.0	4.9
18	$54\frac{5}{8}$	0.990	1,200	65.6	5,197.5	5.0
19	$55\frac{7}{8}$	1.000	1,000	55.9	5,258.3	5.1
20	$57\frac{1}{4}$	1.000	0	0.0	5,263.4	

TABLE 13.3 Simulation of Delta Hedging; Option
Closes out-of-the-Money; Cost of Hedging = $256,600

Week	Stock Price	Delta	Shares Purchased	Cost of Shares Purchased (thousands of dollars)	Cumulative Cost (incl. interest in thousands of dollars)	Interest Cost (thousands of dollars)
0	49	0.522	52,200	2,557.8	2,557.8	2.5
1	$49\frac{3}{4}$	0.568	4,600	228.9	2,789.1	2.7
2	52	0.705	13,700	712.4	3,504.2	3.4
3	50	0.579	(12,600)	(630.0)	2,877.6	2.8
4	$48\frac{3}{8}$	0.459	(12,000)	(580.5)	2,299.8	2.2
5	$48\frac{1}{4}$	0.443	(1,600)	(77.2)	2,224.8	2.1
6	$48\frac{3}{4}$	0.475	3,200	156.0	2,383.0	2.3
7	$49\frac{5}{8}$	0.540	6,500	322.6	2,707.8	2.6
8	$48\frac{1}{4}$	0.420	(12,000)	(579.0)	2,131.4	2.0
9	$48\frac{1}{4}$	0.410	(1,000)	(48.2)	2,085.2	2.0
10	$51\frac{1}{8}$	0.658	24,800	1,267.9	3,355.1	3.2
11	$51\frac{1}{2}$	0.692	3,400	175.1	3,533.5	3.4
12	$49\frac{7}{8}$	0.542	(15,000)	(748.1)	2,788.7	2.7
13	$49\frac{7}{8}$	0.538	(400)	(20.0)	2,771.5	2.7
14	$48\frac{3}{4}$	0.400	(13,800)	(672.7)	2,101.4	2.0
15	$47\frac{1}{2}$	0.236	(16,400)	(779.0)	1,324.4	1.3
16	48	0.261	2,500	120.0	1,445.7	1.4
17	$46\frac{1}{4}$	0.062	(19,900)	(920.4)	526.7	0.5
18	$48\frac{1}{8}$	0.183	12,100	582.3	1,109.5	1.1
19	$46\frac{5}{8}$	0.007	(17,600)	(820.6)	290.0	0.3
20	$48\frac{1}{8}$	0.000	(700)	(33.7)	256.6	

shares at a price of $49. An interest cost of $2,500 is incurred in the first week. The stock price falls by the end of the first week to $48\frac{1}{8}$. This reduces the delta to 0.458, and 6,400 of shares are sold to maintain the hedge. This realizes $308,000 in cash and the cumulative borrowings at the end of week 1 are reduced to $2,252,300. During the second week the stock price reduces to $47\frac{3}{8}$ and delta declines again; and so on. Toward the end of the life of the option it becomes apparent that the option will be exercised and delta approaches 1.0. By week 20, therefore, the hedger has a fully covered position. The hedger receives $5,000,000 for the stock held, so that the total cost of writing the option and hedging it is $263,400.

Table 13.3 illustrates an alternative sequence of events which are such that the option closes out of the money. As it becomes progressively clearer that the option will not be exercised, delta approaches zero. By week 20 the hedger has a naked position and has incurred costs totaling $256,600.

In tables 13.2 and 13.3 the costs of hedging the option, when discounted to the beginning of the period, are close to but not exactly the same as the Black–Scholes price of $240,000. If the hedging scheme worked perfectly, the cost of hedging would, after discounting, be exactly $240,000 on every simulation. The reason that there is a variation in the cost of delta hedging is that the hedge is rebalanced only once a week. As rebalancing takes place more frequently, the variation in the cost of hedging is reduced.

Table 13.4 shows statistics on the performance of delta hedging from 1,000 simulations of stock price movements for our example. As in Table 13.1, the performance measure is the ratio of the standard deviation of the cost of hedging the option to the Black–Scholes price of the option. It is clear that delta hedging is a great improvement over the stop-loss strategy. Unlike the stop-loss strategy, the performance of delta hedging gets steadily better as the hedge is monitored more frequently.

Delta hedging aims to keep the total wealth of the financial institution as close to unchanged as possible. Initially, the value of the written option is $240,000. In the situation depicted in Table 13.2, the value of the option can be calculated as $414,500 on week 9. Thus, the financial institution has lost $174,500 on its option position. Its cash position, as measured by the cumulative cost, is $1,442,700 worse in week 9 than in week 0. However, the value of the shares held has increased from $2,557,800 to $4,171,100. The net effect of all this is that the overall wealth of the financial institution has changed by only $3,900.

WHERE THE COST COMES FROM

The delta-hedging scheme in tables 13.2 and 13.3 in effect creates a long position in the option synthetically. This neutralizes the short position arising from the option that has been written. The scheme generally involves selling stock just

TABLE 13.4 Performance of Delta Hedging

Time Between Hedge Rebalancing (weeks)	5	4	2	1	0.5	0.25
Performance Measure	0.43	0.39	0.26	0.19	0.14	0.09

after the price has gone down and buying stock just after the price has gone up. It might be termed a buy high, sell low scheme! The cost of $240,000 comes from the average difference between the price paid for the stock and the price realized for it. Of course, the simulations in tables 13.2 and 13.3 are idealized in that they assume that the volatility is constant, and that there are no transactions costs.

DELTA OF OTHER EUROPEAN OPTIONS

For European call options on a stock index paying a dividend yield q,

$$\Delta = e^{-q(T-t)} N(d_1)$$

where d_1 is defined in Equation (11.1). For European put options on the stock index,

$$\Delta = e^{-q(T-t)}[N(d_1) - 1]$$

For European call options on a currency,

$$\Delta = e^{-r_f(T-t)} N(d_1)$$

where r_f is the foreign risk-free interest rate and d_1 is defined as in Equation (11.3). For European put options on a currency,

$$\Delta = e^{-r_f(T-t)}[N(d_1) - 1]$$

For European futures call options,

$$\Delta = e^{-r(T-t)} N(d_1)$$

where d_1 is defined as in Equation (11.8), and for European futures put options,

$$\Delta = e^{-r(T-t)}[N(d_1) - 1]$$

Example 13.1

A bank has written a 6-month European option to sell £1,000,000 at an exchange rate of 1.6000. Suppose that the current exchange rate is 1.6200, the risk-free interest rate in the United Kingdom is 13% per annum, the risk-free interest rate in the United States is 10% per annum, and the volatility of sterling is 15%. In this case $S = 1.6200$, $X = 1.6000$, $r = 0.10$, $r_f = 0.13$, $\sigma = 0.15$, and $T - t = 0.5$. The delta of a put option on a currency is

$$[N(d_1) - 1]e^{-r_f(T-t)}$$

where d_1 is given by Equation (11.3).

$$d_1 = 0.0287$$

$$N(d_1) = 0.5115$$

and the delta of the put option is -0.458. This is the delta of a long position in one put option. The delta of the bank's total short position is $+458,000$. Delta hedging therefore requires a short sterling position of £458,000 be set up initially. This short sterling position has a delta of $-458,000$ and neutralizes the delta of the option position. As time passes, the short position must be changed.

USING FUTURES

In practice, delta hedging is often carried out using a position in futures rather than one in the underlying asset. The contract that is used does not have to mature at the same time as the derivative security. For ease of exposition we assume that a futures contract is on one unit of the underlying asset.

Define:

T^*: Maturity of futures contract

H_A: Required position in asset at time t for delta hedging

H_F: Alternative required position in futures contracts at time t for delta hedging

If the underlying asset is a non-dividend-paying stock, the futures price, F, is from Equation (3.5) given by

$$F = Se^{r(T^*-t)}$$

When the stock price increases by ΔS, the futures price increases by $\Delta Se^{r(T^*-t)}$. The delta of the futures contract is therefore $e^{r(T^*-t)}$. Thus $e^{-r(T^*-t)}$ futures contracts have the same sensitivity to stock price movements as one stock. Hence

$$H_F = e^{-r(T^*-t)}H_A$$

When the underlying asset is a stock or stock index paying a dividend yield q, a similar argument shows that

$$H_F = e^{-(r-q)(T^*-t)}H_A \qquad (13.2)$$

When it is a currency

$$H_F = e^{-(r-r_f)(T^*-t)}H_A$$

Example 13.2

Consider again the option in Example 13.1. Suppose that the bank decides to hedge using 9-month currency futures contracts. In this case $T^* - t = 0.75$ and

$$e^{-(r-r_f)(T^*-t)} = 1.0228$$

so that the short position in currency futures required for delta hedging is $1.0228 \times 458,000 = £468,442$. Since each futures contract is for the purchase or sale of £62,500, this means that (to the nearest whole number) 7 contracts should be shorted.

It is interesting to note that the delta of a futures contract is different from the delta of the corresponding forward. This is true even when interest rates are constant and the forward price equals the futures price. Consider the situation where the underlying asset is a non-dividend-paying stock. The delta of a futures contract on one unit of the asset is $e^{r(T^*-t)}$ whereas the delta of a forward contract on one unit of the asset is as discussed earlier 1.0.

DELTA OF A PORTFOLIO

When a portfolio of options and other derivative securities on an asset are held, the delta of the portfolio is simply the sum of the deltas of the individual derivative securities in the portfolio. If a portfolio, Π, consists of an amount, w_i, of derivative security i $(1 \leq i \leq n)$, the delta of the portfolio is given by

$$\Delta = \sum_{i=1}^{n} w_i \Delta_i$$

where Δ_i is the delta of ith derivative security. This can be used to calculate the position in the underlying asset, or in futures contract on the underlying asset, necessary to carry out delta hedging. When this position has been taken, the delta of the portfolio is zero and the portfolio is referred to as being delta neutral.

Example 13.3

Consider a financial institution that has the following three positions in options to buy or sell German marks:

1. A long position in 100,000 call options with exercise price 0.55 and exercise date in 3 months. The delta of each option is 0.533.
2. A short position in 200,000 call options with exercise price 0.56 and exercise date in 5 months. The delta of each option is 0.468.
3. A short position in 50,000 put options with exercise price 0.56 and exercise date in 2 months. The delta of each option is -0.508.

The delta of the whole portfolio is

$$0.533 \times 100{,}000 - 200{,}000 \times 0.468 - 50{,}000 \times (-0.508) = -14{,}900$$

This means that the portfolio can be made delta neutral with a long position of 14,900 marks.

A 6-month futures contract could also be used to achieve delta neutrality in this example. Suppose that the risk-free rate of interest is 8% per annum in the United States and 4% per annum in Germany. The number of marks that must be sold forward for delta neutrality is

$$14{,}900e^{-(0.08-0.04)\times 0.5} = 14{,}605$$

13.6 THETA

The *theta* of a portfolio of derivative securities, Θ, is the rate of change of the value of the portfolio with respect to time with all else remaining the same.[6] It

---

[6]More formally, $\Theta = \partial\Pi/\partial t$, where Π is the value of the portfolio.

is sometimes referred to as the *time decay* of the portfolio. For a European call option on a non-dividend-paying stock,

$$\Theta = -\frac{SN'(d_1)\sigma}{2\sqrt{T-t}} - rXe^{-r(T-t)}N(d_2)$$

where d_1 and d_2 are defined as in Equation (10.27) and

$$N'(x) = \frac{1}{\sqrt{2\pi}}e^{-x^2/2}$$

For a European put option on the stock,

$$\Theta = -\frac{SN'(d_1)\sigma}{2\sqrt{T-t}} + rXe^{-r(T-t)}N(-d_2)$$

For a European call option on a stock index paying a dividend at rate q,

$$\Theta = -\frac{SN'(d_1)\sigma e^{-q(T-t)}}{2\sqrt{T-t}} + qSN(d_1)e^{-q(T-t)} - rXe^{-r(T-t)}N(d_2)$$

where d_1 and d_2 are defined as in Equation 11.1. The formula for $N'(x)$ is given in Section 10.10. For a European put option on the stock index

$$\Theta = -\frac{SN'(d_1)\sigma e^{-q(T-t)}}{2\sqrt{T-t}} - qSN(-d_1)e^{-q(T-t)} + rXe^{-r(T-t)}N(-d_2)$$

With q equal to r_f, these last two equations give thetas for European call and put options on currencies. With q equal to r and S equal to F, they give thetas for European futures options.

Example 13.4

Consider a 4-month put option on a stock index. The current value of the index is 305, the strike price is 300, the dividend yield is 3% per annum, the risk-free interest rate is 8% per annum, and the volatility of the index is 25% per annum. In this case, $S = 305$, $X = 300$, $q = 0.03$, $r = 0.08$, $\sigma = 0.25$, and $T - t = 0.3333$. The option's theta is

$$-\frac{SN'(d_1)\sigma e^{-q(T-t)}}{2\sqrt{T-t}} - qSN(-d_1)e^{-q(T-t)} + rXe^{-r(T-t)}N(-d_2) = -18.15$$

This means, if 0.01 year (or 2.5 trading days) passes with no changes to the value of the index or its volatility, the value of the option declines by 0.1815.

Theta is almost always negative for an option.[7] This is because, as the time to maturity decreases, the option tends to become less valuable. The variation of Θ with the stock price for a call option on a stock is shown in Figure 13.5. When

---

[7]An exception to this could be an in-the-money European put option on a non-dividend-paying stock or an in-the-money European call option on a currency with a very high interest rate.

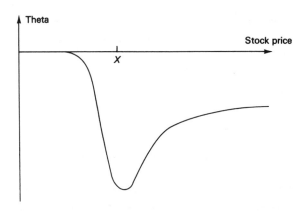

Figure 13.5   Variation of Theta of a European Call Option with Stock Price

the stock price is very low, theta is close to zero. For an at-the-money option, theta is relatively large and negative. As the stock price becomes larger, theta tends to $-rXe^{-r(T-t)}$. Figure 13.6 shows the variation of Θ with the time to maturity for an in-the-money, at-the-money, and out-of-the-money option.

Theta is not the same type of hedge parameter as delta and gamma. This is because, although there is some uncertainty about the future stock price, there is no uncertainty about the passage of time. It does not make sense to hedge against

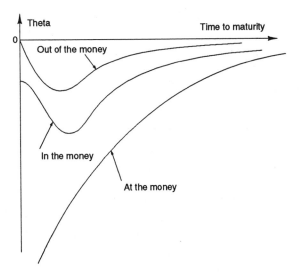

Figure 13.6   Variation of Theta of a European Call Option with Time to Maturity

the effect of the passage of time on an option portfolio. As we will see in Section 13.7, if theta is large in absolute terms, either delta or gamma must be large. If both the delta and gamma of an option position are zero, theta indicates that the value of the position will grow at the risk-free rate.

13.7 GAMMA

The *gamma*, Γ, of a portfolio of derivative securities on an underlying asset is the rate of change of the portfolio's delta with respect to the price of the underlying asset.[8] If gamma is small, delta changes only slowly and adjustments to keep a portfolio delta neutral need only be made relatively infrequently. However, if gamma is large in absolute terms, delta is highly sensitive to the price of the underlying asset. It is then quite risky to leave a delta-neutral portfolio unchanged for any length of time. Figure 13.7 illustrates this point. When the stock price moves from S to S', delta hedging assumes that the option price moves from C to C' when in actual fact it moves from C to C''. The difference between C' and C'' leads to a hedging error. The error depends on the curvature of the relationship between the option price and the stock price. Gamma measures this curvature.[9]

Suppose that ΔS is the change in the price of an underlying asset in a small interval of time, Δt, and $\Delta \Pi$ is the corresponding change in the price of the portfolio. If terms such as Δt^2, which are of higher order than Δt, are ignored, Appendix 13A shows that for a delta-neutral portfolio,

$$\Delta \Pi = \Theta \, \Delta t + \frac{1}{2} \Gamma \, \Delta S^2 \tag{13.3}$$

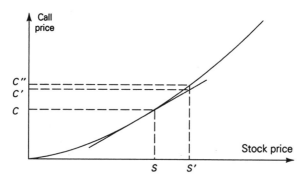

Figure 13.7   Illustration of Error in Delta Hedging

[8]More formally, $\Gamma = \partial^2 \Pi / \partial S^2$, where Π is the value of the portfolio.

[9]Indeed the gamma of an option is sometimes referred to by practitioners as its curvature.

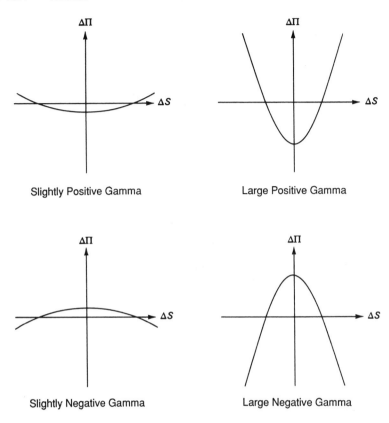

Figure 13.8 Alternative Relationships between $\Delta\Pi$ and ΔS for a Delta-neutral Portfolio

where Θ is the theta of the portfolio. Figure 13.8 shows the nature of this relationship between $\Delta\Pi$ and ΔS.[10] It can be seen that, when gamma is positive, the portfolio declines in value if there is no change in the S, but increases in value if there is a large positive or negative change in S. When gamma is negative the reverse is true; the portfolio increases in value if there is no change in S, but decreases in value if there is a large positive or negative change in S. As the absolute value of gamma increases, the sensitivity of the value of the portfolio to S increases.

---

[10]Figure 13.8 assumes that Θ has the opposite sign to Γ. This is usually, but not always, the case. It will be shown in Section 13.8 that

$$\Theta + \frac{1}{2}\sigma^2 S^2 \Gamma = r\Pi$$

for a delta-neutral portfolio.

MAKING A PORTFOLIO GAMMA NEUTRAL

A position in the underlying asset or in a futures contract on the underlying asset has zero gamma. The only way a financial institution can change the gamma of its portfolio is by taking a position in a traded option. Suppose that a delta-neutral portfolio has gamma equal to Γ and a traded option has a gamma equal to Γ_T. If the number of traded options added to the portfolio is w_T, the gamma of the portfolio is

$$w_T \Gamma_T + \Gamma$$

Hence the position in the traded option necessary to make the portfolio gamma neutral is $-\Gamma/\Gamma_T$. Of course, including the traded option is liable to change the delta of the portfolio, so the position in the underlying asset (or futures contract on the underlying asset) then has to be changed to maintain delta neutrality. Note that the portfolio is only gamma neutral instantaneously. As time passes, gamma neutrality can be maintained only if the position in the traded option is adjusted so that it is always equal to $-\Gamma/\Gamma_T$.

Example 13.5

Suppose that a portfolio is delta neutral and has a gamma of $-3,000$. The delta and gamma of a particular traded call option are 0.62 and 1.50, respectively. The portfolio can be made gamma neutral by including a long position of

$$\frac{3,000}{1.5} = 2,000$$

traded call options in the portfolio. However, the delta of the portfolio will then change from zero to $2,000 \times 0.62 = 1,240$. A quantity, 1,240, of the underlying asset must therefore be sold from the portfolio to keep it delta neutral.

Making a delta-neutral portfolio gamma neutral can be regarded as a first correction for the fact that the position in the underlying asset (or futures contracts on the underlying asset) cannot be changed continuously when delta hedging is used.

CALCULATION OF GAMMA

For a European call or put option on a non-dividend-paying stock, the gamma is given by

$$\Gamma = \frac{N'(d_1)}{S\sigma \sqrt{T-t}}$$

where d_1 is defined as in Equation (10.27) and $N'(x)$ is given in Section 10.10. This is always positive and varies with S in the way indicated in Figure 13.9.

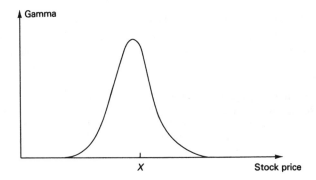

Figure 13.9   Variation of Gamma with Stock Price for an Option

The variation of gamma with time to maturity for out-of-the-money, at-the-money, and in-the-money options is shown in Figure 13.10. For an at-the-money option, gamma increases as the time to maturity decreases. Short-life at-the-money options have very high gammas—which means that the value of the option holder's position is highly sensitive to jumps in the stock price.

For a European call or put option on a stock index paying a continuous dividend at rate q,

$$\Gamma = \frac{N'(d_1)e^{-q(T-t)}}{S\sigma\sqrt{T-t}}$$

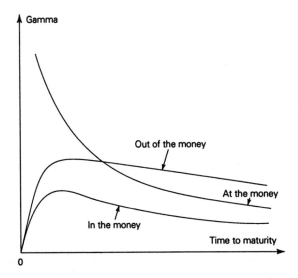

Figure 13.10   Variation of Gamma with Time to Maturity for a Stock Option

where d_1 is defined as in Equation (11.1). This formula gives the gamma for a European option on a currency when q is put equal to the foreign risk-free rate and gives the gamma for a European futures option with $q = r$ and $S = F$.

Example 13.6

Consider a 4-month put option on a stock index. Suppose that the current value of the index is 305, the exercise price is 300, the dividend yield is 3% per annum, the risk-free interest rate is 8% per annum, and volatility of the index is 25% per annum. In this case, $S = 305$, $X = 300$, $q = 0.03$, $r = 0.08$, $\sigma = 0.25$, and $T - t = 0.3333$. The gamma of the index option is given by

$$\frac{N'(d_1)e^{-q(T-t)}}{S\sigma\sqrt{T-t}} = 0.00857$$

Thus an increase of 1 in the index increases the delta of the option by approximately 0.00857.

13.8 THE RELATIONSHIP BETWEEN DELTA, THETA, AND GAMMA

The Black–Scholes equation (10.20) which must be satisfied by the price, f, of any derivative security on a non-dividend-paying stock is

$$\frac{\partial f}{\partial t} + rS\frac{\partial f}{\partial S} + \frac{1}{2}\sigma^2 S^2 \frac{\partial^2 f}{\partial S^2} = rf$$

Since

$$\Theta = \frac{\partial f}{\partial t}, \qquad \Delta = \frac{\partial f}{\partial S}, \qquad \Gamma = \frac{\partial^2 f}{\partial S^2}$$

it follows that

$$\Theta + rS\Delta + \frac{1}{2}\sigma^2 S^2 \Gamma = rf \tag{13.4}$$

This is true for portfolios of derivative securities on a non-dividend-paying security as well as for individual derivative securities.

For a delta-neutral portfolio, $\Delta = 0$ and

$$\Theta + \frac{1}{2}\sigma^2 S^2 \Gamma = rf$$

This shows that when Θ is large and positive, gamma tends to be large and negative, and vice versa. This is consistent with the way in which Figure 13.8 has been drawn.

13.9 VEGA

Up to now we have implicitly assumed that the volatility of the asset underlying a derivative security is constant. In practice, volatilities change over time. It means that the value of a derivative security is liable to change because of movements in volatility as well as because of changes in the asset price and the passage of time.

The *vega* of a portfolio of derivative securities, Λ, is the rate of change of the value of the portfolio with respect to the volatility of the underlying asset.[11] If vega is high in absolute terms, the portfolio's value is very sensitive to small changes in volatility. If vega is low in absolute terms, volatility changes have relatively little impact on the value of the portfolio.

A position in the underlying asset or in a futures contract has zero vega. However, the vega of a portfolio can be changed by adding a position in a traded option. If Λ is the vega of the portfolio and Λ_T is the vega of a traded option, a position of $-\Lambda/\Lambda_T$ in the traded option makes the portfolio instantaneously vega neutral. Unfortunately, a portfolio that is gamma neutral will not in general be vega neutral, and vice versa. If a hedger requires a portfolio to be both gamma and vega neutral, at least two traded derivative securities dependent on the underlying asset must usually be used.

Example 13.7

Consider a portfolio that is delta neutral, has a gamma of $-5,000$ and a vega of $-8,000$. Suppose that a traded option has a gamma of 0.5, a vega of 2.0, and a delta of 0.6. The portfolio can be made vega neutral by including a long position in 4,000 traded options. This would increase delta to 2,400 and require that 2,400 units of the asset be sold to maintain delta neutrality. The gamma of the portfolio would change from $-5,000$ to $-3,000$.

To make the portfolio gamma and vega neutral, we suppose that there is a second traded option with a gamma of 0.8, a vega of 1.2, and a delta of 0.5. If w_1 and w_2 are the amounts of the two traded options included in the portfolio, we require that

$$-5,000 + 0.5w_1 + 0.8w_2 = 0$$

$$-8,000 + 2.0w_1 + 1.2w_2 = 0$$

The solution to these equations is $w_1 = 400$, $w_2 = 6,000$. The portfolio can therefore be made gamma and vega neutral by including 400 of the first traded option and 6,000 of the second traded option. The delta of the portfolio after the addition of the positions in the two traded options is $400 \times 0.6 + 6,000 \times 0.5 = 3,240$. Hence 3,240 units of the asset would have to be sold to maintain delta neutrality.

For a European call or put option on a non-dividend-paying stock, vega is given by

$$\Lambda = S \sqrt{T - t}\, N'(d_1)$$

---

[11]More formally, $\Lambda = \partial \Pi / \partial \sigma$, where Π is the value of the portfolio. Vega is also sometimes referred to as lambda, kappa, or sigma.

where d_1 is defined as in Equation (10.27). The formula for $N'(x)$ is given in Section 10.10. For a European call or put option on a stock or stock index paying a continuous dividend yield at rate q,

$$\Lambda = S\sqrt{T-t}\,N'(d_1)e^{-q(T-t)}$$

where d_1 is defined as in Equation (11.1). This equation gives the vega for a European currency option with q replaced by r_f. It also gives the vega for a European futures option with q replaced by r, and S replaced by F. Using these formulas implicitly assumes that the price of an option with a variable volatility is the same as the price of an option with constant volatility. To a reasonable approximation this appears to be the case.[12] The vega of an option is always positive. The general way in which it varies with S is shown in Figure 13.11.

Gamma neutrality corrects for the fact that time elapses between hedge rebalancing. Vega neutrality corrects for a variable σ. As might be expected, whether it is best to use an available traded option for vega or gamma hedging depends on the time between hedge rebalancing and the volatility of the volatility. This issue is discussed in some detail by Hull and White.[13]

Example 13.8

Consider again the put option in Example 13.5. Its vega is given by

$$S\sqrt{T-t}\,N'(d_1)e^{-q(T-t)} = 66.44$$

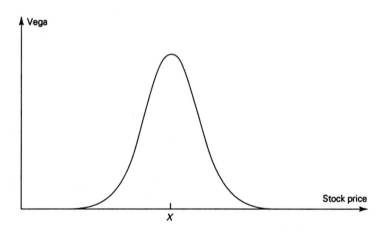

Figure 13.11   Variation of Vega with Stock Price for an Option

[12]See J. Hull and A. White, "The Pricing of Options on Assets with Stochastic Volatilities," *Journal of Finance*, 42 (June 1987) 281–300.

[13]See J. Hull and A. White, "Hedging the Risks from Writing Foreign Currency Options," *Journal of International Money and Finance*, 6 (June 1987), 131–52.

Thus a 1% or 0.01 increase in volatility (from 25% to 26%) increases the value of the option by approximately 0.6644.

13.10 RHO

The *rho* of a portfolio of derivative securities is the rate of change of the value of the portfolio with respect to the interest rate.[14] It measures the sensitivity of the value of a portfolio to interest rates. For a European call option on a non-dividend-paying stock,

$$\text{rho} = X(T - t)e^{-r(T-t)}N(d_2)$$

and for a European put option on the stock,

$$\text{rho} = -X(T - t)e^{-r(T-t)}N(-d_2)$$

where d_2 is defined as in Equation (10.27). These same formulas apply to European call and put options on stocks and stock indices paying a dividend yield at rate q, and to European call and put options on futures contracts, when appropriate changes are made to the definition of d_2.

Example 13.9

Consider again the 4-month put option on a stock index. The current value of the index is 305, the strike price is 300, the dividend yield is 3% per annum, the risk-free interest rate is 8% per annum, and the volatility of the index is 25% per annum. In this case, $S = 305$, $X = 300$, $q = 0.03$, $r = 0.08$, $\sigma = 0.25$, $T - t = 0.333$. The option's rho is

$$-X(T - t)e^{-r(T-t)}N(-d_2) = -42.57$$

This means that for a one-percentage-point or 0.01 change in the risk-free interest rate (from 8% to 9%), the value of the option decreases by 0.4257.

In the case of currency options, there are two rhos corresponding to the two interest rates. The rho corresponding to the domestic interest rate is given by the previous formulas. The rho corresponding to the foreign interest rate for a European call on a currency is given by

$$\text{rho} = -(T - t)e^{-r_f(T-t)}SN(d_1)$$

while for a European put it is

$$\text{rho} = (T - t)e^{-r_f(T-t)}SN(-d_1)$$

---

[14]More formally, rho equals $\partial \Pi / \partial r$, where Π is the value of the portfolio.

13.11 HEDGING OPTION PORTFOLIOS IN PRACTICE

It would be wrong to give the impression that option traders are continually re-balancing their portfolios to maintain delta neutrality, gamma neutrality, vega neutrality, and so on. In practice, transaction costs make frequent rebalancing very expensive. Rather than trying to eliminate all risks, an option trader therefore usually concentrates on assessing risks and deciding whether they are acceptable.

Option traders tend to use delta, gamma, and vega measures to quantify the different aspects of the risk inherent in their option portfolios. They then consider different possible future scenarios for movements in the stock price and the stock price volatility. If the downside risk is acceptable, no adjustment is made to the portfolio; if it is unacceptable, they take an appropriate position in either the underlying security or a traded portfolio.

13.12 PORTFOLIO INSURANCE

Portfolio managers holding a well-diversified stock portfolio are sometimes interested in insuring themselves against the value of the portfolio dropping below a certain level. One way of doing this is by holding, in conjunction with the stock portfolio, put options on a stock index. This strategy was discussed in Chapter 11.

Consider, for example, a fund manager with a $30 million portfolio whose value mirrors the value of the S&P 500. Suppose that the S&P 500 is standing at 300 and the manager wishes to insure against the value of the portfolio dropping below $29 million in the next 6 months. One approach is to buy 1,000 6-month put option contracts on the S&P 500 with an exercise price of 290 and a maturity in 6 months. If the index drops below 290, the put options will become in the money and provide the manager with compensation for the decline in the value of the portfolio. Suppose, for example, that the index drops to 270 at the end of 6 months. The value of the manager's stock portfolio is likely to be about $27 million. Since each option contract is on 100 times the index, the total value of the put options is $2 million. This brings the value of the entire holding back up to $29 million. Of course, insurance is not free. In this example the put options could cost the portfolio manager as much as $1 million.

CREATING OPTIONS SYNTHETICALLY

An alternative approach open to the portfolio manager involves creating the put options synthetically. This involves taking a position in the underlying asset (or futures on the underlying asset) so that the delta of the position is maintained equal to the delta of the required option. If more accuracy is required, the next step is to use traded options to match the gamma and vega of the required option. The position necessary to create an option synthetically is the reverse of that necessary to hedge it. This is simply a reflection of the fact that a procedure for hedging an option involves the creation of an equal and opposite option synthetically.

There are two reasons why it may be more attractive for the portfolio manager to create the required put option synthetically than to buy it in the market. The first is that options markets do not always have the liquidity to absorb the trades that managers of large funds would like to carry out. The second is that fund managers often require strike prices and exercise dates that are different from those available in traded options markets.

The synthetic option can be created from trades in stocks themselves or from trades in index futures contracts. We will first examine the creation of a put option by trades in the stocks themselves. Consider again the fund manager with a well-diversified portfolio worth $30 million who wishes to buy a European put on the portfolio with a strike price of $29 million and an exercise date in 6 months. Recall that the delta of a European put on an index is given by

$$\Delta = e^{-q(T-t)}[N(d_1) - 1] \tag{13.5}$$

where, with the usual notation,

$$d_1 = \frac{\ln(S/X) + (r - q + \sigma^2/2)(T - t)}{\sigma\sqrt{T - t}}$$

Since, in this case, the fund manager's portfolio mirrors the index, this is also the delta of a put on the portfolio when it is regarded as a single security. The delta is negative. Accordingly, in order to create the put option synthetically, the fund manager should ensure that at any given time a proportion

$$e^{-q(T-t)}[1 - N(d_1)]$$

of the stocks in the original $30 million portfolio have been sold and the proceeds invested in riskless assets. As the value of the original portfolio declines, the delta of the put becomes more negative and the proportion of the portfolio sold must be increased. As the value of the original portfolio increases, the delta of the put becomes less negative and the proportion of the portfolio sold must be decreased (i.e., some of the original portfolio must be repurchased).

Using this strategy to create portfolio insurance means that at any given time funds are divided between the stock portfolio on which insurance is required and riskless assets. As the value of the stock portfolio increases, riskless assets are sold and the position in the stock portfolio is increased. As the value of the stock portfolio declines, the position in the stock portfolio is decreased and riskless assets are purchased. The cost of the insurance arises from the fact that the portfolio manager is always selling after a decline in the market and buying after a rise in the market.

USE OF INDEX FUTURES

Using index futures to create portfolio insurance can be preferable to using the underlying stocks, as the transactions costs associated with trades in index futures are generally less than those associated with the corresponding trades in the underlying stocks. The portfolio manager considered earlier would keep the $30 million stock portfolio intact and short index futures contracts. The dollar amount of futures contracts shorted as a proportion of the value of the portfolio should from equations (13.2) and (13.5) be

$$e^{-q(T-t)}e^{-(r-q)(T^*-t)}[1 - N(d_1)] = e^{q(T^*-T)}e^{-r(T^*-t)}[1 - N(d_1)]$$

where T^* is the maturity date of the futures contract. If the portfolio is worth K_1 times the index and each index futures contract is on K_2 times the index, this means that the number of futures contracts shorted at any given time should be

$$e^{q(T^*-T)}e^{-r(T^*-t)}[1 - N(d_1)]\frac{K_1}{K_2}$$

Example 13.10

In the example given at the beginning of this section, suppose that the volatility of the market is 25% per annum, the risk-free interest rate is 9% per annum, and the dividend yield on the market is 3% per annum. In this case, $S = 300$, $X = 290$, $r = 0.09$, $q = 0.03$, $\sigma = 0.25$, and $T - t = 0.5$. The delta of the option that is required is

$$e^{-q(T-t)}[N(d_1) - 1] = -0.322$$

Hence if trades in the portfolio are used to create the option, 32.2% of the portfolio should be sold initially. If 9-month futures contracts on the S&P 500 are used, $T^* - T = 0.25$, $T^* - t = 0.75$, $K_1 = 100,000$, $K_2 = 500$, so that the number of futures contracts shorted should be

$$e^{q(T^*-T)}e^{-r(T^*-t)}[1 - N(d_1)]\frac{K_1}{K_2} = 61.6$$

An important issue when put options are created synthetically for portfolio insurance is the frequency with which the portfolio manager's position should be adjusted or rebalanced. With no transaction costs, continuous rebalancing is optimal. However, as transactions costs increase, the optimal frequency of rebalancing declines. This issue is discussed by Leland.[15]

Up to now we have assumed that the portfolio mirrors the index. As discussed in Chapter 11, the hedging scheme can be adjusted to deal with other situations. The strike price for the options used should be the expected level of the market index when the portfolio's value reaches its insured value. The number of index

---

[15]See Hayne E. Leland, "Option Pricing and Replication with Transactions Costs," *Journal of Finance*, 40 (December 1985), 1283–1301.

options used should be β times the number of options that would be required if the portfolio had a beta of 1.0.

Example 13.11

Suppose that the risk-free rate of interest is 5% per annum, the S&P 500 stands at 500, and the value of a portfolio with a beta of 2.0 is $10 million. Suppose that the dividend yield on the S&P 500 is 3%, the dividend yield on the portfolio is 2%, and that the portfolio manager wishes to insure against a decline in the value of the portfolio to below $9.3 million in the next year. If the value of the portfolio declines to $9.3 million at the end of the year, the total return (after taking account of the 2% dividend yield) is approximately –5% per annum. This is 10% per annum, worse than the risk-free rate. We expect the market to perform 5% worse than the risk-free rate (i.e., to provide zero return) in these circumstances. Hence we expect a 3% decline in the S&P 500 since this index does not take any account of dividends. The correct exercise price for the put options which are created is therefore 485. The number of put options required is beta times the value of the portfolio divided by the value of the index or 40,000 (i.e., 400 contracts).

To illustrate that this answer is at least approximately correct, suppose that the portfolio's value drops to $8.3 million. With dividends it provides a return of approximately –15% per annum. This is approximately 20% per annum, worse than the risk-free rate. The S&P 500 plus dividends on the S&P 500 can be expected to provide a return that is 10% per annum worse than the risk-free rate. This means that the index will reduce by 8%, to 460. The 40,000 put options with an exercise price of 485 will pay off $1 million, as required.

When β is not equal to 1.0 and the fund manager wishes to use trades in the portfolio to create the option, the portfolio can be regarded as a single security. As an approximation, the volatility of the portfolio can be assumed to be equal to β times the volatility of the market index.[16]

OCTOBER 19, 1987 AND STOCK MARKET VOLATILITY

Creating put options on the index synthetically does not work well if the volatility of the index changes rapidly or if the index exhibits large jumps. On Monday, October 19, 1987, the Dow Jones Industrial Average dropped by over 500 points. Portfolio managers who had insured themselves by buying traded put options survived this crash well. Those who had chosen to create put options synthetically found that they were unable to sell either stocks or index futures fast enough to protect their position.

We have already raised the issue of whether volatility is caused solely by the arrival of new information or whether trading itself generates volatility. Portfolio insurance schemes such as those just described have the potential to increase

---

[16]This is only exactly true if beta is calculated on the basis of the returns in very small time intervals. By contrast, the argument in Example 13.11 is only exactly true if beta is calculated on the basis of returns in time intervals of length equal to the life of the option being created.

volatility. When the market declines, they cause portfolio managers either to sell stock or to sell index futures contracts. This may accentuate the decline. The sale of stock is liable to drive down the market index further in a direct way. The sale of index futures contracts is liable to drive down futures prices. This creates selling pressure on stocks via the mechanism of index arbitrage (see Chapter 3) so that the market index is liable to be driven down in this case as well. Similarly, when the market rises, the portfolio insurance schemes cause portfolio managers either to buy stock or to buy futures contracts. This may accentuate the rise.

In addition to formal portfolio insurance schemes, we can speculate that many investors consciously or subconsciously follow portfolio insurance schemes of their own. For example, an investor may be inclined to enter the market when it is rising, but will sell when it is falling, to limit his or her downside risk.

Whether portfolio insurance schemes (formal or informal) affect volatility depends on how easily the market can absorb the trades that are generated by portfolio insurance. If portfolio insurance trades are a very small fraction of all trades, there is likely to be no effect. But, as portfolio insurance becomes more widespread, it is liable to have a destabilizing effect on the market.

BRADY COMMISSION REPORT

The report of the Brady commission on the October 19, 1987 crash provides some interesting insights into the effect of portfolio insurance on the market at that time.[17] The Brady commission estimates that $60 billion to $90 billion of equity assets were under portfolio insurance administration in October 1987. During the period Wednesday, October 14, 1987, to Friday, October 16, 1987, the market declined by about 10 percent with much of this decline taking place on the Friday afternoon. This should have generated at least $12 billion of equity or index futures sales as a result of portfolio insurance schemes.[18] In fact, less than $4 billion were sold, which means that portfolio insurers approached the following week with huge amounts of selling already dictated by their models. The Brady commission estimated that on Monday, October 19, sell programs by three portfolio insurers accounted for almost 10 percent of the sales on the New York Stock Exchange, and that portfolio insurance sales amount to 21.3 percent of all sales in index futures markets. It seems likely that portfolio insurance caused some downward pressure on the market. It is significant that in aggregate, portfolio insurers executed only a relatively small proportion of the total trades generated by their models. Needless to say, the popularity of portfolio insurance schemes that are based on dynamic trading in stocks and futures has declined considerably since October 1987.

---

[17]See "Report of the Presidential Task Force on Market Mechanisms," January 1988.

[18]To put this in perspective, on Monday, October 19, all previous records were broken when 604 million shares worth $21 billion were traded on the New York Stock Exchange. Approximately $20 billion of S&P 500 futures contracts were traded on that day.

13.13 SUMMARY

Financial institutions offer a variety of option products to their clients. Often the options do not correspond to the standardized products traded by exchanges. This presents the financial institutions with the problem of hedging their exposure. Naked and covered positions leave them subject to an unacceptable level of risk. One strategy that is sometimes proposed is a stop-loss strategy that involves holding a naked position when an option is out of the money and converting it to a covered position as soon as the option moves in the money. Surprisingly, the strategy does not work at all well.

The delta, Δ, of an option is the rate of change of its price with respect to the price of the underlying asset. Delta hedging involves creating a position with zero delta (sometimes referred to as a delta-neutral position). Since the delta of the underlying asset is 1.0, one way of doing this is to take a position of $-\Delta$ in the underlying asset for each long option being hedged. The delta of an option changes over time. This means that the position in the underlying asset has to be frequently adjusted.

Once an option position has been made delta neutral, the next stage is often to look at its gamma. The gamma of an option is the rate of change of its delta with respect to the price of the underlying asset. It is a measure of the curvature of the relationship between the option price and the asset price. The impact of this curvature on the performance of delta hedging can be reduced by making an option position gamma neutral. If Γ is the gamma of the position being hedged, this is usually achieved by taking a position in a traded option that has a gamma of $-\Gamma$.

Delta and gamma hedging are both based on the assumption that the volatility of the underlying asset is constant. In practice, volatilities do change over time. The vega of an option, or an option portfolio, measures the rate of change of its value with respect to volatility. If a trader wishes to hedge an option position against volatility changes, he or she can make the position vega neutral. Like the procedure for creating gamma neutrality, this usually involves taking an offsetting position in a traded option. If the trader wishes to achieve both gamma and vega neutrality, two traded options are usually required.

Two other measures of the risk of an option position are theta and rho. Theta measures the rate of change of the value of the position with respect to the passage of time with all else remaining constant, rho measures the rate of change of the value of the position with respect to the short-term interest rate with all else remaining constant.

Portfolio managers are sometimes interested in creating put options synthetically for the purposes of insuring an equity portfolio. They can do this either by trading the portfolio or by trading index futures on the portfolio. Trading the portfolio involves splitting the portfolio between equities and risk-free securities.

As the market declines, more is invested in risk-free securities. As the market increases, more is invested in equities. Trading index futures involves keeping the equity portfolio intact and selling index futures. As the market declines, more index futures are sold; as it rises fewer are sold. This works well in normal market conditions. However, on Monday October 19, 1987, when the Dow Jones Industrial Average dropped by over 500 points, it worked badly. Portfolio insurers were unable to sell either stocks or index futures fast enough to protect their positions.

SUGGESTIONS FOR FURTHER READING

On Hedging Option Positions

BOYLE, P. P., and D. EMANUEL, "Discretely Adjusted Option Hedges," *Journal of Financial Economics*, 8 (1980), 259–82.

DILLMAN, S., and J. HARDING, "Life after Delta: the Gamma Factor," *Euromoney*, Supplement (February 1985), pp. 14–17.

FIGLEWSKI, S., "Options Arbitrage in Imperfect Markets," *Journal of Finance* 44 (December 1989), 1289–1311.

GALAI, D., "The Components of the Return from Hedging Options Against Stocks," *Journal of Business*, 56 (January 1983), 45–54.

HULL, J., and A. WHITE, "Hedging the Risks from Writing Foreign Currency Options," *Journal of International Money and Finance*, 6 (June 1987), 131–52.

On Portfolio Insurance

ASAY, M., and C. EDELBERG, "Can a Dynamic Strategy Replicate the Returns on an Option," *Journal of Futures Markets*, 6 (Spring 1986), 63–70.

BOOKSTABER, R., and J. A. LANGSAM, "Portfolio Insurance Trading Rules," *Journal of Futures Markets*, 8 (February 1988) 15–31.

ETZIONI, E. S., "Rebalance Disciplines for Portfolio Insurance," *Journal of Portfolio Insurance*, 13 (Fall 1986), 59–62.

LELAND, H. E., "Option Pricing and Replication with Transactions Costs," *Journal of Finance*, 40 (December 1985), 1283–1301.

LELAND, H. E., "Who Should Buy Portfolio Insurance," *Journal of Finance*, 35 (May 1980), 581–94.

RUBINSTEIN, M., "Alternative Paths for Portfolio Insurance," *Financial Analysts Journal*, 41 (July–August 1985), 42–52.

RUBINSTEIN, M., and H. E. LELAND, "Replicating Options with Positions in Stock and Cash," *Financial Analysts Journal*, 37 (July–August 1981), 63–72.

SCHWARTZ, E. S., "Options and Portfolio Insurance," *Finanzmarkt und Portfolio Management*, 1 (1986), 9–17.

TILLEY, J. A., and G. O. LATAINER, "A Synthetic Option Framework for Asset Allocation," *Financial Analysts Journal*, 41 (May–June 1985), 32–41.

QUESTIONS AND PROBLEMS

13.1. What does it mean to assert that the delta of a call option is 0.7? How can a short position in 1,000 call options be made delta neutral when the delta of each option is 0.7?

13.2. Calculate the delta of an at-the-money 6-month European call option on a non-dividend-paying stock when the risk-free interest rate is 10% per annum and the stock price volatility is 25% per annum.

13.3. What does it mean to assert that the theta of an option position is –0.1 when time is measured in years? If a trader feels that neither a stock price nor its implied volatility will change, what type of option position is appropriate?

13.4. What is meant by the gamma of an option position? Consider the situation of an option writer when the gamma of his or her position is large and negative and the delta is zero. What are the risks?

13.5. "The procedure for creating an option position synthetically is the reverse of the procedure for hedging the option position." Explain this statement.

13.6. Why did portfolio insurance not work well on October 19, 1987?

*13.7. A deposit instrument offered by a bank guarantees that investors will receive a return during a 6-month period that is the greater of (a) zero; and (b) 40% of the return provided by a market index. An individual is planning to invest $100,000 in the instrument. Describe the payoff as an option on the index. Assuming that the risk-free rate of interest is 8% per annum, the dividend yield on the index is 3% per annum, and the volatility of the index is 25% per annum, is the product a good deal for the individual?

13.8. The Black–Scholes price of an out-of-the-money call option with an exercise price of $40 is $4.00. A trader who has written the option plans to use the stop-loss strategy in Section 13.3. The trader's plan is to buy at 40\frac{1}{8}$ and to sell at 39\frac{7}{8}$. Estimate the expected number of times the stock will be bought or sold.

*13.9. Use the put–call parity relationship to derive for a non-dividend-paying stock the relationship between:
   (a) The delta of a European call and the delta of a European put;
   (b) The gamma of a European call and the gamma of a European put;
   (c) The vega of a European call and the vega of a European put;
   (d) The theta of a European call and the theta of a European put.

13.10. Suppose that a stock price is currently $20 and that a call option with exercise price $25 is created synthetically using a continually changing position in the stock. Consider the following two scenarios:
   (a) Stock price increases steadily from $20 to $35 during the life of the option;
   (b) Stock price oscillates wildly ending up at $35.

Which scenario would make the synthetically created option more expensive? Explain your answer.

13.11. What is the delta of a short position in 1,000 European call options on silver futures? The options mature in 8 months and the futures contract underlying the option matures in 9 months. The current 9-month futures price is $8.00 per ounce, the exercise price of the options is $8.00, the risk-free interest rate is 12% per annum, and the volatility of silver is 18% per annum.

13.12. In Problem 13.11, what initial position in 9-month silver futures is necessary for delta hedging? If silver itself is used, what is the initial position? If 1-year silver futures are used, what is the initial position? Assume no storage costs for silver.

13.13. A company uses delta hedging to hedge a portfolio of long positions in put and call options on a currency. Which of the following would give the most favorable result?
(a) A virtually constant spot rate;
(b) Wild movements in the spot rate.
Explain your answer.

13.14. Repeat Problem 13.13 for a financial institution with a portfolio of short positions in put and call options on a currency.

13.15. A financial institution has just sold some 7-month European call options on the Japanese yen. Suppose that the spot exchange rate is 0.80 cent per yen, the exercise price is 0.81 cent per yen, the risk-free interest rate in the United States is 8% per annum, the risk-free interest rate in Japan is 5% per annum, and the volatility of the yen is 15% per annum. Calculate the delta, gamma, vega, theta, and rho of the option. Interpret each number.

13.16. A financial institution has the following portfolio of over-the-counter options on sterling:

Type	Position	Delta of Option	Gamma of Option	Vega of Option
Call	−1,000	0.50	2.2	1.8
Call	−500	0.80	0.6	0.2
Put	−2,000	−0.40	1.3	0.7
Call	−500	0.70	1.8	1.4

A traded option is available which has a delta of 0.6, a gamma of 1.5, and a vega of 0.8.
(a) What position in the traded option and in sterling would make the portfolio both gamma neutral and delta neutral?
(b) What position in the traded option and in sterling would make the portfolio both vega neutral and delta neutral?

13.17. Consider again the situation in Problem 13.16. Suppose that a second traded option with a delta of 0.1, a gamma of 0.5, and a vega of 0.6 is available. How could the portfolio be made delta, gamma, and vega neutral?

*13.18. Under what circumstances is it possible to make a position in an over-the-counter European option on a stock index both gamma neutral and vega neutral by introducing a single traded European option into the portfolio?

13.19. A fund manager has a well-diversified portfolio that mirrors the performance of the S&P 500 and is worth $90 million. The value of the S&P 500 is 300 and the portfolio manager would like to buy insurance against a reduction of more than 5% in the value of the portfolio over the next 6 months. The risk-free interest rate is 6% per annum. The dividend yield on both the portfolio and the S&P 500 is 3%, and the volatility of the index is 30% per annum.

   (a) If the fund manager buys traded European put options, how much would the insurance cost?

   (b) Explain carefully alternative strategies open to the fund manager involving traded European call options, and show that they lead to the same result.

   (c) If the fund manager decides to provide insurance by keeping part of the portfolio in risk-free securities, what should the initial position be?

   (d) If the fund manager decides to provide insurance by using 9-month index futures, what should the initial position be?

13.20. Repeat Problem 13.19 on the assumption that the portfolio has a beta of 1.5. Assume that the dividend yield on the portfolio is 4% per annum.

13.21. Show by substituting for Θ, Δ, Γ, and f that the relationship in Equation (13.4) is true for:

   (a) A single European call option on a non-dividend-paying stock;

   (b) A single European put option on a non-dividend-paying stock;

   (c) Any portfolio of European put and call options on a non-dividend-paying stock.

13.22. What is the equation corresponding to Equation (13.4) for a portfolio of derivative securities on a currency?

13.23. Suppose that $70 billion of equity assets are the subject of portfolio insurance schemes. Assume that the schemes are designed to insure that the value of the assets do not decline by more than 5% within one year. Making whatever estimates you find necessary, calculate the value of the stock or futures contracts that the administrators of the portfolio insurance schemes will attempt to sell if the market falls by 23% in a single day.

APPENDIX 13A: TAYLOR SERIES EXPANSIONS AND HEDGE PARAMETERS

The various hedging alternatives open to the manager of a portfolio of derivative securities can be illustrated using a Taylor series expansion of the change in the value of the portfolio in a short period of time.

    If the volatility of the underlying asset is assumed to be constant, the value of the portfolio, Π, is a function of the asset price, S, and time t. The Taylor series expansion gives

$$\Delta\Pi = \frac{\partial\Pi}{\partial S}\Delta S + \frac{\partial\Pi}{\partial t}\Delta t + \frac{1}{2}\frac{\partial^2\Pi}{\partial S^2}\Delta S^2 + \frac{1}{2}\frac{\partial^2\Pi}{\partial t^2}\Delta t^2 + \frac{\partial^2\Pi}{\partial S\partial t}\Delta S\Delta t + \cdots \quad (13A.1)$$

where $\Delta\Pi$ and ΔS are the change in Π and S in a small time interval Δt. Delta hedging eliminates the first term on the right-hand side. The second term is non-stochastic. The third term (which is of order Δt) can be made zero by ensuring that the portfolio is gamma neutral as well as delta neutral. Other terms are of higher order than Δt.

For a delta-neutral portfolio, the first term on the right-hand side of Equation (13A.1) is zero, so that

$$\Delta\Pi = \Theta\,\Delta t + \frac{1}{2}\Gamma\,\Delta S^2$$

when terms of higher order than Δt are ignored. This is Equation (13.3).

When the volatility of the underlying asset is assumed to be variable, Π is a function of σ, S, and t. Equation (13A.1) then becomes

$$\Delta\Pi = \frac{\partial\Pi}{\partial S}\Delta S + \frac{\partial\Pi}{\partial\sigma}\Delta\sigma + \frac{\partial\Pi}{\partial t}\Delta t + \frac{1}{2}\frac{\partial^2\Pi}{\partial S^2}\Delta S^2 + \frac{1}{2}\frac{\partial^2\Pi}{\partial\sigma^2}\Delta\sigma^2 + \cdots$$

where $\Delta\sigma$ is the change in σ in time Δt. In this case, delta hedging eliminates the first term on the right-hand side. The second term is eliminated by making the portfolio vega neutral. The third term is nonstochastic. The fourth term is eliminated by making the portfolio gamma neutral. Other terms are generally fairly small.

14

Numerical Procedures

In this chapter we discuss three numerical procedures that can be used to value derivative securities when exact formulas are not available. The first of these procedures involves Monte Carlo simulation and is useful for derivative securities where the payoff is dependent on the history of the underlying variable or where there are several underlying variables. The last two procedures involve the use of trees and finite difference methods. Unlike Monte Carlo simulation, they can be used for derivative securities where the holder has early exercise decisions or other types of decisions to make prior to maturity. The chapter shows how all the procedures can be used to calculate hedge parameters such as delta, gamma, and vega. It also presents some approximate valuation formulas for American options.

Up to now we have denoted the current time by t. When presenting the three numerical procedures we will, for ease of exposition, assume that the current time is zero.

14.1 MONTE CARLO SIMULATION

We will use the term *European-style derivative security* to describe a derivative security where the holder has no decisions to make during its life, and the term

American-style derivative security to refer to a derivative security where there are early exercise or other decisions that may have to be made. Consider a European-style derivative security that pays off f_T at time T. From Equation (12.15), its value at time zero is given by

$$f = \hat{E}[f_T e^{-\bar{r}T}] \tag{14.1}$$

where $\hat{E}$ denotes expectations in a risk-neutral world and $\bar{r}$ is the average instantaneous risk-free interest rate between time zero and time T. If the risk-free interest rate is assumed to be known with certainty, Equation (14.1) simplifies to

$$f = e^{-\bar{r}T} \hat{E}(f_T) \tag{14.2}$$

and $\bar{r}$ equals the yield on a zero-coupon bond maturing at time T.

ONE UNDERLYING VARIABLE

Monte Carlo simulation is a procedure for estimating the value of a European-style derivative security from either Equation (14.1) or (14.2). Consider first the situation where there is only one underlying stochastic variable and suppose that this is not an interest rate, so that Equation (14.2) can be used. One possible path for the variable is simulated in a risk-neutral world using a method similar to that described in Section 9.4 for simulating a stock price. This enables a terminal value of the derivative security to be calculated. This terminal value can be regarded as a random sample from the set of all possible terminal values. A second path for the variable is sampled and a second sample terminal value obtained. Further sample paths give further sample terminal values. After a large number, say 10,000, terminal values have been calculated, $\hat{E}(f_T)$ can be estimated as the arithmetic average of them. The current value of the derivative security can then be calculated using Equation (14.2). The calculation of a single terminal value or discounted terminal value will be referred to as a *simulation run*. Thus the simulation just described consists of 10,000 simulation runs.

The sample paths for the underlying variable must correspond to the stochastic process that the state variable would follow in a risk-neutral world. From Section 12.3 this means that, for the purposes of the simulation, the proportional drift rate of each variable must be reduced by $\lambda\sigma$, where λ is the market price of risk of the variable and σ is the volatility of the variable. If the variable is the price of a traded security, the effect of this adjustment is to set the drift rate equal to the risk-free interest rate less the instantaneous dividend yield.

If there is only one variable and this is the short-term risk-free interest rate, r, or some variable related to r, the Monte Carlo simulation procedure is similar to that just described except that the discount rate is different for each run. Paths for r in a risk-neutral world are simulated. On each simulation run, the average value of r during the life of the derivative security must be calculated. Before proceeding to the next simulation run, the terminal value of the derivative security must be discounted at this average rate and the result stored. After a large number of simulation runs, the arithmetic average of the discounted terminal values is calculated. This, from Equation (14.1), provides an estimate of f.

To describe Monte Carlo simulation more formally when there is one underlying variable, we suppose that the variable is θ. Define s as the volatility of θ and $\hat{m}$ as its growth rate in a risk-neutral world. For the purposes of carrying out the simulation, the life of the derivative security is divided into N subintervals of length Δt. As discussed in Section 9.4, the discrete version of the process for θ in a risk-neutral world is

$$\Delta\theta = \hat{m}\theta\,\Delta t + s\theta\epsilon\,\sqrt{\Delta t} \qquad (14.3)$$

where $\Delta\theta$ is the change in θ in time Δt and ϵ is a random sample from a standardized normal distribution.[1] To carry out one simulation run, N independent random samples must be drawn from a standardized normal distribution. When these are substituted into Equation (14.3), the values of $\Delta\theta$ at times $0, \Delta t, 2\,\Delta t, \ldots, T$ are calculated. These provide a simulated path for θ and enable a sample terminal value of the derivative security to be calculated.

SEVERAL UNDERLYING VARIABLES

When there are several variables, the paths of each one must be sampled on each simulation run. The terminal value of the derivative security is calculated on each simulation run from the sample paths. If the instantaneous risk-free interest rate, r, is a function of the state variables, the average value of r, $\bar{r}$, must also be calculated on each simulation run. The terminal value is discounted at $\bar{r}$ before the next simulation run is begun. Again it should be emphasized that the stochastic processes for all variables, including r, must, for the purposes of the simulation, be the processes that the variables would follow in a risk-neutral world.

Suppose there are n variables, θ_i $(1 \leq i \leq n)$. Define s_i as the volatility of θ_i, $\hat{m}_i$ as the expected growth rate of θ_i in a risk-neutral world, and ρ_{ik} as the instantaneous correlation between θ_i and θ_k. As in the single-variable case, the life of the derivative security must be divided into N subintervals of length Δt. The discrete version of the process for θ_i is then

$$\Delta\theta_i = \hat{m}_i\theta_i\,\Delta t + s_i\theta_i\epsilon_i\,\sqrt{\Delta t} \qquad (14.4)$$

---

[1]When θ follows geometric Brownian motion, it is slightly more accurate to assume that $(\theta + \Delta\theta)/\theta$ is lognormally distributed. Using the results in Section 10.2, it can be shown that Equation (14.3) becomes

$$\theta + \Delta\theta = \theta \exp\left[\left(\hat{m} - \frac{s^2}{2}\right)\Delta t + s\epsilon\,\sqrt{\Delta t}\right]$$

where $\Delta\theta_i$ is the change in θ_i in time Δt and ϵ_i is a random sample from a standardized normal distribution. The coefficient of correlation between ϵ_i and ϵ_k is ρ_{ik} for $1 \leq i, k \leq n$. One simulation run involves obtaining N samples of the ϵ_i ($1 \leq i \leq n$) from a multivariate standardized normal distribution. These are substituted into Equation (14.4) to produce simulated paths for each θ_i and enable a sample value for the derivative security to be calculated.

GENERATING THE RANDOM SAMPLES

Most programming languages incorporate routines for sampling a random number between 0 and 1. An approximate sample from a univariate standardized normal distribution can be obtained from the formula

$$\epsilon = \sum_{i=1}^{12} R_i - 6 \tag{14.5}$$

where the R_i are independent random numbers between 0 and 1 ($1 \leq i \leq 12$) and ϵ is the required sample from $\phi(0, 1)$. This approximation is satisfactory for most purposes.

If samples from a standardized bivariate normal distribution are required, an appropriate procedure is as follows. Independent samples x_1 and x_2 are drawn from a univariate standardized normal distribution as previously described. The required samples ϵ_1 and ϵ_2 are then calculated as follows:

$$\epsilon_1 = x_1$$

$$\epsilon_2 = \rho x_1 + x_2 \sqrt{1 - \rho^2}$$

where ρ is the correlation between the variables in the bivariate distribution.

For an n-variate normal distribution where the coefficient of correlation between variable i and variable j is ρ_{ij}, we first sample n independent variables x_i ($1 \leq i \leq n$) from univariate standardized normal distributions. The required samples are ϵ_i ($1 \leq i \leq n$) where

$$\epsilon_i = \sum_{k=1}^{k=i} \alpha_{ik} x_k$$

For ϵ_i to have the correct variance and the correct correlation with the ϵ_j ($1 \leq j < i$) we must have

$$\sum_k \alpha_{ik}^2 = 1$$

and

$$\sum_k \alpha_{ik}\alpha_{jk} = \rho_{ij}$$

The first sample, ϵ_1, is set equal to x_1. These equations enable ϵ_2 to be obtained from ϵ_1, ϵ_3 to be obtained from ϵ_1 and ϵ_2, and so on.

The number of simulation runs carried out depends on the accuracy required. If M is the number of independent runs and ω is the standard deviation of the values of the derivative security calculated from the simulation runs, the standard error of the estimate of f is $\omega/\sqrt{M}$.

VARIANCE REDUCTION PROCEDURES

If no adjustments are made to the sampling procedures, a very large value of M is usually necessary to estimate f with reasonable accuracy. However, two variance reduction procedures, known as the *antithetic variable technique* and the *control variate technique*, can be used to produce a significant reduction in the required value of M.

In the antithetic variable technique, a simulation run involves calculating two values of the derivative security. The first value, f_1, is calculated in the usual way; the second value, f_2 is calculated by changing the sign of all the samples from standard normal distributions. (If ϵ is the sample used to calculate the first value, $-\epsilon$ is used to calculate the second value.) The estimate of the value of the derivative security calculated from the simulation run is the average of the two calculated values. This works well because when one value is above the true value, the other tends to be below and vice versa. Denote $\overline{f}$ as the average of f_1 and f_2

$$\overline{f} = \frac{f_1 + f_2}{2}$$

The final estimate of the value of the derivative security is the average of the $\overline{f}$'s. If ω is the standard deviation of the $\overline{f}$'s, and M is the number of simulation runs (that is, the number of pairs of values calculated), then the standard error of the estimate is, as before, $\omega/\sqrt{M}$.

The control variate technique is applicable when there are two similar derivative securities, A and B. Security A is the security under consideration; security B is a security that is similar to security A and for which an analytic solution is available. Two simulations using the same random number streams and the same Δt are carried out in parallel. The first is used to obtain an estimate, f_A^*, of the value of A; the second is used to obtain an estimate, f_B^*, of the value of B. A better estimate of the value of A, f_A, is then obtained using the formula

$$f_A = f_A^* - f_B^* + f_B \tag{14.6}$$

where f_B is the known true value of B.[2]

APPLICATIONS

Compared to other procedures, Monte Carlo simulation is numerically efficient when there are several variables. This is because the time taken to carry out a Monte Carlo simulation increases approximately linearly with the number of variables, whereas the time taken for most other procedures increases exponentially with the number of variables. It also has the advantage that it provides a standard error for the estimates that are made. One limitation of the Monte Carlo simulation approach is that it can be used only for European-style derivative securities. But it is an approach that can accommodate complex payoffs and complex functional forms for the $\hat{m}_i$ and s_i. In particular, it can be used when the payoff depends on some function of the whole path followed by a variable, not just its terminal value.

Monte Carlo simulation has been used to analyze options where the volatility of the underlying stock is stochastic.[3] Paths for both the stock price and the volatility are jointly simulated. The value of the volatility at any given time determines the probability distribution from which the stock price is sampled.

Hedge parameters can be calculated using Monte Carlo simulation. Suppose that we are interested in the rate of change of f with q, where f is the value of the derivative security and q is the value of an underlying variable or a parameter. First, Monte Carlo simulation is used in the usual way to calculate an estimate, f, for the value of the security. A small increase, Δq, is then made in the value of q, and a new value for the security, f^*, is calculated *using the same random number streams* as for f. An estimate for the hedge parameter is given by

$$\frac{f^* - f}{\Delta q}$$

The number of intervals, N, should be kept the same for estimating both f and f^*.

---

[2]For a further discussion of variance reduction procedures, see J. M. Hammersley and D. C. Handscomb, *Monte Carlo Methods* (London: Methuen, 1964); P. P. Boyle, "Options: A Monte Carlo Approach," *Journal of Financial Economics*, 4 (1977), 323–38; J. Hull and A. White, "The Pricing of Options on Assets with Stochastic Volatilities," *Journal of Finance*, 42 (June 1987), 281–300.

[3]See H. E. Johnson and D. Shanno, "Option Pricing When the Variance is Changing," *Journal of Financial and Quantitative Analysis*, 22 (July 1987), 143–51; J. Hull and A. White, "The Pricing of Options on Assets with Stochastic Volatilities," *Journal of Finance* 42 (June 1987), 281–300.

14.2 BINOMIAL TREES

In Chapter 10 we used a simple binomial model when explaining the nature of the arguments underlying the Black–Scholes model. In the model it was assumed that only two stock prices were possible at the end of the life of the option. This model is clearly unrealistic and was used only for illustrative purposes. A more realistic assumption is that stock price movements are binomial in a short period of time of length Δt. This is the assumption that underlies a widely used numerical procedure that was first proposed by Cox, Ross, and Rubinstein.[4]

Consider the evaluation of an option on a non-dividend-paying stock. We start by dividing the life of the option into a large number of small time intervals of length Δt. We assume that in each time interval the stock price moves from its initial value of S to one of two new values, Su and Sd. This model is illustrated in Figure 14.1. In general, $u > 1$ and $d < 1$. The movement from S to Su is therefore an "up" movement and the movement from S to Sd is a "down" movement. The probability of an up movement is assumed to be p and the probability of a down movement is assumed to be $1 - p$.

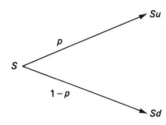

Figure 14.1 Stock Price Movements in Time Δt under the Binomial Model

RISK-NEUTRAL VALUATION

In Chapter 10 we introduced what is known as the risk-neutral valuation principle. This states that any security dependent on a stock price can be valued on the assumption that the world is risk neutral. It means that for the purposes of valuing an option (or any other derivative security), we can assume that

1. The expected return from all traded securities is the risk-free interest rate;
2. Future cash flows can be valued by discounting their expected values at the risk-free interest rate.

---

[4]See J. C. Cox, S. A. Ross, and M. Rubinstein, "Option Pricing: A Simplified Approach," *Journal of Financial Economics*, 7 (October 1979), 229–63.

When using the binomial model we will make use of the risk neutral valuation principle and assume that the world is risk neutral.

DETERMINATION OF p, u, AND d

The parameters p, u, and d must give correct values for the mean and variance of stock price changes during a time interval Δt. Since we are working in a risk-neutral world, the expected return from a stock is the risk-free interest rate, r.[5] Hence the expected value of the stock price at the end of a time interval Δt is $Se^{r\Delta t}$, where S is the stock price at the beginning of the time interval. It follows that

$$Se^{r\Delta t} = pSu + (1 - p)Sd \tag{14.7}$$

or

$$e^{r\Delta t} = pu + (1 - p)d \tag{14.8}$$

It will be recalled from the stock price model assumed in Chapter 10 that the variance of the change in the stock price in a small time interval Δt is $S^2\sigma^2\Delta t$. Since the variance of a variable Q is defined as $E(Q^2) - [E(Q)]^2$, where E denotes expected value, it follows that

$$S^2\sigma^2\Delta t = pS^2u^2 + (1 - p)S^2d^2 - S^2[pu + (1 - p)d]^2$$

or

$$\sigma^2\Delta t = pu^2 + (1 - p)d^2 - [pu + (1 - p)d]^2 \tag{14.9}$$

Equations (14.8) and (14.9) impose two conditions on p, u, and d. A third condition that is usually used is

$$u = \frac{1}{d}$$

It can be shown that the three conditions imply[6]

$$p = \frac{a - d}{u - d} \tag{14.10}$$

$$u = e^{\sigma\sqrt{\Delta t}} \tag{14.11}$$

$$d = e^{-\sigma\sqrt{\Delta t}} \tag{14.12}$$

---

[5]In practice, r is usually chosen as a constant equal to the zero-coupon yield on a bond maturing at the same time as the option.

[6]See footnote 5 in Chapter 9 with $\mu = r$.

where

$$a = e^{r \Delta t} \tag{14.13}$$

provided Δt is small.[7]

THE TREE OF STOCK PRICES

The complete tree of stock prices that is considered when the binomial model is used is illustrated in Figure 14.2. At time zero, the stock price, S, is known. At time Δt, there are two possible stock prices, Su and Sd; at time $2\Delta t$, there are three possible stock prices, Su^2, S, and Sd^2; and so on. In general, at time $i\Delta t$, $i + 1$ stock prices are considered. These are

$$Su^j d^{i-j} \qquad j = 0, \ 1 \ldots, \ i$$

Note that the relationship $u = 1/d$ is used in computing the stock price at each node of the tree in Figure 14.2. For example, $Su^2 d = Su$. Note also that the tree recombines in the sense that an up movement followed by a down movement leads to the same stock price as a down movement followed by an up movement. This considerably reduces the number of nodes on the tree.

WORKING BACKWARD THROUGH THE TREE

Options are evaluated by starting at the end of the tree (time T) and working backward. The value of the option is known at time T. For example, a put option

---

[7]This approximation is reasonable for most purposes. However, these values of p, u, and d are only correct in the limit as $\Delta t \longrightarrow 0$. It is slightly more accurate to solve

$$pu + (1 - p)d = a$$

$$pu^2 + (1 - p)d^2 - a^2 = b^2$$

$$u = \frac{1}{d}$$

where a and b are the mean and variance of the (lognormal) distribution of $S(t + \Delta t)/S(t)$ in a risk-neutral world. This gives

$$u = \frac{(a^2 + b^2 + 1) + \sqrt{(a^2 + b^2 + 1)^2 - 4a^2}}{2a}$$

$$p = \frac{a - d}{u - d}$$

From equations (10.8) and (10.9),

$$a = e^{r \Delta t}$$

$$b^2 = a^2(e^{\sigma^2 \Delta t} - 1)$$

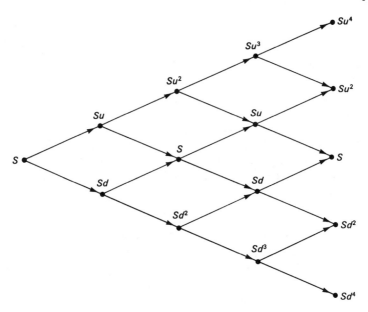

Figure 14.2   Tree Used to Value a Stock Option

is worth max $(X - S_T, 0)$ and a call option is worth max $(S_T - X, 0)$, where S_T is the stock price at time T and X is the strike price. Since a risk-neutral world is being assumed, the value at each node at time $T - \Delta t$ can be calculated as the expected value at time T discounted at rate r for a time period Δt. Similarly, the value at each node at time $T - 2\Delta t$ can be calculated as the expected value at time $T - \Delta t$ discounted for a time period Δt at rate r, and so on. If the option is American, it is necessary to check at each node to see whether early exercise is preferable to holding the option for a further time period Δt. Eventually, by working back through all the nodes, the value of the option at time zero is obtained.

Example 14.1

Consider a 5-month American put option on a non-dividend-paying stock when the stock price is $50, the strike price is $50, the risk-free interest rate is 10% per annum, and the volatility is 40% per annum. With our usual notation, this means that $S = 50$, $X = 50$, $r = 0.10$, $\sigma = 0.40$, and $T = 0.4167$. Suppose that we divide the life of the option into five intervals of length 1 month (= 0.0833 year) for the purposes of constructing a binomial tree. Then $\Delta t = 0.0833$ and using equations (14.10) to (14.13)

$$u = e^{\sigma\sqrt{\Delta t}} = 1.1224, \qquad d = e^{-\sigma\sqrt{\Delta t}} = 0.8909$$

$$a = e^{r\Delta t} = 1.0084, \qquad p = \frac{a - d}{u - d} = 0.5076$$

$$1 - p = 0.4924$$

Figure 14.3 shows the binomial tree. At each node there are two numbers. The top one shows the stock price at the node; the lower one shows the value of the option at the node. The probability of an up movement is always 0.5076; the probability of a down movement is always 0.4924.

The stock price at the jth node ($j = 0, 1 \ldots, i$) at time $i \Delta t$ is calculated as $Su^j d^{i-j}$. For example, the stock price at the node labeled A ($i = 4, j = 1$) is $50 \times 1.1224 \times 0.8909^3 =$ $39.69. The option prices at the final nodes are calculated as $\max(X - S_T, 0)$. For example, the option price at node G is $50 - 35.36 = 14.64$.

The option prices at the penultimate nodes are calculated from the option prices at the final nodes. First, we assume no exercise of the option at the nodes. This means that the option price is calculated as the present value of expected option price in time Δt. For example, at node E the option price is calculated as

$$(0.5076 \times 0 + 0.4924 \times 5.45)e^{-0.10 \times 0.0833} = 2.66$$

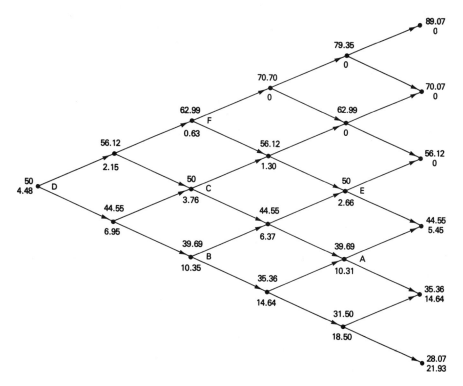

Figure 14.3   Binomial Tree for American Put on Non-Dividend-Paying Stock (Example 14.1)

while at node A it is calculated as

$$(0.5076 \times 5.45 + 0.4924 \times 14.64)e^{-0.10 \times 0.0833} = 9.90$$

We then check to see if early exercise is preferable to waiting. At node E, early exercise would give a value for the option of zero since both the stock price and strike price are $50. Clearly it is best to wait. The correct value for the option at node E is therefore $2.66. At node A it is a different story. If the option is exercised it is worth $50.00 − $39.69 or $10.31. This is more than $9.90. If node A is reached, the option should therefore be exercised and the correct value for the option at node A is $10.31.

Option prices at earlier nodes are calculated in a similar way. Note that it is not always best to exercise an option early when it is in the money. Consider node B. If the option is exercised, it is worth $50.00 − $39.69 or $10.31. However, if it is held, it is worth

$$(0.5076 \times 6.37 + 0.4924 \times 14.64)e^{-0.10 \times 0.0833} = 10.35$$

The option should therefore not be exercised at this node, and the correct option value at the node is $10.35.

Working back through the tree, we find the value of the option at the initial node to be $4.48. This is our numerical estimate for the option's current value. In practice, a smaller value of Δt, and many more nodes, would be used. The true value of the option, obtained using a very small value of Δt, is $4.29.

Expressing the Approach Algebraically

Suppose that the life of an American put option on a non-dividend-paying stock is divided into N subintervals of length Δt. Define f_{ij} as the value of an American option at time $i\Delta t$ when the stock price is $Su^j d^{i-j}$ for $0 \leq i \leq N$, $0 \leq j \leq i$. We will refer to this as the value of the option at the (i, j) node. Since the value of an American put at its expiration date is $\max(X - S_T, 0)$, we know that

$$f_{Nj} = \max[X - Su^j d^{N-j}, 0] \qquad j = 0, 1 \ldots, N$$

There is a probability, p, of moving from the (i, j) node at time $i\Delta t$ to the $(i + 1, j + 1)$ node at time $(i + 1)\Delta t$, and a probability $1 - p$ of moving from the (i, j) node at time $i\Delta t$ to the $(i + 1, j)$ node at time $(i + 1)\Delta t$. Assuming no early exercise, risk-neutral valuation gives

$$f_{ij} = e^{-r\Delta t}[pf_{i+1,j+1} + (1 - p)f_{i+1,j}]$$

for $0 \leq i \leq N - 1$ and $0 \leq j \leq i$. When early exercise is taken into account, this value for f_{ij} must be compared with the option's intrinsic value, and we obtain

$$f_{ij} = \max\{X - Su^j d^{i-j}, e^{-r\Delta t}[pf_{i+1,j+1} + (1 - p)f_{i+1,j}]\}$$

Note that because the calculations start at time T and work backward, the value at time $i\Delta t$ captures not only the effect of early exercise possibilities at time $i\Delta t$, but also the effect of early exercise at subsequent times. In the limit as Δt tends to zero, an exact value for the American put is obtained. In practice, $N = 30$ usually gives reasonable results.

ESTIMATING DELTA AND OTHER HEDGE PARAMETERS

It will be recalled that the delta, Δ, of an option is the rate of change of its price with respect to the underlying stock price. In other words,

$$\Delta = \frac{\Delta f}{\Delta S}$$

where ΔS is a small change in the stock price and Δf is the corresponding small change in the option price. At time Δt we have an estimate, f_{11}, for the option price when the stock price is Su; and an estimate, f_{10}, for the option price when the stock price is Sd. In other words, when $\Delta S = Su - Sd$, $\Delta f = f_{11} - f_{10}$. An estimate of Δ at time Δt is therefore:

$$\Delta = \frac{f_{11} - f_{10}}{Su - Sd}$$

To determine gamma, Γ, we note that we have two estimates of Δ at time $2\Delta t$. When $S = (Su^2 + S)/2$ (half way between the second and third node), delta is $(f_{22} - f_{21})/(Su^2 - S)$; when $S = (S + Sd^2)/2$ (half way between the first and second node) delta is $(f_{21} - f_{20})/(S - Sd^2)$. The difference between the two values of S is h where

$$h = 0.5(Su^2 - Sd^2)$$

and gamma is the change in delta divided by the change in h

$$\Gamma = \frac{[(f_{22} - f_{21})/(Su^2 - S)] - [(f_{21} - f_{20})/(S - Sd^2)]}{h} \tag{14.14}$$

These procedures provide estimates of delta at time Δt and of gamma at time $2\Delta t$. In practice, these are often used as estimates of delta and gamma at time zero as well. If slightly more accuracy is required for delta, it makes sense to start the binomial tree at time $-2\Delta t$ and assume that the stock price is S at this time. The required estimate of the price of the option is then f_{21} (rather than f_{00}). More nodes have to be evaluated, but three different values of S are considered at time zero: Sd^2, S, and Su^2. An estimate of delta is

$$\Delta = \frac{f_{22} - f_{20}}{Su^2 - Sd^2} \tag{14.15}$$

and Equation (14.14) provides the estimate of gamma.

A further hedge parameter that can be obtained directly from the tree is theta, Θ. This is the rate of change of the option price with time when all else is kept constant. If the tree starts at time zero, an estimate of theta is

$$\Theta = \frac{f_{21} - f_{00}}{2\Delta t}$$

If the tree starts at time $-2\Delta t$, a symmetrical estimate of theta can be obtained

$$\Theta = \frac{f_{42} - f_{00}}{4\Delta t} \tag{14.16}$$

Vega can be calculated by making a small change, $\Delta\sigma$, in the volatility and constructing a new tree to obtain a new value of the option (Δt should be kept the same). The estimate of vega is

$$\text{vega} = \frac{f^* - f}{\Delta\sigma}$$

where f and f^* are the estimates of the option price from the original and the new tree, respectively. Rho can be calculated similarly.

Example 14.2

Consider a 3-month American put option on a non-dividend-paying stock when the stock price is \$50, the strike price is \$50, the risk-free interest rate is 10% per annum, and the volatility is 40% per annum. In this case, $S = 50$, $X = 50$, $r = 0.10$, $\sigma = 0.4$, and $T = 0.25$. The option is exactly the same as the option considered in Example 14.1 except that it lasts for 3 months instead of 5 months. Choosing Δt equal to 1 month (= 0.0833 year), an estimate of the value of the option is the value of being at point C in Figure 14.3, that is, \$3.76.

In the context of our new example, Figure 14.3 starts at time $-2\Delta t$. From Equation (14.15), an estimate of delta can be obtained from the values at nodes B and F as

$$\frac{0.63 - 10.35}{62.99 - 39.69} = 0.42$$

From Equation (14.16), an estimate of the gamma of the option can be obtained from the values at nodes B, C, and F as

$$\frac{[(0.63 - 3.76)/(62.99 - 50.00)] - [(3.76 - 10.35)/(50.00 - 39.69)]}{11.65}$$

From Equation (14.10), an estimate of the theta of the option can be obtained from the values at nodes D and E as

$$\frac{2.66 - 4.48}{0.333} = -5.5$$

These are of course only rough estimates. They would be improved if a tree with a smaller Δt were constructed.

14.3 USING THE BINOMIAL TREE FOR OPTIONS ON INDICES, CURRENCIES, AND FUTURES CONTRACTS

The binomial tree approach to valuing options on non-dividend-paying stocks can easily be adapted to valuing American calls and puts on a stock paying a continuous dividend yield at rate q.

Since the dividends provide a return of q, the stock price itself must on average in a risk-neutral world provide a return of $r - q$. Hence Equation (14.7) becomes:

$$Se^{(r-q)\Delta t} = pSu + (1 - p)Sd$$

so that (14.8) becomes

$$e^{(r-q)\Delta t} = pu + (1 - p)d$$

It turns out that equations (14.10), (14.11), and (14.12) are still correct but with

$$a = e^{(r-q)\Delta t} \tag{14.17}$$

The binomial tree numerical procedure can therefore be used exactly as before with this new value of a.

It will be recalled from Chapter 11 that stock indices, currencies, and futures contracts can, for the purposes of option evaluation, be considered as stocks paying continuous dividend yields. In the case of a stock index, the relevant dividend yield is the dividend yield on the stock portfolio underlying the index; in the case of a currency, it is the foreign risk-free interest rate; in the case of a futures contract, it is the domestic risk-free interest rate. The binomial tree approach can therefore be used to value options on stock indices, currencies, and futures contracts.

Example 14.3

Consider a 4-month American call option on index futures where the current futures price is 300, the exercise price is 300, the risk-free interest rate is 8% per annum, and the volatility of the index is 40% per annum. We divide the life of the option into four 1-month periods for the purposes of constructing the tree. In this case, $F = 300$, $X = 300$, $r = 0.08$, $\sigma = 0.4$, $T = 0.3333$, and $\Delta t = 0.0833$. Since a futures contract is analogous to a stock paying dividends at a continuous rate r, q should be set equal to r in Equation (14.17). This gives $a = 1$. The other parameters necessary to construct the tree are

$$u = e^{\sigma\sqrt{\Delta t}} = 1.1224, \qquad d = \frac{1}{u} = 0.8909$$

$$p = \frac{a - d}{u - d} = 0.4713, \qquad 1 - p = 0.5287$$

The tree is shown in Figure 14.4. (The upper number is the futures price; the lower number is the option price.) The estimated value of the option is 25.54.

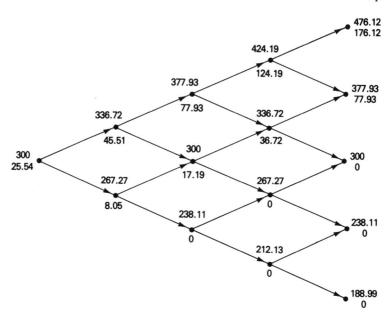

Figure 14.4 Binomial Tree for American Call Option on an Index Futures Contract (Example 14.3)

Example 14.4

Consider a 1-year American put option on the British pound. The current exchange rate is 1.6100, the strike price is 1.6000, the U.S. risk-free interest rate is 8% per annum, the sterling risk-free interest rate is 10% per annum, and the volatility of the sterling exchange rate is 12% per annum. In this case, $S = 1.61$, $X = 1.60$, $r = 0.08$, $r_f = 0.10$, $\sigma = 0.12$, and $T = 1.0$. We divide the life of the option into four 3-month periods for the purposes of constructing the tree so that $\Delta t = 0.25$. In this case, $q = r_f$ and Equation (14.17) gives

$$a = e^{(0.08-0.10)\times 0.25} = 0.9950$$

The other parameters necessary to construct the tree are

$$u = e^{\sigma\sqrt{\Delta t}} = 1.0618, \qquad d = \frac{1}{u} = 0.9418$$

$$p = \frac{a-d}{u-d} = 0.4433, \qquad 1 - p = 0.5567$$

The tree is shown in Figure 14.5. (The upper number is the exchange rate; the lower number is the option price.) The estimated value of the option is \$0.0782.

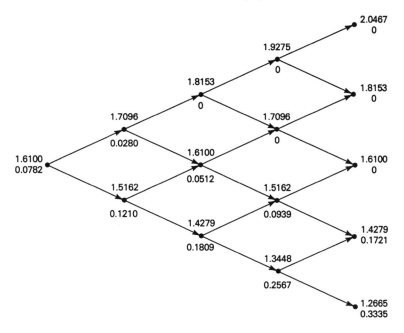

Figure 14.5 Binomial Model for American Put Option on a Currency (Example 14.4)

14.4 THE BINOMIAL MODEL FOR A DIVIDEND-PAYING STOCK

We now move on to the more tricky issue of how the binomial model can be used for a dividend-paying stock. As in Chapter 10, the word "dividend" will, for the purposes of our discussion, be used to refer to the reduction in the stock price on the ex-dividend date as a result of the dividend.

KNOWN DIVIDEND YIELD

If it is assumed that a known dividend yield, δ, is to be paid at a certain time in the future, the tree takes the form shown in Figure 14.6 and can be analyzed in a way that is analogous to that just described. If the time $i\Delta t$ is prior to the stock going ex-dividend, the nodes on the tree correspond to stock prices

$$Su^j d^{i-j} \qquad j = 0,\ 1,\ldots,\ i$$

where u and d are defined as in equations (14.11) and (14.12). If the time $i\Delta t$ is after the stock goes ex-dividend, the nodes correspond to stock prices

$$S(1-\delta)u^j d^{i-j} \qquad j = 0,\ 1,\ldots,\ i$$

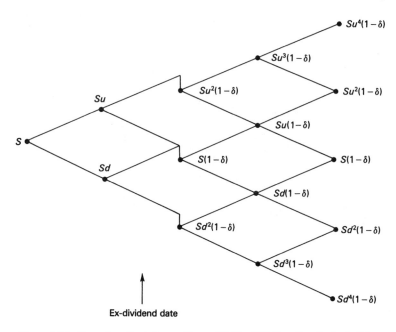

Figure 14.6 Tree when Stock Pays a Known Dividend Yield at One Particular Time

Several known dividend yields during the life of an option can be dealt with similarly. If δ_i is the total dividend yield associated with all ex-dividend dates between time zero and time $i\Delta t$, the nodes at time $i\Delta t$ correspond to stock prices

$$S(1 - \delta_i)u^j d^{i-j}$$

KNOWN DOLLAR DIVIDEND

In some situations, the most realistic assumption is that the dollar amount of the dividend rather than the dividend yield is known in advance. If the volatility of the stock, σ, is assumed constant, the tree then takes the form shown in Figure 14.7. It does not recombine, which means that the number of nodes that have to be evaluated, particularly if there are several dividends, is liable to become very large. Suppose that there is only one dividend; that the ex-dividend date, τ, is between $k\Delta t$ and $(k+1)\Delta t$; and that the dollar amount of the dividend is D. When $i \leq k$, the nodes on the tree are as in Figure 14.2. When $i = k+1$ the nodes at time $i\Delta t$ correspond to stock prices

$$Su^j d^{i-j} - D \qquad j = 0,\ 1,\ 2,\ldots,\ i$$

as before. When $i = k + 2$, the nodes on the tree correspond to stock prices

$$(Su^j d^{i-1-j} - D)u \qquad \text{and} \qquad (Su^j d^{i-1-j} - D)d$$

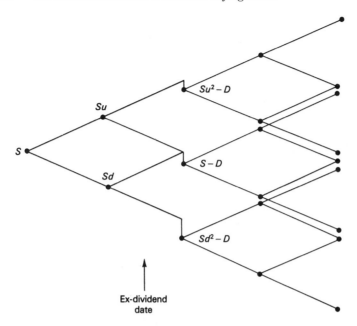

$Su^2 - D$

Su

S

Sd

$S - D$

$Sd^2 - D$

Ex-dividend
date

Figure 14.7   Tree when Dollar Amount of Dividend Is Assumed Known and Volatility
Is Assumed Constant

for $j = 0, 1, 2, \ldots, i - 1$, so that there are $2i$ rather than $i + 1$ nodes. At time
$(k + m)\Delta t$ there are $m(k + 1)$ rather than $k + m + 1$ nodes.

The problem can be simplified by assuming, as in the analysis of European
options in Chapter 10, that the stock price has two components: a part that is
uncertain and a part that is the present value of all future dividends during the life
of the option. Suppose, as before, that there is only one ex-dividend date, τ, during
the life of the option and that $k\Delta t \leq \tau \leq (k + 1)\Delta t$. The value of the uncertain
component, S^*, at time x is given by

$$S^*(x) = S(x) \qquad \text{when } x > \tau$$

and

$$S^*(x) = S(x) - De^{-r(\tau - x)} \qquad \text{when } x \leq \tau$$

where D is the dividend. Define σ^* as the volatility of S^* and assume that σ^*
rather than σ is constant. (In general $\sigma^* > \sigma$). The parameters p, u, and d can be
calculated from equations (14.10), (14.11), (14.12), and (14.13) with σ replaced
by σ^* and a tree can be constructed in the usual way to model S^*. By adding to
the stock price at each node the present value of future dividends (if any), the tree
can be converted into another tree that models S. At time $i\Delta t$, the nodes on this

tree correspond to the stock prices

$$S^*(t)u^j d^{i-j} + De^{-r(\tau - i\Delta t)} \qquad j = 0, 1, \ldots, i$$

when $i\Delta t < \tau$ and

$$S^*(t)u^j d^{i-j} \qquad j = 0, 1, \ldots, i$$

when $i\Delta t > \tau$. This approach, which involves a perfectly reasonable assumption about the stock price volatility, succeeds in achieving a situation where the tree recombines so that there are $i + 1$ nodes at time $i\Delta t$. It can be generalized in a straightforward way to deal with the situation where there are several dividends.

Example 14.5

Consider a 5-month put option on a stock that is expected to pay a single dividend of $2.06 during the life of the option. The initial stock price is $52, the strike price is $50, the risk-free interest rate is 10% per annum, the volatility is 40% per annum, and the ex-dividend date is in $3\frac{1}{2}$ months.

We first construct a tree to model S^*, the stock price less the present value of future dividends during the life of the option. Initially, the present value of the dividend is

$$2.06e^{-0.2917 \times 0.1} = 2.00$$

The initial value of S^* is therefore 50.0. Assuming that the 40% per annum volatility refers to S^*, Figure 14.3 provides a binomial tree for S^*. (S^* has the same initial value and volatility as the stock price upon which Figure 14.3 was based.) Adding the present value of the dividend at each node leads to Figure 14.8, which is a binomial model for S. The probabilities at each node are, as in Figure 14.3, 0.5076 for an up movement and 0.4924 for a down movement. Working back through the tree in the usual way gives the option price as $4.43.

14.5 EXTENSIONS TO THE BASIC TREE APPROACH

Unlike Monte Carlo simulation, tree approaches can be used for an American-style as well as for a European-style derivative security. However, the approach as it has been outlined here is appropriate only when the value of the derivative security depends on the current values of the underlying variables, not when it depends on their past history.

The tree approach can be used for a wide range of underlying variables. The parameters u, d, and p are calculated from equations (14.10), (14.11), and (14.12) with

$$a = e^{\hat{m}\Delta t}$$

where $\hat{m}$ is the growth rate of the variable in a risk-neutral world. Situations where there are modest changes in $\hat{m}$ can be accommodated by the tree approach. Equations (14.10), (14.11), and (14.12) show that u and d do not change, while p

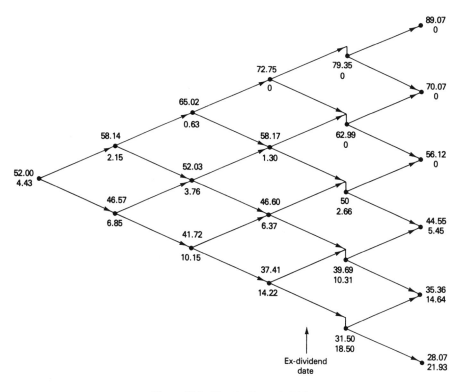

Figure 14.8   Tree for Example 14.5

becomes a function of time. The value of $\hat{m}$ for a commodity can be calculated in the way described in Section 12.4.

Tree approaches can be used when there is more than one underlying variable. The tree then unfolds in several dimensions. The probabilities at each node must be chosen so that each variable has the correct expected growth rate and standard deviation in a risk-neutral world, and so that the coefficient of correlation between any two variables is correct.[8]

When there is only one underlying variable, a binomial tree may not give the best numerical procedure. Boyle considers a trinomial tree where there are three possible price movements during each time interval Δt to be potentially more efficient.[9]

---

[8] See P. P. Boyle, "A Lattice Framework for Options Pricing with Two State Variables," *Journal of Financial and Quantitative Analysis*, 23 (March 1988), 1–12; J. C. Hull and A. White, "The Use of the Control Variate Technique in Option Pricing," *Journal of Financial and Quantitative Analysis*, 23 (September 1988), 237–51.

[9] See P. P. Boyle, "Option Valuation Using a Three Jump Process," *International Options Journal*, 3 (1986), 7–12.

In Chapter 15 we will describe how trinomial trees can be used to model interest rates.

THE CONTROL VARIATE TECHNIQUE

It is worth noting that the control variate technique mentioned in Section 14.2 can be used in conjunction with the tree approach. This point has been made by Hull and White.[10] The same tree is used to evaluate two similar derivative securities A and B. Security A is the derivative security under consideration; security B is a similar security whose value is known analytically. Equation (14.6) is then used. An example of a situation where this technique is appropriate is the evaluation of an American put option. Security B can be chosen as the corresponding European put option.

To illustrate the use of the control variate technique, Figure 14.9 values the option in Figure 14.3 on the assumption that it is European. The price obtained is $4.31. From the Black–Scholes formula, the true European price is $4.08. The

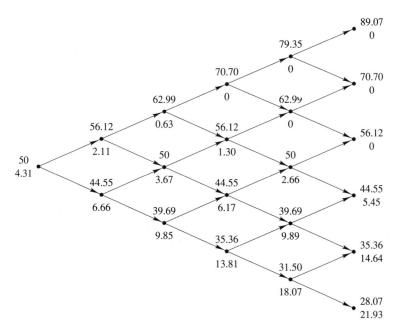

Figure 14.9   Tree for European Version of Option in Figure 14.3. At Each Node, Upper Number Is Stock Price, and Lower Number Is Option Price

[10]See J. C. Hull and A. White, "The Use of the Control Variate Technique in Option Pricing," *Journal of Financial and Quantitative Analysis*, 23 (September 1988), 237–51.

estimate of the American price in Figure 14.3 is $4.48. The control variate estimate of the American price is therefore

$$4.48 + 4.08 - 4.31 = 4.25$$

The true American price, as mentioned earlier, is 4.29. The control variate approach does therefore produce a considerable improvement over the original estimate of 4.48 in this case.

The calculation of the delta, gamma, and theta of the derivative security was discussed at the end of Section 14.2 and in Example 14.2. Other hedge parameters are obtained by first calculating the price of the derivative security, f, using the tree in the usual way. A small change, Δq, is then made to the parameter in question and the *same tree* is used to reevaluate the price of the derivative security. Suppose that the new price of the derivative security is f^*. The required partial derivative can be estimated as

$$\frac{f^* - f}{\Delta q}$$

14.6 AVOIDING NEGATIVE PROBABILITIES

The procedures that have been described so far produce a satisfactory tree in most circumstances. However, when σ is very small, they sometimes lead to one of the two probabilities being either very small or negative. For example, if r is 12% per annum, σ is 1% per annum, and $\Delta t = 0.1$, equations (14.10) to (14.12) give:

$$a = e^{0.1 \times 0.12} = 1.0121$$

$$u = e^{0.01 \times \sqrt{0.1}} = 1.0032$$

$$d = \frac{1}{u} = 0.9968$$

$$p = \frac{1.0121 - 0.9968}{1.0032 - 0.9968} = 2.39$$

$$1 - p = -1.39$$

The probabilities are in this case meaningless!

Define S as the spot price of the asset underlying the option and F as the asset's futures price for a contract expiring at the same time as the option. When the tree is used to model F, the procedures that have been described in this chapter never give rise to negative probabilities. (This is because the parameter a always equals 1.0.) This suggests a way of overcoming the negative probabilities problem. Regardless of whether the option is on F, we construct the tree to model F. At each node we can calculate S from F using

$$S = Fe^{-(r-q)(T-\tau)} \tag{14.18}$$

where τ is the time to which the node corresponds and T is the expiration of the option and futures contract. [See Equation (3.10).]

Example 14.6

Consider a 1-year American call option on the Canadian dollar. The current exchange rate is 0.7900, the strike price is 0.8000, the U.S. risk-free interest rate is 6% per annum, the Canadian risk-free interest rate is 10% per annum, and the volatility of the exchange rate is 4% per annum. In this case, $S = 0.79$, $X = 0.80$, $r = 0.06$, $r_f = 0.10$, $\sigma = 0.04$, and $T = 1$. We divide the life of the option into 3-month periods for the purposes of constructing the tree so that $\Delta t = 0.25$. When using the tree to model the futures price for a contract maturing in 1 year

$$a = 1$$

$$u = e^{0.04 \times \sqrt{0.25}} = 1.0202$$

$$d = \frac{1}{u} = 0.9802$$

$$p = \frac{a - d}{u - d} = 0.4950$$

$$1 - p = 0.5050$$

The initial futures price is, from Equation (3.10)

$$0.79e^{(0.06-0.10) \times 1} = 0.7590$$

The tree for the futures price is shown in Figure 14.10. At each node, the middle number shows the futures exchange rate, the upper number shows the spot exchange rate [calculated using Equation (14.18)] and the lower number shows the option price. The tree gives the value of the option as $0.0016.

14.7 FINITE DIFFERENCE METHODS

Finite difference methods value a derivative security by solving numerically the differential equation that the derivative security satisfies. The differential equation is converted into a set of difference equations and the difference equations are solved iteratively.

To illustrate the approach, we consider how it might be used to value an American put option on a non-dividend-paying stock. The differential equation

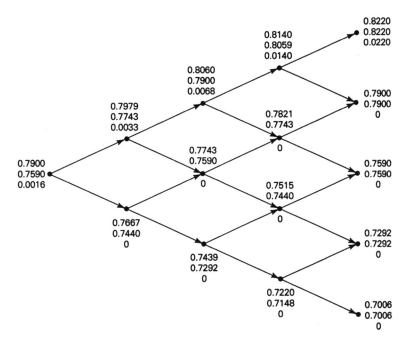

Figure 14.10 Binomial Tree for American Call Option on a Low Volatility Currency; at Each Node, Uppermost Number Is Spot Exchange rate, Middle Number Is Futures Exchange Rate, and Lower Number Is Option Price

that the option must satisfy is

$$\frac{\partial f}{\partial t} + rS\frac{\partial f}{\partial S} + \frac{1}{2}\sigma^2 S^2 \frac{\partial^2 f}{\partial S^2} = rf \qquad (14.19)$$

A finite number of different, equally spaced times between the current time, zero, and the maturity of the option, T, are chosen. We suppose that $\Delta t = T/N$ and that total of $N + 1$ times are considered:

$$0, \Delta t, 2\Delta t, \ldots, T$$

A finite number of different, equally spaced stock prices are also chosen. We suppose that S_{max} is a stock price which is sufficiently high that, when it is reached, the put has virtually no value. We define $\Delta S = S_{max}/M$ and consider a total of $M + 1$ stock prices:

$$0, \Delta S, 2\Delta S, \ldots, S_{max}$$

One of these is assumed to be the current stock price.

This general approach is represented diagrammatically in Figure 14.11. A grid consisting of a total of $(M + 1)(N + 1)$ points is constructed. The (i, j) point

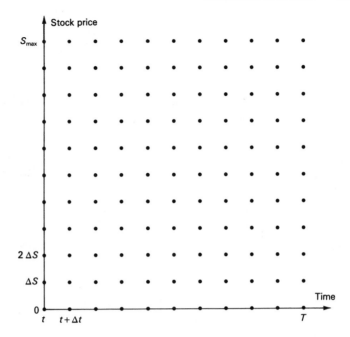

Figure 14.11   Grid for Finite Difference Approach.

on the grid is the point that corresponds to time $i\,\Delta t$ and stock price $j\,\Delta S$. We will use the variable, f_{ij}, to denote the value of the option at the $(i,\ j)$ point.

IMPLICIT FINITE DIFFERENCE METHOD

For an interior point $(i,\ j)$ on the grid, $\partial f/\partial S$ can be approximated as

$$\frac{\partial f}{\partial S} = \frac{f_{i,j+1} - f_{ij}}{\Delta S} \tag{14.20}$$

or as

$$\frac{\partial f}{\partial S} = \frac{f_{ij} - f_{i,j-1}}{\Delta S} \tag{14.21}$$

Equation (14.20) is known as the *forward difference approximation*; equation (14.21) is known as the *backward difference approximation*. In the *implicit finite difference method* we use a more symmetrical approximation by averaging the two:

$$\frac{\partial f}{\partial S} = \frac{f_{i,j+1} - f_{i,j-1}}{2\,\Delta S} \tag{14.22}$$

For $\partial f / \partial t$ we will use a forward difference approximation so that the value at time $i \, \Delta t$ is related to the value at time $(i + 1) \, \Delta t$:

$$\frac{\partial f}{\partial t} = \frac{f_{i+1,j} - f_{ij}}{\Delta t} \tag{14.23}$$

The backward difference approximation for $\partial f / \partial S$ at the (i, j) point is given by Equation (14.21). The backward difference at the $(i, j + 1)$ point is

$$\frac{f_{i,j+1} - f_{ij}}{\Delta S}$$

Hence a finite difference approximation for $\partial^2 f / \partial S^2$ at the (i, j) point is

$$\frac{\partial^2 f}{\partial S^2} = \left(\frac{f_{i,j+1} - f_{ij}}{\Delta S} - \frac{f_{ij} - f_{i,j-1}}{\Delta S} \right) \Big/ \Delta S$$

or

$$\frac{\partial^2 f}{\partial S^2} = \frac{f_{i,j+1} + f_{i,j-1} - 2f_{ij}}{\Delta S^2} \tag{14.24}$$

Substituting equations (14.22), (14.23), and (14.24) into the differential equation (14.19) and noting that $S = j \, \Delta S$ gives

$$\frac{f_{i+1,j} - f_{ij}}{\Delta t} + rj \, \Delta S \frac{f_{i,j+1} - f_{i,j-1}}{2 \, \Delta S} + \frac{1}{2} \sigma^2 j^2 \, \Delta S^2 \frac{f_{i,j+1} + f_{i,j-1} - 2f_{ij}}{\Delta S^2} = r f_{ij}$$

for $j = 1, 2 \ldots, M - 1$ and $i = 0, 1 \ldots, N - 1$. Rearranging terms, we obtain

$$a_j f_{i,j-1} + b_j f_{ij} + c_j f_{i,j+1} = f_{i+1,j} \tag{14.25}$$

where

$$a_j = \frac{1}{2} rj \, \Delta t - \frac{1}{2} \sigma^2 j^2 \, \Delta t$$

$$b_j = 1 + \sigma^2 j^2 \, \Delta t + r \, \Delta t$$

$$c_j = -\frac{1}{2} rj \, \Delta t - \frac{1}{2} \sigma^2 j^2 \, \Delta t$$

We now use the boundary conditions for an American put. The value of the put at time T is $\max[X - S_T, 0]$ where S_T is the stock price at time T. Hence

$$f_{Nj} = \max[X - j \, \Delta S, 0] \qquad j = 0, 1 \ldots, M \tag{14.26}$$

The value of the put option when the stock price is zero is X. Hence

$$f_{i0} = X \qquad i = 0, 1 \ldots, N \tag{14.27}$$

The value of the option tends to zero as the stock price tends to infinity. We therefore use the approximation

$$f_{iM} = 0 \qquad i = 0, 1 \ldots, N \tag{14.28}$$

Equations (14.26), (14.27), and (14.28) define the value of the put option along the three edges of the grid in Figure 14.11, where $S = 0$, $S = S_{max}$ and $t = T$. It remains to use Equation (14.25) to arrive at the value of f along the left edge of the grid. First the points corresponding to time $T - \Delta t$ are tackled. Equation (14.25) with $i = N - 1$ gives $M - 1$ simultaneous equations:

$$a_j f_{N-1,j-1} + b_j f_{N-1,j} + c_j f_{N-1,j+1} = f_{Nj} \tag{14.29}$$

for $j = 1, 2 \ldots, M - 1$. The right-hand sides of these equations are known from Equation (14.26). Furthermore, from equations (14.27) and (14.28),

$$f_{N-1,0} = X \tag{14.30}$$

$$f_{N-1,M} = 0 \tag{14.31}$$

Thus equations (14.29) are $M - 1$ equations which can be solved for the $M - 1$ unknowns: $f_{N-1,1}, f_{N-1,2}, \ldots, f_{N-1,M-1}$.[11] After this has been done, each value of $f_{N-1,j}$ is compared with $X - j\Delta S$. If $f_{N-1,j} < X - j\Delta S$, early exercise at time $T - \Delta t$ is optimal and $f_{N-1,j}$ is set equal to $X - j\Delta S$. The nodes corresponding to time $T - 2\Delta t$ are handled in a similar way, and so on. Eventually, $f_{01}, f_{02}, f_{03}, \ldots, f_{0,M-1}$ are obtained. One of these is the option price of interest.

The control variate technique can be used in conjunction with finite difference methods. The same grid is used to value an option that is similar to the one under consideration but for which an analytic valuation is available. Equation (14.6) is then used.

Example 14.7

Table 14.1 shows the result of using the implicit finite difference method as just described for pricing the option in Example 14.1. Values of 20, 10, and 5 were chosen for M, N, and ΔS, respectively. Thus the option price is evaluated at $5 stock price intervals between $0 and $100, and at half-month time intervals throughout the life of the option. The option price given by the grid is $4.07. The same grid gives the price of the corresponding European option as $3.91. The true European price given by the Black–Scholes formula is $4.08. The control variate estimate of the American price is therefore

$$4.07 + 4.08 - 3.91 = \$4.24$$

This is reasonably close to the true value of $4.29.

THE EXPLICIT FINITE DIFFERENCE METHOD

The implicit finite difference method has the advantage that it is very robust. It always converges to the solution of the differential equation as ΔS and Δt

---

[11]This does not involve inverting a matrix. The first equation in (14.29) can be used to express $f_{N-1,2}$ in terms of $f_{N-1,1}$; the second equation can be used to express $f_{N-1,3}$ in terms of $f_{N-1,1}$; and so on. The final equation provides a value for $f_{N-1,1}$ which can then be used to determine the other $f_{N-1,j}$.

TABLE 14.1 Grid to Value Option in Example 14.1 Using Implicit Finite Difference Methods

Stock Price (dollars)	Time to Maturity (Months)										
	5	$4\frac{1}{2}$	4	$3\frac{1}{2}$	3	$2\frac{1}{2}$	2	$1\frac{1}{2}$	1	$\frac{1}{2}$	0
100	0.00	0.00	0.00	0.00	0.00	0.00	0.00	0.00	0.00	0.00	0.00
95	0.02	0.02	0.01	0.01	0.00	0.00	0.00	0.00	0.00	0.00	0.00
90	0.05	0.04	0.03	0.02	0.01	0.01	0.00	0.00	0.00	0.00	0.00
85	0.09	0.07	0.05	0.03	0.02	0.01	0.01	0.00	0.00	0.00	0.00
80	0.16	0.12	0.09	0.07	0.04	0.03	0.02	0.01	0.00	0.00	0.00
75	0.27	0.22	0.17	0.13	0.09	0.06	0.03	0.02	0.01	0.00	0.00
70	0.47	0.39	0.32	0.25	0.18	0.13	0.08	0.04	0.02	0.00	0.00
65	0.82	0.71	0.60	0.49	0.38	0.28	0.19	0.11	0.05	0.02	0.00
60	1.42	1.27	1.11	0.95	0.78	0.62	0.45	0.30	0.16	0.05	0.00
55	2.43	2.24	2.05	1.83	1.61	1.36	1.09	0.81	0.51	0.22	0.00
50	4.07	3.88	3.67	3.45	3.19	2.91	2.57	2.17	1.66	0.99	0.00
45	6.58	6.44	6.29	6.13	5.96	5.77	5.57	5.36	5.17	5.02	5.00
40	10.15	10.10	10.05	10.01	10.00	10.00	10.00	10.00	10.00	10.00	10.00
35	15.00	15.00	15.00	15.00	15.00	15.00	15.00	15.00	15.00	15.00	15.00
30	20.00	20.00	20.00	20.00	20.00	20.00	20.00	20.00	20.00	20.00	20.00
25	25.00	25.00	25.00	25.00	25.00	25.00	25.00	25.00	25.00	25.00	25.00
20	30.00	30.00	30.00	30.00	30.00	30.00	30.00	30.00	30.00	30.00	30.00
15	35.00	35.00	35.00	35.00	35.00	35.00	35.00	35.00	35.00	35.00	35.00
10	40.00	40.00	40.00	40.00	40.00	40.00	40.00	40.00	40.00	40.00	40.00
5	45.00	45.00	45.00	45.00	45.00	45.00	45.00	45.00	45.00	45.00	45.00
0	50.00	50.00	50.00	50.00	50.00	50.00	50.00	50.00	50.00	50.00	50.00

approach zero.[12] One of the disadvantages of the implicit finite difference method is that $M - 1$ simultaneous equations have to be solved in order to calculate the f_{ij}'s from the $f_{i+1,j}$'s. The method can be simplified if the values of $\partial f/\partial S$ and $\partial^2 f/\partial S^2$ at point (i, j) on the grid are assumed to be the same as at point $(i + 1, j)$. Equations (14.22) and (14.24) then become

$$\frac{\partial f}{\partial S} = \frac{f_{i+1,j+1} - f_{i+1,j-1}}{2 \Delta S}$$

$$\frac{\partial^2 f}{\partial S^2} = \frac{f_{i+1,j+1} + f_{i+1,j-1} - 2 f_{i+1,j}}{\Delta S^2}$$

and Equation (14.25) becomes:

$$f_{ij} = a_j^* f_{i+1,j-1} + b_j^* f_{i+1,j} + c_j^* f_{i+1,j+1} \tag{14.32}$$

where

$$a_j^* = \frac{1}{1 + r \Delta t} \left(-\frac{1}{2} rj \, \Delta t + \frac{1}{2} \sigma^2 j^2 \, \Delta t \right)$$

$$b_j^* = \frac{1}{1 + r \Delta t} (1 - \sigma^2 j^2 \, \Delta t)$$

$$c_j^* = \frac{1}{1 + r \Delta t} \left(\frac{1}{2} rj \, \Delta t + \frac{1}{2} \sigma^2 j^2 \, \Delta t \right)$$

This creates what is known as the *explicit finite difference method*. Figure 14.12 shows the difference between the two methods. The implicit method leads

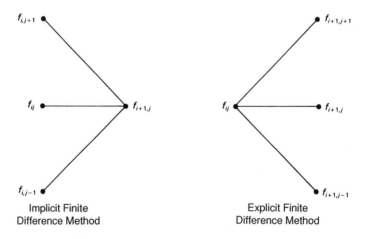

Implicit Finite
Difference Method   Explicit Finite
                                               Difference Method

Figure 14.12   Difference between Implicit and Explicit Finite Difference Methods

[12]A useful rule of thumb for finite difference methods is that ΔS should be kept proportional to $\sqrt{\Delta t}$ as they approach a zero.

to Equation (14.25), which gives a relationship between three different values of the option at time $i \Delta t$ (i.e., $f_{i,j-1}$, f_{ij}, and $f_{i,j+1}$) and one value of the option at time $(i + 1) \Delta t$ (i.e., $f_{i+1,j}$). The explicit method leads to Equation (14.32), which gives a relationship between one value of the option at time $i \Delta t$ (i.e., f_{ij}) and three difference values of the option at time $(i + 1) \Delta t$ (i.e., $f_{i+1,j-1}$, $f_{i+1,j}$, $f_{i+1,j+1}$).

Example 14.8

Table 14.2 shows the result of using the explicit version of the finite difference method for pricing the option in Example 14.1. As in Example 14.7, values of 20, 10, and 5 were chosen for M, N, and ΔS, respectively. The option price given by the grid is \$4.26.[13]

Finite difference methods are often used with $\ln S$ rather than S being the underlying variable.[14] The grid then evaluates the derivative security for equally spaced values of $\ln S$ rather than for equally spaced values of S. This is slightly more efficient computationally. Also, it has the advantage that a_j, b_j, and c_j in Equation (14.29), as well as a_j^*, b_j^*, and c_j^* in Equation (14.32) are independent of j.

RELATION TO TREE APPROACHES

The explicit finite difference method is very similar to the tree approach. In the expressions for a_j^*, b_j^*, and c_j^* in Equation (14.32), we can interpret terms as follows:

$-\frac{1}{2}rj \Delta t + \frac{1}{2}\sigma^2 j^2 \Delta t$: probability of stock price decreasing from $j \Delta S$ to $(j - 1) \Delta S$ in time Δt

$1 - \sigma^2 j^2 \Delta t$: probability of stock price remaining unchanged at $j \Delta S$ in time Δt

$\frac{1}{2}rj \Delta t + \frac{1}{2}\sigma^2 j^2 \Delta t$: probability of stock price increasing from $j \Delta S$ to $(j + 1) \Delta S$ in time Δt

This interpretation is illustrated in Figure 14.13. The three probabilities sum to unity. They give the expected increase in the stock price in time Δt as $rj \Delta S \Delta t = rS \Delta t$. This is the expected increase in a risk-neutral world. For small values of Δt, they also give the variance of the change in the stock price in time Δt as $\sigma^2 j^2 \Delta S^2 \Delta t = \sigma^2 S^2 \Delta t$. This corresponds to the stochastic process followed by

---

[13] The negative numbers and other inconsistencies in the top left-hand part of the grid will be explained later.

[14] If $X = \ln S$, it can be shown that Equation (14.19) becomes

$$\frac{\partial f}{\partial t} + \left(r - \frac{\sigma^2}{2}\right)\frac{\partial f}{\partial X} + \frac{1}{2}\sigma^2\frac{\partial^2 f}{\partial X^2} = rf$$

TABLE 14.2 Grid to Value Option in Example 14.1 Using Explicit Finite Difference Method

Stock Price (dollars)	Time to Maturity (Months)										
	5	$4\frac{1}{2}$	4	$3\frac{1}{2}$	3	$2\frac{1}{2}$	2	$1\frac{1}{2}$	1	$\frac{1}{2}$	0
100	0.00	0.00	0.00	0.00	0.00	0.00	0.00	0.00	0.00	0.00	0.00
95	0.06	0.00	0.00	0.00	0.00	0.00	0.00	0.00	0.00	0.00	0.00
90	-0.11	0.05	0.00	0.00	0.00	0.00	0.00	0.00	0.00	0.00	0.00
85	0.28	-0.05	0.05	0.00	0.00	0.00	0.00	0.00	0.00	0.00	0.00
80	-0.13	0.20	0.00	0.05	0.00	0.00	0.00	0.00	0.00	0.00	0.00
75	0.46	0.06	0.20	0.04	0.06	0.00	0.00	0.00	0.00	0.00	0.00
70	0.32	0.46	0.23	0.25	0.10	0.09	0.00	0.00	0.00	0.00	0.00
65	0.91	0.68	0.63	0.44	0.37	0.21	0.14	0.00	0.00	0.00	0.00
60	1.48	1.37	1.17	1.02	0.81	0.65	0.42	0.27	0.00	0.00	0.00
55	2.59	2.39	2.21	1.99	1.77	1.50	1.24	0.90	0.59	0.00	0.00
50	4.26	4.08	3.89	3.68	3.44	3.18	2.87	2.53	2.07	1.56	0.00
45	6.76	6.61	6.47	6.31	6.15	5.96	5.75	5.50	5.24	5.00	5.00
40	10.28	10.20	10.13	10.06	10.01	10.00	10.00	10.00	10.00	10.00	10.00
35	15.00	15.00	15.00	15.00	15.00	15.00	15.00	15.00	15.00	15.00	15.00
30	20.00	20.00	20.00	20.00	20.00	20.00	20.00	20.00	20.00	20.00	20.00
25	25.00	25.00	25.00	25.00	25.00	25.00	25.00	25.00	25.00	25.00	25.00
20	30.00	30.00	30.00	30.00	30.00	30.00	30.00	30.00	30.00	30.00	30.00
15	35.00	35.00	35.00	35.00	35.00	35.00	35.00	35.00	35.00	35.00	35.00
10	40.00	40.00	40.00	40.00	40.00	40.00	40.00	40.00	40.00	40.00	40.00
5	45.00	45.00	45.00	45.00	45.00	45.00	45.00	45.00	45.00	45.00	45.00
0	50.00	50.00	50.00	50.00	50.00	50.00	50.00	50.00	50.00	50.00	50.00

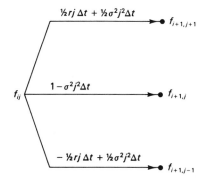

Figure 14.13 Interpretation of Explicit Finite Difference Method as a Trinomial Tree.

S. Equation (14.32) in effect moves from time $(i + 1)\,\Delta t$ to time $i\,\Delta t$ using a trinomial tree. The value of f at time $i\,\Delta t$ is calculated as the expected value of f at time $(i + 1)\,\Delta t$ in a risk-neutral world discounted at the risk-free rate.

For the explicit version of the finite difference method to work well, the three "probabilities"

$$-\frac{1}{2}rj\,\Delta t + \frac{1}{2}\sigma^2 j^2\,\Delta t$$

$$1 - \sigma^2 j^2\,\Delta t$$

$$\frac{1}{2}rj\,\Delta t + \frac{1}{2}\sigma^2 j^2\,\Delta t$$

should all be positive. In Example 14.8, $1 - \sigma^2 j^2\,\Delta t$ is negative when $j \geq 13$ (i.e., when $S \geq 65$). This explains the negative option prices and other inconsistencies in the top left-hand part of the grid. This example illustrates the main problem associated with the explicit finite difference method: because the probabilities in the associated tree may be negative, it does not necessarily produce results which converge to the solution of the differential equation.[15]

APPLICATIONS OF FINITE DIFFERENCE METHODS

Finite difference methods can be used for the same types of derivative security pricing problems as tree approaches. They can handle American-style as well as European-style derivative securities but cannot easily be used in situations where the payoff from a derivative security depends on the past history of state variable. Finite difference methods can, at the expense of a considerable increase in computer

---

[15] J. Hull, and A. White, "Valuing Derivative Securities Using the Explicit Finite Difference Method", *Journal of Financial and Quantitative Analysis*, 25 (March 1990), 87–100, show how this problem can be overcome. In the situation considered here it is sufficient to construct the grid in ln S rather than S.

time, be used when there are several state variables. The grid in Figure 14.11 then becomes multidimensional.

Geske and Shastri[16] provide a careful comparison of finite difference methods and tree approaches. They conclude that "researchers computing a smaller number of option values may prefer binomial approximation, while practitioners in the business of computing a larger number of option values will generally find that finite difference methods are more efficient."

The method for calculating hedge statistics is similar to that used for trees. Delta, gamma, and theta can be calculated directly from the f_{ij} values on the grid. For vega, it is necessary to make a small change to volatility and recalculate the value of the derivative security using the same grid.

14.8 ANALYTIC APPROXIMATIONS IN OPTION PRICING

As an alternative to the numerical procedures described so far in this chapter, a number of analytic approximations to the valuation of American options have been suggested. The best known of these is a quadratic approximation approach originally suggested by Macmillan, and extended by Barone-Adesi and Whaley.[17] It can be used to value American calls and puts on stocks, stock indices, currencies, and futures contracts. It involves estimating the difference, v, between the European option price and the American option price. Since both the European and American option satisfy the same differential equation, v must also satisfy the differential equation. Macmillan, and Barone-Adesi and Whaley, show that when an approximation is made, the differential equation can be solved using standard methods. More details on the approach are presented in Appendix 14A.

14.9 SUMMARY

In this chapter we have presented three different numerical procedures for valuing derivative securities when no analytic solution is available. These involve Monte Carlo simulation, binomial trees, and finite difference methods.

---

[16] See R. Geske and K. Shastri, "Valuation by Approximation: A Comparison of Alternative Option Valuation Techniques," *Journal of Financial and Quantitative Analysis*, 20 (March 1985), 45–71.

[17] L. W. Macmillan, "Analytic Approximation for the American Put Option," *Advances in Futures and Options Research*, Vol. 1 (1986), 119–39; G. Barone-Adesi and R. E. Whaley, "Efficient Analytic Approximation of American Option Values," *Journal of Finance*, 42 (June 1987), 301–20.

Monte Carlo simulation involves using random numbers to sample many different paths that the variables underlying the security could follow in a risk-neutral world. For each path the payoff is calculated and discounted at the risk-free interest rate. The arithmetic average of the discounted payoffs is the estimate of the value of the security.

Binomial trees assume that in each short interval of time, Δt, a stock price either moves up by a proportional amount, u, or down by a proportional amount, d. The sizes of u and d and their associated probabilities are chosen so that the change in the stock price has the correct mean and standard deviation in a risk-neutral world. Option prices are calculated by starting at the end of the tree and working backwards. For an American option, the value at a node is the greater of the value if it is exercised immediately and the discounted expected value if it is held for a further period of time Δt.

Finite difference methods solve the underlying differential equation by converting it to a difference equation. They are similar to tree approaches in that the computations work back from the end of the life of the option to the beginning. The implicit finite diffence method is more complicated than the explicit method, but has the advantage that the user does not have to take any special precautions to ensure convergence.

The method that is chosen in practice is likely to depend on the characteristics of the derivative security being evaluated and the accuracy required. Monte Carlo simulation, which works forward from the beginning to the end of the life of a security, can only be used for European-style options but can cope with a great deal of complexity as far as the payoffs are concerned. It becomes relatively more efficient as the number of underlying variables increases. Tree approaches and finite difference methods, which work from the end of the life of a security to the beginning, can accommodate American-style as well as European-style derivative securities. However, they are very difficult to apply when the payoffs depend on the past history of the state variables as well as on their current values. Also, they are liable to become computationally quite time consuming when three or more variables are involved. As an alternative to numerical procedures a number of analytic approximations have been suggested. The most well known of these was suggested by Macmillan and extended by Barone-Adesi and Whaley. It is described in Appendix 14A.

SUGGESTIONS FOR FURTHER READING

On Monte Carlo Simulation

BOYLE, P. P., "Options: A Monte Carlo Approach," *Journal of Financial Economics*, 4 (1977), 323–38.

On Tree Approaches

BOYLE, P. P., "A Lattice Framework for Option Pricing with Two State Variables," *Journal of Financial and Quantitative Analysis*, 23 (March 1988) 1–12.

COX, J., S. ROSS, and M. RUBINSTEIN "Option Pricing: A Simplified Approach," *Journal of Financial Economics*, 7 (October 1979), 229–64.

HULL, J. C., and A. WHITE, "The Use of the Control Variate Technique in Option Pricing," *Journal of Financial and Quantitative Analysis*, 23 (September, 1988), 237–51.

On Finite Difference Methods

BRENNAN, M. J., and E. S. SCHWARTZ, "Finite Difference Methods and Jump Processes Arising in the Pricing of Contingent Claims: A Synthesis," *Journal of Financial and Quantitative Analysis*, 13 (September 1978), 462–74.

BRENNAN, M., and E. S. SCHWARTZ, "The Valuation of American Put Options," *Journal of Finance*, 32 (May 1977), 449–62.

COURTADON, G., "A More Accurate Finite Difference Approximation for the Valuation of Options," *Journal of Financial and Quantitative Analysis*, 17 (December 1982), 697–705.

HULL, J., and A. WHITE, "Valuing Derivative Securities Using the Explicit Finite Difference Method", *Journal of Financial and Quantitative Analysis*, 25 (March 1990), 87–100.

SCHWARTZ, E. S., "The Valuation of Warrants: Implementing a New Approach," *Journal of Financial Economics*, 4 (1977), 79–94.

On Analytic Approximations

BARONE-ADESI, G., and R. E. WHALEY, "Efficient Analytic Approximation of American Option Values," *Journal of Finance*, 42 (June 1987), 301–20.

GESKE, R., and H. E. JOHNSON, "The American Put Valued Analytically," *Journal of Finance*, 39 (December 1984), 1511–24.

JOHNSON, H. E., "An Analytic Approximation to the American Put Price," *Journal of Financial and Quantitative Analysis*, 18 (March 1983), 141–48.

MACMILLAN, L. W., "Analytic Approximation for the American Put Option," *Advances in Futures and Options Research*, 1 (1986), 119–39.

QUESTIONS AND PROBLEMS

14.1. Which of the following can be estimated for an American option by constructing a single binomial tree: delta, gamma, vega, theta, rho?

14.2. Calculate the price of a 3-month American put option on a non-dividend-paying stock when the stock price is $60, the strike price is $60, the risk-free interest rate is 10% per annum, and the volatility is 45% per annum. Use a binomial tree with a time interval of 1 month.

14.3. Explain how the control variate technique is implemented when a tree is used to value American options.

14.4. Calculate the price of a 9-month American call option on corn futures when the current futures price is 198 cents, the strike price is 200 cents, the risk-free interest rate is 8% per annum, and the volatility is 30% per annum. Use a binomial tree with a time interval of 3 months.

14.5. Consider an option that pays off the amount by which the final stock price exceeds the minimum stock price achieved during the life of the option. Can this be valued using the binomial tree approach? Explain your answer.

14.6. "For a dividend-paying stock, the tree for the stock price does not recombine; but the tree for the stock price less the present value of future dividends does recombine." Explain this statement.

14.7. Under what circumstances are the probabilities in a binomial tree negative? How can this problem be overcome?

14.8. How would you use the binomial tree approach to value an American option on a stock index when the dividend yield on the index is a function of time?

14.9. Explain why the Monte Carlo simulation approach cannot be used for American-style derivative securities.

14.10. A 1-year American put option on a non-dividend-paying stock has an exercise price of $18. The current stock price is $20, the risk-free interest rate is 15% per annum, and the volatility of the stock price is 40% per annum. Divide the year into four 3-month time intervals and use the tree approach to estimate the value of the option. Use the control variate technique to improve this estimate.

14.11. A 1-year American call option on silver futures has an exercise price of $9. The current futures price is $8.50, the risk-free rate of interest is 12% per annum, and the volatility of the futures price is 25% per annum. Divide the year into four 3-month time intervals and use the tree approach to estimate the value of the option. Use the control variate technique to improve this estimate. Extend the tree to estimate the delta of the option.

14.12. A 2-month American put option on the Major Market Index has an exercise price of 480. The current level of the index is 484, the risk-free interest rate is 10% per annum, the dividend yield on the index is 3% per annum, and the volatility of the index is 25% per annum. Divide the life of the option into four half-month periods and use the tree approach to estimate the value of the option.

14.13. A 6-month American call option on a stock is expected to pay dividends of $1 per share at the end of the second month and the fifth month. The current stock price is $30, the exercise price is $34, the risk-free interest rate is 10% per annum, and the volatility of the part of the stock price that will not be used to pay the dividends is 30% per annum. Divide the life of the option into six 1-month periods and use the tree approach to estimate the value of the option. Compare your answer to that given by Black's approximation (see Section 10.12). Estimate the delta and theta of the option from your tree.

14.14. How can the control variate approach improve the estimate of the delta of an American option when the tree approach is used?

*14.15. Suppose that Monte Carlo simulation is being used to evaluate a European call option on a non-dividend-paying stock when the volatility is stochastic. How could the control variate and antithetic variable technique be used to improve numerical efficiency?

*14.16. Explain how Equation (14.19) and equations (14.25) to (14.28) change when the finite difference method is being used to evaluate an American call option on a currency.

*14.17. Suppose that the explicit version of the finite difference method is used to value an American put option on a non-dividend-paying stock, with $\ln S$ being used instead of S as the underlying variable. Derive a relationship between f_{ij}, $f_{i+1,j-1}$, $f_{i+1,j}$, and $f_{i+1,j+1}$ where the notation is as in sections 14.7 and 14.8. (*Hint*: See footnote 14)

*14.18. An American put option on a non-dividend-paying stock has 4 months to maturity. The exercise price is $21, the stock price is $20, the risk-free rate of interest is 10% per annum, and the volatility is 30% per annum. Use the explicit version of the finite difference approach to value the option. Use stock price intervals of $4 and time intervals of 1 month.

*14.19. The current value of the British pound is $1.60 and the volatility of the pound–dollar exchange rate is 15% per annum. An American call option has an exercise price of $1.62 and a time to maturity of 1 year. The risk-free rates of interest in the United States and the United Kingdom are 6% per annum and 9% per annum, respectively. Use the explicit finite difference method to value the option. Consider exchange rate intervals of 0.20 and time intervals of 3 months. (*Hint*: Only exchange rates between 0.80 and 2.40 need to be considered).

*14.20. Suppose that, as an approximation, it is assumed that the term structure of interest rates is flat for 1 year and that

$$dr = (a - r)b \, dt + rc \, dz$$

where a, b, and c are known constants; r is the interest rates for maturities up to 1 year; and dz is a Wiener process. Discuss the problems in using the binomial tree approach to value a 6-month European option on a T-bill.

14.21. The spot price of copper is $0.60 per pound. Suppose that the futures prices (dollars per pound) are as follows:

3 months	0.59
6 months	0.57
9 months	0.54
12 months	0.50

The volatility of the price of copper is 40% per annum and the risk-free rate is 6% per annum. Use a binomial tree to value an American call option on copper with an exercise price of $0.60 and a time to maturity of 1 year. Divide the life of the option into four 3-month periods for the purposes of constructing the tree. (*Hint*: As explained in Chapter 12, futures prices can be used to estimate the process followed by a commodity price in a risk-neutral world.)

14.22. Use the binomial tree in Problem 14.21 to value a security that pays off x^2 in 1 year where x is the price of copper.

*14.23. When do the boundary conditions for $S = 0$ and $S \longrightarrow \infty$ affect the estimates of derivative security prices in the explicit finite difference method?

*14.24. How can finite difference methods be used when there are known dividends?

*14.25. A company has issued a 3-year convertible bond that has a face value of $25 and can be exchanged for 2 of the company's shares at any time. The company can call the issue forcing conversion when the share price is greater than or equal to $18. Assuming that the company will force conversion at the earliest opportunity, what are the boundary conditions for the price of the convertible? Decribe how you would use finite difference methods to value the convertible assuming constant interest rates.

14.26. Provide formulas that can be used for obtaining three random samples from standard normal distributions when the correlation between sample i and sample j is ρ_{ij}.

APPENDIX 14A: THE ANALYTIC APPROXIMATION TO AMERICAN OPTION PRICES OF MACMILLAN, AND BARONE-ADESI AND WHALEY

Consider an option on a stock paying a continuous dividend yield at rate q. We will denote the difference between the American and European option price by v. Since both the American and the European option prices satisfy the Black–Scholes differential equation, v also does so. Hence

$$\frac{\partial v}{\partial t} + (r - q)S\frac{\partial v}{\partial S} + \frac{1}{2}\sigma^2 S^2 \frac{\partial^2 v}{\partial S^2} = rv$$

For convenience we define

$$\tau = T - t$$

$$h(\tau) = 1 - e^{-r\tau}$$

$$\alpha = \frac{2r}{\sigma^2}$$

$$\beta = \frac{2(r - q)}{\sigma^2}$$

We also write, without loss of generality,

$$v = h(\tau)g(S, h)$$

With appropriate substitutions and variable changes, this gives

$$S^2 \frac{\partial^2 g}{\partial S^2} + \beta S \frac{\partial g}{\partial S} - \frac{\alpha}{h} g - (1 - h)\alpha \frac{\partial g}{\partial h} = 0$$

The approximation which is used involves assuming that the final term on the left-hand side is zero, so that

$$S^2 \frac{\partial^2 g}{\partial S^2} + \beta S \frac{\partial g}{\partial S} - \frac{\alpha}{h} g = 0 \qquad (14A.1)$$

The term that is ignored is generally fairly small. When τ is large, $1 - h$ is close to zero; when τ is small, $\partial g/\partial h$ is close to zero.

The American call and put prices will, as usual, be denoted by $C(S)$ and $P(S)$, where S is the stock price, and the corresponding European call and put prices will be denoted by $c(S)$ and $p(S)$. Equation (14A.1) can be solved using standard techniques. After boundary conditions have been applied, it is found that

$$C(S) = \begin{cases} c(S) + A_2 \left(\frac{S}{S^*}\right)^{\gamma_2} & \text{when } S < S^* \\[2mm] S - X & \text{when } S \geq S^* \end{cases}$$

The variable S^* is the critical price of the stock above which the option should be exercised. It is estimated by solving the equation

$$S^* - X = c(S^*) + \left\{1 - e^{-q(T-t)} N[d_1(S^*)]\right\} \frac{S^*}{\gamma_2}$$

iteratively. For a put option, the valuation formula is

$$P(S) = \begin{cases} p(S) + A_1 \left(\frac{S}{S^{**}}\right)^{\gamma_1} & \text{when } S > S^{**} \\[2mm] X - S & \text{when } S \leq S^{**} \end{cases}$$

The variable S^{**} is the critical price of the stock below which the option should be exercised. It is estimated by solving the equation

$$X - S^{**} = p(S^{**}) - \left\{1 - e^{-q(T-t)} N[-d_1(S^{**})]\right\} \frac{S^{**}}{\gamma_1}$$

iteratively. The other variables that have been used here are

$$\gamma_1 = \left[-(\beta - 1) - \sqrt{(\beta - 1)^2 + \frac{4\alpha}{h}} \right] \bigg/ 2$$

$$\gamma_2 = \left[-(\beta - 1) + \sqrt{(\beta - 1)^2 + \frac{4\alpha}{h}} \right] \bigg/ 2$$

$$A_1 = -\left(\frac{S^{**}}{\gamma_1} \right) \left\{ 1 - e^{-q(T-t)} N[-d_1(S^{**})] \right\}$$

$$A_2 = \left(\frac{S^{*}}{\gamma_2} \right) \left\{ 1 - e^{-q(T-t)} N[d_1(S^{*})] \right\}$$

$$d_1(S) = \frac{\ln(S/X) + (r - q + \sigma^2/2)(T - t)}{\sigma \sqrt{T - t}}$$

As pointed out in chapters 11 and 12, options on stock indices, currencies, and futures contracts can be regarded as analogous to options on a stock paying a continuous dividend with the dividend yield constant. Hence the quadratic approximation approach can easily be applied to all of these types of options.

15 *Interest Rate Derivative Securities*

Interest rate derivative securities are securities whose payoffs are dependent in some way on the level of interest rates. In recent years they have become increasingly popular. This chapter starts by describing the range of different products that are traded over the counter and on exchanges. It then moves on to discuss valuation issues. The models that are considered can be divided into three categories. Those in the first category are extensions of Black–Scholes. Those in the second category are the equilibrium models that have been traditionally favored by researchers. Those in the third category are no-arbitrage models, designed in such a way that they are exactly consistent with the term structure observed in the market at the time the model is built.

15.1 EXCHANGE–TRADED BOND OPTIONS

The most popular exchange-traded interest rate options are those on Treasury bond futures, Treasury note futures, and Eurodollar futures. Table 11.4 in Chapter 11 shows the closing prices for these securities on February 3, 1992. The prices are quoted as a percentage of the principal amount of the underlying debt security. For options on Eurodollar futures, the price is quoted to two decimal places and one contract is for the delivery of futures contracts with a face value of $1 million. For options on Treasury bond and Treasury note futures, the price is quoted to the nearest $\frac{1}{64}$ of 1 percent and one contract is for the delivery of futures contracts with a face value of $100,000. Thus Table 11.4 gives the price of the IMM September call futures option on Eurodollars as 0.14 percent of the debt principal when the strike price is 95.75 (implying that one contract would cost $1,400). It also gives the price of the September call futures option on Treasury bonds as $4\frac{6}{64}$ percent of the debt principal when the strike price is 96 (implying that one contract would cost $4,093.75).

When interest rates rise, bond prices fall; when interest rates fall, bond prices rise. An investor who thinks that short-term interest rates will rise can speculate by buying put options on Eurodollar futures, while an investor who thinks that they will fall can speculate by buying call options on Eurodollar futures. An investor who thinks that long-term interest rates will rise can speculate by buying put options on Treasury notes or Treasury bonds, while an investor who thinks they will fall can speculate by buying call options on these instruments.

Suppose that it is August and the futures price for the December Treasury bond contract traded on the CBOT is 96-09 (or $96\frac{9}{32} = 96.28125$). The yield on long term government bonds is about 8.4 percent per annum. An investor who feels that this yield will fall by December might choose to buy December calls with a strike price of 98. Assume that the price of these calls is 1-04 (or $1\frac{4}{64} = 1.0625\%$ of the principal). If long-term rates fall to 8 percent per annum, the Treasury bond futures price will rise to 100-00 and the investor will make a net profit per $100 of bond futures of

$$100.00 - 98.00 - 1.0625 = 0.9375$$

Since one option contract is for the purchase or sale of instruments with a face value of $100,000, the investor would make a profit of $937.50 per option contract bought.

15.2 EMBEDDED BOND OPTIONS

Some bonds contain embedded call and put options. For example, a callable bond contains provisions that allow the issuing firm to buy back the bond at a predetermined price at certain times in the future. The holder of such a bond has sold a call option to the issuer. The value of the call option is reflected in the yields on bonds so that bonds with call features provide an investor with a higher yield than bonds with no call features. A puttable bond contains provisions that allow the holder to demand early redemption at a predetermined price at certain times in the future. The holder of such a bond has purchased a put option on the bond as well as the bond itself. Since the put option increases the value of the bond to the holder, bonds with put features provide lower yields than bonds with no put features.

A number of other instruments have embedded bond options. For example, early redemption privileges on fixed rate deposits are analogous to the put features of a bond. Prepayment privileges on fixed rate loans are analogous to the call features of a bond. Also, mortgage commitments made by a bank or other financial institution are put options. Consider, for example, the situation where a bank quotes a 5-year mortgage rate of interest of 12 percent per annum to a client and states that the rate is good for the next 2 months. The client has in effect obtained the right to sell a 5-year bond with a 12 percent coupon to the financial institution for its face value any time within the next 2 months.

15.3 MORTGAGE-BACKED SECURITIES

A type of interest rate option is embedded in what is known as a *mortgage-backed security* (MBS). This security has become very popular in recent years. It is created when a financial institution decides to sell part of its residential mortgage portfolio to investors. The mortgages sold are put into a pool and investors acquire a stake in the pool by buying units. The units are known as mortgage-backed securities. A secondary market is usually created for the units so that investors can sell them to other investors as desired. An investor who owns units representing X percent of a certain pool is entitled to X percent of the principal and interest cash flows received from the mortgages in the pool.

The mortgages in a pool are generally insured so that investors are protected against defaults. This makes an MBS sound like a regular fixed income security. But there is one important complicating feature. The mortgages in an MBS pool have certain prepayment privileges. This means that the holder of an MBS has granted a series of interest rate options to the borrowers of the mortgage funds.[1] In general, investors require a higher rate of interest on an MBS than on other fixed income securities to compensate for these prepayment options.

15.4 SWAPTIONS

Swaptions or swap options are options on interest rate swaps and are another increasingly popular type of interest rate option. They give the holder the right to enter into a certain interest rate swap at a certain time in the future. (The holder

---

[1]These options are not pure interest rate options in the sense that the decision to exercise may depend on more than just the level of interest rates. For example, a family might prepay a mortgage when rates are relatively high simply because it is moving house—not because it can refinance more cheaply.

does not, of course, have to exercise this right.) Many large financial institutions that offer interest rate swap contracts to their corporate clients are also prepared to sell them swaptions or buy swaptions from them.

To give an example of how a swaption might be used, consider a company that knows it will enter into a 5-year floating rate loan agreement in 6 months and knows that it will wish to swap the floating interest payments for fixed interest payments in order to convert the loan into a fixed rate loan. (See Chapter 5 for a discussion of how swaps can be used in this way.) At a cost the company could enter into a swaption and obtain the right to swap the floating interest payments for a certain fixed interest payment, say 12 percent per annum, for a 5-year period starting in 6 months. If the fixed rate on a regular 5-year swap in 6 months turns out to be less than 12 percent per annum, the company will choose not to exercise the swaption and will enter into a swap agreement in the usual way. However, if it turns out to be greater than 12 percent per annum, the company will choose to exercise the swaption and will obtain a swap at more favorable terms than those available in the market.

Swaptions provide companies such as the one just considered with an alternative to forward swaps (sometimes called deferred swaps). Forward swaps involve no up-front cost but have the disadvantage that they obligate the company to enter into a certain swap agreement. With a swaption, the company is able to benefit from favorable interest rate movements while acquiring protection from unfavorable movements. The difference between a swaption and a forward swap is analogous to the difference between an option on foreign exchange and a forward contract on foreign exchange.

RELATION TO BOND OPTIONS

It will be recalled from Chapter 5 that an interest rate swap can be regarded as an agreement to exchange a fixed rate bond for a floating rate bond. At the start of a swap, the value of the floating rate bond always equals the principal amount of the swap. A swaption can therefore be regarded as an option to exchange a fixed rate bond for the principal amount of the swap. If a swaption gives the holder the right to pay fixed and receive floating, it is a put option on the fixed rate bond with strike price equal to the principal. If a swaption gives the holder the right to pay floating and receive fixed, it is a call option on the fixed rate bond with a strike price equal to the principal.

15.5 INTEREST RATE CAPS

Another type of over-the-counter interest rate option offered by financial institutions is an interest rate cap. Caps are designed to provide insurance against the rate of interest on a floating rate loan rising above a certain level. This level is known as the *cap rate*. When a cap on a loan and the loan itself are both provided by the same financial institution, the cost of the options underlying the cap is often incorporated into the interest rate charged. When they are provided by different financial institutions, an up-front payment for the cap is likely to be required.

The operation of a cap is illustrated in Figure 15.1. A cap guarantees that the rate charged on a loan at any given time will be the lesser of the prevailing rate and the cap rate. Suppose that the rate on a loan, where the principal amount is $10 million, is reset every 3 months equal to 3-month LIBOR, and that a financial institution has provided an interest rate cap of 10 percent per annum. To fulfill its obligations under the cap agreement, the financial institution must pay to the borrower at the end of each quarter (in millions of dollars),

$$0.25 \times 10 \times \max(R - 0.1, 0)$$

where R is the 3-month LIBOR rate at the beginning of the quarter. For example, when the 3-month LIBOR rate at the beginning of the quarter is 11 percent per annum, the financial institution must pay $0.25 \times 10,000,000 \times 0.01 = \$25,000$ at the end of the quarter. When it is 9 percent per annum, the financial institution is not required to pay anything. The expression $\max(R - 0.1, 0)$ is the payoff from a call option on R. The cap can therefore be viewed as a portfolio of call options on R with the payoffs from the options occurring 3 months in arrears. The individual options comprising a cap are sometimes referred to as *caplets*.

In general if the cap rate is R_X, the principal is L, and interest payments are made at times τ, 2τ, $\ldots$, $n\tau$ from the beginning of the life of the cap, the writer of the cap is required to make a payment at time $(k + 1)\tau$ given by

$$\tau L \max(R_k - R_X, 0) \tag{15.1}$$

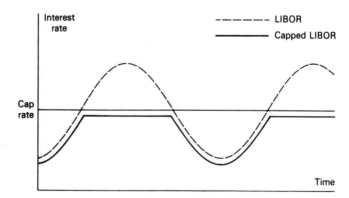

Figure 15.1 Borrower's Effective Interest Rate with a Floating Rate Loan and an Interest Rate Cap

where R_k is the value at time $k\tau$ of the rate being capped. Suppose that F_k is the forward interest rate for the time period between $k\tau$ and $(k+1)\tau$ and that the rates R_X, R_k, and F_k are all expressed with a compounding frequency of τ. As an approximation, we can use F_k as the discount rate between times $k\tau$ and $(k+1)\tau$ so that the payment in (15.1), which is made at time $(k+1)\tau$, becomes equivalent to a payment of

$$\frac{\tau L}{1 + \tau F_k} \max(R_k - R_X, 0) \tag{15.2}$$

at time $k\tau$. The advantage of doing this is that it enables us to regard each caplet as a European call option on a τ-period interest rate with the payoff occurring at the maturity of the option rather than one period later. The principal amount for each option is $\tau L/(1 + \tau F_k)$.

A SIMPLE MODEL FOR VALUING CAPS

Equation (15.2) leads to a commonly used valuation model. At time $k\tau$, $F_k = R_k$. We can therefore regard the caplet corresponding to the period between $k\tau$ and $(k+1)\tau$ as a European call option on F_k rather than R_k. If we assume that the forward interest rate, F_k, has a constant volatility, σ_F, Black's model, introduced in Section 11.4, gives the price of the option as

$$\frac{\tau L}{1 + \tau F_k} e^{-rk\tau} [F_k N(d_1) - R_X N(d_2)] \tag{15.3}$$

where

$$d_1 = \frac{\ln(F_k/R_X) + \sigma_F^2 k\tau/2}{\sigma_F \sqrt{k\tau}}$$

$$d_2 = \frac{\ln(F_k/R_X) - \sigma_F^2 k\tau/2}{\sigma_F \sqrt{k\tau}} = d_1 - \sigma\sqrt{k\tau}$$

and r is the risk-free interest rate for an instrument that matures at time $k\tau$. If r is defined as the risk-free rate for an instrument maturing at $(k+1)\tau$, an expression equivalent to (15.3) for the value of a caplet is

$$\tau L e^{-r(k+1)\tau} [F_k N(d_1) - R_X N(d_2)]$$

Example 15.1

Consider a contract that caps the interest on a $10,000 loan at 8% per annum (with quarterly compounding) for 3 months starting in 1 year. This could be one element of a cap. Suppose that the forward interest rate for a 3-month period starting in 1 year is 7% per annum (with quarterly compounding); the current 1-year interest rate is 6.5% per annum (with continuous compounding); and the volatility of the 90-day forward rate is 20% per annum. In Equation

(15.3), $F_k = 0.07$, $\tau = 0.25$, $L = 10,000$, $R_X = 0.08$, $r = 0.065$, $\sigma = 0.20$, and $k\tau = 1.0$.

$$\frac{\tau L}{1 + \tau F_k} = \frac{0.25 \times 10,000}{1 + 0.25 \times 0.07} = 2,457$$

Since

$$d_1 = \frac{\ln 0.875 + 0.02}{0.20} = -0.5677$$

$$d_2 = d_1 - 0.20 = -0.7677$$

the cap price is

$$2457e^{-0.065}[0.07N(-0.5677) - 0.08N(-0.7677)] = 5.19$$

or $5.19.

Black's model involves the assumption that σ_F is constant. This assumption is at best only a rough approximation to the truth. When the time to the maturity of the forward contract is long, F_k is relatively insensitive to current interest rate movements and has a low volatility. However, as the time to maturity becomes smaller, F_k is more affected by changes in the current level of interest rates and its volatility increases. Figure 15.2 shows the general way in which the appropriate σ_F varies with the maturity of the option being considered. Black's model when applied to valuing caps can also be criticized for being inconsistent in its treatment of interest rates. The rate, r, which is used for discounting is assumed to be constant. But the forward rates, F_k, are assumed to be stochastic.

In practice, the following procedure is sometimes adopted to overcome the weaknesses in Black's model. First, the model is used to calculate implied volatilities for forward interest rates from traded Eurodollar futures options. These implied

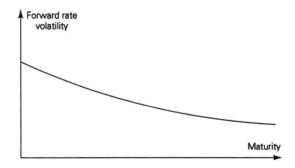

Figure 15.2 Variation of Forward Rate Volatility with Maturity of Caplet when Black's Model Is Used

volatilities are then used to value the options underlying interest rate caps. A 3-month option is valued on the basis of the volatility implied by the price of a Euro-dollar futures option with approximately 3 months to maturity; a 6-month option is valued on the basis of the volatility implied by the price of a Eurodollar futures option with approximately 6 months to maturity; and so on. This twofold use of the model (to calculate implied volatilities for exchange-traded options and to calculate prices of over-the-counter options from the implied volatilities of exchange-traded options) tends to reduce errors caused by the use of an imperfect model and to ensure that calculated option prices are reasonably consistent with exchange-traded option prices. The interest rate volatilities implied by the market prices of Euro-dollar futures options of different maturities are regularly quoted by traders and published by investment houses. Since most caps last beyond the longest maturity of traded Eurodollar options, the relationship between volatility and maturity which is observed for traded Eurodollar options must be extrapolated in some way.

Traders applying Black's model using the approach just discussed would change the volatility, σ_F, according to the caplet considered. The volatilities are then referred to as *forward forward volatilities*. An alternative approach is to use the same volatility for all the caplets comprising any particular cap, but to vary this volatility according to the life of the cap. The volatilities used are then referred to as *forward volatilities*.

A CAP AS A PORTFOLIO OF BOND OPTIONS

An more precise characterization of a cap is as a portfolio of put options on discount bonds. The payoff in (15.1) at time $(k + 1)\tau$ is equivalent to

$$\frac{\tau L}{1 + \tau R_k} \max(R_k - R_X, 0)$$

at time $k\tau$. A few lines of algebra shows that this reduces to

$$\max \left[L - \frac{L(1 + R_X \tau)}{1 + \tau R_k}, 0 \right] \tag{15.4}$$

The expression

$$\frac{L(1 + R_X \tau)}{1 + \tau R_k}$$

is the value at time $k\tau$ of a discount bond that pays off $L(1 + R_X \tau)$ at time $(k+1)\tau$. The expression in (15.4) is therefore the payoff from a put option with maturity $k\tau$ on a discount bond with maturity $(k + 1)\tau$ when the face value of the bond is $L(1 + R_X \tau)$ and the strike price is L. This proves the assertion that an interest rate cap is a portfolio of European put options on discount bonds.

FLOORS AND COLLARS

Interest rate floors and interest rate collars (which are sometimes called floor-ceiling agreements) can be defined analogously to caps. A *floor* places a lower limit on the interest rate that will be charged. *Collars* specify both the upper and lower limits for the rate that will be charged. Similarly to an interest rate cap, an interest rate floor is a portfolio of put options on interest rates or a portfolio of call options on discount bonds. It can be valued in an analogous way to an interest rate cap. It is often written by the borrower of floating rate funds. A collar is a combination of a long position in a cap and a short position in a floor. It is usually constructed so that the price of the cap equals the price of the floor. The net cost of the collar is then zero.

15.6 SIMPLE APPROACHES TO VALUING BOND OPTIONS

We now move on to valuing bond options. The simplest model is the Black–Scholes model described in Chapter 10. Define

B: Current bond price
T: Maturity date of option
σ: Volatility of bond price
X: Strike price of option
R: Current interest rate applicable to a risk-free investment maturing at time T[2]

In the case of a zero-coupon bond, the Black–Scholes model gives the European call and put prices, c and p, at time t as

$$c = BN(d_1) - e^{-R(T-t)}XN(d_2) \tag{15.5}$$

and

$$p = e^{-R(T-t)}XN(-d_2) - BN(-d_1) \tag{15.6}$$

where

$$d_1 = \frac{\ln(B/X) + (R + \sigma^2/2)(T - t)}{\sigma\sqrt{T - t}}$$

$$d_2 = \frac{\ln(B/X) + (R - \sigma^2/2)(T - t)}{\sigma\sqrt{T - t}} = d_1 - \sigma\sqrt{T - t}$$

---

[2]As mentioned in Chapter 10, when Black–Scholes and similar models are implemented, the risk-free interest rate is usually chosen to correspond to an investment maturing at the end of the life of the option.

An argument similar to that in Chapter 7 shows that an American call on a bond that pays no coupons should never be exercised early and can be treated as a European option.

If coupon payments are due to be received during the life of the option, they can be treated like the dividends on a stock (see Section 10.14). The present value of the coupons should be subtracted from B before equations (15.5) and (15.6) are used. The volatility parameter, σ, should be the volatility of the bond price net of the present value of these coupons.

The precise terms of the option are important when the bond pays coupons. If the strike price is the cash amount that is exchanged for the bond when the option is exercised, X should be put equal to this strike price in equations (15.5) and (15.6). If the strike price is the quoted price applicable when the option is exercised (as it is in exchange-traded bond options), X should be set equal to the strike price plus accrued interest at the expiration date of the option in equations (15.5) and (15.6).

Example 15.2

Consider a 10-month European call option on a 9.75-year bond with a face value of $1,000. Suppose that the cash bond price is $960, the strike price is $1,000, the 10-month risk-free interest rate is 10% per annum, and the volatility of the bond price is 9% per annum. The bond pays a semiannual coupon of 10% and coupon payments of $50 are expected in 3 months and 9 months. The 3-month and 9-month risk-free interest rates are 9.0% and 9.5% per annum, respectively. The present value of the coupon payments is

$$50e^{-0.25 \times 0.09} + 50e^{-0.75 \times 0.095} = 95.45$$

or $95.45.

(a) If the strike price is the cash price that would be paid for the bond on exercise, the parameters for Equation (15.5) are $B = 960 - 95.45 = 864.55$, $X = 1000$, $R = 0.1$, $\sigma = 0.09$, and $T - t = 0.8333$. The price of the call option is $9.49.

(b) If the strike price is the quoted price that would be paid for the bond on exercise, one month's accrued interest must be added to X. This produces a value for X of

$$1,000 + 50 \times 0.16667 = 1,008.33$$

The values for the other parameters in Equation (15.5) are unchanged (i.e., $B = 864.55$, $R = 0.1$, $\sigma = 0.09$, and $T - t = 0.8333$). The price of the option is $7.97.

PROBLEMS IN APPLYING THE BLACK–SCHOLES MODEL TO BOND
PRICES

The Black–Scholes model that has just been described assumes that the volatility of a bond's price is constant. In practice, a bond's price volatility is dependent on its time to maturity. The longer the time to maturity, the greater a bond's price volatility. Schaefer and Schwartz argue that a bond's price volatility is roughly proportional to its duration.[3] This means that the volatility of a bond with a duration of 10 years is twice the volatility of a bond with a duration of 5 years, and so on. This idea seems to be reasonably well supported by empirical studies.

When the life of the option is short in relation to the life of the underlying bond (as it is in the case of most exchange-traded bond options), it can be assumed that the volatility of the bond is constant during the life of the option. The duration argument can then be used as an approximation. For example, suppose we wish to value a 3-month option on a bond with a duration of 4 years and a 1-month option on a bond with a duration of 8 years. The volatility used in Black–Scholes when the first option is valued should be roughly half that used when the second option is valued.

For longer-term options, the assumption that the volatility of a bond is constant during the life of the option is no longer reasonable. A natural suggestion is to make the bond's price volatility proportional to the average duration of the bond during the life of the option. However, this approach overstates the values of long-dated options because it does not capture one key aspect of the behavior of bond prices. This is that the price of a bond must equal its face value at its maturity. This is sometimes referred to as the *pull-to-par phenomenon*. Figure 15.3 illustrates the phenomenon by showing how the standard deviation of the future price of a bond and a stock change as we look further ahead. The stock's price becomes progressively more uncertain, but our uncertainty about the bond's price first increases and then decreases.

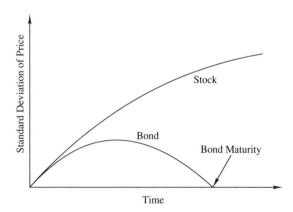

Figure 15.3   Standard Deviation of a Future Bond Price and a Future Stock Price

[3]See S. M. Schaefer and E. S. Schwartz, "Time-Dependent Variance and the Pricing of Bond Options," *Journal of Finance*, 42 (December 1987), 1113–28.

USING FORWARD BOND PRICES

One approach to valuing European options when the life of the option is significant in relation to the life of the underlying bond is to regard the option as being written on the forward price of the bond that will be delivered if the option is exercised. This is the forward price of a bond lasting between the end of the life of the option and the end of the life of the bond. When the option matures, the forward bond price equals the price of the underlying bond—which means that the forward bond option being considered is the same as the spot bond option whose value is required. This approach enables Black's model, which was discussed in Section 11.4, to be used. The correct volatility to use for the forward bond price will depend on the time between the end of the life of the option and the end of the life of the bond. It also tends to depend on the life of the option itself. The longer the option lasts, the lower the volatility. The valuation formulas are

$$c = e^{-R(T-t)}[FN(d_1) - XN(d_2)] \tag{15.7}$$

and

$$p = e^{-R(T-t)}[XN(-d_2) - FN(-d_1)] \tag{15.8}$$

where

$$d_1 = \frac{\ln(F/X) + \sigma^2(T-t)/2}{\sigma\sqrt{T-t}}$$

$$d_2 = \frac{\ln(F/X) - \sigma^2(T-t)/2}{\sigma\sqrt{T-t}} = d_1 - \sigma\sqrt{T-t}$$

F is the forward bond price, σ is its volatility, and other variables are defined as before.

The forward bond price can be calculated using Equation (3.7)

$$F = (B - I)e^{R(T-t)}$$

where I is equal to the present value of the coupons during the life of the option. Substituting for F into Equations (15.7) and (15.8) shows that there is in essence no difference between the forward bond approach and the Black–Scholes approach just mentioned. Like the Black-Scholes approach the forward bond approach therefore has the drawback of not modeling the pull to par. A point in favor of both approaches is that they give results that satisfy the put-call parity condition for bond option prices:

$$c + Xe^{-R(T-t)} = p + Fe^{-R(T-t)} \tag{15.9}$$

Example 15.3

Consider a 3-year European call option on a 5-year bond with a face value of $100 and a coupon of 10% per annum. We suppose that the forward price of the bond that would be delivered if the option were exercised is $95. We also suppose that the strike price is $98, the 3-year risk-free interest rate is 11% per annum, and the volatility of the forward bond price is 2.5% per annum. This means that $F = 95$, $X = 98$, $R = 0.11$, $\sigma = 0.025$, and $T = 3.0$. Equation (15.7) gives the call price as $0.42.

MODELING FORWARD BOND YIELDS

One attempt to overcome the pull-to-par problem in modeling bond prices is to regard a bond option as a yield option. We define the strike yield, Y_X, as equal to the continuously compounded yield on the bond at the option's maturity if the bond's price equals the strike price. From Equation (4.8) in Section 4.5, an approximate relationship between the bond price, B_T, and its yield, Y_T, at the option's maturity is

$$\frac{B_T - X}{X} = -D(Y_T - Y_X)$$

where D is the bond's duration at the maturity of the option. Using this formula

$$B_T - X = DX(Y_X - Y_T)$$

The payoff on a call option can be written as

$$\max[DX(Y_X - Y_T), \, 0]$$

and the payoff from a put option on the bond can be written as

$$\max[DX(Y_T - Y_X), \, 0]$$

These equations convert a call option on a bond price into a put option on a bond yield and a put option on a bond price into a call option on a bond yield. If forward bond yield volatilities are assumed constant, Black's model can be used to value the option.

This approach, although simple, has a weakness. As explained in Section 4.5, the duration of a bond measures the sensitivity of the bond's price to bond yields for only very small changes in the yield. The expressions just given for the payoffs in terms of yields are therefore approximations. A problem related to this weakness is that the option prices produced using the approach do not satisfy put-call parity.

The assumption that the forward yield on the bond underlying an option is attractive to many practitioners. To overcome the weakness just mentioned, some practitioners use numerical procedures to convert the lognormal yield disribution into a price distribution. The center of the distribution is chosen so that it represents a possible behavior for bond prices in a risk-neutral world. Option prices are then obtained numerically.

15.7 LIMITATIONS OF SIMPLE MODELS

The models for pricing interest rate options that have been presented so far have been versions of the Black and Black–Scholes models. They have provided ways of valuing caps and European bond options, but have the disadvantage that the volatility used must in general be different for different deals. It is not easy to find a way of relating the volatility used for one option to that used for another. A further serious drawback of the models is that they can only be used for European options. American bond options and other types of interest rate derivative securities cannot be valued.

The reason why the models cannot be used for American options is as follows. If we are valuing a European bond option, we are interested in the standard deviation of the bond's price at just one time in the future (the maturity of the option). There is always some volatility for a stock that would cause it to have the same standard deviation as the bond at this time. Once this volatility has been identified, we can treat the bond option as though it were an option on the stock and use Black–Scholes. If we are interested in valuing an American bond option this approach does not work because the possibility of early exercise means that we must represent bond price uncertainty at all times during the life of the option, not just at the end. As Figure 15.3 shows, the evolution of uncertainty for a bond's price is quite different to that for a stock's price.

YIELD CURVE MODELS

A more sophisticated approach to valuing interest rate derivative securities involves constructing what is known as a *yield curve model* or *term structure model*. This is a model that describes the probabilistic behavior of the yield curve over time. Yield curve models are more complicated than the models used to describe the movements of a stock price or currency exchange rate. This is because they are concerned with movements in a whole curve—not with changes to a single variable. As time passes, the individual interest rates in the term structure change. In addition, the shape of the curve itself is liable to change.

15.8 TRADITIONAL APPROACH USED BY RESEARCHERS TO MODEL THE TERM STRUCTURE

The traditional approach used by researchers to model the term structure involves starting with a plausible stochastic process for the short-term rate, r, in a risk-neutral world and exploring what the process implies for bond prices and option prices. It is important to emphasize that it is not the process for r in the real world that matters. As discussed in Chapter 12, bond prices, option prices, and other derivative security prices depend only on the process followed by r in a risk-neutral world.

In a number of the models that have been developed by researchers there is assumed to be only one underlying stochastic variable (or factor), so that the risk-neutral process for r is of the form

$$dr = m(r)\,dt + s(r)\,dz \tag{15.10}$$

The instantaneous drift, m, and instantaneous standard deviation, s, are assumed to be functions of r, but independent of time. The assumption of a single factor is not as restrictive as it might at first sight appear. It does not, as is sometimes supposed, imply that the term structure always has the same shape. A fairly rich pattern of term structures can occur under a one-factor model. The essence of a one-factor model is that it implies that all rates move in the same direction in any short time interval; it does not imply that all rates move by the same amount.

From the analysis in Chapter 12, the value of an interest-rate derivative security is

$$\hat{E}\left[e^{-\bar{r}(T-t)} f_T\right] \tag{15.11}$$

where $\bar{r}$ is the average value of r in the time interval between t and T, and $\hat{E}$ denotes expected value in a risk-neutral world.

Define $P(t, T)$ as the price at time t of discount bond that pays off \$1 at time T. From Equation (15.11),

$$P(t, T) = \hat{E}\left[e^{-\bar{r}(T-t)}\right] \tag{15.12}$$

If $R(t, T)$ is the continually compounded interest rate at time t for a term of $T - t$,

$$P(t, T) = e^{-R(t,T)(T-t)} \tag{15.13}$$

so that

$$R(t, T) = -\frac{1}{T-t} \ln P(t, T) \tag{15.14}$$

and from Equation (15.12),

$$R(t, T) = -\frac{1}{T-t} \ln \hat{E}\left[e^{-\bar{r}(T-t)}\right] \tag{15.15}$$

This equation enables the term structure of interest rates to be obtained from the risk-neutral process for r in Equation (15.10).

The functions $m(r)$ and $s(r)$ typically involve several parameters. In practice, the trial-and-error procedure indicated in Figure 15.4 must be used to choose these

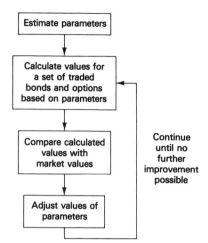

Figure 15.4   Procedure for Estimating the Parameters in an Interest Rate Model

parameters so that the values of bonds and options calculated from the model are as close as possible to those observed in the market. The procedure is similar to that used to calculate implied volatilities from option prices. The only difference is that more than one parameter is being estimated.

15.9 THE RENDLEMAN AND BARTTER MODEL

Rendleman and Bartter make particularly simple assumptions about $m(r)$ and $s(r)$ in Equation (15.10).[4] They assume that $m(r) = Mr$ and $s(r) = Sr$ where M and S are constants. This means that r follows geometric Brownian motion. It has a constant expected growth rate of M and a constant volatility of S in a risk-neutral world. It can be modeled using a binomial tree similar to the one used for stocks in Chapter 14. The parameters u, d, and p chosen are as follows:

$$u = e^{S\sqrt{\Delta t}}$$

$$d = e^{-S\sqrt{\Delta t}}$$

$$p = \frac{a - d}{u - d}$$

where

$$a = e^{M\Delta t}$$

[4]See R. Rendleman and B. Bartter, "The Pricing of Options on Debt Securities," *Journal of Financial and Quantitative Analysis*, 15 (March 1980), 11–24.

To illustrate the approach, suppose that $\Delta t = 1$ year, $M = 0.05$, $S = 0.15$, and we wish to model interest rates over a 5-year period. It follows that $u = 1.1618$, $d = 0.8607$, $a = 1.0513$, and $p = 0.6329$. Since the time step on the tree is 1 year, we define the short-term interest rate, r, as the 1-year rate. If the initial value of r is 10 percent per annum, the tree that is obtained is shown in Figure 15.5. It should be emphasized that this is a tree representing interest rate movements in a risk-neutral world rather in the real world. In this respect it is analogous to the trees for stock prices in Chapter 14.

Assume that we wish to value a 4-year American call option on a bond maturing in 5 years that pays an 8 percent coupon at the end of each year and has a face value of $1,000. Suppose that the exercise price of the option is $1,000. The first step in the analysis is to calculate the bond's price at each node of the tree. The bond is worth $1,000 at the end of year 5. The value of the bond at earlier times can be obtained by working backward through the tree. Define $r_{ij} = r u^j d^{i-j}$

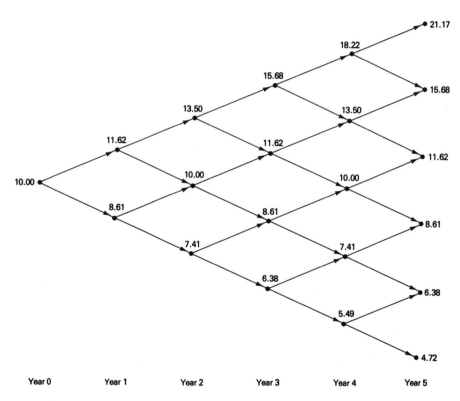

| Year 0 | Year 1 | Year 2 | Year 3 | Year 4 | Year 5 |

Figure 15.5 Binomial Tree of Interest Rate Movements in a Risk-Neutral World Using Rendleman and Bartter Model

and P_{ij} as the value of the bond at time $t + i \, \Delta t$ when the interest rate is r_{ij}. It
follows that

$$P_{ij} = e^{-r_{ij} \Delta t} \left[p P_{i+1,j+1} + (1 - p) P_{i+1,j} + c \right] \qquad (15.16)$$

where c is the coupon paid at the end of each year. Figure 15.6 shows the results
of these calculations.

The next stage is to use the tree to calculate the option price. If f_{ij} denotes
the value of the option at time $t + i \, \Delta t$ when the interest rate is r_{ij},

$$f_{4j} = \max \left[P_{4j} - 1000, \, 0 \right]$$

and when $i < 4$,

$$f_{ij} = \max \left[P_{ij} - 1000, \, e^{-r_{ij} \Delta t} \left(p f_{i+1,j+1} + (1 - p) f_{i+1,j} \right) \right]$$

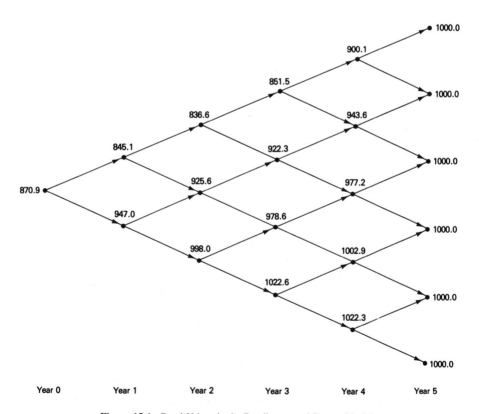

Figure 15.6   Bond Values in the Rendleman and Bartter Model

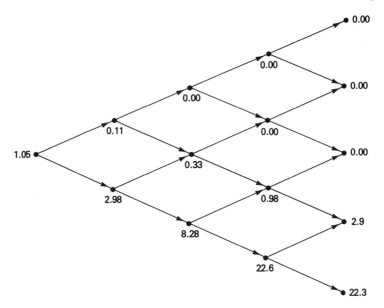

Figure 15.7   Using the Rendleman and Bartter Tree to Determine the Values of a Call Option on the Bond.

The results of these calculations are shown in Figure 15.7. The value of the option is $1.05.

It will be noted that the way of rolling back through an interest rate tree is similar to that for a stock price tree. The chief difference is that in the interest rate tree, the interest rate used for discounting varies from node to node.

15.10 MEAN REVERSION

Rendleman and Bartter assume that the short-term interest rate behaves like a stock price. One important difference between the interest rates and stock prices is that interest rates appear over time to be pulled back to some long-run average level. This phenomenon known as *mean reversion* and is not captured by the Rendleman and Bartter model. When r is high, mean reversion tends to cause it to have a negative drift; when r is low, mean reversion tends to cause it to have a positive drift. Mean reversion is illustrated in Figure 15.8.

There are compelling economic arguments in favor of mean reversion. When rates are high the economy tends to slow down and there is less requirement for funds on the part of borrowers. As a result, rates decline. When rates are low, there tends to be a high demand for funds on the part of borrowers. As a result, rates tend to rise.

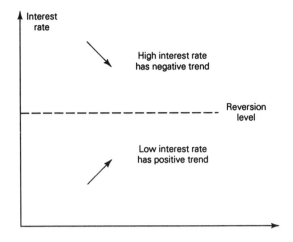

Figure 15.8   Mean Reversion

One effect of mean reversion is to make the volatility of interest rates a decreasing function of maturity. The 10-year spot interest rate tends to have a lower volatility than the 5-year spot interest rate, the 5-year spot interest rate tends to have a lower volatility than the 1-year spot interest rate, and so on.

Mean reversion can be shown to be responsible for the fact that a forward rate volatility tends to decline as the maturity of the forward contract increases. The volatility of the 3-month forward interest rate starting in 3 months is greater than the volatility of the 3-month forward interest rate starting in 2 years; this in turn is greater than the volatility of the 3-month forward rate starting in 5 years; and so on. Finally, mean reversion has some impact on bond price volatilities. It can be shown that when there is mean reversion, the relationship between volatility and a discount bond maturity has the curvature shown in Figure 15.9. This is not consistent with the hypothesis presented earlier that bond price volatility is proportional to duration.

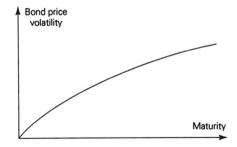

Figure 15.9   Relationship between Volatility of Discount Bond and Maturity When There Is Mean Reversion

15.11 THE VASICEK MODEL

Vasicek has proposed a model where $m(r) = a(b - r)$ and $s(r) = \sigma$ in Equation (15.10) when a, b, and σ are constants.[5] This model incorporates mean reversion. The risk-neutral process for the short rate, r, is

$$dr = a(b - r) \, dt + \sigma \, dz \tag{15.17}$$

The short rate is pulled to a level b at rate a. Superimposed upon this "pull" is a normally distributed stochastic term $\sigma \, dz$.

Vasicek solves Equation (15.12) to obtain the following analytic expression for the price of a discount bond paying \$1 at maturity in terms of r

$$P(t, T) = A(t, T)e^{-B(t,T)r} \tag{15.18}$$

where, when $a \neq 0$

$$B(t, T) = \frac{1 - e^{-a(T-t)}}{a} \tag{15.19}$$

and

$$A(t, T) = \exp\left[\frac{(B(t, T) - T + t)(a^2 b - \sigma^2/2)}{a^2} - \frac{\sigma^2 B(t, T)^2}{4a}\right] \tag{15.20}$$

When $a = 0$, $B(t, T) = T - t$ and $A(t, T) = \exp[\sigma^2(T - t)^3/6]$

Using Equation (15.14), the whole term structure can be determined as a function of r once a, b, and σ have been chosen. The shape can be upward sloping, downward sloping, or slightly "humped" (See Figure 15.10).

VALUING EUROPEAN OPTIONS ON DISCOUNT BONDS

Jamshidian has shown that the prices of options on discount bonds can be obtained using Vasicek's model.[6] The price at time t of a European call option maturing at time T on a discount bond with principal \$1 and maturing at time s is

$$P(t, s)N(h) - XP(t, T)N(h - \sigma_P) \tag{15.21}$$

where

$$h = \frac{1}{\sigma_P} \ln \frac{P(t, s)}{P(t, T)X} + \frac{\sigma_P}{2}$$

$$\sigma_P = v(t, T)B(T, s)$$

---

[5]See O. A. Vasicek, "An Equilibrium Characterization of the Term Structure," *Journal of Financial Economics*, 5 (1977), 177–88.

[6]See F. Jamshidian, "An Exact Bond Option Pricing Formula," *Journal of Finance*, 44 (March 1989), 205–9.

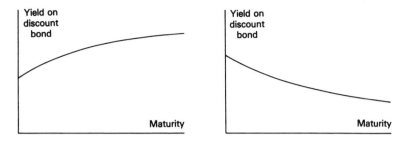

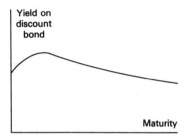

Figure 15.10   Possible Shapes of Term Structure When Vasicek's Model Is Used

$$v(t, T)^2 = \frac{\sigma^2(1 - e^{-2a(T-t)})}{2a}$$

and X is the strike price. The price of a European put option on the bond is

$$XP(t, T)N(-h + \sigma_P) - P(t, s)N(-h) \tag{15.22}$$

When $a = 0$, $v(t, T) = \sigma\sqrt{T - t}$ and $\sigma_P = \sigma(s - T)\sqrt{T - t}$.

VALUING EUROPEAN OPTIONS ON COUPON-BEARING BONDS:
   JAMSHIDIAN'S APPROACH

In the same paper, Jamshidian shows that the prices of options on coupon-bearing bonds can be obtained from the prices of options on discount bonds in a model such as Vasicek's where there is only one stochastic variable. Consider a European call option with exercise price X and maturity T on a coupon-bearing bond. Suppose that the bond provides a total of n cash flows after the option matures. Let the ith cash flow be c_i and occur at s_i ($1 \leq i \leq n$; $s_i > T$). Define

r^*: Value of r at time T that causes the coupon-bearing bond price to equal the strike price

X_i: Value at time T of a discount bond paying off \$1 at time s_i when $r = r^*$

When bond prices are known analytically as a function of r (as they are in Vasicek's model), r^* can be obtained by trial and error.

The payoff from the option is

$$\max\left[0,\ \sum_{i=1}^{n} c_i P(T, s_i) - X\right]$$

Since there is only one stochastic variable, all bond prices are decreasing functions of r. This means that the coupon-bearing bond is worth more than X at time T and should be exercised if and only if $r < r^*$. Furthermore, the discount bond maturing at time s_i that underlies the coupon-bearing bond is worth more than $c_i X_i$ at time T if and only if $r < r^*$. It follows that the payoff from the option is

$$\sum_{i=1}^{n} c_i \max\left[0,\ P(r, T, s_i) - X_i\right]$$

This shows that the option on the coupon-bearing bond is the sum of n options on the underlying discount bonds. A similar argument applies to European put options on coupon-bearing bonds.

Example 15.4

Suppose that $a = 0.1$, $b = 0.1$, and $\sigma = 0.02$ in Vasicek's model. Consider a 3-year European put option with a strike price of \$98 on a bond that will mature in 5 years. Suppose that the bond has a face value of \$100 and pays a coupon of \$5 every 6 months. At the end of 3 years the bond can be regarded as the sum of four discount bonds. If the short-term interest rate is r at the end of the 3 years, the value of the bond is from Equation (15.18)

$$5A(3, 3.5)e^{-B(3,3.5)r} + 5A(3, 4)e^{-B(3,4)r} + 5A(3, 4.5)e^{-B(3,4.5)r} + 105A(3, 5)e^{-B(3,5)r}$$

Using the expressions for $A(t, T)$ and $B(t, T)$ in equations (15.19) and (15.20), this becomes:

$$5 \times 0.9988e^{-0.4877r} + 5 \times 0.9952e^{-0.9516r} + 5 \times 0.9895e^{-1.3929r} + 105 \times 0.9819e^{-1.8127r}$$

To apply Jamshidian's procedure, we must find, r^*, the value of r for which this bond price equals the strike price of 98. Trial and error shows that $r^* = 0.10952$. When r has this value, the values of the four discount bonds underlying the coupon-bearing bond are 4.734, 4.484, 4.248, and 84.535. The option on the coupon-bearing bond is therefore the sum of four options on discount bonds:

1. A 3-year option with strike price 4.734 on a 3.5-year discount bond with a face value of 5

2. A 3-year option with strike price 4.484 on a 4-year discount bond with a face value of 5

3. A 3-year option with strike price 4.248 on a 4.5-year discount bond with a face value of 5

4. A 3-year option with strike price 84.535 on a 5-year discount bond with a face value of 105

Using equation (15.22) and assuming an initial r of 10%, the prices of these options are, respectively, 0.0125, 0.0228, 0.0314, and 0.8085. The price of the option under consideration is therefore $0.8752.

THE USE OF TRINOMIAL TREES

Hull and White have shown how trinomial trees can be used to value American bond options and other interest rate contingent claims in Vasicek's model.[7]

The value of r on the tree at time zero is the initial short rate, r_0. The values of r considered at other nodes have the form $r_0 + k\Delta r$ where k is a positive or negative integer. The relationship between Δr and the time step, Δt, is

$$\Delta r = \sigma \sqrt{3\Delta t}$$

The trinomial tree is constructed so that the change in r has the correct mean and standard deviation over each time interval Δt. The tree is more complicated than the binomial tree considered in Chapter 14 in three ways:

1. There are three branches emanating from each node, not two
2. The probabilities on the branches are different in different parts of the tree
3. A branching process is liable to vary from node to node

The alternative branching processes are illustrated in Figure 15.11. Figure 15.11(a) is the normal branching process. The alternative changes in r are: move up by Δr, stay the same, and move down by Δr. When r is high, it is sometimes necessary to use the branching process in Figure 15.11(c). The alternative changes in r are:

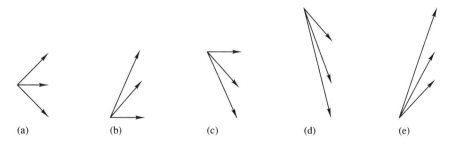

(a)   (b)   (c)   (d)   (e)

Figure 15.11   Alternative branching processes in trinomial tree

[7]See J. Hull and A. White, "Valuing Derivative Securities Using the Explicit Finite Difference Method," *Journal of Financial and Quantitative Analysis*, 25 (March 1990), 87–100.

stay the same, move down by Δr, and move down by $2\Delta r$. When r is low, it is sometimes necessary to use the branching process in Figure 15.11(b). The alternative changes in r are then: move up by $2\Delta t$, move up by Δt, and stay the same. Other branching processes that are occasionally necessary in applications of the trinomial tree approach are indicated in Figure 15.11(d) and 15.11(e).

Consider the node at time $i\Delta t$ where $r = r_0 + j\Delta r$. To choose a branching process, we first calculate the expected value of r at time $(i+1)\Delta t$ given that we start at this node. We then choose the value of k which makes $r_0 + k\Delta r$ as close as possible to this expected value of r and draw the tree so that the three possible values of r that can be reached at time $(i+1)\Delta t$ are $r_0 + (k-1)\Delta r$, $r_0 + k\Delta r$, and $r_0 + (k+1)\Delta r$. If the drift in r is such that the expected change in r in time Δt is between $-\Delta r/2$ and $+\Delta r/2$, the normal branching process in Figure 15.11(a) is appropriate; if the expected change is between $\Delta r/2$ and $3\Delta r/2$, the branching process in Figure 15.11(b) is appropriate; and so on.

Bond prices are known analytically at each node of the tree. When an American bond option is being valued, it is therefore necessary for the tree to extend only to the end of the life of the option (not to the end of the life of the bond as in the Rendleman and Bartter model).[8]

AN ILLUSTRATION

To illustrate the construction of the tree, suppose that $a = 0.2$, $b = 0.125$, and $\sigma = 0.01$ so that

$$dr = 0.2(0.125 - r)\,dt + 0.01\,dz$$

and we wish to build a tree with $\Delta t = 0.25$ years. We suppose r_0, the initial value of r, is 0.05.

In this case $\Delta r = 0.01\sqrt{3 \times 0.25} = 0.0087$. Figure 15.12 shows the tree that is constructed for the first three time steps. At the initial node A, $r = 0.05$. The expected change in r in the next time interval Δt is

$$a(b - r)\Delta t = 0.00375$$

and the standard deviation is $0.01\sqrt{0.25} = 0.005$. Since the expected change is between $-\Delta r/2$ and $+\Delta r/2$, the normal branching process is appropriate and the three possible changes in the value of r in time Δt are –0.0087, 0, and +0.0087. The probabilities are chosen on the branches to give the correct mean and standard deviation for the changes. Define p_u, p_m, and p_d as the probabilities associated

---

[8]There are two types of American bond options. The underlying bond can have a fixed life measured from today or a fixed life measured from the time the option is exercised. Both types can be valued using the tree.

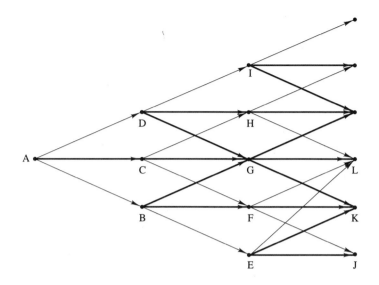

Node	A	B	C	D	E	F	G	H	I
$r\%$	5.00	4.13	5.00	5.87	3.26	4.13	5.00	5.87	6.74
p_u	0.474	0.521	0.474	0.428	0.039	0.521	0.474	0.428	0.385
p_m	0.483	0.439	0.483	0.525	0.453	0.439	0.483	0.525	0.561
p_d	0.043	0.040	0.043	0.047	0.508	0.040	0.043	0.047	0.054

Figure 15.12   Trinomial Tree for Vasicek's Model

with the upper, middle, and lower branches, respectively. They must satisfy

$$p_d + p_m + p_u = 1$$

$$0.0087 p_u - 0.0087 p_d = 0.00375$$

$$0.0087^2 p_u + (-0.0087)^2 p_d = 0.005^2 + 0.00375^2$$

The solution to these equations is $p_d = 0.043$, $p_m = 0.483$, and $p_u = 0.474$. The probabilities at all other nodes are calculated similarly.

At node E, the branching process proves to be nonstandard. The value of r at this node is 0.0326 and the expected change in r in the next time interval Δt is

$$a(b - r)\Delta t = 0.00462$$

As at other nodes, the standard deviation of the change is 0.005. Since the value of the expected change is between $\Delta r/2$ and $3\Delta r/2$, the branching process used is the one shown in Figure 15.11(b). The three possible changes in the value of r

in the next time interval Δt are 0, +0.0087, +0.0174. The probabilities, p_u, p_m, and p_d must satisfy the equations

$$p_d + p_m + p_u = 1$$

$$0.0174 p_u + 0.0087 p_m = 0.00462$$

$$0.0174^2 p_u + 0.0087^2 p_m = 0.005^2 + 0.00462^2$$

The solution is $p_u = 0.039$, $p_m = 0.453$, and $p_d = 0.508$.

Rolling Back through the Tree

Once the tree has been constructed, the prices of all bonds at each node can be calculated using Equation (15.18). The procedure for rolling back through the tree is similar to that used for the binomial tree in the Rendleman and Bartter model. The difference is that the discounted expected value at each node has to be calculated over three possible branches rather than two. When we roll back through the tree we assume that the interest rate at a node applies for the whole of the following time step. Thus, if f_G, f_H, and f_I are the value of a derivative security at nodes G, H, and I, respectively, then assuming no early exercise, the value at node D is

$$e^{-0.0587 \times 0.25}[0.428 f_I + 0.525 f_H + 0.047 f_G]$$

With a similar notation, the value at node E, assuming no early exercise, is

$$e^{-0.0326 \times 0.25}[0.039 f_L + 0.453 f_K + 0.508 f_J]$$

Checks for the desirability of early exercise must be made as in binomial trees.

15.12 THE COX, INGERSOLL, AND ROSS MODEL

One of the theoretical disadvantages of Vasicek's model is that interest rates can become negative. Cox, Ingersoll, and Ross have proposed an alternative model that overcomes this problem.[9] The risk-neutral process for r in their model is

$$dr = a(b - r)\, dt + \sigma \sqrt{r}\, dz$$

This has the same mean-reverting drift as Vasicek, but the stochastic term has a standard deviation proportional to $\sqrt{r}$. This means that as the short-term interest rate increases its standard deviation increases.

---

[9]See J. C. Cox, J. E. Ingersoll, and S. A. Ross, "A Theory of the Term Structure of Interest Rates," *Econometrica*, 53 (1985), 385–407.

Cox, Ingersoll, and Ross show that, in their model, bond prices have the same general form as in Vasicek's model:

$$P(t, T) = A(t, T)e^{-B(t,T)r}$$

but the functions $B(t, T)$ and $A(t, T)$ are different:

$$B(t, T) = \frac{2(e^{\gamma(T-t)} - 1)}{(\gamma + a)(e^{\gamma(T-t)} - 1) + 2\gamma}$$

and

$$A(t, T) = \left[\frac{2\gamma e^{(a+\gamma)(T-t)/2}}{(\gamma + a)(e^{\gamma(T-t)} - 1) + 2\gamma} \right]^{2ab/\sigma^2}$$

where $\gamma = \sqrt{a^2 + 2\sigma^2}$. As in the case of Vasicek's model, upward-sloping, downward-sloping, and slightly humped yield curves are possible.

Cox, Ingersoll, and Ross provide formulas for European call and put options on discount bonds. These involve integrals of the noncentral chi-square distribution. European options on coupon-bearing bonds can be valued using Jamshidian's approach in a similar way to that described for Vasicek's model. American options can be valued using the trinomial tree approach described for European options. The trick is to use the tree to model $x = 2\sqrt{r}$ rather than r itself. From Ito's lemma, the process followed by x is

$$dx = 2 \left[\frac{a(b - x^2/4)}{x} - \frac{\sigma^2}{4x} \right] dt + \sigma \, dz$$

At each node of the tree, r is calculated using the inverse transformation $r = (x/2)^2$. The procedure works in circumstances where $4ab > \sigma^2$ so that the drift in x is positive as x approaches zero.

15.13 TWO-FACTOR MODELS

The models considered assume that the whole term structure depends on a single stochastic variable or factor. A number of researchers have investigated the properties of two-factor models. For example, Brennan and Schwartz have developed a model where the process for the short rate reverts to a long rate which in turn follows a stochastic process.[10] The long rate is chosen as the yield on a perpetual consol bond. Since the yield on a consol bond is the reciprocal of the price of the bond, the two variables in the model can therefore be regarded as the short-term

---

[10] See M. J. Brennan and E. S. Schwartz, "A Continuous Time Approach to Pricing Bonds," *Journal of Banking and Finance*, 3 (July 1979), 133–55; M. J. Brennan and E. S. Schwartz, "An Equilibrium Model of Bond Pricing and a Test of Market Efficiency," *Journal of Financial and Quantitative Analysis*, 17, 3 (September 1982), 301–29.

rate r and the price of a consol bond. The fact that a consol bond is a traded security simplifies the analysis since we know that its drift in a risk-neutral world must be the risk-free interest rate less the yield on the bond.

Another two-factor model has been proposed by Longstaff and Schwartz.[11] These authors start with a general equilibrium model of the economy and derive a term structure model in which there is a stochastic volatility. The model proves to be analytically quite tractable.

15.14 NO–ARBITRAGE MODELS

The disadvantage of the term structure models presented in the the previous few sections is that they do not automatically fit today's term structure. By choosing the parameters judiciously in the way indicated in Figure 15.4, they can be made to provide an approximate fit to many of the term structures that are encountered in practice. But the fit is not usually an exact one and in some cases there are significant errors. Most traders find this unsatisfactory. Not unreasonably, they argue that they can have very little confidence in the price of a derivative security when the model does not price the underlying correctly. A 1 percent error in the price of the underlying can lead to a 50 percent error in an option price.

In this section, we present some general theoretical background material on what are known as *no-arbitrage models*. These are models which are designed so that they are exactly consistent with today's term structure. We will assume that the term structure depends on only one factor, but the results can be extended to accommodate several factors.

We will adopt the following notation:

$P(t, T)$: Price at time t of a discount bond with principal \$1 maturing at time T

$v(t, T)$: Volatility of $P(t, T)$

$f(t, T_1, T_2)$: Forward rate as seen at time t for the period between time T_1 and time T_2

$F(t, T)$: Instantaneous forward rate as seen at time t for a contract maturing at time T

$r(t)$: Short-term risk-free interest rate at time t

$dz(t)$: Wiener process driving term structure movements

The variable $F(t, T)$ is the limit of $f(t, T, T + \Delta t)$ as Δt tends to zero.

[11]See F. A. Longstaff and E. S. Schwartz, "Interest Rate Volatility and the Term Structure: A Two Factor General Equilibrium Model," Working Paper, November 1990, Ohio State University and UCLA.

THE PROCESSES FOR DISCOUNT BOND PRICES AND FORWARD RATES

We start with the risk-neutral process for $P(t, T)$:

$$dP(t, T) = r(t)P(t, T)dt + v(t, T)P(t, T)dz(t) \qquad (15.23)$$

This equation reflects the fact that, since a discount bond is a traded security providing no income, its expected return in a risk-neutral world must be $r(t)$. The volatility, $v(t, T)$, can in the most general form of the model be any well-behaved function of past and present P's, but, since a bond's price volatility declines to zero at maturity, we must have[12]

$$v(t, t) = 0$$

The forward rate, $f(t, T_1, T_2)$, can be related to discount bond prices as follows

$$f(t, T_1, T_2) = \frac{\ln[P(t, T_1)] - \ln[P(t, T_2)]}{T_2 - T_1} \qquad (15.24)$$

From (15.23)

$$d\ln[P(t, T_1)] = \left[r(t) - \frac{v(t, T_1)^2}{2} \right] dt + v(t, T_1)dz(t)$$

and

$$d\ln[P(t, T_2)] = \left[r(t) - \frac{v(t, T_2)^2}{2} \right] dt + v(t, T_2)dz(t)$$

so that

$$df(t, T_1, T_2) = \frac{v(t, T_2)^2 - v(t, T_1)^2}{2(T_2 - T_1)} dt + \frac{v(t, T_1) - v(t, T_2)}{T_2 - T_1} dz(t) \qquad (15.25)$$

Equation (15.25) shows that the risk-neutral process for f depends only on the v's. It depends on r and the P's only to the extent that the v's themselves depend on these variables.

When we put $T_1 = T$ and $T_2 = T + \Delta T$ in (15.26) and then take limits as ΔT tends to zero, $f(t, T_1, T_2)$ becomes $F(t, T)$, the coefficient of $dz(t)$ becomes $v_T(t, T)$, and the coefficient of dt becomes

$$\frac{1}{2} \frac{\partial \left[v(t, T)^2 \right]}{\partial T} = v(t, T)v_T(t, T)$$

where subscripts denote partial derivatives. It follows that

$$dF(t, T) = v(t, T)v_T(t, T)\, dt - v_T(t, T)\, dz(t)$$

---

[12] $v(t, t) = 0$ is equivalent to the assumption that all discount bonds have finite drifts at all times. This is because, if the volatility of the bond does not decline to zero at maturity, an infinite drift may be necessary to ensure that the bond's price equals its face value at maturity.

Since we may without loss of generality change the sign of $dz(t)$, we can write this

$$dF(t, T) = v(t, T)v_T(t, T)\, dt + v_T(t, T)\, dz(t) \tag{15.26}$$

Once $v(t, T)$ has been specified for all t and T, the risk-neutral processes for the $F(t, T)$'s are known. The $v(t, T)$'s are therefore sufficient to fully define a one-factor interest rate model.

Equation (15.26) shows that there is a link between the drift and standard deviation of an instantaneous forward rate. Heath, Jarrow, and Morton were the first to point this out.[13] Integrating $v_T(t, \tau)$ between $\tau = t$ and $\tau = T$ we obtain

$$v(t, T) - v(t, t) = \int_t^T v_T(t, \tau)\, d\tau$$

Since $v(t, t) = 0$, this becomes

$$v(t, T) = \int_t^T v_T(t, \tau)\, d\tau$$

If $m(t, T)$ and $s(t, T)$ are the instantaneous drift and standard deviation of $F(t, T)$, it follows from (15.26) that

$$m(t, T) = s(t, T) \int_t^T s(t, \tau)d\tau \tag{15.27}$$

A similar result holds where there is more than one factor.

THE PROCESS FOR THE SHORT RATE

We now move on to derive the risk-neutral process for $r(t)$ from bond price volatilities and the initial term structure. Since

$$F(t, t) = F(0, t) + \int_0^t dF(\tau, t)$$

and $r(t) = F(t, t)$ it follows from (15.26) that[14]

$$r(t) = F(0, t) + \int_0^t v(\tau, t)v_t(\tau, t)d\tau + \int_0^t v_t(\tau, t)dz(\tau) \tag{15.28}$$

---

[13] See D. Heath, R. Jarrow, and A. Morton, "Bond Pricing and the Term Structure of Interest Rates; A New Methodology," *Econometrica*, 60, 1 (1992), 77–105.

[14] The stochastic calculus in equations (15.28) and (15.29) may be unfamiliar to some readers. To interpret what is going on we can replace integral signs with summation signs and d's with Δ's. For example, $\int_0^t v(\tau, t)v_t(\tau, t)d\tau$ becomes $\sum_{i=1}^n v(i\Delta t, t)v_t(i\Delta t, t)\Delta t$ where $\Delta t = t/n$.

Differentiating with respect to t and using the result that $v(t, t) = 0$

$$dr(t) = F_t(0, t)dt + \left\{ \int_0^t [v(\tau, t)v_{tt}(\tau, t) + v_t(\tau, t)^2] d\tau \right\} dt$$

$$+ \left\{ \int_0^t v_{tt}(\tau, t) \, dz(\tau) \right\} dt + [v_t(\tau, t)|_{\tau=t}] dz(t)$$

(15.29)

It is interesting to examine the terms on the right hand side of (15.29). The first and fourth terms are straightforward. The first term shows that one component of the drift in r is the slope of the initial forward rate curve. The fourth term shows that the instantaneous standard deviation of r is $v_t(\tau, t)|_{\tau=t}$. The second and third terms are more complicated, particularly when v is stochastic. The second term depends on the history of v because it involves $v(\tau, t)$ when $\tau < t$. The third term depends on the history of both v and dz. The two terms are therefore liable to cause the process for r to be non-Markov.

15.15 THE HEATH, JARROW, AND MORTON APPROACH

The Heath, Jarrow, and Morton (HJM) approach is to specify the volatilities of all instantaneous forward rates at all future times. This is sometimes referred to as the *volatility structure*. Equation (15.27) is then used to calculate the drift of each instantaneous forward rate and a binomial tree describing the evolution of the term structure of forward rates is constructed.

Unfortunately, the HJM tree is, in general, nonrecombining in the sense that an up movement followed by a down movement does not lead to the same term structure as a down movement followed by an up movement. Figure 15.13 shows a typical HJM tree for one factor and three time steps. In general, after n time steps there are 2^n nodes. This severely limits the number of time steps that can be used and makes computations extremely slow.

Since a complete knowledge of the behavior of the short rate is sufficient to determine the initial term structure and how it can evolve, we can regard the HJM tree as a tree in the short rate. Our discussion of the process for the short rate, r, in the previous section explains why the HJM tree does not necessarily recombine. In the general HJM model, the process for r is non-Markov. In order to know the stochastic behavior of r over a short period of time in the future, we need to know not only the value of r at the beginning of the period but also the path it followed in reaching that value.[15]

A numerical procedure that can be used fairly easily in conjunction with the general HJM model is Monte Carlo simulation. This can be used to test the

---

[15]Note that this does not lead to a market inefficiency since r is not the price of a traded security.

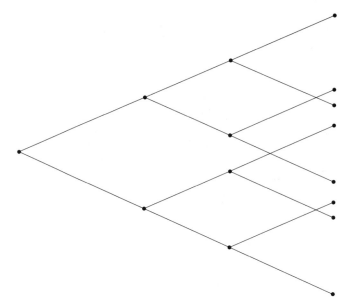

Figure 15.13   A Nonrecombining Tree

effect of different volatility structures on European option prices. Unfortunately, American-style options cannot be priced with Monte Carlo simulation.

MARKOV VERSIONS OF THE MODEL

Markov models of the short rate can be represented using recombining trees and have the advantage that they use far less computer time than non-Markov models. As a practical matter, it makes sense to try to find particular cases of the general HJM model where r is Markov. Note that when we are developing a no-arbitrage model, we cannot simply write down a process for r such as the one in Equation (15.10). This is because there is no guarantee that the model will fit the initial term structure.

This shows that there is a key difference between modeling r and modeling either bond prices or instantaneous forwards. When we model bond prices or instantaneous forwards, the initial values of the variables ensure that we are consistent with the initial term structure, but we have no easy way of knowing whether the process for r is Markov. When we model r directly, we know immediately whether the process is Markov, but the initial value of the variable only ensures that we are consistent with the short end of the term structure.

We now examine in some detail two no-arbitrage Markov models of the short rate.

15.16 THE HO AND LEE MODEL

Ho and Lee proposed the first no-arbitrage model of the term structure in a paper in 1986.[16] They presented the model in the form of a binomial tree where there were two parameters, one concernerned with volatility the other concerned with the market price of risk. It has since been shown that the continuous time limit of the model is

$$dr = \theta(t)\,dt + \sigma\,dz$$

where σ, the instantaneous standard deviation of the short rate, is constant and $\theta(t)$ is a function of time chosen to ensure that the model fits the initial term structure. The equation for $\theta(t)$ is

$$\theta(t) = F_t(0, t) + \sigma^2 t$$

It is interesting note that Ho and Lee's parameter concerned with the market price of risk is a redundant variable. This is analogous to risk preferences being irrelevant in the pricing of stock options.

In the Ho and Lee model, discount bonds and European options on discount bonds can be valued analytically. The expression for the price of a discount bond at time t in terms of the short rate is

$$P(t, T) = A(t, T)e^{-r(T-t)}$$

where

$$\ln A(t, T) = \ln \frac{P(0, T)}{P(0, t)} - (T - t)\frac{\partial \ln P(0, t)}{\partial t} - \frac{1}{2}\sigma^2 t(T - t)^2$$

The price of a European call and put options on a discount bond is given by equations (15.21) and (15.22) where

$$\sigma_P = \sigma(s - T)\sqrt{T - t}$$

European options on coupon-bearing bonds can be valued by decomposing them into a portfolio of European options on discount bonds using the approach suggested by Jamshidian that was described in Section 15.11. American options can be valued by drawing a tree in either the way described by Ho and Lee or by using trinomial trees as will be described later in this chapter.

The Ho and Lee model has the advantage that it is a Markov analytically tractable model. It easy to apply and provides an exact fit to the current term structure of interest rates. One disadvantage of the model is that it gives the user very little flexibility in choosing the volatility structure. All spot and forward rates have the same instantanous standard deviation, σ. Another related disadvantage

[16] See T. S. Y. Ho and S.-B. Lee, "Term Structure Movements and Pricing Interest Rate Contingent Claims," *Journal of Finance*, 41 (December 1986), 1011–29.

of the model is that it has no mean reversion. This means that regardless of how high or low interest rates are at a particular point in time, the average direction in which interest rates move over the next short period of time is always the same.

15.17 THE HULL AND WHITE MODEL

In a paper published in 1990, Hull and White explored extensions of the Vasicek and Cox, Ingersoll, and Ross models that provide an exact fit to the initial term structure.[17] One version of the extended Vasicek's model is

$$dr = (\theta(t) - ar)\, dt + \sigma\, dz \qquad (15.30)$$

where a and σ are constants. We will refer to this as the Hull–White model. It can be characterized as the Ho and Lee model with mean reversion at rate a. Alternatively it can be characterized as the Vasicek model with a time-dependent reversion level. The Ho and Lee model is a particular case of this Hull–White model with $a = 0$.

The model has the same amount of analytic tractability as Ho and Lee. The bond price at time t can be determined analytically as a function of the short rate.

$$P(t, T) = A(t, T)e^{-B(t,T)r}$$

where

$$B(t, T) = \frac{1 - e^{-a(T-t)}}{a}$$

and

$$\ln A(t, T) = \ln \frac{P(0, T)}{P(0, t)} - B(t, T)\frac{\partial \ln P(0, t)}{\partial t} - \frac{1}{4a^3}\sigma^2(e^{-aT} - e^{-at})^2(e^{2at} - 1)$$

The formulas for European option prices on discount bonds are the same as those given for the Vasicek model in equations (15.21) and (15.22). European options on coupon-bearing bonds can be valued using the Jamshidian decomposition into options on discount bonds described in Section 15.11.

The volatility structure in the Hull–White model is determined by both σ and a. The model can represent a wider range of volatility structures than Ho and Lee. The volatility at time t of a bond of maturing at time T is

$$\frac{\sigma}{a}[1 - e^{-a(T-t)}]$$

---

[17]See J. Hull and A. White, "Pricing Interest Rate Derivative Securities," *Review of Financial Studies*, 3, 4 (1990), 573–92.

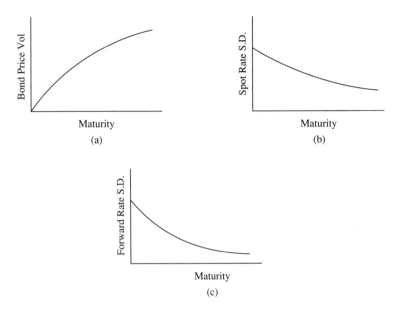

Figure 15.14   The Volatility Structure in the Hull–White Model

The instantaneous standard deviation at time t of the zero-coupon interest rate maturing at time T is

$$\frac{\sigma}{a(T-t)}[1 - e^{-a(T-t)}]$$

and the instantaneous standard deviation of the T-maturity instantaneous forward rate is $\sigma e^{-a(T-t)}$. These functions are shown in Figure 15.14. The parameter σ determines the short rate's instantaneous standard deviation. The reversion rate parameter, a, determines the curvature in Figure 15.14(a) and the rate at which standard deviations decline with maturity in Figure 15.14(b) and 15.14(c). The higher a, the greater the curvature and the greater the decline. When $a = 0$, discount bond price volatilities are a linear function of maturity and the instantaneous standard deviations of both zeroes and forward rates are constant.

Using Trinomial Trees

A trinomial tree can be used to value American options and other more complicated derivative securities in the Hull and White model. The details are explained in a paper by Hull and White.[18] The geometry of the tree is similar to

---

[18] See J. Hull and A. White, "One-Factor Interest Rate Models and the Valuation of Interest Rate Derivative Securities," forthcoming, *Journal of Financial and Quantitative Analysis.*

the geometry of the tree used for Vasicek's model in Section 15.11. However, there is one important difference. When implementing Vasicek's model, the process for r is known and the tree is chosen so that it matches the process as closely as possible. Here there is an unknown function $\theta(t)$ and part of the objective of the process used to construct the tree is to determine $\theta(t)$ so that all discount bonds are priced correctly.

The short rate, r, on the tree is defined as the continuously compounded yield on a discount bond maturing in time Δt. The values of r on the tree are equally spaced and have the form $r_0 + j\Delta r$ for some Δr where r_0 is the current value of r and j is a positive or negative integer. The time values considered by the tree are also equally spaced having the form $i\Delta t$ for some Δt where i is a non-negative integer. The variable Δr is related to Δt using $\Delta r = \sigma\sqrt{3\Delta t}$.

For convenience, the node on the tree where $t = i\Delta t$ and $r = r_0 + j\Delta r$ ($i \geq 2$) will be referred to as the (i, j) node. We use the following notation:

$R(i)$: Yield at time zero on a discount bond maturing at time $i\Delta t$

r_j : $r_0 + j\Delta r$

$\mu_{i,j}$: Drift rate of r at node (i, j)

We suppose that the tree has already been constructed up to time $n\Delta t$ ($n \geq 0$) so that it is consistent with the $R(i)$ and show how it can be extended one step further. Since the interest rate, r, at time $i\Delta t$ is assumed to apply to the time period between $i\Delta t$ and $(i + 1)\Delta t$, a tree constructed up to time $n\Delta t$ reflects the values of $R(i)$ for $i \leq n + 1$. In constructing the branches comprising the tree between times $n\Delta t$ and $(n + 1)\Delta t$, we must choose a value of $\theta(n\Delta t)$ so that the tree is consistent with $R(n + 2)$. The equation for doing this is

$$\theta(n\Delta t) = \frac{1}{\Delta t}(n+2)R(n+2) + \frac{\sigma^2\Delta t}{2} + \frac{1}{\Delta t^2}\ln\sum_j Q(n, j)e^{-2r_j\Delta t + ar_j\Delta t^2} \quad (15.31)$$

where $Q(i, j)$ is the value of a security that pays off \$1 if node (i, j) is reached and zero otherwise. The $Q(i, j)$'s can be calculated as the tree is constructed using

$$Q(i, j) = \sum_{j^*} Q(i - 1, j^*)q(j^*, j)e^{-r_{j^*}\Delta t} \quad (15.32)$$

where $q(j^*, j)$ is the probability of moving from node $(i - 1, j^*)$ to node (i, j) (For any given j^*, this is zero for all except three of the j's.)

Once $\theta(n\Delta t)$ has been determined, the drift rates $\mu_{n,j}$ for r at the nodes at time $n\Delta t$ are calculated using

$$\mu_{n,j} = \theta(n\Delta t) - a(r_0 + j\Delta r) \quad (15.33)$$

The branches emanating from the nodes at time $n\Delta t$ and their associated probabilities are then chosen to be consistent with the $\mu_{n,j}$'s and with σ in a similar way to that described for Vasicek's model in Section 15.11.

Example 15.5

Figure 15.15 shows the tree that is constructed for the Hull–White model in Equation (15.30) when $a = 0.1$, $\sigma = 0.014$, and $\Delta t = 1$. The term structure is assumed to be upward sloping with the yields on 1-, 2-, 3-, 4-, and 5-year discount bonds being 10 percent, 10.5 percent, 11.0 percent, 11.25 percent, and 11.5 percent, respectively.

The first step in constructing the tree is to calculate $\theta(0)$. Since $Q(0,0) = 1$, $r_0 = 0.1$, and $R(2) = 0.105$, Equation (15.31) gives $\theta(0) = 0.0201$. From Equation (15.33) calculate

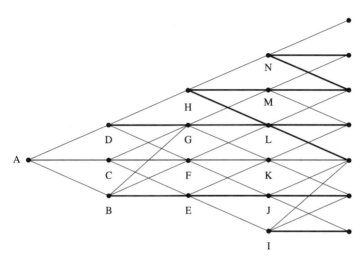

Table of rates and probabilities

Node	A	B	C	D	E	F	G
Rate	10.00	7.58	10.00	12.42	7.58	10.00	12.42
p_u	0.462	0.044	0.507	0.415	0.286	0.221	0.166
p_m	0.493	0.477	0.451	0.534	0.627	0.657	0.667
p_d	0.045	0.479	0.042	0.051	0.087	0.122	0.167

Node	H	I	J	K	L	M	N
Rate	14.85	5.15	7.58	10.00	12.42	14.85	17.27
p_u	0.121	0.042	0.455	0.370	0.293	0.228	0.171
p_m	0.657	0.426	0.499	0.570	0.623	0.654	0.667
p_d	0.222	0.532	0.046	0.060	0.084	0.118	0.162

Figure 15.15   Tree for Hull–White Model

the drift of r at the $(0,0)$ node is 0.0101. The mean and standard deviation of r on the nodes that can be reached from node $(0,0)$ is therefore 0.0101 and 0.014. This leads to the probabilities, 0.045, 0.493, and 0.462, for the first three branches in Figure 15.15. Equation (15.32) shows that $Q(1, -1)$, $Q(1, 0)$, and $Q(1, 1)$ are 0.041, 0.446, and 0.418 respectively. This completes calculations for the first time step. Equation (15.31) can now be used again to calculate $\theta(\Delta t)$ as 0.0213. This leads to the probabilities shown on the branches corresponding to the second time step in Figure 15.15; and so on. For accurate calculations a computer should be used as rounding errors build up fast when only a 3 or 4 decimal places are stored.

OTHER MARKOV MODELS

The tree procedure that has just been described can be used to construct other one-factor Markov models of the term structure that are consistent with the initial term structure. Consider, for example, the model

$$d \ln r = [\theta(t) - a \ln r] \, dt + \sigma \, dz \qquad (15.31)$$

This is similar to models proposed by Black, Derman, and Toy, and Black and Karasinski.[19] A trinomial tree is constructed in $\ln r$ rather than r. At each step, $\theta(t)$ is chosen so that the tree prices discount bonds correctly. The procedure that must be followed is explained by Hull and White.[20]

The advantage of the Hull–White model over alternatives is its analytic tractability. Bond prices and European option prices are known analytically. By contrast, other models such as the one in Equation (15.31) have no analytic tractability. This means that trees for r must be constructed out to the end of the life of the underlying asset—not just to the end of the life of the option. This can be computationally quite time consuming.

15.18 HEDGING

The hedge statistics calculated for a portfolio of interest rate derivative securities are generally more extensive from those calculated for a portfolio of derivative securities dependent on a stock or a currency. Often practitioners choose to divide the yield curve into sections or "buckets." They make a small parallel shift in one section keeping the rest of the yield curve unchanged and observe the effect on the

---

[19] See F. Black, E. Derman, and W. Toy, "A One-Factor Model of Interest Rates and its Application to Treasury Bond Options," *Financial Analysts Journal*, (January–February, 1990), 33–39; F. Black and P. Karasinski, "Bond and Option Pricing When Short Rates are Lognormal," *Financial Analysts Journal*, (July–August, 1991), 52–59.

[20] See J. Hull and A. White, "One-Factor Interest Rate Models and the Valuation of Interest Rate Derivative Securities," forthcoming, *Journal of Financial and Quantitative Analysis*.

value of their portfolio. A well-hedged portfolio is not unduly sensitive to changes in any of the buckets. If the hedge statistics indicate an unacceptable exposure, trades are done to reduce the exposure.

This approach corresponds to the GAP management approach that is often used by financial institutions to manage their assets and liabilities. Note that in any model for r that we use, there are only certain ways that the term structure can evolve. Purists might argue that we should hedge against only these particular movements rather than all possible movements. In practice, however, the approach previously described is usually adopted even though it is somewhat inconsistent with the model being used. We can draw an analogy with the Black–Scholes model as far as this is concerned. When pricing equity options, analysts usually assume that volatility is constant, but, when hedging, they recognize that this model is imperfect and hedge against volatility changes by calculating vega measures.[21]

15.19 SUMMARY

Interest rate options arise in practice in many different ways. For example, options on Treasury bond futures, Treasury note futures, and Eurodollar futures are actively traded by exchanges. Many traded bonds include features that are options. The loans and deposit instruments offered by financial institutions often contain hidden options. Mortgage-backed securities contain embedded interest rate options. Options on swaps (swaptions) and interest rate caps are actively traded over the counter.

Interest rate options are more difficult to value than stock options, currency options, index options, and most futures options. This is partly because we are dealing with a whole term structure—not a single variable. It is also partly because the behavior of interest rates is relatively complicated. For example, interest rates appear to exhibit a phenomenon known as mean reversion. This means that they have a drift rate that always tends to pull them back towards some central value. Superimposed upon this mean reversion is a volatility.

Caps are frequently valued by assuming that each element of the cap is an option on a forward interest rate and by using Black's model. The appropriate forward rate volatility to use in the model tends to decline as the maturity of the forward contract increases.

European bond options are frequently valued by assuming that either bond prices or bond yields are lognormal at the time when the option matures. This approach cannot be extended to American bond options and other interest rate

---

[21]For a fuller discussion of hedging issues, see J. Hull and A. White, "Modern Greek," *RISK*, (December 1990), 65–67.

derivative securities because the pattern of our uncertainty about a bond's price during its life has features that are not well represented by the Black–Scholes model. To overcome this problem, a yield curve model is required.

Many of the yield curve models that have been proposed have the disadvantage that they are not consistent with the term structure of interest rates at the time the model is built. This has led Ho and Lee; Heath, Jarrow, and Morton; Hull and White; and others to suggest ways in which yield curve models can be constructed so that they are automatically consistent with the initial yield curve. The Heath, Jarrow, and Morton model has the advantage that it can fit all forward rate volatilities at all times. But this advantage is achieved at considerable cost. The process for the short rate, r, is in general non-Markov. This means that the tree for r is nonrecombining and, even with only one factor, there are 2^n nodes at the nth time step, making the model very slow computationally. A number of Markov no-arbitrage models of the short rate have been suggested to overcome this problem. Amongst these are the Ho and Lee model; the Hull–White model; the Black, Derman, and Toy model; and the Black and Karasinski model. The Ho and Lee model has the advantage that it is analytically tractable. Its disadvantage is that it implies that all rates are equally variable at all times. The Hull–White model is a version of the Ho and Lee model that includes mean reversion. This allows a richer description of the volatility environment while preserving the analytic tractability of Ho and Lee. The Black, Derman, and Toy model and Black and Karasinski model avoid the possibility of negative interest rates, but have no analytic tractability.

SUGGESTIONS FOR FURTHER READING

Traditional Approaches to Modeling the Term Structure

BRENNAN, M. J. and E. S. SCHWARTZ, "An Equilibrium Model of Bond Pricing and a Test of Market Efficiency," *Journal of Financial and Quantitative Analysis*, 17, 3 (September 1982), 301–29.

COURTADON, G., "The Pricing of Options on Default-free Bonds," *Journal of Financial and Quantitative Analysis*, 17 (March 1982), pp. 75–100.

COX, J. C., J. E. INGERSOLL, and S. A. ROSS, "A Theory of the Term Structure of Interest Rates," *Econometrica*, 53 (1985), 385–407.

JAMSHIDIAN, F., "An Exact Bond Option Pricing Formula," *Journal of Finance*, 44 (March 1989), 205–9.

RENDLEMAN, R., and B. BARTTER, "The Pricing of Options on Debt Securities," *Journal of Financial and Quantitative Analysis*, 15 (March 1980), 11–24.

SCHAEFER, S. M., and E. S. SCHWARTZ, "Time-Dependent Variance and the Pricing of Options," *Journal of Finance*, 42 (December 1987), 1113–28.

VASICEK, O. A., "An Equilibrium Characterization of the Term Structure," *Journal of Financial Economics*, 5 (1977), 177–88.

No-Arbitrage Models

BLACK, F., E. DERMAN, and W. TOY, "A One-Factor Model of Interest Rates and its Application to Treasury Bond Options," *Financial Analysts Journal*, (January–February 1990), 33–39.

BLACK, F. and P. KARASINSKI, "Bond and Option Pricing When Short Rates are Lognormal," *Financial Analysts Journal*, (July–August, 1991), 52–59.

HEATH, D., R. JARROW, and A. MORTON, "Bond Pricing and the Term Structure of the Interest Rates: A New Methodology," *Econometrica*, 60,1 (1992), 77–105.

HO, T. S. Y., and S.-B. LEE, "Term Structure Movements and Pricing Interest Rate Contingent Claims," *Journal of Finance*, 41 (December 1986), 1011–29.

HULL, J., and A. WHITE, "Coming to Terms," *RISK*, December 1989, 21–25.

HULL, J., and A. WHITE, "Modern Greek," *RISK*, December 1990, 65–67.

HULL, J., and A. WHITE, "Pricing Interest Rate Derivative Securities," *The Review of Financial Studies*, 3, 4 (1990), 573–92.

HULL, J., and A. WHITE, "Valuing Derivative Securities Using the Explicit Finite Difference Method," *Journal of Financial and Quantitative Analysis*, 25 (March 1990), 87–100.

HULL, J., and A. WHITE, "In the Common Interest," *RISK*, March 1992, 64–68.

HULL, J., and A. WHITE, "One-Factor Interest Rate Models and the Valuation of Interest Rate Derivative Securities," forthcoming, *Journal of Financial and Quantitative Analysis*.

QUESTIONS AND PROBLEMS

15.1. A company caps 3-month LIBOR at 10% per annum. The principal amount is $20 million. On a reset date, 3-month LIBOR is 12% per annum. What payment would this lead to under the cap? When would the payment be made?

15.2. Explain what mortgage-backed securities are. Explain why mortgage-backed securities are more risky than regular fixed income instruments such as government bonds.

15.3. Explain why a swaption can be regarded as a type of bond option.

15.4. Use the Black–Scholes model to value a 1-year European put option on a 10-year bond. Assume that the current value of the bond is $125, the strike price is $110, the 1-year interest rate is 10% per annum, the bond's price volatility is 8% per annum, and the present value of the coupons that will be paid during the life of the option is $10.

15.5. Explain carefully why the Black–Scholes approach is inappropriate for valuing European bond options when the life of the option is a significant proportion of the life of the bond. What other approaches can be used?

15.6. Calculate the price of an option that caps the 3-month rate starting in 18 months time at 13% (quoted with quarterly compounding) on a principal amount of $1,000.

The relevant forward interest rate for the period in question is 12% per annum (quoted with quarterly compounding), the 18-month risk-free interest rate (continuously compounded) is 11.5% per annum, and the volatility of the forward rate is 12% per annum.

15.7. What are the advantages of yield curve models over the use of the Black and Black–Scholes models for valuing caps and bond options?

15.8. Suppose that an implied volatility for a 9-month Eurodollar futures option is calculated using Black's model and that this volatility is then used to value an 18-month Eurodollar futures option. Would you expect the resultant price to be too high or too low? Explain.

15.9. Consider an 8-month European put option on a Treasury bond that currently has 14.25 years to maturity. The current bond price is $910, the exercise price is $900, and the volatility of the bond price is 10% per annum. A coupon of $35 will be paid by the bond in 3 months. The risk-free interest rate is 8% for all maturities up to 1 year. Use the Black–Scholes model to determine the price of the option. Consider both the case where the strike price corresponds to the cash price of the bond and the case where it corresponds to the quoted price.

15.10. Calculate delta, gamma, and vega in Problem 15.9 when the strike price corresponds to the quoted price. Explain how they can be interpreted.

15.11. Calculate the price of a cap on the 3-month LIBOR rate in 9 months' time when the principal amount is $1,000. Use Black's model and the following information:

Quoted 9-month Eurodollar futures price = 92

Interest-rate volatility implied by a 9-month Eurodollar option = 15% per annum

Current 9-month interest rate with continuous compounding = 7.5% per annum

Cap rate = 8% per annum

15.12. Calculate delta, gamma, and vega in Problem 15.11. Explain how they can be interpreted.

15.13. Calculate the value of a 4-year European call option on a 5-year bond using Black's model. The 5-year bond price is $105, the price of a 4-year bond with the same coupon is $102, the strike price is $100, the 4-year risk-free interest rate is 10% per annum with continuous compounding, and the volatility of the forward price of 1-year bond whose life starts in 4 years is 2% per annum.

15.14. Does a European interest rate option always increase in value as the time to maturity increases, with all else being held constant? Explain your answer.

15.15. What other instrument is the same as a 5-year zero-cost collar where the strike price of the cap equals the strike price of the floor? What does the common strike price equal?

*15.16. Can Jamshidian's approach for converting an option on a coupon-bearing bond into a portfolio of options on discount bonds be used in conjunction with a two-factor model? Explain your answer.

15.17. "The lognormal bond price model allows negative interest rates." Discuss.

*15.18. Suppose that the yield, R, on a discount bond follows the process

$$dR = \mu \, dt + \sigma \, dz$$

where μ and σ are functions of R and t, and dz is a Wiener process. Show that the volatility of the discount bond declines to zero as it approaches maturity.

15.19. Use a binomial tree as in Section 15.9 to evaluate a put option on a 6% coupon bond with a face value of $1,000 that matures at the end of year 6. The option is American and expires at the end of year 4. Assume that coupons are paid at the end of each year, the exercise price is $900, the initial short-term interest rate is 8%, the volatility of interest rates is 20%, the real-world drift in interest rates is zero, and the market price of interest rate risk is –0.4. Use a time interval of 1 year.

15.20. In the Hull–White model $a = 0.08$ and $\sigma = 0.01$. Calculate the price of a 1-year European call option on a discount bond that will mature in 5 years when the term structure is flat at 10%, the face value of the bond is $100, and the strike price $60.

15.21 In the Hull–White model $a = 0.1$ and $\sigma = 0.015$. Calculate the price of a 3-month European put option on a 15-month bond with a 12% (semiannual) coupon. Assume that the bond principal is $100, the cash strike price is $100, and the yield curve is

$$y(t) = 0.09 + 0.02t$$

Exotic Options

Derivative securities with more complicated payoffs than the standard European or American calls and puts are sometimes referred to as *exotic options*. Most exotic options trade over the counter. They are designed by a financial institution to meet a particular need in the market. Sometimes they are added to a bond issue to make it more attractive in the market.[1] Some financial institutions market exotic options very aggressively and are prepared to quote a price for almost any deal proposed by a client. In this chapter, we describe some of the different exotics that exist in the market and present one or two new valuation techniques.

Unless otherwise stated we consider options on stocks paying a continuous dividend yield at rate q. As discussed in Chapter 11, for an option on a currency we set q equal to the foreign risk-free rate; for an option on a futures contract we set q equal to the domestic risk-free rate. The arguments in Chapter 12 show that for an option on a commodity we can set q equal to the convenience yield net of storage costs; equivalently we can set $r - q$ equal to the rate at which futures prices grow as we look at longer and longer maturity contracts.

---

[1]Examples of bond issues incorporating options are given in Section 1.4.

16.1 TYPES OF EXOTIC OPTIONS

In an excellent series of articles that appeared in *RISK* magazine in 1991 and 1992, Mark Rubinstein divides exotics into a number of categories. The categorization in this section is similar to his.

PACKAGES

A package is a portfolio consisting of standard European calls, standard European puts, forward contracts, cash, and the underlying asset itself.[2] We discussed a number of different types of packages in Chapter 8: bull spreads, bear spreads, butterfly spreads, straddles, strangles, and so on.

Often financial institutions like to design a package so that it has zero initial cost. The product is then similar to a forward contract or a swap in that it can lead to a positive or negative payoff. One example of a zero-cost package is a *range forward contract*.[3] This was mentioned in Chapter 1. It consists of a long forward contract combined with a long position in a put and a short position in a call (see Figure 16.1). The strike prices are chosen so that the value of the call equals the value of the put. Since the value of the forward contract is zero, the value of the whole package is also zero. A range forward contract has a similar type of payoff pattern to a bull spread, which was discussed in Chapter 8.

A regular option can be converted into a zero-cost product by deferring payment for the option until maturity. If c is the cost of the option when payment is made up front, then $A = ce^{r(T-t)}$ is the cost when payment is made at maturity of the option. The payoff is then $\max(S - X, 0) - A$ or $\max(S - X - A, -A)$. When the strike price, X, equals the forward price, other names for a deferred payment option are break forward, Boston option, forward with optional exit, and cancellable forward.

NONSTANDARD AMERICAN OPTIONS

In a standard American option, exercise can take place at any time during the life of the option and the exercise price is always the same. In practice, the American options that trade do not always have these standard features.

One type of nonstandard American option is known as a *Bermudan option*. In this, early exercise is restricted to certain dates during the life of the option.

---

[2]We could omit standard European puts from the list of securities in a package since put–call parity shows that a standard European put can always be created from a standard European call, cash, and the underlying asset. Similarly, we could omit forward contracts since they can be created from a position in the underlying asset.

[3]Other names used for a range forward contract are zero-cost collar, flexible forward, cylinder option, option fence, min-max, and forward band.

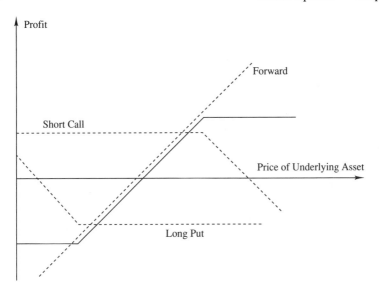

Figure 16.1   Construction of a Range Forward Contract

An example of a Bermudan option would be an American swap option that can be exercised only on reset dates.

Other types of nonstandard American options sometimes occur in the warrants issued by a company on its own stock. It is often the case that early exercise is possible during part of the life of the option, but not during all of its life. Sometimes the strike price increases with the passage of time. For example, in a 5-year warrant the strike price might be $30 during the first 2 years, $32 during the next 2 years, and $33 during the final year.

FORWARD START OPTIONS

Forward start options are options that are paid for now but will start at some time in the future. They are sometimes used in employee incentive schemes. The terms of the option are usually chosen so that the options will be at the money at the time they start.

Consider a forward start call option that will start at the money at time t_1 and mature at time t_2 when the underlying asset is a non-dividend-paying stock . Suppose that the current time is t, the current stock price is S, and the stock price at time t_1 is S_1. To value the option, we note from the Black–Scholes formula that the value of an at-the-money call option is proportional to the stock price. The value of the forward start option at time t_1 is therefore cS_1/S where c is the value today of an at-the-money option that lasts for $t_2 - t_1$. Using risk-neutral valuation, the value of the forward start option today is

$$e^{-r(t_1-t)}\hat{E}\left[c\frac{S_1}{S}\right]$$

where $\hat{E}$ denotes expectations in a risk-neutral world. Since c and S are known and $\hat{E}[S_1] = Se^{r(t_1-t)}$, it follows that the value of the forward start option is c. In other words, the value of the forward start option is exactly the same as the value of a regular at-the-money option with the same life as the forward start option.

If the stock is expected to pay dividends at rate q, then $\hat{E}[S_1] = Se^{(r-q)(t_1-t)}$ and the previous analysis shows that the value of the forward start option is $ce^{-q(t_1-t)}$.

COMPOUND OPTIONS

Compound options are options on options. There are four main types of compound options: a call on a call, a put on a call, a call on a put, and a put on a put. Compound options have two strike prices and two exercise dates. Consider, for example, a call on a call. On the first exercise date, T_1, the holder of the compound option is entitled to pay the first strike price, X_1 and receive a call option. The call option gives the holder the right to buy the underlying asset for the second strike price, X_2 on the second exercise date, T_2. The compound option will only be exercised on the first exercise date if the value of the option on that date is greater than the first strike price.

When the usual geometric Brownian motion assumption is made, European-style compound options can be valued analytically in terms of integrals of the bivariate normal distribution.[4] With our usual notation the value at time zero of a European call option on a call option is

$$Se^{-qT_2}M(a_1, b_1; \sqrt{T_1/T_2}) - X_2e^{-rT_2}M(a_2, b_2; \sqrt{T_1/T_2}) - e^{-rT_1}X_1N(a_2)$$

where

$$a_1 = \frac{\ln(S/S^*) + (r - q + \sigma^2/2)T_1}{\sigma\sqrt{T_1}}; \qquad a_2 = a_1 - \sigma\sqrt{T_1}$$

$$b_1 = \frac{\ln(S/X_2) + (r - q + \sigma^2/2)T_2}{\sigma\sqrt{T_2}}; \qquad b_2 = b_1 - \sigma\sqrt{T_2}$$

The function M is the cumulative bivariate normal distribution function; S^* is the stock price at time T_1 for which the option price at time T_1 equals X_1. If the actual

[4]See R. Geske, "The Valuation of Compound Options," *Journal of Financial Economics*, 7 (1979), 63–81; M. Rubinstein, "Double Trouble," *RISK*, December 1991–January 1992.

stock price is above S^* at time T_1, the first option will be exercised; if it is not above S^*, the option expires worthless.

With similar notation the value of a European put on a call is

$$X_2 e^{-rT_2} M(-a_2, b_2; -\sqrt{T_1/T_2}) - S e^{-qT_2} M(-a_1, b_1; -\sqrt{T_1/T_2}) + e^{-rT_1} X_1 N(-a_2)$$

The value of a European call on a put is

$$X_2 e^{-rT_2} M(-a_2, -b_2; \sqrt{T_1/T_2}) - S e^{-qT_2} M(-a_1, -b_1; \sqrt{T_1/T_2}) - e^{-rT_1} X_1 N(-a_2)$$

The value of a European put on a put is

$$S e^{-qT_2} M(a_1, -b_1; -\sqrt{T_1/T_2}) - X_2 e^{-rT_2} M(a_2, -b_2; -\sqrt{T_1/T_2}) + e^{-rT_1} X_1 N(a_2)$$

A procedure for computing M is in Appendix 10B.

"As You Like It" Options

An "as you like it" option has the feature that, after a specified period of time, the holder can choose whether the option is a call or a put. Suppose that the time at which the choice is made is t_1. The value of the "as you like it" option at this time is
$$\max(c, \ p)$$
where c is the value of the call underlying the option and p is the value of the put underlying the option.

If the options underlying the "as you like it" option are both European and have the same strike price, put–call parity can be used to provide a valuation formula. Suppose that S_1 is the stock price at time t_1, X is the strike price, t_2 is the maturity of the options, and r is the risk-free interest rate. Put–call parity implies that

$$\max(c, \ p) = \max(c, \ c + X e^{-r(t_2-t_1)} - S_1 e^{-q(t_2-t_1)})$$

$$= c + e^{-q(t_2-t_1)} \max(0, \ X e^{-(r-q)(t_2-t_1)} - S_1)$$

This shows that the "as you like it" is a package consisting of

1. A call option with strike price X and maturity t_2; and
2. $e^{-q(t_2-t_1)}$ put options with strike price $X e^{-(r-q)(t_2-t_1)}$ and maturity t_1.

As such it can be readily valued.

More complex "as you like it" options can be defined where the call and the put do not have the same strike price and time to maturity. They are then not packages, but have the same types of features as compound options.

Barrier Options

Barrier options are options where the payoff depends on whether the underlying asset's price reaches a certain level during a certain period of time. In

Chapter 11 we met one particular type of barrier option: the CAPS that trade on the CBOT. These are options designed so that the payoff cannot exceed $30. A call CAP is automatically exercised on a day when the index closes more than $30 above the strike price. A put CAP is automatically exercised on a day when the index closes more than $30 below the strike price. Capped European and capped American options similar to those traded by the CBOT are regularly traded over the counter.

Another type of barrier option is a *knockout option*. This is similar to a regular option except that, when the underlying asset's price reaches a certain barrier, H, the option ceases to exist. In the case of a call knockout, the barrier is generally below the strike price ($H < X$). The option is then sometimes referred to as a *down-and-out option*. In the case of a put knockout, $H > X$ and option is sometimes referred to as an *up-and-out option*. A *down-and-in option* is a call that comes into existence only when the barrier, H ($H < X$), is reached. Similarly an *up-and-in option* is a put that comes into existence only when the barrier H ($H > X$) is reached.

When the usual geometric Brownian motion assumption is made and our usual notation is used, the value of a European down-and-in call option at time zero is

$$Se^{-qT}(H/S)^{2\lambda}N(y) - Xe^{-rT}(H/S)^{2\lambda-2}N(y - \sigma\sqrt{T})$$

and the value of a European up-and-in put option is

$$Xe^{-rT}(H/S)^{2\lambda-2}N(-y + \sigma\sqrt{T}) - Se^{-qT}(H/S)^{2\lambda}N(-y)$$

where

$$\lambda = \frac{r - r_f + \sigma^2/2}{\sigma^2}$$

$$y = \frac{\ln[H^2/(SX)]}{\sigma\sqrt{T}} + \lambda\sigma\sqrt{T}$$

A regular call option is the sum of the price of a corresponding down-and-out and down-and-in options. A price of a European down-and-out call is therefore the price of a regular European call less the price of the corresponding down-and-in call. Similarly the price of a European up-and-out put option is the price of a regular European put option less the price of the corresponding up-and-in put option.

A convertible bond usually contains a type of barrier option. This is because there is generally a clause which allows the issuing company to call the bond, thereby forcing conversion, if the stock price crosses some barrier.

A important issue for barrier options is the frequency with which the asset price, S, is observed for the purposes of testing whether the barrier has been reached. The analytic formulas given above assume that S is observed continuously. Often the terms of a contract state that S is observed once a day. For example in S&P CAPS, S is observed at the close of trading each day.

BINARY OPTIONS

Binary options are options with discontinuous payoffs. A simple example of a binary option is *cash or nothing call*. This pays off nothing if the stock price ends up below the strike price and pays a fixed amount, Q, if it ends up above the strike price. In a risk-neutral world, the probability of the stock price being above the strike price at the maturity of an option is, with our usual notation, $N(d_2)$. The value of a cash or nothing call is therefore $Qe^{-r(T-t)}N(d_2)$.

Another type of binary option is an *asset or nothing call*. This pays off nothing if the underlying stock price price ends up below the strike price and pays an amount equal to the stock price itself if it ends up above the strike price. With our usual notation, the value of an asset or nothing call is $SN(d_1)$. A regular option is equivalent to a long position in an asset or nothing call, and a short position in a cash or nothing call where the cash payoff equals the strike price.

LOOKBACK OPTIONS

The payoffs from lookback options depend on the maximum or minimum price reached during the life of the option. If S_1 is the minimum price reached, S_2 is the maximum price reached, and S_T is the final price reached, the payoff from a lookback call is

$$\max(0, \ S_T - S_1)$$

or simply $S_T - S_1$, and the payoff from a lookback put is

$$\max(0, \ S_2 - S_T)$$

or simply $S_2 - S_T$

Valuation formulas have been produced for European lookbacks.[5] The value of a European lookback call at time zero is

$$Se^{-qT}N(a_1) - Se^{-qT}\frac{\sigma^2}{2(r-q)}N(-a_1) - S_{\min}e^{-rT}\left[N(a_2) - \frac{\sigma^2}{2(r-q)}e^{Y_1}N(-a_3)\right]$$

[5]See B. Goldman, H. Sosin, and M. A. Gatto, "Path-Dependent Options: Buy at the Low, Sell at the High," *Journal of Finance*, 34 (December 1979), 1111–27.; M. Garman, "Recollection in Tranquility," *RISK*, March 1989.

where S_{min} is the minimum value achieved to date and

$$a_1 = \frac{\ln(S/S_{min}) + (r - q + \sigma^2/2)T}{\sigma\sqrt{T}}$$

$$a_2 = a_1 - \sigma\sqrt{T}$$

$$a_3 = \frac{\ln(S/S_{min}) + (-r + q + \sigma^2/2)T}{\sigma\sqrt{T}}$$

$$Y_1 = -\frac{2(r - q - \sigma^2/2)\ln(S/S_{min})}{\sigma^2}$$

The value of a European lookback put is

$$S_{max}e^{-rT}\left[N(b_1) - \frac{\sigma^2}{2(r-q)}e^{Y_2}N(-b_3)\right] + Se^{-qT}\frac{\sigma^2}{2(r-q)}N(-b_2) - Se^{-qT}N(b_2)$$

where S_{max} is the maximum price achieved to date and

$$b_1 = \frac{\ln(S_{max}/S) + (-r + q + \sigma^2/2)T}{\sigma\sqrt{T}}$$

$$b_2 = b_1 - \sigma\sqrt{T}$$

$$b_3 = \frac{\ln(S_{max}/S) + (r - q - \sigma^2/2)T}{\sigma\sqrt{T}}$$

$$Y_2 = \frac{2(r - q - \sigma^2/2)\ln(S_{max}/S)}{\sigma^2}$$

A call lookback is, in essence, a way in which the holder can buy the underlying asset at the lowest price achieved during the life of the option. Similarly, a put lookback is a way in which the holder can sell the underlying asset at the highest price achieved during the life of the option. The underlying asset in a lookback option is often a commodity. As with barrier options, the value of a lookback is liable to be sensitive to the frequency with which the asset price is observed for the purposes of computing the maximum or minimum. The above formulas assume that the asset price is observed continuously.

ASIAN OPTIONS

Asian options are options where the payoff depends on the average price of the underlying asset during at least some part of the life of the option. The payoff from an *average price call* is max$(0, S_{ave} - X)$, and that from an *average price put* is max$(0, X - S_{ave})$ where S_{ave} is the average value of the underlying asset calculated over some predetermined averaging period. Average price options are less expensive than regular options and are arguably more appropriate than regular options for meeting some of the needs of corporate treasurers. Suppose that a U.S. corporate treasurer expects to receive from the company's German subsidiary a cash flow of 100 million deutschemarks spread evenly over the next year. The treasurer is likely to be interested in an option that guarantees that the average exchange rate realized during the year is above some level. An average price put option can achieve this more effectively than regular put options.

Another type of Asian option is an average strike option. An *average strike call* pays off $\max(0, S - S_{ave})$ while an *average strike put* pays off $\max(0, S_{ave} - S)$. Average strike options can guarantee that the average price paid for an asset in frequent trading over a period of time is less than the final price. Alternatively, it can guarantee that the average price received for an asset in frequent trading over a period of time is greater than the final price.

If the underlying asset price, S, is assumed to be lognormally distributed, and S_{ave} is a geometric average of the S's, analytic formulas are available for valuing European average price options.[6] This is because the geometric average of a set of lognormally distributed variables is also lognormal. In a risk-neutral world it can be shown that the probability distribution of the geometric average over a certain period is the same as that of a stock at the end of the period when the stock's expected growth rate is $(r - q - \sigma^2/6)/2$ and its volatility is $\sigma/\sqrt{3}$. A geometric average price option can therefore be treated like a regular option with the volatility set equal to $\sigma/\sqrt{3}$ and the dividend yield equal to

$$r - \frac{1}{2}\left(r - q - \frac{\sigma^2}{6}\right) = \frac{1}{2}\left(r + q + \frac{\sigma^2}{6}\right)$$

When, as it more common, Asian options are defined in terms of arithmetic averages, analytic pricing formulas are not available. This is because the distribution of the arithmetic average of a set of lognormal distributions does not have analytically tractable properties. However, there is an analytic approximation for valuing options on the arithmetic average. This involves calculating the first two moments of the probability distribution of the arithmetic average exactly and then assuming that distribution of the arithmetic average is lognormal with same first two moments.[7]

---

[6]See A. Kemna and A. Vorst, "A Pricing Method for Options Based on Average Asset Values," *Journal of Banking and Finance*, 14 (March 1990), 113–29.

[7]See S. M. Turnbull and L. M. Wakeman, "A Quick Algorithm for Pricing European Average Options," *Journal of Financial and Quantitative Analysis*, 26 (September 1991), 377–89.; Levy E., "A Note on Pricing European Average Options," Working Paper, Nomura Bank International plc, 1991; P. Ritchken, L. Sankarasubramanian, A. M. Vijh, "The Valuation of Path Dependent Contracts on the Average," Working Paper, Case Western Reserve University and University of Southern California, 1989.

Define

$$M_1 = \frac{e^{(r-q)T} - 1}{(r-q)T}$$

and

$$M_2 = \frac{2e^{[2(r-q)+\sigma^2]T}}{(r-q+\sigma^2)(2r-2q+\sigma^2)T^2}$$
$$+ \frac{2}{(r-q)T^2}\left[\frac{1}{2(r-q)+\sigma^2} - \frac{e^{(r-q)T}}{r-q+\sigma^2}\right]$$

The first and second moments of the arithmetic average as seen at time zero for a period of time T are SM_1 and S^2M_2 It follows from equations (10.8) and (10.9) that if we make the lognormal approximation we should treat an average price option like a regular option with dividend yield q_A and volatility σ_A where

$$e^{(r-q_A)T} = M_1; \qquad e^{[2(r-q_A)+\sigma_A^2]T} = M_2$$

These two equations can be solved to yield

$$q_A = r - \frac{\ln M_1}{T}; \qquad \sigma_A^2 = \frac{\ln M_2}{T} - 2(r - q_A)$$

OPTIONS TO EXCHANGE ONE ASSET FOR ANOTHER

Options to exchange one asset for another arise in various contexts.   An option to buy deutschemarks with Swiss francs is, from the point of view of a U.S. investor, an option to exchange one foreign currency asset for another foreign currency asset. A stock tender offer is an option to exchange shares in one stock for shares in another stock.

A formula for valuing a European option to give up an asset worth S_1 and receive in return an asset worth S_2 were first produced by Margrabe.[8] Suppose S_1 and S_2 both follow geometric Brownian motion with volatilities σ_1 and σ_2. Suppose further that the instantaneous correlation between S_1 and S_2 is ρ, and the yields provided by S_1 and S_2 are q_1 and q_2. The value of the option is:

$$S_2 e^{-q_2(T-t)} N(d_1) - S_1 e^{-q_1(T-t)} N(d_2)$$

where

$$d_1 = \frac{\log(S_2/S_1) + (q_1 - q_2 + \sigma^2/2)(T-t)}{\sigma\sqrt{T-t}}$$

$$d_2 = d_1 - \sigma\sqrt{T-t}$$

---

[8] See W. Margrabe, "The Value of an Option to Exchange One Asset for Another," *Journal of Finance*, 33 (March 1978), 177–86.

and

$$\sigma = \sqrt{\sigma_1^2 + \sigma_2^2 - 2\rho\sigma_1\sigma_2}$$

It is interesting to note that these formulas are independent of the risk-free rate r. This is because, as r increases, the growth rate of both asset prices in a risk-neutral world increases, but this is offset by an increase in the discount rate. The variable σ is the volatility of S_2/S_1. Comparisons with the formulas in Chapter 11 show that this option price is the same as the price of S_1 European call options on an asset worth S_2/S_1 when the strike price is 1, the risk-free interest rate is q_1, and the dividend yield on the asset is q_2. Mark Rubinstein shows that the American version of this option can be characterized similarly for valuation purposes.[9] It can be regarded as S_1 American options to buy an asset worth S_2/S_1 for 1 when the risk-free interest rate is q_1 and the dividend yield on the asset is q_2. The option can therefore be valued as described in Chapter 14 using a binomial tree.

It is worth noting that an option to obtain the better or worse of two assets can be regarded as a position in one of the assets combined with an option to exchange it for the other asset:

$$\min(S_1, S_2) = S_2 - \max(S_2 - S_1, 0)$$

$$\max(S_1, S_2) = S_1 + \max(S_2 - S_1, 0)$$

OPTIONS INVOLVING SEVERAL ASSETS

Sometimes options involving two or more risky assets are traded. One example is the bond futures contract traded on the CBOT that was described in Chapter 4. The party with the short position is allowed to choose between a large number of different bonds when making delivery. Another example arises in some of the models that are used to take credit into account in the valuation of a regular option. The valuation of the option depends not only on the value of the assets on which the option is written, but also on the value of the assets of the option writer.[10]

Most options involving several underlying assets cannot be valued analytically. An exception is a European option on the maximum or minimum of two assets. Stulz has provided valuation formulas involving integrals of the bivariate normal distribution for this particular case.[11]

---

[9]See M. Rubinstein, "One for Another," *RISK*, July–August 1991.

[10]See H. Johnson and R. Stulz, "The Pricing of Options Under Default Risk," *Journal of Finance*, 42 (1987), 267–280, and J. Hull and A. White, "The Impact of Default Risk on the Prices of Options and Other Derivative Securities," Working Paper, University of Toronto, 1991.

[11]See R. Stulz, "Options on the Minimum or Maximum of Two Assets," *Journal of Financial Economics*, 10 (1982), 161–85.

16.2 BASIC VALUATION TOOLS

In Chapter 14 we introduced a number of numerical procedures for valuing derivative securities. We now discuss how some of these can be adapted to cope with exotics.

MONTE CARLO SIMULATION

Monte Carlo simulation is the natural tool to use for lookback options and Asian options when analytic results are not available. This is because the payoff received from the option at the end of its life depends on the whole path followed by the price of the underlying asset. The basic procedure is described in Chapter 14. We simulate many paths followed by the underlying asset in a risk-neutral world. The estimate of value of the option is the average of the payoffs, discounted from the end of the life of the option to the beginning at the risk-free interest rate. To make the approach computationally feasible, it is important to use it in conjunction with antithetic variable and (where possible) control variate procedures.

In the case of average price or average strike European options, where the average is an arithmetic average, the natural option to use as the control variate option is the corresponding option on a geometric average since analytic formulas exist for this case. The procedure is as follows:

1. Use Monte Carlo simulation to estimate the value of both the arithmetic average option and the corresponding geometric average option. (Use the antithetic variable technique and the same random numbers in obtaining each estimate.)
2. Calculate the difference between the simulated price of the geometric average option and its analytic price.
3. Modify the estimate of the price of the arithmetic average option by adding to the simulation estimate the amount by which the analytic geometric average price exceeds the simulation estimate of the geometric average option.

This is an alternative to the analytic approximation mentioned when Asian options were considered earlier in this chapter.

TREES

A binomial or trinomial tree can be used in a straightforward way to value all the options discussed in Section 16.1 except for Asian options, lookback options, and options involving several risky assets. The nature of the option governs the rules that should be used when we roll back through the tree. For example, in a knockout option the rules are as for a regular option except that the value of the option is set equal to zero when underlying asset's price is below the knockout barrier; in a Bermudan option we only test for early exercise at time t when the time interval between t and $t + \Delta t$ includes a date where early exercise is allowed; and so on. An "as you like it" option where the underlying options are American has the complication that, when rolling back through the tree, we must value both a call and a put. For the nodes which correspond to the date where the choice is made, the value of the security is set equal to the greater of the value of the call and the value of the put. We roll back from these nodes to the present in the usual way.

The accurate valuation of barrier options tends to require many more time steps than regular options. This is because it is important to know with some degree of precision whether the barrier has been hit. Often the terms of a option are such that the parties check whether the barrier has been passed only at the end of each trading day—not during the day. The tree calculations should reflect this.

16.3 AMERICAN PATH-DEPENDENT OPTIONS

American options where the payoff depends on the path followed by the underlying asset as well as its current value present a real challenge to analysts. We cannot use Monte Carlo simulation because when a simulation run has reached a certain point we have no way of knowing whether early exercise is optimal. Also, we cannot use trees in the usual way because the payoff at a node depends on more than just the price of the underlying asset at the node.

Suppose that the payoff from an American option depends on a function, F, of the path followed by the underlying asset. Suppose further that when a tree is drawn, the value of F at time $t + \Delta t$ can be calculated from the value of F at time t and the value of the underlying asset at time $T + \Delta t$. One valuation approach is to draw a tree for the underlying asset in the usual way and keep track at each node of all the different values of F that might occur. Associated with each value of F is a different value of the security.

To illustrate the approach, we suppose we are interested in valuing an American lookback put option on a non-dividend-paying stock which, if exercised at time τ, pays off the amount by which the maximum stock price between time 0 and time τ exceeds the current stock price. We suppose that the initial stock price is \$50, the stock price volatility is 40 percent per annum, the risk-free interest rate is 10 percent per annum, and the total life of the option is 3 months. We consider a three time step tree. Using the notation in Chapter 14, this means that $S = 50$, $\sigma = 0.4$, $r = 0.10$, $\Delta t = 0.08333$, $u = 1.1224$, $d = 0.8909$, $a = 1.0084$, and $p = 0.5076$ and leads to the tree shown in Figure 16.2. (The parameters used in constructing the tree are the same as those used to construct the tree for Example 14.1.) The top number at each node is the stock price. The next level of numbers

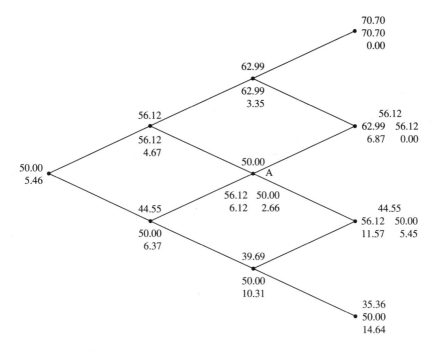

Figure 16.2 Tree for Valuing an American Lookback Option

at each node shows the possible maximum stock prices achievable on paths leading to the node. The final level of numbers show the values of the derivative security corresponding to each of the possible maximum stock prices.

The values of the derivative security at the final nodes of the tree are calculated as the maximum stock price less the actual stock price. To illustrate the roll back procedure, suppose we are at node A where the stock price is $50. The maximum stock price achieved so far is either 56.12 or 50. Consider first the situation where it is 50. If there is an up movement, the maximum stock price becomes 56.12 and the value of the derivative security becomes zero. If there is a down movement, the maximum stock price stays at 50 and the value of the derivative security becomes 5.45. Assuming no early exercise, the value of the derivative security at A when the maximum achieved so far is 50 is therefore

$$(0 \times 0.5076 + 5.45 \times 0.4924)e^{-0.1 \times 0.08333} = 2.66$$

Clearly it is not worth exercising at node A in these circumstances since the payoff from doing so is zero. A similar calculation for the situation where the maximum value at node A is 56.12 gives the value of the derivative security at node A, without early exercise, to be

$$(0 \times 0.5076 + 11.57 \times 0.4924)e^{-0.1 \times 0.08333} = 5.65$$

In this case, early exercise is optimal since it gives a value of 6.12 and is the optimal strategy. Rolling back through the tree in this way gives the value of the derivative security as \$5.46.

In our example, the F-values considered at each node are the alternative maximum values of the stock price achievable between time zero and the node. With n time steps, the total number of different possible maximum values at a node is always less than $n + 1$. This makes the approach computationally feasible for large values of n. By contrast, consider the possibility of using the approach to value American options on the arithmetic average. The number of different arithmetic averages that can exist at a node increases exponentially as we advance through a tree making it computationally infeasible to use trees of any size. It can be applied to American options on the geometric average since the number of alternative geometric averages after n time steps is quite manageable ($< n^3/6$). This has led Ritchken, Sankarasubramanian, and Vijh to propose that American options on the arithmetic average can be valued by assuming that the difference between the values of American and European options on the arithmetic average is the same as the difference between the values of American and European options on the geometric average.[12] Their value for an American option on the arithmetic average is

$$C_{ea} + C_{ag} - C_{eg}$$

where C_{ea} is the value of a European option on the arithmetic average, C_{ag} is the value of an American option on the geometric average, and C_{eg} is the value of a European option on the geometric average. C_{ag} is calculated using the tree technology just described, C_{ea} and C_{eg} are calculated using Monte Carlo simulation or the analytic approximation described earlier in this chapter. An alternative to this, which involves an extension of the approach in Figure 16.2, is suggested by Hull and White.[13]

16.4 OPTIONS ON TWO CORRELATED ASSETS

Another tricky numerical problem is that of valuing American options on two or more assets. A general approach for handling this type of problem was suggested by Hull and White.[14] Their approach involves defining new uncorrelated variables.

---

[12]See P. Ritchken, L. Sankarasubramanian, A. M. Vijh, "The Valuation of Path Dependent Contracts on the Average," Working Paper, Case Western Reserve University and University of Southern California, 1989.

[13]See J. Hull, and A. White, "Extensions of the Binomial Tree Approach for Valuing Path-Dependent Options," Working Paper, University of Toronto, 1992.

[14]See J. Hull and A. White, "Valuing Derivative Securities Using the Explicit Finite Difference Method," *Journal of Financial and Quantitative Analysis*, 25 (1990), 87–100.

Consider two assets, S_1 and S_2, with the following processes in a risk-neutral world

$$dS_1 = rS_1\,dt + \sigma_1 S_1\,dz_1$$

$$dS_2 = rS_2\,dt + \sigma_2 S_2\,dz_2$$

where the instantaneous correlation between the Wiener processes, dz_1 and dz_2, is ρ. This means that

$$d \ln S_1 = (r - \sigma_1^2/2)\,dt + \sigma_1\,dz_1$$

$$d \ln S_2 = (r - \sigma_2^2/2)\,dt + \sigma_2\,dz_2$$

We define two new uncorrelated variables:

$$x_1 = \sigma_2 \ln S_1 + \sigma_1 \ln S_2$$

$$x_2 = \sigma_2 \ln S_1 - \sigma_1 \ln S_2$$

These variables follow the processes

$$dx_1 = [\sigma_2(r - \sigma_1^2/2) + \sigma_1(r - \sigma_2^2/2)]\,dt + \sigma_1\sigma_2\sqrt{2(1 + \rho)}\,dz_A$$

$$dx_2 = [\sigma_2(r - \sigma_1^2/2) - \sigma_1(r - \sigma_2^2/2)]\,dt + \sigma_1\sigma_2\sqrt{2(1 - \rho)}\,dz_B$$

where dz_A and dz_B are uncorrelated Wiener processes. The variables can be modeled using two separate binomial trees where, in time Δt, x_i has a probability p_i of increasing by h_i and a probability $1 - p_i$ of decreasing by h_i. The variables h_i and p_i are chosen so that the tree gives correct values for the first two moments of the distribution of x_1 and x_2. Since the variables are uncorrelated, the two binomial trees can be combined together to form a three-dimensional tree where the probabilities of movements in x_1 and x_2 in time Δt are as follows:

$p_1 p_2$: x_1 increases by h_1 and x_2 increases by h_2
$p_1(1 - p_2)$: x_1 increases by h_1 and x_2 decreases by h_2
$(1 - p_1)p_2$: x_1 decreases by h_1 and x_2 increases by h_2
$(1 - p_1)(1 - p_2)$: x_1 decreases by h_1 and x_2 decreases by h_2.

At each node of the tree, S_1 and S_2 can be calculated from x_1 and x_2 using the inverse relationships:

$$S_1 = \exp\left[\frac{x_1 + x_2}{2\sigma_2}\right]$$

$$S_2 = \exp\left[\frac{x_1 - x_2}{2\sigma_1}\right]$$

To value a derivative security we roll back through the tree in three dimensions.

16.5 HEDGING ISSUES

Before trading an exotic option it is important for a financial institution to assess not only how it should be priced, but also the difficulties that are likely to be experienced in hedging it.

Some exotics are easier to hedge using the underlying than the corresponding plain vanilla option. An example is an average price option where the averaging period is the whole life of the option and the underlying asset is a stock price. As time passes, we observe more of the stock prices that will constitute the final average upon which the payoff is based. This means that our uncertainty about the payoff decreases with the passage of time. As a result, the option becomes progressively easier to hedge. In the final few days, the delta of the option always approaches zero since price movements in the final few days have very little impact on the payoff.

Barrier options can in certain circumstances be significantly more difficult to hedge than regular options. Consider a knockout call option on a currency when the exchange rate is 0.0005 above the barrier. If the barrier is hit, the option is worth nothing. If the barrier is not hit, the option may prove to be quite valuable. The delta of the option is discontinuous and hedging is difficult.

16.6 SUMMARY

Exotic options are options with rules governing the payoff that are more complicated than standard options. We have discussed 11 different categories of exotic options: packages, nonstandard American options, forward start options, compound options, "as you like it" options, barrier options, binary options, lookback options, Asian options, options to exchange one asset for another, and options involving several assets. Some can be valued using straightforward extensions of the procedures we have developed for European and American calls and puts. Some can be valued analytically, but using much more complicated formulas than those for regular European calls and puts. Some require special numerical procedures.

American-style options where the payoff depends on the whole path followed by the underlying asset as well as its final value are particularly challenging for the analyst. If the payoff depends on one particular function of the path followed by the underlying asset and the number of alternative values for this function at each node of the tree does not grow too quickly, it is possible to adapt the binomial tree approach presented in Chapter 14 to cope with the problem. American lookback options and American options on the geometric average price of an asset can be valued in this way.

A convenient way of valuing options dependent on the prices of two correlated asset prices, is to apply a transformation and create two new uncorrelated start variables. These two variables are each modeled with binomial trees. The binomial trees are then combined together to form a three-dimensional tree. At each node of the tree, the inverse of the transformation gives the asset prices.

Some exotic options are easier to hedge than the corresponding regular options; others are more difficult. In general, Asian options are easier to hedge because the payoff becomes progressively more certain as we approach maturity. Barrier options are liable to be more difficult to hedge because delta is liable to be discontinuous.

SUGGESTIONS FOR FURTHER READING

BLAZENKO, G., P. BOYLE, and K. NEWPORT, "Valuation of Tandem Options," Working Paper, University of Waterloo.

BOYLE, P. P., and D. EMANUEL, "Mean Dependent Options," Working Paper, University of Waterloo, 1985.

BOYLE, P. P., J. EVNINE, and S. GIBBS, "Numerical Evaluation of Multivariate Contingent Claims," *Review of Financial Studies*, 2 no. 2 (1989), 241–50.

GARMAN, M., "Recollection in Tranquility," *RISK*, March 1989.

GESKE, R., "The Valuation of Compound Options," *Journal of Financial Economics*, 7 (1979), 63–81.

GOLDMAN, B., H. SOSIN, and M. A. GATTO, "Path Dependent Options: Buy at the Low, Sell at the High," *Journal of Finance*, 34 (Dec 1979), 1111–27.

HUDSON, M., "The Value of Going Out," *RISK*, March 1991.

HULL, J., and A. WHITE, "Extensions of the Binomial Tree Approach for Valuing Path-Dependent Options," Working Paper, University of Toronto, 1992.

JOHNSON, H., "Options on the Maximum and Minimum of Several Assets," *Journal of Financial and Quantitative Analysis*, 22 no. 3 (September 1987), 277–83.

KEMNA, A., and A. VORST, "A Pricing Method for Options Based on Average Asset Values," *Journal of Banking and Finance*, 14 (March 1990), 113–29.

LEVY, E., "A Note on Pricing European Average Options," Working Paper, Nomura Bank International plc, 1991.

MARGRABE, W., "The Value of an Option to Exchange One Asset for Another," *Journal of Finance*, 33 (March 1978), 177–86.

RITCHKEN, P., L. SANKARASUBRAMANIAN, A. M. VIJH, "The Valuation of Path Dependent Contracts on the Average," Working Paper, Case Western Reserve University and University of Southern California, 1989.

RUBINSTEIN, M., and E. REINER, "Breaking Down the Barriers," *RISK*, September 1991.

RUBINSTEIN, M., "Double Trouble," *RISK*, December, 1991–January, 1992.

RUBINSTEIN, M., "One for Another," *RISK*, July–August, 1991.

RUBINSTEIN, M., "Options for the Undecided," *RISK*, April 1991.

RUBINSTEIN, M., "Pay Now, Choose Later," *RISK*, February, 1991.

RUBINSTEIN, M., "Somewhere Over the Rainbow," *RISK*, November, 1991.

RUBINSTEIN, M., "Two in One," *RISK*, May, 1991.

RUBINSTEIN, M., and E. REINER, "Unscrambling the Binary Code," *RISK*, October 1991.

STULZ, R., "Options on the Minimum or Maximum of Two Assets," *Journal of Financial Economics*, 10 (1982), 161–85.

TURNBULL, S. M., and L. M. WAKEMAN, "A Quick Algorithm for Pricing European Average Options," *Journal of Financial and Quantitative Analysis*, 26 (September 1991), 377–89.

QUESTIONS AND PROBLEMS

16.1. Explain the difference between a forward start option and an "as you like it" option.

16.2. Describe the payoff from a combination of a lookback call and a lookback put.

16.3. Explain the purpose of the call feature in convertible bonds.

16.4. Consider an "as you like it" option where the holder has the right to choose between a European call and a European put at any time during a 2-year period. The maturity dates and strike prices for the calls and puts are the same regardless of when the choice is made. Is it ever optimal to make the choice before the end of the 2-year period? Explain your answer.

16.5. Suppose c_1 and p_1 are the prices of a European average price call and a European average price put with strike X and maturity T; c_2 and p_2 are the prices of a European average strike call and European average strike put with maturity T; and c_3 and p_3 are the prices of a regular European call and a regular European put with strike price X and maturity T. Show that

$$c_1 + c_2 - c_3 = p_1 + p_2 - p_3$$

16.6. The text derives a decomposition of a particular type of "as you like it" option into a call maturing at time t_2 and a put maturing at time t_1. Derive an alternative decomposition into a call maturing at time t_1 and a put maturing at time t_2.

16.7. Use a three time step tree to value an American lookback call option on a currency when the initial exchange rate is 1.6, the domestic risk-free rate is 5% per annum, the foreign risk-free interest rate is 8% per annum, the exchange rate volatility is 15%, and the time to maturity is 18 months.

16.8. Use a three time step tree to value an American put option on the geometric average of the price of a non-dividend-paying stock when the stock price is $40, the strike price is $40, the risk-free interest rate is 10% per annum, the volatility is 35% per annum, and the time to maturity is 3 months. The geometric average is measured from today until the option matures.

16.9. Suppose that the strike price of an American call option on a non-dividend paying stock grows at rate g. Show that if g is less than the risk-free rate, r, it is never optimal to exercise the call early.

16.10. How can the value of a forward start put option on a non-dividend paying stock be calculated if it is agreed that the strike price will be 10% greater than the stock price at the time the option starts?

16.11. If a stock price follows geometric Brownian motion, what process does $A(t)$ follow where $A(t)$ is the arithmetic average stock price between time zero and time t?

16.12. Explain why Asian options are much easier to hedge using the underlying than barrier options.

16.13. Calculate the price of a 1-year European option to give up 100 ounces of silver in exchange for 1 ounce of gold. The current prices of gold and silver are $380 and $4 respectively; the risk-free interest rate is 10% per annum; the volatility of each commodity price is 20%; and the correlation between the two prices is 0.7. Ignore storage costs.

16.14. Is a European down-and-out option on an asset worth the same as a European down-and-out option on the asset's futures price for a futures contract maturing at the same time as the option?

16.15. (a) What put–call parity relationship exists between the price of a European call on a call and a European put on a call? Show that the formulas given in the text satisfy the relationship.
(b) What put–call parity relationship exists between the price of a European call on a put and a European put on a put? Show that the formulas given in the text satisfy the relationship.

16.16. Does a lookback call become more valuable or less valuable as we increase the frequency with which we observe the asset price in calculating the minimum?

16.17. Does a down-and-out call become more valuable or less valuable as we increase the frequency with which we observe the asset price in determining whether the barrier has been crossed? What is the answer to the same question for a down-and-in call?

16.18. Explain why a regular European call option is the sum of a down-and-out European call and a down-and-in European call.

16.19. How can the formulas in the text be used to value an arithmetic average option when part of the average has already been seen?

17 *Alternatives to Black–Scholes for Option Pricing*

In this chapter we consider a number of alternatives to the usual assumption of geometric Brownian motion for stock prices. We start by considering the adjustments that must be made to the Black–Scholes model when the volatility and the interest rate are known functions of time. We then move on to consider a variety of other models. These include models where the underlying variable follows a jump process rather than a continuous process and models where the volatility is stochastic. We discuss the pricing biases that will be observed if the Black–Scholes formula is used when, in reality, stock price movements correspond to one of these other models. The chapter concludes with a brief review of some of the empirical research on option pricing and a brief discussion of the way in which practitioners allow for model imperfections in the way they use Black–Scholes. For ease of exposition, most of the results in this chapter are presented in the context of valuing options on non-dividend-paying stocks, but much of the discussion of pricing biases is equally applicable to options on stock indices, currencies, and futures contracts.

17.1 KNOWN CHANGES IN THE INTEREST RATE AND VOLATILITY

When the risk-free interest rate is a known function of time, the Black–Scholes formulas for valuing European call and put options on a stock are correct with r replaced by the average instantaneous risk-free rate during the remaining life of the option. Similarly, when the volatility is a known function of time, the Black–Scholes formulas are true with the variance rate, σ^2, replaced by its average value during the remaining life of the option.

These results can be derived using risk-neutral valuation. They are useful in some situations. If the volatility of a stock is expected to rise steadily from 20% to 30% during the life of an option (perhaps because of uncertainties associated with a forthcoming presidential election), it would be appropriate to use a volatility of about 25% when valuing the option.[1] Also, if the term structure of interest rates indicates that interest rates are likely to change during the life of an option, this can be taken into account when choosing r. Usually r is, as a matter of course, set equal to the rate of interest on a risk-free security that matures at the same time as the option, rather than as the current instantaneous interest rate.

17.2 MERTON'S STOCHASTIC INTEREST RATE MODEL

The valuation of options when the interest rate is stochastic has been considered by Merton.[2] Define $B(t)$ as the value of a discount bond that matures at the same time as the option and pays \$1 to the holder at maturity. Merton assumes that B follows the process

$$\frac{dB}{B} = \mu_B \, dt + \sigma_B \, dz_B$$

The variable μ_B is the growth rate in the bond price, which is stochastic; σ_B is the volatility of B, which is assumed to be a known function of time; dz_B is a Wiener process. The model is consistent with the Vasicek, Ho–Lee, and Hull–White interest rate models in Chapter 15. Merton shows that the European call and put prices are given by

$$c = SN(d_1) - BXN(d_2)$$

$$p = BXN(-d_2) - SN(-d_1)$$

---

[1] Setting σ^2 equal to the average variance rate during the life of an option is not quite the same as setting σ equal to the average volatility, but in practice there is very little difference between the two. If, in this example, the volatility increases linearly from 20% per annum to 30% per annum, the correct value to use for σ can be shown to be 25.17% per annum.

[2] See R. C. Merton, "Theory of Rational Option Pricing," *Bell Journal of Economics and Management Science*, 4 (Spring 1973), 141–83.

where

$$d_1 = \frac{\ln(S/X) - \ln B + (\hat{\sigma}^2/2)(T - t)}{\hat{\sigma}\sqrt{T - t}}$$

$$d_2 = d_1 - \hat{\sigma}\sqrt{T - t}$$

$$\hat{\sigma}^2(T - t) = \int_t^T (\sigma^2 + \sigma_B^2 - 2\rho\sigma\sigma_B)\, dt \tag{17.1}$$

The parameter, σ, is the volatility of the stock and ρ is the instantaneous correlation between the stock and bond prices.

The variable $B(t)$ is given by

$$B(t) = e^{-R(T-t)}$$

where R is the rate of interest on a riskless bond that matures at time T. Merton's model is therefore the same as the Black–Scholes model with:

1. The instantaneous interest rate, r, replaced by the rate of interest, R, on a riskless bond maturing at the same time as the option
2. The stock price volatility, σ, replaced by $\hat{\sigma}$ [see Equation (17.1)]

Merton's model provides support for using R rather than r in the Black–Scholes model. For most traded options it can be shown that $\hat{\sigma}$ is close to σ.[3] The volatility adjustment therefore has little effect on the option price.[4]

Merton's model has one theoretical drawback. It requires the volatility of a discount bond to be a known function of time. Under many of the models that have been proposed for interest rates (e.g., the Cox, Ingersoll, and Ross model presented in Chapter 15), the volatility of bond prices is a function of both the bond price itself and time.

17.3 PRICING BIASES

The critical determinant of the price of a European stock option is the terminal stock price distribution. Up to now we have assumed that this is lognormal. In

---

[3] This is because σ_B is always very much smaller than σ. For a 1-year option on a stock, a high initial value for σ_B would be 2% per annum, and this would decline to zero during the life of the option. Typically, σ is about 30%.

[4] Stock and bond prices are generally positively correlated so that $\rho > 0$. If $\sigma_B < 2\rho\sigma$, it follows from Equation (17.1) that $\hat{\sigma} < \sigma$. The effect of the volatility adjustment is then to reduce the price of the option.

this section we consider the effects of departures from lognormality. The general approach is similar to that taken by Jarrow and Rudd.[5]

Figure 17.1 shows four ways in which the true terminal distribution can be different from a lognormal distribution while still giving the same mean and standard deviation for the stock price return. In Figure 17.1(a), both tails are thinner than the lognormal distribution; in Figure 17.1(d), both tails are fatter; in Figure 17.1(b) and (c), one tail is thinner and the other is fatter.

It is instructive to consider the biases that would be observed if the Black–Scholes model were used to price options in the four situations. Consider first a call option that is significantly out of the money. It has a positive value only if there is a large increase in the stock price. Its value therefore depends only on the right tail of the terminal stock price distribution. The fatter this tail, the more valuable the option is. Consequently, Black–Scholes will tend to underprice out-of-the-money calls in Figure 17.1(c) and (d), and overprice out-of-the-money calls in Figure 17.1(a) and (b). Consider next a put option that is significantly out

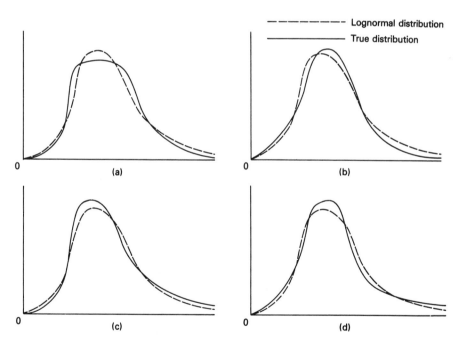

Figure 17.1   Alternative Terminal Stock Price Distributions. Dashed Line, Lognormal Distribution; Solid Line, True Distribution

[5]R. Jarrow and A. Rudd, "Approximate Option Valuation for Arbitrary Stochastic Processes," *Journal of Financial Economics*, 10 (November 1982), 347–69.

of the money. It has a positive value only if there is a large decrease in the stock price. Its value therefore depends only on the left tail of the terminal stock price distribution. The fatter this tail, the more valuable the option is. Black–Scholes will therefore tend to underprice out-of-the-money puts in Figure 17.1(b) and (d), and overprice out-of-the-money puts in Figure 17.1(a) and (c).

To obtain the biases for in-the-money options, we can use put–call parity. With the usual notation, put–call parity (see Section 7.6) gives

$$p + S = c + Xe^{-r(T-t)}$$

This relationship is independent of the shape of the terminal stock price distribution. If the European call with price c is out of the money, the corresponding European put with price p is in the money, and vice versa. Consequently, an in-the-money European put must exhibit the same pricing biases as an out-of-the-money European call. Similarly, an in-the-money European call must exhibit the same pricing biases as an out-of-the-money European put. The biases are therefore as indicated in Table 17.1.

TABLE 17.1   Biases Corresponding to Alternative
Stock Price Distributions in Figure 17.1

Distribution	Characteristics	Biases
Figure 17.1(a)	Both tails thinner	Black–Scholes overprices out-of-the-money and in-the-money calls and puts.
Figure 17.1(b)	Left tail fatter, right tail thinner	Black–Scholes overprices out-of-the-money calls and in-the-money puts. It underprices out-of-the-money puts and in-the-money calls.
Figure 17.1(c)	Left tail thinner, right tail fatter	Black–Scholes overprices out-of-the-money puts and in-the-money calls. It underprices in-the-money puts and out-of-the-money calls.
Figure 17.1(d)	Both tails fatter	Black–Scholes underprices out-of-the-money and in-the-money calls and puts.

17.4 ALTERNATIVE MODELS

In this section we discuss a number of alternatives to the Black–Scholes model and explain how they can give rise to some of the biases mentioned in the previous section.

STOCHASTIC VOLATILITY

Practitioners change the volatility frequently when they use Black–Scholes to value options. It is natural therefore to attempt to develop models which allow the stock price volatility to be stochastic. Hull and White consider this problem.[6] They show that, when the volatility is uncorrelated with the stock price, the European option price is the Black–Scholes price integrated over the distribution of the average variance rate during the life of the option. Thus the European call price is

$$\int c(\overline{V}) g(\overline{V}) \, d\overline{V}$$

where $\overline{V}$ is the average value of the variance rate, σ^2, c is the Black–Scholes price expressed as a function of $\overline{V}$; and g is the probability density function of $\overline{V}$. They show that the Black–Scholes formula overprices options that are at the money or close to the money, and underprices options that are deep in or deep out of the money.

In the case where the stock price and volatility are instantaneously correlated, Hull and White show how either Monte Carlo simulation or a series expansion can be used to obtain option prices.[7] When the correlation is positive, the situation is as in Figure 17.1(c). The Black–Scholes model tends to underestimate the price for out-of-the-money call options and overestimate the price for out-of-the-money put options. The reason is as follows: When the stock price increases, volatility tends to increase. This means that very high stock prices are more likely than under geometric Brownian motion. When the stock price decreases, volatility tends to decrease. This means that very low stock price are less likely than under geometric Brownian motion.

When the correlation is negative, the situation is as in Figure 17.1(b). Black–Scholes tends to overestimate the price of out-of-the-money call options and underestimate the price of out-of-the-money put options. This is because, when the stock price increases, volatility tends to decrease, making it less likely that really high stock prices will be achieved. When the stock price decreases, volatility tends to increase, making it more likely that really low stock prices will be achieved.

---

[6]See J. C. Hull and A. White, "The Pricing of Options on Assets with Stochastic Volatilities," *Journal of Finance*, 42 (June 1987), 281–300.

[7]For this series expansion, see J. C. Hull and A. White, "An Analysis of the Bias in Option Pricing Caused by a Stochastic Volatility," *Advances in Futures and Options Research*, 3 (1988) 27–61.

For options which last less than a year the biases caused by a stochastic volatility are fairly small in absolute terms. In percentage terms the biases can be quite large for deep-out-of-the-money options. The biases become progressively larger as the life of the option increases.

COMPOUND OPTION MODEL

The equity in a levered firm can be viewed as a call option on the value of the firm. To see this, suppose that the value of the firm is V and the face value of outstanding debt is A. Suppose further that all the debt matures at a single time, T^*. If $V < A$ at time T^*, the value of the equity at this time is zero since all the company's assets go to the bondholders. If $V > A$ at time T^*, the value of the equity at this time is $V - A$. Thus the equity is a European call option on V with maturity T^* and exercise price A.

An option on stock of the firm that expires earlier than T^* can be regarded as an option on an option on V or a compound option model (see Chapter 16). This model has been analyzed by Geske.[8] The state variable underlying the value of the stock option is the firm value, V, rather than the stock price, S. Geske assumes that σ_V, the volatility of V, is constant and that the amount of debt, A, is also constant. The volatility of S is then negatively correlated with V. When V decreases, leverage increases and the volatility of S increases. When V increases, leverage decreases and the volatility of S decreases. From the arguments concerning stochastic volatility, this means that the pricing biases correspond to Figure 17.1(b). Relative to Black–Scholes, the compound option model overprices out-of-the-money calls and in-the-money puts. It also underprices in-the-money calls and out-of-the-money puts.

Under Geske's model, the Black–Scholes formula gives S as a function of V:

$$S = V N(d_1) - A e^{-r(T^*-t)} N(d_2) \qquad (17.2)$$

where

$$d_1 = \frac{\ln(V/A) + (r + \sigma_V^2/2)(T^* - t)}{\sigma_V \sqrt{T^* - t}}$$

$$d_2 = d_1 - \sigma_V \sqrt{T^* - t}$$

The formula for pricing a European call option using the compound option model is given in Appendix 17A. It is more complicated than the Black–Scholes formula in that it requires a knowledge of the face value of the debt and the maturity of the debt.

---

[8] See R. Geske, "The Valuation of Compound Options," *Journal of Financial Economics*, 7 (1979), 63–81.

DISPLACED DIFFUSION MODEL

Rubinstein has proposed what is known as a *displaced diffusion model* for stock option pricing.[9] In this model, the firm is assumed to hold two categories of assets: risky assets, which have a constant volatility, and riskless assets, which provide a return, r. There is also assumed to be a certain fixed amount of default-free debt. If α is the initial proportion of the total assets of the firm which are risky and β is the initial debt-to-equity ratio, a key parameter, a, in the model is defined by

$$a = \alpha(1 + \beta)$$

If $a > 1$, the amount of debt in the displaced diffusion model exceeds the riskless assets. Netting the riskless assets off against the debt, the model becomes very similar to the compound option model and leads to biases that correspond to Figure 17.1(b). Unlike the compound option model, the displaced diffusion model does not take into account the possibility of default on the debt. In a situation where the value of the assets is less than the face value of the debt, the model assumes that the value of the equity is negative.

If $a < 1$, the amount of debt is less than the amount of riskless assets. The model then has properties that are markedly different from the properties of the compound option model. Netting off the debt against the riskless assets, we can write

$$S = S_A + S_B$$

where S is the stock price, S_A is the value of the risky assets, and S_B is the value of net riskless assets. When S_A increases quickly, S increases and the volatility of S also increases. This is because risky assets have become a proportionately larger part of S. Similarly, when S_A decreases quickly, both S and the volatility of S decrease. It follows that the volatility and stock price are positively correlated. From the arguments concerning stochastic volatility, this means that the biases correspond to Figure 17.1(c).

The formula for pricing a European call under the displaced diffusion model is given in Appendix 17A. It will be recalled that in valuing options on stocks paying known dividends, we assumed that the stock price can be divided into a riskless component which is used to pay the dividends and a risky component with a constant volatility. This is a version of the displaced diffusion model with zero debt.

---

[9]See M. Rubinstein, "Displaced Diffusion Option Pricing," *Journal of Finance*, 38 (March 1983), 213–17.

CONSTANT ELASTICITY OF VARIANCE MODEL

The constant elasticity of variance model was proposed by Cox and Ross.[10] In this model the stock price has a volatility of $\sigma S^{-\alpha}$ for some α where $0 \leq \alpha \leq 1$.[11] Thus the volatility decreases as the stock price increases.

The rationale for the constant elasticity of variance model is that all firms have fixed costs that have to be met regardless of the firm's operating performance. When the stock price declines, we can presume that the firm's operating performance has declined and the fixed costs have the effect of increasing volatility. When the stock price increases, the reverse happens and the fixed costs have the effect of decreasing volatility. One type of fixed cost is that arising from financial leverage. In general concept, the constant elasticity of variance model is therefore similar to the compound option model. The formulas for pricing options under the general constant elasticity of variance model are relatively complicated and are not reproduced in this book. Since the volatility is negatively related to the stock price, the arguments in Section 17.3 show that the biases correspond to Figure 17.1(b).

When $\alpha = 1$, the stock price volatility is inversely proportional to the stock price. This gives rise to a simple version of the constant elasticity of variance model known as the *absolute diffusion model*. The formula for pricing a European call under the absolute diffusion model is given in Appendix 17A. The model is easy to apply. Unfortunately, it has a weakness in that it allows stock prices to become negative.

THE PURE JUMP MODEL

The models in the preceding three sections have involved the stock price changing continuously. We now consider a model where the stock price follows a jump process. This was first suggested by Cox and Ross and elaborated on in a later paper by Cox, Ross, and Rubinstein.[12] The model is illustrated in Figure 17.2. In each small interval of time, Δt, the stock price has a probability $\lambda \, \Delta t$ of moving from S to Su and a probability of $1 - \lambda \, \Delta t$ of moving from S to $Se^{-w \Delta t}$. Most of the time, the stock price declines at rate w. However, occasionally it exhibits jumps equal to $u - 1$ times the current stock price.

[10] See J. C. Cox and S. A. Ross, "The Valuation of Options for Alternative Stochastic Processes," *Journal of Financial Economics*, 3 (March 1976), 145–66.

[11] More formally, the model for the stock price is

$$dS = \mu S \, dt + \sigma S^{1-\alpha} dz$$

[12] See J. C. Cox and S. A. Ross, "The Pricing of Options for Jump Processes," Working Paper no. 2-75, Rodney L. White Center for Financial Research, University of Pennsylvania, April 1975; J. C. Cox, S. A. Ross, and M. Rubinstein, "Option Pricing: A Simplified Approach," *Journal of Financial Economics*, 7 (September 1979), 229–63.

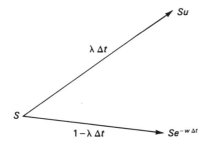

Figure 17.2   Stock Price Changes Under the Pure Jump Model

In the limit as $\Delta t \longrightarrow 0$, jumps occur according to a Poisson process at rate λ. The terminal stock price distribution is log-Poisson and the price of a call is as given in Appendix 17A. It is easy to see that the pure jump model leads to the situation in Figure 17.1(c). Arguably, the model is unrealistic in that jumps can only be positive.

THE JUMP DIFFUSION MODEL

Merton has suggested a model in which the stock price has jumps superimposed upon a geometric Brownian motion.[13] Define

μ: Expected return from stock

λ: Rate at which jumps happen

k: Average jump size measured as a proportional increase in the stock price

The proportional jump size is assumed to be drawn from a probability distribution in the model. The average growth rate from the jumps is λk. This means that the expected growth rate provided by the geometric Brownian motion is $\mu - \lambda k$.[14]

The key assumption made by Merton is that the jump component of the stock's return represents nonsystematic risk (i.e., risk not priced in the economy).[15] This means that a Black–Scholes type of portfolio, which eliminates the uncertainty

[13]See R. C. Merton, "Option Pricing When Underlying Stock Returns are Discontinuous," *Journal of Financial Economics*, 3 (March 1976), 125–44.

[14]More formally, the model is

$$\frac{dS}{S} = (\mu - \lambda k)\, dt + \sigma\, dz + dq$$

where dz is a Wiener process, dq is the Poisson process generating the jumps, and σ is the volatility of the geometric Brownian motion. The processes dz and dq are assumed to be independent.

[15]This assumption is important because it turns out that we cannot apply risk-neutral valuation to situations where the size of the jump is systematic. For a discussion of this point, see E. Naik and M. Lee, "General Equilibrium Pricing of Options on the Market Portfolios with Discontinuous Returns," *Review of Financial Studies*, 3 (1990), 493–521.

arising from the geometric Brownian motion, must earn the riskless rate. This leads to the pricing formula in Appendix 17A.

As one might expect jump processes give rise to fatter tails than do continuous processes. In Merton's model, jumps can be either positive or negative. The model therefore leads to the situation in Figure 17.1(d). Black–Scholes formulas underprice calls and puts when they are either significantly in the money or significantly out of the money.

17.5 OVERVIEW OF PRICING BIASES

Table 17.2 summarizes the results from the last few sections. In addition to being categorized according to the terminal stock price distribution, the various models can be categorized according to whether the bias increases or decreases as the time to maturity increases. The biases caused by a stochastic volatility become a larger percentage of the option price as the time to maturity increases. The reason for this is easy to understand. Just as the effect of volatility on the standard deviation of the stock price distribution increases as we look farther ahead, so the distortions to that distribution caused by uncertainties in the volatility become greater as we look farther ahead. For a similar reason, the biases in the compound option model become more pronounced as the time to maturity increases.

Jumps are different in that they produce proportionately greater effects when the time to maturity of the option is small. When we look sufficiently far into

TABLE 17.2 Categorization of Models According
to Shape of Terminal Stock Price Distribution

Figure 17.1(b)	Figure 17.1(c)	Figure 17.1(d)
Compound option model	Displaced diffusion model when $a < 1$	Jump diffusion model
Displaced diffusion model when $a > 1$	Pure jump model	Stochastic volatility model when stock price and volatility
Constant elasticity of variance model	Stochastic volatility model when stock price and volatility	have zero correlation
Stochastic volatility model when stock price and volatility are negatively correlated	are positively correlated	

the future, jumps tend to get "averaged out" so that the stock price distribution arising from jumps is almost indistinguishable from that arising from continuous changes.

17.6 EMPIRICAL RESEARCH

There are a number of problems in carrying out empirical research to test the Black–Scholes and other option pricing models. The first problem is that any statistical hypothesis about how options are priced has to be a joint hypothesis to the effect that (1) the option pricing formula is correct; and (2) markets are efficient. If the hypothesis is rejected, it may be the case that (1) is untrue; (2) is untrue; or both (1) and (2) are untrue. A second problem is that the stock price volatility is an unobservable variable. One approach is to estimate the volatility from historical stock price data. Alternatively, implied volatilities can be used in some way. A third problem for the researcher is to make sure that data on the stock price and option price are synchronous. For example, if the option is thinly traded, it is not likely to be acceptable to compare closing option prices with closing stock prices. This is because the closing option price might correspond to a trade at 1:00 P.M., while the closing stock price corresponds to a trade at 4:00 P.M.

Black and Scholes and Galai have tested whether it is possible to make excess returns above the risk-free rate of interest by buying options that are undervalued by the market (relative to the theoretical price) and selling options that are overvalued by the market (relative to the theoretical price).[16] A riskless delta-neutral portfolio is assumed to be maintained at all times by trading the underlying stocks on a regular basis as described in Section 13.5. Black and Scholes used data from the over-the-counter options market where options are dividend protected. Galai used data from the Chicago Board Options Exchange (CBOE) where options are not protected against the effects of cash dividends. Galai used Black's approximation as described in Section 10.14 to incorporate the effect of anticipated dividends into the option price. Both of the studies showed that, in the absence of transactions costs, significant excess returns over the risk-free rate could be obtained by buying undervalued options and selling overvalued options. It is possible that these excess returns were available only to market makers, and that when transactions costs are considered, they vanish.

A number of researchers have chosen to make no assumptions about the process followed by stock prices and have tested whether arbitrage strategies can be used to make a riskless profit in options markets. Garman provides a very

---

[16]See F. Black and M. Scholes, "The Valuation of Option Contracts and a Test of Market Efficiency," *Journal of Finance*, 27 (May 1972), 399–418; D. Galai, "Tests of Market Efficiency and the Chicago Board Options Exchange," *Journal of Business*, 50 (April 1977), 167–97.

efficient computational procedure for finding any arbitrage possibilities that exist in a given situation.[17] One study by Klemkosky and Resnick which is frequently cited tests whether the relationship in Equation (7.9) is ever violated.[18] It concludes that some small arbitrage profits were possible from using the relationship. These were due mainly to the overpricing of American calls.

Chiras and Manaster have carried out a study using CBOE data which compares the weighted implied standard deviation from options on a stock at a point in time with the standard deviation calculated from historical data.[19] They found that the former provides a much better forecast of the volatility of the stock price during the life of the option. The study has been repeated by other authors using other data and has always given similar results. We can conclude that option traders are using more than just historical data when determining future volatilities. Chiras and Manaster also tested to see whether it was possible to make above-average returns by buying options with low implied standard deviations and selling options with high implied standard deviations. This strategy showed a profit of 10 percent per month. The Chiras and Manaster study can be interpreted as providing good support for the Black–Scholes model while showing that the CBOE was inefficient in some respects.

MacBeth and Merville have tested the Black–Scholes model using a different approach.[20] They looked at different call options on the same stock at the same time and compared the volatilities implied by the option prices. The stocks chosen were AT&T, Avon, Kodak, Exxon, IBM, and Xerox, and the time period considered was the year 1976. They found that implied volatilities tended to be relatively high for in-the-money options and relatively low for out-of-the-money options. A relatively high implied volatility is indicative of a relatively high option price and a relatively low implied volatility is indicative of a relatively low option price. Therefore, if it is assumed that Black–Scholes prices at-the-money options correctly, it can be concluded that out-of-the-money call options are overpriced by Black–Scholes and in-the-money call options are underpriced by Black–Scholes. These effects become more pronounced as the time to maturity increases and the degree to which the option is in or out of the money increases. MacBeth and Merville's results are consistent with the displaced diffusion model when $a > 1$, the compound option model, the absolute diffusion model, and the stochastic volatility model when the stock price and volatility are negatively correlated.

[17]Garman, M. B., "An Algebra for Evaluating Hedge Portfolios," *Journal of Financial Economics*, 3 (October 1976), 403–27.

[18]R. C. Klemkosky and B. G. Resnick, "Put-call Parity and Market Efficiency," *Journal of Finance*, 34 (December 1979), 1141–55.

[19]D. Chiras and S. Manaster, "The Information Content of Stock Prices and Test of Market Efficiency," *Journal of Financial Economics*, 6 (September 1978), 213–34.

[20]See J. D. MacBeth and L. J. Merville, "An Empirical Examination of the Black–Scholes Call Option Pricing Model," *Journal of Finance*, 34 (December 1979), 1173–86.

Rubinstein has carried out a study similar to the MacBeth and Merville study, but using a far larger data set and a different time period.[21] He looked at all reported trades on the 30 most active Chicago Board Option Exchange options classes between August 23, 1976 and August 31, 1978. Special care was taken to incorporate the effects of dividends and early exercise. Rubinstein compared implied volatilities of matched pairs of call options which differed either only as far as exercise price was concerned or only as far as maturity was concerned. He found that his time period could be conveniently divided into two subperiods: August 23, 1976 to October 21, 1977 and October 22, 1977 to August 31, 1978. For the first period, his results were consistent with those of MacBeth and Merville. However, for the second period, the opposite result from MacBeth and Merville was obtained; that is, implied volatilities were relatively high for out-of-the-money options and relatively low for in-the-money options. Throughout the entire period Rubinstein found that for out-of-the-money options, short-maturity options had significantly higher implied volatilities than long-maturity options. The results for at-the-money and in-the-money options were less clear cut.

No single alternative to the Black–Scholes model seems superior for both of Rubinstein's time periods. Indeed, it is difficult to imagine a model that leads to the changes in the biases that were observed between the first time period and the second time period. Possibly macroeconomic variables affect option prices in a way that is as yet not fully understood. At present, there does not seem to be any really compelling arguments for using any of the models introduced earlier in this chapter in preference to Black–Scholes.

A number of authors have researched the pricing of options on assets other than stocks. For example, Shastri and Tandon, and Bodurtha and Courtadon have examined the market prices of currency options;[22] Shastri and Tandon in another paper have examined the market prices of futures options;[23] Chance has examined the market prices of index options.[24] The authors find that the Black–Scholes model and its extensions misprice some options. There appears to be some evidence, for example, that currencies follow jump processes. However, the mispricing was not sufficient in most cases to present profitable opportunities to investors when

[21] See M. Rubinstein, "Nonparametric Tests of Alternative Options Pricing Models Using All Reported Trades and Quotes on the 30 Most Active CBOE Options Classes from August 23, 1976 through August 31, 1978," *Journal of Finance*, 40 (June 1985), 455–80.

[22] See K. Shastri and K. Tandon, "Valuation of Foreign Currency Options: Some Empirical Tests," *Journal of Financial and Quantitative Analysis*, 21, (June 1986), 145–60; J. N. Bodurtha and G. R. Courtadon, "Tests of an American Option Pricing Model on the Foreign Currency Options Market," *Journal of Financial and Quantitative Analysis*, 22 (June 1987), 153–68.

[23] See K. Shastri and K. Tandon, "An Empirical Test of a Valuation Model for American Options on Futures Contracts," *Journal of Financial and Quantitative Analysis*, 21 (December 1986), 377–92.

[24] See D. M. Chance, "Empirical Tests of the Pricing of Index Call Options," *Advances in Futures and Options Research*, 1, pt. A (1986), 141–66.

transactions costs and bid–ask spreads were taken into account. In their two papers, Shastri and Tandon point out that even for a market maker, some time must elapse between a profitable opportunity being identified and action being taken. This delay, even if it is only to the next trade, can be sufficient to eliminate the profitable opportunity.

In an interesting study, Lauterbach and Schultz investigated the pricing of warrants.[25] They conclude that the biases are consistent with Figure 17.1(b). The constant elasticity of variance model with $\alpha = 0.5$ gave a better fit to the data than did the Black–Scholes model. From Table 17.2 we see that Lauterbach and Schultz's results are also consistent with the the compound option pricing model, the displaced diffusion model where $a > 1$, and the stochastic volatility model where the stock price and interest rate are negatively correlated. Their results were found to persist throughout a 10-year time period.

17.7 HOW THE MODELS ARE USED IN PRACTICE

Practitioners when using Black–Scholes recognize that it is a less than perfect model. A common approach is to construct a matrix of volatilities, one dimension of the matrix being strike price, the other being time to maturity. For actively traded options, volatilities are implied from market prices. This provides some of the points in the matrix. The rest of the matrix is then determined using an interpolation procedure.

When the matrix shows that biases corresponding to Figure 17.1(d) are observed, practitioners sometimes refer to the phenomenon as the *volatility smile*. The reason for this will be clear from Figure 17.3, which plots implied volatility against strike price.

How important is the pricing model being used if practitioners are prepared to use a different volatility for every deal? It can be argued that the model is simply a tool for understanding the volatility environment and for pricing illiquid securities consistently with the market prices of actively traded securities. If practitioners stopped using Black–Scholes and switched to the constant elasticity of variance model, the matrix of volatilities would change and the shape of the smile would change—but arguably the prices quoted in the market would not change appreciably.

17.8 SUMMARY

The Black–Scholes model and its extensions assume that the probability distribution of the stock price at any given future time is lognormal. If this assumption is

---

[25] See B. Lauterbach and P. Schultz, "Pricing Warrants: An Empirical Study of the Black–Scholes Model and its Alternatives," *Journal of Finance*, 4 no. 4 (Sepember 1990), 1181–1210.

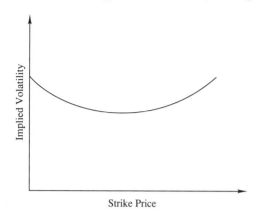

Strike Price   **Figure 17.3**   The Volatility Smile

incorrect, there are liable to be biases in the prices produced by the model. If the right tail of the true distribution is fatter than the right tail of the lognormal distribution, there will be a tendency for the Black–Scholes model to underprice out-of-the-money calls and in-the-money puts. If the left tail of the true distribution is fatter than the left tail of the lognormal distribution, there will be a tendency for the Black–Scholes model to underprice out-of-the-money puts and in-the-money calls. When either tail is too thin relative to the lognormal distribution, the opposite biases are observed.

A number of alternatives to the Black–Scholes model have been suggested. These include models where the future volatility of a stock price is uncertain, models where the company's equity is assumed to be an option on its assets, and models where the stock price experiences occasional jumps rather than continuous changes. The models can be categorized according to the biases they give rise to. It is interesting to note that biases arising from jumps become less pronounced as an option's life increases, while biases arising in other ways become more pronounced as the option life increases.

Generally, the empirical research that has been done is supportive of the Black–Scholes model. It is a model that has stood the test of time. Differences between market prices and the Black–Scholes prices have been observed. However, these differences have usually been small when compared to transactions costs.

SUGGESTIONS FOR FURTHER READING

On Alternative Models

BLACK, F., "How to Use the Holes in Black–Scholes," *RISK*, (March 1988).

Cox, J. C., and S. A. Ross, "The Valuation of Options for Alternative Stochastic Processes," *Journal of Financial Economics*, 3 (March 1976), 145–66.

Cox, J. C., S. A. Ross, and M. Rubinstein, "Option Pricing: A Simplified Approach," *Journal of Financial Economics*, 7 (September 1979), 229–63.

Geske, R., "The Valuation of Compound Options," *Journal of Financial Economics*, 7 (1979), 63–81.

Hull, J. C., and A. White, "The Pricing of Options on Assets with Stochastic Volatilities," *Journal of Finance*, 42 (June 1987), 281–300.

Merton, R. C., "Option Pricing When Underlying Stock Returns are Discontinuous," *Journal of Financial Economics*, 3 (March 1976), 125–44.

Merton, R. C., "Theory of Rational Option Pricing," *Bell Journal of Economics and Management Science*, 4 (Spring 1973), 141–83.

Rubinstein, M., "Displaced Diffusion Option Pricing," *Journal of Finance*, 38 (March 1983), 213–17.

On Empirical Research

Black, F., and M. Scholes, "The Valuation of Option Contracts and a Test of Market Efficiency," *Journal of Finance*, 27 (May 1972), 399–418.

Bodurtha, J. N., and G. R. Courtadon, "Tests of an American Option Pricing Model on the Foreign Currency Options Market," *Journal of Financial and Quantitative Analysis*, 22 (June 1987), 153–68.

Chance, D. M., "Empirical Tests of the Pricing of Index Call Options," *Advances in Futures and Options Research*, vol 1 pt. A (1986), 141–66.

Chiras, D., and S. Manaster, "The Information Content of Option Prices and a Test of Market Efficiency," *Journal of Financial Economics*, 6 (September 1978), 213–34.

Galai, D., "Tests of Market Efficiency and the Chicago Board Options Exchange," *Journal of Business*, 50 (April 1977), 167–97.

Klemkosky, R. C., and B. G. Resnick, "Put–Call Parity and Market Efficiency," *Journal of Finance*, 34 (December 1979), 1141-55.

Lauterbach, B., and P. Schultz, "Pricing Warrants: An Empirical Study of the Black–Scholes Model and its Alternatives," *Journal of Finance*, 4 no. 4 (September 1990), 1181–1210.

MacBeth, J. D., and L. J. Merville, "An Empirical Examination of the Black–Scholes Call Option Pricing Model," *Journal of Finance*, 34 (December 1979), 1173–86.

Rubinstein, M., "Nonparametric Tests of Alternative Option Pricing Models Using All Reported Trades and Quotes on the 30 Most Active CBOE Option Classes from August 23, 1976 through August 31, 1978," *Journal of Finance*, 40 (June 1985), 455–80.

Shastri, K., and K. Tandon, "Valuation of Foreign Currency Options: Some Empirical Tests," *Journal of Financial and Quantitative Analysis*, 21 (June 1986), 145–60.

Shastri, K., and K. Tandon, "An Empirical Test of a Valuation Model for American Options on Futures Contracts," *Journal of Financial and Quantitative Analysis*, 21 (December 1986), 377–92.

QUESTIONS AND PROBLEMS

17.1. What option pricing biases are likely to be observed when
(a) both tails of the stock price distribution are thinner than those of the lognormal distribution?
(b) the right tail is thinner, and the left tail is fatter, than that of a lognormal distribution?

17.2. What biases are caused by an uncertain volatility when the stock price is positively correlated with volatility?

17.3. What biases are caused by jumps in the movements of a stock price? Are these biases likely to be more pronounced for a 6-month option than for a 3-month option?

17.4. Assume that a stock price follows the compound option model. The Black–Scholes model is used to calculate implied volatilities for call and put options with different exercise prices and different times to maturity. What patterns would you expect to observe in the implied volatilities?

17.5. Why are the biases (relative to Black–Scholes) for the market prices of in-the-money call options usually the same as the biases for the market prices of out-of-the-money put options?

17.6. A stock price is currently $20. Tomorrow, news is expected to be announced that will either increase the price by $5 or decrease the price by $5. What are the problems in using Black–Scholes to value options on the stock?

17.7. What are the major problems in testing a stock option pricing model empirically?

*17.8. At time t a stock price is S. Suppose that the time interval between t and T is divided into two subintervals of length t_1 and t_2. During the first subinterval, the risk-free interest rate and volatility are r_1 and σ_1, respectively. During the second subinterval, they are r_2 and σ_2, respectively. Assume that the world is risk neutral.
(a) Use the results in Chapter 10 to determine the stock price distribution at time T in terms of r_1, r_2, σ_1, σ_2, t_1, t_2, and S.
(b) Suppose that $\bar{r}$ is the average interest rate between time t and T, and that $\overline{V}$ is the average variance rate between times t and T. What is the stock price distribution at time T in terms of $\bar{r}$, $\overline{V}$, $T - t$, and S?
(c) What are the results corresponding to (a) and (b) when there are three subintervals with different interest rates and volatilities?
(d) Show that if the risk-free rate, r, and the volatility, σ, are known functions of time, the stock price distribution at time T in a risk-neutral world can be calculated using Equation (10.7) on the assumption that (1) the risk-free rate is constant and equal to the average value of r; and (2) the variance rate is constant and equal to the average value of σ^2.
(e) Prove the result in Section 17.1.

17.9. A company has two classes of stock, one voting and one nonvoting. Both pay the same dividends and the voting stock always sells for a 10% premium over the nonvoting stock. If the volatility of the total equity is constant, is the Black–Scholes formula correct for valuing European options on the voting stock? Explain your answer.

17.10. Assume that a stock price follows the jump diffusion model. The Black–Scholes model is used to calculate implied volatilities for call and put options with different exercise prices and different times to maturity. What patterns would you expect to observe in the implied volatilities?

17.11. Repeat Problem 17.10 assuming that the stock price follows a stochastic volatility model with the stock price and its volatility positively correlated.

17.12. Suppose that a foreign currency exchange rate follows a jump process and has a stochastic volatility that is uncorrelated with the exchange rate. What sort of biases would you expect in the option prices observed in the market relative to those given by the Black–Scholes formulas? Assume that implied volatilities are calculated on the basis of at-the-money options.

17.13. Consider a firm with no riskless assets and a certain amount of debt. Does the displaced diffusion model or the compound option model give a higher value for a call option? Which model gives a higher value for a put option? Explain your answer.

17.14. Option traders sometimes refer to deep out-of-the-money options as being options on volatility. Why do you think they do this?

APPENDIX 17A: PRICING FORMULAS FOR ALTERNATIVE MODELS

In this appendix, we present for reference European call option pricing formulas for some of the models considered in the chapter. European put option prices can be obtained from the call prices using put–call parity.

COMPOUND OPTION MODEL

The value of a European call on a non-dividend-paying stock is given by

$$c = VM\left(a_1, b_1; \sqrt{\frac{\tau_1}{\tau_2}}\right) - Ae^{-r\tau_2}M\left(a_2, b_2; \sqrt{\frac{\tau_1}{\tau_2}}\right) - Xe^{-r\tau_1}N(a_2)$$

where

$$a_1 = \frac{\ln(V/V^*) + (r + \frac{1}{2}\sigma_V^2)\tau_1}{\sigma_V\sqrt{\tau_1}}$$

$$b_1 = \frac{\ln(V/A) + (r + \frac{1}{2}\sigma_V^2)\tau_2}{\sigma_V\sqrt{\tau_2}}$$

$$a_2 = a_1 - \sigma_V\sqrt{\tau_1}$$

$$b_2 = b_1 - \sigma_V\sqrt{\tau_2}$$

$$\tau_1 = T - t$$

$$\tau_2 = T^* - t$$

The function $M(a, b; \rho)$ is the cumulative probability in the standardized bivariate normal distribution that the first variable is less than a and the second variable is less than b when the coefficient of correlation between the variables is ρ. A procedure for evaluating it numerically is given in Appendix 10B. The variable V^* is the value of V at time T, which gives $S = X$. This can be determined numerically from Equation (17.2). Other notation is defined in Section 17.4.

DISPLACED DIFFUSION MODEL

The price of a European call option on a stock using the displaced diffusion model is

$$c = aSN(d_1) - (X - bS)e^{-r(T-t)}N(d_2)$$

where

$$d_1 = \frac{\ln[aS/(X - bS)] + \left(r - \sigma_R^2/2\right)(T - t)}{\sigma_R \sqrt{T - t}}$$

$$d_2 = d_1 - \sigma_R \sqrt{T - t}$$

$$a = \alpha(1 + \beta)$$

$$b = (1 - a)e^{r(T-t)}$$

In this formula, α is the initial proportion of the total assets that are risky, β is the initial debt-to-equity ratio, and σ_R is the volatility of the risky assets. If there are known dividends, their value compounded to time T at the risk-free rate should be subtracted from b.

ABSOLUTE DIFFUSION MODEL

The price of a European call option on a stock using the absolute diffusion model is

$$c = (S - Xe^{-r(T-t)})N(y_1) + (S - Xe^{-r(T-t)})N(y_2) + v[n(y_1) - n(y_2)]$$

where

$$v = \sigma\sqrt{\frac{1 - e^{-2r(T-t)}}{2r}}$$

$$y_1 = \frac{S - Xe^{-r(T-t)}}{v}$$

$$y_2 = \frac{-S - Xe^{-r(T-t)}}{v}$$

$$n(y) = \frac{1}{\sqrt{2\pi}}e^{-y^2/2}$$

Pure Jump Model

Using the pure jump model the European call option price is given by

$$c = S\Psi(x;\ y) - Xe^{-r(T-t)}\Psi(x,\ \frac{y}{u})$$

where

$$\Psi(\alpha;\ \beta) = \sum_{i=\alpha}^{\infty} \frac{e^{-\beta}\beta^i}{i!}$$

$$y = \frac{(r+w)(T-t)u}{u-1}$$

and x is the smallest nonnegative integer which is greater than

$$\frac{\ln(X/S) + w(T-t)}{\ln u}$$

Jump Diffusion Model

The simplest form of Merton's jump diffusion model is when the logarithm of the size of the proportional jump has a normal distribution. Assume that the standard deviation of the normal distribution is δ. The European call option price can then be written

$$c = \sum_{n=0}^{\infty} \frac{e^{-\lambda'\tau}(\lambda'\tau)^n}{n!} f_n$$

where $\tau = T - t$ and $\lambda' = \lambda(1+k)$. The variable f_n is the Black–Scholes option price when the instantaneous variance rate is

$$\sigma^2 + \frac{n\delta^2}{\tau}$$

and the risk-free rate is

$$r - \lambda k + \frac{n\gamma}{\tau}$$

where $\gamma = \ln(1+k)$.

18
Credit Risk

When valuing a derivative security, it is customary to assume that there is no risk of default. For an exchange-traded option, this assumption is usually a reasonable one since most exchanges have been very successful in organizing trading to ensure that their contracts are always honored. Unfortunately, the no-default assumption is far less defensible in the over-the-counter market. In recent years, this market has become increasingly important. Dealing with credit risk issues has become a major activity for both banks and bank regulators.

The main overall concern of bank regulators is to ensure that a bank's capital reflects the risks it is bearing. The traditional approach they have adopted has been to specify minimum levels for balance sheet ratios such as equity:total assets. This has become inappropriate in recent years because derivative securities such as swaps and options, which do not appear on the balance sheet, have begun to account for a significant proportion of the total risk. A new scheme, proposed by the Bank for International Settlements (BIS), has achieved widespread acceptance by central banks throughout the world.[1] In this scheme, each on- and off-balance

---

[1] Bank for International Settlements, "Proposals for International Convergence of Capital Adequacy Standards," July 1988.

sheet item is assigned a weight reflecting its relative credit risk and minimum levels are set for the ratio of bank capital to total risk-weighted exposure.

In addition to ensuring that they satisfy the new capital requirements, financial institutions are faced with the problem of adjusting the prices of off-balance sheet items to reflect credit risk. They must ensure that their bid-offer spreads are large enough to provide compensation for possible defaults. In many financial institutions there has been a tendency to categorize credit risks as either acceptable or unacceptable and then to price all acceptable credit risks in much the same way. It seems likely that this will change as methods for quantifying the impact of credit risk become more widely accepted.

This chapter discusses the impact of credit risk on the pricing of derivative securities and provides some details concerning the BIS regulatory requirements.

18.1 THE NATURE OF THE EXPOSURE

For a financial institution to make a credit loss on a derivative security, two conditions must be satisfied:

1. The counterparty must default; and
2. The no-default value of the contract to the financial institution must be positive.

There is no ambiguity about whether the second condition is satisfied when we are considering the possibility of a credit loss on an option since this is always an asset to one party (the purchaser) and a liability to the other party (the writer). The second condition is relevant for contracts such as swaps and forward contracts that can become either assets or liabilities to a financial institution. If a counterparty gets into financial difficulties when a contract has a positive value to the counterparty and a negative value to the financial institution, it is reasonable to assume that the contract will be sold to another party or taken over by the liquidator in such a way that there is no real change in the financial institution's position. On the other hand, if the counterparty gets into financial difficulties when the contract has a negative value to the counterparty and a positive value to the financial institution, the financial institution is liable to make a loss equal to the positive value it has in the contract. This situation is illustrated in Figure 18.1. The financial institution's possible loss (i.e., exposure) at any given time is an option-like function of the value of the contract. Expressed algebraically the exposure is

$$\max(V, 0)$$

where V is no-default value of the contract to the financial institution.

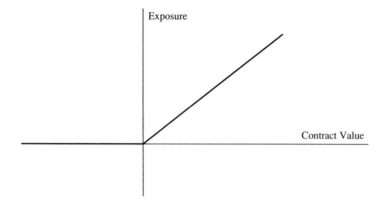

Figure 18.1   Exposure as a Function of Contract Value

THE INDEPENDENCE ASSUMPTION

When defaults are possible, there are two groups of variables affecting the value of a derivative security to a financial institution:

1. The variables affecting its value in a no-default world; and
2. The variables affecting the occurrence of defaults by the counterparty and the proportional recovery made by the financial institution in the event of a default.

Hull and White examine a general model for pricing the option in terms of these two sets of variables.[2]   The results in this chapter are largely based on their analysis.

The most general case of the model is quite cumbersome and requires a full specification of the relationships between the two sets of variables. An assumption that considerably simplifies the analysis is that the variables in 1 are independent of the variables in 2. Unless otherwise mentioned we make this assumption throughout the rest of this chapter. We will refer to the assumption as the *independence assumption.*

How realistic is the independence assumption? Underlying the assumption is the requirement that the value of the contract under consideration has a negligible bearing on the ability of the counterparty to meet its liabilities as they become due. This means that the contract must be a very small part of the counterparty's port folio of assets and liabilities or that the contract's risk must entirely hedged by

---

[2]See J. Hull and A. White, "The Impact of Default Risk on the Prices of Options and Other Derivative Securities," Working Paper, University of Toronto, 1991, and "The Price of Default," *Risk,* September 1992.

the counterparty. The variables which actually cause defaults are also assumed to be uncorrelated with the variables affecting the no-default value of the derivative security.

The independence assumption is defensible when the counterparty is a large financial institution. The variables underlying a typical over-the-counter derivative are interest rates, exchange rates, stock prices, and commodity prices. Most large financial institutions have sophisticated systems for ensuring that they are not unduly exposed to movements in the values of any of these variables. If they run into financial difficulties, these are likely to arise from other factors such as their third world debt exposure, their real estate exposure or their exposure to some other sector of the world economy. Market variables, particularly interest rates, do of course affect the performance of particular sectors of the world economy. But a great deal of time generally elapses between a problem being caused and any resultant difficulties being experienced by financial institutions. Defaults by a financial institution can therefore be expected to be only very weakly related to the values of market variables at the time when the default occurs. (An example may help to illustrate the point being made here. High interest rates in the early 1980s caused problems in many sectors, but they did not lead to serious difficulties for financial institutions until a few years later – when rates were much lower.)

In the case where the counterparty is a corporate, the reasonableness of the independence assumption is likely to depend on the particular circumstances. If the fortunes of the corporate are closely tied to the price of a commodity and the derivative is also contingent on the commodity's price the assumption is questionable. For a routine interest rate swap, it is likely to be quite reasonable.

Arguably the independence assumption provides a good robust starting point for an evaluation of the impact of credit risk and to provide a basis for incorporating credit risk into the systems used by financial institutions. In particular cases where the assumption is clearly inappropriate a trader can use judgement to adjust the assessment of the credit risk upwards or downwards.

EQUAL-RANKING BONDS

Hull and White define a bond as ranking equally with a derivative security if the recovery made in the event of a default, as a proportion of the exposure, is always the same for both the derivative security and the bond. They assume that the yields are known or can be estimated on a wide range of bonds that rank equally with the derivative security. In fact, a necessary preliminary to the analysis is that a zero-coupon yield curve for bonds with different credit ratings be constructed.

It is sometimes argued that yields on corporate bonds reflect more than just the term structure or interest rates and default risk. Altman's research, for example, shows that the excess yields of corporate bonds over Treasuries are higher than can be justified by their default experience.[3] This may be because of market inefficiency, illiquidity or some other factor that we do not wish to reflect in the way we adjust the prices of derivatives for credit risk. To overcome this problem, the analysis can be based on notional bond prices, calculated from the actual default experience on bonds with a credit rating similar to that of the counterparty, rather than on bond prices in the market.

18.2 CONTRACTS THAT ARE UNAMBIGUOUSLY ASSETS

In this section we consider the impact of credit risk on the value of a contract that is always an asset to the financial institution. For convenience we will assume that the contract under consideration is a long position in an option, but the arguments we use can be extended to other contracts that are unambiguously assets, both those on the balance sheet and those off the balance sheet. We will use the term *vulnerable* to describe an option or other security that is subject to default risk.

A RULE FOR EUROPEAN OPTIONS

Consider first European options. Define

f: Price of vulnerable European option

f^*: Price of similar no-default option

B: Price of a zero-coupon bond issued by the option writer maturing at the same time as the option and ranking equally with the option in the event of a default

B^*: Price of a similar riskless bond

The pricing rule is

$$f = f^* \frac{B}{B^*}$$

If y and y^* are the yields on B and B^*, respectively, this reduces to

$$f = f^* e^{-(y-y^*)(T-t)}$$

where T is the option maturity date. The yield y can be estimated either from the yields on bonds issued by the option writer or from the yields on bonds issued by companies that have a similar credit risk to the option writer.

---

[3] See E. I. Altman, "Measuring Corporate Bond Mortality and Performance," *Journal of Finance* (1989) 44, 902-22.

As an example of the pricing rule, consider a 2-year OTC option with a default-free value of $3. Suppose that a 2-year bond issued by the option writer that would rank equally with the option in the event of a default yields 150 basis points over similar Treasury issues. Default risk has the effect of reducing the option price to

$$3e^{-0.015 \times 2} = 2.911$$

or by about 3 percent.

This simple adjustment for credit risk is appropriate for all European-style derivative securities that provide a payoff at one particular point in time. Thus, in our example, default risk has the effect of reducing the price of any security that promises a payoff in 2 years by about 3 percent.

ALTERNATIVE INTERPRETATIONS OF THE RULE

One interpretation of the adjustment rule is that we should use the "risky" discount rate, y, instead of the risk-free discount rate, y^*, when discounting payoffs from the derivative security. Some care must be taken here. The risk-free interest rate enters into the calculation of a Black–Scholes option price in two ways: It is used to define the expected return from the underlying asset in a risk-neutral world and it is used to discount the expected payoff. We should change the risk-free rate to a risky rate for discounting purposes, but not when determining expected returns in a risk-neutral world.

For another interpretation of the adjustment rule, define

$w^*(t, \tau)$: The instantaneous forward rate at time τ, as seen at time t, calculated from the risk-free yield curve

$w(t, \tau)$: The instantaneous forward rate at time τ, as seen at time t, calculated from the yield curve corresponding to bonds that have the same default risk as the option

$\alpha(t, \tau)$: The forward rate differential, $w(t, \tau) - w^*(t, \tau)$

It can be shown that a vulnerable European option is equivalent to a similar no-default option where the holder is required to make payments at rate $\alpha(t, \tau)$ times the option value at time τ ($t \leq \tau \leq T$). The forward rate differential is therefore an important indicator of the expected cost of future defaults.

AMERICAN OPTIONS

The impact of default risk on American options is more complicated than on European options. This is because the option holder's decision on early exercise may be influenced by new information, received during the life of the option, on the fortunes of the option writer. An example may help to illustrate the point here.

Suppose that bank X sells a 1-year call option on a non-dividend-paying stock to bank Y and that during the following 6 months bank X experiences a series of well-publicized large loan losses. Normally the option would not be exercised early. But, if the option is somewhat in the money at the end of the 6 months, bank Y might choose to exercise the option at this time rather than wait and risk bank X being liquidated before the option matures.

The proportional impact of default risk on the price of an American option is less than that for a similar European option. This is because early exercise shortens the life of an American option, making a loss from defaults less likely. Another general result is that American options subject to default risk are always exercised earlier than similar no-default options. It is interesting to note that options, such as calls on non-dividend-paying stocks, that are never exercised early in a no-default world, should sometimes be exercised early when there is default risk. When the independence assumption is made, a lower bound to the value of a vulnerable American option can be obtained by using the binomial tree in the usual way, but with the discount rate at time τ being increased by $\alpha(t, \tau)$.

18.3 CONTRACTS THAT CAN BE ASSETS OR LIABILITIES

Contracts such as swaps that can become either assets or liabilities are more complicated to analyze than those considered in the previous section. One popular approach for swaps that has been used by regulatory authorities is to compare the average expected exposure on a swap with the average expected exposure on a loan that has the same principal as the swap. If the average expected exposure on the swap is, say, 5 percent of that on the loan, this is an indication that the financial institution should require the swap to contribute about 5 percent as much as towards profits as a loan with the same counterparty.

The average expected exposure on a swap during its life can be calculated using Monte Carlo simulation. Consider first an interest rate swap where the financial institution is receiving fixed and paying floating. The exposure at a future time is equal to

$$\max(B_{\text{fixed}} - B_{\text{floating}}, \, 0)$$

where B_{fixed} is the price of the fixed bond underlying the swap, and B_{floating} is the price of the floating rate bond underlying the swap. Since B_{floating} is relatively constant, this is similar to the payoff from a call option on the fixed-rate bond. Consider next a currency swap when the financial institution is receiving the domestic interest and principal while paying the foreign interest and principal. The exposure at a future time is equal to

$$\max(B_D - B_F S, \, 0)$$

or

$$B_F \max \left[\frac{B_D}{B_F} - S, \, 0 \right] \tag{18.1}$$

where B_F is the price of the foreign bond underlying the swap and B_D is the price of the domestic bond underlying the swap. If interest rates are assumed constant, B_D and B_F are relatively constant and this is similar to the payoff from a put option on the currency.

Figure 18.2 compares the expected exposure on a matched pair of interest rate swaps with the expected exposure on a matched pair of currency swaps. The expected exposure on a matched pair of interest rate swaps starts at zero, increases, and then decreases to zero. By contrast, the expected exposure on a matched pair of currency swaps increases steadily with the passage of time.

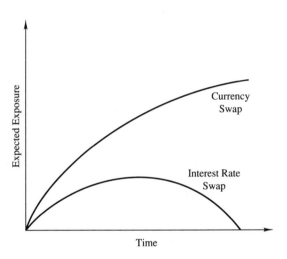

Figure 18.2   Expected Exposure on Matched Pairs of Interest Rate Swaps and Currency Swaps

A MORE PRECISE APPROACH

There are theoretical problems in assessing the impact of credit risk on a contract by looking at the average expected exposure during the life of the contract. For a start, it is difficult to know whether we should evaluate exposures in a risk-neutral world or the real world. A risk-neutral world is easier, but the real world is arguably more relevant. It is also difficult to know whether we should take a straight average of the exposures or weight them in some way. Arguably more weight should be given to later exposures because some time must elapse for the fortunes of the company to decline sufficiently for default to occur.[4]

A more precise approach to the problem of quantifying the impact of default risk can be developed by extending the results in the previous section. Hull and White show that when the independence assumption is made[5]

$$f^* - f = \int_t^T v(\tau) e^{-(y_\tau - y_\tau^*)(\tau - t)} \alpha(t, \tau) d\tau \qquad (18.2)$$

where

$$v(\tau) = \hat{E}[e^{-\bar{r}(\tau - t)} \max(f_\tau^*, 0)],$$

y_τ and y_τ^* are the yields on vulnerable and riskless bonds maturing at time τ, $\bar{r}$ is the average interest rate between t and τ, and f_τ^* is the no-default value of the security at time τ. The term $v(\tau)$ is the present value of a claim that pays off the exposure at time τ.

The function $v(\tau)$ can be valued by using Monte Carlo simulation or one of the other derivative security pricing procedures that have been discussed in this book. The value of $f^* - f$ can then be calculated from Equation (18.2) using numerical integration.

AN EXAMPLE

Consider a fixed-for-fixed foreign currency swap in which interest in sterling at the sterling risk-free rate is exchanged for interest in dollars at the dollar risk-free rate. Principals are also exchanged at the end of the life of the swap. Suppose that the swap details are as follows

Life of swap: 5 years
Frequency of payments: Annual
Sterling Principal: £100 million
Dollar Principal: $100 million
Initial exchange rate: 1.0000
Dollar riskless rate: 5% per annum (assumed constant)

---

[4]Figure 18.2 shows that the exposure on a matched pair of currency swaps increases with time whereas the exposure on an interest rate swap first increases and then decreases. Moving to a scheme where more weight is given to later exposures therefore increases the credit risk of a currency swap relative to that of an interest rate swap.

[5]See J. Hull and A. White, "The Impact of Default Risk on the Prices of Options and Other Derivative Securities," Working Paper, University of Toronto, 1991. We are here assuming that the counterparty may default, but that the company from whose viewpoint the derivative security is being valued will not default.

Sterling riskless rate: 10% per annum (assumed constant)

Volatility of exchange rate: 15%

We suppose that 1-, 2-, 3-, 4-, and 5-year zero coupon bonds issued by the counterparty would have yields that are 25, 50, 75, 85, and 95 basis points above the corresponding riskless rate.

When the company is receiving domestic and paying fixed, Equation (18.2) shows that the cost of defaults is $0.73 million; when it is receiving foreign and paying domestic the cost of defaults is $0.13 million.[6] In total, the impact of credit risk on the value of a matched pair of swaps is 0.73+0.13=$0.86 million. The financial institution should therefore require a spread that has a present value equal to at least $0.86 million. Using a discount rate of 5 percent per annum, an annuity of $0.198 million for 5 years has a present value of $0.86 million. Since the principal is $100 million, this indicates that a total spread of at least 19.8 basis points is required on the matched pair of swaps.

The impact of default risk on interest rate swaps is generally considerably less than that on currency swaps. Using the similar data to that for the currency swap, the required total spread for a matched pair of interest rate swaps is only 2 to 3 basis points.

18.4 THE BIS CAPITAL REQUIREMENTS

Regulatory authorities require that the following BIS requirements be satisfied:

$$\frac{\text{Tier One Capital}}{\text{Risk-adjusted Exposure}} > 4\%$$

$$\frac{\text{Tier One plus Tier Two Capital}}{\text{Risk-adjusted Exposure}} > 8\%$$

Tier One capital is shareholder's equity not including goodwill. Tier Two capital consists of subordinated debt, loan reserves, and other sorts of long term capital.

Risk-adjusted exposure equals the total of risk-adjusted on-balance exposure and risk-adjusted off-balance exposure. Risk-adjusted on-balance sheet exposure equals to the sum of

$$\text{Principal} \times \text{Risk Weight}$$

---

[6]In general, a financial institution has more credit risk when it is receiving a low-interest currency and paying a high-interest currency. This is because the low-interest currency is expected to appreciate over time.

for each asset. The risk weight for a commercial loan is 1.0, the risk weight for some other types of assets is less than 1.0. For example, residential mortgages have a risk weight of 0.5; Treasury bills have a risk weight of 0.0; loans to banks have a risk weight of 0.2; and so on. Consider a bank with the following on-balance sheet assets

Commercial Loans $10 million

Residential Mortgages $30 million

The risk-adjusted exposure is $10 + 0.5 \times 30 = \$25$ million. The Tier One (equity) capital required to support the assets would be $0.04 \times 25 = \$1$ million. In addition, Tier One plus Tier Two capital would have to be greater that $0.08 \times 25 = \$2$ million.

For off-balance sheet contracts there are a variety of rules. Consider interest rate swaps. The first step is to calculate

Current Exposure + Add-on Factor

The current exposure is the greater of the current value of the swap and zero (see Figure 18.1). The add-on factor, as a percentage of the notional principal, is calculated as indicated in Table 18.1. The current exposure + add-on factor is multiplied by the risk weight of the counterparty to give the risk-adjusted exposure. For this purpose corporate counterparties are given a risk weight of 0.5 rather than 1.0. As an example, consider a 3-year interest rate swap with a corporate counterparty that has a current value of $10,000 and a notional principal of $1 million. The add-on factor is $5,000 and the risk-adjusted exposure would be calculated as $15,000 \times 0.5 = \$7,500$. If the swap were with a bank (risk weight $= 0.2$), the risk-adjusted exposure would be $15,000 \times 0.2 = \$3,000$.

When a swap or other derivative security is being negotiated, it is important to realize that it is not only the capital requirement at the time the contract is negotiated that is important. We must also calculate the average of the expected capital requirements during the life of the derivative security. Many financial institutions carry out Monte Carlo simulations to determine how the capital requirements on their derivatives book are likely to change over time.

TABLE 18.1 Percent of Notional Principal Added to
Current Exposure to Obtain Capital Requirements for Swaps

Residual Maturity	Interest-Rate Contracts	Single Currency Floating/Floating Swaps	Exchange-Rate Contracts
< 1 yr	nil	nil	1.0%
> 1 yr	0.5%	nil	5.0%

The BIS capital requirements do not distinguish between different corporate counterparties. A counterparty with a AAA rating is treated the same as one with a BBB rating. For internal use, some financial institutions have developed more sophisticated capital allocation procedures. An amount of capital is allocated to each deal entered into by the financial institution and traders are evaluated on the basis of their return on capital employed. This has the advantage that it motivates traders to take credit risk into account when quoting prices. One way of allocating capital internally is to charge a trader an amount of capital proportional to $f^* - f$. The constant of proportionality should be chosen so that the total capital allocated equals or exceeds the BIS requirements.

NETTING

A contentious issue in the evaluation of credit risk concerns what is known as *netting*. Most swap contracts state that if a counterparty defaults on one contract it must default on all contracts. This has led banks to argue that, when exposures and capital requirements are calculated, a swap with a negative value should be allowed to offset a swap with a positive value when the counterparty is the same in the two cases. Consider all the swaps that a bank has with a particular counterparty. Without netting the bank's exposure at a future time is the payoff from a portfolio of options. With netting it is the payoff from an option on a portfolio. The latter is never greater than, and is often considerably less than, the former.

18.5 REDUCING DEFAULT RISK

If a financial institution is unwilling to accept the default risk in a contract, it may propose an arrangement where the counterparty provides collateral. The amount of the collateral required changes as the financial institution's exposure changes. This arrangement is similar to that used for futures contracts traded on exchanges (see Chapter 2) and has the effect of eliminating virtually all credit risk.

Sometimes default risk can be reduced by the way in which a contract is designed. Consider for example a financial institution wishing to buy an option from a counterparty with a lower credit risk. It might insist on a zero-cost package that involved the option premium being paid in arrears (see Chapter 16).

AAA-rated companies are in a strong negotiating position in derivatives markets. This has led some financial institutions, which do not themselves have AAA ratings, to set up subsidiaries with AAA ratings for the purposes of trading derivative securities. The parent company guarantees the subsidiary, but the subsidiary does not guarantee the parent company.

18.6 SUMMARY

As the volume of trading in the over-the-counter markets has increased, it has become important to assess the effect of default risk on derivative security prices. This chapter has presented some of the ways in which this can be done. If we are prepared to assume that the variables concerned with defaults are independent of the variables determining the value of the security in a no-default world, analytic results comparing the impact of defaults on derivatives to the impact of defaults on bonds are available. For example, in the case of contracts that are unambiguously assets, credit risk is taken into account by increasing the interest rate that is used for discounting.

Capital requirements for banks throughout the world are determined using the Bank for International Settlements proposals. In these, each on- and off-balance sheet item is assigned a weight reflecting its relative credit risk. This weight depends on both the nature of the contact and the counterparty. Minimum levels are set for the ratio of capital to risk-weighted exposure.

SUGGESTIONS FOR FURTHER READING

ALTMAN, E. I., "Measuring Corporate Bond Mortality and Performance," *Journal of Finance*, (1989) 44, 902–22.

BANK FOR INTERNATIONAL SETTLEMENTS, "Proposals for International Convergence of Capital Adequacy Standards," July 1988.

BELTON, T. M., "Credit Risk in Interest Rate Swaps," Working Paper, Board of Governors of Federal Reserve System, 1987.

HULL, J., "Assessing Credit Risk in a Financial Institution's Off-Balance Sheet Commitments," *Journal of Financial and Quantitative Analysis,* 24 (1989), 489–501.

HULL, J., and A. WHITE, "The Impact of Default Risk on the Prices of Options and Other Derivative Securities," Working Paper, University of Toronto, March 1991.

HULL, J., and A. WHITE, "The Price of Default," *Risk,* September 1992.

JOHNSON, H., and R. STULZ, "The Pricing of Options Under Default Risk," *Journal of Finance*, 42 (1987), 267–80.

JONKHART, M. J. L., "On the Term Structure of Interest Rates and the Risk of Default: An Analytical Approach," *Journal of Banking and Finance*, 3 (1979), 253–62.

RODRIGUEZ, R. J., "Default Risk, Yield Spreads, and Time to Maturity," *Journal of Financial and Quantitative Analysis*, 23 (1988), 111–17.

WALL, L. D., and K.-W. FUNG, "Evaluating the Credit Exposure of Interest Rate Swap Portfolios," Working Paper 87-8, Federal Reserve Board of Atlanta, (1987).

YAWITZ, J. B., K. J. MALONEY, and L. H. EDERINGTON, "Taxes, Default Risk, and Yield Spreads," *Journal of Finance*, 4 (1985), 1127–40.

QUESTIONS AND PROBLEMS

18.1. Suppose that the spread between the yield on a 3-year zero-coupon riskless bond and a 3-year zero-coupon bond issued by a corporation is 1%. By how much does Black–Scholes overstate the value of a 3-year option sold by a corporation?

18.2. "A vulnerable long forward contract is a combination of a short position in a no-default put and a long position in a vulnerable call." Discuss this statement.

18.3. Explain why the credit exposure on a matched pair of forward contracts resembles a straddle.

18.4. Explain why the impact of credit risk on a matched pair of interest rate swaps tends to be less than that on a matched pair of currency swaps.

18.5. A bank has the following assets: $200 million of Treasury bills; $100 milllion of loans to corporations; $50 million of residential mortgages; $150 million of loans to other banks. What are the capital requirements?

18.6. "When a bank is negotiating currency swaps, it should try to ensure that it is receiving the lower interest rate currency from a company with a low credit risk." Explain.

*18.7. Show that the expression $f = f^* e^{-(y-y^*)(T-t)}$ for options in Section 18.2 is a particular case of Equation 18.2.

18.8. Does put–call parity hold when there is default risk? Explain your answer.

Review of
Key Concepts

Although much of this book has focussed on options, the reader should by now have realized that there are certain key concepts that are important in the analysis of all derivative securities. In this final chapter we review some of these concepts.

19.1 RISKLESS HEDGES

The pricing of derivative securities involves the construction of riskless hedges from traded securities. For a hedge to be riskless, it must be totally independent of any stochastic variables. If the prices of two traded securities depend on one underlying stochastic variable, it is possible to set up a hedge, consisting of a position in the two securities, which is riskless. More generally, if the prices of $N + 1$ traded securities depend on N underlying stochastic variables, it is possible to set up a hedge, consisting of a position in the $N + 1$ traded securities, which is independent of all N stochastic variables and is therefore riskless.

A riskless hedge must earn the risk-free rate of interest. This fact can be used to obtain a differential equation that derivative securities must satisfy. In the situation where all the stochastic variables underlying a derivative security are the prices of traded securities, a riskless hedge can be set up using these securities together with the derivative security. In the situation where some or all of the underlying state variables are not the prices of traded securities, the riskless hedge must consist of a position in several different derivative securities.

It is important to realize that a differential equation which is derived by setting up riskless hedges does not have a unique solution. Indeed, any security that is contingent on the stochastic variables under consideration must satisfy the same differential equation. The particular security that is obtained is determined by the specification of the boundary conditions.

Derivative securities can be classified according to whether the riskless hedges that are set up are permanently riskless or only instantaneously riskless. For forward contracts on a traded security, a permanently riskless hedge can be set up consisting of the forward contract and the underlying security. In the case of options and other more complicated derivative securities, the hedge that is set up is only instantaneously riskless. To remain riskless it must be continuously rebalanced. It is interesting to note that a futures contract can in this context be viewed as being intermediate between forward contracts and options. A hedge that is set up between a futures contract and the underlying security is not permanently riskless, but it needs to be rebalanced only once per day to remain riskless.

19.2 TRADED SECURITIES VERSUS OTHER UNDERLYING VARIABLES

In the context of pricing derivative securities, a traded security can be defined as any asset that is held solely for investment purposes by a significant number of investors. Silver is a traded security according to this definition, while copper is not. There is an important difference between the situation where a derivative security depends only on the prices of traded securities and the situation where it depends on the values of other variables. When an underlying variable is a traded security, the price of an option is independent of the expected drift rate of the underlying variable and the market price of its risk. When the underlying variable is not a traded security, these parameters become important. This difference arises from the fact that only traded securities can be included in the construction of a riskless hedge.

19.3 RISK-NEUTRAL VALUATION

The risk-neutral valuation argument is a very simple argument that is at the heart of much of the analysis of derivative securities. If a derivative security depends only on the prices of traded securities, the differential equation for its price does not involve parameters that are affected by risk preferences. It follows that the price of the derivative security in a world where all investors are risk neutral must be the same as its price in the real world. For the purposes of valuing the derivative security, it is therefore permissible to assume that all investors are risk neutral.

This assumption considerably simplifies the analysis. In a risk-neutral world, the expected return from any traded security is the risk-free rate. Furthermore, the expected payoffs from any derivative security are discounted at the risk-free rate to get its present value. It should be emphasized that the risk-neutrality assumption does not mean that the derivative security is being valued only for the case of a risk-neutral world. Its value in a risk-neutral world happens to be the same as its value in other worlds where investors are risk averse.

It turns out that when some or all of the variables underlying a derivative security are not the prices of traded securities, an extension of the risk-neutral valuation argument can be used. It is still permissible to assume that the world is risk neutral. However, the expected growth rate in each variable must be reduced by the product of the market price of its risk and its volatility for the purposes of the analysis. If the variable happens to be the price of a traded security, this adjustment changes the drift rate to a level where the variable's expected return is the risk-free rate.

19.4 A FINAL WORD

I hope that this book has stimulated the reader's interest in derivative securities. I have certainly found the task of organizing my own knowledge of the subject to write this book a rewarding one.

What does the future hold for the analysis of derivative securities? It is always tempting to answer a question such as this by saying that all the important discoveries have already been made. I do not think this is true for the analysis of derivative securities. A great deal of research—both theoretical and empirical—is carried out each year by financial institutions and by academics. New derivative securities are being developed at an exciting pace. There can be little doubt that important new ideas and new results will continue to emerge.

Table For N(x) When x ≤ 0

This table shows values of $N(x)$ for $x \leq 0$. The table should be used with interpolation. For example

$$N(-0.1234) = N(-0.12) - 0.34[N(-0.12) - N(-0.13)]$$
$$= 0.4522 - 0.34 \times (0.4522 - 0.4483)$$
$$= 0.4509$$

x	.00	.01	.02	.03	.04	.05	.06	.07	.08	.09
−0.0	0.5000	0.4960	0.4920	0.4880	0.4840	0.4801	0.4761	0.4721	0.4681	0.4641
−0.1	0.4602	0.4562	0.4522	0.4483	0.4443	0.4404	0.4364	0.4325	0.4286	0.4247
−0.2	0.4207	0.4168	0.4129	0.4090	0.4052	0.4013	0.3974	0.3936	0.3897	0.3859
−0.3	0.3821	0.3783	0.3745	0.3707	0.3669	0.3632	0.3594	0.3557	0.3520	0.3483
−0.4	0.3446	0.3409	0.3372	0.3336	0.3300	0.3264	0.3228	0.3192	0.3156	0.3121
−0.5	0.3085	0.3050	0.3015	0.2981	0.2946	0.2912	0.2877	0.2843	0.2810	0.2776
−0.6	0.2743	0.2709	0.2676	0.2643	0.2611	0.2578	0.2546	0.2514	0.2483	0.2451
−0.7	0.2420	0.2389	0.2358	0.2327	0.2296	0.2266	0.2236	0.2206	0.2177	0.2148
−0.8	0.2119	0.2090	0.2061	0.2033	0.2005	0.1977	0.1949	0.1922	0.1894	0.1867
−0.9	0.1841	0.1814	0.1788	0.1762	0.1736	0.1711	0.1685	0.1660	0.1635	0.1611
−1.0	0.1587	0.1562	0.1539	0.1515	0.1492	0.1469	0.1446	0.1423	0.1401	0.1379
−1.1	0.1357	0.1335	0.1314	0.1292	0.1271	0.1251	0.1230	0.1210	0.1190	0.1170
−1.2	0.1151	0.1131	0.1112	0.1093	0.1075	0.1056	0.1038	0.1020	0.1003	0.0985
−1.3	0.0968	0.0951	0.0934	0.0918	0.0901	0.0885	0.0869	0.0853	0.0838	0.0823
−1.4	0.0808	0.0793	0.0778	0.0764	0.0749	0.0735	0.0721	0.0708	0.0694	0.0681
−1.5	0.0668	0.0655	0.0643	0.0630	0.0618	0.0606	0.0594	0.0582	0.0571	0.0559
−1.6	0.0548	0.0537	0.0526	0.0516	0.0505	0.0495	0.0485	0.0475	0.0465	0.0455
−1.7	0.0446	0.0436	0.0427	0.0418	0.0409	0.0401	0.0392	0.0384	0.0375	0.0367
−1.8	0.0359	0.0351	0.0344	0.0336	0.0329	0.0322	0.0314	0.0307	0.0301	0.0294
−1.9	0.0287	0.0281	0.0274	0.0268	0.0262	0.0256	0.0250	0.0244	0.0239	0.0233
−2.0	0.0228	0.0222	0.0217	0.0212	0.0207	0.0202	0.0197	0.0192	0.0188	0.0183
−2.1	0.0179	0.0174	0.0170	0.0166	0.0162	0.0158	0.0154	0.0150	0.0146	0.0143
−2.2	0.0139	0.0136	0.0132	0.0129	0.0125	0.0122	0.0119	0.0116	0.0113	0.0110
−2.3	0.0107	0.0104	0.0102	0.0099	0.0096	0.0094	0.0091	0.0089	0.0087	0.0084
−2.4	0.0082	0.0080	0.0078	0.0075	0.0073	0.0071	0.0069	0.0068	0.0066	0.0064
−2.5	0.0062	0.0060	0.0059	0.0057	0.0055	0.0054	0.0052	0.0051	0.0049	0.0048
−2.6	0.0047	0.0045	0.0044	0.0043	0.0041	0.0040	0.0039	0.0038	0.0037	0.0036
−2.7	0.0035	0.0034	0.0033	0.0032	0.0031	0.0030	0.0029	0.0028	0.0027	0.0026
−2.8	0.0026	0.0025	0.0024	0.0023	0.0023	0.0022	0.0021	0.0021	0.0020	0.0019
−2.9	0.0019	0.0018	0.0018	0.0017	0.0016	0.0016	0.0015	0.0015	0.0014	0.0014
−3.0	0.0014	0.0013	0.0013	0.0012	0.0012	0.0011	0.0011	0.0011	0.0010	0.0010
−3.1	0.0010	0.0009	0.0009	0.0009	0.0008	0.0008	0.0008	0.0008	0.0007	0.0007
−3.2	0.0007	0.0007	0.0006	0.0006	0.0006	0.0006	0.0006	0.0005	0.0005	0.0005
−3.3	0.0005	0.0005	0.0005	0.0004	0.0004	0.0004	0.0004	0.0004	0.0004	0.0003
−3.4	0.0003	0.0003	0.0003	0.0003	0.0003	0.0003	0.0003	0.0003	0.0003	0.0002
−3.5	0.0002	0.0002	0.0002	0.0002	0.0002	0.0002	0.0002	0.0002	0.0002	0.0002
−3.6	0.0002	0.0002	0.0001	0.0001	0.0001	0.0001	0.0001	0.0001	0.0001	0.0001
−3.7	0.0001	0.0001	0.0001	0.0001	0.0001	0.0001	0.0001	0.0001	0.0001	0.0001
−3.8	0.0001	0.0001	0.0001	0.0001	0.0001	0.0001	0.0001	0.0001	0.0001	0.0001
−3.9	0.0000	0.0000	0.0000	0.0000	0.0000	0.0000	0.0000	0.0000	0.0000	0.0000
−4.0	0.0000	0.0000	0.0000	0.0000	0.0000	0.0000	0.0000	0.0000	0.0000	0.0000

Table For N(x) When x ≥ 0

This table shows values of $N(x)$ for $x \geq 0$. The table should be used with interpolation. For example

$$N(0.6278) = N(0.62) + 0.78[N(0.63) - N(0.62)]$$
$$= 0.7324 + 0.78 \times (0.7357 - 0.7324)$$
$$= 0.7350$$

x	.00	.01	.02	.03	.04	.05	.06	.07	.08	.09
0.0	0.5000	0.5040	0.5080	0.5120	0.5160	0.5199	0.5239	0.5279	0.5319	0.5359
0.1	0.5398	0.5438	0.5478	0.5517	0.5557	0.5596	0.5636	0.5675	0.5714	0.5753
0.2	0.5793	0.5832	0.5871	0.5910	0.5948	0.5987	0.6026	0.6064	0.6103	0.6141
0.3	0.6179	0.6217	0.6255	0.6293	0.6331	0.6368	0.6406	0.6443	0.6480	0.6517
0.4	0.6554	0.6591	0.6628	0.6664	0.6700	0.6736	0.6772	0.6808	0.6844	0.6879
0.5	0.6915	0.6950	0.6985	0.7019	0.7054	0.7088	0.7123	0.7157	0.7190	0.7224
0.6	0.7257	0.7291	0.7324	0.7357	0.7389	0.7422	0.7454	0.7486	0.7517	0.7549
0.7	0.7580	0.7611	0.7642	0.7673	0.7704	0.7734	0.7764	0.7794	0.7823	0.7852
0.8	0.7881	0.7910	0.7939	0.7967	0.7995	0.8023	0.8051	0.8078	0.8106	0.8133
0.9	0.8159	0.8186	0.8212	0.8238	0.8264	0.8289	0.8315	0.8340	0.8365	0.8389
1.0	0.8413	0.8438	0.8461	0.8485	0.8508	0.8531	0.8554	0.8577	0.8599	0.8621
1.1	0.8643	0.8665	0.8686	0.8708	0.8729	0.8749	0.8770	0.8790	0.8810	0.8830
1.2	0.8849	0.8869	0.8888	0.8907	0.8925	0.8944	0.8962	0.8980	0.8997	0.9015
1.3	0.9032	0.9049	0.9066	0.9082	0.9099	0.9115	0.9131	0.9147	0.9162	0.9177
1.4	0.9192	0.9207	0.9222	0.9236	0.9251	0.9265	0.9279	0.9292	0.9306	0.9319
1.5	0.9332	0.9345	0.9357	0.9370	0.9382	0.9394	0.9406	0.9418	0.9429	0.9441
1.6	0.9452	0.9463	0.9474	0.9484	0.9495	0.9505	0.9515	0.9525	0.9535	0.9545
1.7	0.9554	0.9564	0.9573	0.9582	0.9591	0.9599	0.9608	0.9616	0.9625	0.9633
1.8	0.9641	0.9649	0.9656	0.9664	0.9671	0.9678	0.9686	0.9693	0.9699	0.9706
1.9	0.9713	0.9719	0.9726	0.9732	0.9738	0.9744	0.9750	0.9756	0.9761	0.9767
2.0	0.9772	0.9778	0.9783	0.9788	0.9793	0.9798	0.9803	0.9808	0.9812	0.9817
2.1	0.9821	0.9826	0.9830	0.9834	0.9838	0.9842	0.9846	0.9850	0.9854	0.9857
2.2	0.9861	0.9864	0.9868	0.9871	0.9875	0.9878	0.9881	0.9884	0.9887	0.9890
2.3	0.9893	0.9896	0.9898	0.9901	0.9904	0.9906	0.9909	0.9911	0.9913	0.9916
2.4	0.9918	0.9920	0.9922	0.9925	0.9927	0.9929	0.9931	0.9932	0.9934	0.9936
2.5	0.9938	0.9940	0.9941	0.9943	0.9945	0.9946	0.9948	0.9949	0.9951	0.9952
2.6	0.9953	0.9955	0.9956	0.9957	0.9959	0.9960	0.9961	0.9962	0.9963	0.9964
2.7	0.9965	0.9966	0.9967	0.9968	0.9969	0.9970	0.9971	0.9972	0.9973	0.9974
2.8	0.9974	0.9975	0.9976	0.9977	0.9977	0.9978	0.9979	0.9979	0.9980	0.9981
2.9	0.9981	0.9982	0.9982	0.9983	0.9984	0.9984	0.9985	0.9985	0.9986	0.9986
3.0	0.9986	0.9987	0.9987	0.9988	0.9988	0.9989	0.9989	0.9989	0.9990	0.9990
3.1	0.9990	0.9991	0.9991	0.9991	0.9992	0.9992	0.9992	0.9992	0.9993	0.9993
3.2	0.9993	0.9993	0.9994	0.9994	0.9994	0.9994	0.9994	0.9995	0.9995	0.9995
3.3	0.9995	0.9995	0.9995	0.9996	0.9996	0.9996	0.9996	0.9996	0.9996	0.9997
3.4	0.9997	0.9997	0.9997	0.9997	0.9997	0.9997	0.9997	0.9997	0.9997	0.9998
3.5	0.9998	0.9998	0.9998	0.9998	0.9998	0.9998	0.9998	0.9998	0.9998	0.9998
3.6	0.9998	0.9998	0.9999	0.9999	0.9999	0.9999	0.9999	0.9999	0.9999	0.9999
3.7	0.9999	0.9999	0.9999	0.9999	0.9999	0.9999	0.9999	0.9999	0.9999	0.9999
3.8	0.9999	0.9999	0.9999	0.9999	0.9999	0.9999	0.9999	0.9999	0.9999	0.9999
3.9	1.0000	1.0000	1.0000	1.0000	1.0000	1.0000	1.0000	1.0000	1.0000	1.0000
4.0	1.0000	1.0000	1.0000	1.0000	1.0000	1.0000	1.0000	1.0000	1.0000	1.0000

World Exchanges

Major Exchanges Throughout the World Trading Futures
and Options and the Average Number of Contracts
Traded Daily Between January and August 1990

Chicago Board of Trade	CBOT	609,139
Chicago Board Options Exchange	CBOE	523,098
Chicago Mercantile Exchange	CME	403,455
San Paulo Mercantile & Futures Exchange	BOVESPA	196,364
New York Mercantile Exchange	NYMEX	175,069
American Stock Exchange	AMEX	169,822
London International Financial Futures Exchange	LIFFE	139,538
Marché à Terme International de France	MATIF	114,599
Tokyo International Financial Futures Exchange	TIFFE	91,837
Philadelphia Stock Exchange	PHLX	89,540
Osaka Securities Exchange	OSA	85,461
Commodity Exchange, New York	COMEX	82,469
Pacific Stock Exchange	PSE	57,025
Coffee, Sugar & Cocoa Exchange	CSCE	53,205
London Metal Exchange	LME	49,593
Sydney Futures Exchange	SFE	46,950
European Options Exchange	EOE	42,979
Australian Stock Exchange Sydney	AUS	41,870
Swiss Options and Financial Futures Exchange	SOFFEX	35,438
London Traded Options Market	LTOM	33,018
San Paulo Mercantile & Futures Exchange	BM&F	31,714
Stockholm Options Market	OM	29,425
Deutsche Termin Börse	DTB	26,810
International Petroleum Exchange	IPE	24,095
Singapore Mercantile Exchange	SIMEX	21,543
London Futures and Options Exchange	FOX	19,257
Marché de Options Négociables de Paris	MONEP	18,478
Rio Janeiro Stock Exchange	BVRJ	14,147
New York Stock Exchange	NYSE	12,587
Toronto Stock Exchange	TSE	9,137
New York Cotton Exchange	NYCE	9,021
New York Futures Exchange	NYFE	6,681
Montreal Exchange	ME	5,639
Winnipeg Commodity Exchange	WCE	4,848
Financial Instruments Exchange	FINEX	3,714
Finnish Options Market	FOM	3,070

Source: European Options Exchange Bulletin, September 1990

Glossary of Notation

A guide to the main ways in which symbols are used in this book is given below. Symbols which appear in only one small part of the book may not be listed here, but are always defined at the time they are first used.

a: Growth rate of underlying variable in a risk-neutral world in binomial model during time Δt. For example, when the underlying variable is a non-dividend paying stock $a = e^{r\Delta t}$; when it is a currency $a = e^{(r-r_f)\Delta t}$; and so on. The variable a is also used in chapters 9 and 10 as the drift rate in a generalized Wiener process. In Chapter 15, it is the reversion rate in an interest rate process.

A: Principal amount of bond.

b: In Chapter 9, b^2 is the variance rate in a generalized Wiener process. In Chapter 15, b is the reversion level in an interest rate process.

B: Value of a bond.

c: Price of European call option.

c_i: ith cash payment on a bond.

C: Price of American call option.

d_1, d_2: Parameters in option pricing formulas. See, for example, equations (10.27) and (11.3).

d: Proportional down movement in binomial model. If $d = 0.9$, value of variable moves to 90% of its previous value when there is a down movement.

D: In chapters 7 and 8, D is the present value of dividends on a stock. In Chapter 10, D is the cash dividend and D_i is used for the ith cash dividend payment. In chapters 4 and 15, D is used to denote duration.

$E(\cdot)$: Expected value of variable.

$\hat{E}(\cdot)$: Expected value of variable in a risk-neutral world.

f: Value of derivative security. The symbol, f_i, is the value of the ith derivative security. The symbol, f_T, is the value of the derivative security at time T. The symbol f_{ij} is the jth price of the derivative security at time $i \, \Delta t$ in binomial models.

F: Forward or futures price. The symbol F_T is the forward or futures price at time T. In Appendix 3A, F_i is the futures price at the end of day i.

G: G_i is used in Appendix 3A for the forward price at the end of day i. Also, G is used as an arbitrary function of a stochastic variable in Chapter 10.

h: Hedge ratio

H_A: Position in asset for delta hedging.

H_F: Position in forward or futures contracts for delta hedging.

I: Present value of income on a security.

K: Delivery price in forward contract.

L: Principal amount in interest-rate cap contract.

m: Expected growth rate of stochastic variable, θ. The symbol m_i is the expected growth rate of θ_i; $\hat{m}$ is the expected growth rate of θ in a risk-neutral world; and so on. In chapter 15, m is the expected growth rate of r.

$M(x, y, \rho)$: Cumulative probability in a bivariate normal distribution that the first variable is less than x and the second variable is less than y when the coefficient of correlation between the variables is ρ.

$N(x)$: Cumulative probability that a variable with a standardized normal distribution is less than x. A standardized normal distribution is a normal distribution with a mean of zero and standard deviation of 1.0. Thus $N(0) = 0.5$.

p: This is used in two major ways: (1) value of European put option (see Chapter 10); and (2) probability of an up movement in binomial models (see Chapter 14).

The meaning will be clear from the context.

P: Value of American put option. Also $P(t, T)$ is used as the price at time t of a discount bond maturing at time T.

q: Dividend yield rate.

Q: Notional principal in interest rate swap in Chapter 5.

r: Risk-free interest rate. Note that in chapters 3, 4, 7, and 8, r is the risk-free rate between times t and T. Elsewhere in the book, it should be interpreted as the instantaneous (i.e., very short term) risk-free interest rate.

r_f: Instantaneous risk-free interest rate in foreign country.

$\bar{r}$: Average instantaneous risk-free rate of interest during life of derivative security.

r^*: Risk-free interest rate between times t and T^*.

$\hat{r}$: Forward interest rate between times T and T^*.

R_k: Interest rate between time $k\tau$ and $(k+1)\tau$ on a LIBOR-based loan (Chapter 15).

R_X: Cap rate in an interest-rate cap agreement.

$R(t, T)$: Risk-free interest rate at time t for an investment maturing at time T.

$\hat{R}(t, T, T^*)$: Forward interest rate at time, t, for period between T and T^*.

s: Volatility of θ.

s_i: Volatility of θ_i.

S: Price of asset underlying derivative security. In different parts of the book S is used to refer to the price of a currency, the price of a stock, the price of a stock index, and the price of a commodity.

S_T: Value of S at time T.

t: Current time.

T: Time at maturity of derivative security.

T^*: Time at maturity of futures contract or bond underlying derivative security.

u: Proportional up movement in binomial model. For example, $u = 1.2$ indicates that the variable increases by 20% when an up movement occurs. The symbol u is also used to denote the storage costs per unit time as a proportion of the price of an asset.

U: Present value of storage costs.

v: Variance

V: Value of swap

w_i: Number owned of ith security.

w_T: Number owned of traded security.

X: Strike price of option.

y: Convenience yield. Also used for yield on a bond.

z: Variable following a Wiener process.

β: Beta. This is the slope of the line obtained when returns from a portfolio (or from an individual stock) are plotted against returns from the market.

Γ: Gamma of derivative security or portfolio of derivative securities.

Δ: Delta of derivative security or portfolio of derivative securities.

Δx: Small change in x for any variable x.

ϵ: Random sample from standardized normal distribution.

η: Continuously compounded return on a stock.

θ: Stochastic variable underlying a derivative security; θ_i is the ith stochastic variable underlying a derivative security.

Θ: Theta of derivative security or portfolio of derivative securities.

λ: Market price of risk; λ_i is market price of risk of variable i.

Λ: Vega of derivative security or portfolio of derivative securities.

μ: Expected growth rate in price of asset (for a non-dividend-paying stock, μ is expected return).

μ_F: Expected growth in F.

Π: Value of portfolio.

ρ: Coefficient of correlation; ρ_{ij} is coefficient of correlation between θ_i and θ_j.

σ: Volatility of asset. In Chapter 2, σ_S and σ_F are standard deviations.

σ_F: Volatility of F.

$\phi(m, s)$: Normal distribution with mean m and standard deviation s.

Author Index

Subject Index